IN EUROPE'S NAME

Timothy Garton Ash is a Fellow of St Antony's College,
Oxford. After reading Modern History at Oxford, his
research into the German resistance to Hitler took him to
Berlin, where he lived, in both the western and the eastern halves of the divided city, for several years. From
there, he started to travel widely behind the iron curtain.

Throughout the nineteen eighties, he reported and
analysed the emancipation of Central Europe from communism in contributions to the *Spectator*, the *Independent*, the *New York Review of Books* and other journals.
In 1989 he was awarded the David Watt Memorial Prize
for his commentaries on international affairs and named
'Commentator of the Year' in the Granada television
What The Papers Say awards.

He is the author of '*Und willst Du nicht mein Bruder
sein...*' *Die DDR heute*, a book published in West Ger-
many about what was then still East Germany; *The
Polish Revolution: Solidarity*, which won the Somerset
Maugham Award; *The Uses of Adversity: Essays on the
Fate of Central Europe*, for which he was awarded the
Prix Européen de l'Esssai; and *We the People: The Rev-
olution of '89 Witnessed in Warsaw, Budapest, Berlin &
Prague*, which has now appeared in fourteen languages.

In Europe's Name was first published in Germany,
where it became a bestseller and provoked wide debate.
It has since appeared in Dutch and Italian, and is currently being translated into French, Polish and Japanese.

Timothy Garton Ash

IN EUROPE'S NAME

Germany and the Divided Continent

VINTAGE

Published by Vintage 1994

2 4 6 8 10 9 7 5 3 1

First published in Great Britain
by Jonathan Cape Ltd. 1993

Vintage
Random House, 20 Vauxhall Bridge Road,
London SW1V 2SA

Random House Australia (Pty) Limited
20 Alfred Street, Milsons Point, Sydney
New South Wales 2061, Australia

Random House New Zealand Limited
18 Poland Road, Glenfield, Auckland 10,
New Zealand

Random House South Africa (Pty) Limited
PO Box 337, Bergvlei, South Africa

Random House UK Limited Reg. No. 954009

A CIP catalogue record for this book
is available from the British Library

ISBN 0 09 982050 1

Printed and bound in Great Britain by
Cox & Wyman, Reading, Berkshire

Contents

Author's Note

To keep the main text readable, all sources, some caveats and many interesting further details have been consigned to the notes and other appendices. To avoid littering the text with superscript numbers, each note is keyed to a few words from the passage to which it relates. The top of each page of notes tells you to which pages of text those notes refer. This sounds complicated, but in practice it is not.

Informed criticism, questions and corrections really are welcome, but would-be critics, questioners and rectifiers are asked to look in these notes and appendices as well as at the main text. I hope other readers, too, may find the notes, with their guidance to sources and further reading, and the carefully conceived maps, tables and chronology, both useful and stimulating. However, the book can be read without any reference to the supporting apparatus.

TGA, Oxford,
May 1993

Prologue

European Question

Which question?

Once, Europe was cut in two. The two parts were called West and East. The division itself was often labelled 'Yalta'. It was set in concrete in the Berlin Wall.

In the early 1980s, this 'Yalta' divide became the subject of intense international debate. The legitimacy and permanence of the East-West division of Europe were questioned from the left and from the right, by the Presidents of the French Republic and of the United States, by opposition activists in Eastern Europe and peace movement activists in Western Europe, by Nato and by the Pope.

Of course the issue had never quite disappeared from the international agenda since 1945, and certainly not from the German and East European agendas. Yet the catalysts for this wider popular discussion were the declaration of a 'state of war' to crush the Solidarity movement in Poland, in December 1981, and the controversy about the deployment of new American nuclear missiles in West Germany, in the years 1980–83. The former turned attention to the external, geopolitical conditions that then precluded success for the Polish revolution, and particularly to the position of the Soviet Union in East Central Europe. The latter turned attention to the subject of European security, and particularly to the position of the United States in West Central Europe. The two debates — about freedom and about peace — then clashed and combined in convoluted ways, with many variations according to country, creed and political affiliation.

In these debates there were not a few who publicly, and even more who privately defended the 'Yalta' division, arguing that it had brought peace and stability to Europe. 'The peace of Europe,' wrote a well-known German commentator in 1983, 'depends for longer than we can foresee on the system of Yalta . . .' More diplomatic versions of this view could be heard in high places in many capitals of the West. Looking back in December 1989, the British Foreign Secretary, Douglas Hurd, said that this was a system 'under which we've lived quite happily for forty years'.

The sense that there were others who had not lived quite so happily under this system, and that their lack of happiness might materially affect our own, nonetheless clearly grew through the first half of the decade. By 1985 the goal of overcoming, or at least, reducing the division of Europe was a staple ingredient of the rhetoric of most Western governments, as well as of independent activists from Eastern and Western Europe.

Thus, for example, on the fortieth anniversary of the end of the Second World War, the leaders of the group of seven leading industrial countries (the so-called G7), together with the President of the Commission of the European Community, issued a solemn declaration in which they said: 'We deplore the division of Europe. In our commitment to the ideals of peace, freedom and democracy, we seek by peaceful means to lower the barriers that have arisen within Europe.' In the same year, the Czechoslovak civil rights movement Charter 77 issued a 'Prague Appeal' which identified the division as the root-cause of tension in Europe, and called for a gradual, peaceful transformation of the underlying 'political reality'. The concluding resolution of an international human rights conference in Kraków in 1988 all-embracingly declared that 'the goal of Europeans is to overcome the division of the continent, to unite Europe'.

In the second half of the 1980s, this debate was then transformed by the 'new thinking' on Soviet foreign policy under Mikhail Gorbachev, and by the way in which the peoples of Eastern Europe seized the opportunities that it offered. Even before he became Party leader in 1985, Gorbachev had spoken of his vision of a 'common Europe home'. Yet this image had already been used by Brezhnev on a visit to Bonn in November 1981. In the mid-1980s there was still a considerable gap between what Gorbachev seemed — at least from his public statements — to have in mind, and what either Western leaders or the European citizens advocating 'détente from below' had in mind when they spoke of 'overcoming the division of Europe'.

Here we encounter a problem that will recur throughout this book: that of distinguishing between what people said in public, what they said or merely thought in private, and, not least, what they think or say now that they thought or said then. Gorbachev made an explicit public commitment to overcoming the division in a Joint Declaration with Chancellor Helmut Kohl during the Soviet leader's visit to Bonn in June 1989. This Declaration stated that 'the Federal Republic of Germany and the Soviet Union consider the foremost task of their policy to be to draw on the historically developed European traditions and so to contribute to overcoming the partition of Europe'. Yet even here the Russian text used the more vague and general term, *razobshchennosty*, that is, 'disunity', by contrast with the specific German *Trennung*. Soviet commentators talked of overcoming the continent's economic and 'military-political' divides. One even described the Berlin Wall as a 'relic of the Cold War'. Yet, at least in public, they nonetheless still envisaged the co-existence of states with different 'social systems' — to use the misleading Soviet term.

Gorbachev himself put this quite starkly in his speech to the Council of Europe at Strasbourg in July 1989, just three weeks after his visit to Bonn:

I know that many in the West see the presence of two social systems as the major difficulty. But the difficulty actually lies elsewhere — in the widespread conviction (sometimes even a policy objective) according to which overcoming the split (*raskol*) in Europe means 'overcoming socialism'. But this is a policy of confrontation, if not worse. No European unity will result from such approaches.

The reference to two social systems is significant. Gorbachev did not say that there were many social systems in Europe: the Swedish social system, for example, as opposed to the Swiss social system, the Danish and the Polish, the Hungarian and the Dutch. He said that there were just two, East and West, 'socialist' and not. By implication, the common European home should be built in spite of, and around, this central difference.

President Bush, by contrast, had declared in a speech at Mainz in West Germany, in May 1989: 'Let Europe be whole and free.' This, he averred, was 'the new mission of Nato'. 'In the East,' he said, 'brave men and women are showing us the way. Look at Poland, where Solidarity — Solidarność — and the Catholic Church have won legal status. The forces of freedom are putting the Soviet status quo on the defensive.' And the first of his four proposals 'to heal Europe's tragic division' was to 'strengthen and broaden the Helsinki process to promote free elections and political pluralism in Eastern Europe'. He went on to underline this message by demonstrative visits to Poland and Hungary, the two East European countries furthest down that path.

Thus, while the gap between the Soviet leader's proclaimed vision of a 'common European home' and the American leader's proclaimed vision of 'overcoming the division' was much narrower in summer 1989 than it had been in 1985, let alone in 1981, it was still perceptible and important. What changed this decisively in the second half of 1989 was not further movement from above on either side, but movement from below, in the centre. In events which, taken together, may be called a revolution, the countries of Eastern Europe took matters into their own hands. They did this in different ways, with varying degrees of élite and popular participation, and diverse outcomes — but all rejected the previous system, which had described itself as socialism.

While these changes certainly went faster and farther than Gorbachev and his closest associates had hoped or expected, they accepted them with quite extraordinary grace. Above all, they steadfastly refused all siren calls to preserve the 'Yalta' order by means of the instrument with the help of which it had been imposed in the first place, and then restored in 1953, 1956, 1968, and even, indirectly, in 1981: the Red Army. This renunciation of what had been known as the Brezhnev Doctrine had emerged slowly and painfully in the evolution of the 'new thinking'. The new doctrine of free choice and renunciation of force had been expressed in general terms in Gorbachev's speech to the United Nations in December 1988. Still, at the beginning of 1989 no one could be quite sure that when put to the hard test it would actually be applied to Eastern Europe. In October 1989, on American television, the Soviet Foreign Ministry spokesman Gennady Gerasimov then gave a colourful name to the successor to the Brezhnev Doctrine: 'We now have the Frank Sinatra Doctrine. He had a song, "I had it my way" (sic). So every country decides, on its own, which way to take.'

In January 1945, anticipating a preliminary Anglo-American summit meeting on Malta, to precede the Yalta conference in February of that year, Churchill jovially telegraphed to Franklin Roosevelt: 'No more let us falter! From Malta to Yalta! Let nobody alter!' In one of history's nicer coincidences, it was again on Malta, in December 1989, that there took place the Soviet-American informal summit which was an important milestone on Europe's road from Yalta. 'The post-war split of the continent,' said Gorbachev in his 1990 New Year's address, 'is receding into the past.' The Soviet Union's acceptance of the end of communism in Eastern Europe, the demise of the Warsaw Pact and the unification of Germany then marked the decisive breakthrough. By the beginning of 1991, it was no longer appropriate to talk of the 'Yalta' division of Europe. Many lines of division in Europe remained, and new ones would emerge, but this single, central divide was finished. The 'iron curtain' was no more. The Berlin Wall would soon be rubble and rusty wire.

If one argued in the 1980s that the question 'how, by peaceful means, might the "Yalta" division of Europe be overcome?' was the European question, this was considered by many to be a rhetorical exaggeration. Some said that the European question was that of how the relative economic decline of (Western) Europe, 'Eurosclerosis', might be halted or reversed. Others said that the European question was that of the development and further integration of the (West) European Community — sometimes called the 'construction of Europe'. Others again said that the European question concerned the future relationship of this community with the United States of America, especially in defence arrangements: in other words, that hardiest perennial, 'whither Nato?'

So it would perhaps be more modest and precise to talk of the Central European question. Yet throughout modern European history, the Central

European question has had a habit of becoming, sooner or later, the central European question; and this is what happened again in the 1980s.

Yalta

Two key terms emerged, or rather re-emerged, in these debates: 'Central Europe' and 'Yalta'. The matter of Central Europe is present throughout this book. A word should be said about Yalta. That Yalta became the prevailing shorthand for the division of Europe there can be no doubt. When President Mitterand wished to express indignation at the imposition of martial law in Poland he said 'anything that helps us to get out of Yalta (*sortir de Yalta*) is good', although he warily concluded 'so long as we never confuse our desires with today's reality.' When Zbigniew Brzezinski wrote about the United States and the European question, his chosen title was 'The Future of Yalta'. The notion of 'Yalta' was equally prominent in East European opposition thinking, usually in the forms 'post-Yalta' or 'anti-Yalta'.

One might ask why Yalta, rather than Potsdam, or Tehran, or, for that matter, 'Hitler' or 'Stalin', became the all-European symbol of partition. It is also important to ask what relation Yalta — the Crimean conference of 4–11 February 1945 — bears to 'Yalta'. Almost certainly, earlier political-military decisions in the Second World War, including those at the Tehran summit conference of 1943, were more fateful even for Poland than the confused and ambiguous conclusions of the Crimean conference. In fact, 'Yalta' is drastic and misleading shorthand for the results of a long historical process, whose beginnings have to be traced back at least to August 1914, and which was not finally completed until August 1961, when the partition was set in the concrete of the Berlin Wall. The history of the Cold War is an essential part of this story, but so is that of the 'Thirty Years' War' of 1914 to 1945 — of what the historian Hajo Holborn called 'the political collapse of Europe'.

This history was retold as myth in the debates of the 1980s. Assertions about the solely negative impact of the Cold War underpinned West European social democrats' arguments for détente. Assertions about Western failures over Yalta figured largely in American neo-conservatives' criticism of détente. Some of the professional historiography, too, had a sharp political edge, which usually consisted in the explicit or implicit posing of 'if' questions ('what would have happened if . . .?'), or the canvassing of alleged 'missed opportunities'.

One of the most characteristic fallacies of this politicised if-historiography was the silent projection of certain conditions of the present into the past. A good example was furnished by the German historian Rolf Steininger. In the conclusion to his influential and well-documented book about Stalin's March 1952 offer of German reunification in return for

German neutrality, Steininger quoted a 1984 West German poll according to which fifty-three per cent of those asked were in favour of reunification in a 'bloc-free' Germany: 'a Germany,' Steininger wrote, 'such as Stalin offered in 1952'. As if the West Germany to which Stalin made his offer was the West Germany of 1984 — prosperous, stable, experienced in democracy, embedded in countless non-military structures of Western association and co-operation. Here the historian's task is to point out how different things then were.

Yet as one explores the putative alternatives of the 1940s and 1950s one sometimes feels that there is nothing new under the sun. It is remarkable how few arguments of the 1980s were not anticipated in some form — and often more eloquently and concisely — in the arguments of those earlier years. Writing in 1981, John Lewis Gaddis observed that, due to Washington's institutional amnesia, 'debates over the future of containment tend to be little more than reruns of those between George Kennan and Paul Nitze three decades ago.' *Mutatis mutandis*, much the same might be said of European debates about disengagement.

When a Christian Democrat member of the Bundestag, Bernhard Friedmann, emerged in 1987 with a proposal to put the German question on the superpowers' disarmament agenda, one of West Germany's most experienced retired ambassadors, Wilhelm Grewe, exploded in a letter to the *Frankfurter Allgemeine Zeitung*:

> How can one explain that an active politician . . . should put on paper reflections, questions and proposals without noticing that everything, but *everything* that he says, has already been said, written, proclaimed, doubted, answered countless times in the course of the last forty years — and then put aside for the time being as unreal, utopian and impractical?'

Of course we cannot here begin to explore all those historical 'ifs'. Yet it is essential to bear in mind the questions that the Yalta shorthand begs. Even if the conclusion of such an exploration were to be that, indeed, there were no real 'missed opportunities', that already in 1945 the division of Europe was as near inevitable as anything ever is in human history, it would still clearly be true that the way in which the division was completed, sealed and acknowledged, between 1945 and 1961, must have shaped the nature of the division and the way in which the division was subsequently regarded.

A unique divide

'The United States and its allies have always insisted,' the US Secretary of State, George Shultz, said before an East European tour in 1985, 'that the division of Europe is artificial, unnatural and illegitimate.' As an historical statement this is seriously open to question. There had been times since 1945 when the United States' 'insistence' on this point was less than audible, and it was more as a critic than as an ally of the United States that Charles de Gaulle insisted on Europe 'from the Atlantic to the Urals'. But if 'always' is taken to mean 'for a few years' — a fairly usual meaning of 'always' in politics — then the assertion was true. As we have already observed, by 1985 some version of this formula had become a staple ingredient of Western rhetoric. But what on earth did it mean?

If the division of Europe was 'unnatural' then what was Europe's natural state? Unity? If yes, in what form? Or was it rather — and more plausibly — that this particular division was unnatural as compared with other past or putative forms of division: for example, the 'Westphalia' division, the 'Vienna' division, the 'Versailles' division, the division into multi-national empires or the division into sovereign nation-states, each enjoying government of the people by the people for the people? Even if the last is what was meant, one is bound to say that Europe has never been natural yet.

The objection is not a frivolous one. While a Pole, a Hungarian, a Czech, a German and an American might all have heartily assented to the proposition that the division of Europe was 'unnatural', each would have meant something different by it. An older German, for example, might have taken this to mean that the division of the German nation into more than one state was unnatural. A younger West German might have regarded as the most unnatural thing the presence of American nuclear missiles on German soil.

And what would a Pole, Hungarian or Czech have meant by this proposition? Probably, some variant or combination of the following: what was 'unnatural' was that he as an individual, his society and/or his nation were denied certain rights, freedoms, opportunities and/or powers that individuals, societies and nations enjoyed elsewhere (chiefly, in 'the West', meaning essentially Western Europe and North America) and/or that his compatriots, his society and his nation had enjoyed — or were fondly believed to have enjoyed — in the past. There were thus two fundamental reference points: the real or imagined present-day West, on the one hand, the real or imagined past on the other. Different people would stress different aspects and use different vocabularies. One Polish acquaintance would use the traditional imagery of romantic nationalism, another, concepts from Hegel. One Hungarian would stress the violation of individual human and civil rights as defined in Anglo-American political thought, and find his model for a natural and truly European order in the (West) European Community. Another would consider that Europe fell from its natural state with the Treaty of Trianon.

Plainly, this division of Europe was not easy to define. And plainly it changed over time. Relations between the governments and peoples of, say,

Hungary and Austria, were not the same in 1988 as they were in 1968. Nonetheless, a rudimentary working definition — a rough sketch map — is important for our purpose.

Many attempts have been made to correlate this division with earlier and, it has sometimes been said, deeper or underlying divisions of Europe, starting with the *limes* of the Roman empire. The boundaries of the original European Community (or strictly, European Communities) of six member-states can be shown to correspond quite closely to those of Charlemagne's empire in the year 814. Several economic historians have argued that the lands to the east of the River Elbe took a different, and tendentially more 'backward' course of economic development from the sixteenth century onward. The cautious empiricist will note signal exceptions on both sides of such boldly drawn lines: with, for example, developed Silesia and Bohemia to the east, and less developed Spain and Portugal to the west. Moreover, one can point to what are arguably even deeper lines of division — such as that between Western and Eastern Christianity — running far to the east of the Yalta line.

Whatever the validity of these deeper correlations, this division of Europe was distinguished from — and at least arguably more 'artificial' and 'illegitimate' than — earlier divisions of Europe, by virtue of its historical arbitrariness, its absoluteness, the asymmetrical roles of partly extra-European, nuclear-armed superpowers, and the congruence of military, political and economic differences.

Many border lines in European history have been drawn arbitrarily, but few more so than those of which the last details were finally agreed by the Soviet representatives in the so-called European Advisory Commission on 13 August 1945, and which became the Berlin Wall on 13 August 1961. Frontiers have always divided peoples, but no frontier in modern European history has divided peoples as completely as did those between Eastern and Western Europe at their most impenetrable. The cliché once expressed a truth: these frontiers were like an 'iron curtain'. While the movement of people between Eastern and Western Europe did increase as the iron curtain grew more permeable, this was as nothing compared with the increased movement of people within each part of Europe.

Both West and East European states depended, in ways they had not before 1945, on partly extra-European, nuclear-armed superpowers. But the westward and eastward dependencies were far from symmetrical. East European states depended on their immediate continental neighbour; West European states depended on a power removed from them by several thousand miles of ocean. France and Britain had their own nuclear weapons; no East European state did. Nato defended West European states against a real or imagined Soviet threat; the Warsaw Pact defended East European states against a real or imagined Western threat, but above all against their own peoples.

West European states had a larger combined population than the United States; East European states, taken all together, had less than half the population of the Soviet Union. According to Western specialists, what the Soviet Union took out of the East European economies in the first decade after 1945 was roughly equivalent to what the United States put in to West European economies through Marshall Aid. Comecon and the European Community were no less asymmetrical. The former included the superpower, the latter did not. The EC was increasingly a genuine common market; Comecon never was.

Most East European states had been poorer than most West European states before the war. Most East European states were poorer than most West European states at the beginning of the 1980s. Despite the indubitable fact of industrial development in Eastern Europe since the war, most of these countries' relative economic position vis-à-vis Western Europe had not significantly improved. In some cases — notably that of East Germany — it had actually worsened, and in all cases it threatened to worsen still further. Although the statistics in this field were even more treacherous than usual, the economic gap between East and West in Europe, as experienced in everyday life, was plainly visible in the figures for the provision of telephones or car-ownership.

In the internal orders of the European states there had also been asymmetrical developments. At Stalin's death, East European states were clearly more like each other, more closely integrated (at least formally) both with each other and with the 'protecting' superpower, than were those of Western Europe. Since that time, however, East European states had tended to diverge whereas West European states tended to converge. By the beginning of the 1980s, virtually all the states of Western Europe were combined in or closely associated with an historically unprecedented form of European Community, to which they had voluntarily sacrificed part of their sovereignty. Whereas for much of the post-war period several of them had been dictatorships (Spain, Portugal) all of them were now liberal (or 'bourgeois' or 'capitalist') democracies. In their internal political, economic and legal orders they were at once increasingly alike and increasingly interdependent. If they were economically and politically more dependent on each other they were also less dependent on the United States. The one — signal — exception to this rule was defence.

East European states, by contrast, had diverged not only from the Soviet model but also from each other. Although on paper their political systems might still look very similar, in practice their real internal political and economic structures had become increasingly diverse, complex and difficult to categorise. No single term — 'totalitarianism', 'authoritarianism', 'state capitalism', 'really existing socialism', 'dictatorship over needs' — was adequate to embracing this diversity and complexity. With apologies to William Empson, one might describe the East European states in the

1980s as six types of ambiguity. If West European states had voluntarily surrendered part of their sovereignty to the European Community, East European states had generally attempted to claw back some of the sovereignty which they involuntarily surrendered in the 1940s and 1950s. While these states were to a significant degree economically dependent on each other, they had not made any major virtue out of this necessity. By contrast with Western Europe, their own bi- and multilateral associations in the region had not made them, individually or collectively, economically or politically, less dependent on their superpower 'protector'.

Things were even less clear at the level of society and culture. Was there ever such a thing as an 'East European society'? Did East German society have more in common with Polish society than with West German society? Or Hungarian with Romanian rather than Austrian? Was there any meaningful sense in which one could talk of an individual man or woman as 'an East European' as opposed to 'a West European'? When Czech, Hungarian and Polish intellectuals initiated a cultural-historical revival of the idea of 'Central Europe' in the early 1980s, they aimed to challenge precisely these simplistic dichotomies.

Nonetheless, for all this complexity and diversity, and for all the relative softening over time, there was still, even in the 1980s, one great divide. Every ordinary first-time visitor in either direction could tell you that. There was a reality of 'Eastern Europe', a reality of 'Western Europe', and you knew when you had crossed the line. You knew it at the line. Even if you did not actually see the 'iron curtain' with barbed wire and guard dogs, there were — coming from the West — the stricter border controls, the politically determined import restrictions, the compulsory exchange of hard currency. Beyond the line, there were a hundred aspects of everyday life, large and small — the cheap paper forms in quadruplicate, the queues, the newspapers, the smell of the air — in which, for all the differences, Budapest was still more like Warsaw or even Bucharest than it was like Vienna. And that was even more true as you penetrated into the individual's experience, not only in politics and direct relations with the state, but at the workplace, in hospital, at school or university.

In historical perspective, what was most remarkable about this divide was the congruence of military, political, economic, ideological, cultural and social differences. To be sure, after the Peace of Augsburg the rule in Central Europe was *cuius regio, eius religio*. But under 'Yalta' it was much more than just *religio*. Never before had so much flowed from so little. If you happened to live at the bottom end of the Friedrichstrasse in central Berlin, you got liberal democracy, the Americans, the European Community, the Costa del Sol, the Volkswagen and McDonald's. Your brother, who lived three blocks up the street, got communism, the Russians, Comecon, the Black Sea, the Trabant and *soljanka*.

One final remark is necessary to complete this rudimentary sketch map.

The description of Europe as being cut in half by one great divide should not obscure an important eastern sub-divide. Without venturing into the inspissated jungle of cultural-historical argument about the eastern frontiers of Europe, whether Russia is part of Europe, or where historic Central Europe begins and ends, let it simply be stated that there were major parts of the Soviet Union — for example, the Baltic republics — which were historically and culturally European. Those parts of Europe, or elements of 'Europeanness', inside the Soviet Union were, however, in a different political position from, say, Hungary or Czechoslovakia. Although their fundamental aspirations might be the same, their possibilities for realising them were not.

For the period covered in the main part of this book — until 1989–90 — it is meaningful to talk of 'the Soviet Union' as one thing, and of 'Eastern Europe' as another. This political 'Eastern Europe' may briefly be defined as those parts of historic Central, East Central and South Eastern Europe which in the 1940s and 1950s were organised into party-states on the Soviet model, with limited sovereignty, closely tied to the Soviet Union by public and secret arrangements, and incorporated into Comecon and the Warsaw Pact.

Here then is what we mean by the 'Yalta' division of Europe: distinguished from previous divisions of Europe by its historical arbitrariness, its absoluteness, the asymmetrical roles of partly extra-European, nuclear-armed superpowers, and the congruence of military, political and economic differences.

Healing?

What would it mean to 'overcome' this division? What, to use more emotive words, was to be understood by the 'restoration', 'reunification' or 'healing' of Europe? It will already be apparent that very different answers could be — and were — offered to these questions. American policymakers suggested that the healing of Europe meant ending communism in Eastern Europe while preserving Nato in Western Europe. Soviet policymakers suggested ending Nato while preserving communism.

Clearly, overcoming the division had an external and an internal aspect. The external aspect, concerning relations between Western and Eastern Europe, had two main dimensions. First, there was the relationship between Western and Eastern states, and perhaps between Western and Eastern groupings of states such as the OECD, the European Community and Comecon. Secondly, there was the relationship between peoples and between individual people: possibilities of travel, emigration, family reunification, cultural, academic, commercial or technological exchanges, and so forth. The internal aspect concerned relations inside the two parts, and this might also be said to have two dimensions. Firstly, there were the relationships of states with their nuclear-armed superpower and with other states in their own part. Secondly, there were the relationships of states to their own societies and to their own citizens.

Even if the basic terms of this crude outline were accepted by most West and East European participants in the debates of the 1980s, very different emphases were placed, and radically divergent accounts were given of the connections between different points on the agenda. Thus it was, for example, a matter of the hottest dispute, how much and what change was needed in Western Europe as against how much and what change in Eastern Europe, and what the causal relationship might be between the one and the other. With a few exceptions, even those who saw a deep symmetry between the situation of Western and Eastern Europe within their respective 'blocs' would have agreed that, however imperfect the relations between state and society might be in Western Europe, these relations were worse in Eastern Europe (some would have said 'in degree', most 'in kind'), and that in this regard there was, to put it mildly, more need for change in Eastern than in Western Europe.

Many politicians and commentators in Western Europe did, however, maintain that the position of West European states vis-à-vis the United States was in important respects comparable to the position of East European states vis-à-vis the Soviet Union; that the more independent West European states became from the United States, the more independent East European states might become from the Soviet Union; and that these states, being more independent, would then better be able to satisfy the aspirations of their societies for more freedom, respect for human rights, contacts with Western Europe and so forth, thus 'restoring Europe' internally as well as externally.

Of course this argument came in many variants, from the exaggerated and crudely deterministic version offered by parts of the peace movement and the Greens in the early 1980s to the cautious and statesmanlike German Gaullism of ex-Chancellor Helmut Schmidt. Yet even Schmidt went so far as to say (in 1986) that 'in the second half of the 1980s the extent of Western Europe's standing up for itself is, for West Europeans *and for East Europeans* the measure of Europe's standing up for itself overall' [author's italics].

Independent intellectuals and opposition activists in Eastern Europe, by contrast, tended to argue the case from the other end. East European states, they said, could only be more self-reliant and peaceful partners for Western Europe when they could rely on the support of their own societies. The less these states could depend on their own populations, the more they would have to depend on the Soviet Union. And they could only rely on the support of their own societies when they showed more respect for human rights and popular aspirations.

Since this debate was initially couched in terms of peace rather than European unification, these East Europeans said: Europe has not been at peace since 1945, it has only been in a state of 'non-war', because the countries of Eastern Europe have not enjoyed that 'internal peace' which the countries of Western Europe have, by and large, enjoyed. 'Without internal peace,' wrote Václav Havel in 1985, 'that is, peace among citizens and between citizens and the state, there can be no guarantee of external peace.' And, echoing the reflections of Immanuel Kant nearly two centuries earlier, he went on: 'a state that ignores the will and the rights of its citizens can offer no guarantee that it will respect the will and the rights of other peoples, nations and states'. If West European peace activists said that peace — meaning, in the first place, nuclear disarmament in Western Europe — would bring more respect for human rights in Eastern Europe, East European oppositionists replied that only respect for human rights in Eastern Europe would bring that real condition of European peace in which it would be safe for Western Europe to disarm.

Here too we have simplified a complex argument. The contrasting positions reflected different interests as well as different analyses. Yet this controversy well illustrates the lack of neutral or common definitions. Even with an agreed diagnosis, doctors may propose widely different cures. Here they started with neither a common diagnosis of the sickness nor even a common definition of health.

I

German Answers

The divided centre

Germany was central to this European question in two senses. First, it was central because it was in the centre. There is a long line of German historians who have argued that the most distinctive features of German history, and particularly of German foreign policy, are primarily a consequence of Germany's geographical position without well-defined natural frontiers in the middle of Europe: the famous *Mittellage*. Germany, they say, is only to be understood as a 'land of the centre'. Yet Polish historians have observed that Poland is also a land without well-defined natural frontiers in the middle of Europe; and rather different consequences have flowed for the two countries from this similar, indeed shared, geographical position. Meanwhile Prague has vied with Warsaw and Berlin for the title of 'the heart of Europe'.

Nonetheless, Germany's geopolitical situation in 'Yalta' Europe was unique. No other country had the line between East and West running through its middle. Germany was the divided centre of a divided Europe. Berlin, Germany's once and future capital, was the divided centre of the divided centre.

The second sense in which Germany was central is closely related to this unique geopolitical dilemma, but far from merely determined by it. This is the centrality of Ostpolitik. It is no accident that Ostpolitik is one of relatively few German words to be used in the English language, alongside Weltanschauung, Angst and Schadenfreude. For if one examines the policies of the major Western powers towards Eastern Europe over the twenty years from 1969 to 1989, one soon finds that the policy of the Federal Republic was the most consistent, the most extensive and the most intensive. In relations with the Soviet Union, the United States self-evidently remained in a class of its own, at least until Gorbachev's visit to Bonn in June 1989. But in terms of direct action in Eastern Europe, the Federal Republic was already second to none in the 1980s.

In 1985-86, the then Charter 77 spokesman Jiří Dienstbier wrote a manuscript entitled 'Dreaming of Europe'. He wrote it in his spare time while working as a stoker, for, like many intellectuals who had resisted Gustáv Husák's so-called 'normalisation', he was prevented by the party-state authorities from obtaining any but menial employment. In the Preface to the 1991 German edition of this book, Dienstbier, now, incredibly, Czechoslovakia's Foreign Minister, recalled that as he looked around from his boiler-room in the mid-1980s to see how the dream goal of overcoming the Yalta division might be achieved, he 'found in the West only the positions of individuals and a single larger conception, Brandt's Ostpolitik, which reckoned with a Europe other than the one to which we had all accustomed ourselves during the Cold War'. We shall try to explore, in this book, how accurate that judgement was, in relation both to Brandt's Ostpolitik and to the concepts and policies of other states, governments, movements and individuals, in West and East. But that it looked this way to the intellectual stoker in Prague is itself revealing.

Before turning specifically to Ostpolitik, however, we must look briefly at the general terms and context of German answers to the European question. For no one offered more (or longer) diagnoses of the Yalta sickness than the Germans, and no one was more fertile in proposing cures.

Let us start with the end. What would be the healing or peaceful restoration of Europe? In the 1980s, one mainstream German answer was: the 'normalisation' of relations between Western and Eastern Europe. A notable early use of the term 'normalisation' in this context was in the Soviet Union's diplomatic note of 7 June 1955, proposing the opening of diplomatic relations with the Federal Republic. On his visit to Moscow in September 1955, Adenauer took up the word, at the same time firmly insisting that the division of Germany was 'abnormal'. An important Bundestag resolution of June 1961, based on a report by the Sudeten German Social Democrat, Wenzel Jaksch, called on the federal government 'to seize every available opportunity . . . to achieve a normalisation of relations between the Federal Republic and the East European states'.

Normalisation then became a central term of the social-liberal Ostpolitik of the early 1970s, which the Free Democrat Foreign Minister Walter Scheel described as 'nothing but the attempt at a political normalisation on the basis of the realities that we find here and now.' The term was then used in the Federal Republic's actual treaties with the Soviet Union, Poland and East Germany, the three most important of the so-called 'Eastern treaties'.

This story will be told in more detail below. The point here is simply that by the 1980s the word 'normalisation' had become a regular and central component of German responses to the European question. In a tirelessly repeated formula, West German politicians of all parties said that they wanted to change not the frontiers in Europe but the quality of frontiers in Europe. They wanted to rid the frontiers of their divisive character, to make them ever more permeable. The iron curtain should be turned into one of velvet, or even of lace. The crossing between East and West Germany should be as normal as that between West Germany and Holland. Relations between the Federal Republic and Poland should be as normal as relations between the Federal Republic and France.

This answer was, to use an old schoolteacher's phrase, good as far as it went. But it did not go very far. We may leave aside for the moment the fact that the very term 'normalisation' had a sinister ring for most people in East Central Europe, where it was used in this same period to describe the attempt to return a European society, by force, to Soviet norms: as in Czechoslovakia after 1968. This coincidence — and the relationship between the two kinds of 'normalisation' — is far from irrelevant to some problems in the Federal Republic's relations with those countries, but its significance can only be understood in context.

Immediately relevant, however, is the fact that, by the standard of relations between European states in the past, or by the standard of relations between most states in the world, the relations between the Federal Republic and the French Republic or the Kingdom of the Netherlands were, by the 1980s, very far from normal. They were quite abnormally good. The frontiers were abnormally open and the relations between peoples as well as governments were abnormally close. And the essential precondition for this was not merely the elementary will to reconciliation and co-operation on the part of governments and peoples, but also the basic compatibility of political, economic and social systems.

On reflection, therefore, this was to set a quite exceptionally high standard, since to achieve such an abnormal 'normality' would self-evidently require fundamental political change inside Eastern Europe. Yet at other times the achievement of 'normality' was measured, in German usage, against the exceptionally low standard of freedom of movement between the two German states. By this standard, relations between Austria and Hungary were already almost perfect in the mid-1980s, although at that time Hungary still had a fundamentally different political and economic system. The erratic standard of 'normality' is well illustrated by a passage in Helmut Schmidt's 1978 state of the nation address in which he suggested that the goal for the relationship between the two German states should be that 'gradually a situation of matter-of-course normality should be achieved, such as has so far been achieved for example in our relationship with the Polish People's Republic'. Normality?

European peace order

These ambiguities are still more apparent when one looks at the concept of a 'European peace order' (*Europäische Friedensordnung*). By the end of the 1960s, this phrase had been adopted by politicians of all the major parties as a common formula for the long-term goal of Ostpolitik. It seems to have appeared for the first time in the July 1957 Berlin Declaration of the Federal Republic and its Western allies, the United States, France and Britain. It was used fitfully, but with growing frequency, through the early 1960s, before being accorded prominence in the first government declaration of the 'Grand Coalition' of Christian and Social Democrats, in December 1966. It was then used repeatedly by both the Christian Democrat Chancellor, Kiesinger, and the Social Democrat Foreign Minister, Brandt. It was also taken up in Nato's December 1967 Harmel report, a text which German policymakers would cite religiously for more than two decades thereafter. Helmut Schmidt expresses a sentiment which many, if not all, leading West German policymakers would have endorsed, when he writes in his memoirs that this European peace order 'has seemed to me down all the years to be the most important thing'.

But what did it mean? Here again, there were many versions of the vision, most of them remaining at a high level of conceptual imprecision. Nonetheless, one may tentatively discern two different sorts of public definition, which relate to the broader debate about the healing of Europe. The first was indicated by Walter Scheel in a Bundestag debate in 1970. The objective of the new Ostpolitik, said Scheel, was to bring about a European order 'in which countries of different political orders and social systems are equally members'. The object was not a 'compromise' between liberal and communist orders, but co-operation between countries, organisations or communities with different social and political orders. 'Only thus can there be a European peace order which embraces all of Europe, and not, as some imagine, through "pulling over" one or other side into the political system of the one or the other.'

Seventeen years later, Scheel's successor as Foreign Minister and leader of the Free Democrats, Hans-Dietrich Genscher, declared in a reflective exposition of his foreign policy credo: 'The development is inexorably towards a European peace order, in which peoples, even in different social and state orders, can advance in peaceful competition and without fear of each other.' Writing in early 1988 about this process of knitting together Eastern and Western Europe, the grand old lady of West German liberal journalism, Marion Gräfin Dönhoff, added the following observation: 'last week influential politicians of various affiliations in Vienna assured me that their relations with Budapest are now better than in Austria-Hungary under the Monarchy. So the difference between the social systems need be no obstacle.'

The clearest, though also the most extreme statement of this version of the goal came from the Social Democrat Egon Bahr, one of the most fertile and influential practitioners, strategists and ideologists of Ostpolitik from the early 1960s to the late 1980s. In a little book entitled *Towards European*

Peace. A Response to Gorbachev, published in 1988, Bahr wrote that a system of collective security was the 'necessary structure of international law' for a European peace order. Such a system of collective security, which he suggested could be achieved by the end of the century, 'would be equivalent to European peace.' Although at one point he observed in passing that in this European peace 'the western principles of the Helsinki Final Act . . . would become binding in international law', its achievement was clearly envisaged prior to, and irrespective of, a change of the political system in Eastern Europe.

In this peace, Bahr wrote, the contradictions between East and West would remain 'to be historically resolved'. What the Soviet system might develop in conditions of guaranteed peace 'could be very exciting'. There would be a 'guaranteed peaceful political competition of systems and economic co-operation' for which a proper 'culture of dispute' should be developed. And, in perhaps the clearest statement, he wrote of 'growing co-operation in unchanged political structures. Abnormal normality.'

Now one cannot, of course, simply assume that such public statements reflect the sum total of the private hopes or intentions of the speaker or writer. That states and statesmen should disguise their real goals is hardly a novelty, and in most Western countries there is a continual debate about how loudly and explicitly governments should embrace the goal of political change inside other countries. In an interview in 1973, Egon Bahr quoted von Moltke to the effect that 'everything that one says must be true, but one must not say everything that is true'. 'That,' commented Bahr, 'also applies to politics.' How these public statements related to private intentions is therefore a question that we shall have to consider in more detail below. The point here is simply to sketch the publicly articulated vision.

The vision of a 'European peace order' publicly articulated by leading Christian Democrats in the 1980s made a sharp contrast. From the moment they came to power in 1982, Chancellor Kohl and his closest associates roundly asserted the centrality of the issue of freedom, not merely to the German question, on which they were vocal, but also to the European question, as I have defined it here. The Social Democrats in government had firmly and consistently maintained that the Federal Republic's Western ties in the European Community and Nato were the *sine qua non* of their Ostpolitik. But the Christian Democrats, returning to government, brought a strong public re-emphasis of shared Western values as well.

Indeed, these re-emphasised Western values took centre stage in the rhetoric of their Ostpolitik. People in Central and Eastern Europe, Chancellor Kohl declared simply in his 1984 state of the nation address, wanted to be free, as people in the Federal Republic were free: 'And therein lies the real problem of the German and European division, in the denial of freedom and self-determination for the people in Central and

Eastern Europe.' The European peace order, he said in his 1987 address, would be one in which 'the basic freedoms are realised, undivided and unlimited, for all the peoples of Europe . . .'

'The clear articulation of our own goals and values,' said a key figure in the Kohl Chancellery, Wolfgang Schäuble, 'also serves the predictability of relations [with communist states]. Concealment would more likely be understood as an attempt to deceive, and arouse mistrust.' In the same speech, in 1986, he made a distinction which could have come straight from the writings of independent intellectuals and opposition activists in Poland, Hungary, Czechoslovakia and, not least, the GDR. Talking of the ruling Socialist Unity Party in the GDR he said: 'To be sure, it verbally subordinates its policies to the priority of securing peace. But by "peace" it understands rather the absence of war than the free development of the citizen in a state which is also inwardly at peace.' And Chancellor Kohl might have been quoting the Polish Pope when he declared that 'Peace begins with respect for the absolute and unconditional dignity of every individual human being in all departments of their life.'

So these leading Christian Democrats' public vision of the 'European peace order' explicitly linked the issue of peace between East and West to the question of freedom inside Eastern Europe, marking the symbiotic relationship between external and internal peace, and thus at least implicitly accepting that reducing or overcoming the division of Europe was as much a matter of changing internal relations between state and society inside Eastern Europe as it was of changing external relations between East and West. Freedom is the precondition of unity, they tirelessly repeated, for Germany, but also for Europe. How far their practice reflected this theory is another question, which will also be addressed below.

Two questions or one?

The governments of centre-left and centre-right were at one, however, in proclaiming deep harmony, if not complete identity, between German and European interests. Chancellor Kohl echoed Chancellor Schmidt in observing that 'the division of Germany is simultaneously the division of Europe'. Foreign Minister Genscher said simply: 'the division of Germany is the division of our European continent'. To work by peaceful means for European unity is 'above all a matter for the Germans', said President von Weizsäcker. 'To overcome the division of Germany is simultaneously to overcome the division of Europe', wrote Chancellery Minister Wolfgang Schäuble, 'it is as important for Europe as it is for us Germans.' 'German foreign policy' was always and simultaneously 'European peace policy'. There was no contradiction at all between West European integration and Ostpolitik: each served the other. Ostpolitik, as Walter Scheel most plainly put it, was 'an expression of the identity of our interests with the interests of Europe'.

That the German and European questions were very closely related is obvious. That there was such a sublime harmony of interests is not. There are good reasons for subjecting these claims to a little closer examination. For a start, it is characteristic of most European nation-states in modern history that their representatives assert or assume a harmony, or even identity, between what they see as national interests and what they claim to be European interests. One could cite countless examples from France, Poland, Italy, Russia or Hungary over the last two centuries. It was Bismarck who observed that 'I have always found the word "Europe" in the mouths of those politicians who wanted from other powers something they did not dare to demand in their own name . . .' The all-European phenomenon acquires, however, a particular edge in the case of Germany.

To mention Hitler in this context may seem perverse. Yet it is remarkable to look again into Max Domarus's collection of Hitler's speeches and to find just how often and how eloquently Hitler spoke of Europe: of Europe at peace, of respect and equal rights for European neighbours, of 'European co-operation' and Franco-German reconciliation, and then again of peace and friendship. 'No man ever spoke with greater feeling of the horror and stupidity of war than Adolf Hitler,' wrote his biographer Alan Bullock. One might add: no one spoke more movingly of Europe. All of which is to say only this: that 'Europe' is one of those large words — like 'peace' — which have been so terribly abused in the twentieth century, that it should be a basic intellectual and moral requirement to use them not loosely, vaguely, or instrumentally, but sharply, precisely, and for themselves. Apart from that, any comparison with Hitler is not relevant.

A more relevant comparison is with Gustav Stresemann. Willy Brandt, Helmut Kohl and Hans-Dietrich Genscher themselves all either made or accepted the comparison of their policies with those of the foreign minister of the 1920s. Yet even in the case of Stresemann there was a strong element of using 'Europe' — both semantically and diplomatically — as a means to the achievement of national ends.

So also with Konrad Adenauer. Germany in 1945 was not only physically and morally degraded, it was also totally deprived of sovereignty. Adenauer's first task, the first task of anyone who aspired to the title of German statesman, was therefore, beside the physical and moral restoration, the recovery of sovereignty. The struggle to achieve, first the bare minimum of local self-government, then statehood in part of the nation, then sovereignty for that state (with important powers and prerogatives reserved to France, Britain and the United States), then a growing 'room for manoeuvre' for that sovereign state: this is a leitmotif of the history of the Federal Republic. It runs through all Chancellorships over four decades.

Now the first ladder out of the morass was marked 'Europe'. The conservative historian Michael Stürmer has put it thus: 'The only opportunity left to Germany [after 1945] was to play the Western game, to be the most European nation among the Europeans, and to translate Germany's geostrategic position into political negotiating power.' The Cold War turned Germany's position as the divided centre of the continent from a further liability into a partial asset — although only for the Germans in the Western zones of occupation.

For Adenauer, the enterprise of building Europe clearly had two sides. On the one hand, the Germans, whose capacity to steer their own course he sometimes doubted, were to be bound in to a larger European community, to which they might yield some of the traditional authority and powers of a nation-state. On the other hand, participation in a (West) European community was a way for (part of) Germany to recover such authority and powers. In many respects, West Germany immediately took the West European path. The 1948 Hague Congress on Europe was the first major international meeting where German representatives again took their seats as free and equal partners, democrats among democrats, Europeans among Europeans. The Council of Europe, which grew out of that meeting, was the first body in which the West German state became a full and equal member. The founding of the European Coal and Steel Community in 1951 proved, in the event, to be the first step towards building a political European Community through the pursuit of common commercial and economic policies. In 1952, the treaty which Adenauer hoped would mark the decisive breakthrough to sovereignty was umbilically linked to a treaty forming a European Defence Community. But although Franco-German reconciliation would later became a cornerstone of German policy, in 1954 the plan for a European Defence Community was defeated — in the French National Assembly.

The second ladder out of the morass was therefore marked 'Nato'. Although German membership of Nato was linked to membership of a so-called Western European Union, and with a special, unique commitment of British troops to serve in Germany, the essence of Nato was clearly the alliance with the United States. While Adenauer kept an open mind for all possible tactical and strategic variations, in the German interest, he nonetheless repeatedly insisted on West Germany's need of the United States to counterbalance the Soviet Union in the centre of Europe. For the very survival of the Federal Republic, he argued, the ties with the United States were more important even than those with France. While the renegotiated treaties of the autumn of 1954 were known as the Paris treaties, they linked the recovery of sovereignty and the commitment to a military alliance with the United States.

These Western treaties of the early 1950s were the first great leap on the (West) German path back to independence. The second great leap came twenty years later with the Eastern treaties of the early 1970s. The former enabled the Federal Republic to operate as an independent state in the West; the latter enabled it to operate as an independent state in the East.

One could write the history of Central Europe over the forty years from 1949 to 1989 as the story of attempts by European peoples to become once again the subjects rather than the objects of history. For Poles, Hungarians and Czechs this meant primarily the attempt to regain control over their own internal affairs, for to regain control over their external affairs was hardly to be dreamed of. It meant endeavouring to restore, by reform or revolution, what might be called 'internal sovereignty', with citizens becoming willing, participant and enfranchised subjects rather than un-willing, non-participant and disenfranchised objects of state policy. The key concept which Pope John Paul II used when discussing civic aspira-tions was that of '*podmiotowość*', inadequately translated as 'subjectness' or 'subjectivity', and meaning precisely the condition of being fully a subject rather than an object of history.

The majority of Germans were early given full control over their internal affairs, full 'internal sovereignty'. Like all citizens of liberal democracies, they had to work — sometimes even to struggle — to preserve and enhance this control. But the striving to become subject rather than object found its clearest expression in foreign policy: both in the struggle for external 'freedom of action' as a sovereign state and in deciding how to use that freedom. This is one of many ways in which the recent history of the Germans is at once very similar to and quite different from the recent history of other Central European peoples. The Pope said Solidarity was an expression of the Poles' 'subjectivity'. One might say that Ostpolitik was an expression of the Germans' 'subjectivity'.

This consistent and patient struggle for what Willy Brandt in his seminal government declaration of October 1969 called 'a more self-reliant German policy' required the support of allies and neighbours to an unusual degree. All major Western countries were increasingly interde-pendent in foreign policy (especially in foreign economic policy), and all major West European countries were specifically dependent on the United States for their defence. But West Germany had more ties than any. It had the residual dependencies resulting from defeat and occupation, and the new dependencies of the Cold War, including a direct dependence on the Western allies for the security of West Berlin, and, as a non-nuclear power on the front line of the Cold War, a special dependence on the nuclear-armed superpower to the West to counterbalance the nuclear-armed superpower to the East. At the same time it had the multifarious, voluntary ties and dependencies resulting from its attempt to rehabilitate itself in a larger West European, Atlantic and world community. Europe

was the first ladder out of the morass, but the ladder also became a fence
— as French politicians always intended that it should.

One of the oft-repeated formulae of West German politics was that
German unity could only be achieved with the 'understanding', 'agreement' or 'support' of Germany's neighbours. Like several other command-
ments of Ostpolitik, this combined a political with a moral message. The
implicit moral message was that it would be wrong for Germany to push
through reunification against the will of her neighbours. The political
message was that she hadn't a chance of doing so anyway. The moral and
the political messages were not, however, precisely congruent. For
example, in a somewhat unusual formulation, Chancellor Schmidt declared
in his 1979 state of the nation address that German unity was not to be
had 'without the assent of the East European peoples'. Yet if Moscow,
Washington, Paris and London agreed to German reunification, could
even a unanimous chorus of Poles, Hungarians, Czechs, Slovaks, Romanians, Bulgarians, Albanians, Slovenes, Serbs and Croats do anything at all
to prevent it?

Now clearly no other Western state was as directly interested as the
Federal Republic was in reducing or overcoming the division of Europe.
What is more, those West European countries that did express some
serious interest in reducing the division of Europe were not equally
interested in reducing the division of Germany. Helmut Schmidt writes in
his memoirs that when he became Chancellor in 1974 ' . . . there was
hardly a government in Europe which genuinely regretted the partition
of Germany. That was more the case in Washington or distant Peking.'
In sum: 'The world thus seemed to be quite content with the division
of Germany; illogically it was much less content with the division of
Europe.'

To rebuke the world for being illogical was marvellously characteristic
of Helmut Schmidt. It was also not entirely logical. In other contexts,
Schmidt himself, like Brandt before him, spoke with perfect understanding
of the fears that European neighbours might have of an united Germany
of more than seventy-five million people in the heart of Europe. 'We love
Germany so much that we are glad there are two of them,' as François
Mauriac had famously remarked. The attitude of Germany's European
neighbours, moreover, was shaped not merely by fears of Germany but
also by ties of tradition and affection with other countries. Was there
anything really illogical in Austrians caring more about the lot of Hungarians, or Frenchmen caring more about the lot of Poles than either might
about the lot of Germans?

To say that you could not overcome the division of Europe without
overcoming the division of Germany was, at first glance, iron logic. It was
like saying: the division of an apple is the division of the core. You cannot
have a united apple with a divided core. But Europe is not an apple. In

fact, logically or illogically, both possible variants of a German-European disjuncture — a united Germany in a divided Europe, and even a divided Germany in a united Europe — had at different times been envisaged, not merely in theory, but in the practice of major Western partners of the Federal Republic. There was a time in the 1950s when policymakers in Washington seriously discussed the 'policy of strength' somehow pulling the rest of Germany fully into the West: thus creating, at least temporarily, the variant of 'united Germany in divided Europe'. (The phrase was used in American State Department discussions.) The Gaullist vision of Europe from the Atlantic to the Urals, by contrast, came close to being one of a united Europe around a divided Germany. In general, France, although sporadically interested in overcoming the division of Europe, was also the Western power least interested in overcoming the division of Germany.

The relationship between the German and the European questions was thus extremely complex. They were two questions, but so long as the Federal Republic considered itself to have a basic national interest in overcoming the division of Germany, it had overwhelming national reasons for desiring that the two questions should be taken as one. The Federal Republic therefore wanted its Western neighbours and allies to be as concerned as possible about the European question, while at the same time building the German question into the centre of the European one. In notes for a conversation with de Gaulle in December 1966, Willy Brandt put it simply and eloquently: 'The trench that divides my country also divides Europe. Anyone who fills in that trench also helps my country. We have no other prospect than to overcome the division of Europe.' And twenty years later, Chancellery Minister Wolfgang Schäuble explained: 'Our chance lies in the fact that the division of Germany is simultaneously the division of Europe.'

The rhetorical assertion of sublime harmony between German and European interests was but the most obvious symptom of this national interest, and the simplest means to securing it. This involved at least one major ambiguity in the use of the word 'Europe'. For the phrase 'unifying Europe' was applied both to the process of integration inside the (West) European Community and to the larger enterprise of overcoming the division of Europe. It then became not merely obvious but tautologous to observe that European unification served the cause of European unification. Yet, in practice, the tension between further West European integration and the search for closer ties with Eastern Europe and the Soviet Union was a recurrent theme of German foreign policy debates. The Social Democrats under Kurt Schumacher attacked Adenauer's policy of Western integration for closing the door to the East, and specifically to national reunification. Franz Josef Strauss and others attacked Brandt and Scheel for neglecting the cause of West European integration in pursuit of what Strauss then described as the chimera of a greater Europe (*Grossraum Europa*). When in government, however, each party proclaimed the harmony of interests.

Yet, plainly, rhetoric alone would not suffice. 'The unity of the Germans,' said Willy Brandt in his January 1970 state of the nation address, 'depends ... not in the first place or solely on the wording of treaties, but rather on how far we can win other states as friends, not so much on Potsdam 1945 but much more on overcoming the division of Europe in the 1970s, the 1980s and, if it must be, in the 1990s, Ladies and Gentlemen.' And other states are not won as 'friends' by sweet words alone. In its own interest, the Federal Republic had not only to say but to do things that at least some other states or peoples felt to be in their interest too. But what things, and for which states or peoples?

Of course it would be ungenerous, and against the evidence of deeds as well as words, to imply that German policy-makers or opinion-formers did not have a large measure of disinterested, idealistic, historically informed and morally sensitive concern about the lot of those other Europeans who suffered most from the 'Yalta' division. Most certainly they did. The one by no means precludes the other. But on the evidence of their own authoritative statements, we are certainly obliged to ask how far what happened in the 1970s and 1980s was — to use a formula from the late 1960s — the Europeanisation of the German question, and how far the Germanisation of the European question.

Was Ostpolitik a European answer to the European question, a German answer to the European question, a European answer to the German question, or simply a German answer to the German question? And if, as the architects of Ostpolitik would immediately object, it was all of the above, then in what proportions?

The European interest

Not everything that is called European is, in fact, European, and not everything that is European is so called. The Europeanness of Ostpolitik may be asserted. It has yet to be proved. But how can it be proved or disproved? What are the criteria, and who the judges of Europeanness? One criterion has already been suggested: that of motives. A policy is European because those who practise or support it genuinely believe that they are acting for Europe. But this is a very weak and slippery criterion. For do we really understand even our own motives? And what if others think otherwise? 'Do not do unto others as you would they should do unto you,' said George Bernard Shaw. 'Their tastes may not be the same.'

A second approach would be to try and advance a clear definition of what is European, or in the European interest, and then measure various policies and approaches against this. Thus one could say, for example, that it is European to respect certain, explicitly specified, human and civil rights, protected by due process of law, while it is not European to repress or murder people because of their race, colour or creed. Plainly, such a definition is prescriptive rather than descriptive.

This procedure has the merit of taking the discussion into the sphere of rational argument. The meaning and implications of competing interpretations of Europeanness or the European interest can usefully be explored, and compared with other vital and closely related concepts such as the West, peace, or Thomas Mann's *Humanität*. But logic provides no tools for making a final decision between these rival claims. Assertions about what is European are not falsifiable. There is no philosophical essence of Europeanness. A Christian will mean one thing, an atheist another. There will be a Polish interpretation of the European interest, a French interpretation, and a German interpretation — indeed there will be several Polish, French and German interpretations.

Who decides? After the experience of European barbarism in this century, most inhabitants of Europe could probably now agree on a basic, minimum list of what is not European. But beyond this basic code of irreducible human rights, itself still breached in several European countries, there is a vast area of profound disagreement between people who consider themselves Europeans. How, if at all, are these differences to be resolved or reconciled?

The best answer we can come up with is: liberal democracy as an epistemological principle. Like individual men and women, so also individual states and nations differ. Their interests, perceptions, tastes and aspirations conflict. These differences and conflicts cannot be resolved — although they may be illuminated — by scientific enquiry. Nor can they ever be wholly reconciled. But in deciding between rival claims in any pluralistic community or society, the freely expressed wishes of the majority are a primary criterion of rightness. We do not say 'the majority is always right'. There are certain rights that every minority must always have. But the larger the majority, and the more clearly expressed its wishes, the greater is the burden on the minority to, at the very least, consider its position.

To apply this rough-and-ready criterion to the internal affairs of a state is already difficult. To apply it to international relations is even more so. For here there are at least three sorts of putative majority involved. There is the putative majority of states, where the relevant set of states may range in size from two to nearly two hundred, and the definition of the relevant set will itself be disputed (especially where the boundaries of states and nations do not coincide). There is the will of the majority in the state conducting the policy at issue. Last, but by no means least, there is the will of the majority in the state(s) directly affected by that policy.

Even in democratic Western Europe it was a real question how far the will of the majority was really translated into domestic, let alone into foreign policy. But what about Eastern Europe, where — until 1989 — neither the ballot box nor even the opinion survey came to our aid? There was real meaning in the statement 'Mrs Thatcher speaks for Britain', 'President Mitterrand speaks for France', and even 'Chancellor Kohl speaks for Germany' — much as many Britons, French and Germans would have disputed it. But who spoke for Czechoslovakia in the 1980s? Gustáv Husák or Václav Havel? And who for Poland? Wojciech Jaruzelski? Lech Wałęsa? The Pope?

Yet the fact that a criterion is difficult to apply does not make it less important. To adapt Churchill's famous remark about democracy: this is the worst possible criterion we have, apart from all the other criteria that have been tried from time to time. Thus, to apply it to our theme, if a head of government, a politician or a writer declares 'what we are doing, or propose to do, is in the European interest', but the majority of their European neighbours reply 'no, my friend, that is not in the European interest', then it is not in the European interest. The head of government, politician or writer may passionately believe that it is. He may have powerful arguments to support this belief. He may, he should, attempt to convince his neighbours by the force of these arguments. But if they remain unconvinced, then he must yield — or abandon the claim to be working for Europe. This is the stern criterion that we shall apply to German Ostpolitik.

II

Ostpolitik

Was there one?

Was there one German Ostpolitik? To judge by party-political debates in the Bundestag or the West German media, you might doubt it. Throughout the history of the Federal Republic, from the 1950s to the 1980s, critics inside successive governing coalitions as well as in opposition loudly maintained that the government had no Ostpolitik worthy of the name, that if it existed, it was not consistent, or that, even if it existed and was consistent, it was not in the German interest. This sound and fury demonstrated nothing more nor less than the centrality of Ostpolitik to West German politics. In no other major Western state was policy towards the Soviet Union, let alone that towards Eastern Europe, the subject of such constant attention. The general conduct of East-West relations might be a major issue in an American or French Presidential election, but nothing that any American or French politician said about this issue would be a statement about the future existence of the United States or the French Republic.

German arguments about Ostpolitik have been arguments about the future of Germany. Social Democrats in opposition to Adenauer's Ostpolitik (or lack of one) in the 1950s certainly believed this to be the case. So did Christian Democrats in opposition to the Eastern treaties in the early 1970s. And some Social Democrats and Greens in opposition claimed to believe it still, or again, in the 1980s.

One reason for the persistence of these party-political differences about Ostpolitik was simple. In the 1970s, the Federal Republic had, if one counted the Christian Social Union as a separate party, four political parties that won more than five per cent of the popular vote in federal elections and were therefore represented in the Bundestag. With the arrival of the Greens, who first entered the Bundestag in 1983, this rose to five. At any given moment, two or three of these parties would form a coalition government, and two or three would be in opposition. Each party therefore had to define itself, when in power, against its coalition partners as well as against the opposition and, when out of power, against its opposition rivals as well as against the government. Since there were several state elections every year, as well as the federal election every four years, these differences had constantly to be thrust before the noses of the electors.

If I was a Free Democrat, I had to keep distinguishing myself both from the Social Democrats in opposition and from my Christian Democrat partners in government. If I was a Social Democrat, I had to keep distinguishing myself from both the Free Democrats in government and the Greens in opposition. And so on. Hence one of the most characteristic terms of West German politics '*sich profilieren*', meaning roughly 'to establish your profile', and its derivatives, such as *Profilierungsbedarf* (the need to profile yourself) and *Profilneurose* (profile neurosis). Moreover, each of these parties contained any number of individual rival politicians, many of whom felt themselves particularly qualified to speak out on this or that: either because they were designated national party spokespersons, or in their capacity as heads or members of a state (*Land*) government (some of which came close to conducting their own miniature foreign policies), or simply as backbenchers. Ostpolitik, increasingly popular with the voters, was an attractive subject on which to make your mark. It is always easier to solve the problems of the world than to solve those of your own household.

In the history of Ostpolitik, personal, party-political and electoral motives are therefore constantly intertwined with national and international ones. This was true of Willy Brandt, especially while he was the Social Democrats' candidate for Chancellor in the 1960s. It was eminently true of Hans-Dietrich Genscher, whose statements and moves as Foreign Minister cannot possibly be interpreted without bearing in mind that he was also the leader of a small party which had constantly to struggle to enhance its 'profile' and hence its ability to surmount the five per cent hurdle in successive state and federal elections. It was true of Chancellor Kohl, who, to take an especially piquant example, reportedly had an aide lean on the East German authorities to delay the opening of the Brandenburg Gate at the end of 1989, so that he, rather than Hans-Dietrich Genscher, could get the main television footage and kudos — tele-kudos? — at the opening. Examples could be multiplied.

The major parties had, moreover, to reckon with particular constituencies which directly impinged on their conduct of Ostpolitik. The most important of these constituencies was undoubtedly the millions of Germans who fled or were expelled after the Second World War from their homes east of the Oder and Neisse rivers and south-east of the Erz mountains. In the early years of the Federal Republic, these refugees and expellees made up nearly one fifth of the new state's population. They were a formidable constraint on Konrad Adenauer's freedom of action in relations with the East. At the beginning of the 1960s, the umbrella organisation of the different regional groups of refugees and expellees, the Federation of Expellees, claimed three million members. Thirty years later it would still claim some two million members (although some of these were in fact the children of refugees and expellees, who, in an extraordinary provision, formally inherited 'expellee' status).

Even if the representativeness of some highly active leaders of the Federation of Expellees might seriously be questioned, they remained, even in the 1980s, a significant influence upon the policy of the Christian Democrats. They were a force inside the Christian Democratic Union itself. They were even more of a force inside the Christian Social Union, where Franz Josef Strauss liked to describe the Sudeten Germans as Bavaria's 'fourth tribe'. And they were a force because they could, explicitly or implicitly, threaten to divert their votes to a right-wing party such as the *Republikaner*, or simply to abstain from voting. Even with Germany's system of proportional representation, this two or three per cent of the vote could make a great difference. As we shall see, Chancellor Kohl's public prevarication on full recognition of the Oder-Neisse line is explicable only in relation to this constituency.

The Social Democrats, too, had to pay close attention to the expellees in the 1960s and 1970s. At least one expellee Social Democrat, the Sudeten German Wenzel Jaksch, actually played a notably constructive part in the early years of Ostpolitik. The defection to the Christian Democrats of a leading Social Democrat expellee member of the Bundestag, Herbert Hupka, over the Eastern treaties, helped to undermine the Brandt government's already small parliamentary majority in 1972. But altogether this constituency was not as important to the Social Democrats, and its importance to them diminished further over the 1970s.

The Social Democrats did, however, have to reckon very seriously in the 1980s with another constituency: that of the peace and ecological movements. If expellees could threaten, explicitly or implicitly, to abstain or to vote for the *Republikaner*, those active in the peace and ecological movements could threaten, explicitly or implicitly, to abstain or to vote for the Greens.

There was, in short, a whole domestic politics of Ostpolitik. Yet in the 1980s one increasingly had the impression of rather artificial attempts to suck the politician's nectar of controversy out of what was, in fact, the flower of consensus. This was particularly true of policy towards East Germany. An opposition's business is to oppose. But it is quite difficult to oppose a government for doing almost exactly what you yourself did while in office, and with more immediately visible success. The consensus on policy towards East Germany was in fact reflected in a February 1984 joint resolution of all the main parties in the Bundestag, with only the Greens voting against. The consensus was obviously less complete on other East-West issues, and particularly on defence and disarmament. Yet even here one often had the sense of distinctions without differences and mountains made out of molehills.

We need a 'security partnership' with the East, said the Social Democrats in the 1980s. Impossible, cried Eberhard Diepgen, then Christian Democrat governing mayor of Berlin; but what we could have is a 'security *Teilhaberschaft*'. 'Not to obscure the difference between *Teilhaberschaft* and partnership,' Diepgen solemnly declared in 1987, 'is a matter of openness, which we need between East and West, but also inside the West.' Clearly this is a vital difference. Impatiently we turn to our German-English dictionary and read: '*Teilhaberschaft*: . . . partnership.'

Not all the distinctions are as meretricious as this. Indeed, the precise terms in which German politicians and intellectuals described the Federal Republic's relationship with the East as opposed or compared to its relationship with the West mattered in and for themselves. It makes some difference whether I call a woman my wife, my girl-friend or my mistress. What makes more difference, however, is whether we are married (and to whom). But what matters far more than either of these considerations, the semantic or the legal, is how we actually behave to each other, and to others.

Now in terms of actual behaviour there can be no doubt about the continuity of West German government policy towards East Germany, Eastern Europe and the Soviet Union through the two decades from 1969 to 1989. A crucial test of this continuity was the transition from a social-liberal to a conservative-liberal coalition government in 1982-83. A measure of continuity was guaranteed by the fact that the Free Democrats not merely remained in power, but continued to hold the Foreign Ministry. The phrase 'hold the Foreign Ministry' is chosen advisedly, for Hans-Dietrich Genscher, having been Foreign Minister for eight years already, from 1974 to 1982, and remaining Foreign Minister for a further ten years, until 1992, had an extraordinary influence on the personnel and practices of the West German foreign service. And that was, of course, a very significant part of what people in Eastern Europe saw as Ostpolitik in practice, whatever Chancellors in Bonn might say in theory.

Yet the continuity of Ostpolitik across the change of government was more than just the continuity of Genscherism. As important was the extraordinary degree to which the Christian Democrats took over almost wholesale the policies and approaches that many (though not all) of them had attacked with notable acerbity in the early 1970s. Franz Josef Strauss furnished an example at once extreme and classical. No one had been more eloquent in denouncing the Eastern treaties. No one was now more eager to pick up the threads of friendly intercourse with the communist regimes in East Berlin and Moscow. Within less than a year of returning to power, he could boast of having personally orchestrated a government-guaranteed one billion DM loan to the GDR, on very favourable terms. In 1984, he helped arrange another credit of comparable size. As soon as Mikhail Gorbachev would invite him, he flew himself to Moscow, and few Western visitors were more fulsome in praise of their Soviet host.

We have observed already that the Western treaties of the early 1950s and the Eastern treaties of the early 1970s were two major steps in the external emancipation of the Federal Republic. (A third major step was thus, as it were, chronologically due in the early 1990s.) Each step was fiercely contested at the time, but then accepted by the major party which had opposed it. The Social Democrats' theoretical acceptance of Adenauer's western integration was spelled out by Herbert Wehner in June 1960, in a remarkable speech to the Bundestag which concluded with the words: 'Divided Germany . . . cannot abide an incurable enmity of Christian and Social Democrats . . .' Practical acceptance was then demonstrated by the Social Democrats in government after 1966.

The Christian Democrats' acceptance of Brandt's Ostpolitik is less easy to date precisely. It was a long, complex, not to say confused process. One might argue that theoretical acceptance was expressed already in the May 1972 'Joint Resolution' of all parties in the Bundestag in connection with the ratification of the Moscow and Warsaw treaties. This reaffirmed both the formal legal positions of the Federal Republic on the German question and the basic priorities of the Adenauerian integration of the Federal Republic into the West. Alternatively, one might argue that theoretical acceptance was only finally expressed in an encyclopaedic resolution of the Christian Democrats' June 1988 Wiesbaden party conference, snappily entitled 'Christian Democratic Perspectives on Germany-, Foreign-, Security-, Europe- and Development-policy.'

In between there were many smaller steps. Christian Democrats continued to criticise what they had seen as excessive haste and unnecessary concessions in the negotiation of the Eastern treaties. In 1975, they were the only major parliamentary party in Western Europe to vote against the Helsinki Final Act — something that they would live to regret. By the end of the 1970s, leading Christian Democrats would nonetheless advocate a policy of 'realistic' and 'illusion-free' détente, based on both the letter and, increasingly, the spirit of the Eastern treaties negotiated under Brandt and Scheel. '*Pacta sunt servanda*', Franz Josef Strauss had declared immediately after the ratification of the treaties, and the parties' interpretations of what it meant to keep those treaties gradually converged in the decade between 1972 and 1982.

There was, to be sure, still a significant change of rhetoric at the transition from social-liberal to conservative-liberal government. The new Chancellor brought a blunt neo-Adenauerian reaffirmation of the absolute priority of Western integration, on the one hand, and of the long-term commitment to reunification on the other. An insistence on the restatement of formal, legal positions on the German question was accompanied, as we have already observed, by a public reassertion of Western values, including individual liberty and national self-determination, as the basis of a lasting 'European peace order'. Yet if one looks at what the government actually did in its relations with East Germany, Eastern Europe and the Soviet Union, the continuity was overwhelming.

When Chancellor Kohl paid a long-delayed visit to Moscow in October 1988, one of the country's leading left-liberal commentators, Theo Sommer, was moved to write: 'And there is no break in the continuity of Bonn's Ostpolitik. As Brandt laid it down, and Schmidt played it in, so it is advanced by Kohl.' Earlier in the same year, Chancellor Kohl himself had declared: 'Despite all the party-political disputes of the last decades, we may speak in this connection, with pride, of "our policy".' In a review of the first volume of Helmut Schmidt's memoirs, Franz Josef Strauss observed that 'on the main lines [of West German foreign policy] there are no more differences between him and me.' In a speech to celebrate Willy Brandt's seventy-fifth birthday, President von Weizsäcker said that next to the 'reconciliation with the West, which Konrad Adenauer brought about', Brandt had placed the 'understanding with the East'. The latter did not supersede the former, however. 'Both parts have come together in an integrated whole, which since then has not seriously been put in question — a treasured common good.'

As the Federal Republic celebrated its fortieth birthday in May 1989 it was thus possible to state with confidence: there was *one* Ostpolitik of the Federal Republic of Germany. All the major parties represented in the West German parliament agreed on the main lines of this policy, although the Social Democrats wanted to build on the common foundations in a direction that was not at all agreed. Bonn governments had pursued this policy for two decades with a consistency rare among Western states. This alone seemed sufficient reason for most of Germany's neighbours, in East and West, to describe it as *German* Ostpolitik, much though the other German state might object to such a usage. Leading Bonn politicians themselves spoke of their foreign policy simply as 'German foreign policy', with no qualifying 'West' or 'Federal'. They often referred to their Ostpolitik as 'the German Ostpolitik' — a usage sanctified by *Duden*.

A further good reason for adopting this usage lay in the notion of national interest which informed the basic political consensus about Ostpolitik in Bonn. The concept of 'national interest' is complex even in relatively straightforward cases. It involves objective factors such as natural resources and frontiers, but is never wholly susceptible to objective definition. In Europe in the 1970s and 1980s, the concept was perhaps most simply and clearly applied in France, for here the interests of nation and state might be considered as virtually conterminous. But in Poland, for example, most people would certainly not have considered the interests of the Polish nation to be conterminous with those of the Polish People's Republic.

No case was more complex than that of Germany. What did a West German politician, diplomat or intellectual mean when he talked and thought — or talked without thinking, or thought without talking — about the national interest? Clearly a large part of this meaning had to be: the interests of this state, the Federal Republic. With many politicians an additional, far from trivial, sense was: the interests of his or her state, meaning Bavaria, Baden-Württemberg, Schleswig-Holstein or the Saarland. Yet politicians in divided Germany could not think simply in terms of the interests of the state, traditionally called *Staatsräson*, the German version of *raison d'état*. Virtually all had some larger sense of national interest (Josef Joffe called it *raison de nation*) which included, at a minimum, the interests of the more than sixteen million Germans living inside the frontiers of the German Democratic Republic. This sense was, however, often further extended to include the interests of those several million inhabitants of Eastern Europe and the Soviet Union, from the Banat to the Volga, who were Germans according to the somewhat curious definition in West Germany's Basic Law (see below, p. 234f). But then again, on an extraordinary range of issues this large concept of national interest came down in practice to the interests of one half of one city: West Berlin.

The concept was thus as many-layered as the language used to convey it. Citizens of the United Kingdom might talk of the nation and mean either the state — Britain — or one of four peoples — the English, the Scots, the Welsh or the Irish. On most issues of foreign policy, however, if a Scotsman or a Welshman talked of the 'national interest' he probably meant the interests of the one state — Britain. Germans had to distinguish between *Nation*, *Volk* and two states, between *Staatsnation* and *Kulturnation*, between interests of the nation, the state (Federal Republic), the states (Bavaria, Saarland etc) and the half-city-state (West Berlin). In practice, of course, no one could ever distinguish between all these senses and interests, so they came tangled together in various combinations and usages. That some larger notion of 'German interest' informed all mainstream West German approaches to Ostpolitik cannot, however, seriously be doubted.

In a word

Thus far we have discussed the modifiers — 'one', 'German' — but not the noun. What was Ostpolitik? 'A designation for the policy of the Federal Republic of Germany towards the states of the Warsaw Pact,' said *Meyers Grosses Universal Lexikon* in 1984. *Duden* (1980) had 'the (especially Federal

Republic of Germany): policy towards the socialist states of East Europe and Asia; the German Ostpolitik.' *Brockhaus-Wahrig* (1982) was more precise:

1. ⟨general⟩ policy towards Eastern countries
2.1. ⟨in broader sense⟩ the foreign policy of Western countries towards the East-block states
2.2. ⟨in narrower sense⟩ the policy of the Federal Republic of Germany towards the Soviet Union and its allied states in East and East Central Europe; the Bonn Ostpolitik.

These definitions rightly recognise the transferred usage of the term. For, as mentioned earlier, Ostpolitik has become an English word. *Langenscheidt*'s concise German–English dictionary says simply: '*Ostpolitik* ostpolitik'! *Chambers English Dictionary* (1988) defines this English word as 'the West German policy of establishing normal trade and diplomatic relations with the East European communist countries; any similar policy.' The Second Edition of the *Oxford English Dictionary* (1989) has (somewhat inaccurately): 'German policy towards Eastern Europe, associated mainly with the Federal Republic of Germany's cultivation of good relations with the Communist block during the 1960s, but applied also, by extension, to the policies of other Western countries regarding the East as a whole.'

The OED's first quotation comes from Terence Prittie's *Germany Divided* (1961). Prittie writes that the Russians 'will scarcely overlook Hitler's statement . . . "The goal of Ostpolitik is to open up an area of settlement for one hundred million Germans".' This somewhat disconcerting comment reminds us of earlier, less cosmopolitan usages of the term. Thus in Henry Picker's record of Hitler's *Table Talk* we read, for 31 March 1942: 'Today's German Ostpolitik — the boss remarked at supper, stimulated by a remark of Bormann's about Heinrich I — is without historical parallel.' Indeed.

In his 1971 Nobel Peace Prize address, Willy Brandt said he did not actually like the term 'Ostpolitik' as a label for his own policy, partly because it was poisoned by this earlier German usage. Yet it is striking that, as the dictionary definitions indicate, in German as in international usage, the term 'Ostpolitik', unlike, say, *Lebensraum*, or even *Mitteleuropa*, has been almost entirely disassociated from pre-1945 usage. In West Germany, 1945 was often referred to as the *Stunde Null* ('hour zero') and this it proves to be for the word Ostpolitik. But what, then, to use another favoured West German phrase, was the *Erste Stunde* ('hour one') of the new German Ostpolitik?

'Twenty-five years ago yesterday, on 9 September 1955, the German Ostpolitik began . . .' declared, on 10 September 1980, the outstanding Christian Democrat expert on foreign policy, Alois Mertes. He referred to

Konrad Adenauer's first trip to Moscow, and the opening of diplomatic relations with the Soviet Union. This was, of course, also a party-political statement. For Mertes thus insisted that the Ostpolitik was not, as Social Democrats and Free Democrats generally implied, their patent discovery and, so to speak, intellectual property. Other analysts have placed the milestone at the 13 August 1961, with the shock of the building of the Berlin Wall; others again, in December 1966, with the formation of the Grand Coalition of Christian and Social Democrats in Bonn, including Willy Brandt as Foreign Minister. The historical justification of these claims will be considered more closely below.

Yet whatever the historical reality, for most Germans, and certainly for most of Germany's neighbours, the term 'Ostpolitik' is inextricably associated with the man who said he did not like it. It was, as Jiří Dienstbier wrote from his Prague boiler-room, 'Brandt's Ostpolitik'. There was certainly *an* Ostpolitik of the Federal Republic before 1969. But *the* Ostpolitik means, in the first place, Chancellor Brandt and the social-liberal coalition from 1969. It means the negotiation of the whole complex of the Eastern treaties, and the titanic struggle to win their acceptance in the Bundestag and in the country at large. It means the election of November 1972, which became almost a plebiscite on Brandt's Ostpolitik. It means the hope-filled crowds at Erfurt shouting 'Willy! Willy!', on Brandt's first official visit to East Germany in March 1970. It means Willy Brandt falling to his knees in Warsaw before the monument to the heroes of the ghetto uprising: one of the great symbolic moments of post-war European history. It means the policies of 'normalisation' and the pursuit of a 'European peace order' based on the full diplomatic recognition of the sovereignty and existing frontiers of East European states, and the virtually full recognition of East Germany as an independent state.

In the second half of the 1960s the policy initiated by the Grand Coalition was called the 'new' Ostpolitik, but by the 1980s the adjective 'new' had been silently absorbed into the noun. No serious analyst would deny that major elements of the thinking behind Brandt's 'new' Ostpolitik were present already in the early to mid-1960s, and even in the late 1950s. What Bonn governments did after 1969 cannot be understood without knowing what they tried to do before 1969. Yet for all that, the simple statement can be made: the child German Ostpolitik came into the world in the years 1969–72. The success had many fathers, but the midwives were definitely called Willy Brandt and Walter Scheel.

Ostpolitik was born as the German version of détente. Ostpolitik may therefore also be described as détente policy: *Entspannungspolitik*. Indeed so closely associated is the term Ostpolitik with the years 1969 to 1972, and so important is the notion of *Entspannung* (literally 'relaxation') to an understanding of German policy, that one is almost tempted to use the term *Entspannungspolitik* rather than Ostpolitik to describe our theme. But unlike the word Ostpolitik, the hectasyllabic *Entspannungspolitik* has not made a great international career.

Moreover, just because it is so central, the notion of *Entspannung* is also imprecise and controversial. The word *Entspannung* was used already by Konrad Adenauer in the early 1950s, before de Gaulle had popularised its precise dictionary equivalent *détente*, and well before Americans had turned the French word into an English one. In the 1960s, and in subsequent German usage, it had to serve both as a description of other states' policies of détente, and as a prescription for diverse German versions of détente, which, however, were themselves heavily influenced by the French and American versions that the term was also used to describe. In the early 1970s, it seemed to acquire a clear meaning: *Entspannungspolitik* = (new) Ostpolitik. But already in 1975 the newly arrived Foreign Minister, Hans-Dietrich Genscher, felt it necessary to qualify the noun-prescriptive *Entspannungspolitik* with the adjective 'realistic'.

In West Germany, as in much of the West, the Soviet invasion of Afghanistan, the Polish crisis, and the so-called 'second cold war' between the Reagan administration and the Brezhnev-Andropov-Chernenko leaderships, were said to have spelt an 'end to détente' and even 'the failure of *Entspannungspolitik*'. In a Joint Declaration at the end of Brezhnev's visit to Bonn in 1978, the word *Entspannung* appeared seven times in two pages. In the Kohl-Genscher government's May 1983 'Programme of Renewal', the word *Entspannung* did not appear once. But by the late 1980s it was back again. In an official government documentation of 'The Ostpolitik of the Federal Government', published in 1986, this Ostpolitik was described as a 'realistic and illusion-free *Entspannungspolitik*'.

In sticking to the simpler, internationally recognised term 'Ostpolitik', one should nonetheless keep in mind those intimate and formative ties with the notion of détente in general, and the social-liberal version of détente in particular.

One further caveat is due. In official Bonn usage, a distinction was made between Ostpolitik and Deutschlandpolitik. Ostpolitik was held to denote policy towards Eastern Europe (*Osteuropapolitik*) and the Soviet Union (formerly *Russlandpolitik*) whereas Deutschlandpolitik meant policy towards East Germany (occasionally described simply as *DDR-Politik*) and Berlin, although it also included the Federal Republic's political-theological approach to the whole German question, the unresolved legal-symbolic-political issues arising out of the post-war settlement, the lack of a peace treaty with Germany, and so forth.

The division between Ostpolitik and Deutschlandpolitik was, however, very far from clear. It was unclear because a quarter of what was once Germany was now Poland, or, in the case of the area around Kaliningrad (formerly Königsberg), the Soviet Union. Such crucial issues of *Osteuropapolitik* as the recognition of the Oder-Neisse line, or the status of the remaining German minorities, were thus always and simultaneously issues of Deutschlandpolitik. Secondly, the distinction was unclear because, as we shall see, the concerns of Deutschlandpolitik in the narrower sense remained absolutely central to the whole Ostpolitik. You could not begin to understand the latter without looking at the former. Indeed, one of the salient features of Ostpolitik was precisely that it attempted to integrate into one seamless whole the three areas, Deutschlandpolitik, *Osteuropapolitik* and *Russlandpolitik*.

The term 'Ostpolitik' is therefore used here — as in fact it was often used even in Bonn — to denote all three areas of policy, and the attempt to combine them in one integrated strategy. At the same time, one cannot entirely overlook the distinction, however imprecise. Whereas Soviet and East European policy were clearly regarded as foreign policy, Deutschlandpolitik was treated in Bonn as half-domestic policy. West German leaders repeatedly emphasised that for them East Germany 'could not be a foreign country'.

The distinction was also enshrined in the policymaking process. In the 1950s and 1960s, Deutschlandpolitik, as well as being a central concern of the Chancellery, was the business of a separate ministry, the Ministry for All-German Questions. With the recognition of the GDR in the early 1970s, operative policy towards the GDR came under the direct control of the Chancellery, although there was still significant input from what was now (in 1969) curiously re-named the Ministry for Intra-German Relations and from the Foreign Ministry, as well as from other Ministries on specific subjects. The Federal Republic's 'Permanent Representative' in East Berlin reported directly to the Chancellery, but had to operate within this complex political-bureaucratic geometry. A crucial part was, however, played by informal East German emissaries, direct correspondence and telephone conversations between Erich Honecker and successive Chancellors, as well as similar contacts with other key West German figures such as the Social Democrats' 'Uncle' Herbert Wehner, and the Bavarian premier Franz Josef Strauss.

Soviet and East European policy was, as you would expect, the direct responsibility of the Foreign Ministry. Yet because of the Chancellor's overall responsibility for the main lines of foreign policy — the *Richtlinienkompetenz* laid down in theory by Article 65 of the Basic Law, and in practice by Konrad Adenauer — and because of the crucial permissive function of Soviet and East European policy for the pursuit of Deutschlandpolitik, the Federal Chancellery played a very important part here too. In the record of bilateral relations with the Soviet Union and East European states, the role of the Chancellor and his advisers continued to be crucial. Chancellors from Adenauer to Kohl also used their own unofficial intermediaries and 'back channels' to cultivate direct relations with Soviet and East European leaders.

As the Foreign Ministry had a department for matters concerning Berlin and Germany as a whole, jealously watching the development of Deutschlandpolitik, and not accidentally a school for diplomatic high fliers, so the Federal Chancellery had its own department for foreign affairs, closely observing the conduct of the Foreign Ministry. Naturally enough, the relationship could often be tense. When Egon Bahr moved from the Foreign Ministry to the Chancellery in 1969, the State Secretary of the Foreign Ministry, Ferdinand Duckwitz jokingly observed: 'so now we are setting you down behind enemy lines, in the Chancellery.'

Such rivalries are, of course, nothing peculiar to Germany. One thinks of the tension between National Security Adviser and Secretary of State in the United States, between President and Prime Minister in France, or even between No. 10 Downing Street and the Foreign Office in Britain. What was peculiar to West Germany, however, was the coincidence of the bureaucratic division with a party-political one. In the Grand Coalition, the Christian Democrat Chancellor Kiesinger lived in uneasy *cohabitation* with the Social Democrat Foreign Minister Brandt. After 1969, a Free Democrat held the Foreign Ministry, with a Social or Christian Democrat as Chancellor. As a result, many of the much-publicised differences between Chancellor and Foreign Minister were those of politicians competing to 'win profile', or trimming to their own particular constituencies, rather than differing on issues of substance. By comparison with most other Western states, the West German political process nonetheless secured a high degree of consistency and continuity in Ostpolitik, not least because the same people dealt with the same issues over very long periods, both in the ministries and in the political parties. There was an important contrast here with France, and even more with the United States.

The task of describing this single, consistent, increasingly consensual German Ostpolitik is, however, complicated by another, more general problem. For towards the end of the twentieth century, foreign policy is not what it was. It is no longer the exclusive domain of nation-states. For most European states, and for the Federal Republic more than any, foreign policy was increasingly a matter of working through multilateral institutions. It was a jungle of acronyms: Nato and WEU for security policy; EC, G7, GATT, CoCom, IMF and World Bank for financial and economic policy; the CSCE ('Helsinki process') for almost everything else. In addition, there was the multilateral co-ordination of national foreign policies, in Nato and through the mechanism of European Political Co-operation between the member states of the European Community. All this greatly complicates the life of the diplomat — and of the analyst.

For if we wish to compare the Soviet and East European policy of the Federal Republic with, say, those of France, Britain, or the United States, we have to consider at least four distinct although intersecting planes. First, there is the area in which these states pursue common goals or interests through common instruments (Nato, EC, CoCom etc). Secondly, there are areas in which these states pursue common goals or interests through separate instruments: for example, through their own bilateral relations with this or that East European country. Thirdly, there are areas in which these states pursue different goals or interests through common instruments: or more precisely, through attempting to direct the common instruments in their own direction. Finally, there are the areas in which these states pursue different goals or interests through separate instruments.

The last-mentioned are the most obvious and easily identified differences. But in the 1970s and 1980s, with the progressive 'multilateralisation' of Western foreign policy, the third area became ever more important. Increasingly, differences between the major West European powers were articulated in a complex, political-bureaucratic negotiation of a supposedly common policy, rather than by direct disagreement or simply by going separate ways. The most obvious example in the 1980s was arms control, where specific German interests played a crucial role in the formation of Western positions. One might talk, in this context, of indirect Ostpolitik. This particular kind of difference is, however, especially difficult for the analyst to identify precisely — let alone to trace through the day-to-day rounds of multilateral *engrenage*.

The difficulty is increased by what Hans-Peter Schwarz has described as a hallmark of West German foreign policy: 'an insatiable striving after international harmony on all sides'. This 'harmonisation need' (*Harmonisierungsbedürfnis*), as Schwarz neatly labels it, may to some extent be characteristic of all modern, liberal industrial states, and particularly of those 'trading states' — such as Germany and Japan — whose prosperity depends to an unusual degree on keeping good relations with a wide range of trading partners. But beyond this, certain specific German reasons may be suggested.

One might, for example, regard this as a particular emanation of that general yearning for synthesis which Ralf Dahrendorf and others have argued is characteristic of German political thought as a whole. Schwarz himself stresses a more recent cause. Having by 1945 become enemies of almost everybody, he says, the Germans after 1945 felt an overwhelming need to try to be friends with almost everybody. This psychological explanation can also be expressed in terms of political thought. If the Germany that reached for world power in the first half of the twentieth century was acting (or justifying its acts) on a Social Darwinian understanding of international society, then West Germany in the second half of the twentieth century seemed at times to have gone to another extreme, with an almost utopian vision of international society. In the early twentieth century, the German left used to sing 'You must rule and win,/ Or serve and lose,/ Suffer or triumph,/ Be the anvil or the hammer.' (The words are Goethe's). In the late twentieth century, the (West) German left seemed at times to be reaching for an understanding of politics in which there were simply no hammers at all.

The vision of eternal peace, friendship and harmony, itself most power-fully articulated by German philosophers, was rejected by the historian Heinrich von Treitschke in the 1870s as an 'unmanly dream'. Seeing where manly dreams had led, many Germans in the 1970s re-embraced the older dream of eternal harmony. Here was, so to speak, the negation of Treitschke's negation.

It has also been suggested that this yearning for synthesis may partly result from Germany's position as a 'land of the centre', between East and West. This position, it is suggested, led Germans into the temptation of believing that they could interpret East to West, and West to East, while themselves combining in synthesis the best of both worlds. What is clearly true is that Germany's position as the divided centre of a divided continent after 1945 produced an acute objective need to try and harmonise ties with Eastern and Western partners, as well as a further temptation to see Germany's role, as the Christian Democrat Jakob Kaiser put it in 1947, not in the politics of 'either/or' but in those of *sowohl-als-auch* (roughly: as-well-as-and).

Whatever the precise combination of ingredients, this 'harmonisation need' was a hallmark of German foreign policy in this period. It resulted, as we have seen already, in a constant conflation of German and European or German and Western interests. Thus, for example, West German policymakers never tired of citing Nato's 1967 Harmel report as the bible of East-West relations. Here, they said, was a common definition of common goals to be realised through common instruments. But at least one reason why German policymakers so often cited the Harmel report is that it was a document which placed the division of Germany at the centre of Western concerns. Moreover, coherent as the Harmel concept of a 'double-track' of defence and détente might be, both defence and détente could be variously defined.

In the public presentation of West German foreign policy, it was further suggested that the harmony could extend not only to the interests of other Western states, but to those of the Soviet Union and East European states as well. In the rhetoric of Ostpolitik it was almost implied that the great work of reconciliation, détente and co-operation, the seamless web of ever-closer ties, cultural, economic, human and political, would bring benefits equally to all. There would be, so to speak, all winners and no losers. In more realistic discourse there was talk of an *Interessenausgleich* between West and East in Europe: a reconciliation or balancing of interests. This at least had the merit of recognising that, in international relations as in all human affairs, interests conflict. Part of our task is therefore to peer through the harmonising rhetoric, and through the tangle of acronymic multilateralism, to determine: who gains? Which usually also means: who loses?

Causes and sources

In this attempt we shall have to consider three main kinds of party. First, there is the Federal Republic, and the broader national goals that it defined as 'German interests'. Secondly, there are its Western neighbours and partners, above all the United States, France and Britain. Thirdly, there are East Germany, the Soviet Union and the other East European states. In considering this third category, however, we have to make a further vital distinction between the interests of the (undemocratic) states and those of their societies. This last distinction is all the more vital because West German policymakers themselves sometimes failed to make it very clearly.

Yet one of the most distinctive features of East-West relations in Europe in the 1970s and 1980s was that they increasingly consisted of attempts to influence domestic social and political developments on the other side of the 'Yalta' division. In the early 1970s, Pierre Hassner observed that a sort of 'hot peace' was increasingly replacing the Cold War. 'The main characteristic of the "hot peace",' Hassner wrote, 'is neither force nor co-operation, but the constant reciprocal influence of societies within the framework of a competition whose goals are less and less tangible, whose means are less and less direct, whose consequences are less and less calculable . . .'

Of course these influences, of states on societies, societies on societies, societies on states, worked in both directions. The Soviet Union had certain hopes of the peace movement in West Germany, the United States had certain hopes of Solidarity in Poland. Neither superpower produced, far less controlled, either social movement, but both could hope to influence both. The debate about Western policy towards Eastern Europe at the end of the 1980s was largely a debate about influencing domestic social, economic and political change in those countries. In the event, the whole 'Helsinki process' turned out to be as much about societies as about states. Television, radio and travel were as important as any meetings between statesmen. Yet such influences are extraordinarily difficult to pin down. What was the political effect of cultural exchanges? How did Western economic policies affect Eastern political economies? How does one distinguish between the effect West Germany had on East Germany by virtue of its mere existence, prosperity, democracy etc, and the influence it had by reason of conscious policy?

All assertions about the connections between Western policies and Eastern politics are therefore highly speculative. It was increasingly difficult to disentangle the specific contribution of German policy in the whole multi-dimensional web of East-West relations in Europe. The attempt will nonetheless be made. There was one German Ostpolitik. It was pursued with remarkable consistency for two decades. What did it achieve for Germany, and what for Europe? Having peered at just a few of the fearsome complexities of defining the 'German interest', let alone the 'European interest', the reader will observe that these questions are more easily asked than answered.

Answers may be offered most firmly in the area of West-East German relations. Although the overall East-West context — what Erich Honecker liked to call the *Grosswetterlage* — always remained crucial to German-German relations, the picture is not confused by the substantial impact of a different Western policy directed specifically at the GDR. This is less true of, say, Poland and Hungary, where distinctive American, French, British, Italian or Austrian approaches made a significant impact. It is even less true in the case of the Soviet Union, for which US policy was of the first importance. Reasonably well-founded statements can nonetheless be ventured about the development of bilateral relations between the Federal Republic and the states (and societies) of Eastern Europe and the Soviet Union.

Much more difficult are the areas of multilateral action, whether of Western co-ordination in Nato, European Political Co-operation and the Group of Seven, or of East-West co-operation or negotiation, in Helsinki review conferences, arms control talks and the like. On these there is at once too much and too little information, and the identification of a particular 'German line' is a delicate and questionable operation.

In offering answers so soon after the event, there is also the problem of historical perspective, and the closely related problem of sources. As Reinhart Koselleck has pointed out, from the time of Thucydides until the eighteenth century the fact of having been a witness to events was considered to be an advantage for the historian of those events. In an age when so much of history is made in personal encounters at summit meetings, on the telephone or on television, this may again be considered to be the case. Unlike in the nineteenth century, much of what is most important may actually never be written down. So there is nothing to compare with being there.

The main disadvantage of the witness is that he does not know the long-term consequences of the events he witnesses, and therefore cannot see them in historical perspective. Of course the perspectives do not cease to change with the march of time. 1989 affects our view of 1789. Yet certainly our perspectives on the distant past change more slowly than those on the more recent past. In the case of Ostpolitik, however, the revolution of 1989 and the German unification of 1990 do furnish a perspective unusually well-defined for such recent events. This story has a beginning, a middle and an end. While the Federal Republic of Germany may in future once again have *an* Ostpolitik, *the* Ostpolitik analysed here came to an end in 1989–90, albeit, arguably, with an important epilogue stretching to the final withdrawal of Soviet/Russian troops from German soil.

Yet the very sharpness of this historical break also brings peculiar difficulties of its own. For the historian, there is the danger of what Bergson called 'the illusions of retrospective determinism'. The story of Ostpolitik can so easily be written — or rather, re-written — teleologically, as if it led smoothly, inexorably and majestically to the dual crescendo of revolution and unification. *Post hoc, ergo propter hoc.* For the politicians, such re-writing of history is a matter of self-justification, of winning 'profile' and therefore votes. But one finds that even participants and witnesses no longer active in political life tend, almost without exception, to adjust their memories of their own words and deeds so they fit better into the direction that history has actually taken.

How can one guard against retrospective determinism and the tricks of memory? In the first place, of course, by taking the public record of what people actually said and did at the time. In the case of the Federal Republic's relations with the Soviet Union, Eastern Europe and, above all, East Germany, this public record is very extensive indeed. Between official publications, journals of record, memoirs and the press, German Ostpolitik is exhaustively — not to say, exhaustingly — documented. Yet if one does not find in these acres of paper the views that participants now claim to have held, they have an obvious retort: '*of course* we couldn't say that publicly! It would have alerted the other side to our true intentions. A bridge player does not show all his cards!' This difficulty, which we have touched on already in looking at public definitions of the 'European peace order', is a substantial one. For such tactical caution was a marked characteristic of Ostpolitik in general, and social-liberal Ostpolitik in particular.

In order to establish how much truth there is in retrospective claims of foresight and concealed strategy one would clearly need to examine all the relevant internal government papers, and above all the most secret ones. These papers are, however, mostly closed for thirty years, if not for longer. Even when they are all opened, the participants could still say — from the grave, or the pages of their memoirs — 'yes, to be sure, these thoughts were so secret that we did not even confide them to the most secret of secret papers!' But the credibility of such claims would be, at least, significantly qualified. Unless we want to wait until all the secret records are available, however, we cannot hope to have even this degree of historical certainty.

Public words and deeds have a weight and importance of their own, irrespective of private motives or unspoken calculations. In any case, an open society, participants, witnesses and the media expose between them a good deal of the private and unspoken. After the canonical thirty years, the revelations are generally less revelatory than one might expect. In this case, moreover, we are able to qualify the general disadvantage of the unavailability of official papers by virtue of several circumstances.

Firstly, the two most important addressee states of Ostpolitik, the Soviet Union and the GDR, have ceased to exist. According to legal provisions made by the now all-German Bundestag, the records of East Germany's ruling Communist Party, of its other parties and mass organisations, and of its State Security Service, are supposed to be made available to scholars with no application of the thirty-year rule, although with some important restrictions. (Regrettably, and illogically, such an enlightened provision is apparently not to be applied to the papers of the former East German Foreign Ministry.) For this book, extensive use has been made of such documents from the communist party and State Security Service ('Stasi') archives as were available to the author in this very early stage of the opening of the archives. Yet these already provide fascinating insights into the 'Eastern' side of the story of Ostpolitik. Clearly there is a great deal more to come, and as the documents are worked through so we may hope that the tentative analysis made here of policy towards the GDR will be put on a broader and firmer footing. At the time of writing, both the legal and the practical position with the Soviet and East European archives was less clear.

The demise of these states has meanwhile opened up another, more immediate source. For their former senior functionaries are ready to talk as they would never have done before. Of course their testimony is also full of retrospective self-justification. But fortunately their retrospective self-justification tends to pull in an opposite direction from that of West German politicians and officials. Where, for example, a West German politician may be tempted to play down, with hindsight, the degree of his or her understanding or intimacy with East German leaders, the former East German leader will be inclined to play it up. There is thus a nice compensatory symmetry of German-German memory.

In the West, official papers are generally unavailable for at least the canonical thirty years. But individuals can be more open than governments. This book thus draws on the papers of Willy Brandt, on such of the papers of Helmut Schmidt as are deposited in Bonn, on a small selection from those of Egon Bahr, and on those of two notable critics of the social-liberal Ostpolitik, Alois Mertes and Werner Marx, to name only the most important treasure-troves. Such documents, when augmented by other sources and conversations with the survivors, already give some remarkable glimpses into the inner history of the making of Ostpolitik.

This quantity and quality of evidence is still, of course, unsatisfactory. But assessments of Ostpolitik are wanted now. They might even, in a very modest way, help to save tomorrow's policymakers, certainly not from mistakes, but perhaps from some avoidable confusion.

So in what follows we make, on this admittedly unsatisfactory basis of evidence, and from this admittedly awkward distance of time, a deliberately selective analysis of the three intersecting circles of direct German Ostpolitik: *Russlandpolitik*, Deutschlandpolitik and *Osteuropapolitik*. About these we can gather reasonably full and manageable information. In them we can also find the key to the German approach in Western and multilateral fora: to indirect German Ostpolitik. For obvious reasons, this book emphasises what has been peculiar to German approaches, rather than what has been common to all Western ones.

Chapter Three discusses the early development of Ostpolitik, German-Soviet relations, and the overall 'system' of Ostpolitik as it was established by the Eastern treaties of the early 1970s, with that central triangle whose coordinates were Bonn-Moscow-Berlin. Chapter Four looks specifically at policy towards the GDR. Chapter Five begins by looking more closely at Germany's special historical problems in relations with the lands east of the River Oder, and south-east of the Erz mountains. It goes on to examine a few major leitmotifs of Ostpolitik, with special reference to Poland, Czechoslovakia and Hungary. Chapter Six steps outside the governmental frame to look at the so-called 'second Ostpolitik' of the Social Democrats in the 1980s. All these chapters take the story up to, but not systematically beyond, the year of wonders 1989. All try to avoid the fallacies of teleology or retrospective determinism.

Chapter Seven then looks briefly at the European revolution of 1989 and the German unification of 1990. Chapter Eight then looks again at the subject of causality: how far, and in what ways, did Ostpolitik contribute directly or indirectly to the final success? Noting some salient characteristics of this 'German model' of policy, this chapter returns to the question of how far and in what senses this was indeed a policy 'for Europe'. The Epilogue peers into the future.

One should, however, also emphasise what this book is not. This is not a comprehensive, narrative history of the making of Ostpolitik, including all the personal motives and party-political manoeuvres of its makers. A characteristic feature of German Ostpolitik is the wide variety of biographically-determined motives to be found among its leading actors. One cannot begin to understand the subject simply by looking at the rational surface of official speeches, couched in the relatively neutral language of contemporary international relations, and the deliberately low-key vocabulary of German politics after Hitler. The most important facts here are often the simplest biographical data — date of birth, place of birth, religion, war service — and the historian must be able to discern, behind those dry and cautious speeches, the dark or golden shadows of a Thuringian childhood; an East Prussian youth before the Fall; the language of Luther, heard from a pulpit in Halle; a freezing dawn on the Eastern front in 1943; or the echoes of a Frankfurt student demonstration in 1968. We are condemned to generalise when, as Stendhal once remarked, all the truth and all the pleasure lie in the details.

This is not a treatment of the 'political culture' of West Germany, nor of popular attitudes as revealed in opinion polls. Both 'public opinion' and 'published opinion' clearly had a great influence on Ostpolitik, while Ostpolitik in turn influenced them. With the exception of Chapter Six, which treats the policy of the Social Democrats in opposition, we have concentrated on the words and deeds of those in power. Yet this is certainly not a full account even of West Germany's governmental policy. Still less can it be a comprehensive history of East-West or West-West relations in the 1970s and 1980s. What has been called the 'essential triangle' of post-war European politics — USA-Germany-USSR — is essential background to this study, especially when it deals with the Bonn-Moscow-Berlin triangle which was in manifold ways subsidiary to the larger one. Their full geometry must await another Euclid. Issues of security policy, arms and disarmament, are discussed where they impinge directly on Ostpolitik, but in no way treated comprehensively. New global challenges — the risks of nuclear war or accident, threats to the eco-system, the world population explosion, hunger, poverty, the North-South rather than the East-West divide — are considered here only insofar as they figured in debates about Ostpolitik.

In short, the main part of this book looks at the West German approach to reducing or overcoming the 'Yalta' division of Germany and Europe — Ostpolitik — in the light of other Western, East European and Soviet approaches. While it reaches back well before 1969, it nonetheless concentrates on the two decades from the dramatic public proclamation of what came to be known round the world as Ostpolitik, in 1969/70, to the revolution and unification of 1989/90, which marked the end of that Ostpolitik.

III

Bonn-Moscow-Berlin

'Our most important task'

In the introduction to a collection of his speeches, published in 1983 under
the memorable title *German History Continues*, Richard von Weizsäcker
reflected on Germany's geopolitical situation as the divided centre of
Europe. The Federal Republic, wrote its future President and then
Governing Mayor of Berlin, was 'not just the East of the West, but also
the West of the Centre'. The foreign policy priorities of the western
German state derived from this geopolitical situation. 'On the basis of our
liberty protected in the alliance [i.e. Nato] we must concentrate our efforts
on a good relationship with the Eastern leading power [i.e. the Soviet
Union]. This is our most important task.'

The Christian Democrat von Weizsäcker went on to observe that work
towards this goal was begun by the Christian Democrat Chancellor
Adenauer, and continued by the Christian Democrat Chancellor Kiesinger,
before being given a 'treaty framework' by the Social Democrat Chancellor
Brandt. And the insight into what Chancellor Kohl would repeatedly call
the 'central importance' of the relationship with the Soviet Union was
self-evidently not an afflatus of Willy Brandt. It was as old as the Federal
Republic, indeed older. Relations with Russia had been a vital interest of
the German Reich from 1871 to 1945, and of Prussia before that. Relations
with Russia were even more of a vital interest after 1945, when the Red
Army had occupied almost half of the former Germany.

The origins of the particular form in which von Weizsäcker formulated
this 'most important task' may, however, be traced back, not as far as 1945,
nor as near as 1969, but to 1955. Over the decade after 1945, Soviet
leaders, like their Western counterparts, played with, and in part attempted, various alternative political 'solutions' for the defeated Germany.
So did German politicians, in East and West, albeit with much more
limited possibilities of translating desires into deeds.

The history of these plans and attempts is highly complex, and still controversial, but one essential point is clear. In this very confused situation, Konrad Adenauer decisively chose the variant of first creating out of the Western zones of occupation a separate West German state, which would be at once sovereign and firmly bound into a Western alliance. In pursuing this goal, he declined to explore as fully as many of his fellow German politicians — in all parties — would have liked, the possible alternative represented by the so-called Stalin Notes of March and April 1952, and the policy towards Germany of Stalin's successors during the short period between Stalin's death and the 17 June 1953 rising in East Germany. This possible alternative consisted in some variant of a basic deal: unification (of the territories of the Federal Republic and the GDR) in return for neutrality (or some very similar form of 'security guarantee' for the Soviet Union).

Adenauer feared, on the one hand, that he might forfeit the precious confidence of the Western allies by exploring these Soviet offers, and, on the other hand, that the Western allies might themselves be all too interested in exploring them — over his head. As he remarked in 1953, whereas Bismarck had a 'nightmare of coalitions', he, Adenauer, had his own nightmare: 'it's called Potsdam'. As we now know, Churchill did in fact briefly toy with the idea of an arrangement about Germany with the Russians over Adenauer's head: a new Potsdam. With support from the Eisenhower administration, Adenauer ignored all Russian blandishments and steered his part of Germany firmly through the door marked 'Nato' into a room called 'sovereignty'.

This hard-won sovereignty — although still significantly limited by residual allied rights and new obligations to Nato — was finally achieved when the Paris Treaties, signed in October 1954, came into force on 5 May 1955. Adenauer issued a triumphant declaration. 'We are a free and independent state' it said, and concluded 'Our goal is: in a free and united Europe a free and united Germany.' A German flag was hoisted before the Palais Schaumburg in Bonn to mark the occasion. Adenauer placed a photograph of this ceremony at the beginning of the second volume of his memoirs. Subsequently, this date would officially be referred to as the Federal Republic's 'day of sovereignty'.

Scarcely a month after that flag was hoisted, on 7 June, the Soviet Government sent a diplomatic note to the Federal Government (via the West German embassy in Paris) expressing its view that 'the interests of peace and European security, as well as the national interests of the Soviet and German peoples require the normalisation of relations between the Soviet Union and the German Federal Republic'. 'It is known,' said this remarkable missive, 'that in the years in which there were friendly relations and co-operation between our peoples, both countries derived great advantages.' The development of 'normal relations' would also help towards 'the solution of the all-national main problem of the German people — the restoration of the unity of a German democratic state'. After recalling that in the past, trade with Germany had been as much as one fifth of the total foreign trade of the Soviet Union, the note called for the establishment of diplomatic, trade and cultural relations between the two countries.

Within three months of receiving this note, and scarcely four months after the 'day of sovereignty', Adenauer was in Moscow. At the end of tough and dramatic negotiations, the Federal Republic and the Soviet Union agreed to open diplomatic relations. As we have already observed, this visit may be said to be the beginning of an Ostpolitik of the Federal Republic — although not of that particular version of it which came to be known round the world as 'Ostpolitik'.

Yet it was by what he refused to do as much as by what he did that Adenauer set those most basic terms of West German Ostpolitik, which von Weizsäcker summarised in what, by 1983, seemed like a self-evident, passing phrase. For it was far from self-evident to many in the 1950s that the most important task of German statesmanship should be to establish a good relationship with the Eastern leading power '*on the basis of our liberty protected in the alliance*'.

For thirty-five years, from 1955 until 1990, that would continue to be the basic premiss of the Ostpolitik of successive Federal Governments. Yet by the same token, that basic premiss would again and again be questioned in German politics, with arguments that grew out of the logic and achievements of Ostpolitik, yet often uncannily recalled those of earlier periods.

Adenauer certainly did not belong to those 'Easterners' among the German political and intellectual élite who felt some deep affinities with Russia. 'Asia stands on the Elbe' he famously remarked in 1946. And in the 1960s he was still warmly commending to Kennedy and de Gaulle a book called *The Russian Perpetuum Mobile*, which portrayed the Soviet Union as just the latest expression of old Russian expansionism. Yet he got on quite well with the representatives of what he called 'this terrible power'. He even allowed himself to be drawn into one theatrical-emotional gesture of reconciliation, holding hands with Bulganin at the end of a Bolshoi ballet performance of *Romeo and Juliet*. Above all, he saw the overwhelming imperative of national interest.

The first, immediate purpose of his visit was to secure the release of the German prisoners-of-war still held in Soviet camps, whose suffering he had specifically recalled in his declaration on the 'day of sovereignty'. He was also concerned with the position of other ethnic Germans inside the Soviet Union. Their emigration was to be one of the main subjects of a second round of negotiations, in 1957–58. Then there was his constant concern to increase the independence and widen the room for manoeuvre of the Federal Republic, making a 'new Potsdam' ever more difficult. On his return to Bonn, he explained confidentially to his colleagues in the party leadership: 'until now we were like the growing young man, who would be taken along by the other three or left at home at their pleasure. And now we have put ourselves at a stroke in the same row. In Moscow, too, the three Western ambassadors will be compelled to go hand in hand with the ambassador of the Federal Republic . . .'

Finally, Adenauer could see as well as anyone that Moscow held the key — or at least, the most important single key — to German unification. According to a distinguished specialist on German-Soviet relations, Boris Meissner, in the period before the building of the Berlin Wall there were two main tendencies discernible in West German Ostpolitik: one proposing to develop relations with all East European states, paying particular attention to Poland, the other giving clear priority to relations with Moscow. Adenauer belonged to the latter tendency: Moscow First.

The basic vision from which he started was, however, one in which the West's 'policy of strength', and the magnetism of an increasingly prosperous, free and united Western Europe, would so contrast with the growing weakness of the Soviet system and empire (exacerbated by the threat from China, on which he placed great hopes), that the Soviet leadership would sooner or later feel itself compelled to concede — from a position of weakness — the unification of Germany.

Some would maintain that this is precisely what happened in 1989–90. Yet this was not at all what seemed to be happening in the last years of Adenauer's chancellorship, in the late 1950s and early 1960s. On the contrary, the Soviet Union under Khrushchev seemed to be strengthening its position in central Europe, and, worse still from Adenauer's point of view, the Americans seemed increasingly ready to reach a modus vivendi with the Soviet Union on the basis of this strengthened position. The ultimate and shocking confirmation of this tendency was the building of a wall through the centre of Berlin on 13 August 1961, and the lack of anything more than a verbal protest from the United States, Britain and France. 'The hour of great disillusionment,' noted Heinrich Krone, one of the Chancellor's most important political associates, in his diary. 'The German people expected more than just a protest note from the West.' He might have added that many German people — and particularly the Berliners — also expected a stronger reaction from Konrad Adenauer.

Andrei Gromyko wrote in his memoirs, with sour (yet premature) satisfaction, that 'Adenauer probably did not abandon the idea of a united Germany until the night of 13 August 1961, when measures were taken to strengthen the state borders and sovereignty of the German Democratic Republic.' In fact, it is very doubtful whether Adenauer ever abandoned the idea of a united Germany. Indeed, there is some plausibility in the suggestion that he became more rather than less committed to the goal of reunification in the last years of his life, even as that goal seemed to recede rather than grow closer.

The question of the precise nature of Adenauer's commitment to the proclaimed goal of reunification is, however, a source of continuing controversy among historians, and cannot seriously be weighed here. What is clear and material for our purpose is that, in his operative policy after the building of the Wall, Adenauer placed the goal of securing elementary humanitarian improvements and, if possible, increased freedoms for the Germans now 'behind the Wall' before that of reunification in one state.

In a 'word to the Soviet Union' at the end of his government declaration in October 1962 he said: 'the Federal Government is ready to discuss many things, if our brothers in the Zone [sc. the Soviet Occupied Zone, that is, the GDR] can arrange their lives as they wish. Here considerations of humanity play a larger part for us even than national considerations.' If in the early 1950s he had placed the goal of freedom for West Germany before that of reunification, in the early 1960s he placed the goal of freedom for the East Germans before that of unity. Yet he continued to hold that the main addressee of such endeavours should be the Soviet Union and not the GDR — still referred to, if at all, as 'Pankow', after the borough of East Berlin where the leaders of the party-state then lived. One should talk to the landlord, not the housekeeper.

Even before the building of the Berlin Wall, Adenauer and his close associates had been actively considering schemes for reaching some *modus vivendi* with the Soviet Union, on the basis of accepting — albeit for a limited, specified period — the continued existence of a second German state. In early 1958, he tentatively proposed to the Soviet ambassador an 'Austrian solution' for the GDR. After the building of the Wall, he made further tentative advances to the Soviet side, suggesting, for example, a ten-year 'truce' on the German question. Heinrich Krone records him saying, after a conversation with the Soviet Ambassador in December 1961, that 'for the rest of his life he considers the most important thing that he still wants to do is to bring our relationship with Russia into tolerable order'. This, however, he hardly began to achieve in the less than two years remaining to him as Chancellor.

Even if Adenauer had been ready (and able, in terms of domestic political support) to make the crucial concessions that Brandt made eight years later — recognising the GDR and the Oder-Neisse line — it must be doubted whether the overall context of East-West relations at that time would have permitted him to achieve anything like the same results. Since he was not, this must remain forever an open question.

The period between Adenauer's departure as Chancellor, in October 1963, and Brandt's arrival as Chancellor, in October 1969, witnessed a highly complex transition, both in German and in other Western and European approaches to overcoming or reducing the division of Germany and Europe. Agitated and often contradictory movements were to be observed in at least four distinct, yet constantly interacting fields: the West German body politic narrowly defined, that is, the governing and opposition parties; the wider field of public and published opinion, the latter being particularly important in this period of transition; the policies of the Federal Republic's main Western allies, the United States, France and Britain (in that order); and, last but by no means least, those of the Soviet Union and its dependent East European states.

All we can do here is to indicate a few major lines of development. The first of these is Foreign Minister Gerhard Schröder's 'policy of movement', initiated under Adenauer from late 1961, but more fully developed under Chancellor Erhard, from 1963 to 1966. Following the recommendation of an important all-party Bundestag resolution of June 1961 (based on a report by the Sudeten German Social Democrat Wenzel Jaksch), and directly influenced by Kennedy's 'strategy of peace', Johnson's 'bridge-building', and de Gaulle's advocacy of what he called 'détente', Schröder set out very cautiously to develop a more constructive policy towards Eastern Europe. No major party in Bonn was yet prepared publicly to advocate abandoning the so-called 'Hallstein Doctrine', according to which the Federal Republic would not accord full diplomatic recognition to any state which recognised the GDR, since the Federal Republic alone represented Germany. But Schröder was able to establish trade missions in Poland, Hungary, Romania and Bulgaria.

The 'policy of movement' was, however, based on a number of highly contentious premisses. Its first addressees were the East European states, which it emphatically treated as sovereign partners. Yet at the same time it continued demonstratively to ostracise the GDR. Moreover, even the conciliatory 'peace note' of March 1966 — which for the first time formally proposed renunciation-of-force agreements such as would form the core of the Eastern treaties of the early 1970s — even this began and ended with a loud insistence on the German people's right to self-determination and reunification, and declared that 'in international law Germany continues to exist in the frontiers of 31 December 1937, so long as a freely elected all-German government does not recognise other frontiers'. These terms were unacceptable not only to the Soviet Union but also to Poland, Czechoslovakia and, of course, the GDR.

When the Grand Coalition government of Christian and Social Democrats was formed in December 1966, with the Christian Democrat Kurt-Georg Kiesinger as Chancellor and the Social Democrat Willy Brandt as Foreign Minister, it was clear to everyone that Bonn would have to go a step further. Encouraged by a valedictory speech from Konrad Adenauer, in which the elder statesman informed his party conference that 'Soviet Russia has entered the ranks of peoples who want peace', Chancellor Kiesinger immediately struck a number of new notes.

In his first government declaration, he painted his vision of what he now called a 'European peace order'. He repeated the 'peace 'note offer of renunciation-of-force agreements, this time stressing particularly the offer to the Soviet Union, and offered words of historic reconciliation to Czechoslovakia, and to Poland 'whose desire at last to live in a state area with secure frontiers we now understand better than in earlier times, given the present fate of our own partitioned nation'. He advocated the extensive development of 'human, economic and spiritual ties' with 'our compatriots in the other part of Germany'. But the words 'German Democratic Republic' or 'GDR' could still not be spoken. 'Where the establishment of contacts between authorities of the Federal Republic and those in the other part of Germany is necessary, this does not mean a recognition of a second German state.'

In the next year these points were developed in several ways. As we have already noted, the general commitment to work for 'détente', and towards a 'European peace order' in which the division of Germany would also be overcome, was enshrined in Nato's Harmel report. In April 1967, Kiesinger despatched a friend on a secret mission to Moscow, to explain his approach and explore any possible areas of movement or common ground. In an important speech to the Bundestag on 14 June 1967, Kiesinger then publicly emphasised the clear priority that would be given to relations with Moscow, as against that given to relations with other East European states in Schröder's 'policy of movement'.

'We all know,' he said, 'that the overcoming of the division of our people can indeed only be achieved by an arrangement with Moscow, unless we want to wait for one of the scurrilous and dangerous whims of history . . .' One should not think, he continued, 'above all in Moscow', that Bonn would be so foolish as to believe that it could achieve the European peace order and overcome the division of Germany by 'sowing discontent in the East and stirring up the countries there against Moscow'.

Three days later, in the traditional speech to mark the anniversary of the 17 June 1953 East German rising, he expanded on the relationship between the German and the European questions. 'Germany, a reunited Germany,' he declared,

> has a critical size. It is too big to play no role in the balance of forces, and too small to keep the forces around it in balance by itself. It is therefore hard to imagine that, while the present political structure in Europe continues, the whole of Germany could simply join one or other side. Just for this reason one can only see the growing together of the separated parts of Germany bedded into the process of overcoming the East-West conflict in Europe.

Thus Kiesinger already made the fundamental transition from a strategy that might crudely be summarised as 'détente through reunification' to one of 'reunification through détente'. The overcoming of the division of Germany, it was now argued, required first overcoming — or at least, reducing — the division of Europe.

So far as practical policy was concerned, he advocated 'first to seek ground which one can tread together, initially putting to one side the great issues of dispute'. Specifically this translated into a list of proposals for practical co-operation and communication between 'both parts of Germany' which anticipated a large part of the practical agenda of West German policy towards the GDR right up until the end of 1989. There was, Kiesinger told the Bundestag in October 1967, 'a phenomenon' over there, 'a phenomenon, with the representatives of which I have entered into correspondence'.

A great deal of the 'new' Ostpolitik was thus already in place, as a set of premisses and intentions, in 1967. (It was at this point, indeed, that it was christened 'new'.) This policy had been co-conceived, and was, wherever possible, jointly implemented, by Social Democratic members of the Grand Coalition: above all by Brandt as Foreign Minister, by the formidable figure of Herbert Wehner, as Minister for All-German Questions, and by Helmut Schmidt, as parliamentary floor leader of the Social Democrats. Yet it was eloquently and distinctively presented by the Christian Democrat Kurt-Georg Kiesinger, whose early speeches as Chancellor bear re-reading to this day. Ulrich Sahm, a senior Foreign Ministry official at that time, recalls Kiesinger saying emphatically: 'This is *my* Ostpolitik.'

If Kiesinger is a somewhat neglected figure in the history of Ostpolitik, then this is for a simple reason. In politics, as Disraeli observed, nothing succeeds like success — and nothing fails like failure. Although Brandt would say, in a handwritten letter of respect and thanks to the departing Chancellor, that their joint endeavours in the Grand Coalition 'did not do badly by our fatherland', the plain fact is that the Grand Coalition failed to achieve the desired breakthrough to a new relationship with Germany's neighbours to the East.

In January 1967, diplomatic relations were established with Romania. The governments of Hungary, Czechoslovakia, and Bulgaria showed interest in following suit, while Soviet commentaries were initially restrained. Greatly alarmed, the GDR under Walter Ulbricht moved quickly to block this new West German offensive, and soon won support from the Polish party leader, Władysław Gomułka. Yet the decisive voice was, of course, that of the Soviet Union. After a short hesitation, the Soviet leadership backed Ulbricht and Gomułka.

At a Warsaw Pact meeting in February 1967, Romania was sternly criticised for its lack of fraternal solidarity with the GDR, and the other East European states were urged to sign bilateral friendship treaties with the GDR, as the Soviet Union had already done in 1964. Poland and

Czechoslovakia did so at once, thus forming what was christened the 'iron triangle' (East Berlin-Warsaw-Prague) against Bonn's new Ostpolitik. Hungary and Bulgaria followed later. Against the 'Hallstein Doctrine' of the Federal Republic, the GDR placed what journalists would label the 'Ulbricht Doctrine', according to which no other East European state should move faster than East Germany in establishing ties with West Germany. The correspondence that Kiesinger had initiated with 'representatives of the phenomenon' was terminated, by the East German side.

Soviet leaders were themselves in a phase of conservative retrenchment after the overthrow of Khrushchev. They were concerned by signs of growing unruliness amongst their East European satellites — notably Romania's wilfulness in foreign policy, but also domestic developments in Poland, Hungary and Czechoslovakia. They perhaps genuinely misinterpreted this new Ostpolitik as a continuation of Schröder's 'policy of movement', a German revanchist variant of President Johnson's 'bridge-building', designed to split the Warsaw Pact and subvert its individual socialist states. Whatever the precise mixture of motives, the Soviet Union emphatically supported Ulbricht's defensive action, endeavoured to bring not only the Warsaw Pact but all European communist parties behind this line, at a conference in Karlovy Vary (Karlsbad) in April 1967, and launched a propaganda campaign against the new Ostpolitik as alleged West German 'revanchism'. This propaganda campaign only grew in intensity as ideologically 'revisionist' reform movements developed in Czechoslovakia, Poland and (in the economic field) in Hungary.

Although a West German trade mission was established in Prague, and diplomatic relations with bloc-free Yugoslavia (thus further weakening the 'Hallstein Doctrine'), the central thrust of the Grand Coalition's new Ostpolitik was blocked by Moscow. Full recognition of the 'post-war realities' in Europe, including Poland's western frontier on the Oder-Neisse line, the sovereign statehood of the GDR, and West Berlin as an 'autonomous political unit', was made the precondition for negotiations with the Federal Republic.

As we shall see, the social-liberal coalition government formed by Willy Brandt and Walter Scheel in October 1969 came a decisive step closer to this Soviet demand for 'recognition' of the 'Yalta' realities than the Grand Coalition did. Yet it is important to understand that there was also a very significant shift in Moscow's position. Moscow's formal offer to negotiate came in mid-September 1969, before the narrow election victory of the social-liberal coalition. By 1969 Moscow was prepared to do business with the government in Bonn — any government in Bonn — in a way that it was not prepared to in 1967 or 1968.

A number of reasons may be adduced. First, there was the burgeoning of superpower détente. Already in the early 1960s the double climax of the Berlin and Cuba crises, and the growing realisation that neither superpower could hope to win a nuclear war against the other, had pointed both in this direction. In a lecture delivered in 1971, the then State Secretary of the German Foreign Ministry, Paul Frank, would recall how in 1962, at the height of the Cuban missile crisis, he had heard Adlai Stevenson say that in forty-eight hours the world could either be at the start of the third world war or at the beginning of a period of détente between East and West. Frank dryly observed that the nuclear confrontation of 1962 led to a process of rethinking. 'Détente . . . is compelled by the nuclear stale-mate', Egon Bahr had pithily noted for Willy Brandt as early as 1963.

Now, at the end of the 1960s, the Soviet Union was seen to be approaching nuclear parity with the United States. In the so-called 'Reykjavik signal' of June 1968, Nato had indicated its readiness to engage in talks about mutual balanced force reductions. The Brezhnev leadership responded favourably to the détente initiatives of the new administration of Richard Nixon and Henry Kissinger, not least because arms control agreements might ease the burden of defence spending on the Soviet economy.

Secondly, the Soviet leadership felt itself to be more secure in its own East European empire after crushing the Czechoslovak reform movement of the 'Prague Spring'. This was directly relevant to Germany. Despite Kiesinger's and Brandt's painstaking and repeated assurances to the contrary, in 1967 and 1968 the Soviet leadership had publicly held the 'revanchist' Federal Republic at least partly responsible for the discontents in East Central Europe, and specifically for the Prague Spring. Czech ideological revisionism was blamed on German territorial revisionism. Indeed, alleged West German interference was one of the main Soviet pretexts for the invasion of Czechoslovakia. After the 'success' of the invasion, however, to which the reaction of West German leaders was as painfully low-key as those of American and French leaders, the Soviet leadership soon signalled a readiness to negotiate, notably in the March 1969 Budapest Declaration of the Warsaw Pact.

The desirability of intensified technological and economic co-operation with the West figured prominently in this document. For after the failure of the 1965 Kosygin economic reforms, the Brezhnev leadership hoped to find salvation in an injection of modernity from the West. Whereas for arms control Moscow's main partner was obviously the United States, for direct inputs of trade and technology it would be Germany. Finally, if the United States was weakened by the conflict in South-East Asia, the Soviet Union was unsettled by the growing independent strength and self-confidence of China, and the possibility that Washington or indeed Bonn might seek a classic *alliance à rebours* with Peking. (So Adenauer's hope was partly fulfilled.) For all these reasons, Moscow gave both public and private indications of greater flexibility. Full recognition of the GDR and the Oder-Neisse line were no longer made preconditions for negotiations.

Although there were powerful figures among the Christian Democrats — including Franz Josef Strauss — who seriously contemplated responding positively to such Soviet proposals, the Christian Democrats as a whole could not find it in themselves to go this last kilometre. As the domestic political fronts hardened in the run-up to the September 1969 federal election, it became clear that the partners in the Grand Coalition took different sides on this fundamental issue of German foreign policy. On the one side, Kiesinger and the Christian Democrats stuck to, indeed retreated to, their traditional principled insistence on reunification, starting from the legal position that Germany continued to exist in the frontiers of December 1937, and the non-recognition of the GDR. They feared that the Social Democratic Foreign Minister was too ready to concede what the Christian Democrats regarded as fundamental German positions of principle to communist rulers who had just suppressed the Prague Spring so brutally.

On the other side stood Brandt and the Social Democrats, quite explicitly since their Nuremberg party congress in March 1968; Walter Scheel and most of the Free Democrats; and behind them a large part of the media and the intellectual, cultural, academic, and, not least, ecclesiastical community — 'published opinion' in the widest sense. All pleaded, some on practical grounds, others more on moral ones, for the recognition of the realities of 'Yalta' Europe, including the Oder-Neisse line as the permanent western frontier of Poland, and the existence of a second German state. This was to be the starting point for a new relationship between Germany and the East, indeed altogether between East and West in Europe. Chancellor Kiesinger had sarcastically described this very broad church as 'the party of recognition'.

In the election of 1969, the Social and Free Democrats between them won a narrow parliamentary majority, and formed the first social-liberal coalition government in the history of the Federal Republic. The 'party of recognition' was — just — in power, and now launched that particular version of German eastern policy which came to be known round the world as Ostpolitik.

The road from Berlin

It will be very clear from what has been said so far that many roads led to the new Ostpolitik personified by Willy Brandt: by his grand, emotive speeches and symbolic acts. Christian Democrats had started already under Adenauer, and had gone at least half a step further with Kiesinger. Free Democrats had made a major contribution, with innovative proposals associated with the names of Karl Georg Pfleiderer and Wolfgang Schollwer. Other Social Democrats, notably Herbert Wehner and Helmut Schmidt, had contributed directly to the formulation of Brandt's position.

The influence of 'published opinion' inside Germany should as little be underrated as the international causes: the Western examples, starting with Kennedy and de Gaulle, and the crucial shifts in Eastern positions. All in all, the new Ostpolitik of the early 1970s was much less single-handedly the work of Willy Brandt than the Western integration of the early 1950s was of Konrad Adenauer. Yet Brandt it was who did the thing.

If we were to try fully to understand what moved and informed Willy Brandt's personal conduct of this policy we would also have to go back a long way. He was, after all, fifty-six years of age when he became Chancellor. We would be bound to look at his formative experiences as an illegitimate child in Wilhelmine Germany and as a young revolutionary socialist in the Weimar Republic; at his transition to social democracy in Scandinavian exile; at the hopes of a new, democratic, united Europe — 'left and free' — with which he returned to Germany; at his hard-fought political ascent among the Social Democrats of West Berlin and West Germany; at the arguments among those Social Democrats in the 1950s. But when all that was said we would nonetheless return to one place and one date, the place and date that Brandt himself puts at the opening of both his main volumes of memoirs: Berlin, 13 August 1961.

If the building of the Berlin Wall — in its first days not a wall, just a line of men and barbed wire — was a shock for Adenauer and his associates in Bonn, how much more terrible was the shock for the people of Berlin itself, and for their Governing Mayor, Willy Brandt. 'We consider,' he telexed the next day to the Foreign Minister in Bonn, 'that economic measures are necessary against the initiators of the decrees in East Berlin, as also against the so-called "GDR".' He called, in short, for sanctions against the Soviet Union. 'The barred walls of a concentration camp,' he wrote to Jawaharlal Nehru on 17 August 1961, 'have now been erected inside Berlin.' The horror and the fury come shouting through even the memoirs of the elder statesman, written more than a quarter of century later. Horror, of course, at the human suffering caused by the East German-Soviet action. 'In my Wedding constituency,' Brandt recalls, 'people jumped from houses directly on the sector line into the sheets of the fire brigade. Not all made it.' But fury almost as much at the Western allies, and above all at the Americans, for the weakness of their response.

'Gentlemen,' Brandt told the Western Allied commanders in Berlin, 'last night you let Ulbricht kick you in the arse.' Kennedy, he gathered, had not so much as interrupted his weekend yachting trip. Despite an emotional appeal in a personal letter from Brandt, the American President declined even to take the matter before the United Nations. In a cool response to Brandt's letter, Kennedy promised only to support, with a strengthened garrison, *West* Berlin and the half-city's ties with the West.

'Was it this letter [from Kennedy]', Brandt asks, in his 1989 volume of memoirs, 'which drew back the curtain and revealed the empty stage?' The rather delphic reference is explained in his earlier (1976) memoirs, when, after describing the shock of 13 August, he writes:

> I said later that in August 1961 a curtain was drawn aside to reveal an empty stage. To put it more bluntly, we lost certain illusions that had outlived the hopes underlying them . . . Ulbricht had been allowed to take a swipe at the Western superpower, and the United States merely winced with annoyance. My political deliberations in the years that followed were substantially influenced by this day's experience, and it was against this background that my so-called Ostpolitik — the beginning of détente — took shape.

The conclusion he and his closest associates drew was simple: the Americans are neither all-powerful nor all-willing; if we are to do anything for the inhabitants of our poor divided city (country, continent) we will have to do it ourselves, and we will have to do it by dealing directly with the powers-that-be in the East.

It is interesting to find that Brandt himself makes a connection with 'Yalta'. Discussing what the West might have done to avert the complete division of Germany and Berlin, he comes back to the March 1952 Stalin Note and writes (in his 1976 memoirs): 'I wondered then, not for the first or last time, whether the two superpowers might not, with adamantine consistency, have been pursuing the same principle in Europe since 1945: that, whatever happened, they would respect the spheres of influence broadly agreed at Yalta.' And again: 'The basic principle governing the tacit arrangement between Moscow and Washington remained in force during the construction of the Wall and thereafter.' The real historical process of the division of Europe was a great deal more complicated than this. Yet if one takes 'Yalta' to mean that whole historical process, then one might say that 13 August 1961 was the last day of Yalta and the first of Ostpolitik.

For all the diversity of the German roads that lead to the new Ostpolitik, the single most important road, the historical Autobahn, leads from Berlin. It leads from Berlin in the person of Willy Brandt — first Governing Mayor in Berlin, then Foreign Minister and Chancellor in Bonn. It leads from Berlin in the person of Egon Bahr — first Willy Brandt's press spokesman and close adviser in Berlin, then head of the planning staff in Brandt's Foreign Ministry, then key negotiator of the Eastern treaties. It leads from Berlin in the philosophy and practical policy that these two evolved, together with a tight circle of colleagues in the office of the Governing Mayor, known locally as 'the heavenly family'. Most of them had roots in central or eastern Germany, and all shared a passionate, patriotic concern for the divided city and the divided nation. If one wants to know what makes the West German policy of *Entspannung* different from other versions of détente, Berlin in 1961 is the place to start.

Within months of the building of the Wall, the first, strictly unofficial contact was made between a member of the Brandt team and an emissary of the East German leadership. The latter said, in effect, that a few wives might perhaps be let out through the Wall to rejoin their husbands, a few children to rejoin their parents — if the West Berlin government would pay for those wives and children in hard currency. This it did.

The West Berlin government then tried to negotiate with the East Berlin authorities (but without 'recognising' the GDR) an arrangement by which West Berliners could at least visit their relatives in East Berlin for a day or two over the Christmas holiday. In vain. The emotional pressures they were working under are graphically illustrated by a letter from a doctor (presumably in an East Berlin hospital) that Brandt quoted in a December 1961 speech to the Bundestag:

> Since the total strangulation [i.e. the closing of East Germany's frontiers by the Wall] the desire to get out has taken epidemic form. At least 95 per cent of the escapees are caught and suffer a terrible fate. You should see the bleeding hunks of flesh that are delivered to us here, in ever growing numbers, because the ordinary frontier troops must strike mercilessly with their bayonets . . . otherwise it would be their turn. Give the people here some hope, so that the suicide rate, which grows from week to week, and which leads us to fear the worst for Christmas, will at last begin to fall.

On the 17th of August 1962, an eighteen-year-old building worker, Peter Fechter, was shot by East German border guards while trying to escape over the Wall a short distance from Checkpoint Charlie. He lay amidst the barbed wire at the foot of the Wall for about an hour, bleeding to death, before the guards removed his lifeless body. He cried out for help until he died. A horrified crowd watched from the Western side, just a few metres away. So did American military police. The full implications of what had happened a year before were rammed home to the West Berliners, who responded with angry demonstrations not just against the East but even more against the West, and especially the United States, for its lack of response. Here the 'Yalta' line was drawn in blood, for everyone to see.

Slowly, painfully, Brandt and his team developed what they would call their 'policy of small steps'. For more than two years they struggled, through unconventional, even conspiratorial channels, to restore at least some basic human contacts. On 17 December 1963, Willy Brandt's fiftieth birthday, they finally accomplished that goal. While 'agreeing to differ' about nomenclature, and thus still notionally 'not recognising' the GDR, a representative of the West Berlin city government nonetheless signed with a GDR official — acting 'on the instructions of the deputy chairman of the Council of Ministers of the German Democratic Republic', as the document records — the first so-called 'Permit Agreement'. This enabled West Berliners to visit their relatives in East Berlin for a day at a time over the Christmas and New Year holidays. To the dismay of the East German authorities, and the delighted surprise of Brandt and his team, no less than 790,000 West Berliners — more than one in three — seized the opportunity, many going two or three times.

In interviews, speeches and articles over the next quarter-century, Willy Brandt and Egon Bahr would again and again return to this emotional moment. 'It was then,' declared Bahr in 1987, 'that the foundation-stone was laid for what later became known, also in many foreign languages, as "Ostpolitik".' Nor was it only Brandt and his circle in Berlin who saw the significance of what they had done; and not just with hindsight. Watching suspiciously from Bonn, Adenauer's close associate Heinrich Krone noted in his diary that Brandt and his friends were beginning 'an Ostpolitik of their own'.

But how on earth could a city mayor — in practice, the mayor of just half a city — be developing a foreign policy of his own? The answer lies in the unique significance of Berlin — the divided centre of the divided centre — but also in the unique person of Willy Brandt. Brandt's papers from his time as Governing Mayor reveal a man operating simultaneously on the municipal, federal and world stage. One day Brandt would be dealing with efforts to bring a few children back to their mothers across the Wall. The next he would be discussing the future of the world with Kennedy, Macmillan or de Gaulle. While the elementary human agony of the divided city was sufficient and indeed compelling reason for developing the 'policy of small steps', these two other levels were also vitally important.

At the same time as being Governing Mayor of Berlin, Brandt was the Social Democrats' most popular and attractive national leader, and their candidate for Chancellor. Although he had lost the September 1961 election to Adenauer, his colleagues were still urging him to stand and stand again in order at last to bring the Social Democrats to power in Bonn. 'What you must do, and in this I will gladly try to help you,' Herbert Wehner concluded a seven-page handwritten letter to him at Christmas 1963, 'is a really great political thing for SPD and Germany, for International and Europe-America.' (The order — SPD, Germany, International, Europe-America — is worth noting.) And everything that Brandt and his associates attempted to do in the presentation of their policy for the divided city (country, continent) has also to be seen in the context of this party-political struggle.

In the course of his endeavours in Berlin, Brandt formed the first ever social-liberal coalition in West German politics, a precursor of the federal social-liberal coalition six years later. Just as the 1969 Bonn coalition was forged on the basis of a new, common approach to reducing the division of Germany — and Europe — so this 1963 Berlin coalition was forged on the basis of a new, common approach to reducing the division of Berlin — and Germany. 'Don't believe,' said his Free Democratic partner William Borm, 'that we have gone to such trouble only on account of Berlin. The point is above all to get Deutschlandpolitik on the move again.' And a decade later, after he was triumphantly confirmed in office as the Chancellor of Ostpolitik in the federal election of 19 November 1972, Brandt wrote to the same William Borm: 'What most people don't know or have already forgotten: almost exactly ten years ago we two, by bringing together our two parties in Berlin, set in motion the process that was so emphatically endorsed by the voters of the Federal Republic on 19 November!'

At the same time, Brandt was developing an extraordinary range of international contacts. The most important of these were with the four main victor powers of 1945, who still had theoretically unlimited occupation rights in Berlin and residual rights relating to 'Germany as a whole'. Two planned personal meetings with Khrushchev never happened: one in 1959 met the resistance even of his own party, one in 1963 failed at the last minute because of the opposition of the Christian Democrats in Berlin (at that point still — just — his coalition partners). But he lost no opportunity to take discreet and confidential soundings of the Soviet position, most often through the good offices of Egon Bahr. The Brandt papers contain, for example, a note on the Governing Mayor's 'informal talk' with one Mr Polyanov of *Izvestia* on 16 March 1962. 'The German side,' Bahr records himself as saying in the course of this conversation, 'relied on a certain realism on the part of the Soviet Union, which in the long run could not ignore what 55 million Germans wanted, and that 17 million Germans would not become communists. At this point,' says the minute, 'Mr Polyanov became distinctly emotional.'

Still more stark and dramatic, however, was the message from Moscow to Berlin that Bahr recorded in a confidential memorandum dated 10 July 1962. One 'Herr Eimers ("Kurier")', said this memo, had just returned from Moscow with a message to Brandt from the West German Ambassador, Hans Kroll. The message was: 'Khrushchev wants a Western signature on the frontier of political influence in Europe between East and West. In this, he attaches particular importance to a German signature.' Khrushchev had suggested that Kroll should get together with Semyonov to negotiate on subjects including the withdrawal of American troops from Berlin. 'The Wall had been ordered by him, Khrushchev. This order he could also rescind.'

As a message at fourth hand this is not exactly 'from the horse's mouth'. But the brutal frankness sounds like authentic Khrushchev. In any case this memorandum is a vivid illustration of what Bahr and Brandt understood to be, in a nutshell, the Soviet message. A few years later, shortly before he moved to Bonn as Foreign Minister in 1966, Brandt would have a series of personal meetings with the Soviet ambassador to East Berlin, Piotr Abrassimov.

Most of Brandt's high-level personal contacts at this stage were, however, with Western allies and partners. Meeting with Harold Macmillan in November 1962, Brandt described the tragic human consequences of the Wall. According to the German record, Macmillan replied: 'All this is very stupid.' Rather more helpful, and more important, was General de Gaulle. Even before the building of the Wall, de Gaulle had envisaged the development of practical ties and co-operation between the two halves of Germany: a new Deutschlandpolitik *avant la lettre*. In a series of meetings, de Gaulle now directly encouraged Brandt in his policy of 'alleviation and encouragement for people in the Zone', as he put it in April 1963. 'De Gaulle expressed himself very positively — in German — about the policy of small steps,' says the minute of a conversation in Paris in June 1965.

Most important of all was John F Kennedy. On the one hand, Brandt had clearly resented what he saw as the weakness of the American response to the building of the Wall. On the other hand, American backing for his practical policy was crucially important, both directly in Berlin and in West German politics. Encouraged by his close adviser Klaus Schütz, who had been inspired by the American presidential campaign, Brandt — of the same generation as the American president, young and vigorous by contrast with the 87-year-old Chancellor in Bonn — was also not unhappy to be taken for a German Kennedy.

'Small steps are better than none,' he and his advisers said of their own policy, and: 'small steps are better than big words'. But in fact even the first very small steps of the early 1960s were accompanied by very big words, albeit of a different kind from the reunification rhetoric heard in Bonn. First in Berlin, then with a lecture series at Harvard in the autumn of 1962, subsequently published in German under the title *Co-existence: The Need to Dare*, Brandt began to prepare public opinion for the shift to come. He did so with a kind of inspirational vagueness which was already a hallmark of his political rhetoric. 'Brandt likes to talk a hovering language (*eine schwebende Sprache*)' noted Adenauer's associate, Heinrich Krone, in his diary on 27 December 1959. Willy Brandt, like his fellow journalist Winston Churchill, was a past master of emotive imprecision. In the drafts of his speeches and articles one can follow how, time and again down the years, he substitutes — as any good journalist would — a colourful phrase for a dull one, but also a vague, allusive, delphic formulation for a more precise one. Yet with Brandt, as with Churchill, the private thinking was often much clearer than the public speaking.

In this situation, with even Brandt's close political allies still needing to be persuaded of the wisdom of the new line, President Kennedy suddenly proclaimed his 'strategy of peace' at the American University in Washington in June 1963. The effect of this speech, writes Arthur Schlesinger, was to 'redefine the whole [American] national attitude to the Cold War'. While Brandt and Kennedy had talked about the way forward in the centre of Europe, the President's speech was obviously motivated by larger American concerns. To Brandt and his colleagues in Berlin it came, as Egon Bahr recalls, like 'a gift from heaven'.

Here was the charismatic figure with whom Brandt had politically identified himself, the leader of West Germany's and West Berlin's most important ally, now proclaiming a new direction in East-West relations which magnificently legitimated and, so to speak, covered their own. What is more, later that month Kennedy applied his 'strategy of peace' specifically to Germany in a speech at the Free University in West Berlin. This was the triumphant visit which also saw his famous declaration to a crowd before the city hall: '*Ich bin ein Berliner*' (written phonetically in his notes as 'Ish bin ein Bearleener').

Three weeks after the Kennedy visit, Brandt was scheduled to give a lecture at one of those church academies which played a remarkably important role in the intellectual background of West German politics in general and Ostpolitik in particular — the Protestant Academy in the small Bavarian town of Tutzing. The text of his talk was painstakingly discussed and edited by his close circle of advisers. At the last minute, Egon Bahr was invited by the organisers of the conference to add his own informal presentation. Believing, by his own account, that everything of real importance had been put into Brandt's scrupulously prepared text, he hastily dictated a few remarks. Yet it was Bahr's few informal remarks, not Brandt's finely crafted lecture, which would become famous as 'the Tutzing speech'. And justifiably so. For where Brandt covered the underlying logic of their approach in vague and inspirational rhetoric, Bahr revealed it with brilliant and provocative clarity.

Sketching what he called 'the application of the strategy of peace to Germany', Bahr proclaimed the goal of 'overcoming the status quo, by first not changing the status quo'. Reunification, he argued, would not be a single act but 'a process, with many steps and stops'. He saw no possibility of overthrowing the regime in East Germany, or even changing it against the will of the Soviet Union. Brandt's speech recalled his Harvard plea for 'a policy of transformation' of the other side. Bahr added: 'The Zone [i.e. East Germany] must be transformed with the agreement of the Soviets.' Brandt said: 'The German question can only be solved with the Soviet Union, not against it.' Bahr rammed the message home: 'The preconditions for reunification are only to be created with the Soviet Union. They are not to be had in East Berlin, not against the Soviet Union, not without it.'

The heated discussion about the legal-symbolic importance of not fully 'recognising' the 'GDR' could lead into a cul-de-sac. It was, after all, 'the

Interior Minister of the German Democratic Republic — with no inverted commas –' who on 13 August had forbidden the Western Allies to travel freely into the Eastern sector of the city, and limited them to one crossing at Checkpoint Charlie. No, far more important than the legal-symbolic niceties were the possibilities of practical action, 'beneath the level of juristic recognition', such as had already been ably explored by Dr Kurt Leopold of the Trust Office for Inter-Zonal Trade, the West German agency for trade between the two German states.

And more trade was certainly desirable. An economic blockade would only increase the tensions between the two parts of Germany, and within East Germany: 'Increasing tension strengthens Ulbricht and deepens the division.' Trade and credits, such as the United States had already given to Poland, might help to reduce tensions, both between East and West Germany, and within East Germany. 'A material improvement would be bound to have a tension-relaxing effect in the Zone. A better supply of consumer goods is in our interest.' Some might object that this would lessen popular discontent in East Germany 'but precisely that is desirable' for otherwise there might be 'uncontrolled developments' (like the 17 June 1953 rising or the 1960–61 emigration wave) which would lead to 'inevitable reverses' (such as the crushing of the 17 June rising or the building of the Berlin Wall). No 'practical path' led via attempts to overthrow the regime. 'I see only the narrow path of relief for the people in such homeopathic doses that no danger of a revolutionary turn develops, which would necessarily lead to Soviet intervention out of Soviet interests.'

After citing Adenauer's observation that human considerations should be put before national ones, Bahr summed up his argument.

We have said that the Wall was a sign of weakness. One could also say, it was a sign of the communist regime's fear and urge for self-preservation. The question is whether there are not possibilities gradually to diminish the regime's quite justified fears, so that the loosening up of the frontiers and the Wall will also become practicable, because the risk will be bearable. This is a policy which one could sum up in the formula: *Wandel durch Annäherung* (change through rapprochement).

This speech, and particularly the formula *Wandel durch Annäherung*, provoked a storm of controversy, in the course of which Brandt made some tactical criticism of his press spokesman — the better to defend him. For in fact, as Brandt later admitted, Bahr was presenting their 'common thoughts'. Bahr himself would say that the strategy outlined in this speech was designed for a specific, transitional phase on the way to reunification, and thus made obsolete already by the 1964 long-term bilateral friendship treaty between the Soviet Union and the GDR. Certainly many elements were added to this conception, not least by Bahr himself, before it went up into the Ostpolitik of a Federal Government.

Yet it is remarkable to observe how many characteristic features of the Ostpolitik of the 1970s are already present here: the courtly, almost exaggerated emphasis on harmony with Western, and especially American policy; the insistence nonetheless on West Germany's need to do more for herself; the premiss that nothing could be achieved against the will of the Soviet Union; the belief in trade and economic co-operation as a means to facilitate political détente, both between East and West and within the East; the rejection of destabilisation; the notion rather of achieving relaxation by reassuring the communist powerholders; the curious combination of bold, dialectical, world-historical theory with the perforce extraordinarily modest, limited, quotidian practice of pursuing the most elementary humanitarian goals (the reunification of mother and child); and all this with an acute and palpable consciousness of the weakness of your own bargaining position. For it is only a slight exaggeration to say that the new Ostpolitik began in Berlin as a negotiation to free hostages from state-terrorists.

Statesmen may work with sophisticated and detailed analyses of complex international situations. They have to trim and adapt their policies to those of allies and adversaries. They also respond constantly to domestic political pressures. In democracies, this means above all the pressure of winning the next election, and in the Federal Republic there are federal or state elections almost all the time. Yet in most statesmen worthy of the name there is an emotional and intellectual core, formed by certain key experiences. Without grasping this biographical core one cannot begin to explain their visions or their actions.

Friedrich Naumann said of Bismarck that he 'thought Europe from Prussia out'. Recalling this comment, Arnulf Baring has argued that Adenauer thought Europe from Cologne out. With all due caveats and qualifications one may say of Willy Brandt: he thought Europe from Berlin out.

Treaty work

The road from Berlin led via Bonn to Moscow. As head of the planning staff in the Foreign Ministry, Bahr worked out his concept for negotiations with the governments in Moscow, East Berlin, and other East European capitals. Because he was personally so close to Brandt, and because other senior officials in the ministry were themselves divided on the way forward in East-West relations, the planning staff also became a clearing-house for proposals in this area. Meanwhile, Brandt and his advisers did not hesitate to use — as they had in Berlin — every available channel to sound out, and send signals to, the other side. These contacts ranged from an official top-level meeting at the UN between Brandt and the Soviet Foreign Minister to confidential mediation by Italian communists or a discreet lunch in a journalist's flat in Vienna. The conspiratorial secrecy of some of these private contacts bred a mistrust shared even by Chancellor Kiesinger. Some Christian Democrats anyway inclined to charge Social Democrats with being too close to the communists ideologically. The Free Democrats' new leader, Walter Scheel, by contrast, commented calmly: 'If one wants to maintain and improve security in Europe, then one must know that one will have to talk to communists.'

After the Soviet Union sent its diplomatic note formally offering to negotiate, on 12 September 1969, and just a week before the federal elections on 28 September, Bahr produced for Brandt a working paper entitled 'Reflections on the foreign policy of a future federal government'. This started by reaffirming the central importance of the United States for West Germany, noting the impact of Vietnam and the strong American interest in détente with the Soviet Union. It went on to give a very realistic assessment of the dilemmas of the Soviet leadership. Torn between the need to preserve their own power and that to increase economic efficiency, Soviet leaders would, Bahr argued, continue to alternate between loosening and tightening the leash on Eastern Europe. Much therefore depended on the skill of the Communist leaderships in the individual East European states. In relation to West Germany, however, the GDR hoped to open the path to international recognition without itself making concessions. 'This hope,' wrote Bahr, 'is not unfounded.' That pessimistic assumption was also crucial to the position he adopted.

The second part of the paper, drawing conclusions from this analysis, also began with the clear statement that 'the Atlantic Alliance and the close relationship to the USA must continue to remain the basis of our policy'. However, the Federal Republic should try to remove as much as possible of the Western Allies' residual occupation rights — those 'last relics of the post-war period'. The attempt should be made to use the Soviet proposal of a European security conference 'as an instrument for the realisation of our interests'. It would be highly desirable to negotiate a mutual balanced reduction of conventional forces in Central Europe, not least because the Americans seemed likely to reduce their troop numbers anyway — another important assumption.

So far as Deutschlandpolitik and *Osteuropapolitik* were concerned, his starting-point was that the division of Germany was getting ever deeper and more permanent. 'We must reckon with it for the foreseeable future. The necessity increases to adapt to this position without abandoning the goal of reunification.' The danger, Bahr repeated, was that the GDR would achieve international recognition even against Bonn's will. The central objective should therefore be a 'framework treaty' with the GDR, which would not need to be revised 'until reunification', and meanwhile would preserve at least elements of 'the unity of the nation'.

This framework treaty should be combined with 'a European renunciation-of-force', the recognition of the Oder-Neisse line and signing up to the nuclear non-proliferation treaty. It would clearly be desirable to establish diplomatic relations with the other East European states. This would give the 'pragmatic and co-operative forces' in those states more possibilities for pursuing a more autonomous policy, and increase the all-round pressure on the GDR to adopt a more co-operative attitude to the Federal Republic. But one would have always to keep in mind that West Germany's relations with Eastern Europe could only be developed to the extent that this was tolerated by the Soviet Union. Therefore an improvement in relations with the Soviet Union must be sought, exploiting, in particular, the obvious Soviet interest in closer economic ties.

A shorter version of this paper was then the starting-point for the foreign policy part of Brandt's discussions with the Free Democrats on forming a social-liberal coalition government in October 1969. But on Ostpolitik there were only small disagreements between them. 'Scheel stated in the debate,' says a note of the coalition talks on 1 October 1969, 'that the negotiating partners' ideas on foreign policy largely coincided.' The Free Democrats had already been thinking along very similar lines. Indeed, in January 1969 they had publicly proposed a general treaty with the GDR. Walter Scheel and a party delegation including Hans-Dietrich Genscher had returned from a trip to Moscow in July 1969 with very similar conclusions to those drawn by Helmut Schmidt and his Social Democratic delegation on their visit to Moscow in August 1969. Ostpolitik was the great common ground between the new coalition partners.

The basis on which the new social-liberal coalition then set about negotiating a new set of relationships with the Federal Republic's eastern neighbours was 'Moscow First'. As a paper written by Bahr in October 1968 makes crystal clear, the Soviet invasion of Czechoslovakia had only reinforced the lesson already drawn from the building of the Berlin Wall. A few members of this new government — notably Ralf Dahrendorf — still pleaded for the alternative line of giving priority to talks with Warsaw. But the negotiation with Moscow was given absolute priority, both in time and in importance, and the task was entrusted — in its crucial phase — to Egon Bahr.

Like a greyhound that has been straining at the leash, Bahr shot off to try out his 'concept' with a speed, *élan*, and secrecy that left Christian Democrats — out of power for the first time since the founding of the Federal Republic — spluttering with shock and indignation. For Bahr's talks with the Soviet Foreign Minister, Andrei Gromyko, in early 1970, were indeed the key to the whole complex of what came to be known as the Eastern treaties. This *Vertragswerk* ('treaty work') was to be the subject of the second most acute and prolonged political controversy in the history of the Federal Republic, comparable only to that which attended the negotiation of Adenauer's Western 'treaty work' in the 1950s. The controversy reached its high-point in 1972, in titanic debates over the ratification of the Moscow and Warsaw treaties, but even in the late 1980s any bold assertions or new 'revelations' about this subject were certain to raise temperatures rapidly, as with an old fever in the bones.

The secrecy of the negotiations, the unavailability (or very partial availability) of important sources, the intrinsic legal-political complexity of the 'treaty work', the memories of controversy and the political sensitivity of the central issues: all make simple generalisations more than usually inadvisable. At the same time, from the perspective of a reunited Germany, many of the points so long and so heatedly debated seem not only arcane — they were always that — but also archaic.

With the benefit of hindsight, and with a nod at the whole library of works written on this subject, we shall therefore concentrate on those few central points about this 'treaty work' which would in fact be most germane to the development of Ostpolitik over the next two decades. What did Bonn give and what did it get? In the foreplay to the Moscow Treaty, the Bonn government gave three major sweeteners. Firstly, it signed the nuclear non-proliferation treaty, thus confirming also to Moscow the renunciation of any claim to nuclear weapons which Adenauer had made to the Western allies in the context of his Western treaty work. Secondly, it indicated that, given a satisfactory outcome to this German-Soviet negotiation, it would support the Soviet Union's long-running goal of a European security conference — intended by Moscow to seal and sanction 'Yalta'.

Last but by no means least, it showed that it would respond favourably to Moscow's desire for increased economic and technological ties. Before the political negotiator Egon Bahr, the banker F Wilhelm Christians was in Moscow. While Bahr and Gromyko were still in a very early phase of their exploratory talks, agreements were signed in Essen providing for a large delivery of German steel pipes in return for subsequent supplies of Soviet natural gas through those pipes, the whole to be financed by a government-guaranteed credit on very favourable terms. A taste of things to come.

In the Moscow Treaty itself, the fundamental concession that Bonn made to Moscow was a comprehensive recognition of what the treaty called 'the existing real situation' in Europe, and a solemn commitment to respect the inviolability of the frontiers of all states in Europe 'including the Oder-Neisse line, which forms the Western frontier of the People's Republic of Poland, and the frontier between the Federal Republic of Germany and the German Democratic Republic'. Days and weeks had been spent by the German side, first by Bahr, then in the official negotiations by Walter Scheel, trying to weaken and complicate these commitments, so as to leave open in the wording just the crack of a possibility of peaceful change of frontiers, and, above all, of the reunification of the two German states.

The Russian negotiators had wanted the frontiers to be described as 'unalterable'; the Germans got them down to 'inviolable'. A reference in the preamble of the treaty to the terms of the opening of diplomatic relations in 1955 was held to include the unilateral letter sent by Adenauer to Bulganin, restating the Federal Republic's legal positions, as well as the hope formally expressed in an exchange of letters between the two leaders that this would contribute to 'solving the main national problem of the whole German people — the re-creation of the unity of a democratic German state'.

Less delphically, a 'letter on German Unity', which accompanied the Moscow Treaty, plainly reaffirmed the Federal Republic's commitment 'to work towards a state of peace in Europe in which the German people regains its unity in free self-determination'. (Twenty years later, controversy would still rumble on in Bonn about who was responsible for conceiving this letter.) The letter was accepted but not formally acknowledged or appended to the treaty by the Soviet side. An exchange of diplomatic notes with the United States, Britain and France also confirmed that the 'rights and responsibilities of the four powers relating to Berlin and Germany as a whole' were not affected.

Months, indeed years, were subsequently spent by the German body politic, debating what had or had not been, what should or might not have been conceded of the Federal Republic's legal-political-symbolic positions on these issues. After fierce internal debates, the Christian Democratic opposition insisted on a Common Resolution of the Bundestag, as the price for its mere abstention on the ratification vote in May 1972. This Common Resolution stressed that while the Moscow and Warsaw treaties were important elements of the '*modus vivendi*' which the Federal Republic sought with its eastern neighbours, they were in no sense part of any final, legally binding peace settlement for Germany. Responding to an appeal from Franz Josef Strauss's Bavarian State Government (formally questioning the constitutionality of the subsequent Basic Treaty with the GDR), the Constitutional Court averred, in a profoundly convoluted judgement, that legally the German Reich continued to exist in the frontiers of December 1937. These legal-symbolic caveats and qualifications, and the important question of how far they served or hindered the national goals of German Ostpolitik over the next two decades, are considered in more detail later on (see pp. 223ff).

In sum, the recognition of the 'existing real situation' contained in the Moscow Treaty — and in the whole 'treaty work' that followed, including the Warsaw and Prague treaties and the treaty with the GDR — was not quite so complete and unconditional as the Soviet leadership would have wished, and especially, as the East German leadership would have wished. Yet it was a crucial and decisive step further than any previous Bonn government had been prepared to go.

In the first place, there was the basic recognition of the existence of the other German state. 'Even if two states in Germany exist,' Brandt had declared in his first government declaration as Chancellor, 'they are nonetheless not "foreign countries" (*Ausland*) for each other . . .' This distinctly backhanded acknowledgement of the existence of two states in Germany — after just twenty years of their existence! — was, as Richard von Weizsäcker observed at the time, 'the constitutive political statement on which the government's further measures of Ostpolitik are based'.

Beyond this, however, there was the recognition of the Soviet Union's control over the whole of what had come to be called 'Eastern Europe'. Here was the 'German signature' which Khrushchev had demanded in that confidential message to Brandt back in 1962. As Peter Bender, a knowledgeable and enthusiastic supporter of the new Ostpolitik, plainly puts it: 'When on 12 August 1970 Brandt and Scheel signed the Moscow Treaty, the Soviet Union had achieved what it had been working towards for fifteen years: German recognition of its Central European empire.' Thus it was in a treaty with the Soviet Union, not with the GDR, that the Federal Republic first expressed its recognition of the GDR. It was in a treaty with the Soviet Union, not with Poland, that the Federal Republic first expressed its recognition of Poland's post-1945 Western frontier. That result was, of course, fervently desired by the Poles. But the form in which it was achieved was resented even by the communist leadership of Poland. Germany and Russia agreed Poland's frontiers.

Leaked extracts from the German records of Egon Bahr's conversations with Gromyko note the following contribution from the Bonn government's chief negotiator on 21 February 1970:

> We had to make sure that the process which we were now beginning would remain under full control the whole time . . . Here we would have a common interest. The Federal Republic was prepared to do everything it could to help with this. The Minister [i.e. Gromyko] would be informed that the Federal Government had been attacked in the Bundestag with the argument that the policy of the Federal Government would lead to a recognition of the special role — or 'predominance', as it was put there — of the Soviet Union among the socialist states. The Federal Chancellor had said that we would carry on our policy irrespective of these or other attacks. He, State Secretary Bahr, would be pleased if these remarks of his should be understood in their full meaning.

In a further exchange on 10 March, Gromyko showed that he had understood. The minutes record him saying: 'We [i.e. the Germans] should have no particular worry about the behaviour of third states — Poland and the GDR — with which the Soviet Union would talk . . .' And Bahr's response, again according to these leaked and fragmentary protocols: 'He [Bahr] did not have the worry which Minister Gromyko believed oppressed him. Quite the contrary. He [Bahr] would really like to negotiate everything with him [Gromyko].'

At the end of their preliminary talks, on 22 May 1970, Bahr and Gromyko agreed a ten-point working paper, which was soon leaked to the West German press, and dubbed the 'Bahr paper'. Its first four points became, with only relatively minor alterations, the first four points of the Moscow Treaty. The fifth point explicitly stated that this treaty together with 'matching agreements of the Federal Republic of Germany with other socialist countries, especially . . . with the German Democratic Republic (see point 6), the People's Republic of Poland and the Czechoslovak Socialist Republic (see point 8), form a single whole'. The subsequent points spelled out what the Federal Republic would undertake to do in its relationship with the GDR and Czechoslovakia, expressed the intention to expand economic and other ties with the Soviet Union, and committed both states to doing everything they could to advance the Conference on Security and Co-operation in Europe. Although these last six points were not formally incorporated into the treaty, they were solemnly exchanged as joint 'declarations of intent' on the occasion of its signing. The *Ost* in Ostpolitik therefore meant a camp of socialist states dominated by the Soviet Union.

Willy Brandt declared in a memorable television address from Moscow after signing the treaty in August 1970: 'Twenty-five years after the capitulation of the German Reich destroyed by Hitler, and fifteen years after Konrad Adenauer, here in Moscow, agreed the opening of diplomatic relations, the time has come to found our relationship with the East anew — that is, on unconditional mutual renunciation of force, on the basis of the political situation as it exists in Europe.' And, in a phrase that was to become famous, he observed: 'with this treaty nothing is lost that had not long since been gambled away'.

The gambler in this image was Hitler. Without Hitler, Germany might still have had its former territories east of the Oder and Neisse rivers, just as Poland might have had its former territories east of the river Bug. After signing the Warsaw Treaty, Brandt would aver, in another memorable phrase, that his government 'accept[ed] the results of history'. While he might elsewhere suggest that there were missed opportunities in Adenauer's policy towards the East, he left no shadow of doubt that the 'history' at issue here was that of the years before 1945. In his television address from Warsaw, he recalled the image of 'gambled away', and added: 'gambled away by a criminal regime, by National Socialism.' The 'results of history' therefore meant what Hitler had enabled Stalin to take, with a little help — or even, on some interpretations, a lot of help — from Roosevelt and Churchill.

What the Brandt government clearly did not 'accept', however, was that 'the results of history' meant the Germans to the west of the Oder-Neisse line could never be united in one state rather than two. Indeed, in official documents which accompanied the formal proposal for ratification of the Moscow and Warsaw treaties, they took the highly unusual step of publishing (with informal Soviet agreement) their own excerpts from statements made by the Soviet Foreign Minister in his negotiations with Walter Scheel. On the question of peaceful, voluntary changes of frontiers, Gromyko was recorded as saying:

> If two states agree of their own free will to unite, or correct frontiers, as we ourselves have done with Norway, Afghanistan and Poland — there indeed several times — or when two states want, for example, to give up their common frontier and to unite, like Syria and Egypt, it would not occur to us to criticise, for this is an expression of sovereignty and belongs to the inalienable rights of states and peoples.

(The reference — in the course of a German-Soviet negotiation — to Poland's 'voluntary' changes of frontier with the Soviet Union might be taken as a piece of black humour.)

Of course anyone who had suggested at this moment that in just twenty years' time the two German states would be uniting by mutual agreement, with Moscow's assent, would have been laughed out of the room — by German leaders as much as by Soviet ones. Yet the importance attached by the Brandt government to publishing this statement does indicate more than just their desperate desire to get the treaties ratified against furious opposition from Christian Democrats, who accused them of closing the door to German reunification. It also shows, what anyone who examined their earlier record would never doubt, that they cared passionately about bringing the Germans in East and West back together again. In recognising the end of Germany east of the Oder-Neisse line they drew a long-term conclusion from a terrible 'history' — which Brandt had actively opposed. In recognising the second German state, by contrast, they hoped to initiate a long-term process which would lead to fundamental change. While the two 'recognitions' came as one, their quality and thrust differed fundamentally.

Critics said they had conceded too much to Soviet demands, through over-hasty and ill-prepared negotiation by the armchair Metternich, Egon Bahr. Boris Meissner, a leading specialist on German-Soviet relations, described the Moscow Treaty as 'a notable success of Soviet diplomacy'. And while Gromyko at the time suggested the Soviet side had made 'painful' concessions, in his memoirs he writes complacently: 'Consistently in favour of a treaty with the Federal Republic, the USSR was, of course, largely responsible for its character.' There can be no doubt that the explicit recognition of the hard reality of post-Yalta 'Eastern Europe' — where recognition meant not just acknowledgement of *faits accomplis* but also acceptance as the basis for future relations — was profoundly welcome to the Soviet leadership.

Yet to treat this as merely a 'concession' by the German side would be to miss the essential point of what Brandt and Bahr were trying to do. For Bahr's 'concept' was to use this Soviet domination to force the reluctant East German satellite state into closer ties with West Germany, as well as securing vital improvements for West Berlin. As in a judo throw, Bonn would help its much larger opponent to swing in the direction he wanted to go, and then use the Soviet Union's weight for Germany's purpose. Berlin and East Germany were the prizes. Brandt's handwritten notes for his talks with Brezhnev in Moscow on the occasion of signing the treaty start with the question 'Who gets what?' The German side of his list begins: '-*Bln*, -*DDR*'. (Interestingly, the third point is '*Repar. tot*', and he would later note that the annulment of any potential reparations claims was the one and only thing which the Moscow Treaty had in common with Rapallo.)

Bonn insisted that it could not formally negotiate with Moscow over Berlin, since this would tempt the Soviets to resume their old game of trying to undermine the position of the Western Allies in West Berlin. But already in his preliminary talks with Gromyko, Bahr emphasised that Berlin — 'the heart of Europe', as he called it — was a vital German interest. And before signing the Moscow Treaty, the Brandt-Scheel government made an explicit linkage between the ratification of that treaty and the succesful conclusion of a new détente agreement between the four powers over Berlin. In notes scribbled for his response to Brezhnev during their talks in Moscow on 12 August 1970, Brandt listed three 'hopes' '*Ml-Eur* [*Mitteleuropa*], *DDR*, *Berlin*'. From '*Berlin*' he drew an arrow to the lapidary annotation: '*Beding. Ego*'. That is, 'condit[ion] me'.

This so-called *Berlin-Junktim* was, again, a gamble, since it put the fate of West Germany's Ostpolitik in the hands of the three Western allies as well as the Soviet Union. Immensely intricate and delicate negotiations followed, involving, crucially, Henry Kissinger and Egon Bahr — the two Metternichs of détente. But this gamble also paid off, partly because all four powers had a general interest in reducing tensions around Berlin in a period of burgeoning East-West détente, yet more specifically because the Soviet Union faced a hard double linkage: that made by Bonn with the ratification of the Moscow treaty, and that made by Washington with progress in American-Soviet relations, notably over the Strategic Arms Limitation Talks and the arrangement of a Nixon-Brezhnev summit.

The resulting Quadripartite Agreement of September 1971 was, of course, a compromise, which left open or ambiguous a few issues which were to be the source of much diplomatic agony over the next two decades, notably the exact nature and limits of the Federal presence in West Berlin and the inclusion of Berlin in West German treaties or agreements with the Soviet Union and Eastern Europe. Yet the compromise was, on balance, decidedly to the advantage of the West. Looking at the draft agreement worked out through American-German-Soviet back-channels, the American ambassador to Bonn, Kenneth Rush, wrote to Kissinger: 'it is still difficult for me to believe that it is as favorable as it is'.

Brandt's close aide and successor as Governing Mayor of Berlin, Klaus Schütz, had formulated the desiderata for his city as 'three Zs': *Zuordnung* (that is, *assignment* to the Federal Republic, including the right for Federal institutions to be present in West Berlin, and for West Berlin to be represented in and by Federal bodies), *Zugang* (that is, *access* from West Germany to West Berlin, and vice versa), and *Zutritt* (that is, the right of West Berliners to *entry* into East Berlin and the rest of East Germany). On the first point there was some improvement on the status quo, since the Soviet side accepted a formulation in the treaty whereby the 'ties' between West Berlin and West Germany would be 'maintained and developed'. Clear progress was made on the second and third points, since the Soviet Union formally resumed overall responsibility for securing Western civilian access through East Germany to West Berlin, and for ensuring that 'communications' between West Berlin and the surrounding territory (i.e. East Berlin and East Germany) would be 'improved'.

The practical realisation of these commitments of course depended on agreements between what the Quadripartite Agreement called 'the competent German authorities'. Reaching *West* Berlin via Moscow was thus only half the diplomatic journey on which Brandt, Bahr and Scheel had embarked at the end of 1969. The other, and in the longer-term the more important half, was to reach *East* Berlin via Moscow. Brandt mentioned one further anniversary in his television speech from Moscow, beside the twenty-five years since 1945, and the fifteen years since Adenauer's visit. 'Tomorrow [i.e. 13 August 1970],' he said, 'it will be nine years since the Wall was built. Today we have, so I confidently hope, made a beginning, so that the fracturing can be worked against, so that people no longer need to die on barbed wire, until the division of our people can hopefully one day be overcome.' Would Moscow now, as Gromyko had promised Bahr, 'talk to' the leaders of the GDR, pressuring them to open up to the Federal Republic? Here was the vital third side of the Bonn-Moscow-Berlin triangle.

From the Brandt papers we get glimpses of the Chancellor trying to, as it were, work the triangle. Thus, following the signature of the Quadripartite Agreement on Berlin and his controversial summit meeting with

Brezhnev at Oreanda in the Crimea in September 1971, where Berlin and the GDR had been top of his personal agenda, Brandt emphatically informs Brezhnev — in a letter dated 9 February 1972 — that he 'regards the creation of a *modus vivendi* with the GDR . . . as [a? the?] central task of our policy'. And in a message sent with Egon Bahr to Moscow in October 1972 he discreetly appeals for Soviet help in pushing the GDR to conclude negotiations on the Basic Treaty with the Federal Republic, *before* the federal election in November. He links this appeal, in the most delicate way, to the prospect of the GDR entering the United Nations, progress towards a Conference on Security and Cooperation in Europe, improved relations between the Soviet Union and the European Economic Community and, not least, the strengthening of German-Soviet economic ties. *Quid pro quo*. Armed with this letter, Bahr spent four hours talking to Brezhnev.

To see precisely what direct effect such appeals had on the East German position — whether Brezhnev, as it were, picked up the telephone or dashed off a note to Erich Honecker — we will, of course, need to study the top-level documents from the third side of the triangle. A few of these documents are, in fact, already accessible, and we may hope that more will follow. What appear to be Honecker's own notes of two sets of talks between the East German leadership and Brezhnev in December 1969 and May 1970 suggest a deep Soviet suspicion of the West German leader's intentions — 'one must unmask him' — but also a determination to press ahead with negotiations.

Most revealing in this connection are the notes on a one-to-one conversation between Brezhnev and Honecker on 28 July 1970, at the very moment when Walter Scheel was also in Moscow negotiating the last small amendments to the (West) German-Soviet treaty. The main subject of this conversation was the unacceptable arrogance and pig-headedness of the veteran East German Party leader, Walter Ulbricht, and the possibility of Brezhnev's replacing him with the younger and more flexible Erich Honecker. '*I tell you quite openly*,' the German record has Brezhnev saying, '*it will not be possible for him [Ulbricht] to rule without us, to take ill-considered steps against you [Honecker] or other comrades in the Politburo. After all, we have troops in your country*.' (Emphasis in original, presumably by Honecker). In the midst of this frank, comradely exchange, Brezhnev mentions that Scheel is in Moscow, and that a treaty will be signed. 'This will not solve all problems, *but the conclusion of this treaty will be a success for us, for the SU, the socialist countries. The GDR will gain from this treaty*. Its international authority will be increased. Its frontiers, its existence will be confirmed for all the world to see, its inviolability. This will consolidate the position inside the GDR.'

'To be sure,' Brezhnev went on, 'Brandt also expects advantages. He wants to penetrate you. But with time he will find that ever harder.' And in what seems to be an earlier rough note of the same conversation, Brezhnev is recorded as saying: 'Brandt is under double pressure. He must come to agreements with us. He hopes in this way to realise his goals in relation to the GDR. Socialdemocratisation [of the] GDR.' In the course of the conversation, Brezhnev urges Honecker to do everything to resist these influences: 'It . . . must not come to a process of rapprochement between the FRG and the GDR.' So, he says, 'concentrate everything on the all-sided strengthening of the GDR, as you call it.'

The mistrust of, and even hostility to Brandt which speaks from the records of 1969–70 was obviously moderated, at the very least, by their subsequent encounters. Talking to Honecker in Moscow in June 1974, shortly after Brandt's resignation, Brezhnev said 'objectively one must pay him tribute'. The tribute was nonetheless double-edged: 'For thirty years we˗have fought to realise our political goals in Europe. This man has risked pursuing such an Ostpolitik. Have we lost by it? No. The socialist countries and in the first place the GDR have won˗by it.'

Altogether, these documents show, in an uncommonly direct and vivid way, that Brezhnev had a quite shrewd idea of what Brandt was up to; that he felt the Soviet Union had the upper hand in the initial negotiations with the Federal Republic; and that — although not without considerable misgivings — he judged that a new East German leader, more flexible but also more closely tied to Moscow, should be able to control the effects of West German influence inside the GDR.

How far that was in fact the case — whether Brandt's gamble or Brezhnev's paid off — we shall examine in the next chapter. But it is a matter of chronological record that the opening of negotiations between Egon Bahr, for the Federal Republic, and Michael Kohl, for the GDR, followed three and a half months after the signature of the Moscow Treaty; that only following the removal of the recalcitrant Walter Ulbricht and the appointment of Erich Honecker as Party leader in May 1971 did these negotiations bear fruit, first in two minor agreements (made necessary by the Quadripartite Agreement on Berlin), then in a Traffic Treaty, then in the full Treaty on the Bases of Relations, which was initialled, as Brandt had requested, before the federal election of November 1972; and that, in these early years as Party leader, Honecker both publicly and privately emphasised the unbreakable and exemplary closeness of his relations with Moscow.

So Brandt, Bahr and Scheel did indeed make concessions, or diplomatic down payments, to the 'Eastern leading power'. But what they gave in Moscow was intrinsically and, so to speak, umbilically linked to what they hoped to get in the centre of Germany and Europe. Their long-term aim was not to cement the existing reality in Central Europe, but to transform it. As they themselves averred, a shade dialectically: one had to recognise the status quo in order to overcome it.

It is, however, equally important to note what they did not give. What they did not give was any immediate weakening of the Federal Republic's ties with, indeed its Adenauerian anchoring in, the West. Publicly and privately, Brandt and Scheel never tired of repeating the message that Ostpolitik did not diminish their commitment to further steps of economic-political integration in the (West) European Community, on the one hand, and to continued military-political integration in Nato on the other. They devoted considerable diplomatic efforts to reassuring their Western partners on this point. Nor did Brandt omit to mention it in his talks in the East. His scribbled notes for his response to Brezhnev in Moscow in August 1970 say: 'Alliances, us: Rome, loyal'. (There had been an important Nato meeting in Rome in May 1970.) And in his notes for their Crimean summit he writes 'Basic principle: in loyalty to allies and not at the cost of others.' In his Nobel Peace Prize lecture, Brandt said he did not like the very term 'Ostpolitik' not only because it was poisoned by earlier usage but also because it suggested that foreign policy was like a chest of drawers, in which one could pull out now one and now the other drawer. 'In reality it is thus: our détente policy began in the West and remains anchored in the West.'

Yet, as we have indicated already, this profound harmony was far from self-evident, not only to West Germany's Western partners, not just to the social-liberal government's Christian Democratic critics, but also to at least one of the main architects of the Ostpolitik. In his time as head of the planning staff in the Foreign Ministry, Egon Bahr produced two working papers which he considered to be of fundamental importance. As we have seen, the second of these, dating from September 1969, sketched the overall concept of 'normalising' West Germany's bilateral relations with the East: a concept that he himself put into practice in the crucial negotiations with Moscow and the GDR.

The first working paper attempted, in June 1968, to 'analyse German interests in the discussion about the shaping of European security'. The goal of the Federal Republic was here defined as 'the overcoming of the status quo through a European peace order', at the centre of which it clearly placed 'the overcoming of the division of Germany'. Sketching three different 'conceptions' of European security, the paper argued that German interests, thus defined, would best be served by 'Conception C': an entirely new European security system, replacing Nato and the Warsaw Pact. (The suggestion had been made in the 1966 Bucharest declaration of the Warsaw Pact.)

This entirely new European security system, whose headquarters were to be in Berlin, would consist of a central zone of non-nuclear states, including the two German states, the Benelux countries, Poland and Czechoslovakia. They would have no foreign troops on their soil, but their collective security would be guaranteed by the nuclear-armed superpowers.

This system would 'to be sure, concede Soviet demands (recognition of the GDR and the Oder-Neisse line, probably also weakening of our ties to Berlin), but only uses them to create the preconditions for reunification'. The communist leadership of the GDR would fear for its own survival without the presence of Soviet troops, but 'higher Soviet interests' would compel them to accept it. Judo again.

The paper conceded, however, that such a system did not seem achievable for the foreseeable future. In the meantime, it argued, the best variant for Germany would be to continue to work for the greatest possible détente between the existing alliances ('Conception A'), and, in particular, to press for substantial reductions of conventional forces in Central Europe. The clear implication was, nonetheless, that if it ever became possible, Germany should attempt to move from Conception A to Conception C. The notion of a dynamic sequence — from A to C — was spelled out even more clearly in a conversation which Bahr had with an American political scientist, Walter Hahn, in January 1969.

Conception C was more sophisticated than the crude deal proposed in the early 1950s: unity in return for neutrality. But it was still, in its basic premises, closer to that than it was to the Adenauerian commitment, in which the political-military alliance with the United States was as important as the political-economic integration in the European Community. The result would be Germany between East and West rather than Germany as part of the West. This was, of course, precisely what the Federal Republic's Western allies feared.

Now one should not make too much of a single planning staff paper. Planners are there to think the unthinkable. Yet this was more than a mere *jeu d'esprit*. There was a hard and powerful logic of national interest to these arguments, a logic that had persuaded many national-minded Christian and Free Democrats as well as Social Democrats in the early years of the Federal Republic. As we shall see, the Social Democrats returned to these ideas, and developed them further, while in opposition in the 1980s. The other working paper of Bahr's planning staff was largely put into practice in the foreign policy of the Federal Republic. And in a letter to Brandt dated 14 November 1972, anticipating the social-liberal coalition's return to office for another term, Bahr wrote:

> in foreign policy the government can ensure that until the end of the next term the first steps of troop reductions are implemented. I would happily take on this task, neglecting the CSCE. The sainted planning staff has, as you know, already for this term too its papers, which, by the way, in the last three years have proved to be quite workable.

In the event, however, the Brandt government in its second term did no more that attempt to put into practice the — for Germany — most desirable variant of Conception A. In particular, they pressed hard, but unsuccessfully, for rapid progress on conventional troop reductions in Central Europe. 'We deflected the German initiative,' writes Henry Kissinger in his memoirs, 'by supporting a Canadian set of general MBFR [Mutual Balanced Force Reductions] principles of inspired vagueness.' Bahr himself would clearly have liked to do more, but, as he recalls, for the first half of 1973 he was simply exhausted after the huge endeavour of negotiating the treaty work. By the time he recovered, the government was already shaking under other problems. Moreover, in this first phase of the new Ostpolitik, most policymakers agreed that it would be disastrous to be seen in the West to put in question the basic lines of Nato strategy and policy. It is far from certain that even Willy Brandt would at this time have fully endorsed Bahr's analysis of where long-term German interests lay. Walter Scheel and the then Defence Minister, Helmut Schmidt, certainly did not. As we have noted before, the motives and attitudes of the main architects of social-liberal Ostpolitik were quite diverse.

There were three main arguments for making the Nato connection non-negotiable. The first was, so to speak, existential. After the erratic course it had steered in the past, Germany required this heavy anchor in the West to prevent it straying once again between East and West, and losing its balance, as the post-Bismarckian Reich had lost its balance, in the tangle of competing ties, aspirations and demands.

The second was strategic. So long as Germany (West) was threatened by a nuclear-armed superpower in the East, it required the protection of a nuclear-armed superpower in the West. This 'balance of power' argument was urged most forcefully by Helmut Schmidt, who was much less inclined than Bahr or Brandt to believe that the relaxation of tensions, and the development of new forms of political, economic, cultural and other ties with the Soviet Union and its allies, could be a substitute for military defences against what he saw as an historically expansionist Russia.

Finally, there was the tactical argument: in order to gain and retain the support of Germany's Western partners, Bonn could not be seen to put those Western ties in question. On the contrary, she must redouble her insistence on their importance.

The existential argument was probably accepted by only a minority of those who made Ostpolitik. Most of them thought Germany was now big enough and wise enough to do more looking after herself. That was, indeed, a leitmotif of the new policy. The strategic argument was probably accepted by most, albeit with some reluctance. The tactical argument was endorsed by all without exception.

As a result, the diplomatic 'system' which Brandt, Bahr and Scheel built in the years 1970–73 contained no new security components — a fact which Bahr would subsequently regard as a crucial omission (see Chapter Six). It was also erected on the clear understanding that the Federal Republic would not diminish, but would rather redouble, its efforts to push ahead with political integration of the (West) European Community. Following the important Hague summit of December 1969, the EC — enlarged to include Britain, Ireland and Denmark — began the practice of regular consultation on foreign policy, later formalised as European Political Cooperation. 'I think it is no exaggeration to say that the European ship has only set sail again following the Hague conference', Willy Brandt wrote in an eloquent personal letter to the sceptical former US High Commissioner in Germany, John McCloy, pleading for acceptance of the Ostpolitik. Like the commitment to the Atlantic Alliance, this commitment to the European Community was tactical for some, but strategic or existential for most.

The last year and a half of Brandt's Chancellorship, after the double triumph of his re-election and the signature of the Basic Treaty with the GDR at the end of 1972, saw the installation of the last bilateral components of Ostpolitik, and the beginnings of what was always meant to be its multilateral development. Bilaterally, Brezhnev's successful state visit to Bonn in 1973 confirmed the new quality of German-Soviet relations, while placing particular emphasis, predictably enough, on economic ties. In his thank-you letter, Brezhnev wrote: 'After public opinion in our country has made itself thoroughly acquainted with the work done together with you during the visit, I can now tell you with absolute certainty that the Party and the Soviet people fully endorse and support the course of improvement and development of relations between the USSR and the Federal Republic.' Handing over this letter, the Soviet ambassador to Bonn, Valentin Falin, said he had the impression that a 'remarkable personal contact' had developed between the Chancellor and the Soviet leader.

Responding, a few months later, to Brezhnev's message of greetings on his sixtieth birthday, Brandt passed in review the development of German-Soviet relations, emphasised particularly the tripling of trade, touched on problems connected with West Berlin, and then, once again, appealed directly to Brezhnev to make the GDR more co-operative with the Federal Republic. He was particularly concerned, he wrote, about the doubling of the minimum amount that visitors from West Germany and West Berlin were compelled to exchange on every visit to the GDR: 'The Soviet side may not realise how negative is the impression made by this and other measures taken by the GDR on our public opinion.' (If Brezhnev could cite his 'public opinion' so, with considerably more justification, could Brandt.)

The situation which has emerged compels me to draw your attention to the danger that such a negative development could significantly endanger the efforts of my government to widen the policy of détente. I should be most grateful, dear General Secretary, if you could also turn your attention to this problem. It must surely be possible that, for example, the GDR finds a way to compensate the negative effects of its order on the minimum exchange.

Working the triangle again.

At the same time, the bilateral East European network was completed with the relatively easy establishment of diplomatic relations with Hungary and Bulgaria, and the much more difficult conclusion of a treaty with Czechoslovakia. Negotiated with Husák's 'normalising' regime in the shadow of the Soviet invasion, and plagued by legal arguments about whether the 1938 Munich Agreement should be considered invalid from the outset (*ex tunc*) or merely from now on (*ex nunc*), the Prague Treaty of 1973 left unclarities which would return to trouble relations between Prague and Bonn in the early 1990s. Meanwhile, both German states finally became full members of the UN. Multilaterally, both the talks of Mutual Balanced Force Reductions (MBFR) in Vienna and the Conference on Security and Co-operation in Europe (CSCE) got under way, with active German participation. Public statements and private papers make it clear that Brandt regarded the two sets of talks as intimately linked, and that he looked for the completion of those on conventional troop reductions in a time-scale of five years. But these plans were to remain on paper.

Already drained by the Herculean effort of putting this system into place, and much less effective in domestic than in foreign policy, Willy Brandt was toppled, ironically enough by the exposure of one of his aides as an East German spy. Walter Scheel became Federal President. It therefore fell to Brandt's successor as Social Democratic Chancellor, Helmut Schmidt, and Scheel's successor as Free Democratic Foreign Minister, Hans-Dietrich Genscher, to try and 'make work' the complex and delicate diplomatic system that Brandt, Bahr and Scheel had built.

System and crisis

At the time, an outstanding historian of German foreign policy, Waldemar Besson, commented that two fundamentally different traditions had now to be combined: the Adenauerian tradition of unambiguous commitment to Western Europe, and the Bismarckian tradition of standing free in the centre of Europe while attempting to keep a balance with and between the states around Germany. Adenauer met Bismarck.

It was not to Besson alone that the comparison with Bismarck occurred. Henry Kissinger, in his memoirs, compared Bahr's approach to that of Bismarck. When the comparison was put by an interviewer to Bahr himself, he said: 'I have been fascinated, really for as long as I can remember, by Bismarck's foreign policy, and I consider him to have been one of the real greats that we had.' Yet as that interviewer observed, Bismarck had begun a juggling act with many balls, a game which was very complicated, indeed 'too complicated'. Yes, agreed Bahr, 'the real mastery is showed when one has a system that continues to work even without its inventors'. Spoke the latter-day Bismarck.

It is also interesting to find that in a statement to mark the centenary of the proclamation of the German Reich, on 18 January 1971, Chancellor Brandt described Bismarck as 'one of the great statesmen of our nation'. 'The solution of 100 years ago,' he wrote, 'reflected the insights and possibilities of the time. The world-political situation today requires new forms of the Germans' political living and working together . . .', and hence 'the event of 1871 can be no model today'. But 'the work and achievements of Bismarck are nonetheless a lasting illustration of the fact that only skilful and courageous action, not passive waiting, bring us closer to the given goals' — a side-swipe, of course, at the Christian Democratic opposition.

Plainly the analogy can be pushed too far. But with all due caveats, the diplomatic system that Schmidt and Genscher inherited did have elements of a neo-Bismarckian juggling act. Indeed, in one vital respect it was even more complicated. For at its centre was not a static but a dynamic task: not the defence of the state unity already achieved in Bismarck's Reich, but the business of trying to keep alive a cultural and human unity of the nation in two opposed states, and, in the longer term, even of working towards some kind of political unity, albeit in constitutional forms and geographical boundaries quite different from those of the Bismarckian Reich.

To achieve this, the system demanded — or was thought to demand — what might be called horizontal synchronisation of the whole Ostpolitik. The failure of Foreign Minister Schröder's 'policy of movement' was held to have shown that Bonn could not hope to develop closer ties with East European states without Moscow's assent. Moscow's assent depended on recognition of the GDR, and Moscow's weight was at first needed to bring the GDR itself to the negotiating table — the Bahr-judo. But as relations with the GDR warmed up, so it was felt that relations with East European states and with the Soviet Union itself must also be enhanced, so that neither Moscow nor its East European allies (who might then complain to Moscow) would feel threatened by the German-German rapprochement. Whereas the United States' Ostpolitik was based on the principle of 'differentiation' — rewarding those Soviet bloc states that 'behaved well' in domestic or foreign policy, punishing those that behaved badly — the Federal Republic's Ostpolitik was thus based on a principle of synchronisation.

Yet this horizontal or eastward synchronisation, complicated enough in itself, was only half the juggling act. For given the continued, Adenauerian, commitments to the West, a complementary, westward or vertical synchronisation was needed. If the Federal Republic was to carry on integrating into Western Europe as well as thickening its ties with Eastern Europe, then the rest of Western Europe must also go on thickening its ties with Eastern Europe. Otherwise the tension between the two, between Ostpolitik and Europapolitik (a term used in Bonn essentially to describe EC-policy), would become unbearable. An untoward development in any one East European country, or Soviet reaction to such a development, would be threatening to Bonn's policy not only because it might impel Moscow to tighten the imperial leash on the GDR, but also because it might incline Bonn's West European partners to retaliate against Moscow.

Similarly, but *a fortiori*, Bonn could only develop its relations with Moscow (the key to Berlin and the GDR) and maintain its intimate political-military integration in the US-led alliance, if the United States and the Soviet Union continued to have 'détente' relations as good or preferably better than they had when the system was erected. If US-Soviet relations worsened, then Bonn would be torn between the two. The system thus demanded vertical as well as horizontal synchronisation. The national, regional and global levels of détente had somehow all to be kept in harmony. This was a very tall order for what was still only a medium-sized European power, economically stronger than France or Britain, to be sure, but also with unique historical and diplomatic handicaps.

Moreover, this complex task had to be attempted at a time when the Federal Republic faced other major challenges in its external relations. Brandt, Bahr and Scheel had concentrated on Ostpolitik, and to a lesser degree on Europapolitik, to the disadvantage of, indeed even to the neglect of, other areas. One of these was the turbulence in the world economy following the collapse of the Bretton Woods international monetary order and the shock of drastically increased oil prices. For the Federal Republic, a 'trading state' *par excellence*, this was a challenge of the first order. Here was, without question, the first external preoccupation of the new Chancellor, Helmut Schmidt.

In a long, confidential *tour d'horizon* drafted during his Christmas holiday at the end of 1976, and hence known internally as the 'Marbella paper', Schmidt wrote: 'Never since the world economic crisis of the thirties have domestic political, foreign political, and political-economic actions of the rulers (and of parliament) in Germany had such a strong mutual dependency . . . as in the last years. That would seem to be no less true, indeed perhaps more so, for *the year 1977, which will again stand under the primacy of economic policy*' (italics in original). And it is perhaps for his achievements in organising world economic crisis management, and European economic co-operation, that Schmidt will be remembered. Meanwhile his new Foreign Minister, the Free Democratic Hans-Dietrich Genscher, although deeply committed to increasing contacts with the part of Germany from which he himself came, 'profiled' himself (and his party) in this period above all by cultivating the relationship with the United States.

The relative importance of Ostpolitik in the foreign policy of the Federal Republic under Chancellor Schmidt was therefore less than it had been under Brandt. But it would be wrong to suggest that Schmidt neglected or did not care about it. To argue, as did his sometime private archivist, Hans Georg Lehmann, that Schmidt had actually been the true architect of the Social Democratic concept of Ostpolitik which Brandt and Bahr implemented, would be, to put it mildly, an overstatement. But Schmidt had been actively involved in the Social Democrats' public discussion of Ostpolitik since an important speech he delivered at the Dortmund party conference in 1966, a year in which he also travelled privately to Eastern Europe. As parliamentary floor leader, he had been intimately involved in the formulation of Ostpolitik in the late 1960s. As we have noted already, he led a parliamentary delegation on an important trip to Moscow in 1969.

If childhood and family ties gave Hans-Dietrich Genscher a very special interest in East Germany, Helmut Schmidt shared with many of his generation a very specific and complex emotional involvement in relations with the East that derived from having fought as a soldier on the Eastern front in the Second World War. He was, typically, almost archetypically, a representative of this *Frontgeneration*, combining a sombre intellectual and emotional reading of the lessons of that terrible experience ('never again') with a strong residual liking for the methods and manners of a General Staff.

Like all his predecessors, Schmidt also saw very clearly the intimate link between the relationship to the East and the Federal Republic's real freedom of action as a sovereign state. 'We seek,' he wrote in the 1970 Preface to the English edition of his book *The Balance of Power*, 'to use Germany's present scope for taking action. If that attempt is successful it will change and improve the part of the world we live in. If it should fail the partition of Europe will become more permanent. . . . This book basically deals with the scope of action of German foreign policy.' As Chancellor, he self-consciously and self-confidently used the enlarged room for manoeuvre, the greater *de facto* sovereignty, that the Eastern treaty work gave to the Federal Republic. Yet, as with all his predecessors, there were two sides to this coin.

On the one hand, he could on occasion quite directly and even aggressively assert German interests, and German views of European, Western or global interests, notably in his bilateral discussions with the United States and above all with President Jimmy Carter. On the other hand, he was concerned to enmesh German interests, policies and perspectives in the increasingly multilateral frameworks of Western foreign policy-making. Indeed, he was very active in promoting this multilateral co-ordination, whether in the EC, Nato, or the new Group of Seven (G7) top industrial states which held a notable summit in Bonn in 1978. Partly, of course, this was because he thought such multilateral co-ordination was good in itself, good for the world. But there was also, as with his predecessors, a special German motive.

In his confidential Marbella paper he argued that the Federal Republic had become 'in the eyes of the world *de facto* economically the second world power of the West'. This 'unwanted and dangerous rise to second world power of the West in the consciousness of other governments — including especially the Soviet leadership! –' would arouse concerns, and could have negative effects, notably for Berlin. There could be 'a revival of memories not only of Auschwitz and Hitler but also of Wilhelm II and Bismarck . . . perhaps as much in the West as in the East.' It was therefore, he went on, 'necessary for us, so far as at all possible, to operate not nationally and independently but in the framework of the European Community and of the Alliance. This *attempt to cover [abdecken] our actions multilaterally will only partially* succeed, because we will (necessarily and against our own will) become a leadership factor in both systems' [italics in original]. One could write a small essay on the nuances of the word *abdecken* in this sentence. For multilateralism was to 'cover' the growth of German power in many senses: to camouflage, but also to control; to manage, but also to permit; to facilitate, but also to palliate.

In relations with the East, too, the period of Schmidt's Chancellorship, from 1974 to 1982, was one of burgeoning multilateralism. There were the multilateral talks on Mutual Balanced Force Reductions. There were, increasingly, multilateral consultations about economic relations with the East, in the Group of Seven, the International Monetary Fund, the World Bank, the so-called CoCom, controlling the export of Western high technology to the East, and later in the Paris and London 'clubs' of the Western governments and banks to whom Eastern states were increasingly indebted. There was the growth of the EC member states' European Political Cooperation, particularly in connection with the preparations for, and then the follow-up to, the Helsinki Conference on Security and Cooperation in Europe. Above all, there was that whole 'Helsinki process' itself. Yet beside this novel style of institutionalised, ongoing multilateralism there was some quite old-fashioned bilateralism as well.

For Schmidt had in many ways a very old-fashioned view of history being made by what history teachers used to call 'great men'. He regarded summit meetings between those whom he described as *Staatslenker* (roughly: state-pilots) as the key to the development of bilateral relations between states. Accordingly, he systematically went down the list of East European leaders, organising visits from and to Bonn. Plainly, these meetings had an importance of their own. Thus he established a particularly close rapport with the Polish Party leader Edward Gierek: a friendship that combined the profound desire of a member of the *Frontgeneration* for 'reconciliation' with personal liking, but resulted in economic, political and even moral misjudgement (see Chapter Six). Yet all these East European ties were clearly subordinated to those with Moscow, Schmidt's first Eastern port of call in 1974.

On a return visit to Bonn, in May 1978, Brezhnev cannily observed that (as the interpreter's protocol records) 'the role of the Federal Republic of Germany as a state which pursues a distinct and independent policy had begun when the door had been opened to a rapprochement (*Annäherung*) with the Soviet Union and the other socialist states: when what in the Federal Republic was called Ostpolitik had begun.' West Germany, he implied, had its own very special interest in the continuation of détente. In his response, Schmidt said (again according to the interpreter's record) that 'the General Secretary was right when he said that the international weight of the Federal Republic had grown since the Moscow Treaty. This weight had been used to further détente. . . . Visits and the exchange of visits had taken place with Gierek, Kádár, Zhivkov, Ceauşescu. Dr Husák had visited his country as the first Western country [i.e. to give Husák that opportunity].' (The favour was more warmly appreciated by the rulers in Moscow than by the ruled in Prague.) But, Schmidt went on, 'naturally German-Soviet relations stood at the centre of Ostpolitik. This would be so for the next 30 years.'

Schmidt established a good and even sentimental relationship with Brezhnev, based, as more than once between Germans and Russians of their generation, on the experience of having fought each other on the Eastern Front. When they first met, during Brezhnev's first visit to Bonn in May 1973, Schmidt responded to Brezhnev's remarks about the suffering of the Soviet people in the Great Patriotic War with a long and very personal explanation of the schizophrenia of those young soldiers who had fought for Germany by day, yet at night privately wished for Hitler to fail. Willy Brandt, with the exile's quite different perspective on that war, comments drily that 'when war reminiscences are exchanged, the false and the genuine lie very close together'. Yet though Schmidt also recognises the element of calculation in Brezhnev's regular vodka-and-tears turns, he records that he felt genuine sorrow on receiving news of Brezhnev's death. Indeed, he sometimes believed himself better understood by Leonid Brezhnev than by Jimmy Carter.

Like Brandt and Bahr, Schmidt tried to work the Bonn Moscow-Berlin triangle for the benefit of West Berlin and West German policy towards the GDR. Thus, for example, in the record of a conversation with the Soviet Ambassador to Bonn, Valentin Falin, in the run-up to Schmidt's visit to Moscow in October 1974, we find the Chancellor once again raising the subject of the increased compulsory minimum exchange of hard currency for Western visitors to the GDR. Three days before Schmidt flew to Moscow, the GDR announced a reduction of the minimum exchange. A purely sovereign East German decision, of course.

A more explicit subject of debate between Bonn and Moscow was the interpretation of the Quadripartite Agreement on Berlin, which occupied a great deal of time in German-Soviet talks. In a conversation with the Chancellor in 1974, Gromyko spoke dismissively of the idea that Berlin could be a 'barometer' for the state of East-West relations, since the Soviet Union 'wanted détente and peace for the whole world. For this, Berlin was hardly an impressive quantity.' Berlin might not be a barometer, Schmidt replied, but the ties to Berlin were a 'central interest' of the Federal Republic, which was — he modestly observed — 'a power of middling importance, limited to Central Europe, and thus the [Berlin] problem was much more significant for us.'

In the event, Schmidt, Genscher and their diplomats would have to argue again and again and again for what Brezhnev and Brandt had agreed to call the 'strict observance and full application' of the Quadripartite Agreement. In a personal letter to Brezhnev in April 1975, Schmidt wrote that relations between the Federal Republic and the Soviet Union could not be better than the state of affairs around Berlin. However, Schmidt subsequently concluded — somewhat at odds with the Foreign Ministry — that the interests of Berlin would best be served in the long-term by an indirect strategy of all-round improvement of relations with the Soviet Union, and above all of economic relations, rather than by tactics of constant, direct confrontation on issues such as the presence of Federal Government institutions in West Berlin.

The key-word that recurs constantly in the public statements and private papers of his Chancellorship is 'stability'. As we shall see, this key-word had many meanings, but in this context the primary meaning was: stability of the overall diplomatic system of Ostpolitik, with its dual imperative of vertical and horizontal synchronisation. Thus he was, for example, openly and contemptuously dismissive of Jimmy Carter's missionary campaign to secure more respect for human rights in the Soviet Union and Eastern Europe. As he himself observed retrospectively in a lecture in 1991, he — or, as he put it, 'we Europeans' — had in the 1970s placed the principle of stability before human rights. His book, published in 1969, was called *The Balance of Power. German peace policy and the superpowers*. That, in a nutshell, was what he was about. Like Henry Kissinger (and partly influenced by him) he regarded the balance of power as the key to preserving peace in Europe, and international order more generally. At the same time, he saw détente at the superpower and European levels as the necessary condition for working incrementally to reduce (or at the very least, to prevent the deepening of) the division of Berlin and Germany.

In pursuing these twin goals, he gave priority to two classical instruments. The foreign policy of a state, a French president is reported to have said, consists of arms and then money. In the relationship with the Soviet Union, at least, Schmidt acted pretty much in line with that classical dictum, concentrating heavily on the economic-political and the military-political aspects of the German-Soviet relationship. As a former Defence and then Finance and Economics Minister these were, of course, his own personal specialities. Yet it would be superficial to suggest that he considered them to be crucial because they were his own specialities. It was rather that he had made them his specialities because he considered them to be crucial.

As we have noted already, the hope of modernising the Soviet economy through imports of technology, joint projects and expanded trade had been a major Soviet motive for détente with the West in general, and West Germany in particular. It was, in fact, a key element in that Westpolitik of Brezhnev without which the Ostpolitik of Brandt could never have succeeded. In one of the lighter symbolic moments of Brezhnev's first visit to Bonn, in 1973, the Soviet leader jumped into a gleaming new Mercedes sports car presented to him by the Chancellor and roared off down the road, to the consternation of his security guards. He spoke to his German partners in glowing terms of the prospects for great co-operative ventures and joint exploitation of the Soviet Union's natural resources.

Schmidt took up this ball and ran with it. Already, in a conversation with Gromyko in September 1974, he observed that two motives were especially important for the German side: 'the political motive of stabilisation in Europe and the economic motive of expanding economic co-operation with the Soviet Union'. To describe the latter as an 'economic motive' was a diplomatic simplification. Certainly, the Federal Republic had some economic motives. Its expanding economy had growing energy requirements and, especially following the sharp increases in the price of oil from the Middle East, it seemed attractive to supply more of these from Soviet sources. There was a clear complementarity between a Soviet Union rich in raw materials but poor in quality manufactured goods, and a Federal Republic poor in the former but rich in the latter. The Soviet Union was a genuinely important market for a few particular sectors of German industry. In the 1976 election, the government claimed that trade with the East overall secured some 300,000 jobs, although that number was cut in three by more sober analysis.

Yet private papers and even public statements make it clear that Schmidt's primary motive for expanding economic ties was political. He saw, as he writes in his memoirs, that this Soviet economic interest could be used for advancing German national interests. A memorandum in preparation for a 1977 brainstorming session with leading bankers and industrialists dealing with the East observed that the political aim was 'the long-term securing of détente-policy: increasing Soviet interest in good relations with the West'.

Accordingly, Schmidt was prepared to countenance the barter deals frowned upon by sober-minded industrialists, and the low interest rates deplored by sober-minded bankers. With Brezhnev he discussed grandiose projects such as a state-of-the-art nuclear power station in Kaliningrad (formerly Königsberg), and a huge steel mill at Kursk. Where the Germans and Russians of Schmidt and Brezhnev's generation had fought one of the greatest tank-battles of the Second World War, they would now work peacefully together turning crude Russian ore into shining German steel.

Schmidt himself produced the grandest idea of all: an economic co-operation agreement to run for no less than twenty-five years. The Soviet Union, he told the industrialists and bankers assembled in the 'Chancellor bungalow' for that 1977 brainstorming session, must be convinced that Germany was a peaceful neighbour in the long-term. The point was to create trust 'into the third millennium'. So when Brezhnev came to Bonn in May 1978, he and Schmidt signed a very broadly framed agreement on economic and industrial co-operation with a term (*Laufzeit*) of twenty-five years — although its 'initial period of validity' (*Geltungsdauer*) was only ten years, after which it was to be 'continued' by mutual agreement for five years at a time. According to a government spokesman, the Chancellor saw this as a 'political act without parallel in the recent history of the world'. The businessmen were noticeably more reticent. Otto Wolff von Amerongen, the Nestor of West Germany's eastern trade, observed drily: 'It is not a historic accord.'

Nonetheless, the results of Schmidt's efforts in this area were significant. The total volume of German-Soviet trade in 1979 was six times that of 1969. At the beginning of the decade the Soviet Union accounted for thirty-two per cent of the Federal Republic's eastern trade; by the end of the decade it accounted for forty-five per cent. German policymakers never tired of pointing out that West German exports to the Soviet Union were still much less than those to Austria or Switzerland. Yet some important specialist firms and branches of German heavy industry were very dependent on this trade, while under the commitments entered into during the Schmidt period, Soviet natural gas was to provide nearly thirty per cent of West Germany's natural gas supplies (up to five per cent of its total energy imports) by the end of the 1980s. The Soviet Union was altogether much less dependent on foreign trade than West Germany. But West Germany had become by the end of the decade both quantitatively and qualitatively its most important Western trading partner.

There can be little doubt that these burgeoning economic ties, and the perspective of their grandiose expansion, contributed to the goodwill that is apparent in confidential personal letters from Brezhnev to Schmidt, and that the already seriously ill Soviet leader publicly displayed on his May 1978 visit to Bonn. Indeed, this summer of 1978 was arguably the foreign policy high-point of Schmidt's Chancellorship, with the G7 summit in Bonn following two months after the Soviet leader's visit. Yet even as he and Brezhnev publicly celebrated the achievements of détente, in a Joint Declaration liberally studded with the word, Schmidt knew that the overarching 'stability' of the permissive framework of détente was under serious threat.

Now the reasons for what would be called (prematurely) the 'end of détente' and (overdramatically) the 'second Cold War' were, of course, many and controversial. Indeed, at the time there was a sharp polarisation of opinion in the West, with some portraying Brezhnev's Soviet Union as pursuing Stalinist expansionism under the cloak of 'peaceful co-existence', while others placed the blame equally on both superpowers or mainly on the United States. Yet the new makers of Soviet foreign policy under Gorbachev would themselves subject the Brezhnevite version of détente to withering criticism. No doubt their criticism was in some points exaggerated, as that of political successors and historical revisionists tends to be. Nonetheless, when Soviet policymakers said that certain faults lay with Soviet policy, they surely knew what they were talking about.

First of all, and despite repeated American warnings, the Brezhnev leadership continued to treat détente as divisible. It actively extended its influence in the Third World, using the military and security forces of such close allies as Cuba and East Germany. In itself, this did not worry the Bonn government half so much as it worried the United States. For the Federal Republic was, as Schmidt told Gromyko, a power confined to Central Europe. Indeed, in one of his confidential private letters to Brezhnev, in February 1976, Schmidt had gone so far as to remark that 'in my view the quarrel of both world-powers over Angola is not so important that the confidence of other peoples in the durability of détente should be allowed to suffer from it'. But even if Bonn policymakers thought that American concerns were exaggerated, they had to be worried about the increasingly negative effect of those concerns on American-Soviet relations, and hence on their own Ostpolitik. This was the imperative of vertical synchronisation.

Secondly, the Brezhnev leadership continued its formidable arms build-up, and in particular brought on a new middle-range nuclear missile, known in the West as the SS-20. Whereas Schmidt saw the extension of Soviet power and influence in the Third World only as an indirect challenge, this he saw as a direct threat to vital German interests. There is a deep irony in the military-political story of the German-Soviet relationship in the Schmidt era. 'Altogether, the political part of détente must be complemented by a comprehensive military part', Schmidt told Brezhnev in 1978, and that had been a central tenet of his personal approach to East-West relations for nearly twenty years. As he told Gromyko in their private talks in 1974: 'he liked to think that he was one of the inventors of the principle that was today called MBFR. In 1959 he [had] published a carefully prepared book the central subject of which was mutual balanced arms limitations.' That book, *Defence or Retaliation*, was actually first published in 1961, but Schmidt could justly claim that this had been one of his leitmotifs since 1959, when he delivered a memorable speech to the Bundestag on the need for regional arms control in Central Europe. When Bahr wrote in his 1968 planning staff working paper on European security that 'no account [would be] given of the military aspects', Schmidt underlined the sentence and scribbled in the margin: 'Why?'

It was, therefore, precisely because he attached such importance to balanced arms reductions that Schmidt was so exercised by unbalanced arms increases. That the MBFR talks on conventional forces actually made so little progress, since Nato and the Warsaw Pact could not even agree how many arms and men each side had, was certainly no fault of his. On the other hand, when the superpowers did make slow progress towards a second treaty on strategic arms limitation, the SALT II treaty finally signed by Carter and Brezhnev in June 1979, the West German leader had serious concerns about the weapons it did not cover. In the 'grey area' between SALT and MBFR, containing what Schmidt liked to call 'Eurostrategic weapons', he believed both that German interests were directly affected and that German policy could have some effect.

By his own account, Schmidt first raised this problem on his visit to Moscow in October 1974. When the Soviet Union began to build up its arsenal of SS-20 missiles at considerable speed; Schmidt was increasingly alarmed by this development, as well as being infuriated by what he saw as the inconsistency of Jimmy Carter's leadership. In what was to become a famous speech at the International Institute of Strategic Studies in London in 1977 — and even more in conversation over dinner following the speech — he suggested, among many other points about the economic and political aspects of security, that the West would have to consider restoring the military balance in this area too. There followed what one of the guests at the dinner, the historian Michael Howard, would describe as a transatlantic comedy of errors, with American leaders thinking 'the Europeans' needed more American weapons to reassure them of the American commitment, while 'the Europeans' — and above all the West Germans — felt they should accept these weapons to reassure the Americans, although in fact aiming all the time at arms reductions to be negotiated with the Soviet Union.

In any case, as the culmination of this complex transatlantic conversation, the leaders of the United States, West Germany, France and Britain, meeting on the island of Guadeloupe in January 1979, agreed to produce a 'two-track' proposal according to which, if satisfactory reductions in this area could not be negotiated with the Soviet Union by a given date, Nato would deploy new, modernised American Pershing II and land-based Cruise missiles in Western Europe. This decision was then formalised in Nato's 'double-track' resolution of December 1979, with the date for deployment if negotiations failed set for 1983. In Schmidt's view this was still intended as a contribution to creating the vital military component of détente. It was to be a step towards a SALT III. In the event, however, the SS-20s and the double-track decision proved to be, at least in the short term — and the qualification is an important one — a major blow to what Schmidt had understood to be, and what, from the point of view of German Ostpolitik, was most important about, the thing called détente.

The next blow followed within weeks, although no direct causal connection between the two has credibly been established. This was the Soviet invasion of Afghanistan. Schmidt's reaction was cautious to a fault. With his close political ally and friend Valéry Giscard d'Estaing he issued a declaration which said that 'détente could not survive another blow' such as this. By implication, détente could survive this blow. Yet given the quite different reaction in the United States, and to some extent also in Britain, the whole permissive framework of global détente was actually shaken to its foundations. The Carter administration suspended the ratification process for the SALT II Treaty and imposed sanctions on the Soviet Union, including a boycott of the Moscow Olympics which it called on its allies to join. From this time forward, Schmidt and Genscher looked increasingly like jugglers whose balls were beginning to wobble. Now they travelled tirelessly between Washington and Moscow, attempting to persuade both sides to behave more 'reasonably': that is, to negotiate on arms control and not to allow their extra-European conflicts to interfere with the continuation of intra-European détente.

At the end of June 1980, Schmidt became the first Western head of government to visit Moscow after the Soviet invasion of Afghanistan, although Giscard d'Estaing had, independently — and without prior consultation with his allies in Bonn or anywhere else — gone to meet Brezhnev in Warsaw six weeks before. Schmidt's was a high-risk visit which brought Soviet agreement in principle to negotiate with the United States about intermediate nuclear forces. In his last hours in the Chancellery, in the autumn of 1982, he would look back to this as one of the high points of his Chancellorship. 'The dialogue on nuclear disarmament could continue,' noted his close associate Klaus Bölling. 'There [in Moscow in summer 1980] the first lieutenant of the Greater German Wehrmacht, who in 1941 had come close to Moscow, had undertaken a highly successful reconnaissance mission for the West.'

But then came the emergence of Solidarity in Poland in August 1980. The Polish revolution directly threatened both the horizontal and the vertical synchronisation of Ostpolitik. It made the GDR clamp down not only on any stirrings of dissent at home (it was doing that anyway) but also on the developing relationship between the Germans in East and West. Already in August, Schmidt felt obliged to cancel his planned visit to East Germany because of the strikes in Poland. Then, in October, the GDR increased that compulsory minimum exchange of hard currency which both Brandt and Schmidt had devoted so much diplomatic effort to reducing in the 1970s. The challenge of Solidarity, of the 'Polish disease' as they saw it, clearly frightened all the other East European communist leaderships. Above all, it brought heavy Soviet pressure and the real threat of an armed intervention, such as had ended the Prague Spring.

Even if some in Germany might have wanted to continue the détente with the Soviet Union — in the national interest — even after such an intervention, this could only have been done at the cost of untold damage to Germany's Western ties, both those with her West European neighbours and those with the United States. 'If the Russians invade, everything is *kaputt*' was the succinct analysis of a Schmidt confidant. The imperatives of horizontal and vertical synchronisation therefore demanded that Bonn should, first, do everything in its power to persuade the Soviet Union not to intervene directly; second, do everything it could to limit the damage done by the Polish crisis, both to its own relations with the Soviet Union and the rest of Eastern Europe, and to the permissive environment of regional and global détente; and, third, do what little it could to help towards a 'peaceful' solution in Poland. When General Jaruzelski declared a 'state of war' in Poland on 13 December 1981 — while Schmidt was actually making his long-delayed visit to East Germany, and urging Erich Honecker to use his influence in Moscow — the Bonn government was not entirely clear whether it had failed or succeeded.

The government in Washington, by contrast, had no such doubts: this was neither a peaceful nor an internal Polish solution; it was another August 1968; the thing called détente had failed. For this Washington government was that of Ronald Reagan, which came into office in January 1981 with a strong ideological commitment to stop what it saw as the expansion of the Soviet 'evil empire' by a decisive build-up of American military force. The crisis of the East therefore also became a crisis of the West, with the fiercest argument running between Bonn and Washington. This was the last straw. At the end of Schmidt's Chancellorship, in the autumn of 1982, it looked very much as if the diplomatic house that Brandt, Scheel and Bahr had built, the 'system' of West German Ost-politik, was, if not in ruins, then at least seriously damaged.

In the gathering storm, the Bonn government tried desperately to keep the lines of communication open between the superpowers, and more generally between East and West. When Giscard d'Estaing went to Warsaw in 1980 to meet Brezhnev, François Mitterrand memorably described him as '*le petit télégraphiste de Varsovie*'. Though a scorching insult in the terms of the *grande nation*, Schmidt would probably have had no great problem with such a description. Indeed, in his talks in Moscow in the summer of 1980 he reportedly described himself as 'only a postman'.

He was not, he insists in retrospect, attempting to be a mediator or broker, just an interpreter in the elementary sense of helping the American and Soviet leaders to understand each other when 'the one was talking Eskimo, the other Japanese'. Where Bismarck had described his own and Germany's role as that of an 'honest broker' between the great powers to East and West, Schmidt modestly described his own and the Federal Republic's role as that of 'honest interpreters', but honest interpreters '*of Western policy*' [author's italics]. Yet to make the self-description exact one would have to add 'and of German interests'. Perhaps also: 'in Europe's name'.

At the same time, the German adoption of this role clearly had a special significance. No other Western state's vital interests were so directly involved. Other Western states, starting with the United States, had policies of 'bridge-building'. Only Germany might itself be the bridge — a traditional self-image of late nineteenth- and early twentieth-century German policy, revived by Chancellor Kiesinger in 1966, and on occasion used by Schmidt himself.

The pressures on, and temptations for, German policy in these last years of the Schmidt Chancellorship were very great. For beside this woeful external constellation, there were all the associated domestic pressures. All over Protestant north-west Europe the proposed deployment of new Nato missiles provoked a wave of fear and protest, but nowhere was the fear and the protest more extreme than in Germany. It reached deep into Schmidt's own party. Leading Social Democrats took part in a demonstration of more than a quarter of a million people in Bonn in October 1981 — a demonstration against the new American missiles.

The Soviet Union and East Germany tried both overtly and covertly to encourage these protests. The Social Democrat, Horst Ehmke, wryly remarked to a senior East German functionary in 1981 that the peace movement was growing apace 'with God's and your help'. Yet the more important causal connection went in the other direction. For these essentially indigenous protests encouraged the key foreign-policy decision-makers in Moscow — which now meant Gromyko, Ustinov, Andropov and Suslov as much as the terminally sick Brezhnev — to believe that if they played their cards right they might be able to prevent the new Nato deployment, and thus drive a deep wedge between the United States and West Germany.

At the Social Democrats' party conference in April 1982, the leadership could not be sure of getting a majority for the deployment of American missiles if negotiations failed. Instead, this decision was put off to a special conference in 1983. At the same time the Schmidt government was racked by deepening economic and financial difficulties, and by the increasing fragility of the coalition with the Free Democrats. The way in which all these internal and external concerns came together in the formulation of foreign policy positions is vividly illustrated by an internal Chancellery planning staff paper, leaked in the spring of 1982.

This paper proposed 'for substantive, electoral and coalition-political reasons' that the Chancellor should 'set new and controversial accents' in the discussion of foreign policy. The intended controversy was not with the East but with the West: to be precise, with the new right-wing governments of the United States and Great Britain. Public opinion polls, argued the paper, showed that the majority of the population — and particularly of Social and Free Democratic voters — was for a continuation of détente, for increased economic co-operation with the Soviet Union, and 'for a mediator-role of Europe/the Federal Republic between the United States and the Soviet Union, even if this could lead to dissonance with the United States'. (Note the conflation of 'Europe' and 'Federal Republic', even in an internal analysis.) A forcefully expressed claim for 'more autonomy for Europe/the Federal Republic . . . and thereby conflicts with the neo-conservative ideology and the Reagan-Thatcher administrations' would divert public attention from domestic problems and put the Free Democrats on the spot.

The paper went on to spell out elements of the proposed 'controversial' argument. For example: 'Large groups in the USA and GB are in the process of turning away from the common policy and the common values of the West. They endanger the social-political attractiveness of the West in competitition with the communists. They endanger détente (*Entspannungspolitik*).' So far as the Soviet Union was concerned, there had also to be a clear ideological argument: 'clear distance to Soviet bureaucratism; this is not what socialism looks like,' and furthermore: 'clear distance to overarmament; clear distance to imperialist elements in Soviet policy (Afghanistan)'. Yet at the same time there should be a continuation of the long-term policy of economic and political co-operation and 'careful handling of the Polish crisis with the protection of special German interests'. 'To count on the collapse of the Eastern bloc makes no sense for a number of reasons.' 'Altogether,' the paper went on, 'the impression of equidistance should be avoided; however the impression of a "third way" is important.' But a 'third way' for whom? For Germany? For Eastern Europe? For Central Europe? For Europe altogether?

Now clearly this was just one think-piece from one section of the Chancellery, and a deliberately provocative one at that. As in the case of Egon Bahr's planning staff paper on European security, one has to emphasise that planners are there to think the unthinkable. And all political leaders in democracies do mix party, domestic and foreign policy.

Nonetheless, the fact that such an option in public policy could seriously be contemplated at a high level in the Chancellery indicates both the pressures and temptations of the period and — as important for our theme — the possibilities for German policy which more than a decade of Ostpolitik had, or seemed to have, opened up.

Chancellor Schmidt, it must plainly be stated, did not adopt the proposed public posture. He would do all he could to contribute to an arms control agreement between the superpowers, although all that was strictly limited by his disagreements with the American leadership on the one side, and by the senility and miscalculated inflexibility of the Soviet leadership on the other. He would do everything in his power to preserve the developing relationship with the GDR against pressures from both East and West. He would accept and even encourage 'stabilisation' in the rest of Eastern Europe. He would not allow Germany's economic, political or cultural ties with the East to be cut, and certainly not from across the Atlantic. But if it came to the crunch, he would cleave to the West. To be more precise: he would hold to a particular idea of the West which, in the conditions of Yalta Europe, involved shared weapons as well as common values, Pershing missiles and Popperian open societies, Kant but also Cruise.

He told Brezhnev on the latter's last, painful visit to Bonn in November 1981: 'if an agreement cannot be reached, despite all efforts, then my country will certainly meet its obligations from the other half of the two-track decision, in the security interest of my country and of the Western alliance'. On this position he stood, and on this position he fell. Not just or even mainly for this reason, to be sure: there were other, more direct causes of his fall from power. Yet ironically, given the attitudes now prevalent in his own party and even, as we have seen, in his own Chancellery, to lose power was perhaps the best thing he could have done for the basic 'two-track' approach to German foreign policy which he had so long and so consistently represented. Although no one can ever prove 'what would have happened if' — in this case, what would have happened if a social-liberal coalition had remained in power in the autumn of 1982 — there are strong grounds for arguing that the larger continuity of German foreign policy was in fact only assured by the discontinuity in domestic politics. There is a real sense in which Schmidt won by losing.

A new book

When discussing the period of centre-right coalition government which began in the autumn of 1982 the temptations of retrospective determinism are particularly strong. Since this period culminated in a breakthrough in German-Soviet relations more significant even than that of 1970, it is tempting — above all for the politicians and policymakers involved — to read developments in German-Soviet relations and the overall system of German Ostpolitik as somehow leading logically and even inexorably towards that outcome.

We are, of course, bound to examine Western policy and East-West relations more generally for putative causes, or at least contributing causes, of the spectacular events of 1989–91, from the revolution in Eastern Europe through German unification to the end of the Soviet Union. At the same time, it is important to recapture the sense of what people did not know, to note the guesses that were proved wrong, the visions that turned out to be illusions, and to chart those paths of real policy that led either to nowhere or to somewhere quite different from the place the driver thought he was heading.

The search for both sides of this history — the unexpected that happened and the expected that did not — is hampered by the paucity of high-quality unpublished sources for such a recent period, although some very revealing individual items can already be found. It is made doubly difficult by the internal and the external complexity of the context in which German Ostpolitik was made.

The internal complexity of coalition politics and inter-agency rivalry had, of course, been there already under Schmidt and under Brandt. But it was arguably more important in the Kohl-Genscher years. This was a coalition not just of two but of three parties. Not only did the Free Democrats have elaborate coalition talks with the Christian Democrats. The Christian Democrats — that is, Helmut Kohl's Christian Democratic Union and Franz Josef Strauss's Christian Social Union — had first to agree among themselves. Even after their coalition agreements were written down, in considerable detail, Franz Josef Strauss continued to be a significant individual — often highly individual — actor in the field of Ostpolitik.

Meanwhile Hans-Dietrich Genscher, by now beginning to earn the sobriquet of 'veteran' Foreign Minister, had a much more distinctive position in the making of Ostpolitik under Chancellor Kohl than he had under Chancellor Schmidt. While Schmidt had taken the leading part in attempting to develop Germany's relations with the East, and above all with Moscow, Genscher had, partly for substantive, partly for party-political reasons, established himself as the high-priest and guardian of Germany's relations with the West, and above all with Washington. When Kohl set out to re-emphasise West Germany's vital relationship with the West, Genscher presented himself as the high-priest and guardian of Germany's relations with the East.

He did so with growing confidence through the 1980s, skilfully deploying his experience, connections and prestige as Foreign Minister, and the leverage power of his small party, so that German Ostpolitik in the late 1980s came to be known as 'Genscherism', not 'Kohlism'. This in turn was misleading, since it underrated both the strategic and the direct operative contribution of the Chancellor and his foreign policy advisers, notably Horst Teltschik. In short, the changing shape of German Ostpolitik in these years was the product of a complex internal interaction between, as it were, Kohlism and Genscherism, with a rich dash of Strausserie.

The external complexity was also, self-evidently, there in earlier years. We have seen already how the system of German Ostpolitik was always, to put it somewhat mechanistically, a sub-system of the larger system of East-West relations, with its regional and above all its superpower levels. What happened in the triangle Bonn-Moscow-Berlin always depended crucially on what was happening along the Soviet-American side of the larger triangle America-Germany-Soviet Union. And these were years of truly unprecedented movement in American-Soviet relations, from the depths of what was described in the early 1980s as a 'new Cold War', with Ronald Reagan's 'evil empire' speech, his Strategic Defence Initiative and the bitter polemics around the Soviet shooting down of a Korean airliner, to the heights of summitry in the second half of the decade. From the Geneva summit in 1985 to that in Washington (and Camp David) in 1990, the United States and the Soviet Union finally went beyond even the most optimistic versions of détente to a mutual celebration of the end of the Cold War. At the same time, these changes in East-West relations were to a large extent driven by internal developments inside the Soviet Union and in Eastern Europe, which have their own separate and intricate history. It is impossible to explain the evolution of German-Soviet relations without frequent reference to this larger context.

At the outset, while affirming the continuity of German foreign policy — from Genscher to Genscher — the Kohl government made three clear, strong, central commitments. First, it reaffirmed the central importance of the relationship with the United States, and the Federal Republic's full commitment to Nato's double-track resolution, including, if need be, the deployment of Cruise and Pershing II missiles on German soil. 'The Alliance,' said Kohl in his government declaration of October 1982, 'is the core of German *raison d'état*.' The Bundestag protocols record restlessness and heckling from Social Democrats. Second, it reaffirmed West Germany's commitment to move towards what it called 'European Union' inside the existing (that is, West) European Community.

Finally, it roundly reasserted the Federal Republic's commitment to the goal of German unity. This meant, in the words of the Spring 1983 coalition agreement between the Christian Social and Christian Democratic Union, 'not only to keep the German question theoretically open, but also to be actively engaged for the German right to unity in freedom'. What such an active engagement would look like in practice was another question, but the emphatic reassertion of the goal was itself a political act.

These three basic positions could be described, with some oversimplification, as the short, the medium and the long-term foreign policy priorities of the Kohl government. All three reflected long-held convictions of Helmut Kohl. All three would displease Moscow. There is a certain irony — but also a certain logic — in the fact that the Chancellor under whom Germany's breakthrough with the East was achieved was the one who had the least experience of, and personal relationship to, the East. Helmut Kohl, the Catholic from the Rhineland-Palatinate, too young to have fought on the Eastern front (as Schmidt, Weizsäcker and Strauss had done), inspired as a young man by the lifting of frontier barriers between France and Germany, deeply and simply committed to an increasingly united, federal (that is, German-style federal) Europe built around the Franco-German axis, was an archetypal 'Westerner' in West German politics.

Yet of course this did not mean he was blind to the importance of the Soviet Union for German foreign policy. The politician from Germany's western borders had first visited Moscow as a still inexperienced party leader in September 1975, armed with some cautionary notes from a colleague who was at once protégé and mentor, Richard von Weizsäcker. The record of his meeting with Alexei Kosygin reveals a slightly chaotic conversation, in which Kohl emphasised that, being Konrad Adenauer's 'great-grandson in office', he had learned from the old man that after the Nazi period 'the most important thing is that after this period the Germans win back trust'. In this connection he stressed that the Christian Democrats would adhere to the treaties signed, including the Helsinki Final Act, which they had just voted against. As Weizsäcker sophistically suggested in his notes: 'We wouldn't dream of regarding the Final Act as questionable and dubious just because we criticised its negotiation and signature'!

Earlier in the conversation, recalling that Kosygin had enquired after Strauss at the very beginning of their talk, Kohl observed 'he [Strauss] had with good reason said, and I am wholly of his opinion, "*Pacta sunt servanda*" . . .' To which Kosygin rather surprisingly replied: 'I didn't specially put it first. My concern is not Herr Strauss. But I looked at you and thought that you look in very good health. That reminded me of Strauss. You have a similar figure.' Kohl replied that he was 'fully in agreement with this interpretation'. Thus, almost in burlesque, began Helmut Kohl's dealings with the Kremlin. (Yet in a curious way, Kosygin had surely identified one of Helmut Kohl's real political strengths: his sheer physical bulk and stamina.) It is however worth noting that in this first conversation with a Soviet leader, as in many subsequent ones, Kohl spoke clearly and with personal conviction about 'the wish of the German people once again to be united', albeit 'in [a] historical perspective, which may last generations'.

We cannot trace here all the stages in the evolution of his own and his party's understanding of Ostpolitik over the eight years until he became Chancellor. But the general direction was plain: towards acceptance of the basic lines of social-liberal Ostpolitik, but only on the foundations of unqualified adherence to the West (in values and in security policy), full commitment to European Union, and the long-term goal of German unity. Horst Teltschik, already Kohl's key foreign policy adviser, was a specialist on Soviet foreign policy and East-West relations, who had studied and taught in Berlin under Richard Löwenthal, the outstanding Social Democratic authority on international relations. With more detailed knowledge and analytical refinement than Kohl, Teltschik both understood, accepted and wished to develop the overall system of Ostpolitik they inherited from Brandt and Schmidt, with the central triangle (Bonn-Moscow-Berlin) inside a larger triangle (America-Germany-Soviet Union), the priority for relations with Moscow, and the imperative of synchronisation.

While Genscher and Strauss might squabble, the Free Democrats' own record of the coalition talks on foreign policy in March 1983 record none other than Strauss declaring that 'the object in East-West relations was a realistic détente policy' (thus using Gencher's own phrase from 1975). In his own unconventional way, Strauss was to be almost as active as Genscher in advancing Bonn's double-track strategy over the next four years. The idea of an overall double-track Western strategy towards the East, resolute in deterrence but also in détente, was of course embodied already in Nato's Harmel report, to which Chancellor Kohl referred as reverently as his predecessor had done. The specific version of the double-track strategy in Nato's December 1979 resolution was: negotiation about reducing intermediate-range nuclear forces, but also readiness to deploy them by a stated date if no agreement could be reached. Now, as it became apparent that the Soviet-American negotiations would not succeed before the deadline for deployment, the Bonn government pursued its own particular double-track.

On the one hand, despite massive and emotional domestic opposition, and the heaviest intimidation from Moscow, it steeled itself to go ahead with deployment of the new American missiles on German soil, starting in the autumn of 1983. On the other hand, like the Schmidt government before it, it did everything in its power to continue the détente track with the Soviet Union, Eastern Europe and, above all, East Germany, in political, social, cultural and — its strongest card — economic relations. Thus, for example, it paid the most solicitous attention to the development of German-Soviet economic ties, despite heavy pressure from the Reagan administration to curb them. Meanwhile, in the most spectacular single move, Strauss negotiated the first government-guaranteed billion DM credit for East Germany in the summer of 1983, at a stroke restoring the GDR's international creditworthiness.

In July 1983, while Strauss prepared for meetings with Honecker and Jaruzelski on a 'private' East European tour, Kohl and Genscher visited Moscow. The confidential note on these talks sent from the Soviet to the East German Party leaderships plainly records how the Soviet side, now led by the dying Andropov instead of the dying Brezhnev, threatened the West Germans with negative consequences for their relationship with East Germany: 'The Germans in the FRG and the GDR would have to look at each other through a thick fence of missiles.' The note records how the Bonn duo stuck to the American position, although the Soviet side claimed to detect a lack of deep conviction. At the same time, 'Kohl and Genscher assured us in every register of the loyality of the FRG government to a policy of peace, of détente and of stability'.

While the Chancellor once again presented what the Soviet note called 'the FRG's well-known revanchist concept of the "unity of the German nation" ', he also emphasised the need for practical co-operation between the two German states, notably in increasing contacts "between people on both sides of the frontier" (quotation marks in the original). Further: 'noteworthy is the Chancellor's statement that the FRG's decision to give a bn. Mark credit to the GDR was to some extent a signal "to our compatriots, that we don't want to have any missileatomicweapon(sic)-fence between us".'

The conclusion of this Soviet interpretative missive was revealing: 'Although the present government, as the visit showed once again, takes a more strongly pro-American position than the Schmidt cabinet, the possibilities of continuing to work with it, in order to pin it down to the basic principles of the treaties signed in the 1970s, continue to exist. We believe it is important to continue actively to work on Bonn on the question of the intermediate-range missiles and to make clear how the "*Nachrüstung*" of Nato can affect the interests of the FRG itself, including also its bilateral relations to individual socialist countries.' A veiled threat to the GDR! Thus a report on the Bonn-Moscow line of the Ostpolitik triangle, sent down the Moscow-East Berlin line, ends with a clear hint for action on the East Berlin-Bonn line.

Yet at the same time, Kohl, like Schmidt before him, was also trying to work the triangle the other way. Bonn tried to encourage and give incentives to Honecker both to influence Moscow (insofar as that was at all possible) to be more conciliatory in relations with the West, and (more realistically) to maintain good relations with West Germany, despite heavy breathing down the line from Moscow. In the latter, much more than the former, it had some success. While the geriatric progression from the dying Brezhnev to the dying Andropov to the dying Chernenko produced a mixture of stubbornness and irresolution in Soviet policy, the increasingly self-confident East German leader risked a cautious public dissonance with Moscow.

Following the Bundestag's vote in November 1983 to deploy the Cruise and Pershing II missiles, Honecker, instead of freezing relations with West Germany, immediately proclaimed the need to 'limit the damage' done by this deplorable decision, and to pursue a 'coalition of reason' with the West. While Soviet negotiators walked out of the Geneva arms control talks and Soviet propaganda stormed, the GDR (joined in this by Hungary) continued to urge the need for dialogue and practical (above all, economic!) co-operation with the West. Honecker also resolved to take up the invitation to visit West Germany, extended by Schmidt in 1981 and explicitly renewed by Helmut Kohl. As Honecker himself recalled in a retrospective conversation with the author, he was particularly encouraged in this by his first personal meeting with Kohl, in a guesthouse in Moscow's Lenin Hills on the occasion of Andropov's funeral. Only after a stormy meeting with the Soviet leadership in the Kremlin in August 1984 did he decide to call off the planned visit, although continuing in practice to develop the relationship with the Federal Republic. (This remarkable episode, and its significance for German-German relations, are considered in more detail in Chapter Four.)

After the cancellation of Honecker's visit, Willy Brandt read Helmut Kohl a public lesson, in the Bundestag, about the laws of Ostpolitik geometry. You could not, he said, expect to improve relations with the GDR without simultaneously improving relations with the Soviet Union, nor while playing one East European state against the other. Ostpolitik could not merely be a series of bilateral relations but had to be based on an overall concept of a systematic, synchronised approach to West-East relations: a *Gesamtkonzept*. Rejecting the criticism, Kohl nonetheless took Brandt's point. 'The Soviet Union is our most important and most powerful neighbour in Central and Eastern Europe,' he observed, using the word neighbour in an imprecise yet revealing way. 'We know very well that all conceivable bilateral possibilities, whether in talks with the GDR, whether with Poland, Hungary, with Romania or with whoever, can ultimately only be successful if they are bound in to the overall conversation (*Gesamtgespräch*) with the Soviet Union.' Horst Teltschik, playing Bahr to Kohl's Brandt, would spell the lesson out even more clearly: Moscow First.

Yet, as Ronald Reagan remarked, it took two to tango. The dying Konstantin Chernenko, and the obdurate Gromykos and Ustinovs, were plainly not ready for the dance. Kohl, Genscher, Strauss and Weizsäcker, were all eager to start, if not perhaps a vulgar American tango, then certainly an old European waltz. All that was needed were the partners in Moscow. Now with hindsight it is apparent that the new Soviet Party leader who emerged in March 1985, Mikhail Gorbachev, and the colleague he appointed as Foreign Minister in July of that year, Eduard Shevardnadze, were those partners. But hindsight can mislead, and actually the waltz was very slow to begin. For this there were general and specific reasons.

The general reason was that Soviet foreign policy in Gorbachev's first years was concentrated on the relationship with the United States and issues of arms and disarmament. From Geneva in November 1985, through the extraordinary Reykjavik summit/non-summit of October 1986, down to the signature of the treaty agreeing not only to reduce but to destroy intermediate-range nuclear forces, at the Washington summit in December 1987, the superpower relationship and hard security issues headed the new Soviet leaders' agenda. For all Gorbachev's visionary talk of the 'common European home', for all the genuine identification with Europe among many who were close to him, Europe remained a subsidiary theatre.

Within that theatre, moreover, Moscow initially concentrated on improving relations with France, Britain and Italy, rather than with West Germany. This was the price that the Kohl government paid for its combination of demonstrative loyalty to the West, above all in the Nato deployment, and forceful reassertion of the German claim to unity, including easily misunderstood statements about the continued legal existence of the German Reich in the frontiers of 1937. Such statements were grist to the Soviet propaganda mill. In the run-up to the fortieth anniversary of the end of the Second World War, the Soviet Union whipped up a gale of propaganda against the alleged threat of German 'revanchism', with a line being drawn from Hitler's *Wehrmacht* to Helmut Kohl. This was clearly meant to win domestic support in both the Soviet Union and Eastern Europe, and to bring back into line those wilful East European regimes which were trying to save their own ties with Western Europe, and above all with West Germany. Even if this propaganda campaign did not reflect the real convictions of the younger generation of Soviet leaders, it was, for reasons of domestic as well as foreign policy, difficult to change overnight.

German-Soviet economic relations continued despite the rhetorical storm raging overhead, and within weeks of becoming Party leader, Gorbachev summoned F Wilhelm Christians of the Deutsche Bank for a long conversation. Two months later he received Willy Brandt. Altogether, the Soviet leadership continued to cherish and nourish its ties to the German Social Democrats. Gorbachev twice met the Social Democrats' candidate for Chancellor, Johannes Rau, before the January 1987 federal elections. For the Bonn government this was a distinctly ambiguous development. On the one hand, in such difficult times it was helpful to have any high-level German-Soviet contacts. On the other hand, the Social Democrats could score domestic political points by being seen as the people with whom Moscow would talk. There are some indications that Moscow did drag its feet in relations with the centre-right government in the hope of having more congenial partners — say a Rau-Genscher government — in Bonn after the elections. Arguably, it was only after the Kohl-Genscher government was clearly confirmed in office for another four years that Moscow sat down to deal with it in earnest.

If so, this was not for want of trying by the Bonn government. For example, in a ten-page letter to Gorbachev dated 30 January 1986, opening with the slightly unusual greeting 'Highly esteemed (*Hochverehrter*) Mr General Secretary', Kohl started by welcoming the Geneva summit and the progress of talks on reducing intermediate-range nuclear forces. 'In the course and results of the Geneva meeting,' he wrote, 'the Federal Government sees confirmation of the rightness of its own policy. For years it has urged a continuation and intensification of the dialogue between the United States and the Soviet Union at the highest level. It has deliberately worked in this direction in the framework of the North Atlantic Alliance and with the Government of the United States of America.' It is, in fact, questionable what the real impact of West German representations in Washington had been, but in claiming credit in Moscow for services as what Schmidt had called the 'honest interpreter', Kohl stood in the clear continuity of Ostpolitik.

After going on to interpret SDI as a response to existing Soviet defence systems, and making a clear connection between security and human rights, Kohl carefully pressed the special German interests. Picking up Gorbachev's image of the common European home, he wrote: 'I am convinced that life in a common European home with fewer tensions will only be possible when relations between the two German states, too, are constantly stimulated as a stabilising element in the context of the overall process of development between West and East.' A very cautious formulation, showing clearly that he respected the imperative of synchronisation. After pointing to the prospects for improved economic relations he returned to special German interests in connection with the forthcoming Helsinki follow-up meeting in Bern. 'Important subjects there must be particularly the humanitarian aspects of relations between the two German states and the quantitative reduction in the field of family reunification and the possibilities for Soviet citizens of German nationality to emigrate.'

After referring back to an earlier letter, in which he had proposed a Helsinki follow-up conference on economic co-operation — the German carrot again! — he concluded: 'The Federal Republic of Germany wishes, and this goes for all political forces, a deepening and widening of relations with the Soviet Union. If the Soviet side shares this wish, nothing should prevent us from going down the path of a more intensive political dialogue and the consolidation of co-operation.'

Six months later, in July 1986, Genscher was able to visit Moscow. He recalls that Gorbachev began by giving him a long lecture about the wrongness of West Germany's Nato deployment. But then, putting that argument aside, Gorbachev spoke for even longer about his vision of the common European home and the possibilities for East-West, and specifically German-Soviet co-operation. At the end, they agreed that the two states should 'open a new page' in their relations.

This page was, however, then almost torn by an extraordinary gaffe. In an interview with journalists from *Newsweek*, before a visit to the United States, Helmut Kohl compared Gorbachev's public relations skills to those of Joseph Goebbels. Instead of deleting this passage from the version sent for authorisation, the Government spokesman merely edited it so the published version read: 'He [Gorbachev] is a modern communist leader who understands public relations. Goebbels, one of those responsible for the crimes of the Hitler era, was an expert in public relations, too.' This comparison so infuriated the Soviet leadership that the Politburo actually decided to freeze all political contacts with the Federal Republic for a time. The January 1987 federal election results showed that if they wanted to deal with West Germany they would have to deal with Kohl, but for at least a year the leading role in developing relations with the Soviet Union was played by others.

The first of these was Hans-Dietrich Genscher. Having come through the January 1987 election with an improved vote for his party, and successfully fended off a challenge to his position as Foreign Minister from Franz Josef Strauss, almost the first thing Genscher did was to deliver a widely reported speech to the annual meeting of the World Economic Forum at Davos. Warning against the danger of being lamed by 'worst case analysis' — such as could still often be heard in Washington, Paris and London — he concluded with a ringing appeal for the West to 'take Gorbachev seriously, take him at his word!' The two key areas in which the West should 'take Gorbachev at his word' were, of course, disarmament and economic co-operation.

Following the Davos speech, Genscher played a part which was sometimes described as that of 'pacemaker' between East and West. This vanguard role, actually one of relatively few exposed positions that Genscher took in his political career, earned him much criticism, and the initially sceptical tag of 'Genscherism'. Yet his optimistic working hypothesis, inspired by his first long conversation with Gorbachev, was, in the event, triumphantly vindicated.

Secondly, Richard von Weizsäcker, once Kohl's protégé in domestic politics and mentor in foreign policy, now as much a rival as anything else, stepped into the breach. Even before he actually became President, Weizsäcker had emphatically informed two members of the East German Politburo, in a meeting in the summer of 1984, that he wished to visit Moscow. 'However,' as one of his hosts recorded him saying, 'he would need to know whether he was welcome there.' In the summer of 1987 he finally was welcome there — although preceded two months earlier by another German visitor, a young man called Matthias Rust, who piloted his Cessna airplane undetected through Soviet air defences to land on Red Square, thus giving Gorbachev a marvellous pretext to purge and establish full control over his military. Weizsäcker's more conventional visit in July 1987 was important less for his encounters with his formal counterpart and host, President Andrei Gromyko, than for his meeting with Gorbachev.

Greeting Weizsäcker, and Genscher who accompanied him, Gorbachev recalled his agreement with Genscher a year before to 'open a new page' in German-Soviet relations: 'for the time being, however, it had remained unwritten, and for a time there was even a danger that it would be closed. Fortunately this had not happened'. As in his conversations with Brandt, Gorbachev stressed that he had always distinguished between the German people and the Nazi regime. He then spoke at length about the 'realistic' possibilities for an all-round improvement of relations between the two states. At one point in the conversation, Richard von Weizsäcker raised — 'almost just for the record', as he later explained to the author — the question of German unity. He elicited an unexpected response that was rapidly to become famous. The political reality, said Gorbachev, was the existence of two German states with different social orders. Both had learned lessons from history and each could make its own contribution to Europe and the world. And — in the wording of the published Soviet report — history would decide what would happen in a hundred years . . .

Weizsäcker recalls at this point interjecting 'or perhaps fifty?', and receiving an indication of assent from Gorbachev, thus, as Weizsäcker wryly observes, negotiating a fifty per cent cut. But the significant point was less the time period than the fact that Gorbachev did not say 'never'. This requires a little exploration. Whatever the innermost thoughts of the Brezhnev generation of Soviet leaders, whatever the earlier experiments in Soviet policy which they had witnessed or participated in, their public position from the mid-1960s to the mid-1980s had been unequivocal. The division of Germany and Europe into two groups of states with different 'social systems' was permanent. Yalta was for ever. As in the old Soviet bloc joke, the past might be unpredictable but the future was certain. So the mere public acknowledgment that the future was open, that 'history', 'time' or 'life itself', to use three of Gorbachev's favourite philosophical terms, might have other plans than those scientifically discovered by the Communist Party of the Soviet Union, was a significant departure.

But was there not more to it than that? In his memoirs, Eduard Shevardnadze recalls being asked by Genscher — after Germany was united — when he had first come to view German unification as inevitable, and records his own very surprising answer: 'Already in 1986.' In discussion with a leading Soviet expert on Germany, he had then expressed the view that this issue would soon come centre stage in Europe. Asked about this by the author in 1992, Shevardnadze not only repeated his version, with circumstantial detail, but averred that by 1987 both he and Gorbachev had come to the conclusion that German unification was inevitable. Of course the time-scale was unknown but, said Shevardnadze, Gorbachev's formula of 'a hundred years' was a tranquilliser for domestic public opinion, which was not ready for the radicalism of the top leaders' private thinking.

Talking in 1992, Anatoly Chernyaev, one of Gorbachev's closest aides, also averred that 'in his heart' Gorbachev was already convinced at the time of the Weizsäcker visit that 'without a resolution of the German question and without the establishment of historically conditioned normal relations between the two great peoples, no recovery would occur in Europe or the world'. In a separate conversation, another very senior figure close to Gorbachev, Alexander Yakovlev, made the even more surprising statement that Gorbachev probably reckoned with German unification from the very outset, from 1985. But the exigencies of politics did not allow Gorbachev to say what he thought.

These retrospective claims are remarkable. They cannot simply be ignored. There are certainly more to come. But one has with them the same problem as with the West German Ostpolitiker's retrospective claims of deep foresight. In the absence of precise documentary corroboration from records made at the time (which may yet be forthcoming) these tantalising statements are simply what policymakers say now that they thought then.

It is, however, fairly well established that Vyacheslav Dashitschev, a privileged maverick policy intellectual in the important institute headed by Oleg Bogomolov, made a presentation to an advisory council of the Foreign Ministry in November 1987, in which he argued that it was in the vital interest of the Soviet Union to go beyond the Cold War to a fully co-operative relationship with the West — and that the price for this might even eventually include the sacrifice of the separate East German state. Moreover, in obviously embittered recollections, Erich Honecker remembered the East German ambassador to the Soviet Union reporting serious discussions in Moscow about 'overcoming Germany's dual statehood' in 1987. In a television interview, Honecker further claimed that he had raised this issue with Gorbachev, and received firm contrary assurances.

And there's the rub. There is enough retrospective and circumstantial evidence to suggest that by 1987, in the context of a general questioning and rethinking of all the basic positions of Soviet foreign policy, even the question of eventually overcoming the division of Germany into two states was privately discussed at a high and even at the highest level in Moscow. But there is no evidence whatsoever that this was translated into operative policy. Quite the contrary. Dashitschev himself says that his speculative proposals were roundly repudiated by virtually the whole foreign policy apparatus of the Soviet party-state. On a day-to-day basis that apparatus continued to make Soviet foreign policy. When detailed German-Soviet negotiations began in earnest in 1988, the West German negotiators found themselves, like their predecessors in the 1970s, spending weeks and months wrangling over the inclusion of West Berlin in German-Soviet agreements.

As for the Moscow-East Berlin side of the triangle, political relations might be sour, but comprehensive assurances of fraternal solidarity were still repeatedly given. Thus the East German record of a top-level consultation in July 1987 between Hermann Axen, Honecker's Central Committee Secretary for international relations, and the new heads of the Soviet Central Committee departments for international relations and relations with Socialist countries, Anatoly Dobrynin and Vadim Medvedev, has Dobrynin glossing the Weizsäcker-Gorbachev conversation thus: 'Weizsäcker raised the question of the German nation. Comrade M Gorbachev reacted as is known. The USSR would allow no speculation about the "German nation". The defence of the interests of the GDR was a cornerstone of Soviet policy.'

Dobrynin also emphasised that the Soviet Union would continue to look critically at Kohl and the Christian Democrats. 'The policy of the USSR towards Kohl would depend on what policy he pursued towards the Soviet Union. This was the Politburo's opinion.' Kohl therefore still had his work cut out. Not only did the Soviet Union turn to West Germany last among the major powers of Western Europe. Among West German leaders, Gorbachev turned last of all to Kohl.

At the end of December 1987 he received Franz Josef Strauss in Moscow. Strauss, who — like Matthias Rust — had piloted himself to Moscow, and landed perilously in a storm, was euphoric. He came away, he said, 'with the most agreeable feelings', having concluded that East and West might be standing 'on the eve of a new age'. Strauss's visit was actually quite useful for Kohl, securing his right (or southern) flank at home, but it left the Chancellor as almost the only top West German politician who had not had a summit meeing with Gorbachev.

While the evidence is fragmentary, it appears that it was only after the Washington summit and the signature of the INF Treaty in December 1987 that Gorbachev and Shevardnadze turned their full attention to what was clearly their most important potential partner in Western Europe. In January 1988 Shevardnadze visited Bonn, the first time he had done so, and the first visit of a Soviet Foreign Minister for five years. He warmly congratulated the Bonn government on its contribution to the INF treaty. Apart from the 'honest interpreting' and 'pacemaking', this contribution consisted concretely in the Chancellor's decision to sacrifice West Germany's own little stock of 72 Pershing 1A missiles, very much against the better judgement of some of the Christian Democrats' leading defence experts.

Shevardnadze went on to plead for a 'third zero' in arms reductions —

that is, for the removal from Central Europe of those short-range nuclear missiles which, in practice, could only be fired from West Central Europe to hit East Central Europe or vice versa. At the same time, he signed a protocol on bilateral consultation, such as Britain and France had long had with the Soviet Union, and an extension of the 1978 Schmidt-Brezhnev economic co-operation agreement for a further five years.

In February, the Christian Democrat premier of Baden-Württemberg, Lothar Späth, visited Moscow and was received by Gorbachev. The Soviet information note sent to the party leadership in East Berlin records that Späth was told 'that the Soviet Union wishes to bring about a decisive turn for the better in relations with the FRG'. However, it was still concerned that the Federal Republic was dragging its feet. According to the Soviet note (clearly not a wholly reliable record) Späth attempted to explain this by referring to the West Germans' problems with their 'national identity and national consciousness'; to the fact that West Germany belonged to Nato, 'a bloc in which a state which lies on the other side of the Atlantic Ocean takes the leading position'; and to Bonn's fears of arousing the suspicions of its Western partners. But Chancellor Kohl was personally determined to open a new page in relations with Moscow, and 'for many important reasons,' Späth continued, 'the West Germans could not live calmly without good relations with the Soviet Union'.

'At Kohl's request,' the Soviet note reports, 'Späth addressed the question of a meeting between the Chancellor and the General Secretary of the CC of the CPSU . . . In this connection he observed that the Chancellor would react very sensitively if Mikhail Gorbachev, who had already been in France and Great Britain, would leave the FRG to one side. It was agreed that Helmut Kohl would visit the Soviet Union this year. A visit by Mikhail Gorbachev to the FRG would take place next year [i.e. 1989].' This laconic statement concealed the fact that in protocol terms Gorbachev should first have visited Bonn, since Kohl had come to Moscow in 1983 (as well as to the 'working funerals' of Andropov in 1984 and Chernenko in 1985). The Bonn government only agreed to this double visit on condition that it was treated as one whole. 'For our part,' the Soviet note continued, 'it was emphasised that the forthcoming encounter should have the political importance worthy of this level. It should be concluded by a weighty common document, which would clearly express the will of both sides to achieve a qualitative renewal of their relations as well as their responsibility for the future of their peoples and for the whole world.'

With that characteristically deep note, the long-sought, long-delayed, German-Russian waltz could begin in earnest. But while the negotiators got down to the painstaking preparatory work, there was one more move to be made on the West German home front. Nikolai Portugalov, an important messenger and interpreter of Soviet policy towards Germany in these years, had in late 1987 summed up Soviet concerns about the Christian Democrats in a striking phrase. 'The CDU,' he said, 'lacks its Ostpolitik Bad Godesberg.' As the Social Democrats had signalled their acceptance of the basic elements of the Adenauerian integration in the West in their Bad Godesberg programme of 1959, so now the Christian Democrats should signal their acceptance of the basic elements of Brandtian Ostpolitik, in a programmatic statement. And this was exactly what the Christian Democrats did. As we have noted already, at their Wiesbaden party conference in June 1988, the Christian Democratic Union agreed a programmatic foreign policy statement which went farther than the party had ever gone before to codify its practical acceptance of the main lines of Ostpolitik.

Thus it was by no means only the Soviet side that moved in the six years between Kohl's accession in Bonn and his October 1988 visit to Moscow. The centre-right government had began by defiantly restating the Federal Republic's attachment to the West, with Nato missiles and common values, to West European integration, and to the long-term goal of German unity. But while sticking to these three fundamentals, it had come a very long way to meet Soviet concerns and to woo the new Soviet leaders with all the charms at its disposal. As we shall see, the Social Democrats were by now prepared to go several steps further (see Chapter Six). But it is probably true to say that by 1988 leading Christian Democrats had come close to the positions taken up by leading Social Democrats twenty years before. With all their firmly restated Western, European and national principles, Kohl and Teltschik, like Brandt and Bahr two decades before, found themselves accepting the status quo — in order to overcome it.

It was on this basis, then, that Kohl at last visited Moscow. The Chancellor was accompanied by a huge party of ministers, officials, businessmen and bankers. The latter, led as usual by the Deutsche Bank, arranged a credit of DM 3 billion, earmarked for the purchase of machinery for Soviet light industry. Six inter-governmental agreements were signed, covering such subjects as nuclear safety, co-operation in environmental protection, food production and the first formal programme of cultural exchanges between the two states. 'Now,' said Gorbachev, 'we have very many German friends,' referring to the GDR as well as West Germany. Kohl had some ten hours of talks with the Soviet leader. The atmosphere was somewhat frigid at first, but Gorbachev later said that the ice had been broken. In fact, according to Anatoly Chernyaev, Teltschik's counterpart as notetaker at these talks, there were already the beginnings of a strong personal rapport. At the concluding press conference, Kohl ventured to suggest that this was not merely a new page but the beginning of a 'new chapter' in German-Soviet relations.

This important visit was as nothing, however, compared with the Soviet leader's visit to West Germany in June 1989. 'Gorbymania' was not peculiar to Germany. Great popular enthusiasm was manifested on the streets of Washington, London and Paris. But even by those standards, the reception given to Gorbachev by the crowds, the media, the politicians and the business community in West Germany was extraordinary.

One former government spokesman described it, crudely but not innacurately, as a 'Gorbasm'. The tabloid daily *Bild* ran a cover photo of a schoolgirl being embraced by the Soviet leader with the headline: 'A kiss for Annette, a kiss for Germany'. The alternative daily *taz* wryly described Gorbachev as 'the object of desire'. German commentators compared his visit to that of John F Kennedy. High-level Soviet commentators, working the German media with great smoothness, compared it to the historic reconciliation between France and Germany under Adenauer and de Gaulle. West German policymakers reasonably asked to be judged by their own words and deeds, not those of schoolgirls and tabloids. Yet this emotional charge, amounting almost to euphoria, reached to the very top, and should not be underrated.

'After a good sowing in the autumn,' said Chancellor Kohl, 'we can now bring in the harvest.' And what a harvest it was. This time there were no less than eleven agreements, ranging from such major economic items as investment protection and management training, through school and youth training to an agreement on the establishment of a 'hot line' between Bonn and Moscow. A government spokesman pointed to similar connections with Washington and East Berlin.

'We are drawing the line under the post-war period' said Gorbachev in his formal response to Chancellor Kohl. Referring to the Joint Declaration that they were to sign, he observed: 'This must be the first document of such a character and such dimensions in which two great European states belonging to different systems and alliances make an attempt to reflect philosophically upon the meaning of the moment presently being experienced by the world community, and together to lay down the goals of their policy.'

This remarkable document, informally known as the Bonn Declaration, started with the grandiose statement that the two states 'agree that humanity stands before new challenges on the eve of the third millennium', and proceeded to spell out the common principles on which the two states would respond to those challenges. 'The Federal Republic and the Soviet Union,' it said, 'consider it a paramount objective of their policy to continue Europe's historical traditions and thus to contribute to overcoming the division of Europe. They are determined to work together on concepts of achieving this goal through the building of a Europe of peace and co-operation — of a European order of peace or of a common European home — in which the USA and Canada also have a place.'

It then listed a number of 'building bricks' for this Europe of peace and co-operation, including further steps of disarmament, intensified dialogue at all levels, economic, technological and ecological 'co-operation', and exchanges of all possible kinds. In a section devoted specifically to security policy, the declaration said, amongst other things: 'The Federal Republic of Germany and the Soviet Union advocate

– a fifty per cent reduction of the strategic nuclear offensive weapons of the USA and the Soviet Union

– agreed American-Soviet solutions at the nuclear and space talks; this also applies to observance of the ABM Treaty . . .'

The Bonn Declaration thus explicitly equated the overarching long-term goal of Ostpolitik, a 'European order of peace', with Gorbachev's vision of a 'common European home'. It spoke of West Germany and the Soviet Union, each in its alliance, having a common policy ('their policy') for working towards this goal or vision, albeit one in which the United States would 'also' have a place. It went on to list vital steps of disarmament which the Soviet Union and the Federal Republic agreed the Soviet Union should take with the United States.

It therefore ascribed an extraordinary place to the Federal Republic in European and world affairs. 'The Federal Republic of Germany,' it said, 'and the Soviet Union realise, in view of Europe's history and its position in the world as well as the weight that each side has in its alliance, that a positive development of their relationship has central importance for the situation in Europe and East-West relations as a whole.' The two states therefore wished to build on the 'good traditions of their centuries-long history'. (The Federal Republic was founded in 1949, the Soviet Union in 1922.) In one of his keynote speeches, Gorbachev averred that the co-operation between Moscow and Bonn could serve as 'a catalyst for new relations between East and West altogether'.

Bonn had come a very long way since Adenauer's first trip to Moscow in 1955, after which he proudly explained to his Christian Democratic colleagues that the 'growing young man' Federal Republic had put itself 'in the same row' as the 'other three' — meaning the United States, France and Britain. Now the Federal Republic was in the middle of a new and even more exclusive row, which might be described as the new 'Big Three': the United States, (West) Germany, the Soviet Union. Adenauer's 'nightmare called Potsdam' was but a distant memory. In 1945, the United States and the Soviet Union had decided what should happen to Germany. Now West Germany and the Soviet Union were making a joint statement about what the United States should do! The implicit change in Bonn's relationship with the United States was quite as dramatic as the explicit change in its relationship with the Soviet Union. In fact, President Bush had already acknowledged the (re)emergence of (West) Germany as a major, even a leading power in (not just Western) Europe. In a speech at Mainz just two weeks earlier, he declared that the United States and the Federal Republic should now be 'partners in leadership'.

This new position for (West) Germany was not just a matter of the changing balance of power between states. It also concerned what Gorbachev called the 'philosophical' approach to East-West relations. West German officials were at pains to stress the Western values and West German positions that they had persuaded the Soviet leader to endorse: for example, the references to 'the human person with his dignity and rights . . . stand[ing] at the centre of policy', to the cultural value of national minorities, to the supremacy of international law in domestic and international affairs and above all to the right of self-determination. Connoisseurs pointed out the significance of a change of one letter in the Russian-language text. For decades, the Soviet side had described the Federal Republic as the *Federativnaya Respublika Germanyii* (i.e. the German Federal Republic) while the West German Foreign Ministry had tried to persuade them to call it the *Federativnaya Respublika Germaniya* (i.e. the Federal Republic of Germany). Now, at long last, the Russians had changed the 'i' to 'a'.

If one looks closely, however, the 'philosophical' balance of the document was a little more complicated. It certainly incorporated those elements of Western thinking about international relations which had already been adopted as part of Soviet 'new thinking'. Unlike the only comparable bilateral document — the 1972 Soviet-American Agreement on Basic Principles of Relations — it did not contain the compromised Soviet notion of 'peaceful co-existence'. On the other hand, it also included crucial Soviet reservations. For example, the reference to self-determination as a 'building brick' of the new Europe read as follows: 'The unlimited respect for the integrity and security of each state. Each [i.e. state] has the right freely to choose its own political and social system. The unlimited respect for the principles and norms of international law, especially respect for the right to self-determination of peoples (*Völker*).'

Two crucially different notions were thus conflated: the right of peoples to self-determination and the right of states to choose their own political system without outside interference. Thus, applied to Germany, it could be taken to mean two diametrically opposed things: (1) the GDR — as a state — has the right to choose its own political system, and to demand umlimited respect for the integrity and security of the state built on that system, or (2) the Germans — as a people — have the right to choose unity in freedom, thus spelling the end of the GDR as a state!

The commitment to self-determination in the Bonn Declaration was further qualified by two references to the continued existence of different systems. 'Continuing differences in values and in political and social orders are no obstacle to future-shaping policy across the system-frontiers', it said. And again: 'Europe, which suffered most from two World Wars, must give the world an example of stable peace, good neighbourliness and constructive co-operation, which brings together the productive abilities of all states, *irrespective of different social systems*' (author's italics). This was of course one of the crucial premisses of the original social-liberal vision of a 'European order of peace', as articulated by Brandt, Scheel and Bahr in 1969 — but here it was being underwritten by a Christian Democratic Chancellor in the year 1989. Small wonder that Egon Bahr said he could not have formulated it better himself. 'I must admit,' Bahr observed, 'that I am immensely taken with this Bonn Declaration.'

Now it may be recalled that the Soviet-American Agreement on Basic Principles contained an almost identical formula: 'Differences in ideology and in the social systems of the USA and the USSR,' it said, 'are not obstacles to the bilateral development of normal relations based on the principles of sovereignty, equality, non-interference in internal affairs and mutual advantage.' But that was May 1972, not June 1989.

In June 1989 the peoples of two East European states were already well on the way to changing their systems. Just one week before Gorbachev arrived in Bonn, the Poles had, following the Round Table talks between Solidarity and the authorities, voted in the first half-free election in Eastern Europe since the imposition of the Soviet-type 'social system'. The result was a landslide victory for Solidarity which led, within three months, to the appointment of a non-communist prime minister. As Gorbachev was feted in Bonn, another set of round table talks was beginning, in Budapest. The day after he left, the Hungarians gave a ceremonial reburial to the leader of the 1956 revolution, Imre Nagy, thus putting the last nail in the coffin of the ruling Hungarian Socialist Workers' Party. Responding to these developments, the American President had proposed in his Mainz speech that the Helsinki process should be strengthened and broadened 'to promote free elections and political pluralism in Eastern Europe', a message that he subsequently took to Warsaw and Budapest.

This is the context in which the German-Soviet commitment to shaping together a new Europe 'across the system-frontiers', 'irrespective of the differences between social systems' must be seen. Of course all such documents contain ambiguities and compromises. (This is one argument against producing such documents.) And Chancellor Kohl articulated Western values and specific German interests much more clearly in his keynote speech to the Soviet leader. The continuing division of Germany, he said, was 'an open wound'. The Berlin Wall should be pulled down. West Germany's ties with the European Community and Nato were non-negotiable. 'From the decision for freedom and democracy followed the decision to ally ourselves in Nato with the states which recognise the same values.'

Yet at the same time he observed that this Bonn Declaration should 'set the course' for German-Soviet relations 'in the perspective of the year 2000'. His adviser on foreign affairs, Horst Teltschik, one of the architects of the Bonn Declaration, would subsequently write that it might be regarded as 'guidelines for the course of European politics in the coming decades'. So it was certainly not meant to be taken lightly.

Not just in power-political terms but also 'philosophically' Bonn had taken a public position between Washington and Moscow: incomparably closer to Washington as regards the fundamentals of the internal political, economic and social system, but less so in the vision and the priorities of East-West relations. In fact, between Kohl's visit to Moscow and Gorbachev's visit to Bonn, Bonn had been involved in a major controversy with Washington. It concerned Nato's front-line, short-range nuclear missile system, known as Lance. The United States and Britain wanted to modernise this, seeing it as the last surviving link in the Nato chain from conventional to nuclear weaponry. The Soviet Union wanted it removed altogether, as part of the 'third zero' solution.

True to form, Kohl had initially accepted the American argument. But Genscher strongly opposed it. In the spring of 1989 he succeeded in bringing the Federal Government on to his line, with two main arguments. First, these missiles could only be fired from Germany (West) to hit Germany (East). 'The shorter the range the deader the Germans', as West German politicians pithily put it. Second, it might jeopardise the unique chance of a dramatic improvement in East-West, and specifically German-Soviet relations. This was a major row, with even the Federal President talking loftily of the superior wisdom of 'the continental Europeans', while American congressmen muttered the old refrain 'no nukes, no troops'. And it was a row which Genscherist Bonn effectively won, with a compromise hastily patched together for Nato's fortieth anniversary summit in May. When Bush said 'partners in leadership', he was talking from hard experience.

The Bonn Declaration with Gorbachev was not, of course, a pure summary of Bonn's real position. But nor was Nato's fortieth anniversary declaration. Both were compromises. The former spoke of building a new Europe based on the different social systems, but not as unambiguously as Moscow (let alone East Berlin) would have liked. The latter spoke of support for 'the opening of Eastern societies' and encouragement of 'reforms that aim at positive political, economic and human rights developments' — but not as forcefully as Washington (and many East Europeans) would have desired. In both, there was a large element of Bonn's own distinctive approach to East-West relations, with its vision of spinning a web of dialogue, exchange and co-operation across a divided continent (see p. 258f).

But was this all? Were there not private understandings which went beyond the public statements and impressions? Chancellor Kohl suggests that there were. He recalls, in particular, a conversation with Mikhail Gorbachev one evening, in the garden of the Chancellor's bungalow, overlooking the Rhine. After a heart-to-heart talk about their childhood experiences of the war, and after discussing what Germany and the Soviet Union might do together in a better future, Helmut Kohl raised the subject of German unity. The river of history, he said, was flowing towards German unity, as the Rhine before them flowed down to the sea. You could try to dam the Rhine, but the mighty river would flood its banks and find a way round the dam. So also with German unity. Gorbachev could of course stop it for many years, in which case he, Helmut Kohl, would not live to see the day. But the day of German unity — and that of European unity! — would surely come, as the Rhine flowed down to the sea.

In Kohl's recollection, Gorbachev silently registered this weighty statement, expressing neither assent nor contradiction. Then he spoke of the Soviet Union's economic difficulties. If he had, at some point, to request urgent economic help, he asked, would the Chancellor be able and willing to give it? Kohl said yes. This conversation in the garden of the Chancellor's bungalow, looking over the Rhine, was, says Kohl, 'the decisive moment' on the road to German unity.

Now of course this account must be treated critically. Before making a serious judgement one would want to read the interpreters' records in both Moscow and Bonn. But it does seem that Kohl and Gorbachev, despite or perhaps partly because of earlier slights and outright insults ('Goebbels'), established a remarkable rapport. Almost exactly the same age, provincial politicians both, they displayed a rather similar mixture of toughness and sentimentality, and a shared taste for rambling discourse on history, time and life itself. They would subsequently go over to the familiar '*Du*' form, at a time when Kohl was still using the more formal '*Sie*' with George Bush. It is credible that Kohl would have talked with real conviction — and not 'just for the record' — about the rightness and inevitability of German unification, because he had a long track-record of doing just that in all his conversations with Soviet leaders.

The gist of Gorbachev's response, as recalled by Kohl, is also both plausible and revealing. It suggests that even in Bonn he was still overwhelmingly preoccupied with his problems back home, and that he was looking to Germany above all, with something now amounting almost to desperation, for economic help. In looking to Germany for long-term help in tackling the Herculean task of modernising Russia, he stood in a tradition that stretched back at least to Peter the Great. But he was also looking for short-term help to alleviate the deepening economic crisis which had arisen precisely from his own attempt to modernise the Soviet Union, after seventy years of a command economy, with half-measures of perestroika.

It, is course, quite impossible to summarise here the whole story of developments in the Soviet Union, in Eastern Europe and in East-West relations over the previous four years. But to avoid tunnel vision and retrospective determinism it is important to try and work out what point Gorbachev himself had reached in the summer of 1989, and to ask what larger factors — beyond the specific history of German-Soviet relations — had brought him to that memorable moment on the Rhine.

Willy Brandt, in his 1989 volume of memoirs, poured gentle scorn on the idea that a Western policy of military strength brought Gorbachev to power. In the same volume, he highlighted the influence of the Olof Palme commission, and of his own Brandt commission, on Gorbachev's 'new thinking' in foreign and security policy. He thus touched on two opposite claims for the impact of Western policy on Soviet politics in the 1980s. On the one side, a straight line is drawn from Palme to Gorbachev, on the other, from Pershing to Gorbachev. On a larger canvas, there are those who argue that it was Reagan's new-old policy of Cold War, rearmament and, yes, the Strategic Defence Initiative — 'star wars' — that compelled the decisive turn in Soviet foreign policy. And there are those who argue that, on the contrary, the true sources of 'new thinking' are to be found in Western détente policies, in impulses that came from the peace movement and the parties gathered in the Socialist International. So was it SDI or SI?

Evidence and testimony for each partisan claim is sought, and can be found, from Soviet sources. Thus it is demonstrably the case that some of the concepts and terms of Soviet 'new thinking' — especially in security policy — came from left-wing or left-liberal foreign policy debate in Western Europe and North America. Brandt and Bahr can trace a direct line from the Palme commission via Georgi Arbatov to Gorbachev. And they quote Valentin Falin: 'without Ostpolitik no Gorbachev!' Yet this same Falin could say, in an interview with *Die Zeit* in 1992, that the Americans had arms-raced the Soviets to death. Did that mean, came the alarmed question of *Die Zeit*'s publisher and chief editor, that Reagan was right? 'In this sense, yes', Falin replied, although he went on to observe that the deeper cause was not just Reagan but American policy since the war (in other words, containment).

So far as Germany was concerned, Schmidt, Kohl and Genscher all stressed, in retrospective conversations with the author, the crucial part which they now believe their resolve to go ahead with the deployment of Pershing and Cruise missiles had played in compelling a revision of Soviet policy. Had anyone from the Soviet side endorsed this interpretation? Yes, said Chancellor Kohl, Gorbachev had. But had anyone on the Soviet side endorsed Willy Brandt's contrary interpretation? Yes, said ex-Chancellor Brandt, Gorbachev!

At the risk of sounding more harmonisingly dialectical than the most seasoned Ostpolitiker, one is bound to say that there are probably two realistic answers to the simplistic and partisan question of whether it was Cold War or détente that led to the fundamental change in Soviet policy. The first answer is: both. The second is: neither.

120 · *In Europe's Name*

The manifestation of the West's military strength, political solidarity and economic and technological superiority, the hallmark of Reagan's and to a lesser extent of Kohl's first term(s) in office, may have convinced the new Soviet leadership that they could neither out-arm nor split the West. The Soviet Union's achievement of rough nuclear-strategic parity in the 1960s had been a fundamental precondition for the first main period of détente, in which — to paint with a very broad brush — the West moved towards the East. Now the West's demonstration that it could, if it wanted, not only match but beat anything the Soviet Union could do — however large a proportion of public spending the Kremlin devoted to defence — was, arguably at least, a precondition for this second period of détente, in which the East moved towards the West. Yet in this painful and contested realignment of Soviet policy, it was important for Gorbachev and his always small group of firm allies in Soviet politics to be able to show that there were partners in the West, people ready to co-operate without compelling the Soviet Union utterly to lose face. To recall the simplistic dichotomy: if Pershing and SDI showed the impasse, perhaps Palme and SI pointed to a possible way out.

This may be too harmonic an interpretation. It is, as we have seen, also possible to argue that hopes of dealing with the Social Democrats in power in West Germany, and thereby also of driving wedges between Western Europe and the United States, actually retarded the rapprochement between Moscow and Bonn in 1985 and 1986. One might go further and say that the people who showed Gorbachev the way out of the impasse were not the opponents of Reagan and Kohl, but Reagan and Kohl themselves, each in their second terms. It was, after all, the Reagan of the Reykjavik summit who underwrote the most sweeping proposals for nuclear disarmament, to the dismay of many in Western Europe, and especially in West Germany. And was not the Kohl of the Bonn summit a very paragon of détente? Yet the line taken by the opposition, and supported by much of public and published opinion, had helped to modify that government policy, not least through that high-performance semi-conductor called Hans-Dietrich Genscher.

The fact is that, both within the Western alliance and within West Germany itself, the two tracks of the overall Harmel strategy were sustained through argument as much as though consensus: argument within the government coalition, argument between government and opposition, argument between Bonn and Washington. It is therefore impossible to give any clear answer to the question 'who was right?' because both sides ended up doing both. With many alarums and diversions, the Western alliance as a whole pursued both Cold War and détente. Within that overall double-track, the Bonn government had developed a particular double-track of its own.

It challenged the Soviet Union with its allegiance to Nato, and the deployment of missiles that threatened the Soviet Union directly. It challenged the Soviet Union with the development of the Franco-German relationship and the European Community's project of a single market ('1992') and political union, all of which alarmed and goaded the Gorbachev leadership. It defied the Soviet Union by upholding the claim to German unity, which threatened the cornerstone of Moscow's external empire in Eastern Europe. But for each of these sticks, brandished most visibly in the Kohl-Genscher government's first term, it held up a matching carrot, waved most alluringly in the Kohl-Genscher government's second term.

Just because it was so firmly in Nato, it could plead forcefully and successfully for further arms reductions based on an optimistic hypothesis about Soviet policy. Just because it was such a strong player in the EC and other structures of Western economic and political co-operation, it could become the most important advocate in the West of 'helping Gorbachev to succeed', arguing forcefully for the shortening of the Cocom list restricting West-East technology transfer and for expanded economic ties between the EC and Comecon countries. As Kohl remarked in Moscow in October 1988, 'our firm anchoring in the West increases the value of our offer of fair partnership'. Finally, just because it had a major potential to destabilise East Germany, its restraint in operative policy towards East Germany, its reception of Honecker, its anxious solicitude not to 'destabilise' the rest of Eastern Europe, was of real importance to Moscow. The Federal Government spokesman summarised Kohl and Gorbachev's discussions of Eastern Europe at the Bonn summit in two words: 'no destabilisation'.

This double-track could also be described as a balancing act: between Cold War and détente, between Moscow and Washington, between Eastern and Western Europe, between preserving the favourable and changing the unfavourable parts of the status quo. Taken all in all, Bonn governments had not seriously lost their balance in walking this tightrope over the twenty years since 1969, although they had wobbled more than once. With Gorbachev in Bonn, they could congratulate themselves on a success for the combination of Westpolitik and Ostpolitik.

Yet there is a danger of retrospective *hubris* here, especially since unjustified self-congratulation is part of the politician's stock in trade. It is time to remember the other answer to the crude question whether Cold War or détente had brought Gorbachev to this point. That answer is: neither! The primary causes of the changes that led to the end, first of the Soviet Union's external empire in Eastern Europe, then of the Soviet Union, are to be found inside the Soviet Union, in Eastern Europe, and in the nature of Communism. The fundamental contribution of the West was simply to be, and to enhance, what it was: the West. Compared with this, everything it did in direct policy towards the East was of secondary importance.

Writing in 1975, Boris Meissner observed that the strategy of the social-liberal coalition marked a profound change in German Ostpolitik, and then cautiously speculated thus: 'a commensurate change on the Soviet side over a longer period cannot be excluded. It could be the result of a process of development in the Soviet Union which gives domestic renewal the priority over the unfolding of external power.' Was not that, in a nutshell, what happened ten years later? Arguably the evolution of Soviet foreign policy under Gorbachev is a classic example of what in German historiography has been called the *Primat der Innenpolitik*, the primacy of domestic political imperatives.

Gorbachev and his associates, with the pent-up frustration of what many of them saw as ten, some even as twenty lost years of Soviet policy, grasped what they felt was their last chance to modernise the Soviet Union. As they proceeded, they realised that the task was much larger, the problems much deeper, than they had feared. To address this Herculean task, they needed to cut defence spending and establish a co-operative relationship with the West. We have noted already some of the steps they took to achieve this. It also required a fundamental revision of the ideological bases of Soviet foreign policy.

In the Soviet system, such an ideological revision had an autonomous importance which should by no means be underrated. By the time of Gorbachev's speech to the United Nations in December 1988, the main components of 'new thinking' were firmly in place. The 'all-human' replaced the class-based interpretation of international relations. The common problems of humankind should take priority over systemic differences. Most important, the principles of renunciation of force, non-interference and 'freedom of choice' should apply to relations between all states. There was no longer to be a special set of rules governing relations between socialist states. Yet more than a shadow of doubt still remained, especially when it came to Germany.

Domestically, Gorbachev, having become President in the autumn of 1988, was by the summer of 1989 more clearly in command of the partly reformed structure of the Soviet party-state than before. At the same time, however, the half-measures of perestroika had first revealed and then exacerbated the disastrous condition of the economy. As his evening conversation with Kohl indicated, this economic crisis preyed on his mind. Meanwhile, the progress of glasnost strengthened demands for democratic participation and, more threateningly still, fanned the flames of national-ism in what Seweryn Bialer has called the 'internal empire' — that is, the non-Russian republics of the Soviet Union itself. Gorbachev came to Bonn hot foot from a stormy session of the Congress of People's Deputies. From Bonn, he had to keep in daily touch with developments at home, not least because of an acute nationality conflict in Uzbekistan. A small taste of things to come. The quest for a new quality of relations with the

West was thus also, increasingly, a 'flight forward' from mounting problems at home.

Mid-way between the revision of external policy and the ructions of internal politics, and directly affected by both, was Eastern Europe. A new line of more permissive Soviet policy towards Eastern Europe was formally enshrined in a short memorandum to the Politburo in the autumn of 1986, and privately communicated in general terms to East European leaders at that time. But the practice of Soviet policy towards Eastern Europe lagged a long way behind the theory. Gorbachev himself was extremely cautious about undermining the position of East European leaders by unambiguous public articulation of what in the West would be called the 'renunciation of the Brezhnev Doctrine'.

By early 1989, however, Gorbachev had two concrete proposals from East European leaders for changes which went farther than anything he was publicly advocating at home. General Jaruzelski, probably his most trusted East European partner, initiated the Round Table talks with Solidarity. A little later, in March, the new Party leadership in Hungary told him they were preparing to move towards a multi-party system. Gorbachev gave his assent to both experiments. By June, with Solidarity's election triumph and the reburial of Imre Nagy, he was beginning to see where they might lead.

So was the United States. After taking several months in a comprehensive policy review, President Bush had launched his proposals to go 'beyond containment' in a series of speeches leading up to Nato's fortieth anniversary. Fascinated by these developments in Poland (where he had paid a moving visit in 1987) and in Hungary, he went on to make trips to those two countries and to encourage them down the road from Communism to democracy. While his Secretary of State, James Baker, had assured Shevardnadze that 'this isn't meant to create problems for you' he also warned that if the Soviet Union tried to stop these changes it would endanger the new co-operative relationship. Thus, at this crucial juncture, the United States linked the development of its relationship with the Soviet Union to Soviet conduct in East Central Europe.

So in the summer of 1989 Gorbachev was, for all the sunny appearances and the adulation, a politician under immense pressure with very limited options. If Kohl was walking a tightrope, Gorbachev was riding a tiger along a tightrope. What, then, did the Soviet leadership anticipate at this crucial juncture? Defending the loss of Eastern Europe against furious criticism a year later, at the twenty-eighth (and last) congress of the Soviet Communist Party, Shevardnadze said: 'Yes, we had in principle predicted this . . . In principle, we sensed this, we knew this. We felt that if serious changes did not take place, then tragic events would follow.' In his memoirs, he recalls a report from the Soviet ambassador to Bonn as early as April saying that East Germany could collapse within days.

Similar warnings were made by other specialists in the spring and early summer.

Sergei Tarasenko, one of Shevardnadze's closest aides in the Foreign Ministry, recalls a confidential discussion in a small circle around the Foreign Minister, after the dramatic outcome of the Polish elections in June 1989. The conclusion, as he recalls it, was that Eastern Europe would probably 'go'. Although they foresaw grave repercussions, not least inside the Soviet Union, they felt Moscow had no serious alternative to letting it go. For to intervene to prevent this would be to ruin everything they had worked for over the previous four years, at home as well as abroad. And Shevardnadze reportedly told Baker, in a meeting in late July, that for the Soviet Union to use force to stop the changes in Eastern Europe 'would be the end of perestroika'. There are thus significant indications, to put it no stronger, of a pessimistic realism — or realistic pessimism — at a very high level in Moscow.

On the other hand there are also indications of an optimistic idealism which would prove to be unrealistic. After all, the basic starting point of Gorbachev and his closest associates was that the Soviet Union could be modernised while remaining the Soviet Union, and that socialism could be reformed while remaining socialism — that is, a system qualitatively distinct from even the social democratic variant of capitalism. Many of them had been strongly influenced by the Prague Spring. Asked what was the difference between what was happening in Moscow and what had happened in Prague in 1968, the Foreign Ministry spokesman, Gennady Gerasimov, had memorably replied 'nineteen years'. Gorbachev himself said in early 1989 that the aim of perestroika was to 'reveal the human face of socialism', thus taking up the key phrase of 1968. As we have noted already, in his speech to the Council of Europe in July 1989 Gorbachev clearly envisaged the continued existence of two distinct 'social systems' in East and West.

So he probably still hoped that reformed communist leaders — little Gorbachevs, so to speak — could continue to play the leading role in states that would continue to be in some sense socialist. In Czechoslovakia's velvet revolution a few months later, home-made posters would appear showing '89' as '68' upside down. But the people who really believed that '89 might be another '68 were, arguably, the middle-aged reformers in Moscow. These were illusions. But they were, for Eastern Europe, helpful illusions. For if Soviet leaders had foreseen exactly what would happen in Eastern Europe, they might after all have been tempted to draw back. The people of Eastern Europe were thus the beneficiaries not just of the Soviet leaders' realism but also of their illusions — which were, in one of history's nicer ironies, in some measure the East Europeans' own illusions of twenty years before.

If we are right — and such a reconstruction is of course speculative —

then Gorbachev, Shevardnadze and their closest associates were, in that early summer of 1989, hovering between illusory hopes and realistic fears. And what of Kohl, Genscher and their closest associates? Everyone could see that relations between Bonn and Moscow were now better than they had ever been in the history of the Bonn republic. After a long, painful prologue the new page had became a new chapter, and the new chapter now looked like a new book. In economics, at least, Bonn was now Moscow's single most important partner in the West. It was equally plain that what Bonn wanted in return was progress in Deutschlandpolitik. For Kohl and Genscher, as for all their predecessors, the end of the road from Bonn to Moscow was Berlin. For a time, in the mid-1980s, they had got farther along the German-German side of the triangle than along the German-Soviet side. But now they were almost back to the original Brandt-Bahr geometry, working through Moscow to put pressure on a recalcitrant East Berlin.

Reflecting on the significance of the Gorbachev visit, Horst Teltschik wrote that the Bonn Declaration took on 'a particular significance, and in a certain sense even political explosiveness' against the background of Gorbachev's reforms at home. 'If German unification is principally understood to be the means to realise human rights and the right of self-determination for all Germans,' he wrote, 'it can only have a chance if such rights are also realised in the Soviet Union *and if this development then spreads to its allies*' (author's italics). Like Bahr, Teltschik saw change coming from the centre of the Soviet empire and from above. The 1989 version of Bahr-judo was: Moscow must help bring reforms to East Berlin. This was perhaps not so far from what Gorbachev himself envisaged.

However, the time-scale Teltschik then imagined for such changes was still one of many years, probably of decades. If anything, Gorbachev, Shevardnadze and their closest advisers may have had a slightly more realistic idea of how quickly East Germany might collapse than Kohl, Genscher and their colleagues in Bonn. Policymakers in Bonn had worked for so long with Soviet power in Central Europe as a fact almost of physical geography that to anticipate its collapse was almost like anticipating the dissolution of the Alps. Soviet policymakers, by contrast, knew from inside just how rotten the mountains were. What is more, they could sense — even if they did not positively know, let alone publicly admit — how they themselves would react to an avalanche.

The Chancellor and his Foreign Minister had a sense — perhaps scarcely more than a hope against hope — that the German question really might be coming 'open' again, in a way that it had not been for decades. Like any good politician, they were ready to seize the main chance if it came. But nobody knew exactly when or how it would come. That now depended on the workings of what Gorbachev rather mystically described as 'history' or 'life itself', in a state called the GDR.

IV

Germany and Germany

Foundations

In a sense, all Ostpolitik was Deutschlandpolitik. Reducing and eventually overcoming the division of Berlin and Germany was not the only objective of Bonn's new opening to the Soviet Union and Eastern Europe, but it was the single most important one. Increasing the Federal Republic's freedom of action was an end in itself, but also a means to this larger end. Relations with Moscow, above all, but also, to a lesser degree, with Warsaw, Prague or Budapest, were seen to have a crucial permissive function for the pursuit of Deutschlandpolitik. The affairs of Berlin still directly involved the four powers. However, that involvement became less intense, and West Germany's dependence on the Western Allies accordingly less acute, as a result both of the calming effect of the Quadripartite Agreement and of the development of direct relations between the two states in Germany.

It was these direct relations which after 1969 became the central stuff of Deutschlandpolitik. As part of the initial 'recognition' of the GDR, the Brandt government renamed the Ministry for All-German Questions the Ministry for Intra-German Relations, and that deliberately awkward term henceforth became official parlance. A description more widely used, with conscious paradox, was 'German-German relations'. Whatever the label, they were relations and no longer merely questions.

Egon Bahr memorably commented, after signing the Basic Treaty with the GDR in December 1972, that whereas previously the two German states had had no relations they would now at least have bad ones. To say that the two states had previously had no relations was of course a characteristic overstatement. So far as trade was concerned, the two states in Germany had recognised each other from the very beginning. With only minor amendments, the Berlin Agreement of September 1951 remained the contractual basis of what the Federal Republic referred to as 'intra-German trade', right up until 1990. In the crucial area of humanitarian help for political prisoners in the GDR and families divided by the Wall, the efforts not just of the West Berlin city government but also of the West German federal government went back to the early 1960s. Starting in 1963, under the Christian Democrat Rainer Barzel, the All-German and then Intra-German Ministry oversaw these secret and extraordinary humanitarian actions for twenty-seven years.

Moreover, Chancellor Kiesinger's April 1967 declaration on the principles of the government's Deutschlandpolitik, a declaration shaped both by the Social Democrat Herbert Wehner, as Minister for All-German Questions, and by his predecessor Rainer Barzel, reads almost like a check list for the operative Deutschlandpolitik of the 1970s and 1980s. Among the possibilities of 'alleviating the burden of the division of our people (*Volk*)', in order 'to create the preconditions for a détente inside Germany', this listed 'I. Measures to alleviate everyday life for the people (*die Menschen*) in both parts of Germany, such as (a): improved travel opportunities, above all for relatives, with the goal of developing normal communications'. I(b) was 'permit agreements' for Berlin and areas along the frontier, and I(e) the reunification of families (*Familienzusammenführung*), especially the return of children separated from their parents by the division (*Kinderrückführung*).

Sections II and III then listed diverse measures of economic co-operation, improved transport connections, post and telephone links, academic, cultural, youth and sporting exchanges. In proposing the 'creation of a rational electricity network economy' it even anticipated arrangements for the exchange of surplus electricity between East and West Germany which were finally agreed twenty-one years later: if not a *Zollverein*, then at least a *Stromverbund*. (The first part of this cross-border power grid was finished just a month before the opening of the Berlin Wall.)

Yet as we have seen, the Kiesinger government did not manage even to begin the realisation of this practical agenda. It was only after further change in the positions of Moscow, Washington and Bonn, only after the government declaration of October 1969, recognising the existence of 'two states in Germany', that Willy Brandt and the East German Prime Minister Willi Stoph would meet, in two fraught and deeply emotional encounters, first in the East German town of Erfurt and then in the West German town of Kassel. It was only after the Moscow Treaty was signed and the Warsaw Treaty initialled that Egon Bahr could sit down formally to negotiate with State Secretary Michael Kohl of the GDR. It was only after Walter Ulbricht was replaced by Erich Honecker, with a little brotherly help from Moscow, that these negotiations began to bear fruit.

It was only following the Quadripartite Agreement on Berlin that the first, very modest, German-German agreements, on post and telephone links, and transit to and from West Berlin, would be signed. It was only after the ratification of the Moscow and Warsaw treaties, and the blossom-

ing of American-Soviet détente with President Nixon's visit to Moscow
and the signing of the SALT I arms control treaty, that Bahr and Michael
Kohl could sign the first formal bilateral treaty between the two German
states; modestly enough, a treaty about traffic (albeit in a broad sense).
And it was only after all this, and some heavy use of the Bonn-Moscow-
Berlin triangle, that Bahr and Michael Kohl could, at long last, reach
agreement on 'A Treaty on the Bases of Relations between the Federal
Republic of Germany and the German Democratic Republic'.

These three pioneering years of German-German relations saw one of
the most awkward and yet deeply emotional *pas de deux* in diplomatic
history; or rather, a *pas de deux* inside a foursome reel, for the Soviet
Union, the United States, Britain and France were intimately involved at
every stage; and everyone was dancing on a minefield. The summit
meetings in Erfurt, where Willy Brandt was greeted by crowds chanting
'Willy to the window!', and in Kassel, where Willi Stoph was greeted by
right-wing extremists, were the great symbolic moments. 'The day of
Erfurt,' wrote Brandt, looking back from old age, 'was there any in my life
that was more laden with emotion?' Both sides made extraordinary
preparations. Reckoning with listening devices in the hotel at Erfurt, the
West German delegation had a briefing book with numbered alternative
formulations and in their internal discussions merely exchanged numbers.
The Politburo briefing book for Stoph's trip to Kassel runs to more than
one hundred pages, with detailed arguments for every eventuality.

Quite as remarkable, in a less public and dramatic way, were the long
drawn-out negotiations between Bahr and Kohl. Here too every tiny detail
was prescribed and analysed to exhaustion. When an East German official
forgot to remove his hat as he greeted Egon Bahr on a wet and windy day
at the airport, West German analysts speculated that this was a deliberate
affront. But when that same official waited to receive Bahr inside the foyer
of the Council of Ministers, instead of stepping out to greet him, it
actually was a deliberate gesture. And so on and so forth. Only if one
recalls the fantastic hypersensitivity of these early years, and the years of
megaphone diplomacy that preceded them, can one understand the standards by which West German policymakers judged the progress of later
years. It should also soon be possible, drawing on the wealth of documents
which are just becoming available, to make a serious assessment of the
achievement of Egon Bahr in his negotiations for Germany. What was in
many ways the high-point of Bahr's personal diplomacy can only be the
starting-point of our analysis here.

The Treaty on the Bases of Relations (*Grundlagenvertrag*), sometimes
loosely referred to as the Basic Treaty, was at once wholly unique and
supremely typical of the Ostpolitik as conceived and implemented by Willy
Brandt and Egon Bahr. It was, more directly than all the rest, the
culmination of the work they had begun in cruelly divided Berlin a decade

before. We have suggested that the hallmarks of that embryonic Ostpolitik were not, as they put it, 'small steps instead of big words', but rather small steps *and* big words, though of a different kind from Adenauer's. Nowhere were the steps smaller, or the words bigger, than in German-German relations.

Thus the '20 points' which Willy Brandt presented to Willi Stoph in Kassel as the basis for negotiating a treaty still included such elementary humanitarian demands as: 'the problems which result from the division of families should be brought to a solution' (point 15). Yet they also included such high-flown, pathos-laden affirmations as: 'the treaty parties declare that never again may war go out from German soil' (point 7). This phrase, over which Brandt and Stoph had already agreed in Erfurt, was not actually included in the treaty, but it was to play a crucial part in German-German relations over the next twenty years.

The treaty itself was the most extreme example of the approach which the other Eastern treaties exemplified to a lesser degree: putting to one side all the irreconcilable differences of principle so as to open the door for the development of a practical *modus vivendi*, under the general headings of 'détente', 'co-operation' and 'normalisation'. Thus the Preamble declared this treaty to be 'without prejudice to the different views of the Federal Republic of Germany and the German Democratic Republic on fundamental questions, including the national question'. The Federal Republic made explicit its different view by handing over, at the point of signature, the same 'Letter on German Unity' that it had handed over on signing the Moscow Treaty.

Concessions made by the West German side included, beyond the basic — yet not, the Bonn government insisted, full — diplomatic recognition of the GDR, a fairly strong statement in Article 6 that the two states 'proceed on the principle that the sovereign jurisdiction of each of the two states is confined to its own territory. They respect the independence and autonomy of each of the two states in their internal and external affairs.' In a laconic accompanying exchange, however, the Federal Republic declared that 'questions of citizenship have not been regulated by the treaty' — meaning that it would continue to regard citizens of the GDR as citizens of the Federal Republic, and hence automatically to give them West German passports, if they got to the West and wanted to take up that distinctly attractive offer.

Article 1 of the treaty said the two states would develop 'normal, good neighbourly relations' although no-one could say exactly what 'normal, good neighbourly' relations would be between two halves of a divided nation, let alone of a divided city. In a statement to mark the initialling of the treaty, Brandt recalled a central passage from his October 1969 government declaration. 'Twenty years after the foundation of the Federal Republic and the GDR,' he had said, 'we must prevent a further drifting apart of the German nation, that is, try to move via a *geregeltes Neben-einander* [roughly: a regulated next-to-each-other] to a *Miteinander* [with-each-other]'. The treaty, Brandt now commented, 'is the instrument to organise the *Miteinander* under the given circumstances'.

Here was another classic piece of Brandtian inspirational vagueness. For who precisely was to be 'next to' whom? Who was 'regulating' what? When, how, by what criteria would who decide that they (the states? their leaders? the people?) were 'with' rather than just 'next to' each other? Clear, unambiguous meanings were precisely what these big words were not to have.

Meanwhile, Brandt and Bahr pointed to the small steps. Beyond the contorted compromise formulae of the agreements, and the vague emotive glosses, what the Bonn government would stress above all was the possibilities the treaty opened up for practical improvements for 'the people' (*die Menschen*) in the two states. Humanitarian improvements that were achieved in direct connection with the treaty included an explicit formal acceptance by the GDR, albeit only in a letter accompanying the treaty, of the need to reunite families, and detailed provision for easier travel into East Germany for West Germans from areas immediately adjoining the borders of the GDR. Article 7 of the treaty said that the two sides 'will make agreements so as to develop . . . co-operation in the areas of the economy, science and technology, transport, legal relations, post and telecommunications, health, culture, sport, environmental protection, and in other fields.'

So the proof of the pudding was to be in the eating. After the Basic Treaty was ratified, against the opposition of the Christian Democrats, and found by the constitutional court to be in accordance with West Germany's Basic Law, Egon Bahr delivered a lecture at the Tutzing Academy, to mark the tenth anniversary of his 1963 'Tutzing speech'. '*Wandel durch Annäherung* (change through rapprochement),' he said, recalling his famous formula of ten years before, 'is the concept for the conduct of the nation, so long as it is divided. It is a concept which, from this summer, having become an effective treaty, has begun its probation.'

However, it took yet another year, until the summer of 1974, before the so-called Permanent Representations — embassies in all but name — were installed at what were carefully described as 'the respective seats of government', for of course neither West Germany nor the Western Allies would ever refer to East Berlin as the 'capital' of the GDR. The West German Permanent Representative reported directly to the Chancellor. The East German Permanent Representative reported formally to his Ministry for Foreign Affairs — for was not West Germany a quite foreign country?

Behind this formal construction, itself anything but simple, there was on both sides a complex politics — and bureaucratic politics — of German-

German relations. In West Germany, leaders of all the main parties — in the government coalition and in opposition — would, as we shall see, get their oar in, while within the bureaucracy the policy had to be co-ordinated between senior officials from at least three departments, and more would be involved in many individual decisions.

In East Germany, the Chancellor's real counterpart, the man who took the key decisions, was clearly the East German party leader, Erich Honecker. But the party-state's economic chief Günter Mittag was also an important actor, while the State Security Service under Erich Mielke had both an active operational interest and a formidable passive *droit de regard*. The unique nature of the relationship to West Germany, combined with Honecker's — and Mittag's — desire to keep control of it to themselves, led to unusual politbureaucratic devices, such as the Politburo's 'Working Group FRG', chaired by Mittag. Most unusual, too, was the lack of any direct control of the Foreign Ministry's 'FRG Department' by a depart-ment of the Central Committee. These factors also favoured a heavy use of unconventional emissaries such as the lawyer Wolfgang Vogel and, above all, Alexander Schalck-Golodkowski — or plain Schalck, as he was known in the GDR.

From 1976 on, Schalck was the single most important East German intermediary in German-German relations. After unification, a Bundestag special committee struggled valiantly to disentangle the web of his politbureaucratic subordination. Was he answerable to Honecker directly? To Honecker via Mittag? To Mielke? But this was to try to disentangle the undisentangleable. For the ambiguous, murky, duplicated and duplici-tous lines of reporting and command reflected not merely the character of Schalck but the reality of his position, and the reality of the party-and police-state he served.

On many issues, above all in relation to Berlin, West Germany had still to consult with its Western Allies. The so-called Bonn Group (or 'Group of Four'), which for many years had regularly brought together senior officials from the American, British and French embassies and the West German Foreign Ministry, remained an important co-ordinating body. This was as nothing, however, compared to the minute consultations which the East Germany Foreign Ministry, Central Committee apparatus and Polit-buro leadership had with Moscow. As the East German party documents now definitely show, even in the 1980s these consultations sometimes still took the form of taking orders. On the other hand, just because of this exacting requirement, the satellite state went to considerable lengths to establish its own discreet channels to Bonn, if only to test the water before putting the issue to Moscow — and especially to Moscow's long-time Ambassador in East Berlin, the high-handed and suspicious Piotr Abrassimov.

Wolfgang Mischnick, then parliamentary leader of the Free Democrats, recalls a conversation with Erich Honecker in 1973 during which, in the course of a walk in the woods(!), the East German leader suggested that some things could be done between the two German states 'without the big brother'. (Mischnick insists that Honecker himself used the phrase 'big brother'.) Direct correspondence and the despatch of informal emissaries, not only to the Chancellor or Chancellery Minister but also to Wehner or Strauss, all served not only to take measures quietly without consulting Moscow but also to prepare the ground before making a case to Moscow.

Wolfgang Schäuble, responsible for relations with the GDR as Chancellery Minister from 1984 until 1989, suggests a further reason for the sometimes secretive and even conspiratorial style of German-German relations. This, he argues, enabled the GDR to discuss subjects that it was not even prepared to discuss in official talks. More important still, it allowed West Germany to raise and East Germany to accept linkages — for example, between hard currency payments and the easing of travel restrictions — that the GDR would never countenance officially. Since these were precisely the subjects and linkages in which the Bonn government was most interested, it had to accept the conspiratorial terms of business.

Looking back in 1992, the East German party leader himself emphasised the particular importance of his personal telephone conversations with Chancellors Schmidt and Kohl. Talking to the author in the hospital of Berlin's Moabit prison, the former General Secretary of the SED and Chairman of the Council of State of the GDR pulled out of the pocket of his prison pyjamas a slightly dog-eared card on which his (former) secretary had once typed for him the direct telephone number to the Chancellor's office in Bonn. They used to call each other quite often, he said. On occasion he had even dialled the number himself. Hence the little card.

Thoughts, words and deeds

The first Permanent Representative of the Federal Republic in the GDR, Günter Gaus, subsequently described the policy conducted through these diverse and curious channels not as Deutschlandpolitik but as *DDR-Politik*. The term was much criticised in West Germany, because it was taken to imply a too substantial recognition of the GDR, at the expense of an operative commitment to working towards unity. Gaus himself would indeed later plead, explicitly and passionately, for what he called an 'inner' recognition of the GDR. At the same time there is no doubt that the primary meaning of 'Deutschlandpolitik' in Bonn over the next fifteen years, until 1989, was dealings with the GDR, a state which was assumed by virtually all policymakers and responsible politicians to be there for the foreseeable future. In this sense, if one can separate the term from the specific implications of the Gausian view, one may usefully describe this policy as *DDR-Politik*.

Yet can one thus separate it? Can one detach what West German policymakers did from what they said or thought they were doing? In what they actually did in policy towards the GDR there was an overwhelming continuity through the 1970s and 1980s. In what they said, there was near-total consensus on the short-term, operative goals. The diversity of publicly stated views grew as one looked to the medium-term, and became even more pronounced in respect of long-term objectives. And what they thought? This is most difficult of all to pin down, especially given the remarkable transformative effect of unification on so many German memories.

In the wake of unification, the immediate West German (party-) political debate concentrated on this issue of long-term goals. Who, it was severely asked, somewhat in the tones of the Spanish Inquisition, had continued through all these years to 'believe in' German unity? Had not Willy Brandt, the symbol of Ostpolitik and now the father-figure of German unification, declared in 1988 that reunification was the *Lebenslüge* (literally: life-lie) of the Federal Republic? Why yes, came the somewhat strained reply, but the term 'life-lie' referred only to the prefix '*re-*', which, please note, was carefully put in italics in the original speech. A new unification was a quite different matter. Had not Helmut Kohl, by contrast, constantly and loudly insisted that reunification was the ultimate goal? Why yes, but at roughly the same time as Brandt spoke of the 'life-lie' Kohl had confessed that he probably would not see German unity in his lifetime. And so on and so forth.

It is a prudent assumption in all human affairs that people do not always think what they say or say what they think. This assumption is particularly prudent in politics, and nowhere more so than in the politics of East-West relations in Germany. Granted this premiss, one has, logically speaking, four possible categories of person: those who both spoke and thought about German unity, those who neither spoke nor thought about it, those who spoke about it without thinking about it, and those who thought about it without speaking about it. One can state with some confidence that in West Germany in the 1980s the first class was very small and the second very large. There were very few people who both spoke and thought about the unification of Germany in one state as a serious objective in the foreseeable future. The few who did thus speak or write were often regarded, even among the Christian Democrats, as somewhat marginal and even slightly irresponsible.

There were, on the other hand, a very great many people who, although if asked in an opinion poll whether they were in favour of German unity would naturally say 'yes', neither spoke nor thought about it otherwise. A leading analyst of public opinion data on this subject records that whereas in the 1950s and 1960s between thirty-five and forty-five per cent of those asked considered reunification to be 'the most important question with which one should generally concern oneself in the Federal Republic today', from the mid-1970s the figure was never more than one per cent.

Most of West Germany's political class, however, fell into the other two, more problematic categories. The problem of defining attitudes is further exacerbated by the party-political divide. There is no doubt that leading Christian Democrats, in opposition and in government, more constantly and loudly reiterated their formal commitment to work towards German unity. Leading Social Democrats accused them of merely paying 'lip-service' to the commitment to unification in the preamble to the Basic Law, of making 'Sunday speeches' for the benefit of their expellee nationalist voters, without thinking very seriously about the implications of what they were saying, not least for the people who actually suffered most from the division.

Christian Democrats, by contrast, accused Social Democrats of no longer even talking about reunification, or, indeed, of talking positively about alternatives to it: models for the long-term co-existence of two states, of a reformed GDR in a European peace order, and so forth. Yet in the case of the Social Democratic architects of Ostpolitik, the fact that they did not talk about unification is no sure indication of what they thought. For, in the 1960s and early 1970s at least, they certainly thought more than they publicly said. It makes more sense, they argued, to talk publicly about the issues on which we have a chance of reaching agreement with the other side than about those on which there is no such chance. 'The time seems to me to have come,' as Brandt put it in a letter to Willi Stoph in February 1970, 'to relegate that which separates and to seek that which joins.'

It was not just in 1988 but already in 1969 that Brandt said 'I must confess that I have stopped speaking about reunification.' In the short-term, this could be seen as responsible, humane pragmatism, in the interests of the individual people in Germany (*die Menschen*). In the long-run, it had more than a touch of Machiavellianism, in the national interest. German unity could only be achieved if one ceased to demand it!

Given this complex starting point, it is very difficult to make any firm judgements about public statements on long-term goals. One may suspect that the private thoughts of leading Social Democrats came somewhat closer to their increasingly reserved public statements over these twenty years, even as the private thoughts of leading Christian Democrats somewhat (or further) diverged from their public statements, so that by the mid-1980s the two sides had perhaps reached, by different routes, a quite similar point of belief, or non-belief, in the real possibility of German unification. This must, however, vary with each individual case, and in no case will one be able to prove it anyway.

One may also ask how important the theological question of whether Mr X or Ms Y truly 'believed' in German unity ultimately is, interesting though it might be, especially for the purposes of party-political polemics. It is useful, and feasible, to record what leading figures actually said on this issue, over the years. It is important, although much more difficult, to enquire what the real effects of what they said were in East and West Germany, and among Germany's neighbours. Methodologically, the rest is little better than a parlour game.

At the other end of the spectrum were the short-term, operative goals. These were well-defined and consensual. Their realisation could be quite precisely charted. Yet perhaps more interesting than either the short or the long-term goals is the question of the medium-term. How did the Bonn government propose to move from the short-term goal — the reunification of families — to the long-term goal — the reunification of Germany? Even if the long-term goal were defined slightly differently — as, say, a genuinely democratic German Democratic Republic, a third version of German-speaking statehood, next to West Germany and Austria — the question remained of how one proposed to get from here to there. We may, of course, find that there was surprisingly little — of deed, word, or even thought — in this middle ground. The most effective politicians often combine a simple, long-term strategic vision with the greatest tactical flexibility and attention to the immediately do-able, leaving the middle-term to the so-called policy intellectuals. Arguably both Brandt and Kohl were, in their very different ways, this kind of politician, while Helmut Schmidt was witheringly dismissive of the 'concepts' of policy intellectuals.

Yet it would be a remarkable feat to conduct a policy of such central importance to your country for twenty years without having at least some underlying notion, however vague and rudimentary, of where it was taking you. So one can reasonably ask: how did West German policymakers think their policies might be changing the policies, and politics, of East Germany? And then: what effects did they actually have? Of course, as we have mentioned earlier, it is extremely difficult to single out the influence of Western policy among the many factors, domestic and international, that determine the political development of a communist state, and no state was more dependent on the international constellation than the GDR. It is also very difficult to distinguish between the influence that West Germany exerted passively, by virtue of its mere existence, prosperity, freedom, openness etc, and that which it exerted actively, by virtue of conscious policy.

Thus the fact that virtually all East Germans regularly watched West German television was endlessly cited as an example of West German influence. Yet West German television beams did not reach East German television screens as a result of West German government policy. This was, as it were, an act of God. On the other hand, the fact that in the

1970s and 1980s the East Germans received from West German television vivid, first-hand, live reports by Western reporters on their own internal affairs was, without question, a fruit of West German policy, since working conditions for Western journalists were the subject of hard-fought negotiations and agreements between the two states. That the East German regime no longer attempted to prevent its citisens watching Western television, as it had done in the 1950s and 1960s; that, on the contrary, in the 1980s it actually had cable laid so that people in the Dresden area, in what was known as 'the valley of the clueless', could properly receive Western broadcasts, rather than applying to emigrate: this was a significant change in Eastern policy. Yet this change cannot simply be described as a direct 'result' of Western policy. Rather it was the result of a complex calculation of political self-interest, in which Western desires were only one element.

Yet, despite these difficulties of analysis, the German-German relationship still offers a unique opportunity to examine the impact of Western policy on Eastern politics. Nowhere else in Europe do we have a case in which essentially just one policy was applied, by one Western state, to one Eastern state, over twenty years. Of the other major Western states, only France may perhaps be said to have had a distinctive policy directed specifically at the East German state. But this consisted in going slightly further than West Germany in recognition of the GDR (to help ensure that there continued to be two Germanies for France to love). Like France, Britain and the United States had interests in East Germany, and American policy was a prime determinant of the 'overall weather conditions' for German-German relations. But neither Britain nor the United States had a distinctive policy directed specifically at the GDR. In direct relations with the GDR, their role was essentially supportive of Bonn's policy.

In what follows we shall look first at the short-term, consensual, operative goals of West German policy and the means by which they were to be realised: permanent negotiation, money and recognition. We shall then turn to the medium-term relationship between policy towards the GDR and the politics of the GDR, looking first at the intended and then at the actual impact of the former on the latter.

For people and the people

'The intra-German treaty policy,' said the common resolution of all the main parties in the Bundestag, in February 1984, 'should make the consequences of partition more bearable for the people in Germany and preserve the unity of the nation.' In Bonn usage, these central purposes were generally referred to under two rubrics, both difficult to translate: *menschliche Erleichterungen* and *der Zusammenhalt der Nation*. The former means literally 'human alleviations', and the latter 'the cohesion of the nation'. *Menschliche* implies more than simply 'humanitarian', so one might more loosely translate this phrase as 'improvements for people', that is, for individual human beings, *die Menschen*. *Nation* in the second phrase implies less than nation-state, so one might more loosely translate it as 'keeping together the people', that is, the ethnic and cultural collectivity, the *Volk* and the *Kulturnation*. In the statements of West German policymakers these two senses of 'helping (the) people' were practically elided, or at the very least a natural continuum was assumed to lead from one to the other.

No one talked more movingly about *die Menschen* than Willy Brandt. In his first state of the nation address as Chancellor, in January 1970, he concluded by answering the charge that his government was proposing to pay in advance for uncertain concessions from the East. There was a time, he said, 'when considerable German payments-in-advance to the West were considered as proof of special statesmanlike wisdom and foresight'. The reference was of course to Adenauer's Western treaties. Then he went on to spell out the potential benefits that justified the opening to the East. 'And will not Germany then herself have more security and a better peace?' he asked.

Will not her people, every single one, profit from it? Let me put it like this: because there will be less fear; because the burdens will be lighter; because people will see each other again, who for years could not see each other; because perhaps two people from the two states in Germany will be able to marry, who today are divided by inhuman duress. These are the standards, great and small, but always related to the people (*die Menschen*), which this government sets . . .

Seventeen years later, Chancellor Kohl set the same standards and made the same elision. 'We are aware,' he said, in his 1987 state of the nation address,

that human alleviations are not the same thing as human rights. It would nonetheless be irresponsible to underestimate the value of human alleviations. So long as the Germans are separated from each other, it is our task to ease the painful consequences of the division of our fatherland, to strengthen the consciousness of belonging together among all Germans, to preserve what unites and to create new commonalities between them. Our effort to facilitate encounters, in growing number and intensity, between the people (*die Menschen*) in both states in Germany, is central.

Most of what the Federal Republic attempted to do in its operative policy could be located somewhere on this assumed continuum between bringing individual people together and keeping the nation together. Over the years, negotiations with the East German authorities covered almost every sort of interchange within a nation: human, legal, financial, academic, social, commercial, cultural, environmental, technical, sporting, scientific; you name it, Bonn would talk about it. The West German government's interest in every case was to preserve and develop all possible kinds of exchange, link, tie or bond between the two parts of Germany, making a web to 'hold the nation together'. The idea of spinning such a web of ties and interdependencies — a process variously described as *Vernetzung*, *Verklammerung* or, most frequently, *Verflechtung* — had been central to the rethinking of Deutschlandpolitik in the 1960s, and was, as we shall see, important for the whole Ostpolitik in the 1970s and 1980s. The East German regime's interest, by contrast, was only to allow the most carefully controlled and selective development of such ties, and to exact for them the maximum price. The negotiations were therefore slow, painful and tortuous.

They were made doubly painful and tortuous by what West Germany saw as the categorical imperative of wherever possible including West Berlin in the West-East German agreements. Moreover, many of the negotiations were concerned exclusively with the special problems of Berlin. No less than fifteen of the seventeen agreements which Günter Gaus negotiated as Permanent Representative related to Berlin. Arrangements for transit travellers between West Germany and West Berlin, the physical improvement of the transit motorways and railway lines, telephone links between West and East Berlin, visits from West Berlin to East Berlin and the rest of East Germany, the anomalous exclaves of West Berlin almost entirely surrounded by the East, the local railway lines (*S-Bahn*) running through West Berlin but still administered by the *Deutsche Reichsbahn* from the East, the disposal of sewage from West Berlin: the list of Berlin issues was almost endless.

In the 1980s, the agenda of the German-German negotiations became rather more diverse and ambitious. There was some co-operation on tackling common problems like the pollution which originated in one part of Germany (mainly the East) but affected the other. A classic case was the River Elbe, which, by the time it had run diagonally across the breadth of the GDR, reached Hamburg as a poisonous sewer. There was the agreement to develop a cross-border power grid, the *Stromverbund* already mentioned. To the earlier (1974) agreement on sporting ties there were now added two on youth exchanges, although the nature of the East German signatory — the Party youth movement (FDJ) — did not bode well for the selection of young people to be sent West.

After just twelve years of negotiation, an agreement on cultural co-operation was signed in 1986. Even then it was little more than a framework agreement of principle, which some artists feared would actually increase the Eastern party-state's control over the cultural exchanges that were already happening from below. The same applied to the agreement on technical and scholarly exchanges, signed in the autumn of 1987. In 1986 there began a wave of 'twinning' between towns and cities in East and West. By the opening of the Berlin Wall, fifty-eight such agreements had been made, with another six in preparation. Although the town councils in the East were also under Party control, these town twinnings at least put the selection of contact persons lower down the hierarchy.

All these negotiations were necessarily conducted with the East German powers-that-be, under the general motto of 'co-operation'. Most West German politicians and policymakers, however, considered themselves to be negotiating on behalf of the people — *die Menschen* — meaning, first, the Germans living in the GDR, second, the Germans living in West Berlin, third, the Germans in West Germany, and fourth, the Germans altogether. The measure of 'success' for the negotiations was therefore, to quote the Bundestag resolution once again, 'directly useful results for the people'. Measured by this standard, it must be said that some of these painfully negotiated agreements produced only relatively small direct benefits, or had only just begun to do so when revolution and unification overtook them.

Yet overall there was, measured against the quite extraordinary low starting-point of post-Wall Germany, very significant progress 'for the people'. The publications of the Ministry for Intra-German relations lovingly recorded the number of letters and parcels sent from West to East and East to West, the growing number of telephone lines, telexes and telegrams, the volume of trade and the volume of people. Whereas in 1969 there had been just half a million telephone calls from West to East Germany, in 1988 (the last 'normal', that is, normalised-abnormal, year in German-German relations) there were some forty million. Whereas in 1969 there were little more than one million visits recorded from West to East Germany, in the mid-1970s the figure reached nearly eight million. In 1980 the GDR tried, as it had in 1973, to stem the presumably subverting flow of Western visitors by sharply increasing the minimum amount of hard currency that the Western visitor was compelled to exchange on each trip across the border. Yet the number of West German visits still remained above five million a year throughout the 1980s.

The improvement was most dramatic where the problem had been most acute: in Berlin. To appreciate this one has to go back for a moment to the early 1960s. With the building of the Wall, the last relatively risk-free escape route out of the GDR was closed. By September 1961 the division of Berlin and Germany was about as absolute as any territorial division in Europe could be. No ordinary German under pensionable age could now travel from East to West, except by risking their lives. Movement from West to East was also desperately restricted. West Germans could still theoretically travel in East Germany, but West Berliners could not so much as enter East Berlin. They could not even telephone to East Berlin. For ordinary people there were no telephone connections at all until 1970. Your brother three blocks up the Friedrichstrasse might just as well have been in Outer Mongolia. The permit agreements negotiated by Brandt and his team in the West Berlin city government brought some limited, temporary relief, but after 1966 the East German authorities hardened their position and demanded fuller 'recognition' as the price for further agreements. There remained only a small office giving permission for visits on 'urgent family affairs', a mere trickle of some 60,000 a year from 1967 to 1969. Even movement between West and West was severely restricted. The transit routes between West Germany and West Berlin remained theoretically open, but the ordinary citizen risked arbitrary harassment if he chose to travel by car rather than plane.

The treaty work, and subsequent German-German negotiations, transformed this situation. The transit journey between West Germany and West Berlin was still an unsettling experience when you made it for the first time, with the frontier fortifications at each end, the special mirrors to search for possible escapees clinging underneath your car, the faint scent of Le Carré in the air. After a few trips it was no more than marginally inconvenient. The transit fees for West Germans and West Berliners were paid in a lump-sum by the Bonn government, which also paid very large sums for distinctly modest improvements in the condition of the roads. Although the East German police collected fines from speeding Mercedes and BMW drivers with vengeful regularity, the risk of serious harassment was reduced to a minimum; unless, of course, one did actually try to help someone to escape. In consequence, the numbers who travelled by land to and from West Berlin increased very significantly, from just over seven million in 1970 to nearly twenty-four million in 1986, while the numbers who went by air actually declined from more than five and a half million to less than four million.

Still more marked was the improvement in access to the East, for this was an improvement virtually 'from scratch'. In March 1972, as the Bundestag began to debate the Moscow and Warsaw treaties, ordinary West Berliners were allowed to visit East Berlin for the first time in six years. Thereafter, such visits became increasingly routine. This traffic was hard hit by increases in the minimum amount of hard currency which Western visitors had to exchange on each visit — the so-called 'compulsory exchange'. But in 1988 there were still some one and a half million visits by West Berliners to East Germany, of which roughly half were day trips to the other half of the divided city. This annual flow was still probably less than the daily flow of commuters between West London and the surrounding area; but it was a great improvement on nothing. And if one did not physically go to make one's calls on relatives and friends, one could now at least call by phone. Where in 1970 there had been no normal phone calls at all between West and East Berlin, in 1988 there were more than ten million.

Behind these dry statistics were real, profound gains for hundreds of thousands of individual men and women. Yet the value to any West German or West Berliner of easier access to the East was as nothing compared to the value for an East German of travelling to the West. To use an image which in West Germany in the 1980s was widely regarded as inappropriate: the chance of visiting or being visited in prison is nothing compared with the chance of leaving prison, even for a short 'leave-out'. The crucial statistics therefore concerned the movement of Germans from East to West. The basic numbers are given in Tables VI and VIII, but so great was the importance attached to these figures by successive governments that it is worth examining them more closely.

From Germany to Germany

There were two kinds of journey 'from Germany to Germany': the temporary and the permanent. In the sixteen years between the end of the war in Europe and the building of the Berlin Wall, some three and a half million Germans moved permanently to the West from what was then still referred to as 'the Zone'. Most would then have said that they 'fled' or 'chose freedom'. The young, the better educated and the enterprising were disproportionately represented in this great movement of people. Many subsequently attained high positions in the Federal Republic, among them Hans-Dietrich Genscher, who, in 1952, at the age of twenty-five, left his native town of Halle to start a new life in the Federal Republic, first as a junior lawyer and then as a politician. Yet as Genscher himself acknowledged, his heart remained in Halle. Together with those who had earlier fled from Germany's former territories east of the Oder-Neisse line, these natives of East Germany would provide a reservoir of passionate, lasting interest in 'the East' at the very highest levels of West German public life.

After the building of the Berlin Wall had stopped the haemorrhage from what some Western observers then sarcastically referred to as 'the disappearing satellite', the flood was reduced to a trickle. In 1962, only some 21,000 Germans managed to move permanently from East to West, and a mere 4,600 did so with the permission of the East German authorities. In the same year, there were only some 27,000 visits from East to West, and even fewer visitors, since most of those who came were pensioners, invalids, businessmen, functionaries or lorry drivers, making several trips a year. For the ordinary man or woman under pensionable age there was simply no chance whatsoever of visiting or moving to West Germany.

Their freedom of movement to the West was reduced to nil, just at the time when it was gradually becoming easier for Poles, Czechs and Hungarians to travel West. The division of Germany was made deeper when the division of Europe, in this elementary sense, was already beginning to ease around it.

To restore the circulation from East to West was to be the top operative priority of the Bonn government's policy towards the GDR, arguably from 1966, and certainly from 1969. Until the mid-1980s its success was, however, very limited. In the sixteen years from 1968 to 1983 less than a quarter of a million people moved permanently from East Germany to the West: that is, just one person for every fourteen who got out between May 1945 and August 1961. One in three of these, moreover, owed their freedom less to any West German policy than to their own courage and daring. They risked life and limb to cross the German-German border, or, as that become ever more difficult and dangerous, trekked across the more loosely guarded borders from Czechoslovakia or Hungary to Austria or Yugoslavia, and thence to the safe refuge of a West German consulate. There, as we have noted already, the East German could instantaneously become a West German. In the early 1980s the West German government lent on the East German authorities to dismantle the most barbaric features on the German-German border, the automatic shooting devices and minefields, although people were still shot by frontier guards. Apart from this, Bonn's contribution was limited to offering automatic citizenship, followed by practical assistance in starting a new life in the West.

If, however, East Germans were caught and sent to prison for the offence of 'attempting to flee the republic'; if they had been sent to prison for another 'political' offence, such as conscientious objection or outright protest; if they took refuge in West Germany's Permanent Representation in East Berlin, or in a West German embassy elsewhere in Eastern Europe; if they merely applied for permission to leave legally; then the West German authorities were directly involved in attempting to win their freedom. Quantitatively, these 'humanitarian efforts' were, by the 1980s, a relatively small part of the whole network of relations with the GDR. Qualitatively, however, they remained at the very heart of the relationship, from the day the Wall was built until the day the Wall was opened. For nearly thirty years many of the details were shrouded in official secrecy, until unification allowed the main participants to start telling their remarkable stories. Only the barest outlines can be sketched here.

It began with the Protestant church. In June 1962, while attempting to secure the release of church workers imprisoned in the East, a legal representative of the (still formally united) German Protestant church made contact with an East Berlin lawyer, one Wolfgang Vogel. They arranged a deal. In return for three lorry loads of potash, prisoners from an agreed short list were released — to the West. A little later, twenty children divided from their parents by the building of the Wall were also released to the West in a similar way.

In 1963, following an intervention by the publisher Axel Springer, overall responsibility for this 'buying free' of prisoners from the GDR — *Freikauf* — was taken over by the Ministry for All-German Questions, under the then Minister, Rainer Barzel. The Ministry's then representative in Berlin, Ludwig Rehlinger, describes in his memoirs his first, agonising choices as he tried to select 1,000 especially acute or deserving cases from a list of 12,000 known political prisoners in the GDR. Then he was compelled to reduce the 1,000 to 500; the 500 to fifty; the fifty to ten. At the end of the day the GDR allowed the Bonn government to 'buy free' just eight prisoners in 1963. Bonn paid in cash. A West Berlin lawyer, Jürgen Stange, travelled across to East Berlin by *S-Bahn*, with the money in a large unmarked envelope.

When the East German authorities saw that Bonn — and the released prisoners — maintained absolute discretion about this channel, they allowed more human material to be exported through it. In August 1964, the first 'regular' transports went by bus to the frontier. A total of 880 political prisoners would be 'bought free' in 1964, and more than 1,000 in 1965. At this time, the negotiations were mainly conducted by Ludwig Rehlinger and the West Berlin lawyer, Jürgen Stange, with the East Berlin lawyer extraordinary, Wolfgang Vogel, and a certain Heinz Volpert, the senior Stasi officer directly responsible. Initially, they negotiated a price on the head of each prisoner, according to his or her prison sentence, qualifications and 'value' to the communist state. Subsequently, a standard price per head was agreed, although there were still special cases.

When the arrangement was regularised, the Bonn government paid the agreed total sums to a charitable trust of the Protestant church (in the West), the Diaconical Work, which kept a detailed record of what it called 'B-deals'. ('A-deals' were the indirect financing of the Church in East Germany through deliveries of goods, for which the East German authorities then paid the Church in the GDR, in East German Marks.) Ludwig Geissel, the man responsible in the Diaconical Work, arranged for the delivery of goods for that sum, in forms and along channels agreed with his negotiating partners in the GDR. In 1966, the GDR created a special agency called simply Commercial Co-ordination — *KoKo* — the main purpose of which was to maximise hard currency income from this and other sources. The head of *KoKo*, Alexander Schalck, and his deputy Manfred Seidel, would be Geissel's main Eastern partners.

The West German side, sensitive to the charge that this was man-trade, fondly hoped that the goods would benefit not just the state but also the people (*die Menschen*) in the East. Yet in later years the main contingents were of oil, copper, silver and industrial diamonds. And the massive investigation of Schalck's work after unification soon revealed that, from the early 1970s, *KoKo* had immediately and secretly resold many or most of these goods, often through a special firm in Liechtenstein. As an internal *KoKo* paper of 1972 noted: 'The sums are realised by deliveries of goods and turned back into hard currency by sale and manipulation.' So the diaconical supplies were laundered.

What is more, much of the hard currency thus realised was transferred to a special bank account personally controlled by Erich Honecker, and used for purposes as diverse as financing the State's thirtieth anniversary celebrations in 1979, importing Citroën cars for senior functionaries (in summer 1989!), but also importing consumer goods for wider distribution. For example, in November 1976 payment was made from this account for 800,000 pairs of shoes — or, as a retrospective report in *Die Zeit* sharply put it, shoes to the value of 1,072 prisoners.

This extraordinary set-up functioned, albeit with numerous hiccups, variations and elaborations, for more than a quarter century. Its Eastern players, Wolfgang Vogel and above all Alexander Schalck, became, in time, key intermediaries between the top political leaders in the two states. The same channels were used to discuss not just the 'buying free' of political prisoners but also the reunification of families, *Familienzusammenführung*. An especially poignant problem was that of the children cut off from their parents by the building of the Wall. Jürgen Stange estimates that in the autumn of 1961 there may have been some 4,000 of them. The release of many was quietly negotiated through the lawyers, with or without payment. But according to a confidential letter to Chancellor Brandt from the then Minister for Intra-German Relations, Egon Franke, eleven years later, in August 1972, the GDR was still holding more than a thousand such children.

After the ratification of the Basic Treaty, the Brandt government suggested to the GDR that in the twentieth century states would not normally expect to pay ransom, as in the Middle Ages. The Treaty did, after all, speak of 'normal, good neighbourly relations', and the Chancellery trio of Egon Bahr, Horst Ehmke and Günter Gaus proposed to take this seriously. Such cases should be handled directly through the Permanent Representation, and without head money. The East German authorities were deeply affronted. What matchless impudence! What Cold War confrontationism! And they broke off the talks on humanitarian cases. Many people were left literally sitting on packed suitcases. According to Wolfgang Vogel, some who had already been issued with passports actually had them withdrawn.

In this tense situation, Herbert Wehner, whose profound commitment in this field was recognised and respected by colleagues in all parties, travelled to East Berlin with the Free Democrat Wolfgang Mischnick — a fellow Dresdener — to conduct what were officially parliamentary talks with a delegation of East German 'People's Deputies'. The next day, thanks to the good offices of Wolfgang Vogel, the two of them had a long private conversation with Erich Honecker, in his house on the Wandlitzsee just outside Berlin. Although the conversation ranged across the whole palette of German-German affairs, these humanitarian issues were at the very centre of Wehner's personal concern.

Three weeks later Wehner wrote to Willy Brandt, after a talk with the man he referred to simply as 'the lawyer' (that is, Wolfgang Vogel): 'They will get serious about concrete steps in humanitarian questions. One transport can come on 11 July and one on 18 July. Children should come, 45 and again 45.' In a memorandum of a conversation on 17 September 1973, in which Wolfgang Vogel appears to have brought a long verbal message from Erich Honecker, Wehner noted:

> Since [Wehner's conversation with Honecker on 31 May] he [Honecker] had ordered and received a report that ca. 300 people have emigrated . . . On 14 September he signed a further list of 178 persons, including 68 children, and ordered that this is to be handled more swiftly than before. He had heard with great concern of the difficulties which had arisen in connection with this humanitarian field, and also for me [Wehner] personally. Here it must not come to any row or break . . .

This from Erich Honecker, who twelve years before had directly overseen the building of the Wall. Oh the humanity of the gaoler!

Talking to Leonid Brezhnev in Moscow a year later, Honecker presented the matter somewhat differently. 'In the matter of family reunification,' he said, according to the East German record,

> we are very restrictive. For this I am directly responsible, and permission to leave the GDR is given only with my signature. It is a closely controlled matter, which we have mainly pushed ahead to show good will. And there are many problems with it. Many children who are meant to be brought to their parents in the FRG don't want to leave the GDR, they go to school here, belong to the Pioneers and the FDJ [the Party's mass youth organisations] and are happy with us. Moreover, with this family reunification we get rid of some criminal elements to the FRG. They are treated in the FRG as political cases but in fact they are criminal elements.

Now it would clearly be wrong to conclude that what Honecker was saying to Brezhnev was the plain truth, and to Wehner, varnished duplicity. He was making a pitch to both. And there is considerable evidence that Honecker had a very emotional relationship to Wehner, in which old respect and old guilt were generously mingled. Neither Vogel nor Schalck will aver, in retrospect, that Honecker was moved by any deep humanitarian concern — except, says Vogel, when an old 'antifascist' was involved. For Honecker, both suggest, this was a chance to win credit in the West, display his personal power, earn some hard currency and get rid of some troublemakers at the same time. As Vogel pithily summarises Honecker's attitude: for him it was 'one class enemy less'.

Of course their evidence, too, must be treated with due scepticism. Whatever the mixture of motives, the fact is that from the summer of 1973 onwards, under Honecker's direct control, the procedures do seem to have run more smoothly. Indeed, over the years, to try to escape from the GDR became almost a calculable risk. Even if you were caught and sent to prison, so long as your case was known in the West you could reasonably hope that in one year, or two, or three, you would be summoned out of your cell, given your own clothes and a piece of paper certifying that you had once been a citizen of the GDR, and driven in an unmarked bus to the frontier. Bought free.

By the early 1970s, the price for a 'normal' *Freikauf* was set at DM 40,000. In 1977 the price per head was increased to DM 95,847. Wolfgang Vogel recalled, in an interview after unification, that they had arrived at a figure of DM 96,000 per head and then 'one of the participants said: we must make that figure uneven, so it doesn't look like a price per head'. The payment in cases of family reunification was generally DM 4,500 a head in the 1980s. Until 1983, the total number of men, women and children for whose freedom the West German state paid the East German state fluctuated between nine and thirteen thousand a year, of whom some one to two thousand a year were political prisoners and the rest cases of family reunification. In 1984, for reasons to be explored in more detail below, the total figure jumped dramatically to more than 37,000, and, with the exception of 1987, remained above 20,000 a year until the opening of the Wall. (See Table VIII)

In sum, over the period from 1963 until 1989 nearly 34,000 political prisoners were 'bought free' by the Bonn government, more than 2,000 children reunited with their parents, and more than 250,000 cases of family reunification 'regulated', as Ludwig Rehlinger puts it, with government help. For these humanitarian services, Bonn paid to East Berlin, in cash or kind, a round total of DM 3.5 billion.

Of course not everyone wanted to leave the GDR permanently; and the Federal Republic would have been hard-pressed to take them even if they had. So beyond the humanitarian imperative of 'buying free', the Bonn government's top priority was to persuade the GDR to permit 'ordinary', that is, temporary, travel from East to West. Whereas the channels of humanitarian relief were already working in the 1960s, improvement in this respect was directly related to the opening of German-German relations. Every year between 1965 and 1971 there had, according to the East German statistics, been more than a million visits (but not visit*ors*) from East to West Germany. Most of these travellers were, however, pensioners, plus a much smaller number of invalids, businessmen, athletes, lorry drivers, functionaries and, of course, spies. The East German authorities were not unduly worried if a pensioner or invalid decided to stay in the West. That individual had already given his useful working life to the East German state. Such a 'defection' would save it the cost of pension, housing and medical care. The real sticking point was people who still had some productive capacity for the state to extract.

Then, in May 1972, Egon Bahr finally negotiated his first full treaty with the GDR, outlining the arrangements for traffic (in a broad sense) between the two states. In an accompanying letter his East German counterpart, Michael Kohl, promised that some sorts of travel would become easier. Mostly he listed forms of travel from West to East, but in the penultimate sentence he wrote: 'The government of the German Democratic Republic will enable citizens of the German Democratic Republic to travel to the Federal Republic of Germany on urgent family matters (*dringende Familienangelegenheiten*).' The formula 'urgent family matters', like so much else, stemmed from the earlier negotiations in a divided Berlin. This central desire of the East German people and the West German government was thus first formally acknowledged in the penultimate sentence of a letter accompanying a treaty about traffic.

Five months later, the East German Interior Minister and Chief of the People's Police issued a directive according to which GDR citizens could in theory be permitted to visit 'non-socialist states' and 'Westberlin', at the invitation of relatives, on urgent family matters. 'Urgent family matters,' declared this directive, ' . . . are births, marriages, life-threatening illnesses and cases of death (*Sterbefälle*). The presence of these grounds is to be proven by legal instruments or official medical attestation.' Relatives were defined as grandparents, parents, children or siblings.

As we have noted already, a letter accompanying the Basic Treaty then had the GDR promising to take further steps to reunite divided families, and to improve the flow of visitors and 'non-commercial goods'. A set of detailed notes explained that silver and golden wedding anniversaries would also count as 'urgent family matters' and that half-sisters or half-brothers *with the same mother* would also count as relatives. (Why not, one wonders, half-sisters or half-brothers with the same father?) In a further directive of June 1973, the East German Interior Minister and Chief of the People's Police generously threw in '60th, 65th and 70th wedding anniversaries'.

According to the official West German statistics, the practical upshot of this grotesque small print was that some thirty to forty thousand East Germans under pensionable age were allowed out in 1973 for short visits to West Germany. The happy few were carefully selected. They almost invariably had to leave their spouse and children behind. The occasion for their going was as likely to be a mother's funeral as a brother's wedding. But still, they went: and often they were travelling 'from Germany to Germany' for the first time in their lives. The numbers remained relatively constant for ten years, until 1982.

In the mid-1980s, however, there was a significant increase in this 'ordinary' travel to the West, facilitated by a new travel decree of February 1982. The numbers rose to more than 60,000 a year, from 1983 to 1985, then quite dramatically to levels undreamed of since the building of the Wall. According to the (incomplete) West German statistics, there were more than a quarter of a million such visits in 1986, and over 1.2 million in 1987 and again in 1988. This meant that something like one in every six East Germans under pensionable age was able to travel to West Germany in 1988. If one included pensioners, then the total number of visits to the West in 1988 was over six million — more than in the other direction!

This 'ordinary' travel still went under the extraordinary rubric of 'urgent family matters'. In fact such high figures were only achieved by an arbitrary, politically ordered 'stretching the rules' by the responsible East German officials. In 1987–88 it was said that you could almost invent a relative in West Germany. The introduction in January 1989 of precise, legal regulations on travel thus threatened initially to be regress rather than progress, and was sharply criticised as such by the Protestant church in East Germany. In the first months of 1989 it emerged that these rules, too, could be stretched. The improvement nonetheless remained arbitrary and reversible — until the opening of the frontier between Hungary and Austria changed not the rules but the whole game.

What had been achieved in this respect by early 1989 was thus still very, very far from 'normality' in any normal usage of the word. According to a thorough survey commissioned by the Bonn government no less than eighty-four per cent of a representative sample of West Germans said they had 'no contacts' with East Germans in 1988. Even among the West Berliners there were many who lived from one year to the next without ever visiting the people next door. For an ordinary East German, travel to the West was still an almost miraculous experience, at once uplifting and deeply disturbing.

The travel possibilities for East Germans were not even 'normal' by the much more modest norms of the rest of Eastern Europe. In this respect, Poland, Hungary and Czechoslovakia had been ahead in the 1960s, and remained ahead, despite political setbacks and currency restrictions, in the 1980s. In early 1989, the possibility of travel to the West remained the exception for most East Germans, whereas it was by now the rule for most Poles and Hungarians. Poles and Hungarians could also routinely take their wives and children with them.

So by comparison with the division of the rest of Europe, the division of Germany in this elementary sense was still exceptionally acute. By comparison with the division of Germany after August 1961, however, the improvement was spectacular.

'For me,' said Chancellor Kohl in his 1987 state of the nation address, 'this development is the most important achievement of our Deutschland-politik so far'. When he said 'our' he surely meant in the first instance his own government. Yet most Christian Democrats would have agreed that the 'our' had also to refer to the whole consistent, patient policy of the Federal Republic, with the operative ends broadly agreed by all the main parties since 1966, while the operative means changed only slightly with the transition from Social to Christian Democrats in 1982.

Permanent negotiation

What, then, were the means by which Bonn attempted to influence Erich Honecker and the rest of his regime to concede these improvements? Indirectly, Bonn's whole Ostpolitik was designed to create an overall atmosphere of East-West détente, and relaxation in the GDR's neighbouring communist states, so that a repressive regime in East Berlin would increasingly stick out like a sore thumb — and feel itself to be so. Implicit or even explicit appeals to Moscow to lean on East Berlin were also an important part of this overall conception.

Directly, Bonn's first means of influencing the East German regime was continuous negotiation. Thus the minute of a 'meeting about GDR-issues' in the Chancellery on 21 June 1974, a month after Helmut Schmidt had become Chancellor and just as the Permanent Representations were beginning their work, is basically a list of subjects for negotiation — the special arrangements for intra-German trade, electricity supplies for Berlin, the 'compulsory exchange' of hard currency for Western visitors, transit to Berlin, humanitarian questions, projects of industrial co-operation. 'Summing up,' the minute notes, 'the Federal Chancellor said it is in our interest to put together relatively soon a palette of points on which we are ready to negotiate. In this we should use to our advantage the well-known interests of the GDR.'

Thereafter the Permanent Representative, and other West German public servants, engaged in innumerable rounds of negotiation between the two states. For hours, days, weeks, they would meet with Schalck, Vogel, or more regular functionaries such as Karl Seidel, the head of the 'FRG Department' in the East German Foreign Ministry. The day-to-day internal minutes and correspondence on Deutschlandpolitik to be found in the Schmidt papers are almost entirely concerned with the modalities and substance of these negotiations. In the 1980s, there were also a growing number of meetings between senior West German politicians and the political leaders of the GDR — above all, Honecker and Mittag.

There was a great deal to talk about. But in Bonn's view the negotiations were not just a means to specific ends. They were, taken altogether, a means to a more general end, indeed almost an end in themselves. This end was to reduce the bristling barriers of hostility, the complexes and neuroses of the powerholders in East Germany, and to replace the confrontation with a stable relationship of calm, reasonable dealing, and eventually, trust and co-operation. Initially, this somewhat resembled one of those conversations over the radio with aircraft hijackers. Whatever you do, say the hijack experts, you must keep them talking. Later, the dialogue became so broad and regular that such a comparison seemed increasingly inappropriate, although the raw resemblance would keep breaking through — when, for example, men, women and children took refuge in the Permanent Representation in East Berlin, or in West German embassies elsewhere in Eastern Europe, pleading for West Germany to set them free.

While the East German side would often capriciously refuse to talk, or suspend existing talks, the West German aim might be summarised as a Permanent Representation engaged in permanent negotiation. Over these years of dialogue and negotiation a certain style developed in the West German approach to German-German relations, a style which was also substance. In internal notes for the preparation of Schmidt's 1981 state of the nation address we read: '1. *Introduction*: 20 years after the Berlin Wall. 10 years after the Basic Treaty and Quadripartite Agreement. Necessary: prudence, persistence, predictability (*Behutsamkeit, Beharrlichkeit, Berechenbarkeit*).' These three key-words sum up the style. The representatives of West Germany would be low-key, modest, careful, cautious, calm, steady, discreet, responsible. The East Germans should know exactly where they stood with them. No surprises! This style was significantly influenced by the leaders of the Protestant church in East Germany, who had themselves 'recognised' the GDR earlier than the Federal Government by forming a separate church structure in the East, defined themselves ideologically as the 'church in socialism', and developed their own top-level dialogue with the Party leadership.

Yet, as we have seen already, this public piety sometimes went together with, and covered, secret and even conspiratorial dealings with the party-state. This was true of some (though not all) of the Bonn government's negotiators, as also of the Protestant church's chief negotiator, Manfred Stolpe. After unification, when Stolpe became the Social Democrat Prime Minister of the new-old state of Brandenburg, the nature of his contacts with the East German regime, and above all with the Stasi, would figure beside the discussion about Schalck as one of the great retrospective test cases of German-German relations — trials in the first place by the media, in the second place by parliamentary commissions, and only thirdly by the courts.

Stolpe's was a 'borderline case' in every meaning of the phrase. Yet it was also of far from marginal importance for the history of German-German relations. 'Stolpe was a détente politician,' wrote Antje Vollmer, in a perceptive comment. And defending the man in whose cabinet he had, after unification, gone to serve, West Germany's former Permanent Representative in East Berlin, Hans Otto Bräutigam, would say: 'I feel myself close to Stolpe's methods.' Whether, at the time Bräutigam made this generous defence, he knew about all of Stolpe's methods, is another question. But it is clearly true that in trying to work 'for the good of the people' key representatives of the Bonn government, as of the Church, often found themselves — *nolens volens* — alone in a misty no-man's land, with nothing but their own internal compass to rely on. Inevitably, some kept their bearings better than others.

The details of these strange encounters have more than a few overtones of black comedy. When Günter Gaus first made contact with Schalck, the East German insisted that they should meet on a parking lot up the road from the Permanent Representation. Gaus recalls telling his secretary: 'if I haven't rung in by six, alert the government!'. On a corner of the parking lot, Schalck waited in his Volvo, flashing his headlights in signal of greeting. As a scene for a spy movie this would hardly have passed muster. Some liked this conspiratorial style, others did not. Hans Otto Bräutigam recalls being heartily relieved when he could pass Schalck on to other partners in Bonn, after one or two meetings. Conspiracy was not his thing — and precisely in this, his methods differed very much from Stolpe's.

Franz Josef Strauss, by contrast, seems to have revelled in it. His secret communications with Schalck are riddled with terms such as 'the acquaintance', 'the partner', 'No.1', and even the 'third man' — a resonant phrase for British spy afficionados. Yet on inspection the German 'third man' turns out to be nothing more mysterious than the Chancellery Minister then responsible for relations with the GDR, Philipp Jenninger. Jenninger's successor, Wolfgang Schäuble, tried to regularise the encounters with Schalck a little, receiving that jovial conspirator quite normally in the Federal Chancellery. But when Schäuble visited East Berlin, he still found himself meeting Schalck semi-secretly in the office of the lawyer extraordinary, Wolfgang Vogel.

In the private as in the public talks, style and substance, medium and message, cannot be entirely separated, and the outward forms of these meetings surely are a legitimate subject of retrospective inquiry. Yet the medium could not be the only message. So what were those 'well-known interests of the GDR' to which Helmut Schmidt referred? For all the complexities of particular negotiations, in general terms one can say that throughout the history of German-German relations, starting already with the first negotiations in Berlin in the early 1960s, the GDR demanded payment in two currencies: DM and recognition. And, again with slight oversimplification, one can say that the payments made to the GDR in both currencies steadily increased from the late 1960s until the late 1980s, reaching a high-point some three years before the GDR ceased to exist.

The German Mark

The economic relations between the two states in Germany were, of course, exceedingly complex, and could not simply be described as Bonn 'paying' East Berlin. At the time, the true facts were very difficult to come by, due to official secrecy, incomplete or positively false statistics, and often inadequate analysis. Even after the end of the GDR, the web is still hard to disentangle. Our account can therefore only be sketchy and provisional, pending the necessary masterwork on this theme. Roughly speaking, one can divide the relationship into four intersecting circles: trade, hard currency transfers to private individuals in the GDR, hard currency transfers to the state, and government-guaranteed credits.

As already mentioned, for purposes of trade the two states in Germany had recognised each other from the very beginning. What is more, a protocol to the Treaty of Rome confirmed that in the new European Communities this 'intra-German trade', as Bonn called it, would continue to be treated as 'a part of German internal trade'. The Federal Republic consistently maintained that position, despite a steady drizzle of discontent from its EC partners, who spoke darkly of East Germany's 'secret membership' of the European Community and sometimes raised quite specific complaints about external goods finding their way on to West European markets through this shady back-door.

For political reasons — 'keeping together the nation' — the Federal Republic consistently encouraged this trade, offering duty-free access to East German goods, tax concessions, and an interest-free overdraft facility, the so-called 'Swing'. For economic reasons, the GDR consistently took advantage of these extraordinary privileges, despite the obvious slight to its sovereignty that they implied. One particular advantage was the ability to obtain urgently needed supplies or services at very short notice. Since, like all planned economies, the East German economy excelled in the production of bottlenecks, this was important. At the same time, for political reasons, the GDR tried hard not to become too exclusively dependent on trade with the Federal Republic.

Yet by the end of the 1980s, West Germany was far and away its largest trading partner in the West. Although its own published statistics deliberately concealed this dependence, more than half of its Western trade was with the Federal Republic. The Leipzig trade fair had become not merely an annual celebration of this trade, but a national political event, regularly attended by the East German party leader and by senior politicians from West Germany.

The Schmidt government did rather cautiously use the renegotiation of the Swing facility in 1974–5 as a card in overall negotiations, and partly for this reason secured a partial reduction of the compulsory exchange tariff for Western visitors, after a sharp increase in 1973. It even more cautiously tried to make such a linkage, with less success, when the Swing facility was renewed in 1980–81. In 1985, the Kohl government privately — that is, in talks between Schäuble and Schalck — made the extension of the Swing dependent on the GDR stopping the flow of Tamil refugees (who were flying into East Berlin airport and then taking the *S-Bahn* to West Berlin, where they asked for asylum). This the GDR did, only to let a flow of refugees from other countries use the same route a few months later. In sum this was hardly a record of very heavy or successful linkage. But for a simple reason: Bonn's own political interest in the maintenance of this trade was as strong as East Berlin's economic interest.

Much more directly connected to the development of German-German relations was the dramatic increase in public and private transfers of hard currency. Again, the picture is a complex one. Many of these transfers directly benefited ordinary people in the GDR (who were first legally permitted to possess DM in 1972). Such was the case, for example, with the 'welcome money' paid to every East German visitor by the West German government, a small enough sum in itself, but a goodly total of some DM 2 billion over the twenty years from 1970 to 1989. So also with the private presents in cash or kind that flowed across the border from West to East.

The party-state took a handsome profit on many of these transfers, when, for example, the money was spent in its hard-currency 'Intershops'. In hard currency terms, it made an even more outrageous profit by selling East German products to East German consumers for hard currency, through the so-called 'Genex' service company, a wholly-owned subsidiary of the communist party. (In particular, this was a way for East Germans to jump the sometimes ten-year-long queue for domestically produced cars.) At the same time, the Federal Republic made generous lump-sum payments to cover the real or alleged postal costs of sending presents from West to East. A leading specialist estimates that the total value of all these direct or indirect transfers to private citizens was a formidable 30 to 40 billion D-mark over the twenty years (1970–89). Yet at the end of the day, benefits clearly were enjoyed not just by the state but by private persons, *die Menschen*.

The substantial transfers from the West to the East German Protestant church — at a cost of DM 2.2 billion from 1970 to 1989, of which roughly half actually came from the Bonn government — also directly benefited the party-state. As the (West German) Protestant Church's middleman,

Ludwig Geissel, himself notes in his memoirs, he was able to arrange for the supply of goods which the GDR would otherwise have had difficulty in obtaining. Many of the goods were also laundered back into cash by *KoKo*. However, the East Marks which the party-state paid the East German Protestant church in return benefited not the Communists but believers in a God that did not fail. All this was also helping the people and holding together the nation. And to keep these large sums in perspective, it must be emphasised that other East European states (and peoples) also benefited very substantially from private or semi-private transfers in the 1980s. Thus, to give just one example, hard-currency transfers to Poland from Poles abroad were estimated to be of the order of $1–1.5 billion a year at the end of the 1980s.

In an intermediate category were the visa fees and the compulsory exchange of currency demanded of Western visitors. West German specialists estimated that the state took some DM 5 billion from this source alone over the two decades, as well as making additional hard-currency income from the 'Intertank' petrol stations which Western visitors were obliged to use, and the Intershops on transit routes. As we have seen, the West German government pressed hard, but with only marginal success, to have the compulsory exchange reduced. This hard currency went straight to the state. But at least the visitors went to the people.

The direct state-to-state transfers were the subject of more direct negotiation. They fell into three main categories. Firstly, there were the payments to buy people free: some DM 3.5 billion in all, of which about DM 3.2 billion was paid in the years 1970–89. Secondly, there were the 'transit fees' for people travelling to and from West Berlin. Following a suggestion originally made by Willy Brandt to Piotr Abrassimov, the Soviet ambassador to East Berlin, the two states agreed in the early 1970s that Bonn should make a lump-sum payment for the transit and other 'road-use' fees exacted by the GDR. In the second half of the 1970s these were DM 400 million a year, in the 1980s DM 575 million a year, and if the GDR had survived into the 1990s it would, under an agreement signed in October 1988, have got no less than DM 915 million a year from 1990 until 1999. The total actually paid over two decades was a round DM 8.3 billion. Thirdly, there were investments in road, rail and canal links between West Germany and West Berlin, as well as such minor details as taking West Berlin sewage or West German rubbish. These payments totalled more than DM 2.4 billion.

Clearly Bonn did not give everything for nothing in these transactions. It paid for the freedom of more than a quarter of a million people in the first case, and for the well-being of the hostage half-city — West Berlin — in the second and third. In the case of the large autumn 1988 agreement on lump-sum transit payments for the 1990s, the papers presented to the Politburo actually include the written draft of an 'informal verbal declaration' — presumably to be made by Schalck to Schäuble — in which the GDR promised to maintain the high level of permissions granted for East Germans to visit the West.

Moreover, the road and rail links were investments in Germany. If ever unification came, they would still be there. Yet even the most passionate advocate could not say with a straight face that Bonn got 'value for money' in any normal sense. It gave at least as much as the investments would have cost in West Germany, while the GDR paid in soft currency for what was usually a worse job. After the demise of the GDR, West German investigators found, not surprisingly, that only a small part of the hard currency payments had gone to the purposes for which they were theoretically provided. So the justification could not be in terms of any normal cost-accounting.

Last but by no means least were the so-called 'billion credits': commercial bank loans of DM 1 billion in summer 1983 and DM 950 million in summer 1984, both initially negotiated by Franz Josef Strauss with Alexander Schalck-Golodkowski, granted on unusually favourable terms by the banks and guaranteed by the Federal Government. At the time, and again after unification, these 'billion credits' provoked a heated discussion about the relationship between money and politics in German-German relations.

Now neither of the Social Democratic Permanent Representatives in East Berlin disputed that Bonn had been financially generous in the period up to 1982. Günter Gaus vigorously argued that it would pay off in other fields over the longer term. Klaus Bölling, Permanent Representative in 1981–82, concluded that 'the principle of a balance of give and take' was not worth much in practical policy. 'If we are serious about national cohesion,' he wrote in 1983, 'we shall always have to give somewhat more than the other side is prepared to. One may call this our vulnerability to blackmail. It is not dishonourable.' At the end of a long decade of Social Democratic policy towards the GDR, Christian Democrats charged them with paying 'cash against hope'. They had given too much for too little, it was said. The Christian Democrats would now look for a strict balance of give and take.

When, therefore, the Christian Democrats not only continued to make all the hard-currency transfers agreed but also negotiated generous new ones, and gave these two unprecedented 'billion credits', the Social Democrats could hardly resist retorting that 'cash against hope' was precisely what the Christian Democrats were now paying. The Christian Democrats replied that, on the contrary, they had secured valuable concessions, although to explain them in detail would be to endanger them. In time, however, they would point to a reduction of the compulsory exchange for pensioners and children, the dismantlement of the automatic shooting devices and some of the minefields along the German-German frontier, a relaxation of the border controls for West German travellers, and, as we have seen, a very significant increase in the numbers of East Germans allowed to travel West. Moreover, the billion credits were, it was argued, a clear and necessary political signal to the GDR that the Federal Republic wished to continue to improve German-German relations even as it deployed the new Nato missiles.

Documents that became available after the end of the GDR do clearly show that Strauss, for all the flattery that he was happy to give (and receive), made these linkages quite plainly in his private talks with Schalck. Thus, for example, Schalck's internal note of their talks in Leipzig in March 1984 refers to 'the complex of problems

— credit offers by West German bank consortia to the Foreign Trade Bank of the GDR.

— decisions of the GDR in the framework of its sovereign rights to determine certain alleviations in travel and visitor traffic.'

Here also are clear references to a reduction in the compulsory exchange, the dismantlement of minefields and automatic shooting devices, keeping open a particular border crossing, as well as the regulation of individual humanitarian cases 'through the well-tried channel Rehlinger/Vogel'.

On the other hand, what also emerged after the end of the GDR was the extent of the hard currency balance of payments deficit which it had run since the early 1970s, and the vital importance of the hard currency transfers and credits from West Germany. There is little doubt that these saved it from having to reschedule its soaring hard-currency debt, as first Poland and then Hungary had to do. The particular significance of the Strauss credits was, Schalck and others now testify, less the actual sums involved than the signal they sent to the international financial markets. In the early 1980s Western banks, having burnt their fingers terribly in Poland, were classifying the whole of Eastern Europe as a bad risk. However, says Schalck, after the announcement of the first Strauss credit, in 1983, the head of the Foreign Trade Bank was soon able to borrow another DM one billion, this time in dollars or yen from commercial banks.

Whether Strauss actually saved the GDR from financial disaster in 1983 is disputed, and, of course, ultimately unprovable. Günter Mittag goes so far as to suggest that without the first Strauss credit there would have been a massive crisis and civil disorders in the GDR, with incalculable consequences. Gerhard Schürer, then head of the GDR's State Plan Commission, and now a calmer and more reliable historical witness, suggests that the most acute crisis actually came earlier, in 1978–81. By 1983, he argues, the GDR had taken strenuous measures to improve its balance of trade and was not on the verge of default, although clearly the Strauss credit did very much help to restore the GDR's financial credibility. As chairman of the key operational Balance of Payments Working Group, he was in a position to know. Yet Schürer also emphatically confirms the growing preoccupation of East Germany's key economic decision-makers with the burgeoning hard-currency debt, and the unique significance of the whole economic and financial relationship with West Germany in attempting to cope with it.

The internal statistics of the GDR in this field are not yet fully available, and when they are it will need a fine combination of auditor, historian and detective to make reliable sense of them. Yet from the available documents and key witnesses we can at least make an informed guess at orders of magnitude. In 1970, the net hard currency debt of the GDR seems to have been about 2 billion Valutamarks (an East German unit of reckoning equal to one DM). By 1980 this 'plinth', as the East German experts called it, had grown to 25 billion Valutamarks.

The main reason for this spectacular growth was Honecker's strategy, drily called 'the unity of economic and social policy', of which more below. Beside other, domestic economic burdens, such as huge basic food price subsidies and a massive housing construction programme, this involved importing significant quantities of goods from the West — and more consumer than producer goods. Not for nothing was Honecker's model of socialism sometimes called 'Jeans and Golf socialism' (where the Golf referred to was not the game but the imported Volkswagen car). The hard currency expended on these imports was not recouped by exports, hence the growing debt.

It should be noted that the strategy which might loosely be described as socialist consumerism was not peculiar to Honecker alone. János Kádár used it in Hungary, although there it was accompanied by genuine (if ultimately insufficient) measures of economic reform. Edward Gierek tried it in Poland, with truly Catholic profligacy, and unaccompanied by any fundamental economic reforms. But nowhere were there more consumer imports, and less substantial reforms, than in the GDR.

The result, for East Germany as for Poland and Hungary, was what might be called a dollar gap (by loose analogy with the dollar gap faced by Western Europe in the late 1940s). Gierek's inability to bridge his dollar gap was one of the main precipitant causes of his fall, and of the birth of Solidarity. Kádár's growing dollar gap ultimately contributed to his fall, and to the more radical reforms initiated by his successors. In fact, Brezhnev was constantly warning Honecker, and other East European leaders, of the dangers of becoming too indebted to the West. The great lesson of what had happened in Poland, he told the Czechoslovak Politburo in spring 1981, was that they should all make sure that their foreign debt 'did not reach a dangerous level'.

A few of Honecker's own colleagues in the Politburo also warned, although the forcefulness and eloquence of those warnings have no doubt grown in fond recollection. Yet Honecker stubbornly refused to change the fundamentals of his political-economic strategy. Mittag, whatever his private reservations, oversaw its implementation. Instead of fundamental reform, or at least a change of strategy, they tried to plug the dollar gap with (West) German marks.

This gap-stopping function of West Germany had a long pre-history. Ludwig Geissel, the West German Protestant church's veteran middleman, recalls the Foreign Trade Minister of the GDR appealing for his help as early as 1958, because the trains were about to stop running in East Germany. Could the church middleman help out, with a rapid delivery of coal? (For which, of course, the GDR would pay in East Marks to the church in the East.) From the mid-1960s, Schalck's *KoKo* had combined the attempt to create an enclave of real-price, market-oriented economic activity with the attempt to exploit the GDR's half-nelson on the Federal Republic. Selling hostages as the first step towards a market economy!

Now Honecker's new domestic political stategy meant a sharply growing need for hard currency. But his new foreign political strategy — above all, in the relationship with West Germany — also offered increasing possibilities of obtaining it. As the need for hard currency grew, so did the responsibility of Schalck, formally in 1972 and again in 1976, *de facto* even more thereafter. Looking back, Karl Seidel, head of the department dealing with West Germany in the East German Foreign Ministry, considers that the need for DM was the single most important driving force behind the GDR's negotiations with the Federal Republic.

How much did they actually get? Here one has first to distinguish between trade conducted by the Foreign Trade Ministry inside the regular framework of the state's economic Plan, and trade, transfers, deals and everything else conducted outside the Plan, mainly in the twilight realms of Schalck. Gerhard Schürer rightly points out that the hard currency earned for the state budget by that ordinary in-Plan trade was, in a given year, between five and eight times as much as the hard currency contributed by Schalck. However, this ordinary trade did clearly benefit very largely from the extraordinary terms of 'intra-German trade'.

So far as the realms of Schalck were concerned, the king of that twilight world would himself claim, after the end of the GDR, that from 1972 to 1989 he 'secured' a remarkable DM 50 billion for the GDR, of which roughly DM 27 billion came from business and DM 23 billion from payments of various kinds from the Federal Republic. However, in conversation with the author Schalck casually mentioned that the figure of DM 23 billion included the DM 9 billion which was agreed for the transit fees for the 1990s, but not actually paid! Making this minor adjustment, we arrive at a round figure of DM 14 billion, which corresponds almost exactly with the total of the West German figures for the actual state-to-state transfers. Beyond this reasonable correlation, however, there is a very large grey area, which contains such elements as Intershop and Intertank, Schalck's subsequently notorious dealings in antiques, weapons, luxuries, the whole web of firms in the West, and a long list of more ordinary goods which were exported by hook or by crook in the increasingly desperate scramble for hard currency.

As we have seen, by no means all of the hard currency Schalck 'secured', to use his own well-chosen term, went into the state budget. The money from the 'church deals' — A, B and C — did not, but much of it went to special accounts used for the purposes of the party leadership. *KoKo* also organised supplies, personally supervised by Mrs Schalck, for the Politburo's residential compound in Wandlitz, a miniature model of socialist consumerism. Other monies clearly went into other holes and pockets. But the contribution of Schalck's whole 'out-of-Plan' area to the state budget was of the order of 2 billion Valutamarks a year in the 1980s. For comparison, this has to be set against a debt service and repayment requirement running at about 5 billion Valutamarks a year.

This was a very substantial contribution to keeping the GDR financially afloat. Taken together with Strauss's billion credits, the income from in-Plan trade with the West, and measures of retrenchment by the GDR itself, it saved the GDR from the kind of financial crunch which contributed so directly to Gierek's downfall. In a broader sense, it contributed to what in the West would be described as the GDR's relative 'stability' — a term whose full meanings, and ambiguities, will be explored more fully later on.

It did not, however, prevent the debt from growing. Exactly how big it grew is not wholly clear. The internal figures used by Schürer and others showed a net debt 'plinth' of nearly 30 billion Valutamarks in 1985 and nearly 35 billion by 1987. A memorandum prepared by Schürer, Schalck and others for the new Party leadership at the end of October 1989 suggested that the net debt could reach a staggering 49 billion Valutamarks by the end of that year. In fact these figures were probably too high. This was partly because Schalck had his own considerable reserves, held mainly in gold, and partly because, since this was a centrally planned economy, the figures were based on fixed, arbitrary exchange rates. While the Valutamark-DM rate was always 1:1, that to the dollar was periodically adjusted. Schalck himself would speak of a final net debt of 38 billion Valutamarks, or some $20 billion. In its own calculations in 1990, the Bundesbank arrived at an even lower figure, of less than 30 billion DM. But in this twilight world, even the Bundesbank could err.

So, amusingly enough, the combination of chronic secrecy and unreal statistics — two characteristic features of communist systems — may actually have made the problem seem even worse than it was. Yet, realistically, it was still bad enough. Meeting weekly, sometimes even daily, in the Balance of Payments Working Group, Schürer, Schalck, the Foreign

Trade Minister Gerhard Beil, and a handful of other key players, found themselves struggling to keep the GDR afloat. In this endeavour, they even sold off many of the GDR's strategic reserves, including arms and ammunition, for hard currency. Yet with every new billion of debt grew their sense of crippling dependency on West Germany.

By 1988, Schürer and Schalck would privately discuss the idea of some sort of 'confederation' with the Federal Republic as the only way out from under this intolerable load. At the same time, Schürer tried — very cautiously — to suggest some correction in the increasingly distorted domestic price and investment policy. Mittag and Honecker slapped down even those modest proposals for change, although Mittag would claim, retrospectively, that he too had been looking for ever closer economic co-operation with West Germany.

When these facts became known in the West, after unification, they were seized on by many as an explanation of the end of the GDR. Quite simply, it was bankrupt! To some extent that was indeed the feeling of those who had to wrestle directly with the problem. And perhaps not only of them. The figures given to the Politburo were slightly less alarming than those known to Schürer, Schalck and their colleagues. Yet Schürer recalls Alfred Neumann, one of very few Politburo members who still spoke his mind, saying to Honecker at a Politburo meeting: 'When you took over the GDR from Walter Ulbricht we had almost no debt, and now we're almost broke!' Egon Krenz knew the true facts directly from Schalck. In a memorandum written as the regime collapsed, in early 1990, the former Politburo member Werner Krolikowski colourfully remarked that the GDR had reached the financial point where an officer in Imperial Germany or Tsarist Russia would have shot himself.

It is indeed plausible to argue that this awareness of crippling debt and dependency undermined any residual faith many East German decision-makers and functionaries may have had in their own system, and hence also undermined their readiness to defend it — especially against a takeover by West Germany, without which the GDR would anyway be broke. The above-mentioned Schürer memorandum of October 1989 predicted that the net debt could soar to as much as 57 billion Valutamarks by the end of 1990.

It is also plausible to argue that among ordinary people in East Germany, the growing role of the DM both in the state's dealings with the West and in their own everyday consumer lives produced an explosive mixture of resentment and longing. Resentment at the double-standards of the rulers and at the new class divide between those who had DM and those who had not. Longing to have not just an Intershop simulacrum of West German consumer society but the real thing: the DM, the whole DM and nothing but the DM. 'Where has all the hard currency gone?' sang the demonstrators in Leipzig in the autumn of 1989, unforgettably, to the tune of 'Where have all the flowers gone?' And then East Germans voted for unification with the DM.

Yet hindsight can also mislead. While this may be the final balance of the financial relations between the two states, it was by no means necessarily the interim, subjective balance drawn up in either state at the time. In particular, we shall have to look more carefully at the attitudes of the man who was clearly the crucial decision-maker. There is much evidence that Honecker always understood little of economics and increasingly lost touch with reality altogether. As in most dictatorships, who would venture to tell him the unvarnished truth? Neumann's outburst in the Politburo was so memorable precisely because it was so exceptional. The capacity of an ageing dictator to repress unpalatable truths should never be underestimated.

Moreover, states do not simply go bankrupt like companies, let alone shoot themselves like honourable Tsarist officers. Honecker and Mittag's political economy was in many ways ruinous and irrational. But considered as a strategy for political survival it was, at some shallower (or was it deeper?) level, quite rational, so long as the Soviet Union was prepared to support the GDR politically, and the Federal Republic was prepared to save it from ruin financially. At least until 1986, those two conditions seemed to apply. And the two were intimately related. West Germany would give its kind of fraternal help to make quite sure that the Soviet Union would not be called on to give its kind of fraternal help.

There is, furthermore, a serious question as to just how realistic a picture West German policy-makers really did have of the depth of East Germany's economic and financial plight. In the early 1980s, those most directly involved clearly saw that the GDR was in a tight spot financially. For the late 1980s, Schäuble recalls Schalck telling him exactly how bad the situation was. Perhaps more important, Schalck recalls Schäuble replying that, if the worst came to the worst, West Germany would help out with another billion credit. So long as the Brezhnev Doctrine still seemed to apply, West Germany would pay to preserve what it called 'stability' in East Germany, although all the time demanding more of those 'improvements for the people' — for the negotiation of which such a stability was held to be a precondition.

Yet outside this very small inner circle, and perhaps even inside it, there were illusions about the economic and financial strength of East Germany — illusions which in turn reinforced Honecker's own. (For surely hardnosed West German businessmen and politicians would not pay homage to a bankrupt?) In a weighty report prepared to accompany the 1987 state of the nation address, some of West Germany's economic experts did document in minute detail the extent of East Germany's relative economic backwardness. They pointed out, for example, that the average East German cow could produce only 82 per cent of the milk pumped out by the average West German cow, while an East German pig could offer only 75.8 per cent of the pork mustered by its West German counterpart. They did also suggest that the total hard currency transfers from West Germany were probably enough to cover the interest payments on the GDR's foreign debt in the years 1981 and 1982. They nonetheless failed to bring home to most policymakers in Bonn the extent to which the East German economy was already on the rocks.

Did not the official statistics show East Germany outperforming the rest of Eastern Europe? Were not the displays at the Leipzig trade fair or in East Berlin shop windows quite satisfactory, by East Bloc standards of course? Was not Mr Mittag really rather impressive and convincing? (Mittag, says Günter Schabowski, was known in the Politburo as the man who could 'choreograph the West German grande bourgeoisie'.) Did not the World Bank say that per capita income in the GDR was higher than in Britain? The East Germans might have a bad economic system, but they were, after all, still Germans.

On balance it seems fair to say that most Bonn policymakers were not fully aware of how desperate the economic and specifically the financial crisis of the GDR was, and of how crucial a difference their transfers and payments actually made. It was only very late in the day that a few of those at the heart of policy-making realised that they were dealing with a state on tick.

The result was curious. In 1986 an American political scientist, James McAdams, published an article in the journal *Foreign Affairs*. He argued that there had been a remarkable reversal in the relationship between the two German states. In German-German bargaining, East Germany now had the upper hand. With hindsight, the argument may seem slightly absurd. Even at the time it seemed overstated. Yet it was based on a careful study of the subject, and conversations with West German policy-makers at that time could indeed give this impression. While the underlying reality may have been that the GDR was getting weaker and more dependent on the Federal Republic, the overlying perception in the mid-1980s was that the GDR was getting stronger, and the Federal Republic therefore needed more than ever to buy its goodwill and co-operation, for the good of the people.

Recognition

This curious reversal brings us to the other currency in which the GDR in general, and Erich Honecker in particular, demanded payment: recognition. The key-word 'recognition' had been the subject of fierce debate in West Germany in the late 1960s and early 1970s. Characteristically, much of the debate had been about fine legal distinctions: the difference, for example, between a recognition in international law and one in constitutional law. But a more important distinction was that between purely diplomatic recognition of the state and a more substantive recognition of the repressive regime.

Christian Democratic opponents of the recognition of the GDR argued passionately that the former necessarily implied, or would almost certainly lead to, the latter. It would therefore be morally unacceptable, an insult to the people suffering under this regime, and an encouragement to that regime to persist in oppressing them. 'We . . . are not prepared,' declared the terminally ill Freiherr von und zu Guttenberg, in a powerful speech to the Bundestag in 1970, 'to heed, respect, let alone recognise realities that bear the name "Injustice".' Was there anyone in the house, he asked, who would seriously maintain that injustice became justice merely because it had lasted for decades? Would anyone in the house have been prepared to make their peace with Hitler, if he had managed to hold on for thirty-seven years? 'I say no, I say three times no. For the same reason there can be no recognition for new injustice on German soil, for Herr Ulbricht.'

Social and Free Democrats replied that the purely diplomatic recognition of the state did not necessarily imply nor automatically lead to political and moral recognition of the system. On the contrary, the recognition of the state was the only practicable way to begin alleviating the hardships imposed by the system. Willy Brandt quoted a remark of the British Prime Minister Harold Wilson to illustrate the difference between the two kinds of recognition. If I go into a zoo and see an elephant, he said, I recognise him as an elephant. But this does not mean that I recognise him in the sense that, say, a scientist, writer or athlete receives 'recognition' for their achievement. The qualified diplomatic recognition of the GDR in 1972 was presented as recognition strictly in the first sense. The elephant was there. He had people under foot. To help those people (*die Menschen*) and keep the people (i.e. the nation) together, one had to do business with the elephant. But one need hang no medals round his neck. Indeed, one might still consider him a monster.

This purely diplomatic recognition was itself sorely desired and highly prized by the GDR, not least because it opened the door to membership of the United Nations and to recognition by the rest of the Western world. Well into the 1980s, East German leaders never tired of trumpeting this achievement. At the celebration of the thirty-fifth anniversary of the GDR, in 1984, Erich Honecker proudly announced that the GDR maintained diplomatic relations with 132 states 'all over the world'. The printed version of his speech actually said 131, but at the last minute the GDR had scored yet another diplomatic triumph, securing recognition from the Ivory Coast.

More seriously, the Honecker regime tried hard to get the Federal Republic to make this diplomatic recognition still more complete. The most important single expression of this was a speech Honecker delivered at Gera in October 1980. Against a background of sharply worsening East-West relations, with the Polish crisis posing a direct challenge to the domestic political stability of the GDR, the East German leader made four demands, of which the most important was that the Federal Republic should fully recognise GDR citizenship. By this, what he actually meant was *de-recognition* of the East Germans' automatic right to West German citizenship, for the Federal Republic already respected anyone's right to keep (or indeed, should they be so curiously inclined, to take) citizenship of the GDR.

The other demands were for the formal conversion of the Permanent Representations into Embassies; the closure of the West German 'Registration Unit' at Salzgitter which recorded incidents in the GDR, including shootings on the border, for which people might one day be prosecuted; and a point about the precise delineation of the border on a stretch in Lower Saxony where it ran along the River Elbe. Although there were important figures, especially among Social Democrats, who advocated conceding at least the lesser of what came to be known as the 'Gera demands', the Bonn government did not change its basic positions, above all on the key question of citizenship.

There was, however, a significant increase in what one might call *de facto* rather than *de jure* recognition. This was not exactly the substantive approval of the communist system which Christian Democrat critics of the new Ostpolitik had feared. But it was a growing substantive approbation, firstly for the humanitarian and other improvements which the Honecker regime had permitted, and secondly for that regime's commitment to preserve what had been achieved in German-German relations at a time of sharply worsening American-Soviet relations. The milestones of this growing political recognition were Helmut Schmidt's meeting with Erich Honecker in East Germany in 1981, and Erich Honecker's visit to West Germany in 1987.

Already in the late 1970s, Herbert Häber, head of the Party's so-called West Department, had extensive informal contacts with politicians of all the main West German parties. Häber's records of his conversations in West Germany, heavily annotated in Honecker's hand and kept in the Politburo's internal archive, suggest a growing ease of intercourse with leading Social Democrats, but also with Free Democrats such as Wolfgang Mischnick and Christian Democrats, such as Walther Leisler Kiep and Lothar Späth. Of course, these records must be handled with care. When Häber reports, for example, the delight expressed by a West German politician on being given a copy of Erich Honecker's autobiography (as published by Robert Maxwell), we clearly need to take this with a large pinch of salt.

Nonetheless, one recurrent and striking feature is the frequency and vehemence with which Haber's interlocutors appear to have criticised American policy, from Carter's human rights campaign to Nato's double-track resolution and from the neutron bomb to Zbigniew Brzezinski — 'a fanatical Polish nationalist', complained the German Social Democrat Hans-Jürgen Wischnewski to the German Communist Herbert Häber. Häber's report after a trip in March 1980, which Honecker circulated to the Politburo, noted that 'there was hardly an interlocutor who did not in some way express distaste for American policy and Carter', although, Häber went on, they also emphasised Bonn's need for alliance solidarity with the United States. From a trip in September 1980, Häber returned to report the characteristically salty observation of the Social Democrat Holger Börner that 'the difference between Carter and Reagan was like that between plague and cholera' — a comment marked in the margin by Honecker.

Formal top-level contacts were, however, still minimal. The first West German minister to visit East Germany officially under the Schmidt government was the Housing Minister in 1978. By the end of the 1970s, the progress made in the continuous negotiation, and the improvements achieved 'for the people', were already felt by many in Bonn to justify a summit meeting. Herbert Wehner, among others, also argued that, for all Honecker's commitment to his political system and the preservation of his own power, the East German leader personally wished to meet certain basic minimum standards of common humanity. Yet Schmidt himself clearly did not attach as high a priority to direct relations with the GDR as his predecessor had done. Despite — perhaps also because of — their conversation in Helsinki in 1975, he at this time still took a fairly contemptuous view of Erich Honecker. Previous East German suggestions of a German–German summit had been brushed aside.

It was only in the run-up to Nato's double-track resolution of December 1979 that Schmidt himself began to push for a summit. If he were to convince colleagues in his own party of the need for the military part of the double-track, he had to demonstrate his own commitment to the détente part. In January 1980, the East German Politburo member and Central Committee Secretary for international relations, Hermann Axen, hurried off to Moscow with a message to Brezhnev and the Soviet leadership. The message was that despite the double-track decision, the East German Politburo wished to go ahead with the planned 'working meeting' between Honecker and Schmidt, 'in order to put pressure on the government of the FRG'. The East German Politburo asked the Soviet Politburo 'for a swift decision on this matter'. So much for the sovereignty of the GDR! A day later, Boris Ponomaryev conveyed the Soviet Politburo's answer to Axen. The answer was no. But, Vadim Zagladin consoled Axen at the airport: in a few weeks things might be different.

Fortunately, the grim reaper then started to come to the aid of

East-West relations, and Tito's death in May 1980 provided for the first of what would come to be known as the 'working funerals'. The East German record of Honecker's conversation with Schmidt, on that occasion, records Schmidt observing that the medium-sized and smaller states, such as the Federal Republic, the French and the British, the GDR, Poland and Hungary, had to watch out that 'the really big brothers don't get nervous'. After discussing whether Schmidt should go to visit Brezhnev in Moscow, Schmidt raised the question of a date for his 'working visit' to the GDR. According to the East German record, Honecker said: 'you visit Brezhnev in Moscow first, then we can arrange it'. Both perfectly understood the Bonn-Moscow-Berlin geometry.

Not so long afterwards the summit was rearranged, for August 1980. But fortune would not smile on the plan. This time it was called off by the West German side, because of uncertainties created by the strikes in Poland that gave birth to Solidarity. The movement for freedom, or, as it was more often put, the 'crisis' and 'instability' in Poland, caused the East German leadership to raise its defences against possible infection from its Western as well as its Eastern neighbour. Honecker's 'Gera demands' and the simultaneous doubling of the compulsory exchange tariff for Western visitors could only be understood in this context.

By the time the summit finally happened another leitmotif had been added to the language of German-German relations. To the shared responsibility for basic, minimum human alleviations was now added a shared responsibility for the fate of humankind. Beside talking about the reunification of families, or road and rail links, or postal agreements, or trade, the two sides would now talk about arms control and disarmament. This theme had been present already in the original German-German debates and agreements a decade before. As we have seen, the formula 'war must never again go out from German soil' had been used in the Erfurt meeting and was one of Willy Brandt's twenty points at Kassel. Article 5 of the Basic Treaty committed both states to work for 'peaceful relations between European states', for 'security and co-operation in Europe', and specifically for arms control and disarmament. Yet Bahr's hope that the treaties might might lead on to major reductions of conventional forces in Central Europe had proved vain. It was only a decade later, as the number of weapons in Central Europe was about to increase rather than decrease, that the subject moved to the top of the German-German agenda.

First, Helmut Schmidt and Erich Honecker solemnly exchanged that code-phrase about war never again 'going out from German soil'. Then, at their summit meeting in December 1981, in a hunting lodge on the Werbellinsee, Schmidt urged Honecker to use his influence to modify and moderate the Soviet position on East-West relations in general, and arms control in particular. 'We have signed the nuclear non-proliferation treaty, you and us,' he said. 'The world powers have an obligation to us. We must press the great powers.' And again: 'We don't want to show off. But in truth we both, both German states, have great weight. I believe, Herr Honecker, that we have a right to throw this weight into the scales.'

Although the declaration of martial law in Poland cast a dark shadow over the last day of the summit, Schmidt felt obliged not only to complete his visit, but also to try to preserve so far as possible, atmospherically as well as substantively, what had been achieved in the German-German relationship. So as the leaders of Solidarity were thrown into camps just over the frontier, the two German leaders threw snowballs together in the small town of Güstrow, surrounded by solicitous Stasi men keeping the people at bay. At parting, Honecker handed Schmidt a boiled sweet for his train journey home.

Thereafter, the trajectories of overall East-West and specifically East-West German relations crossed, going in opposite directions. The 'overall weather conditions' deteriorated, but both German states tried to preserve, even to improve, their relations. Herbert Häber noted the Christian Democrat Walther Leisler Kiep observing in February 1982 that in West Germany there was little readiness to sacrifice the gains of détente on account of Poland. There were real concerns on the East German side following the formation of the Kohl government. But in October 1983, scarcely a month before the vote to deploy Nato missiles, Herbert Häber could record the Christian Democrat Prime Minister of Baden-Württemberg, Lothar Späth, saying cheerfully: 'these days it is almost a personal taint [i.e. for a West German politician] if one has not been to meet Erich Honecker'.

A further, crucial step in substantive recognition came after the Bundestag vote to deploy the Nato missiles. As we have seen, instead of freezing relations with West Germany, as Soviet propaganda and some of his own previous utterances suggested he should, Erich Honecker surprisingly announced that the point now was to 'limit the damage' of this deplorable decision. 'As genuine advocates of peace,' he declared, 'we are always guided by the popular wisdom that to negotiate ten times is always better than to fire a single shot.' The popular wisdom was clearly helped along by Strauss's one billion DM credit, and by other signals the Kohl government gave that it had a double-track strategy of its own: to implement the Nato decision, but also to preserve and develop what had been achieved in the intra-German détente. Yet it was by no means a foregone conclusion that Honecker would accept this de-coupling.

The Bonn government could therefore hardly believe its luck when the GDR went on to hold up such notions as a 'coalition of reason' between the two German states. West German leaders, for their part, spoke of a 'community of responsibility'. 'The two states in Germany,' Chancellor Kohl wrote to Honecker on 14 December 1983, 'stand in their relations with each other in a community of responsibility to Europe and to the

German people. Precisely in difficult times in West-East relations, both [states] can make an important contribution to stability and peace in Europe, if they come closer to each other and carry forward what is possible in co-operation.' After defending the deployment and criticising the Soviet response, Kohl went on to say that the Federal Republic would make a positive contribution to the 'constructive continuation' of West-East relations, and expected 'that the German Democratic Republic, too, will allow itself to be guided by a common interest in co-operation, security and peace'.

Two months later, Honecker replied, thanking Kohl for his letter and referring to their telephone conversation on 19 December. His reply was almost a mirror-image of Kohl's own. 'Community of responsibility,' he wrote, 'to use your expression, or better still security partnership, presently means from our point of view first and foremost what both states actively do to improve again the changed situation which has arisen out of the stationing of American medium-range nuclear missiles in Western Europe, and above all in the Federal Republic of Germany.' After further criticism of the American deployment, he observed 'the German Democratic Republic is attempting as far as possible to limit the damage done by the missile deployment'. Turning to German-German relations, he repeated his four Gera demands but nonetheless averred: 'the point is, despite the tense situation, to preserve what has been achieved and where possible to build on it, not least in economic relations'.

Remarkably, this East German line was maintained after Soviet negotiators had walked out of the Geneva arms control talks and while the Soviet press poured a torrent of execration upon Nato in general and the 'revanchist' Federal Republic in particular. Whereas a decade before it had been Honecker who devoutly reasserted, against Ulbricht, the intimate and irrevocable ties between the GDR and the Soviet Union, now it was Honecker who, like Ulbricht, asserted against the Soviet Union the special interests — and superior virtues — of the German communist state. The GDR was joined by Hungary in urging the continuation of dialogue and practical (not least, economic!) co-operation with the West.

At another 'working funeral', this time of Andropov in February 1984, Kohl and Honecker met for the first time, in a guesthouse in the Lenin Hills. Kohl renewed Schmidt's invitation to pay his first-ever visit to the Federal Republic, and thereafter detailed preparations went ahead. Only in September 1984 did the GDR announce that Honecker's visit had been 'postponed'.

The GDR blamed this postponement on offensive commentaries in West Germany, and particularly the remark of the Christian Democrats' parliamentary leader Alfred Dregger that 'the future of the Federal Republic does not depend on whether Herr Honecker pays us the honour of this visit'. (From the horrified reaction in much of the West German media and politics one might almost have gathered that the future of the Federal Republic did depend on Honecker's visit.) Documents that have become available since unification conclusively show what all realistic analysts at the time understood — that the visit was cancelled because of Moscow's objections. As late as mid-August the East German Politburo still seems to have been working on the assumption that it might be possible to go ahead with the visit, despite a sharply critical leading article in *Pravda*.

A dramatic encounter in Moscow on 17 August between a delegation led by Honecker and a full turn-out of the Soviet leadership (including Gorbachev), formally under the dying Chernenko, drew the line. Looking back in 1992, Honecker recounted proudly how he had argued over the table with Marshal Ustinov, and then in the car with Gorbachev, all the way to the airport. But it was no good. Egon Krenz vividly recalls the painful Politburo meeting in East Berlin three days later, when the Soviet 'no' had to be swallowed yet again. Dregger thus merely provided the pretext for cancellation. The Politburo minutes for 28 August record the formal decision to postpone the visit, 'on account of the policy of the government of the FRG' — a statement which everyone round the table knew to be untrue. Yet the same resolution instructed the Permanent Representative of the GDR in Bonn to continue negotiations on the basis of Foreign Ministry plans. Attached was the draft of a joint communiqué on the visit that never was. The East and West German leaders, it said, had exchanged views 'in a businesslike and open atmosphere'.

This remarkable episode, made especially complex by the confused leadership transition in Moscow, deserves to be treated at length in any history of Soviet-East European relations. Most important for our immediate purposes, however, is the impact it had in West Germany. It seems fair to say that this, combined with the demonstrative continuity of German-German relations, and the slow improvements in people-to-people contacts, produced something like a psychological breakthrough in German-German relations. Honecker was given more credit and sympathy than he had ever enjoyed before.

From this time forward there was a subtle transformation of the language in which official representatives of the two German states talked with, and about, each other: a change in the quality of their mutual recognition. This was then greatly facilitated for the GDR by the fair winds of change from Moscow after 1985, and specifically by Soviet 'new thinking' on foreign policy, with its central emphasis on the priority of 'all-human' over 'class' interests.

Now the language of the 'all-human' was, of course, particularly characteristic of Willy Brandt and the social-liberal version of détente. Indeed, as we have seen, Brandt, Bahr and Olof Palme would claim with some justification that the Soviet 'new thinkers' took much of this language directly from them. At the very heart of this vocabulary was the word 'peace'. Yet it was not Brandt but the Christian Democrat Chancellor Kohl who, at the moment of Gorbachev's succession, after meeting again with Erich Honecker on the occasion of Chernenko's funeral, agreed with the East German leader a joint statement which said: 'From German soil war may never again, from German soil *peace must go out*' (my italics).

What on earth did this mean? How could peace 'go out' from German soil? Germany was, of course, famous for its capacity to export an extraordinary range of products — including a lot of weapons — to all parts of the world. Would consignments of peace now be added to the export balance? At one level this was merely a symbolic affirmation of mutual goodwill, such as are common in international relations. A Brazilian tribe discovered by the English traveller Peter Fleming greeted him enthusiastically with the repeated word '*Ticantó! Ticantó!*'. He had no idea what '*Ticantó*' meant, but he found that it helped a great deal to repeat the word often, smiling. The Brazilian tribe said '*Ticantó!*'. The Germans said '*Frieden!*'

At another level, it reflected a genuine conviction that the Germans, through their terrible experience of both causing and suffering war, and their position at the front line of the East-West conflict, had a special responsibility to urge caution, moderation and restraint upon their respective allies. Yet there was also the special interest born of the insight that while German-German relations could, after all, be slightly better than East-West relations overall, they were still painfully dependent on this general East-West climate.

So while the two states continued to disagree fundamentally about the nation and the political system, they found common ground at the lowest level — concerning the fates of individual human beings (*die Menschen*) — and at the highest level — concerning the fate of humankind. By talking about the fate of humankind, Bonn might help a few more individual human beings in Germany. By talking about the fate of individual human beings in Germany, Bonn and East Berlin might also be helping humankind. Sublime harmony!

The symbolic high-point of this mutual recognition was the official visit that Erich Honecker finally paid to the Federal Republic in September 1987. As late as April 1986, Gorbachev was still objecting. How can I explain to the Soviet people, he asked the East German Politburo, that Erich goes to Bonn before me? In summer 1987, with the 'overall weather conditions' significantly improving, the East German leadership prepared the ground with Moscow most carefully. Shortly after President von Weizsäcker's visit to Moscow, which marked the gradual thaw in Soviet-West German relations, they despatched Hermann Axen to Moscow once again, for a 'consultation' to discuss a long document prepared by the East German leadership and entitled 'Analysis of the situation of the FRG — Conclusions for a common policy'.

Axen noted a significant difference between the positive response from Anatoly Dobrynin, the new head of the Central Committee department for international relations, and that of Vadim Medvedev, head of the department for relations with socialist countries. Medvedev counselled greater vigilance against subversive West German influence. 'That sounded exactly as in the old manuscripts', Axen sourly minuted to Honecker. In response, Axen pulled out all the stops: 'The visit would be one of the strongest blows against revanchism in history. The foundation of the GDR in 1949 was the first heavy blow, the Protective Wall in 1961 the second blow, the Basic Treaty and the GDR's accession to the UN in 1972 the third blow. In September 1987 a fourth blow would follow.'

Returning with 'the most cordial, fraternal fighting greetings (*Kampfesgrüsse*)' to Honecker from Gorbachev, Axen was able to report a mission accomplished. In the new style of Soviet-East European relations, the East German leadership did not then (as in 1980) 'ask for a decision' about the visit, but merely informed the Soviet comrades of the details.

Yet it was not only in Moscow that there were residual doubts. On the West German side, Helmut Kohl was very far from enthusiastic about the visit. By Wolfgang Schäuble's own account it was he who persuaded Kohl that, in the logic of the policy they had adopted, it was both inevitable and essential. And if it were to be done, it had better be done properly. Honecker was therefore received in Bonn with virtually all the honours usually given to the head of a completely sovereign, foreign state. Two different German flags hung before the Federal Chancellery, the West German army band played two different anthems, two German leaders stood to attention side by side.

Kohl began his keynote dinner speech — actually delivered before dinner so that viewers in both German states could watch it on prime-time television — with a powerful reaffirmation of his belief in German unity. Millions of Germans between Stralsund and Konstanz, between Flensburg and Dresden, and in Berlin — he said — were watching, often with divided feelings. 'The awareness of the unity of the nation is as alive as ever,' he went on, 'and the will to preserve it is unbroken.' Recalling the words of the preamble to the Basic Law, he declared that to complete the unity and freedom of Germany in free self-determination remained the goal, 'and we have do doubt that this reflects the wish and the will, yes, the yearning of the people in Germany'. And again: 'the people in Germany suffer from the partition. They suffer from a Wall which literally stands in their way, and repels them.'

The Stasi closely monitored popular reaction in the GDR. Its Central Evaluation and Information Group reported on 9 September that the contents of the dinner speeches had thus far been the centre of attention. 'Progressive forces' were critical of Kohl's 'presumptuous attitude', but 'hostile-negative forces' were encouraged, 'especially by his comments on the human rights problem'. Six months later, talking to the Free Democrat Otto Graf Lambsdorff, Honecker remarked, according to the East German record: 'The GDR shows great patience. He had calmly listened to the speech of Chancellor Kohl at the meal in Bonn. We had even published it.' A testimony to the impact of the speech — but also to the fact that Honecker thought the risk worth taking. For beside making these points, very forcefully indeed, to the united television nation, Chancellor Kohl also said other things.

This visit, he observed, was another step on the way to a *geregeltes Miteinander*, a 'regulated with-each-other'. (In 1969, Brandt had actually spoken of moving from a regulated next-to-each-other to a with-each-other, but perhaps the regulated with-each-other was an intermediate phase, like that of 'developed socialism' in the GDR.) Kohl gave two main reasons for thinking that the two states might now feel themselves to be 'with' rather than merely 'next to' each other. Firstly, there were the fruits of 'practical co-operation' between the two German states over the fifteen years since the Treaty on the Bases of Relations. 'With our practical co-operation despite all differences,' he said, 'we have given an example — for the well-being of people and in the interest of peace.' It behoves 'the people of Lessing, Schiller and Goethe', he explained, to display, in their dealings with each other, *Humanität* — a word beloved of Thomas Mann and only weakly translated as 'humanity' or 'humaneness'.

Secondly, the Germans in East and West had a special obligation to do 'works of peace' because

In this century terrible havoc and suffering has gone out from German soil. For that reason too it is the task of the two states in Germany to contribute to an improvement of the political climate and to confidence-building in West-East relations by the extension of their co-operation. It seems to me obvious that our governments have to press for arms control and disarmament in the framework of overall East-West negotiations.

And then he spoke of realism, recognising the limits of German possibilities, and again of the incompatibility of the political orders in the two states.

Honecker also started with the theme of realism and incompatibility. 'Socialism and capitalism,' he said, 'can no more be combined than fire and water' — a sentence that Chancellor Kohl quoted, with approval, in his state of the nation address a month later. Later in his speech, Honecker made clear his different approach to the German question, though rather by omission than by explicit statement, and to human rights. Kohl had linked the issues of peace and human rights in his almost Papal formulation that 'peace begins with respect for the absolute and unconditional dignity of the individual person in all areas of his life.' Honecker kept the two issues carefully apart, but said that human rights, 'in the complete complex of political, civil, economic and social rights, find their daily realisation in practical life in the German Democratic Republic . . .'

In between these conflicting positions, however, he restated two basic points that Kohl had made. First, that 'co-operation instead of confrontation' had 'brought good results for the states, for the people (*die Menschen*), not least for the two German states and their citizens' — although he ascribed these 'good results' somewhat pointedly to the détente of the 1970s. Secondly, that the two German states had a special responsibility to be particularly active in promoting peace, disarmament and détente.

He declared that in their joint statement of March 1985, and now again, the two leaders had agreed that everything must be done so that 'never again war, but *always only peace* will go out from German soil' (my italics) — a further rise in the rhetorical bidding. Continuing the exchanges of code-phrases, he said 'we are in favour of realising the thesis of "creating peace with ever fewer weapons" (*Frieden schaffen mit immer weniger Waffen*)'. He thus adopted Kohl's slogan for multilateral disarmament in preference to the original formula for unilateral disarmament — 'create peace without weapons' (*Frieden schaffen ohne Waffen*) — coined by the peace movement in West Germany, and then adopted by independent peace initiatives in East Germany.

Their joint communiqué summarised the two main points, saying that the two states 'in the light of a responsibility arising from the common history, must make special efforts for peaceful living-together in Europe'. Then came the familiar pathos-laden sentence: 'From German soil war may never again, from German soil only peace must go out.' The relationship between the two states, 'must remain a stabilising factor for constructive West-East relations'. It should give 'positive impulses for peaceful co-operation and dialogue in Europe and beyond'. There followed a long list of areas in both West-East German relations and the East-West security dialogue where the leaders agreed that progress had been made or could be made.

In one sense, this remarkable consensus and harmony was not surprising, since few official visits in recent history had been prepared with such exhaustive thoroughness. Moreover, most of the ideas expressed, indeed the very phrases used, had been tried out, swapped, trimmed and polished in what one might now call the national political conversation — direct and indirect, official and unofficial — between the two German states. But in the perspective of forty years, or even of fifteen, it was quite extraordinary.

After signing the Basic Treaty, Egon Bahr had remarked that after having no relations the two German states would now at least have bad ones. Fifteen years later this looked remarkably like good relations. Here they were, the man who styled himself 'Adenauer's grandson' and the man who directly supervised the building of the Berlin Wall for Walter Ulbricht, agreeing not only to disagree, and where they disagreed, and roughly why they disagreed — in itself no mean achievement — but further agreeing that the two German states had common interests and common goals. And no minor goals at that: for what could be more important than 'humanity' and 'peace'? Mutual recognition had indeed reached a new stage.

But who would recognise the recognition? Germany's European neighbours, and the part-European superpowers, certainly 'recognised' this remarkable rapprochement in a narrower sense of recognition. They saw it happening. They adjusted to it. The increase in the diplomatic and political attention other Western states paid to East Germany was directly related to the growth in West Germany's engagement there. Over the next year, Honecker would pay official visits to Belgium, Spain, and, most notably, to France. (Despite strenuous East German efforts, the other Western Allies, America and Britain, were less forthcoming.)

Whether they recognised the German-German achievement in the larger sense of substantive approbation, is a different question. The first German-German common goal, that of more practical co-operation 'for the people' was relatively unproblematic. This was not true of the other common theme: that of the two German states as heavenly twins, separately, yet somehow in spirit together, urging 'peace, disarmament and détente' upon their respective alliances and a recalcitrant world.

Far from endorsing this vision, the Polish People's Republic redoubled its efforts to recapture from the GDR the position it had enjoyed in the 1970s as the West's favoured partner in Eastern Europe. The French Republic redoubled its efforts to bind the Federal Republic ever more closely into the West European web, offering hitherto unexposed charms, such as a Franco-German Joint Brigade and Defence Council, with the vague distant promise of something like that (West) European Army which had been vetoed — in Paris — more than thirty years before.

As for the superpowers, they promptly held their own summit, in which there was a great deal of talk about peace, disarmament and détente, but much less about the particular initiatives or aspirations of the European powers, whether West, Central or Eastern. There was, however, one specifically German point on the agenda of the December 1987 Washington summit. Under 'regional issues', point 9, 'Presidential Initiative on Berlin', this recalled President Reagan's dramatic appeal to Gorbachev in June 1987 to open the Brandenburg Gate and 'tear down' the Berlin Wall. Scant recognition there.

Publicistic reaction to the German-German summit was even more mixed. As usual, there was a large dose of exaggerated — if historically explicable — fear and doubt in many of these commentaries. It has been well said of West Germany, and to a lesser degree of the whole of Western Europe, that it was unhappy when the superpowers got too far apart, as in the so-called 'second Cold War' of the early 1980s, but also when they got too close together, as in the Nixon-Brezhnev détente of the early 1970s. Yet the same might be said, as it were in reverse, about the superpowers' attitude to the two German states: worried if they were too far apart, as in the mid-1960s, but equally worried if they got too close together. Yet both sets of fears — those of the small about the large and those of the large about the (relatively) small — had a rational kernel.

The rational kernel of Western doubts about the German-German rapprochement in the 1980s was presciently formulated by Pierre Hassner. As early as 1983 he argued that West Germany, having for a long time denied the very existence of the GDR, seeing its government as wholly unrepresentative of its people and entirely dependent on the Soviet Union, was now in danger of swinging to the opposite extreme, greatly underrating, or at least under*stating*, the differences between state and society, and the degree of the GDR's continued dependency on the Soviet Union. From the absurd extreme of complete non-recognition in the 1950s it was in danger of swinging to the opposite extreme of exaggerated recognition, in the substantive-approbatory as well as the formal-instrumental sense. To recall Willy Brandt's image of the man contemplating an elephant in the zoo: whereas in the 1950s Bonn was absurdly saying 'we see no elephant!', it now seemed almost to be saying 'what a charming eagle!'.

So far as the GDR's real ability — rather than merely wish — to influence its own 'alliance' in the direction of 'peace, disarmament and détente' was concerned, the evidence was slight. In the early 1980s it had come sharply up against the limits of Soviet tolerance, and retreated. Since 1985 it had, in foreign policy, been following Gorbachev's lead, albeit with its own particular emphases carried forward from the earlier period.

To be sure, a frank and intensive 'security dialogue' between governments in East and West had probably helped to keep the GDR, Hungary and Poland firmly behind Moscow's 'new thinking' in foreign policy. In some details of arms control and military doctrine these countries had indeed been marginally more specific, or, from the Western point of view, more 'helpful' than Moscow. Other Western governments therefore agreed on the value of maintaining this dialogue. Yet no one would have dreamed of comparing, say, Poland's role in the Warsaw Pact with Britain's role in Nato.

Now plainly, if pressed, most serious politicians in Bonn would have acknowledged the deep asymmetry between the Federal Republic's role, influence and room for manoeuvre in Nato, and that of the GDR inside the Warsaw Pact. To be sure, there were still unique restrictions on West Germany's sovereignty. But could anyone imagine an American President telling a West German Chancellor not to visit the GDR? The point is, however, that in Bonn it was no longer thought useful to dwell too much on these differences. Just as there should be said and seen to be the greatest possible harmony between German and European interests, so now there should be said and seen to be the greatest possible harmony between West and East German interests in foreign policy. Hence the rhetoric of explicit or implied symmetry. The danger here was that if the differences were not clearly recalled, they might, in time, cease to be seen at all. As the Christian Democratic specialist on foreign policy, Alois Mertes, observed in 1982: 'It's a short step from calling things the same (*Gleichbenennung*) to valuing things the same (*Gleichbewertung*).'

The other, still more serious, reason why this political recognition seemed exaggerated was the internal condition of the GDR. For the main way in which the GDR asserted its limited sovereignty and autonomy from the Soviet Union after 1985 was in resisting the application of Gorbachev's glasnost and perestroika to its own internal affairs. This it did with quite as much passion as it displayed in embracing the 'new thinking' in foreign policy; indeed with extraordinary frankness. In the spring of 1987 the West German magazine *Stern* asked the GDR's elderly chief ideologist, Kurt Hager, whether there would be perestroika in the GDR. At the end of a long answer, Hager made a remark that rapidly became famous: 'Incidentally,' he said, 'if your neighbour put up some new wallpaper, would you feel obliged to do the same in your own apartment?' So according to the chief ideologist of the GDR, Gorbachev's second Russian revolution was no more than wallpapering.

Whatever the improvement in the GDR's foreign policy, whatever the concessions it made on Western contacts, emigration and travel across its frontiers, what still mattered most to most people in East Germany was how the state treated them inside those frontiers.

Liberalisation through stabilisation?

How did West German policymakers hope or imagine their policy towards the GDR would change, or actually was changing, the domestic politics of the GDR? At the very beginning of Ostpolitik there was one rather clear hypothesis, or set of hypotheses, advanced on this crucial question. The basic lesson of the Cold War, it was argued, was that an aggressive posture by the West had led, compelled or at least encouraged the communist rulers in the East to adopt an aggressive posture, not only towards the West but also towards their own people. Such an aggressive 'Cold War' posture therefore produced the precise opposite of the intended effect. Instead of softening the regimes it hardened them. 'Increasing tension strengthens Ulbricht and deepens the division,' as Bahr plainly put it in his Tutzing speech of 1963.

The Berlin Wall was, as Bahr went on to explain, 'a sign of weakness

. . . of the communist regime's fear and urge for self-preservation. The question is whether there are not possibilities gradually to diminish the regime's quite justified fears, so that the loosening up of the frontiers and the Wall will also become practicable, because the risk will be bearable.' This was the policy which, Bahr concluded, 'one could sum up in the formula *Wandel durch Annäherung* (change through rapprochement)'. The underlying assumption was spelled out even more explicitly by Peter Bender, in his book of 1964, *Offensive Détente*. The basic feature of the GDR, he wrote, was its inner weakness. 'This weakness is the crucial reason why those relaxations (*Lockerungen*) which in other states of the Soviet bloc have already, in part, happened years ago, are still missing in the GDR. The weakness of the SED[i.e. Party]-leadership is thus the main cause of everything which urgently needs to be changed in the SED-state.' The logical conclusion was clear. The SED-state must be strengthened, so it could make those changes. 'Liberalisation of the GDR,' wrote Bender, 'requires stabilisation of the GDR.'

One of the keys to stabilisation was obviously the state of the East German economy. 'A material improvement would be bound to have a tension-relaxing effect in the Zone,' argued Bahr. To the objection that this would reduce popular discontent in the GDR he replied: 'but precisely that is desirable'. For otherwise there might be 'uncontrolled developments', like the 17 June 1953 rising or the 1960–61 emigration wave, which would lead to 'inevitable reverses', such as the crushing of the 17 June rising and the building of the Berlin Wall. No 'practical path' led via attempts to overthrow the regime. 'I see only the narrow path of relief for the people in such homeopathic doses that no danger of a revolutionary turn develops, which would necessarily lead to Soviet intervention out of Soviet interests.' So: reform instead of revolution.

Josef Joffe has forcefully argued that the concept advanced by Bahr and Bender in the early 1960s became a central underlying idea, not just of West German policy towards the GDR, but of the whole Ostpolitik in the 1970s and even into the 1980s. He calls it the notion of 'relaxation through reassurance'. Détente — that is, precisely, relaxation, *Entspannung* — between states in East and West should lead to détente between state and society in the East. An aggressive Western posture towards Eastern rulers had led, or at least contributed to, an aggressive approach by Eastern rulers not only towards the West but also towards their own people. If the West were less aggressive so, in time, should those rulers be — towards the West, but also towards their own subjects. By relaxation, and the building of trust and confidence between East and West, we could encourage the rulers to relax at home. And then they might find that this relaxation produced not explosion (as on 17 June 1953) or defection (as in the run-up to 13 August 1961) but a new trust and confidence between the rulers and the ruled.

There would then follow what Joffe nicely describes as a 'virtuous circle'. International relaxation and reassurance would encourage domestic relaxation. Domestic relaxation would produce domestic reassurance, and therefore encourage the rulers to relax still further, producing more domestic reassurance, and more international relaxation, until all sides, East and West, society and state, were so relaxed and so reassured that we could all move slowly, peacefully forward together from a mere regulated next-to-each-other to a with-each-other, and thence to the highest harmony of the European peace order.

Leaving aside the — important — historical question of how far this theory accurately reflected the real history of the Cold War, one can see that it was, in essence, a hypothesis of behavioural psychology. It was, in fact, one of two rudimentary hypotheses of behavioural psychology that underpinned Western thinking about the relationship between Western policy and Eastern politics. With deliberate oversimplification, one might call these the American and the German détente-hypotheses.

The American hypothesis was also first advanced in the early 1960s, and underlay the United States' policy of 'differentiation' to Eastern Europe. East European states were to be rewarded for good behaviour and punished for bad, and this in the short to medium term. Good behaviour was defined mainly politically, in terms of independence from Moscow in foreign policy and/or relative 'liberalism' and respect for human rights in domestic policy. Punishments and rewards were, in practice, mainly economic. The governing metaphor of 'differentiation' was that of 'carrots and sticks'. East European rulers were thus considered to be, at heart, donkeys. In the behavioural psychology of the German idea of détente, by contrast, East European rulers would appear to be, at heart, rabbits. The rabbit will freeze if you fix him in your headlights. If you frighten him too much, he may even bite. But speak to him gently, offer him carrots — above all, lots of carrots — and he will relax, loosen his grip.

These are, of course, rather childish simplifications — although it is a great mistake to believe that because our politicians and statesmen appear sophisticated the basic ideas underlying their policies are in fact sophisticated. In the case of social-liberal Ostpolitik, however, this rudimentary notion of behavioural psychology came wrapped, not merely in more sophisticated language, but in a world-historical dialectic. The central proposition of this dialectic was first publicly formulated by Egon Bahr at Tutzing in 1963, when he attributed to Kennedy the notion of 'overcoming the status quo, by first not changing the status quo'. With Willy Brandt it was extended from Berlin to Germany, and from Germany to Europe. Twenty years later this Berlin dialectic had hardened, in the hands of other leading SPD strategists, into statements such as 'Only the *unconditional* recognition of the status quo creates the precondition for a gradual changing of the status quo'.

What was this 'status quo' which one now so fully, not to say fulsomely 'recognised'? Was it merely the post-war frontiers, and the existence of new East Central European states, including the GDR, inside those frontiers? Or was it rather the 'post-war realities' as Moscow defined them, that is, including the enduring reality of communist systems in those states? In the case of Poland, Hungary or Czechoslovakia, the distinction between state and system was relatively easy to make; much less so in the case of the GDR. For what need would there be for the separate existence of an East German state if it did not have a fundamentally different system from West Germany? The GDR, said one of the Party's leading ideologists, Otto Reinhold, in a radio interview in August 1989, 'is only thinkable as an antifascist, as a socialist state, as a socialist alternative to the FRG [West Germany]. For what justification would a capitalist GDR have next to a capitalist Federal Republic? None of course.' The Bonn government might distinguish between 'recognising' the state and the system, but the GDR's leaders made no such distinction. For them, the state was the system, and the system was the state. 'Recognising' one meant 'recognising' the other.

The notion of 'relaxation through reassurance' seemed to square this circle. It suggested that by strengthening the East German state, through recognition and hard currency, in the interests of 'the people', the Federal Republic could yet also be working towards its internal liberalisation. To the general dialectical principle — accept the status quo in order to overcome it — was added the specific dialectical principle — strengthen the GDR regime in order to liberalise it. A stronger, more secure GDR could also be more acceptable to its own citisens, because, feeling stronger and more secure, it could afford to relax. This, in turn would permit a further 'coming closer' of the two German states. And this in turn . . . 'The more firmly entrenched the SED leadership,' wrote a leading Social Democratic specialist on Deutschlandpolitik in 1978, 'and the more satisfied the GDR population, the more probable is a co-operative relationship between the two German states.' 'Only a consolidation of the GDR,' wrote another sympathetic scholar in 1980, 'offers a promise of easing and overcoming the gruesome realities of barbed wire and death-strips at the intra-German frontier.' Here was the specifically German version of the 'virtuous circle'.

Now it is clearly not the case that all West German policymakers publicly endorsed or privately subscribed to this bold hypothesis. Far from it. Bahr himself modified and qualified the argument significantly over the next quarter-century. Willy Brandt cautioned against attempts at the 'dialectical resolution' of conflicts of interest, power relations and social differences. Helmut Schmidt was, as we have seen, dismissive of such 'concepts'. And many Christian Democrats had fiercely criticised it, then and subsequently. In 1983, the Christian Democrat who was perhaps most sympathetic to the social-liberal approach, Richard von Weizsäcker, described the notion of 'change through rapprochement' as a 'burden' from which Ostpolitik should be freed.

Yet it is remarkable how much of the basic thrust of this theory survived, or resurfaced in different forms and fragments, among those who were involved in policy towards the GDR over the two decades under review. One of its intellectual architects, Peter Bender, wrote in 1988 that Kohl and Strauss 'decisively reject Bahr's formula, and nonetheless pursue the policy that Bahr recommended twenty-five years ago'. This was a partisan and sweeping claim. Yet on all the evidence it is hard to dispute his next, more qualified assertion: 'Above all, they observe the basic law of social-liberal Ostpolitik and respect the status quo, in order gradually to overcome it. They know that their Deutschlandpolitik will only work if they do not attempt to destabilise the GDR, and when the GDR remains certain of that.'

Certainly this is what they said in public. While they did not adopt the explicit dialectics of social-liberal Ostpolitik, while they repeatedly insisted on the fundamental differences between East and West, the Christian Democrats nonetheless went out of their way to emphasise that they, like their predecessors, had no intention of 'destabilising' the GDR, or any other East European state. The Kohl government's Deutschland-politik was 'not aimed at a destabilisation of the GDR,' said Chancellery Minister Wolfgang Schäuble. 'We have no intention of harming or destabilising the GDR,' said the Minister for Intra-German Relations, Heinrich Windelen.

This 'stability commandment', as Eberhard Schulz well described it, for among most practitioners of Ostpolitik it had almost the sacred force of a commandment, proves on closer examination to contain two different, though closely related propositions. The first proposition is that it would be wrong for the West to attempt directly to 'destabilise' the communist state, to encourage discontent, resistance and revolt in East Germany or the rest of Eastern Europe, as had been done — or was said to have been done, and in reality had been said more than done — in the 1950s. It would be wrong politically, because it would only produce 'inevitable reverses'. It would also be wrong morally, because we might encourage people over there to resist, but when it came to the crunch it was they who would pay the price — in blood — while the West would do nothing. That was 'Yalta'.

The second proposition, closely related but not identical, was that it would be a mistake for people over there to attempt to change their government by revolution. Given the overwhelming reality of Soviet power, they would inevitably be crushed. There was thus a deep ambivalence in the West German attitude to the 17 June 1953 uprising. On the one hand it was celebrated as the first major rising for freedom in Eastern

Europe; kept as a public holiday called 'the day of German unity' in West Germany; and marked every year by a ceremonial speech in the Bundestag. On the other hand, most of those ceremonial speakers would have argued privately, and many argued publicly, that what happened after 17 June 1953 proved conclusively that an uprising was quite the wrong way to go about achieving desirable political change in Eastern Europe.

In 1978, when there were first signs of an explicitly political opposition developing in the GDR, Helmut Schmidt cautioned that

> a serious domestic crisis of the GDR, on which some people seemingly speculate, particularly in the opposition [i.e. the West German opposition], could not bring the state unity of our nation one centimetre closer. . . . Expectations of a crisis-like internal development in the GDR, with a consequent political change, derive from a fatal misjudgement of the existing realities and power relations there. No-one should forget the sacrifice of human life which such a misjudgement has already cost.

So rebelling or protesting was not what the East Germans were to be encouraged to do. And not just the East Germans. When, in the summer of 1980, the Poles started protesting once again — continuing the chain begun by Germans on 17 June 1953 — the reaction of the Schmidt government was extremely defensive, and subsequently critical. This was, in the first place, because the Polish protests had a direct negative impact on German-German relations. But it was also because German policymakers simply did not believe Solidarity's attempt could succeed. A contrast was drawn between the 'unrealism' of the Poles around Lech Wałęsa and the 'realistic' German-German policy — where the essential, constitutive part of 'reality' was the Red Army. The declaration of martial law in Poland seemed only to bear out this sober contention. Here was yet another of those 'inevitable reverses'.

So what was needed was not revolution from below but reform from above. West German policy might be made for — that is, on behalf of — the people in the GDR, but they could not be expected to change their own state. Policy for the people therefore had to be made not with the people but with the rulers. There, with the rulers, lay the key not just to short-term alleviations but also to medium-term reforms. Although the assertion cannot be proved, since policymakers can always claim that they thought more than they said, the evidence points to this having been a basic working assumption of the Bonn government's policy towards the GDR, in the 1980s as well as in the 1970s.

Now the political value of this constant reassurance, particularly in Moscow, should not be lightly underrated. Nor should the genuine moral concerns which informed the commandment of 'no destabilisation'. Yet the moral balance of the commandment was not entirely clear. It is one thing to say 'we should not risk other people's lives', but quite another to say 'you, other people, should not risk your lives'. Responding to Bahr's original Tutzing speech, Harold Hurwitz, an American with a deep and somewhat romantic interest in the history of the German left, wrote (in English) to his friend Willy Brandt: 'It is in the liberal and socialist traditions a somewhat disgusting example of "Hochmut" [arrogance, German in the original] to imagine that, knowing best, one has the right to usurp from an enslaved people its right to insurrection.' From a quite different tradition, conservative and Catholic, Alois Mertes would later make a very similar point about what he called 'the important, the many-layered word "destabilisation" '. 'We do not have the right,' he said, 'to stabilise a system that abuses human rights . . .' This was a difficult line to draw for every Western country, for the Americans in relation to Russia or the French in relation to Poland, but it was doubly difficult in the case of Germans dealing with Germany.

The classic image, almost the mandala, of this dilemma is the photograph of Willy Brandt at the window of the hotel in Erfurt on that first, moving official visit to the GDR in 1970. Here was the crowd of ordinary East Germans, full of emotion and hope, chanting 'Willy, Willy!' There he stood, just for a brief moment, with a tense look on his face, making a desperately strained, almost apologetic gesture of pacification, pushing downwards with the hands splayed out and both wrists pressed against the window frame. 'I was moved,' he wrote in his memoirs, 'but I had to consider the fate of these people: I would be back in Bonn next day, they would not . . . I made a gesture urging restraint, and my point was taken. The crowd fell silent. Turning away with a heavy heart, I noticed that many of my aides had tears in their eyes. I was afraid of kindling hopes that could not be fulfilled, so I adopted a suitably low-key manner.' In a sense, the leaders of the Federal Republic were to go on making this gesture to the people of the GDR for the next twenty years: in some cases still with that deep, inner moral and emotional tension, yet in others with what was almost a routine complacency.

If the moral balance of the stability commandment was not quite so clear as was generally claimed, nor was the political balance. This was, in fact, to enter one of the great political arguments of modern Central European history. On the one hand there were those — Poles, Czechs, Hungarians, Germans — who argued that the interests of people and the people, *die Menschen* and the nation, could best be served by accommodating, with many moral compromises, to the 'realities' imposed by outside powers. One should first adapt to the 'realities' in the hope of then gradually, quietly modifying them. On the other hand there were those who argued that it was more important to uphold certain absolute moral principles and national aspirations, to defy 'reality', even if the attempt was doomed in the short term:

> For freedom's battle once begun,
> Bequeathed by bleeding sire to son,
> Though baffled oft is ever won.

In nineteenth-century Poland the latter were described as romantics, the former as 'positivists' (in this special Polish sense). In the twentieth century the conflict has been described as that between 'realism' and 'idealism' (although not in the special German sense).

Now in the latest round of this great Central European argument, the leaders of Solidarność in Poland stood in the latter, romantic or idealist tradition, albeit in a modern, cautious, carefully moderated form, resolutely abjuring violence. Albeit in a modern, cautious, moderated form, carefully restating positions of principle so far as one's own state was concerned, the makers of Ostpolitik stood in the former tradition. They stood, explicitly, for 'realism' — 'German realism' as Brandt put it in a powerful speech on the ratification of the Basic Treaty. But who, in the long run, was more realistic? The romantic idealists or the self-styled realists? The answer to this question certainly looks different after the revolution of 1989 than it did before them, but it is not simple, and can only be given, insofar as it can be given at all, in that full context. What is important for our purpose here is to establish that up until 1989 the 'realist' premiss was dominant in policy towards the GDR.

The 'realities' of communist rule and Soviet domination were held to preclude a success for revolution from below. The key to political change was therefore held to lie in reform from above. 'Stability' was the key-word in this connection. Like other key-words of Ostpolitik, like 'recognition' or 'normalisation', its meanings were many, and not clearly distinguished from each other. In the original détente hypothesis, 'stability' referred to the strength of the communist state, and 'stabilisation' was seen as a means to liberalisation. Over the years, however, the means began to be taken for an end. This was particularly tempting since the term 'stability' — with its connotations of peace, calm, predictability, order — was considered a positive value in West German domestic and foreign policy more generally.

In the early 1980s, as the subject of 'peace' moved to the fore of German politics in general, and German-German relations in particular, the term 'stability' was linked more closely to the concept of peace. Thus, to take an extreme example, Günter Gaus averred in 1983: 'Polish conditions such as [prevailed] in the last three years, such *polnische Wirtschaft* in Central Germany, understood in the sense of the old, evil, arrogant German metaphor — this would be the eve of a war in Europe.' (Incidentally, if the metaphor was old, evil and arrogant, why use it?)

In more sober government usage, the term stability came to be applied increasingly not to the state or regime, but to German-German relations altogether. The Minister for Intra-German Relations talked of the 'stability' of intra-German travel. Hans Otto Bräutigam, Permanent Representative in East Berlin for most of the 1980s, spoke of the 'stability' of the whole relationship. All the leading practitioners of policy towards the GDR agreed on the need for 'stability' in this modest sense. The internal political 'stability' of the GDR was, however, thought to be necessary for the 'stability' of relations, since it was argued that only a strong, secure, self-confident GDR leadership would be a reliable and forthcoming partner in the Permanent Negotiation. If they protested too much, the people in the GDR would therefore get in the way of negotiations on behalf of the people in the GDR. On the hypothesis of 'relaxation through reassurance', neither they nor the West German government should put too much pressure on the communist rulers of East Germany.

For all his impatience with the 'concepts' of policy intellectuals, Helmut Schmidt makes clear in his memoirs that he, too, adhered to the original nostrum of behavioural psychology. Describing his approach to his summit meeting with Erich Honecker he writes: 'I wanted to help to increase the self-respect of Erich Honecker in the international context and reduce the inferiority complexes of the GDR leadership. In this way I hoped to contribute to a growing sovereignty and generosity of the GDR government in its treatment of its citizens. This had been the dominant motive for me since the beginning of the Ostpolitik of the social-liberal coalition.'

Whether or not they analysed it in precisely this way, Chancellor Kohl and his team in practice largely continued this approach, with growing outward 'recognition' of the Honecker regime, up to the remarkable crescendo of the Honecker visit in 1987. After the visit, leading politicians of all the main parties still regularly went to visit Erich Honecker in East Berlin, and to be photographed smilingly shaking his hand. To judge by the available East German records of these meetings — which of course have to be treated with caution — only a few of these prominent West German visitors directly raised issues of human rights, although many discreetly handed over lists of 'humanitarian cases'. All were respectful and polite. For were they not by their very politeness, yes, even by their flattery, 'helping the people'? (What was certain, however, was they were helping their own political 'profile' in the television democracy of the West.) Hermann Axen, summarising the main points of his own conversation in April 1988 with perhaps the most outspoken of all these visitors, Volker Rühe, was still able to write, in an internal memorandum to Honecker: 'CDU not interested in destabilisation GDR'. That was Bonn's message, sent and received.

To be sure, there was also some criticism of this whole approach, notably from those who had some direct, personal experience of the inner workings of the East German system. Wolfgang Leonhard made a powerful critique of the theory of liberalisation through stabilisation, arguing that a degree of pressure on the rulers, both from below and from outside, was not the obstacle to, but rather the essential prerequisite for, change in communist systems. The Federal Republic, he said, should distinguish more clearly between regime and people, and be more explicit in its demands for more respect for human rights, liberalisation and democratisation.

In 1988, the twin brothers Bernd and Peter Eisenfeld, the latter only recently deported from the GDR, made an even more swingeing critique. They argued, like James McAdams, that the GDR had got the upper hand in the German-German relationship. The Federal Republic should, they said, be much tougher in its negotiations with the regime, and more prepared to support independent and oppositional groups. Similar criticisms were made by other disillusioned intellectuals from East Germany, such as Hermann von Berg, Franz Loeser and Wolfgang Seiffert.

Yet these remained isolated voices. At least until 1988, virtually all those who actually made the policy, in government, opposition or civil service, subscribed to the commandment of 'no destabilisation', in both senses analysed above. Not all went to the opposite extreme, arguing that stabilisation was the only path to liberalisation. Yet this remained a powerful underlying notion, if only because no one seemed to have a better hypothesis about the way desirable change might come about in the GDR. Hans Otto Bräutigam, who was in many ways the walking personification of Bonn's GDR-policy, says — looking back — that he never believed that a stabilisation could lead to a liberalisation of the GDR, but he did believe that one might move through stabilisation to a modest humanisation of the GDR.

In any case, stability (inside the GDR) was thought to be a precondition for stability (in the German-German relationship) which was itself felt to be a contribution to stability (in East-West relations) — also known as 'peace'.

Stabilisation without liberalisation

What were the actual effects of policy towards the GDR on the politics of the GDR? The question is not easily answered. As we have noticed already, it is difficult to distinguish between the effects of the active policy and those of the mere, so to speak, passive reality of the Federal Republic, especially since one of the aims of the former was to expose ordinary East Germans to the charms of the latter. How can one summarise the myriad interactions of two societies, let alone of two societies in one nation? How do these relate to the domestic interactions of state and society in the GDR? And those to the influence of developments in the Soviet Union and elsewhere in Eastern Europe? Moreover, all criticism of a given policy is based on assumptions about possible alternatives. But we cannot, by definition, know 'what would have happened if . . .' All we can know is what actually happened, and even that we know only partially.

What is clearly wrong, however, is to judge the policy only by its final ending — revolution and unification. This may be good enough for politicians, but it is not good enough for historians. That outcome was very far from inevitable, and we must look at an interim as well as at the final balance-sheet. Perhaps the best interim vantage-point is the spring of 1986, when the ruling Socialist Unity Party held its eleventh party congress.

The choice of date is not arbitrary. Boring though they might be, Party congresses were very important moments in the life of communist states. They were important even if their message was, as in this case, 'no change'. This was especially important when the simultaneous message from Moscow was 'change!' The year 1986 also marked fifteen years of Honecker's leadership, while the two states in Germany had had 'relations' for nearly as long. Moreover, as we have seen, this year was felt in Bonn to mark something of a breakthrough in the crucial area of travel 'from Germany to Germany', a pleasure Honecker was himself to taste in 1987.

So, taking stock in spring 1986, what do we find? We find, first, a political system which in its fundamentals was quite unchanged. More than in any other East European state, more even than in the Soviet Union, the GDR had preserved and, so far as possible, made more efficient the basic structures of a Leninist-Stalinist one-party state. The pyramid command system of so-called 'democratic centralism', the external mobilisation of a mass membership, the 'language drill' of ideological conformity — all were maintained in the GDR to a degree long since abandoned even in Gustáv Husák's 'normalised' Czechoslovakia, let alone in Hungary or Poland.

The state bureaucracy, the mass organisations and the media all remained correctly subordinated to the leading role of the Party. Last but by no means least, the formidable domestic state security apparatus — the 'Stasi' — was more numerous and more formidable than ever. Although it certainly had very significant elements of operational autonomy, it remained, to use its own self-description, the 'shield and sword of the Party'. The head of its espionage operations, Markus Wolf, well described the Stasi as a 'hypertrophied function of the system'. At the top of this pyramidical party-state was an autocratic form of rule, with the Party leader increasingly making key decisions on his own, or in direct consultation with the Politburo's key functional bosses: Günter Mittag for the economy, Erich Mielke for security, Joachim Herrmann for the media.

The Party leadership had, however, significantly developed and modified the strategies by which it endeavoured to win from its own citizens some active, voluntary support or 'legitimacy'; if not 'legitimacy', then at least loyalty; if not loyalty, then at least acceptance; if not acceptance, then at least the absence of explicit protest — or what in Bonn was called 'instability'.

The central appeal for popular acceptance made by the Party under Honecker was staked out already at the 8th Party congress in 1971, and only re-stated and embellished at this 11th congress, fifteen years later. The appeal came under the awkward ideological formula of 'the unity of economic and social policy', but in plain words what it said to people in the GDR was roughly this: We do not ask you, as we did in the 1950s, to support us just because of our rejection of a terrible past ('anti-fascism') and our promise of a golden future (the communist utopia). Nor do we claim, as Khrushchev and Ulbricht did in the 1960s, that we will 'bury' the West with our superior economic performance. But we do claim that in our 'really existing socialism' we can sustain economic growth while at the same time providing you with an improved standard of living and a social security which you would never get in the West, ridden as it is with unemployment, crime, drugs etc. You will have cheap food, free medical care and education, safe streets, cheap holidays organised by the party-state's mass organisations, and there will be apartments — Honecker's particular concern — for everyone.

Whereas under Ulbricht the motto had been 'as we work today we will live tomorrow', people were now to enjoy more of the benefits today. Socialism was to be made more attractive — or, as the ideologists carefully reformulated the proposition, as attractive as by its nature it was. In 1986 all this was summed up in the key-word *Geborgenheit*, meaning sheltered, cosy safety. This was an understanding of socialism from a man, indeed from a generation of German communists, who knew from personal experience what it meant not to have enough to eat, warm clothes or a dry roof over your head. At the same time, it was, at least in the short-to medium-term, a fairly shrewd strategy for political survival.

It is important to note that the economic growth to underpin this welfare and consumer provision was not to be achieved by further market-oriented economic reforms, such as had been timorously attempted in the 1960s. On the contrary, the 1970s saw a consolidation of traditional, Soviet-type central planning, with some modifications to make it less inefficient, but with nothing that could seriously be spoken of as reform in the sense that Kádár's Hungary had embarked on economic reform. Instead, the underlying economic growth was supposedly to be achieved, first, by making the existing system (and people) work as hard and efficiently as possible; second, by technological innovation — Honecker himself was particularly keen on micro-electronics; and, last but not least, by opening to the West.

Economists talk of a strategy of 'import substitution', when economies in difficulty substitute alternative, domestic products for costly imports.

One might describe this political strategy as one of reform substitution. Social benefits and consumer goods were offered to the people not as complements to a reform of the system but as substitutes for a reform of the system which the Party leadership considered would be too dangerous (for the Party leadership). And one of the main substitutes for reform was — imports. Imports of Western technology, whether obtained legally, or illegally through the efficient espionage of Markus Wolf's intelligence department of the State Security Service. Imports of Western goods. Imports of DM.

As we have noticed already, this political strategy was not peculiar to East Germany. Edward Gierek did the same thing in Poland, albeit with catholic profligacy rather than puritan self-restraint. In Czechoslovakia, Gustáv Husák also offered material and social goods as substitutes for the crushed reforms and stolen freedoms of the Prague Spring, although he was able to do so without incurring large hard-currency debts. Even János Kádár's 'goulash communism' in Hungary tried initially to make economic without political reforms. When the difficulties of combining plan and market became acute, the Hungarian leadership, too, partially substituted foreign credits and imports for further steps of radical economic reform.

Peculiar to the GDR were, however, two features. On the one hand, Honecker was able to sustain this strategy virtually unchanged into the second half of the 1980s, thanks partly to (East) German good housekeeping, efficiency, hard work and so forth, but also crucially, and increasingly, to the financial and economic advantages of the relationship with West Germany. In Poland and Hungary, the hard currency loans which in the 1970s had been to some extent a substitute for reforms became in the 1980s a vital goad to reform. The West made rescheduling and new loans contingent on measures of economic reform, and on respect for human rights and political liberalisation. In the GDR this medium-term effect was lacking, because the very substantial monies from West Germany came with other, less immediately pressing linkages.

On the other hand, the risks of opening to the West were obviously greater for the GDR than for the other East European states, for while they risked subversion of their communist regimes, the GDR risked undermining the very basis of its existence as a state. In response to Bahr's Tutzing speech, the GDR's then Foreign Minister, Otto Winzer, spoke darkly of 'aggression in felt slippers'. The Minister for State Security, Erich Mielke, was constantly warning about the danger of an undermining of socialism in the GDR through contact with the West.

From the outset, therefore, much more than anywhere else in Eastern Europe, the opening to the West was accompanied by redoubled efforts to maintain the Party's political control and ideological rigour. The phase of 'peaceful co-existence' was openly declared to be one of heightened ideological struggle, directed primarily, of course, against the Federal

Republic. In a series of top-level internal briefings in the early 1970s, Mielke would instruct his subordinates in the Ministry for State Security that for them peaceful co-existence meant 'above all struggle'. Every possible operative step should be taken so that what happened at Erfurt should never be repeated. Following the signature of the Basic Treaty he warned that the process of 'normalisation' of relations with the Federal Republic would be a 'hard and complicated' area of class struggle. Visiting West Germans would have to be kept under close observation. The transit routes would have to be 'secured in depth'. Officers would need to investigate the 'whole personality' of East Germans who applied to travel West. And so on and so forth.

Beside this political-police response there was also an ideological escalation of what was officially called *Abgrenzung* (with connotations of 'drawing the line' and 'fencing off'). The escalation of *Abgrenzung* was the ugly twin sister of the opening to West Germany. In ideology and propaganda, this was particularly apparent in the GDR's new line on the national question. The 1968 constitution had declared that 'the GDR and its citizens . . . strive for the overcoming of the division of Germany forced upon the German nation by imperialism, the step-by-step rapprochement (*Annäherung*) of both German states until their unification on the basis of democracy and socialism'. In October 1974 this passage was deleted from the constitution, which now affirmed that the GDR was 'for ever and irrevocably allied with the Union of Soviet Socialist Republics'.

In the same period it was decided that the words of the GDR's 'national anthem' should no longer be sung, since it declared 'let us serve you for the good/Germany, united fatherland'. Indeed the GDR's ideologists now discovered that there were not just two states but actually two nations in Germany. The GDR was a separate 'socialist nation'. As late as 1987 the Party's veteran ideologist, Kurt Hager, could declare — in the interview already quoted — that the GDR was a 'socialist German nation'.

Looking back from 1992, Erich Honecker insisted that this so to speak anti-national *Abgrenzung* had been done largely at Moscow's behest. The assertion will clearly need to be tested against the evidence in the archives in Moscow and East Berlin. Yet what is demonstrably true is that Honecker always left himself an ideological loophole. Although the nation was now socialist, and its people's citizenship that of the GDR, their *nationality* was, he declared, still 'German'. And through this ideological loophole the GDR began, very tentatively at first, then with growing range and confidence in the 1980s, to acknowledge its own indubitable Germanness. When an East German astronaut was taken up in a Soviet spaceship, the East Germans were informed in a banner headline that he was the first *German* in space. Later, more seriously, there were quite spectacular celebrations to mark the 500th anniversary of Martin Luther's birth, and a cautious rehabilitation of Frederick the Great, even of Bismarck. All were now added, albeit with careful reservations, to the previously thin red line of 'progressive' elements in German history.

Again, the basic direction was not peculiar to East Germany. In their quest for new sources of popular support, the regimes in Poland and Hungary, not to mention those in Romania and Bulgaria, engaged in much more vehement appeals to patriotism — and nationalism — in the same period. There, too, the exercise was fraught with ambivalence. In every case, the appeal to patriotism — or nationalism — was used, at least in part, as an alternative to reform, liberalisation, or democratisation. In every case, there were non- or even anti-democratic national traditions to which the regimes could turn, and which found some echoes in the surviving political culture of at least some parts of the population. Thus, for example, it has been argued that parts of the surviving bourgeoisie in Hungary went quite smoothly from Horthyism to Kádárism. In the Balkans, the echoes were even more crass. Yet in every case there was ultimately an ineradicable tension between the regime's reading of national history — its lesson being: support us! — and the readings of national history that independent citizens made for themselves, which rendered lessons such as: give us back our pre-war freedom and independence!

Nowhere was this tension more acute than in East Germany. On the one hand there was much in traditional German political culture that was serviceable for a dictatorship. In the cliché of 'Red Prussia', as in most clichés, there was a grain of truth. The tradition of blind obedience to the state (the *Untertan* mentality), and the inner emigration of the unpolitical German (*machtgeschützte Innerlichkeit*), both survived and could be built on in the East more than in the West. In this sense, too, East Germany was, to repeat another cliché, 'more German' than West Germany. On the other hand, to emphasise national traditions was inevitably to concentrate people's minds on the enduring fact of division. And could even Erich Honecker be certain, in his heart of hearts, that they would then conclude the GDR was the better Germany?

Two other, related modifications of the ideological and political rigour of *Abgrenzung* should be mentioned here. In the 1970s, the opening to the West had been accompanied by redoubled efforts to ensure that young East Germans' readiness to defend the 'socialist fatherland' against the evil, capitalist, militarist, imperialist Federal Republic should not be diminished by actual contact with the beast. 'Defence education' was stepped up, with verses exalting a soldier's readiness to shoot his West German counterpart — 'perhaps my brother but . . . my enemy'. Yet in the 1980s, as we have seen, the official line became, increasingly, that the two German states had a joint responsibility for 'peace', that, indeed, in their 'coalition of reason', they were together helping to keep the peace, despite the less responsible behaviour of outside powers — meaning, above all, the United States.

Now this, too, was double-edged. It could bring the regime some popular appreciation, even active support. Yet it also had worrying implications. As the architects of West German policy towards the GDR had always hoped and intended, it made it increasingly difficult for the regime to present West Germany to its own people with any plausibility as a dangerous enemy or threat. Precisely this concern is reflected in a summary report of the Stasi's central evaluation group on popular reactions to Honecker's visit to Bonn. University and school teachers, said this report, found themselves confronted with such questions as: 'Do we still need an enemy-image (*Feindbild*)? . . . Is the Wall still necessary? Has the imperialism of the FRG changed its character? Western politicians also want peace.' The 'coalition of reason' also brought the risk that some citizens of the GDR, inspired by the images of the West German peace movement brought them every day by television, would start wanting to 'do something for peace' themselves, independently. What is more, they might, like peace activists elsewhere in Eastern Europe, link the theme of peace to that of human rights.

The second important modification concerned relations with the Protestant Church. Here the themes of German history and tradition, peace and human rights all came together, but in ways that were not merely double- but multiple-edged. Indeed, the history of church-state relations inside the GDR is scarcely less complex than that of German-German relations. Crudely stated, the basic political facts are that under Erich Honecker there was a cautious rapprochement between the party-state and the Church. This rapprochement was symbolised by a summit meeting between the head of the Federation of Protestant Churches in the GDR, Bishop Albrecht Schönherr, and Erich Honecker, on 6 March 1978. In the 1980s, there was a more or less permanent dialogue or negotiation between the party-state authorities and the Church, at lower as well as higher levels. There were, however, numerous ups and downs in the relationship, and wide variations between regions, dioceses, and individual parishes.

Whereas the minority Catholic Church was highly centralised and authoritarian, the majority Protestant Church was highly decentralised, with important historical differences between individual regional churches (*Landeskirchen*) and a quite democratic internal structure, with much lay participation in Church councils, synods and the like. In the GDR — unlike in Poland — the Catholic Church mainly concentrated on purely religious themes and ecclesiastical interests, keeping its distance from the regime. The Protestant Church, by contrast, addressed a whole palette of social and political issues. Diversity was therefore its hallmark. With considerable over-simplification one might, however, identify three main strands.

Firstly, there was a small but active minority of priests and lay Christians who saw themselves, in the tradition of Dietrich Bonhoeffer and the *Bekennende Kirche* as working in outright opposition to an evil, dictatorial state — although few would have accepted a direct comparison of the GDR with the Third Reich. Secondly, there was a somewhat larger minority of clergy and laity who, while they would surely have condemned the collaboration of the so-called German Christians with the authorities of the Third Reich, now more or less actively collaborated with the authorities of the GDR.

Thirdly, there were the many who attempted to navigate a path between those two extremes. Sometimes they believed in the genuine possibilities of Christian-Marxist dialogue, leading to a partial agreement on such issues as welfare provision, social justice and, indeed, peace. The formula of 'the Church in socialism' seemed to imply that possibility, while at the same time implicitly denying that this was a regime which intrinsically and necessarily demanded a Christian's outright resistance. (Compare the barely imaginable formula: 'the Church in national socialism'.) Instead, they saw their political function as that of mediators between state and people. In playing that part they developed a style and language which, as we have already suggested, also influenced the style of West German policymakers — prudent, persistent, predictable. As the extent of Stasi penetration of the Church became apparent after unification, so the political and ethical borderline between these last two categories would become the subject of a fierce debate, personified in the case, at once extreme and exemplary, of Manfred Stolpe.

The putative advantages to the regime of this still barbed and cautious rapprochement with the Church were considerable. It widened its potential basis of support. It gained the possibility of more fully engaging the talents of Christians, and the resources of the Church (including its monies for the West), especially in such areas of common interest as social welfare provision. Co-operation with the Churches on such issues as 'peace' gave it badly needed credibility. Through some churchmen, at least, it could also hope to moderate, even to pacify discontented citizens. All this was, to use the West German key-word, 'stabilising'. The political culture of Lutheranism was itself ambivalent, containing the potential for both collaboration and resistance. There was obviously a profound connection between German Protestantism and the substance of the *Kulturnation*, of German cultural unity in music, thought, literature. Yet so long as the political division seemed set in concrete this, too, could work for as well as against the interests of the regime.

Unambiguously negative from the regime's point of view were four things. First, the Church represented a fundamentally different view of the human person, a view which went back slightly further than the Marxist one and might be found to make more sense of the life even of a completely secularised young person in the GDR. Second, the Protestant Church in the GDR was both *de jure* and *de facto* autonomous to a degree unique in Eastern Europe, while the structure of its internal self-government was partly democratic. Third, it formed enclaves of free speech and free association, which the church-state rapprochement made it more difficult to encroach upon.

Finally, the Church could, if it wanted, offer the security of these enclaves to critics and even outright opponents of the regime, some of whom would certainly not otherwise have been regular churchgoers. Here, in churches, church halls and vicarages, they could talk about environmental and social problems, about peace, and about human rights. This they did, in growing numbers, at the beginning of the 1980s. They would, they said, taking their motto from the Bible, beat 'swords into ploughshares'.

Yet as soon as they stepped outside the church doors they were liable to be picked up by the police, harassed or arrested. The Stasi would make difficulties for them at work, or, if they were young, prevent them from going to university — as the children of clergy were still, anyway, regularly prevented from doing. Even the transport police on the trains would stop you just for wearing a 'swords into ploughshares' badge on your denim jacket. So with a touch of that glorious semiotic ingenuity which was to be seen all over East Central Europe in 1989, some young people displayed simply the bare round patch where a badge might have been. Yet the swords remained: in the National People's Army, in which all but a few still had to do armed service, despite the peace movement's demand for civil alternatives, and in the self-styled 'shield and sword of the Party', the Stasi.

The Church-protected groups survived as a small counter-culture, an important fragment of what all over East Central Europe would come to be called 'civil society'. They were dissidents in the original, Latin sense of the word: they 'sat apart' (*dissidere*). But the state successfully prevented them from becoming a lasting democratic opposition. In fact, the authorities dealt decisively with the leading lay activists of the Church-based peace movement; as they had with the leaders of a would-be democratic socialist opposition, the Robert Havemanns and Rudolf Bahros, and with the balladeer Wolf Biermann and other critical writers who had taken seriously Erich Honecker's initial announcement that there would be 'no taboos' in East Germany's cultural life. The methods of dealing with this opposition were, to be sure, less crudely brutal than in the 1950s. People were no longer shot — except at the frontier. But this improvement, this 'humanisation', to recall Hans Otto Bräutigam's term, was common to the whole Soviet bloc, with East Germany still close to the rear of the pack.

When the lesser repertory of intimidation and harassment failed, the dissident activist was faced, sometimes quite explicitly and cynically, with a stark choice. Here, in this room, said the police or state prosecutor, we are preparing the case against you, 'you'll get three years'. (No need to worry about independent judges, the sentence could be predicted in advance.) But there, in the next room, we have a completed application to emigrate, 'just sign and you'll be in the West next week'. It was, as one young Christian put it, like the choice between Heaven and Hell. In the circumstances it is not surprising that, often under acute psychological pressure, most of these courageous men and women chose emigration. And so the opposition was bled, and bled.

In sum, one has to conclude that after some fifteen years of Honecker's rule and West German 'GDR-policy', there had been a significant, although still fragile, stabilisation of the party-state, but no significant liberalisation. If the West German hope had been liberalisation through stabilisation, the interim balance was stabilisation without liberalisation. And our standard of comparison is not, let it be carefully noted, the freedoms of the West, but the much more limited freedoms of the East. In his original Tutzing speech, Bahr had himself observed that the 'Zone' was behind Poland and Hungary in political development, because of the special difficulties posed by the presence of West Germany. Yet on any meaningful measure of 'liberalisation', the GDR was now further behind Poland and Hungary, despite more than fifteen years of a West German policy designed to close that gap.

While people were more able to withdraw into an unpolitical private life — Günter Gaus coined the vivid term 'niche society' — the tribute of external conformity, that is, of public lying, expected even of the ordinary citizen was still much greater in the GDR than in that neighbouring 'niche society', Czechoslovakia. While there were fragments of civil society, above all in the churches, this was nothing to compare with the spectrum of independent activity in culture, the universities, the media, and the explicitly democratic opposition in Poland and Hungary. While there had been important changes in the tactics and even the strategy of the Party leadership, there was nothing that seriously deserved the name of reform in the political, economic or legal system. The Stasi was more numerous and ubiquitous than ever.

This stabilisation without liberalisation was, of course, primarily the achievement of the GDR itself. West German historians agreed with their East German colleagues that the consolidation of the party-state really dated from the building of the Berlin Wall in 1961. Yet both the main instruments of West German policy had contributed to this stabilisation. In the medium term, Bonn's growing transfers of DM and recognition had greatly helped the party-state. The importance of the DM has already been discussed. The importance of the recognition is well illustrated by the notes of one participant in the regular top-level meetings of senior editors with the head of the Agitation department of the Central Committee. 'Important, important strong GDR,' went the propaganda argument at the time of Honecker's visit to West Germany. 'If the GDR were on crutches, the leading representatives of business and politics would not have met with E.H., his delegation and our "captains of industry". We are a stable soc. [ialist] country in the heart of Europe: a political and economic factor.' And even more cheerfully: 'If Bavaria and Baden-Württemberg help us to build socialism — that's just great!'

We have been at pains not to over-simplify this story. The gains were double-edged. The GDR paid both an economic and a political price. The short- to medium-term financial relief to the state brought medium- to long-term financial dependency. The currency and goods that went to the people diminished immediate material dissatisfaction. Yet they also diminished the economic credibility of a state which treated its own currency with such contempt. The main political price the GDR paid was to permit the growth of ties between West Germany and West Berlin, contacts between the Germans in West and East, and slightly more travel (temporarily or permanently) for East Germans to the West. The reports of the Stasi's Central Evaluation and Information Group clearly indicate that ordinary East Germans responded to every major step of German-German summit diplomacy, whether Brandt in Erfurt, the Basic Treaty, Schmidt on the Werbellinsee, Brandt's meeting with Honecker in 1985, or Honecker in Bonn, with hopes of easier travel.

Yet even the balance of these concessions was not simply destabilising. Of course the presence of a prosperous, vital West Berlin in the very heart of the GDR, and visits from thousands of prosperous, vital West Germans, was not liable to increase satisfaction with one's own grey reality — although the vulgar arrogance of some West German visitors could actually prompt a curious defensive loyalty. As for travel to the West: since the lack of that freedom was one of the main grievances of the East Germans — the 'Wall sickness' was universal — the gradual, controlled granting of that freedom could perhaps reduce rather than increase the discontent. And since this freedom was granted not as a right but as a privilege, it was also a means of control. With this instrument, too, the regime could 'divide and rule'.

Even the most sensitive aspect of West Germany's efforts 'for the people' — family reunification and the 'buying free' of political prisoners — was double-edged. To be sure, when too many people applied to leave, as they did, for example, after the text of the Helsinki Final Act was published in *Neues Deutschland* in 1975, then the authorities made strenuous efforts to reduce the pressure. All sorts of intimidation were regularly used for this purpose. Moreover, three former East German intellectuals suggested that the GDR had in the 'emigration movement' something analogous to Solidarity in Poland. Those whose applications were refused swelled the ranks of the discontented at home; those who succeeded made new connections across the frontier and encouraged others to follow; while those short-term visitors to the West who went back to the GDR would spread the word about the attractions of life in West Germany. Ludwig Rehlinger has also argued that the business of 'buying free' must have demoralised the police and judicial authorities who thus routinely subverted the rules by which they supposedly lived.

Yet the effect of emigration and the 'buying free' was also, and more immediately, to demoralise those who probably had rather more morale (and morality) to lose in the first place: the would-be opposition. Asked, in July 1989, what they considered to be the main reason for the relative weakness of the opposition in the GDR, as compared with Poland, Hungary and Czechoslovakia, a circle of dissident activists in East Berlin unanimously gave as their first answer: emigration. Of course many other factors contributed: the efficacy of the Stasi; the relative constancy and cheapness of basic consumer supplies; the continuity of an undemocratic political culture; the lack of support from prominent writers and artists; the attitude of parts of the Church leadership; last but not least, the lack of any direct or explicit support from the Federal Government or any of the main parties in Bonn, with the partial exception of the Greens and a few individual Social Democrats. But the main reason remained: emigration.

After unification, Bärbel Bohley, one of the few who both opposed and stayed (indeed, returned), charged the Federal Republic with the 'slice-by-slice' buying of the opposition. Now it may be objected that the numbers of those actually 'bought free' were relatively small. But if one considers what a difference the one to two thousand members of the democratic oppositions in Hungary and Czechoslovakia were to make to the political life of their countries, then it seems reasonable to suggest that the departure of between one and three thousand of East Germany's brightest and best citizens *each year* must have had some debilitating effect. In fact, General Jaruzelski and Gustáv Husák could have dreamed of nothing better than to export their dissidents for hard currency.

This is not to make a final judgement. It is to explain why, in 1986, Erich Honecker could conclude that the balance of German-German relations was favourable to the stabilisation of his unreformed regime. Taking out that protocol of his memorable conversation with Leonid Brezhnev back in July 1970 (see p. 77f), the 74-year old Party leader might nod and say: 'Yes, indeed, how right you were, dear Comrade Leonid Ilyich, to suggest that Brandt's Ostpolitik would increase our "international authority" and "consolidate the position inside the GDR". And so it has! You rightly warned against Brandt's hopes of "penetrating" us, but on balance I think we have that under control.' Unfortunately the man in Moscow was now called Mikhail Gorbachev, and he was embarking on a course of reform which would have Brezhnev turning in his grave.

Liberation by destabilisation

How should the GDR respond to the challenge from the East? The constitution of 1974 said that the GDR was 'for ever and irrevocably allied to the Soviet Union'. Honecker's wife Margot, the Minister of Education, had the GDR's children taught that 'to learn from the Soviet Union is to learn how to win'. On the other hand, by late 1986 Gorbachev was indicating to East European rulers that they were now much more at liberty than under Brezhnev to pursue their own individual domestic strategies. This could be taken, as it was in Poland and Hungary, as an invitation to try further reforms. But it could also be taken as (albeit grudging) licence to continue as before. Honecker, like Husák, took this latter option. But he did not merely batten down the hatches in hope of calmer seas. Instead, he took what looks in retrospect like a remarkable gamble.

Honecker's last gamble was reform substitution on a grand scale. As in the 1970s, but much more boldly, he would use the burgeoning relationship with West Germany as a substitute for political and economic reform at home. Since, however, the example of reform was now coming from Moscow, and being enthusiastically embraced in Budapest and Warsaw, the further opening to the West was accompanied, not, as in the early 1970s, by a redoubling of fraternal ties with the East, but rather by a limitation of those ties. In the 1970s the opening to the West had been accompanied by *Abgrenzung* against the West. Now the further opening to the West was accompanied by *Abgrenzung* against the East.

In relation to Poland the fences had been up since the birth of Solidarity in 1980. But after 1986 the 'fencing-off' was turned against the Soviet Union itself. A Church weekly was forbidden to reprint an article from *Moscow News* on the grounds that this would be 'interference in the affairs of another state'. The Soviet journal *Sputnik* was banned from circulation in the GDR. Honecker lauded the superior economic and social perform-ance of 'socialism in the colours of the GDR'. Yet along with the rejection of the Soviet reforms went a further intensification of German-German contacts, not only between the political élites — referred to in Politburo minutes as the GDR's *'Dialogpolitik'* — but also between ordinary people. As we have seen, from 1986 onwards the number of ordinary East Germans under pensionable age allowed to travel West increased dramatic-ally.

To describe this as a conscious gamble or strategy is of course a speculative interpretation. Rich as they are in many ways, the archives of the former party-state are poorest precisely in documenting the back-ground to decision-making at the very top. Honecker's sometime crown prince and eventual successor, Egon Krenz, suggests that the whole process was more confused, reactive and improvised. Certainly Honecker did not look like a gambler. Yet others who had been close to him argue that he did have a real political intelligence, and even a penchant for taking risks. What is more, in conversation with the author in late 1992, Erich Honecker himself quite emphatically confirmed that the decision to let more people travel was part of a conscious strategy. It was his own response to the challenge from the East, and a further step to 'normalize' relations between the two German states. He believed that his people would become more not less satisfied if they were allowed to travel.

That this is not merely retrospective rationalisation is suggested by perhaps the most striking of all Honecker's comments during his visit to West Germany. Speaking in the town of Neunkirchen in his native Saarland, he said:

> The German Democratic Republic is an active member of . . . the Warsaw Treaty, and the Federal Republic of Germany is firmly anchored in the Western Alliance. It is only too understandable that under these conditions the frontiers are not as they should be. But I believe that if we act in accordance with the communiqué that we agreed in Bonn, and thereby achieve a peaceful co-operation, then the day will also come on which frontiers no longer divide us, but unite us, as the frontier between the German Democratic Republic and the People's Republic of Poland unites . . .

Since the frontier between the GDR and Poland had been virtually closed since the emergence of Solidarity, this could almost be taken for a bad joke. Yet the message that the frontiers were not 'as they should be', and the clear implication that it was the alliances that prevented them from being so, was still remarkable. If there was to be a new era of East-West détente, then this time East Germany would make sure it was in the vanguard.

What Honecker would still vigorously deny in 1992 was the motive of financial need or dependency on the Federal Republic. For those who actually had to keep the state solvent from day to day, this was clearly a dominant concern. But Gerhard Schürer recalls Honecker treating the issue in Politburo as almost an administrative, departmental problem — as if the 'plinth' of net debt could be halved by decree. Talking to the author in 1992, the deposed leader would refer to the Bonn government's recently announced conclusion that the final net hard-currency debt of the GDR was 'only' about DM 30 billion. This, said Honecker blithely, was a level 'usual in trading relations'. And in a striking display of economic naïvety, he suggested that the GDR's debit balance in hard currency should be set against its credit balance in transferable roubles. So even if the GDR's hard currency debt and financial dependency was an objective reason for the further opening to West Germany, and a conscious ground for some of Honecker's close associates, the balance of the evidence suggests that it was probably not a major motive for him.

Beside the political gamble there were no doubt also more personal and emotional elements in the behaviour of the key decision-maker. In 1985 Willy Brandt called him 'the last all-German' in the East German leadership. Helmut Schmidt observed that over the years Honecker became 'more German'. Perhaps this was partly a result of the increasingly intense German-German conversation. Partly it may have been simply old age. Old men remember, and, in his seventies now, Honecker would often hark back to his early days in the Saarland and the tragic division of the German labour movement between Social Democrats and Communists, which had allowed Hitler to come to power.

This was a leitmotif which can be found as early as his intensely emotional meeting in 1973 with Herbert Wehner, with whom he had worked as a young Communist in the Saarland, and of whom he would often speak with deep respect. In the Brandt papers there is a remarkable text — typewritten by Herbert Wehner himself — of what appears to be a letter which Honecker sent him in February 1974. Thanking Wehner for his summary of and commentary on their previous exchanges, Honecker wrote 'I hope that a man like Herbert Wehner can long go on working for views "which another not yet or no longer has". This will make it possible to discuss questions of mutual interest and bring them to a solution.' After emphasising the closeness of the GDR to the Soviet Union, Honecker wrote that he, like the Brandt government, also wished to fill the German-German treaties with life, 'although I assume that even with the best relations, polemics will not bc wholly avoidable on account of the different social orders' — a quite extraordinarily mild formulation at a time of fierce public *Abgrenzung*. Honecker and Wehner subsequently met a number of times, in or near East Berlin.

Looking back after his fall from power, Honecker again warmly recalled Wehner's role, saying that although Wehner had rejected the Communist Party 'his goal was still the unity of the labour movement and the building of a socialist German republic'. In 1992 he affirmed that this had also been his own goal. Of course one must allow for the colouring of retrospect. But this all-German leftist perspective was certainly there, and grew stronger rather than weaker with advancing age and the development of German-German relations. 'We are going the German way,' he told Willy Brandt in 1985.

At the same time, he visibly enjoyed the 'recognition' that was increasingly accorded his regime and him personally. Trivial though it may sound, the element of simple vanity should never be underrated in explaining the conduct of men and women in power. Honecker's own visit to West Germany would be the crowning glory — especially if it could include a sentimental return to his native Saarland. And if West Germany wanted more ordinary East Germans to travel too: well, the experience of the last fifteen years suggested that the political risk could be worth taking.

As we have seen, one of the underlying ideas of the West German approach was to produce 'relaxation through reassurance'. Arguably, the reassurance did indeed produce relaxation — but not in the intended form of domestic liberalisation. Instead, it came in the classical form of *hubris*. So reassured was Honecker that he miscalculated the strength, popularity and stability of his own regime. As numerous witnesses testify, he was already suffering from that growing distance from everyday reality which affects all long-term rulers in dictatorships. Asked about public attitudes, he would refer to the happy expression on people's faces at the May Day parade.

In an almost touching conversation with the Czechoslovak Communist Party ideologist Jan Fojtík, in January 1989, Honecker observed (according to the East German record) that it was plain 'that the majority of the population prefers the kind of socialism which respects Engels' view that people need food, clothing etc before they talk about politics. Socialism in some other countries was no example for that. Since in the GDR socialism had something to offer people, it was unshakeable.' One could hardly ask for a more pregnant summary of Honecker's basic political philosophy, strategy, and illusions. But West Germany, with its increasingly fulsome 'recognition', reinforced those illusions.

Plainly, any such interpretation of a leader's motives and calculations can never finally be proven. Yet whatever the precise mixture of causes, the results were visible for all. More East Germans than ever since the building of the Wall travelled, like Honecker himself, to West Germany in 1987. More East Germans than ever returned through the Wall to find an unchanged, indeed a worsening state of affairs at home. The young East German writer Gabriele Eckart concluded a moving account of her first trip to West Germany, in 1987, with the words: 'I would wish everyone who rules over us to peer into the heart of a GDR citizen in the hour after their return from West Germany'.

Their reactions to some aspects of West German life might be ambivalent, but they certainly did not conclude on their return that, as the Central Committee of the Socialist Unity Party had only recently informed them, the GDR was 'one of the freest countries in the world'. In fact, as we now know, secret police control was further stepped up in 1986, with the recruitment or infiltration of Stasi 'officers on special duty' in all key areas of East German life, while a further clampdown on dissent followed soon after Honecker's own return from Bonn.

The people of East Germany now lived with a double contrast: that between their own grey, stagnant reality and the West, which more of them had now seen at first hand; and that between their own unreformed, repressive regime and the increasingly daring reforms in the Soviet Union, Hungary and Poland. It is impossible to say which contrast was more important. They came together. In June 1987, young East Berliners gathered at the western end of Unter den Linden to hear the British rock band Pink Floyd playing just across the Wall, in West Berlin. When the police tried to disperse them, they chanted 'Gorbachev! Gorbachev!' The influences of West and East conspired against Honecker.

Talking to Western visitors, Honecker would often insist that youth was behind the party-state. But polls conducted by its own Institute for Youth Research in Leipzig gave a dramatically different result. Whereas in 1985 some 51 per cent of apprentices, 57 per cent of young workers, and no less than 70 per cent of students said that they felt themselves 'strongly or very strongly' tied to (*verbunden mit*) the GDR, by October 1988 the figures had sunk to 18, 19 and 34 per cent respectively. 28 per cent of the apprentices, 23 per cent of young workers and even 15 per cent of students now replied: 'not all all'. In part, these results may reflect less a change in underlying attitudes than a reduction in fears about the consequences of an honest answer. But whether loss of loyalty or simply loss of fear, the results were devastating.

There were two main outward expressions of growing popular discontent. Firstly, the number of applications to emigrate increased. Figures given to the Politburo by Egon Krenz in April 1988 put the number of applications to emigrate at 112,000, compared with 78,000 in 1987, and 87 per cent of the applicants were under the age of forty. Western estimates of the numbers wishing to leave in 1988–9 varied widely, from a quarter of a million to more than a million. Whatever the true figures, the trend was clearly upward. Honecker hoped that freer travel to the West would make people more satisfied, as arguably it had done in the previous fifteen years. But now it made them more dissatisfied. The combination of direct experience of the West, change to the East, and no change at home, turned the safety-valve into a steam-hammer.

Secondly, despite the sharper repression that followed soon after Honecker's return from West Germany, the dissident groups grew in strength and boldness. When an official mass rally in East Berlin to commemorate the murder of Karl Liebknecht and Rosa Luxemburg was joined by independent demonstrators carrying banners with Rosa Luxemburg's words 'freedom is always freedom for those who think differently', they were rounded up by the police. Several leaders of those who thought differently were now more or less compelled to leave the country, albeit in a few cases with the promise that they could subsequently return. Church synods pointedly sang the praises of perestroika. In a striking echo of Martin Luther, a priest from Wittenberg read '20 Theses' for a reformation of the GDR. Then, in May 1989, the dissidence acquired — for the first time — the breadth and quality of a democratic opposition, with a quite widespread action to monitor local elections. While the regime instantly claimed a 98.85 per cent 'yes' vote, the independent monitors could virtually prove that the results were falsified.

202 · *In Europe's Name*

It is important to note that these two tendencies, the growing pressure to emigrate and the growing opposition, were not merely complementary. While they were both expressions of the same discontent, they were in a sense opposite answers to the same challenge. The one said: 'I will stay and fight for improvements here.' The other said: 'that is hopeless, I will leave'. Although would-be emigrants often became oppositionists while they remained, and would-be oppositionists very often ended up as emigrants, it was only in the autumn of 1989 that the two movements really came together as one.

What both indicated was the disappearance of that middle option of steady, controlled reform from above which West German policy had hoped to promote. First the medium-term stabilisation without liberalisation, facilitated by the relationship with West Germany, then the further opening to the West, as a substitute for reform at home, at a time of galloping reform to the East: this sequence had produced a situation which from the viewpoint of the active citizen seemed to offer only two alternatives — resignation (of which emigration could also be an expression) or revolution (to which the wave of emigration finally contributed). From the viewpoint of the state this meant that the domestic political situation was at once very stable — with the combination of state repression and popular resignation — and very unstable.

In June 1989 the Ministry for State Security sent a report to Honecker which estimated the total number of 'hostile, oppositional or other negative forces' in the GDR at about 2,500, with some 600 leaders and a hard core of just sixty 'fanatical . . . unteachable enemies of socialism'. There is no reason to doubt the thoroughness of the Stasi's researches. Two months later Mielke asked a crisis meeting of his regional commanders: 'is it that tomorrow the 17 June will break out?' No, said the commander from Gera. And his colleague from Leipzig averred: 'so far as the power question is concerned, Comrade Minister, we have the thing firmly in hand, *it's stable*' (emphasis added).

Shortly thereafter a '17 June' did begin — in Leipzig — and transformed the GDR out of all recognition. But this was a new 17 June: a peaceful, sustained, candle-bearing 17 June, one which bore the marks not just of the internal learning process of the Church-based opposition in the GDR, but of the much larger East Central European learning curve that began with the German rising of 17 June 1953 and continued through the Hungarian Revolution and the Polish October of 1956, through the Prague Spring of 1968, through the Polish December of 1970, the Polish protests of 1976, the Polish Solidarity born in 1980, the Polish and Hungarian 'refolutions' (reform-revolutions) of the first half of 1989, before returning at last to East Berlin.

Who could but be touched when Willy Brandt declared, in Berlin on the day after the opening of the Wall, 'now what belongs together is growing together'? Who could begrudge Helmut Kohl his moment of glory at the opening of the Brandenburg Gate, or Hans-Dietrich Genscher his triumphant returns to his native Halle? And perhaps most moving of all, to those who knew, was the sight of Willy Brandt once again at the window in Erfurt, twenty years on, this time not pressing his palms downward in that gesture of painful restraint, but raising his arm in a cheerful wave, with the strain only of memories touching the lined familiar face.

Looking at such scenes it seems almost churlish to ask the historian's dry questions about causes and intentions. All's well that ends well. 'The final measure of any policy is its success,' as Adenauer once remarked. And this was an extraordinary success. What need to say more? Yet the question of the real contribution made by Bonn's policy towards the GDR to the end of the GDR is still an interesting one. It might even, perhaps, carry a few indirect lessons for the future. Of course the reasons for the success of the peaceful rebellion and its transformation into unification cannot be understood without looking at the change in Soviet policy, the 'refolutions' and revolutions elsewhere in Eastern Europe, overall developments in East-West relations, and, not least, at the Federal Republic's own relations with the rest of the East. Yet there are some tentative conclusions that may be drawn, and questions still to be asked, about the specific story of policy towards the GDR.

Success and failure

The success was rich in ironies. For a start, the opening of the Berlin Wall was already the fulfilment of the operative goals of the Ostpolitik which began after the building of the Berlin Wall. What followed in 1990 went beyond what the architects of Ostpolitik had thought to be possible. Originally, in the early 1960s, they still hoped for unification in their lifetime. Over the years they gradually, painfully, buried the hope. Now, just as they had thoroughly buried the hope, just as not only they but the Christian Democrats who took over their GDR-policy had become soberly convinced that it would not happen in their lifetime — it happened.

Insofar as they had a concept of promoting desirable political change in the GDR, West German policymakers had aimed at reform from above. Instead, the change came through rebellion from below. As Robert Leicht observed in *Die Zeit*, this was not *Wandel durch Annäherung* (change through rapprochement) but *Wandel durch Auflehnung* (change through rebellion). If the original, and remarkably long-lived, idea had been liberalisation through stabilisation, what actually happened was liberation through destabilisation.

Yet the irony goes deeper still. For we have argued that both the Federal Republic's objective contribution to Honecker's fifteen-year long stabilisation without liberalisation, and the subjective contribution of Bonn's increasing, flattering 'recognition' of Honecker and his fundamentally unchanged party-state, including all those assurances about 'no destabilisation', helped to lull Erich Honecker and his colleagues into taking that final political gamble of opening to the West, instead of reform, while fencing-off to the East.

Now one could, of course, suggest, with hindsight, that this was a magnificent piece of long-term strategic deception by West Germany: a triumph of Machiavellism on a grand scale. Destabilisation through stabilisation! Precisely by allowing the Honecker leadership to continue without reforms, Bonn had actually helped the GDR down the road to ruin. So perhaps Franz Josef Strauss had 'saved' the GDR in 1983 only the better to strangle it in 1989? Yet unless hard evidence is produced to the contrary we must be permitted to doubt that the great Bavarian foresaw what no one else did.

So also with the inventor of *Wandel durch Annäherung*. In a conversation in June 1991, Egon Bahr told the author that when Otto Winzer had warned in response to his 1963 Tutzing speech of 'aggression in felt slippers' that was good enough for him. He, Egon Bahr, could not say anything like this, or it would have the reverse effect. Once, in 1968, he had incautiously told an interviewer that the real hope was that a Prague Spring would break out in Moscow. But fortunately the GDR hadn't noticed.

Yet as late as September 1989, Egon Bahr could say, in a discussion in which there were only Western participants: 'If our demands add up to taking away their state from the people (*die Menschen*) over there, then they will certainly not allow it. In this sense reforms in the GDR are only conceivable if the SED [Party] leadership can be certain that one doesn't want to take away their state.' Here the elision was not of people (*die Menschen*) and nation, but of people and Party leadership. Now the stenographic record of these proceedings was subsequently printed and circulated to a small audience. One could therefore theoretically argue that tactical caution explained even these remarks. After all, perhaps a copy might fall into the hands of the East German leadership, and then, instead of relaxing (because reassured) they would sit up and say 'my goodness, they really want to subvert us!' — and therefore clamp down. But it is more plausible to suggest that these remarks indicated not just tactical caution but also some genuine, substantive misassessment of the nature of the East German state and the intentions of its subjects.

Yet were not precisely these Western misapprehensions in a paradoxical way a contribution to the originally desired, but now largely abandoned, end? Was not the reassurance which contributed to Honecker's hubristic misjudgement the more effective precisely because the West German politicians and policymakers at least partly believed what they were saying?

It was, as we have been at pains to stress, by no means only leading Social Democrats who displayed symptoms of cognitive dissonance in relation to the GDR in the mid-1980s, overrating, or at least overstating, its economic strength and its contribution to 'peace' and *Humanität*. In this sense Honecker was not merely the victim of his own illusions. He was also a victim of the Bonn politicians' illusions.

Paradox was the characteristic intellectual figure of German-German relations (itself a paradoxical phrase): the two-in-one of the 'community of responsibility'; accepting the status quo in order to overcome it; strengthening the regime in order to loosen its grip; not demanding German unity being the only means to achieve it. So perhaps the architects of policy towards the GDR might enjoy this final paradox: they got it right because they got it wrong!

It does not, of course, follow that getting it wrong is an advisable course in future dealings with other dictatorships. The *salto mortale* from stabilisation without liberalisation to liberation by destabilisation only succeeded due to overriding external factors, above all the changes in Soviet policy and East European politics, plus a generous slice of luck. Nor does it follow that everything that was actually done in policy towards the GDR was right only because it was wrong.

At least until 1987, and even up until the summer of 1989, the working hypothesis that protest in the GDR would meet with domestic repression, and outright revolution would be crushed by the Red Army, was justified on the information available to policymakers in the West. That was 'Yalta'. It is entirely reasonable to ask: what would have happened if there had been widespread popular discontent, rebellion even, in the GDR in 1983? But we have tried to suggest that the answer is not quite as simple as is often assumed. Almost certainly the protest would have been violently suppressed, with or without the help of Soviet troops, which did not even need to threaten to invade since they were there *en masse* already. So any such protest would have been defeated. But one should note the curious fact that in East Central Europe people celebrate their greatest defeats — from the battles of Mohács and the White Mountain to the Hungarian Revolution, the Prague Spring and Solidarity.

The great Central European argument between idealism and realism is an argument precisely about the meanings of victory and defeat. Even defeated protests leave their mark, and can sometimes, in the end, become victories. This can never be said of non-existent protests. No one has the right from a position of comfort and safety to encourage others to risk their lives; but equally, no one has the right to deny others that possibility. Treading along the narrow line between not encouraging an oppressed people to revolt, and actively discouraging them from exercising what Harold Hurwitz called their 'right to insurrection', the Federal Republic erred on the side of discouragement. 'German realism' underrated the possible contribution even of apparently failed revolts — like the 17 June 1953 — to a final victory. Until very late in the day, West German policymakers failed to distinguish clearly between the two meanings of 'destabilisation': between West Germany trying to liberate the East Germans and the East Germans trying (albeit step-by-step) to liberate themselves.

If for most of this period the East Germans did not seem to be making many efforts to liberate themselves, the relative passivity of the majority was to some extent an effect of West German policy, while the minority received little or no encouragement from Bonn. The ultimate, external justification — the Red Army — did, however, seem persuasive so long as Moscow's attitude did not change. And in the rest of Ostpolitik Bonn was attempting to change Moscow's attitude, partly by the repeated reassurance of 'no destabilisation'.

One cannot, moreover, simply dismiss the claim that, whatever the stabilising effects on the internal political life of the GDR, this policy was justified by the help it gave individual people, *die Menschen*. How can we possibly put a value on the freedom which the Bonn government bought for nearly 300,000 people? And the temporary freedom for the millions who could travel to the West? Yet one may at least ask if the overall price paid for these gains was not a worse existence at home for the majority.

Here we again enter the treacherous realms of the counter-factual, of 'what would have happened if . . .' If the Bonn government had pursued a somewhat tougher policy in the 1980s, being less generous in its financial dealings, making explicit linkages to respect for human rights inside the GDR, pressing more loudly for reform, 'recognising' the independent groups as fully as it did the regime, could this have resulted in, or at least facilitated, that combination of reforms and the growth of civil society which one saw elsewhere in East Central Europe?

Some have gone a step further and argued that such a combination, if introduced early enough, might even have saved the GDR. In 1990 this argument was made, with different emphases, by leading figures from the younger generation in the Party, by some members of the opposition groups which led the peaceful protests in autumn 1989, and by some sympathetic politicians, scholars and intellectuals in the West. In whatever precise form the argument is made, it assumes that there was a possible 'third way': a system attractive enough to compete with the liberal capitalist democracies of the West, yet different enough from them to justify a separate state. Since it was precisely this hope of a 'third way' which 1989 marked the end of all over Eastern Europe, and 1991 in the Soviet Union, it is difficult to see how it could have survived just in the GDR — for all the considerable resources of ideological ingenuity present in that small space.

Even if there were such a 'third way', which might conceivably have justified a continued division of Germany, it is almost impossible to see how this could have justified the continued division of Berlin. Democratic socialism at one end of the Friedrichstrasse and social democracy at the other? And a state frontier in between? Yet without East Berlin there would hardly be a GDR, and West Berlin could not seriously be expected to risk joining the great new adventure.

Earlier reforms and a stronger civil society might, however, have meant a different end to the GDR: one in which a reformist Party leadership made a more constructive retreat, while the population had its own experienced and sophisticated political counter-élite, its shadow government in waiting. Both were notable features of the 'refolutions' in Poland and Hungary. As a result, the East Germans as a whole might have gone in to the process of unification with somewhat more self-respect and higher morale. In other words, there is a question whether West German policy did not, in some small degree, also contribute to that demoralisation of the people in East Germany which was so apparent during and after unification. Did not the patronising approach (*Bevormundung*) by the government in the West aggravate, at least to some degree, the systematic denial of adult responsibility (*Entmündigung*) by the regime in the East? Yet this is, we must stress again, a suggestion made on a highly speculative basis of 'what if . . ?'

Another, related, speculation concerns the rapid turn in East Germany after the opening of the Wall from the cry of 'we are the people' (*Wir sind das Volk*) to that of 'we are one people' (*Wir sind ein Volk*). Here two claims for West German policy are made. The first is that the defensive Deutschlandpolitik of the Christian Democrats, rhetorically holding high the constitutional claim to unity and jealously guarding the fine legal distinctions that underpinned it, contributed to keeping alive the hope of unification in the hearts of ordinary East Germans. The second claim is that the offensive GDR-policy of promoting contacts of all kinds between the people in the two states, pioneered by Social and Free Democrats, did indeed keep alive among people in the GDR the consciousness of belonging to one nation. Neither claim can be lightly discounted, nor does one contradict the other.

Yet given the context in which revolution turned to unification, some scepticism is in order. The fact is that all over Eastern Europe in 1989, as in 1848, the ideas of liberty and nation went together. Everywhere, but everywhere, the hope of one was seen in the other. Moreover, the common sense case for joining the Federal Republic, as the fastest route to secure prosperity, liberty, democracy, the rule of law — and protection from possible reversals in the East — was so overwhelming, that one may doubt if the earlier nuances of consciousness made a decisive difference. One is tempted to suggest that even if the Federal Republic had totally ignored the German Democratic Republic for the previous twenty years, the East Germans would still have come knocking on West Germany's door.

The degree to which the German nation actually had been 'held together' can also be overstated. We recall the startling figure that eighty-four per cent of a representative sample of West Germans had 'no contacts' with East Germans in 1988. And if one was impressed by the cry of 'we are one people' in East Germany, then one could also be struck by the degree to which profound differences between 'Easterners' and 'Westerners' persisted — and even grew — after unification.

With all these 'if' arguments, however, we still have to bear in mind one rudimentary constraint on West German policy: the position of the hostage city West Berlin. Even if all the criticisms made above were allowed, one could still argue that West Germany had to deal with the GDR in more or less this way because of West Berlin. As we have seen, the largest part of the direct financial transfers to East Berlin was related directly to improving the position of West Berlin.

This position was sometimes compared to that of Hong Kong. Now, in 1991 the British Prime Minister became the first Western leader to pay an official visit to Peking since the massacre of students on Tiananmen Square in June 1989. The Prime Minister had to do this, British officials said, because of the position of Hong Kong. Loud moralising and megaphone diplomacy would not help the people on the spot. Quiet diplomacy was best. The resemblance to the argument made by Brandt and his team from Berlin was very striking. Yet when the Prime Minister actually got to Peking, he spoke out strongly and publicly on human rights — not least because of pressures from public and political opinion at home.

So even in such a tightly constrained policy there is a range of possibilities in what one says and how one says it. When the Mayor of Bonn went to the new partner town of Potsdam in 1988 he pleaded publicly for the release of those arrested after the Luxemburg/Liebknecht demonstration, and declared that he would speak out for human rights 'whether in Potsdam or in South Africa'. Far from Mayor Daniels earning all-round applause from political and public opinion in the Bonn republic, however, he was widely criticised. The Social Democratic Bundestag member for Bonn, Horst Ehmke, suggested that he should apologise to his East German hosts.

The most serious questions about West German policy are perhaps ultimately less about what was done than about what was said — or not said — to the leadership of the GDR and the people of the GDR; and what was said — or not said — about the GDR. For in the condition of permanent communication between the two halves of Germany created above all by television, there was no clear dividing line between speaking to and speaking about.

This is a complex subject, but let us start with a simple assertion: the public picture of the GDR presented by most West German policy makers and opinion-formers in 1987 was hard to reconcile with the public picture of the GDR presented by most West German policy makers and opinion-formers in 1991. The former was remarkably positive and friendly. The negative features of the GDR, and especially of its frontiers, were of course mentioned, but the general syntax of commentary was: *on the one hand* there is the Wall, the Stasi, shortages, greyness etc, but *on the other hand* there are small improvements for *die Menschen*, social security, the rediscovery of Germanness, the commitment to humanity and peace. And 'the other hand', that important but easily abused intellectual instrument, worked overtime.

The commentary in 1991, by contrast, was almost uniformly negative. A whole vocabulary for the description of a dictatorship — starting with the word 'dictatorship' — which had largely disappeared from the polite society of German politics, was rediscovered overnight with the end of the dictatorship. To substantiate this generalisation would of course require extensive documentation, for how otherwise can one show what is 'typical' and what not? Here the reader will simply have to take the generalisation on trust.

Now as we have seen, it is possible, and even, up to a point, plausible to argue that this flattering treatment of the GDR was part of a long-term strategy designed to change the way in which the rulers of the GDR ruled. Here was recognition and reassurance designed to produce relaxation and reform. We have tried to show how oblique and paradoxical were the real effects of this long-term strategy on the GDR. But there remains the question whether West German policymakers did not actually come to believe some of what they said. And even if — as experienced politicians — they did not believe what they said, whether other people in the Federal Republic, especially younger people, did believe it.

An ambassador, according to a famous English definition, is a good man sent to lie abroad for the good of his country. The Federal Republic carefully emphasised that its Permanent Representative in East Berlin was not an ambassador. And his task differed from that of an Ambassador also in this: that he was a good man sent to lie in his own country for the good of his country. And this did not just apply to the Permanent Representative. Because of the condition of permanent communication between the two halves of the divided country, politicians, officials, journalists, academics, priests, writers — all were players in the great game of intra-German relations. All could feel themselves to be, in some small degree, permanent representatives. Their words had political weight. The temptations into which this could lead were strikingly anticipated in a letter which one of West Germany's most famous writers, Günter Grass, wrote to Willy Brandt in February 1970.

'As a result of the new Ost- and Deutschlandpolitik of the social-liberal coalition,' wrote Grass, 'the Stalinism inside the GDR is no longer critically treated and Stalinist attacks from the Honecker camp rightly [*sic*] go unanswered. This behaviour, relaxed and right in itself, can nonetheless lead inside the SPD to the false conclusion that there might soon be a reconciliation with the SED . . . Already the understandable desire for détente is producing curious side-effects.' And then he came to the point, which was that West German television (ARD) was declining to broadcast his play about the 17 June 1953 rising, *The Plebeians Rehearse the Uprising*, on the grounds that this could disturb relations with Moscow and, above all, negotiations with the GDR.

'In other words,' wrote Grass:

> the change of climate in the Federal Republic brought about by the change of government has, beside a whole series of favourable and liberating democratic developments, encouraged increasing uncertainty in the judgement of the social systems in the two German states. Extreme swings in Germany, familiar of old, suggests that the cold warriors of yesterday can in no time transform themselves into effusive peace-apostles . . .

(The letter is marvellously characteristic of the writer's — all writers' — train of thought: there must be something wrong if they won't broadcast my play!)

The development that Grass anticipated, and then at times himself seemed to exemplify, went through self-censorship to relativism. It is important to understand the shape this relativism took in the 1980s. It was not a simple restatement of the 'convergence' theories of the 1960s, according to which communist 'industrial society' and capitalist 'industrial society' would necessarily converge; although if one listened carefully echoes of that theory could still be found. But explicitly and repeatedly the leaders of West German political opinion said that the two systems could not be reconciled, an interpretation heartily endorsed by the East German leadership.

Socialism and capitalism were like fire and water. However, both fire and water have their uses as well as their dangers. This new relativism consisted, firstly, in a concentration on the overarching common problems — the threat of nuclear war, environmental destruction, hunger and overpopulation in the Third World — beside which mere system differences in Central Europe could appear insignificant. Secondly, it was founded on a consistent effort to look at the 'brighter side', the positive qualities, of the East German state and/or society — with the distinction between state and society often being blurred. Out of the attempt at 'normalisation' came, gradually, the conclusion that a certain normality had been achieved, that, for all its faults, the GDR was another possible version of Germany, or at least, that life in the GDR offered another possible way of living as a German.

In place of the clear, and to be sure simplistic, contrast between freedom in the West and dictatorship in the East, there was now talk of the two states' different 'terms of business' (Klaus Bölling), of a 'Peace of Augsburg' between the two systems (Günter Gaus), implying that the difference between communism and liberal democracy was comparable to that between Protestantism and Catholicism. After all, did not both worship the same God, the God of peace? Klaus Bölling wrote in his 1983 memoirs that Erich Honecker's self-confidence had grown because he knew 'that time has passed by all the reunification ideas of the Adenauer era, because it is the general consensus in East and West that peace is after all a higher good than those articles dedicated to the thought of freedom which can also be found in the constitution of the GDR'. So much for freedom.

Of course there were countless variants and gradations of this relativism. And of course it cannot solely be ascribed to the effects of a détente policy towards the GDR. It was certainly more widespread on the left than on the right. The years that saw the birth of the social-liberal Ostpolitik also saw fierce criticism of the real, existing Federal Republic, against which was counterposed the vision of 'another republic'. Not only in the generation of Herbert Wehner but also in the class of '68 were attitudes to *the* other German republic related, albeit in very complex and often contradictory ways, to hopes of *an* other republic at home. Somewhere in both was still the hope of a 'third way'. The specific story of the West German Social Democrats is examined in more detail in Chapter Six.

Almost as important, and overlapping this particular history of the left, was the peculiar history of German Protestantism, in West as well as East. From this quarter, for example, came the notion that the division of Germany was in some way God's punishment for the sins of the fathers. There is a very important book still to be written on the political history of German Protestantism over the whole period from 1933 to 1989.

There is also a distinctive history of journalism, and of scholarship. In journalism, political, ideological and cultural motives mixed with simpler common factors, such as competition for a good story and self-censorship out of the fear of expulsion or visa-refusal — that 'visa syndrome' familiar from writing about the rest of the Soviet bloc. In scholarship, there were also the familiar conflicts of generations and disciplines. A younger generation of scholars embraced a social scientific approach to analysis of the GDR, ostensibly value-free, 'taking the system on its own terms', against an older generation of political scientists and lawyers, with their value-loaded theory of 'totalitarianism'. After anti-communism came anti-anti-communism.

In 1990, once the East had voted for the West, the West generously supplied it with West German schoolbooks, so that young East Germans could learn the true facts about German history and politics. Opening these schoolbooks, the young East Germans — some of whom had just been on the streets demonstrating to get rid of the dictatorship — could read that 'both states [the Federal Republic and the GDR] understand themselves as democracies'. Elsewhere they would learn that the 17 June 1953 was 'the rising of a minority in the GDR, concerned mainly or even exclusively with social questions'. 'Read No. 10.24,' they would be instructed by another textbook, 'and try to explain why many citizens of the GDR are self-confident and proud of their state'.

None of this should be made simpler than it was. In a liberal democracy it should, however, be possible to distinguish clearly between the politicians and the intellectuals: the latter jealously guarding their independence, and attempting, as Havel put it, to 'live in truth', the former necessarily working in half-truth. Yet one of the features of the intra-German détente was that this distinction was very substantially blurred. The intellectuals — writers, journalists, scholars — became participants in the policy. Their analyses were coloured by the hopes or expectations of the policymakers, which their analyses in turn reinforced, which in turn . . .

So far as the politicians and policymakers were concerned, we may point to another palette of special causes. After unification not a few remarked, notably in relation to the economic weakness of the GDR, 'we didn't know . . .'. Although, as we have indicated, their own Western analysts did partly fail them, the strict answer to this must be that they could have known. There were, beyond this, a number of reasons specific to their *métier*. Politicians have to claim success, and that in the fairly short term. Since all parties now practised the policy of small steps, they all had to claim success for it. Small successes, to be sure, but if one goes on claiming small successes for a long time, then a lot of small successes must begin to add up to a larger one.

Secondly, there is the problem of repetition. An associate of Adenauer's has suggested that one of the reasons Adenauer came genuinely to believe in the goal of reunification near the end of his life, having perhaps originally embraced it more tactically, is that it is very difficult to go on repeating something publicly for twenty years without beginning to believe it yourself. Perhaps what happened to Adenauer with the aspiration to reunification happened, in reverse, with some West German politicians in the 1970s and 1980s. Constantly repeating that the GDR was a strong, stable, improving state, worthy of growing recognition, did they not come — just a little — to believe it?

For those most directly involved there was also sometimes an emotional element of discovering that older Germany which lay just under the surface of the Soviet-type state, following the familiar East European paradox of revolutionary conservation. In the case of Günter Gaus —

revealing precisely because it was extreme — it would not be too much to say that he fell in love with the GDR. Indeed, in a curious novella he wrote at the time of unification he portrayed her — if she it was — as a lost woman. While West Germany's leaders constantly insisted that the Federal Republic was not and would never be a 'wanderer between the worlds' (that is, East and West), a veteran practitioner of policy towards the GDR described himself precisely as a 'wanderer between the worlds'. And strange bonds developed between some of these intra-German negotiators, advocates, as they saw it, of elementary humanity, and defenders of the people.

If this sounds fanciful, there is another speculation which may seem even more so. There is a well-known psychological phenomenon — sometimes called the Stockholm Syndrome — in which hostages come to identify with their captors, or at least to show extraordinary appreciation of their 'humanity'. Now West German policymakers, while not themselves hostages, were nonetheless, as we have seen, acutely conscious of negotiating on behalf of hostages — the hostage city West Berlin, and *die Menschen* in the GDR. In a sense, from 1961 to 1989 Germany lived through a twenty-eight year long hostage crisis. It is quite difficult to work with people over many years, smiling for the photographers, doing the honours, sitting at the same table talking about peace and humanity, and still regard them as criminals. For if they are criminals, what am I doing shaking their hand and paying them compliments and hard currency?

In a remarkable article to mark Honecker's visit to Bonn, Helmut Schmidt concluded that the West Germans, having spoken for years of the oppressed East Germans as 'our brothers and sisters', should now welcome Erich Honecker as 'one of our brothers'. But then, in his memoirs, he observed: 'the charge that the Federal Government allowed itself to be blackmailed in the "buying free" of prisoners always angered me, although *or rather because* it was factually correct' (author's italics). Those three little words — 'or rather because' — surely capture an important psychological truth. Trying to make a virtue out of necessity, one ended up ascribing some of the virtue to the necessity. My blackmailer, my brother.

In his valedictory speech to the Bundestag in 1986, Schmidt himself identified the emotional tension that he also exemplified. 'The suffering caused by the partition,' he said, 'brings the recurrent danger that the chronic German inclination to emotional overreaction breaks dangerously through.' Indeed, in looking at the ups and downs of the West German perceptions of East Germany, one thinks of nothing so much as of 'The Marquise von O.' Readers may recall that in Kleist's story the Marquise believes herself to have been saved from a fate worse than death by a noble Russian officer, only to discover that he himself had raped her while she swooned — yet finally marries him. At the end of the story her new husband asks her why, after the discovery, she shrank away from him as if he were a devil. She would not have taken him for a devil, sighs the Marquise, if she had not first taken him for an angel.

In the history of West Germany's relationship to the GDR we see a double reverse Marquise von O. effect. First, in the 1950s, the GDR was demonised. Then, in the 1970s and 1980s, it was increasingly idealised. And then, in the early 1990s, it was demonised once again. Yet through all this the most salient feature of the GDR was just how little it changed: arguably less than any other state in Eastern Europe. Certainly the way the GDR treated its own citizens changed much less than the way the Federal Republic treated the GDR.

Now some might feel that such an impressionistic account of states of mind — and heart — has no place in a serious analysis. How much safer to stick to sober facts about trade and traffic and rail links! And really such statements should only be made biographically, for each individual is a special case. Yet the real dereliction of intellectual duty would be not to mention the emotional depths at all, for, difficult as they are to describe, they were nonetheless very, very important.

After the end of the dictatorship comes the process known in West Germany after 1945 as *Vergangenheitsbewältigung*, that is, overcoming or coming to terms with the past. In the case of the Third Reich, beside self-examination by the Germans there was a less acute self-examination by peoples to the west. How much had Britain, for example, contributed to the horrors, by the policy which gave the previously positive term 'appeasement' a lasting bad name? Should Britain not have done more to encourage, or at least to recognise the efforts of the German resistance to Hitler?

Now the GDR was not the Third Reich. It did not practise genocide and it was in no position to start wars. Its army and security forces took part in one invasion in Europe — that of Czechoslovakia in 1968 — and a few lesser 'advisory' actions in the Third World. Otherwise, its evils were confined to home, and even its domestic evils were, on the whole, lesser evils than those of the Third Reich — although their effects could be more insidious because they lasted so much longer. The self-examination of those who served, or merely accepted, this regime was made in some ways easier, but in many ways more difficult, by the fact that they were doing it no longer 'among themselves', like the Czechs or Hungarians, but in the same house as the West Germans.

Yet there was also a lesser self-examination to be made on the West German side. For the Federal Republic's responsibility for what happened in the GDR was greater than that of any other Western state in relation to any other Eastern state. Did West Germany really do all that was in its power to combat, limit, or at least moderate the everyday evils of the GDR? Was the right balance struck between the interests of West Germany itself, of West Berlin, and of the people in the GDR? Did policymakers distinguish clearly enough between party-state and society? Was 'buying free' the best and only possible way to help those who dared to protest? Did all that negotiation, hard currency, recognition and self-censorship really achieve the desired effects? Even if it did, what was the price, in demoralisation in the East and relativism in the West? Did not some West Germans come, after all, to accept the GDR as another sort of German normality? And if so, what did that say about their own norms?

V

Beyond the Oder

History and frontiers

In a seminal essay on West German foreign policy, the historian Richard Löwenthal once described the Federal Republic as the product of a 'double conflict' with the Soviet Union. There was, he wrote, a common conflict of the West, including the West Germans, based on the shared desire to preserve freedom this side of the 'Yalta' dividing line. But there was also a special conflict of the West Germans, based on the desire for reunification and a refusal to accept the loss of German territories east of the Oder-Neisse line. In this latter conflict, the Federal Republic could count only on limited, and dwindling, support from the West. Writing in 1974, Löwenthal described the Eastern treaties as the Federal Republic's 'liberation' from this special conflict, a liberation that was 'on the whole successful'.

Yet looking at the Federal Republic's relations with Eastern Europe in the 1970s and 1980s, his optimistic verdict seems more than a little premature. For what is most striking about these relations is the extent to which they continued to be shaped both by the legacy of the past and by the Federal Republic's own continued pursuit of a set of special, national goals. West Germany's relations with the states and societies of Eastern Europe since the Eastern treaties cannot possibly be understood without reference to the results of pre-1945 German Ostpolitik, on the one hand, and to the intentions of post-1961 Deutschlandpolitik on the other.

The past did not weigh equally on all the Federal Republic's Eastern ties. West Germany's relations with Hungary, Bulgaria and Romania were markedly easier than her relations with Poland, Czechoslovakia or the Soviet Union. It has been suggested that this is partly because the first-mentioned countries have never had a common frontier with Germany. There is some truth in this. It is a general rule of modern European history – at least until 1945 – that neighbouring states are more likely to be enemies, while the neighbour's neighbour is more likely to be a friend.

Thus Germany goes with Russia against Poland, France with Poland against Germany, and so on. The great Polish-Jewish-British historian Lewis Namier memorably called this 'the rule of odd and even numbers'.

Yet Germany's post-1945 relationship with the neighbour's neighbour Soviet Union and with unadjacent Yugoslavia was heavily burdened, while that with adjacent Switzerland was clearly less so. For beyond, and cutting across, this general factor, the specific causes lie in the period 1938-47, and the question of who did what to whom in that terrible decade. If we look more closely, the crucial difference seems to be that between wartime allies and wartime enemies. Hungary, Bulgaria and Romania were – less or more willingly – allied to, or satellites of, Hitler's Reich for most of the Second World War. They neither suffered so heavily from German occupation, nor inflicted such heavy suffering on Germans in return.

It is no accident that the diplomatic 'normalisation' of relations with just these three countries was accomplished without major, fraught negotiations, and, indeed, without formal treaties. Other factors subsequently made a particular relationship more difficult (e.g. Ceauşescu's dictatorship, and ill-treatment of the German minority), or easier (Hungary's reforms, and good treatment of its German minority). But the history of these countries' relations with Germany and the Germans before the founding of the Federal Republic was not in itself a major, ongoing burden.

It was such a burden with Poland, Czechoslovakia and the Soviet Union. The complex, rich and troubled history of their relations with Germany is reflected in a complex, rich, but also very troubled historiography. Partisan interpretations, polemics, apologies, double standards and special pleading have abounded, even in supposedly scholarly work written decades after the disputed events. There were always notable and honourable exceptions, both in Germany and in Eastern Europe. There has more recently been a general although uneven improvement in standards both of national scholarship and international scholarly exchange. (Each requires the other. Good scholars talk and listen to their foreign peers, but it is no good talking to scholars who are no good.) To attempt to make any concise generalisations or overall judgements nonetheless remains an extremely difficult and risky undertaking.

Insofar as it directly affected Ostpolitik, this history may very crudely be divided into five main chapters: the whole, long period up to the moment of first territorial encroachment by *Wehrmacht* and *SS*; the period of war with Germany and German occupation; the post-war reprisals against, and mass expulsions of, the Germans; the major conflict that still persisted after the founding of the Federal Republic on the issue of the new frontiers drawn in what we call in shorthand 'Yalta' Europe; and, last but not least, the position of the remaining German minorities in what was now called Eastern Europe.

Only in the Polish case was the balance plainly negative even in that first, long chapter. Men and women of goodwill on both sides of the Oder-Neisse line have tried to evoke the happier moments of German-Polish relations. They recall the rich cultural and technological interchange in the late middle ages or the period of German liberal enthusiasm for the cause of Polish independence in the 1830s, when every romantic poet worth his salt (and many not worth it) penned a song for Poland. Yet the sad truth is that long before 1939 the German-Polish relationship was one of the most tense and difficult in Europe.

Both German views of Poles and Polish views of Germans were poisoned by the fact that, from the partitions of the late eighteenth century until 1918, Germans had ruled over Poles, often bringing good administration and economic progress, to be sure, but also crushing the Poles' insurrections and, in the late nineteenth century, attempting to 'Germanise' their children. In this period, too, the whole previous history was rewritten by both sides, in textbook, ballad and historical novel, through a nationalist prism.

The re-creation of an independent Polish state in the bitterly contested Versailles settlement of 1918/19 meant the transfer to Poland of territory in which Germans had not only lived but ruled for more than a century. Co-existence was tense wherever Poles ruled Germans or Germans ruled Poles, not to mention in the Free City of Danzig (Gdańsk). Poles and Germans engaged in armed struggle for control of Upper Silesia, a conflict that was hardly resolved by arbitrary partition. The German minority in Poland was discriminated against by the Polish authorities, who viewed it as a 'fifth column' for the 'revisionist' or 'revanchist' aspirations which German governments, including that of the harmonising Europeanist Gustav Stresemann, did indeed harbour. And then Hitler's Germany and Stalin's Soviet Union joined forces to erase the Polish state from the map of Europe, in what has been called the fourth partition.

'*Placet*', wrote the Habsburg empress Maria Theresa in the margin of the first partition decree of 1772, 'because so many great and learned men wish it so. When I am long dead, people will find out what will come of this violation of everything that up to now was sacred and just.' Writing in 1990, Bishop Josef Homeyer, a dedicated advocate of Polish-German reconciliation, commented wryly: 'We have found out.'

In the Czechoslovak – or rather Czech and Slovak – and Soviet – or rather Soviet-Russian – cases it is possible to derive a less wholly negative balance from at least part of the pre-war chapter. The shared history of Czechs and Germans, in some respects even until 1938, was one of compromise as well as conflict, of mutual enrichment as well as bitter rivalry. The formal renunciation of the Munich Agreement in the 1973 treaty with Czechoslovakia did begin to make it possible for Czechs as well as Germans to start looking back 'before Munich', although the legally qualified nature of that renunciation, combined with the strength and radicalism of the Sudeten German lobby, would combine to reopen the wound after 1989. The Slovaks' historic oppressor was Hungary rather than Germany, and the wartime Slovak republic was another ally of Hitler's Reich, until honour was saved at the eleventh hour by a brief uprising.

The German-Russian relationship is one of the most contorted, and psychologically complex, in all European history. It contains, as Sebastian Haffner has written, almost every conceivable variant of relations between two nations. But throughout, on both sides, there was admiration as well as distrust, fascination as well as repulsion. Germans might be more ready than Russians to recall the part played by Germans, since the eighteenth century, in the attempted modernisation (and westernisation) of Tsarist Russia. Russians might be more ready than Germans to recall the spirit of Rapallo. Neither might like to recall the Hitler-Stalin pact. But none of this shared history, good and bad, could be completely forgotten.

Of course, these pre-war histories were buried under the memory of war, occupation and post-war reprisals. Here, too, the balance was somewhat different in each case. Poland was again the extreme. With the single, unique exception of the Jews, no people suffered more terribly under German occupation than the Poles. Beside three million Polish Jews, some three million ethnic Poles were killed, more than a million were forced to go to work in Germany, hundreds of thousands were driven out of their homes to make way for ethnic Germans from further east, all were deprived and oppressed. But it was then to Poland that nearly a quarter of post-1918 Germany was assigned, at Stalin's behest, with the assent of the United States and Britain. It was then from these territories that the largest number of Germans was expelled, at Stalin's behest, with Roosevelt and Churchill's assent, but also with the direct brutality of Poles taking revenge. The British historian of Eastern Europe, Norman Davies, writes: 'For the first time in their lives, a great mass of ordinary and decent Germans were reduced to the sort of predicament which most ordinary and decent citizens of Central and Eastern Europe had come to regard as normal.' Horror followed horror.

'One ought,' observes the German historian Golo Mann, 'to look upon events and decisions between 1939 and 1947 as a chain of evil actions and evil reactions.' Yet the image of the chain invites the question: where does the chain begin? With Hitler? With Stalin before Hitler? With the First World War before Stalin? And so one enters that historiographical danger zone where the necessary, balanced account of a full historical context can slide into moral relativism and national apologies – a minefield now staked out with signs marked *Historikerstreit*.

Plainly the tangled web of causality and responsibility – more skein than chain – cannot even be properly laid out, let alone disentangled, here. Perhaps the only just comment on this whole terrible last act of Europe's second Thirty Years' War is the verse written in 1939 by the poet W H Auden:

> I and the public know
> What all schoolchildren learn
> Those to whom evil is done
> Do evil in return.

Such light sovereign compassion may be possible for an Englishman, particularly an Englishman watching from New York. It was not possible for those directly involved.

The post-1945 Polish and German historiographies of this period were therefore like distorted mirror images of each other. German historians at once documented, with minute acerbity, the horrors of the Polish expulsions. Only later, in the 1960s, did they move on to document the prior horrors of German occupation. Polish historians at once documented, with minute acerbity, the horrors of German occupation. Only much later did a few independent scholars and intellectuals try to open up the question of the Polish deportations. (The asymmetry was compounded by the asymmetrical position of the two historical professions. From the 1950s, West German scholars were free agents in a way that Polish contemporary historians only began to be in the 1980s).

The Czech case was comparable, if not quite so extreme. The wartime occupation was terrible, but not as comprehensively murderous as in Poland. The post-war reprisals and expulsions were often brutal, and they were carried out not, as in Poland, on the orders of a puppet communist government directly under Stalin's thumb, but on the instructions of a legitimate and still semi-autonomous Czechoslovak government. Here too, the distorted mirror image was broken by free West German scholars in the 1960s, and by independent, isolated – indeed banned – Czech scholars a decade later. The shadow remained, but it was not as long or dark as in the Polish case. Nor did it find quite such persistent expression in official relations, whereas Polish government claims to compensation payments for victims of German occupation, and German government demands on behalf of the remaining German minority, continued to figure high on the Polish-German agenda throughout the 1970s and 1980s.

The Soviet case was different again. Soviet citizens of all nationalities suffered terribly in the war and under German occupation. The totemic phrase 'twenty million Russian war dead' may be allowed to stand for this suffering, even if, as Norman Davies has observed, it was probably not twenty million, many of them were not Russian, and quite a lot were victims of Stalin's dictatorship rather than Hitler's war. Yet the fact that Soviet citizens also suffered terribly under their 'own' dictatorship, both before and after the war, gave the memory at least a different context from the Czech and Polish ones. So did the Hitler-Stalin Pact, and Soviet-German co-operation in the fourth partition of Poland.

Moreover, the Soviet Union won the war – more, it won an empire.

Germany lost a Reich stretching into the east of Europe. The Soviet Union gained an empire stretching into the centre of Germany. The overall German-Soviet balance sheet for the years 1939 to 1949 thus showed huge profits as well as losses on the Soviet side: at least, so long as one considered gaining an empire to be a profit. As we have seen, some West German policymakers, particularly those of the 'front generation', felt a deep psychological need to make moral 'compensation' to the Soviet Union for its wartime losses – a feeling sometimes curiously mixed with the awe of the vanquished for the superior strength of the victor. But Stalin took his 'compensation' at once, in lands and men. What is more, he took it more from Poland than from Germany. This is perhaps the deepest irony of the historical legacy.

The history of wartime diplomacy is exceedingly complex, and in part still unclear due to the shortage of Soviet sources. Yet there is little doubt that the incorporation of eastern Germany into Poland was fundamentally dictated by the incorporation of eastern Poland into the Soviet Union. It is of course true that the Western allies wished to punish, and themselves contemplated dismembering, Germany – and above all Prussia, the imagined heart of darkness. It is true that some Polish leaders saw the more developed territories in the west as, in the circumstances, a good swap for the lost eastern territories, as well as providing a militarily more defensible frontier. But it is also true that in the last years of the war the legitimate Polish Government-in-exile bitterly opposed this westward shift. And Churchill, who in 1943 had encouraged Stalin's scheme, argued at the Potsdam conference that the southern part of Poland's new western frontier should follow the line of the eastern rather than the western River Neisse. (In 1939 some 2.7 million Germans had lived in the large part of Silesia between the two Neisse rivers.) It was Stalin's unbending insistence on keeping almost all the territory that he had first acquired by the Hitler-Stalin pact which led directly to the 'compensation' of Poland in the west, and it was Stalin – speaking both in his own name and through his Polish puppets – who insisted on the western Neisse.

For the Soviet Union, this was a double gain. Not only did it acquire vast new territories, under its direct or indirect control. It also ensured that the new Poland and Germany would be in bitter conflict over the lost German territories, and therefore that the new Poland – whatever the precise complexion of its regime – would be beholden to the Soviet Union for the security of its western frontier, so long as Germany would not accept the permanence of that frontier. For who else would actually defend the Oder-Neisse line? In one move, Stalin destroyed the German Reich, tied Poland to Russia, and added yet one more cause for hatred between Germans and Poles.

Having achieved the new frontiers *de facto*, the Soviet Union then devoted its formidably consistent diplomatic attention to securing full, formal, binding, ceremonial recognition of these frontiers *de jure*. The concluding protocol of the Potsdam conference said that 'the final delimita-tion of the western frontier of Poland should await the peace settlement'. However, the final peace conference, with a formal settlement and treaties, such as had taken place after the First World War, did not happen. It was pre-empted by the Cold War. Beside the legal recognition of frontiers, the Soviet Union wished so far as possible also to secure recognition of the political status quo that it had established behind those frontiers, of all that it comprehensively styled 'the post-war realities'.

In the circumstances of the time, the new East European states had little choice but to recognise both the Soviet Union's new western frontiers, which deprived Hungary, Czechoslovakia and Romania as well as Poland of some of their pre-war territory, and each other's new frontiers. The new German leaders in the Soviet Zone of Occupation were initially loath to recognise the Polish western frontier. (It is sometimes forgotten that they had proportionately almost as many refugees and expellees from the east.) As late as 1947 Otto Grotewohl declared: 'The Socialist Unity Party regrets any change of frontiers. It rejects the Oder-Neisse line as much as frontier changes in the west.' But they were soon drummed into line. In the 1950 Görlitz Agreement between the GDR and the Polish People's Republic, East Germany ceremonially recognised the Oder-Neisse line not just as the frontier between the two socialist states, but as 'the state frontier between Germany and Poland'.

The challenge was, therefore, to secure recognition from the major Western powers and from the new Western Germany, which claimed to be the legal heir of the German Reich and to speak for all Germans. To recall Löwenthal's distinction, this was an issue both in the general East-West conflict and in the special conflict of the Federal Republic with the East.

In the struggle for recognition of the frontiers, the Soviet Union was joined formally by all its East European allies, but with particular emphasis by Czechoslovakia, Poland, and of course the GDR. As we have seen, 'recognition' was, for the East German state, an issue of life or death. The same might almost be said for the new Polish state, and this in a double sense. Given the Soviet incorporation of eastern Poland, the Polish incorporation of eastern Germany was a *sine qua non* for the continued existence of any but a rump Polish state. The Poles deported from eastern Poland physically took the place of the Germans deported from eastern Germany. Polish Lwów moved to German Breslau, and made it Wrocław. At the same time, the Soviet-imposed regime in Poland had a special interest in the Oder-Neisse line, since this was the only issue on which it could firmly reckon with the support both of the mighty Catholic Church and of the majority of the population. Similarly, although with less intensity, all Czechs were interested in a final, definitive recognition of what they saw as the pre-Munich rather than the post-Yalta frontiers of Czechoslovakia.

The story of this 'frontiers issue', the *Grenzfrage*, is one of the most intricate in contemporary European history: a pleasure-ground for connoisseurs of legal and diplomatic detail, and an impenetrable thicket for the layman. For our purpose, the essentials are these. In 1975, Leonid Brezhnev seems to have believed that he had finally achieved definitive Western recognition of the post-war status quo in Eastern Europe, and therewith of the Soviet position in the heart of Europe. The Helsinki Final Act was this recognition from the West as a whole: the sealing of Yalta. The Federal Republic's Eastern treaties were the recognition from West Germany. Both the general and the special conflicts were thus apparently resolved. The fruits of his generation's sacrifice in the Great Patriotic War were now secured 'for ever', as he had candidly expressed the thought to Alexander Dubček when justifying the invasion of Czechoslovakia in August 1968.

The West saw it rather differently. It is true that the Helsinki Final Act contained the most solemn undertakings to 'regard as inviolable . . . the frontiers of all States in Europe', to 'refrain now and in the future from assaulting these frontiers', and to 'respect the territorial integrity of each of the participating states'. But before that it declared, in a formula negotiated by Henry Kissinger on behalf of the Federal Republic, that the signatory states 'consider that their frontiers can be changed, in accordance with international law, by peaceful means and by agreement'.

It is true that the Moscow Treaty emphatically and exhaustively declared that both signatory states 'regard as inviolable now and in the future the frontiers of all states in Europe, as they run on the day of signature of this treaty, including the Oder-Neisse-line, which is the Western frontier of the People's Republic of Poland, and the frontier between the Federal Republic of Germany and the German Democratic Republic'. It is true that the Moscow, Warsaw and Prague treaties all declared that the contracting parties 'have no territorial claims . . . and will not raise any such in future'. But, as we have seen, these commitments were qualified in a number of important ways.

The 'Letter on German Unity', handed over by the Bonn government on signature of each of the main Eastern treaties, asserted that these treaties did not contradict the 'political goal' of the Federal Republic to 'work towards a state of peace in Europe in which the German people regains its unity in free self-determination'. The Bonn government simultaneously assured the Western allies that their 'rights and responsibilities relating to Germany as a whole and Berlin' were not affected by the Moscow Treaty – a contention crucially underlined by the subsequent conclusion of the Quadripartite Agreement on Berlin. The Common Resolution of the Bundestag emphasised that the Eastern treaties were no substitute for that final, binding, legal peace settlement which had obviously been envisaged at Potsdam more than a quarter-century before. The Federal Constitutional Court, in a judgement calculated to confound all but the most hardened jurist, averred that the German Reich continued to exist in the frontiers of December 1937 – the original Allied definition of 'Germany as a whole'. The Federal Republic, said its highest court, was as a state identical with that German Reich but 'so far as its territorial extent is concerned "part-identical", so that to this extent the identity does not aspire to exclusivity'. (Is that clear?)

These reservations were thus at once legal, with reference to past arrangements, and political, with reference to possible future arrangements, where, however, both kinds of reservation were more emphatically expressed by West Germany than by the other major Western powers, while the legal and the political, the past and the future, were all ambiguously intertwined. The diplomatic-political language had to bridge not only differences between East and West, but also differences between West Germany and the rest of the West, and, what is more, significant differences within the West German body politic.

The West German argument of the early 1970s, which continued to rumble on right through the 1980s, might at first sight be described, with obvious and deliberate oversimplification, as one between politician-journalists of the left and politician-jurists of the right. The politician-journalists, typified by Brandt and Bahr, and supported by much of published opinion, argued on grounds of morality and realism. While they acknowledged the formal constitutional and legal position, and had of necessity spent a great deal of time negotiating fine legal and diplomatic details, they were impatient of what Brandt called the *Formelkram* (formula stuff). For them, the Warsaw Treaty was a frontier treaty. That was the reality. Germany had given up the territories east of the Oder-Neisse line. Here was the price, a heavy and bitter price, to be paid for the crimes of Nazi Germany. Morality demanded that this should now be stated clearly.

Yet more even than morality, it was political realism that demanded this. For only by making a clear and explicit statement could one begin bringing the Germans in East and West Germany closer together, with Soviet acceptance, if not approval. Trust – Soviet and East European trust – was a vital part of the political capital that West German Ostpolitik had to build up. The firmer the acceptance of the German-Polish frontier, the greater the chances of opening the German-German frontier.

The position of the politician-jurists of the right was more complex. As late as 1989, a suggestion by a leading German specialist on international relations (and Social Democrat) that Konrad Adenauer had already privately given up the territories east of the Oder-Neisse line for lost in the early 1950s would provoke a storm of controversy. Adenauer's most authoritative biographer, Hans-Peter Schwarz, considers that at the beginning of the 1950s Adenauer was still genuinely a territorial revisionist. Yet as early as 1955, Adenauer reportedly told the leader of the Social Democratic opposition 'Oder-Neisse, Eastern provinces – they're gone! They don't exist any more!' Schwarz also shows that by the late 1950s Adenauer had come privately to accept that, realistically, recognition of the Oder-Neisse line would now be a *quid pro quo* for the Western allies' support for any reunification of the Germans between Rhine and Oder. This had by no means always been the American or British position. Indeed, following Byrnes' Stuttgart speech in 1946 the United States had rather encouraged questioning of the Oder-Neisse line. But at the very beginning of détente, Kennedy and Macmillan as well as de Gaulle made it clear that this now was their common position.

Why, then, attempt to qualify, obscure or even deny this political reality with legalistic paper castles? Three reasons can be adduced. First, the surrender of any claim to the territories east of the Oder-Neisse line was still a diplomatic card for Germany to play. An increasingly faded and dog-eared card, to be sure, but you do not simply throw away a card still notionally representing a quarter of the German Reich without getting something more than promises in return.

Second, the complex legal positions continued to have real political substance inasmuch as they were the only basis in international law for the claim to reunification even of West and East Germany, however remote that prospect might seem. If it ever became possible, the starting point for the international negotiation of unification would still have to be the unfinished post-war settlement, and the fragile origami of international and constitutional law which held that unfinished settlement in permanent suspension over Germany and Europe. Even if one wished to settle the specific Oder-Neisse question finally, one could not excise the part without jeopardising the whole.

Where the politician-journalists of the left said that opening (even a little) the German-German frontier required a final sealing of the Polish-German frontier, the politician-jurists of the Right argued that a final sealing of the Polish-German frontier might actually preclude, or at least make much more difficult, a final opening of the German-German frontier. Where the former spoke in the name of moralism and realism, the latter urged legalism and idealism. The conversion to painstaking legalism came very soon after 1945. (The historian Elizabeth Wiskemann, who had witnessed Nazi Germany trampling all principles of law all across Central Europe, wrote that 'it is difficult for Germany's neighbours not to smile sourly over this post-1945 legalism'.) This legalism was not just the *déformation professionelle* of lawyers or legally trained diplomats and politicians. It was also, as Egon Bahr's closest legal adviser on the Eastern treaties observes, the classic resource of the weak and the defeated.

At the same time, however, there was in the best version of liberal-conservative legalism an element of genuine idealism. Alois Mertes, an outstanding and influential representative of this liberal-conservative tradition, argued that to maintain these legal positions was also to hold up for people in East Germany the prospect – however remote – of free self-determination. The realists, in this view, were thinking too much in the short-term, and not paying sufficient regard to the great imponderables of history. In this sense the position of Germany's liberal-conservative legalists might be compared to that of the Poles who maintained a government-in-exile in London in the 1980s. Unrealistic, anachronistic, absurd – but it was from the President-in-exile and not from President Jaruzelski that President Wałęsa chose to receive the insignia of his new office in 1990, thus asserting the ideal continuity of a legitimate Polish government. Similarly, the balance-sheet of this German upholding of legal principles, in defiance of political realities, might look rather different after 1990 than it did in the late 1980s.

As Alois Mertes expressed it, the liberal-conservative position was that the constitutional claim for the continued existence of the German Reich in the frontiers of December 1937 was the necessary starting-point for any negotiation about German unification, but by no means the target of any such negotiation. On the contrary, he repeatedly emphasised that the quality of the German-German frontier, which divided one people, was now fundamentally different from that of the Polish-German frontier, which now divided two peoples. As Adenauer's close associate Wilhelm Grewe also insisted, reunification therefore meant reunification of East and West Germany. An interesting exchange of letters between Mertes and Egon Bahr in 1984 makes clear that on this basic point those bitter opponents of the early 1970s were actually in agreement, though the journalist Bahr cattily remarked that the jurist Mertes put in 'too much effort' to work out the legal niceties. (The devil, replied Mertes, is in the detail, as Soviet diplomats well knew.) And it was on precisely this point that the liberal conservatives crossed swords with ageing leaders of the expellees like Herbert Hupka and Herbert Czaja, who still somehow wished to regard the frontiers of 1937 as a target, not merely a starting-point.

In the essential substance, then, one might argue that the crucial divide was actually not – as it seemed – between politician-journalists of the left and politician-jurists of the right, but rather between the liberal conservative legalists, on the one hand, and the genuinely revisionist, nationalist right, with its hard core among the expellees, on the other. Yet it required a sharp, informed and dispassionate eye to notice this, especially since neither left nor right was interested in emphasising in public the common ground across party lines, while the more Social Democrats (or Free Democrats) pointed up divisions in the Christian Democrat ranks the more Christian Democrats would be at pains to deny them. Here we come to the third main reason for maintaining these legal-symbolic paper castles: the relationship of the Christian Democratic leadership to its own nationalist right wing, especially in the Bavarian Christian Social Union, to the leaders of the expellee organisations, and to the expellee vote.

West German leaders almost ritually invoked the 'Stuttgart charter' of the German expellees from the East, in which, as early as 1950, the expellees renounced any thought of 'revenge or retaliation'. This is true, and admirable. But it is also true that many of the German refugees and expellees from the East would not, or simply could not, accept the loss of their ancestral homelands as history's last word. (If Poland had been a free country in the 1950s there would surely have been a mighty organisation of Polish expellees.) In the 1950s this was still a burning issue in West German politics. No major German party would dare publicly to declare the territory to the east of the Oder-Neisse for lost, whatever the private conviction of this or that politician might be. (The West German Communists' public support for the Soviet and East German position on this issue was a major step in their self-marginalisation.)

Looking back from the 1970s, Willy Brandt himself observed that the peaceful integration of these millions of refugees and expellees was one of Konrad Adenauer's greatest services to his country. This was a double integration. It was, first, a social and economic integration. With a large initial investment by the state, partly financed by a special tax, the Silesians and Pomeranians and East Prussians and Sudeten Germans were successfully integrated into what then became (partly through this process) West German society. Indeed they contributed much to the so-called 'economic miracle', with the energies of the uprooted. But it was also a party-political integration. In the course of the 1950s, the Christian Democratic Union and the Bavarian Christian Social Union managed to mop up the right-wing expellee vote, squeezing the expellees' and right-wing nationalist parties down below the five per cent hurdle, and thus into parliamentary oblivion. This was a major contribution to the stability of West German democracy. But it also carried a price in the (growing) disparity between the private conviction and the public rhetoric of Christian Democratic leaders on the issue of frontiers, and the dismay this public rhetoric could cause abroad. At the same time, the fear of nationalist splinter parties remained in the bones of the Christian Democrats, revived as it was by electoral challenges from the National Democratic Party in the 1960s, and from the *Republikaner* in the 1980s.

It is only against this background that one can understand the public posture of Chancellor Kohl and his government on this issue. An author who knew Helmut Kohl well recalls that already in 1970, over a glass of good Palatine wine in the cellar of the state chancellery in Mainz, the then Prime Minister of the Rhineland-Palatinate thought of making a public declaration that the Federal Republic should accept the Oder-Neisse line.

This would be the beginning of a German reconciliation with Poland, such as Adenauer had achieved with France, and would enable Warsaw to view the prospect of German unity with greater equanimity. The next morning, however, after telephone conversations with a few prominent colleagues in his own party, including Richard von Weizsäcker, he rapidly concluded that the time was not ripe.

Of Helmut Kohl's private recognition of this frontier there could really be little doubt. Yet again and again, throughout his Chancellorship, right up until the early summer of 1990, he allowed uncertainty and doubt and misunderstanding to arise around the issue. Near the beginning of his Chancellorship, it was Friedrich Zimmermann, the Interior Minister from the Christian Social Union (with particularly strong expellee representation within its ranks), who put the cat among the pigeons by averring, as a political rather than merely a juridical claim, that Germany continued to exist in the frontiers of 1937. In 1985 the Chancellor himself was at the eye of the storm, when he seemed to be about to address a meeting of refugees and expellees from Silesia, on what was billed as the 'fortieth anniversary' of the expulsion, under the remarkable motto 'Silesia remains ours'. Eventually he did address the meeting, under the revised motto 'Silesia remains our future in a Europe of free peoples'.

In his speech, Kohl said that the Federal Government's position was predictable and *unmissverständlich*, that is, literally, unmisunderstandable. He then simply listed, as he had done so often before, the legal bases of his government's position, from the Basic Law to the judgement of the Federal Constitutional Court. These, he blithely repeated, made the German legal position unmisunderstandable. His government could not and would not change this legal position, he said, but it 'constituted no threat to our neighbours'. The expulsion of the Germans was a wrong, but so would another expulsion be – and he was able to quote a resolution of the Silesian association to this effect. Two wrongs would not make a right. 'Today,' he said, 'Silesia is inhabited almost entirely by Polish families, for whom this country has in the meantime become home (*Heimat*). We will respect this and not put it in question.' He went on to say that the real issue was not sovereignty rights but that of freedom for all those who lived beyond the East-West divide in Europe.

Now to deliver this message to an audience which raised banners saying defiantly 'Silesia remains ours', and in which a banner declaring 'Silesia remains Polish' was immediately torn down, was not merely appeasement. But nor was it, to use the Chancellor's own word, unmisunderstandable. Earlier in the year, the foreign affairs spokesman of his own party, Volker Rühe, had made the important statement that the Federal Republic's commitments in the Eastern treaties would also have a 'political binding effect' on a united Germany. Kohl did not venture even that far. And this was a summer in which the whole of Europe reflected on the fortieth anniversary, not just of the expulsion of the Germans but of the end of the Second World War, an occasion memorably and self-critically marked – just six weeks before – in a famous speech by the new Federal President, Richard von Weizsäcker.

What is more, Kohl's appearance before the Silesians came at a time when the Soviet media and Jaruzelski's Polish regime were engaged in a virulent propaganda campaign against West German revanchism. To be sure, the specialists in Moscow and Warsaw could perfectly well tell the difference between the liberal-conservative and the truly revisionist positions: between Helmut Kohl and his host at the meeting of Silesians, Herbert Hupka. But in the political context of the moment their political masters did not want to see that difference. The last revanchists in the West furnished ammunition for the last revanchists in the East. The actual effect on public opinion was probably not very great: even in Poland, where an independent opinion survey showed that only 4.7 per cent of those asked in 1984 saw a threat to Polish independence from the Federal Republic. But the effect on inter-governmental relations was serious. In distancing himself from Kohl's position, Hans-Dietrich Genscher was certainly in part 'winning profile' in the eternal Bonn game of coalition politics. Yet he was also representing real, immediate interests of German foreign policy.

In the second half of the 1980s, the issue faded somewhat from the public (if not from the Polish) eye, especially with the dramatic improvement in German-Soviet relations. It was revived in 1989, once again by a minister from the Christian Social Union talking about Germany in the frontiers of 1937, and not accidentally at a time when the right-wing *Republikaner* were seen to be gaining electoral ground, especially in Bavaria. In an attempt to clear the path for his great symbolic reconciliation with Poland, dreamed of already two decades before in that wine cellar in Mainz, Kohl supported a Bundestag resolution which contained the important new formulation – originally coined by Genscher – that 'the Polish people should know that its right to live in secure frontiers will not be put in question by us Germans now or in the future through territorial claims'.

Yet when the opening of the Berlin Wall, during Kohl's visit to Poland, opened the door also to German unification, the question of the frontier was still there. That it was still there as a point for international legal settlement was clear to all. Although Brezhnev had celebrated the Eastern treaties and Helsinki as the final peace settlement left unfinished in Potsdam, neither West Germany nor the West as a whole had ever accepted that spurious claim of finality. That it was still an issue of actual political controversy was, however, also the result of the specific developments inside West Germany that we have described above, and notably of the neo-Adenauerian domestic political strategy used by Helmut Kohl.

Bronisław Geremek, the outstanding Polish historian, Solidarity adviser and politician, whose own Jewish family was murdered by Germans in the war, records his conversation on this issue with Chancellor Kohl, in the autumn of 1989. 'The Chancellor tried to calm my fears concerning, among other things, the German position on the frontiers issue. I have the impression that he spoke sincerely. But when I asked him if I could make public the substance of our conversation he replied that if I did that he would immediately deny it. The justification given for this position was the realities of German politics.'

In his 'ten-point programme' of November 1989, which laid out steps leading to unification, Kohl did not mention the frontiers issue at all. The absence of this 'eleventh point' was much criticised, and not just in Poland. In March 1990, the Chancellor then surprised and appalled most of the partners with whom he was negotiating the unification of Germany by suggesting that a final treaty on the frontier was conditional on satisfactory binding commitments from the Polish side on the rights of the remaining German minority in Poland, and the renunciation of any further Polish claims to reparations for war damages. While the Chancellor soon retreated from this position, in the '2+4' negotiations for German unity, it was the other five (including Markus Meckel, the Social Democratic Foreign Minister of the now democratised German Democratic Republic), who pressed most forcefully for the unconditional recognition of the frontier precisely as it now ran between Poland and East Germany. For the Federal Republic, the final ratification of the final frontier treaty with Poland in the autumn of 1991 was still linked by the Bonn government to a further bilateral Polish-German treaty in which, among other things, the issue of German minority rights was addressed.

In a retrospective conversation with the author, in the autumn of 1991, the Chancellor left no doubt that this domestic political factor had been very important in his thinking. The strategic purpose had been to show the nationalist right and the last unteachables among the expellees that this was the price which Germany simply had to pay for the unification of the Germans between Oder and Rhine. (By his seemingly insensitive suggestions, provoking a storm of international criticism, he had indeed demonstrated this brilliantly.) He could then say, in effect, to the real nationalist-revisionists: do you wish to be responsible for sabotaging the unification of Germany?

If the liberal-left, as represented supremely by Willy Brandt, worked from the bases of moralism and a realism which included more than a touch of Machiavellism in foreign policy, the liberal-right, as represented by Chancellor Kohl, proceeded not only from legalism and idealism but also from a sort of Machiavellism in domestic politics – a Machiavellism which was in the real tradition of Konrad Adenauer quite as much as the desire for reconciliation with historic enemies. Some would say that without first securing their domestic power base the leaders of democracies will never have the power do the right thing in foreign policy, and the reckoning paid off magnificently in the end. Others would say that this approach helped to keep fading illusions alive, to rub salt in wounds that could have been more quickly healed, and that, in any case, there are issues in international affairs where such domestic political tactics, or even strategies, must yield to higher imperatives. What actually happened is now clear. The judgement must be the reader's.

Compatriots

The past therefore would not pass away, or at least, passed away much more slowly than many had anticipated in the early 1970s. There was another, more direct way in which the Federal Republic's 'special conflict' with the East continued to shape its relations with the Soviet Union and Eastern European. This was what may be called the permissive function of those relations for the Federal Republic's efforts on behalf of the Germans in the East. As we have seen, one of the two most important purposes of developing relations with Moscow was to permit Bonn to deal with the powers-that-were in East Berlin, in the interests of the people. Following the imperative of synchronisation, relations with East European states played an important supporting role in this overall scheme of Ostpolitik.

Yet beside this general, indirect permissive function there was also a specific, direct permissive function. This concerned the treatment by these states of their remaining German minorities. Like the frontiers issue, this is a subject of extraordinary historical complexity and emotional, legal and political sensitivity. Like the frontiers issue, it continued to haunt the Federal Republic's relations with the Soviet Union and Eastern Europe – and above all with Poland – even at the end of the 1980s. Unlike the frontiers issue, it remained a major point on the operative agenda of German Ostpolitik.

The basic outlines of the problem are as follows. After the vast movement of peoples, the modern *Völkerwanderung* across Central and Eastern Europe in the terrible decade from 1939 to 1949; after the expulsion of Slavs from their homes and their replacement by settlers from other parts of Germany or by ethnic Germans (*Volksdeutsche*) summoned by Hitler 'back into the empire' (*Heim ins Reich*); after the flight of millions of Germans before the advancing Red Armies; after the so-called 'wild expulsions' of Germans in the immediate aftermath of war, with Russians, Poles, Czechs, the peoples of Yugoslavia, and, in lesser measure, all the other peoples of Eastern Europe, taking bitter and often brutal revenge, sometimes on guilty but also on quite innocent Germans; after the more systematic 'transfers' of Germans, with the Western allies attempting – often vainly – to ensure that the pious wish expressed in the

Potsdam Agreement that these transfers should be 'orderly and humane' was not entirely ignored; after all this, some four million Germans nonetheless remained in the newly constituted communist states east of the Oder-Neisse line and south-east of the Erz mountains at the beginning of the 1950s.

The background and position of these Germans varied widely. There were German soldiers still held as prisoners of war in Stalin's camps. There were ethnic Germans invited to settle on the Volga and the Black Sea by Catherine the Great and Alexander I, but then deported to Central Asia and Siberia by Stalin during the war, as collective punishment for being German. Of the ancient German settlements in Bohemia, Moravia and Slovakia very little was left after the expulsions. Still intact, though beleaguered in the new Romania, was one of the most ancient of all the German communities in the East: the Germans of Transylvania, the Siebenbürgen Saxons, settled there since the early Middle Ages and described already by the eighteenth-century German historian August Ludwig Schlözer as *Germanissimi Germanorum*, the most German of Germans. Also relatively intact, though also beleaguered, were the more recent settlements at the invitation of the Habsburgs: the Germans in Hungary and the so-called Swabians of the Banat, now in Romania. From what was now Yugoslavia the Germans were almost entirely expunged.

Most complicated of all was the background and position of the remaining Germans within the frontiers of the new Poland. At one extreme there were those who were both indubitably German in culture, language and tradition, and had held German citizenship in the Reich in its frontiers of 1937. At the other extreme there were vaguely Aryan-looking Poles who had taken up the Nazi occupiers' offer to become Germans through the third and fourth categories of the so-called *Volksliste*, but had then smartly become Poles again after 1945. In between there were a great many people, above all in Upper Silesia, who for generations had lived amidst and between Polishness and Germanity, now turning one way, now the other, mixing blood, language, tradition, culture into an identity which was, simply – or rather, not at all simply – Silesian. Most of them were allowed to stay by the Polish communist authorities, being officially classed as 'autochthones'.

Such, then, were the sad puddles of Germanity which were all that was left, at the founding of the Federal Republic, of more than a thousand years of German settlement in the East. Given the real confusion of the time, and the deliberate confusion sown by the communist states' nationality statistics, all figures must be approximate, but of the total, the largest number – perhaps some two million – were in the Soviet Union, another one to two million – depending greatly on definitions – were in Poland, up to half a million in Romania, less than a quarter of a million in Hungary, still fewer in Czechoslovakia.

All Bonn governments, from Adenauer to Kohl, made it their business to help these Germans in the East. Socialists, liberals and conservatives agreed that this was a national duty: to help the Germans who were still suffering most from the consequences of the war and the 'Yalta' division of Europe. This concern, indeed this priority, was understandable. But it also saddled the Federal Republic with difficulties faced by no other Western state. Moreover, contrary to the expectations of 'normalisation' in the 1970s, the problems posed were in some respects actually more acute at the end of the 1980s than they had been at the end of the 1960s.

From the outset, Bonn governments were faced with a choice between two lines of action: to help the Germans in the East to stay there, by working to support their material, cultural, educational and legal position as a group in the given state, or to help them to leave, as individuals. Of course, one could in theory attempt to do both, as Bonn did in relations with East Germany. But there was at the very least a strong tension between the two approaches. Moreover, because of earlier German policies, each course laid Bonn open to suspicions and charges from the East.

Efforts to help the Germans to stay, by improving their lot as a minority, all too swiftly recalled the support given first by the Weimar Republic and even more by the Third Reich to what were then called the *Auslandsdeutsche* in the Versailles successor-states. In that period, German Foreign Ministry support, carefully laundered through foreign bank accounts, to organisations with such innocuous names as the *Konkordia Literarische Gesellschaft*, had paved the way for territorial revisionism. On the other hand, efforts to bring the Germans individually 'home' could be tarred with the brush of Hitler's '*Heim ins Reich*', while at the same time the new East European states feared to lose people who made an important contribution to their economies.

Bonn was thus likely to be damned one way or the other. Yet given the hatred, both popular and manipulated, of Germany and the Germans in the new Eastern Europe, given the obvious determination of the Stalinist leaderships to Polonise, Magyarise or Czechify their remaining Germans, the first option seemed nearly hopeless. In the early years of the Federal Republic, government policy therefore concentrated on helping individual Germans to get out. If in 1945 Germans were expelled against their will, in 1950 Germans were seen to be detained against their will.

This first priority was reflected in the terms applied to the Germans who came to the Federal Republic from the East. The prisoners of war in the East were described as *Spätheimkehrer*, late homecomers, the others as *Spätaussiedler*, literally late out-settlers. So far as prisoners of war were concerned, the term expressed an obvious and terrible truth. They were late homecomers indeed. As we have seen, the main immediate objective of Konrad Adenauer's trip to Moscow in September 1955 – the 'beginning of Bonn's Ostpolitik' – was to free those prisoners. Adenauer remarked that he was ready to talk to the devil's grandmother to get 10,000 people home, ten years after the end of the war. However, this trip also brought significant improvements for the ethnic Germans banished by Stalin to Siberia and Kazakhstan, in many cases releasing them from more than a decade of forced labour. In a second, extremely difficult round of negotiations with the Soviet Union, in 1957–58, the issue of 'repatriation' was a major bone of contention. Yet here it was already questionable whether Germans whose families had been settled in the Baltic states or Russia itself for generations should be described as late leavers. And had the Germans in Transylvania really been sitting on packed bags for eight hundred years?

In the 1960s, West German usage settled down with the simpler, although still curious term out-settlers, *Aussiedler*, not to be confused with the over-settlers, *Übersiedler*, from East Germany. The 1961 Bundestag initiative for a more active Ostpolitik was explicitly linked to the position and concerns of the Germans who remained in the East. The Brandt and Schmidt governments, like their predecessors, continued to press for emigration possibilities for the Germans in the East, and to point to the statistics of out-settlers as a measure of their 'success'. Moreover, they continued to do this using the remarkably generous definition of 'a German' established at the founding of the Federal Republic.

In the official translation, Article 116 of the Basic Law read as follows:

Article 116 (Definition of 'German', Regranting of citizenship)

(1) Unless otherwise provided by law, a German within the meaning of this Basic Law is a person who possesses German citizenship or who has been admitted to the territory of the German Reich within the frontiers of 31 December 1937 as a refugee or expellee of German stock (*Volkszugehörigkeit*) or as the spouse or descendant of such a person.

(2) Former German citizens who, between 30 January 1933 and 8 May 1945, were deprived of their citizenship on political, racial or religious grounds, and their descendants, shall be regranted German citizenship on application. They shall be considered as not having been deprived of their German citizenship if they have established their domicile (*Wohnsitz*) in Germany after 8 May 1945 and have not expressed a contrary intention.

There were thus two key categories, German citizenship (*Staatsangehörigkeit*) and German stock (*Volkszugehörigkeit*). German citizenship was defined according to a modifed version of the 1913 citizenship law of the (second) Reich, which gave central importance to the so-called *ius sanguinis*, that is, citizenship by descent. Whereas in America or Britain the *ius sanguinis* had long been complemented by the *ius soli* – that is, a person was American if born on American soil –, in Germany the emphasis remained on descent. A young Turk born and brought up in Germany had no automatic right to German citizenship, and, indeed, would find that citizenship quite difficult to acquire. On the other hand, a glance at the guidelines drawn up for officials at the Friedland reception camp for out-settlers shows that the descendants of people who had at any time between 1913 and 1945 been declared by the German Reich to be German citizens, whether in the former German eastern territories, the Memel, Danzig, the Sudetenland or even the Reich Commissariat of the Ukraine, would automatically qualify for citizenship of the Federal Republic.

But this was only half the story. The other, even more difficult half concerned the category of German stock. What was this? The Federal Law on Expellees and Refugees said: 'A member of the German *Volk* is . . . one who in his *Heimat* declared himself for Germanity (*deutsches Volkstum*), insofar as this declaration is confirmed by certain attributes such as extraction (*Abstammung*), language, upbringing, culture.' Beside the former German eastern territories (in the frontiers of December 1937), the possible *Heimat* in this definition was held to include Danzig, Estonia, Latvia, Lithuania, the Soviet Union, Poland, Czechoslovakia, Hungary, Romania, Bulgaria, Yugoslavia, Albania and China!

As the 1980 official guidelines for the application of this law indicate, there were thus two essential ingredients: the subjective declaration for Germanity (*deutsches Volkstum*) in your *Heimat*, and objective attributes to confirm this declaration. The guidelines went on to indicate that applicants must have shown 'by their behaviour the consciousness and will to belong to German *Volkstum* and to no other *Volkstum* . . .'

For people who lived in former German areas east of the Oder-Neisse line it would suffice that 'their overall behaviour show[ed] no demonstrative inclination towards another *Volkstum*'. In the case of mixed marriages one had to determine which parent had a dominant influence: 'If the dominant influence of one or the other parent cannot be established, the formative influence of the German parent is to be assumed.' The relevant moment for establishing whether there was a declaration for Germanity was 'immediately before the beginning of the persecution- and deportation-measures directed against the German population' – that is, in late 1944 or early 1945. For *Jewish* applicants, however, the relevant moment was before 30 January 1933, since after that date 'they could not be expected to declare themselves for Germanity'.

At this point the 1980 official guidelines defensively remarked: 'the concept of German stock (*Volkszugehörigkeit*) in the sense of article 6 . . . is fundamentally different from the national-socialist theory of *Volkstum*'. Yet the profoundly embarrassing fact was that, as a result of the definition in the Basic Law, and the way in which it was subsequently interpreted, West German officials at the Friedland reception camp were obliged to accept or reject candidates for German citizenship on the basis not merely of criteria that eerily recalled Nazi criteria (declaration for Germanity *and for no other Volkstum*), but actually on the basis of Nazi selection.

For example, as part of the attempt to Germanise occupied Poland, the Nazis in some places simply, arbitrarily, and often grotesquely declared Poles to be Germans, entering them in groups three or four of the so-called *Volksliste*. Group three membership, accorded to some 1.7 million people between 1941 and 1944, brought the right to citizenship after a period of ten years. So: produce your father's *Volkslistenausweis* in 1989, and you automatically became a West German citizen. Enrolment in the *Wehrmacht*, or other mass organisations of the Third Reich, had generally depended on a certification of Germanity, and was therefore accepted by the Federal Republic as evidence of it. Question 15 of the questionnaire for applicants asked whether you, your spouse, father, or another close relation belonged to the German *Wehrmacht*, *Waffen-SS*, Police, RAD (*Reichsarbeitsdienst*) or the *Organisation Todt*. They did? Welcome to West Germany. One way or another, roughly half of those accepted as out-settlers from Poland in the 1980s came through what one might call the Third Reich route. The others were descended, one way or another, from citizens of the Second Reich.

The general principle remained wholly understandable: the Germans enjoying freedom (and prosperity) should help the Germans who did not. So far as the Germans coming out of Romania were concerned, there was also relatively little difficulty in the concrete application of that general principle, for these people were self-evidently as German in descent, culture, language, upbringing, as any German in the Federal Republic – indeed, in some ways they were more German, *Germanissimi Germanorum*. The same applied to some, though by no means all, of the Germans in the Soviet Union. But for those areas of 'floating nationality' where for centuries people had been sometimes Czech or Polish, sometimes German, always Masurian or Silesian; for those areas, moreover, where, after 1939, the German authorities had tried to turn Poles into Germans, and then, after 1945, the Polish authorities had tried (perhaps less brutally, but more systematically and tenaciously) to turn Germans into Poles: for these areas the specific application of the general principle became simply grotesque.

Young Poles seeking – also quite understandably – a better life for themselves and their families in the West, would scrabble for proof of a Nazi skeleton in the family cupboard. Your father fought for freedom during the war? Conceal it as best you may. Not a family past in the Polish resistance but a past in the *Waffen-SS* would bring you freedom today. That a complete 'German past' could reportedly be bought on the black market in Poland for about $8,000 (1988 prices) seems, in the circumstances, less a criminal subversion of German nationality law than an ironic commentary upon it.

It was the Federal Republic's relationship with Poland, above all, that was bedevilled by this problem throughout the 1970s and 1980s. In the early 1950s the Polish communist authorities had tried to Polonise the remaining Germans within the frontiers of the new state. Following the Polish October of 1956, the Gomułka regime did permit very limited cultural freedoms to German communities in Lower Silesia, although not in Upper Silesia or the former East Prussia. At the same time, it permitted a wave of German emigration: just under a quarter of a million people came out in the years 1956 to 1959, more than one hundred thousand in the course of the 1960s.

When the negotiations for the Warsaw Treaty began in 1970, the Polish authorities at first maintained that there were no longer any Germans living in Poland. The German Red Cross said there were some 400,000 who wanted to leave, and estimates based on the legal definition outlined above brought a figure of more than one million potential German out-settlers. The social-liberal coalition reckoned that it could not get the treaty through parliament without some provision for these Germans to leave. The eventual compromise was a so-called '*Information*' of the Polish government which said that 'some tens of thousands' of Germans might still be found to be living in Poland. Unpublished 'Confidential Notes' confirmed that these persons should be allowed to leave in 'one to two years'. In the event, some 38,500 were allowed out in the next two years, but the flow then dwindled.

After coming into office in 1974, the new Chancellor, Helmut Schmidt, and the new Foreign Minister, Hans-Dietrich Genscher, made a deter-mined effort to resolve the whole complex of problems related to the German minority. Following a long and emotional late-evening talk between Schmidt and Edward Gierek in the margins of the Helsinki Conference in August 1975, their negotiators produced a package of agreements. This included a pension agreement covering the German minority, for which the Bonn government agreed to pay DM 1.3 billion over three years, and an extraordinary miniature treaty for a DM 1 billion loan at an annual interest rate of 2.5 per cent. In an accompanying 'Protocol' the Polish side stated that 'on the basis of investigations by the responsible Polish authorities . . . some 120,000 to 125,000 persons would receive assent to their applications [to leave] in the course of the next four years'.

Like the first Warsaw Treaty, however, this supplementary package was the subject of heated political debate in the Federal Republic, with the right shaping up for the 1976 federal election campaign by accusing the Schmidt government of giving in to communist blackmail and trading money for people. The attack on the billion DM loan was led by Franz Josef Strauss. (The billion DM credit he himself orchestrated for the GDR just seven years later was, of course, something completely different.)

Since the social-liberal coalition did not have a majority in the *Bundesrat* (the second chamber of parliament with representatives of the federal states), it was compelled to lean on the Polish government to make further, quite humiliating public assurances on the issue of German emigration, in order to give more liberal conservatives in Bonn (including Helmut Kohl) sufficient grounds to allow the package through. This done, and the money paid, the Polish authorities did in fact allow roughly the agreed number of people to leave.

Now an economic 'linkage' on the emigration issue was not wholly unknown in the Ostpolitik of other Western countries. The Jackson-Vanik amendment in the United States Congress made the development of US economic relations with any 'nonmarket economy country', and specifically the grant of Most Favored Nation status, dependent on that country allowing its citizens 'the right or opportunity to emigrate'. What had originally raised Senator Jackson's ire was the imposition of a per capita 'exit tax' on Jews wishing to emigrate from the Soviet Union. If the Soviet Union ended the tax, and generally made Jewish emigration easier, then it might get the Most Favored Nation status. In the case of Romania, Most Favored Nation status was awarded by Washington partly as recognition of concessions on Jewish emigration, though also of Romania's maverick stance in foreign policy. Yet this case also showed how difficult this sort of linkage was to make, for in the American political and policy-making process, the MFN status, once granted, proved extraordinarily difficult to withdraw, even when Romania had ceased to offer most of the original favours.

West Germany, by contrast, was effectively paying the 'exit tax' itself – but for those it considered to be its own citizens. As we have seen, this it did, both directly and indirectly, in relation to the GDR. So also with Romania. Here the business of 'buying free' began after a visit to Romania by President Heinemann in 1971. As with the buying free of Germans from the GDR, it began tentatively and conspiratorially, with cash being carried to the border in unmarked envelopes, but then gradually became regularised. Under an agreement reached between Chancellor Schmidt and President Ceauşescu in 1978, the Romanian dictator agreed to allow out at least 12,000 Germans per year for the next five years. The Bonn government agreed to pay a well-rounded per capita sum for these emigrants, a sum increased, when the agreement was renewed for another five years in 1983, to nearly DM 8,000 per head.

The 1975 deal with Poland was, however, uniquely ambiguous. What was this DM 1 billion 'jumbo credit' at knock-down terms being granted for? Was it an act of historic reconciliation or even delayed reparation? Or was it just a thinly disguised exit tax: cash for Germans? Was it a personal declaration of friendship from Schmidt to Gierek? Or was it, as the preamble to the agreement declared, 'to advance the conditions for the development of economic and industrial co-operation'? The problem with the 'jumbo credit' was precisely the cloudy mixture of motives and goals: moral and national, personal, political and economic. The one thing it certainly was not was good business – for either side. Between 1976 and 1980 the West German taxpayer paid DM 290.5 million in interest subsidies for this credit alone. Meanwhile, Gierek and his colleagues so misspent this and other Western credits that they not only ruined the Polish economy but also diminished rather than increased the country's chances of 'economic and industrial co-operation' with the West.

The only people who benefited (presumably) in the longer term were the more than 120,000 Polish Germans or German Poles thus 'bought free'. Yet the problem still would not go away. The more that left, the more there were who wanted to leave. The Germans in Poland multiplied like relics of the true cross: a development not unconnected with Poland's deepening economic crisis. At the end of 1983 the then Minister of State in the Foreign Ministry, Alois Mertes, observed that 'at least 120,000 Germans in the Oder-Neisse area and neighbouring areas of the People's Republic of Poland demonstrably desire to move permanently to the Federal Republic of Germany'. As we have seen this was not merely a practical problem. It was also a symbolic-political one.

In the same document which brought this answer – in the form of a long letter to a parliamentary colleague – Mertes estimated, on the basis of scrupulous calculations, that there were probably some 1.1 million people still living in Poland who were 'Germans' according to German law. He went on, however, to emphasise that 'over ninety per cent of the population' were Poles who 'now regard the Oder-Neisse area as their final *Heimat*'. And he concluded by recalling that liberal-conservative interpretation of Germany's position in international law which clearly indicated that a putative 'reunification' would include only the territory west of the Oder-Neisse line. His intentions were thus of the best. But they were misunderstood – in part deliberately so.

For the Polish authorities took this as a further ground for winding up, entirely in line with Soviet propaganda at that time, their own campaign against alleged West German 'revanchism': a campaign intended to mobilise the Polish population behind the Jaruzelski regime. It was a curious reward for the government which, of all major Western governments had shown most understanding for General Jaruzelski's attempts at 'normalisation' and 'stabilisation'. In this way, the German minorities issue, linked to the frontier question, once again blighted relations between the Polish and West German states.

Nor was it only the Jaruzelski regime. With that exquisite sensitivity to the feelings of other nations which he was later to display in his remarks on Polish-Jewish relations, Primate Glemp preached a sermon in which he said, in effect, that there were no Germans left in Poland, and they should anyway be glad to be Poles. Proudly he reported his retort to an old lady in West Germany who had asked him that no injury should be done to the Germans remaining in Poland. 'What Germans, what injury?' he had replied. This in turn provoked outrage in West Germany. And so, forty years after the end of the war, the bitter cycle of recrimination continued.

In the second half of the 1980s the remaining German minorities produced yet another problem for the Federal Republic. This time, it was a problem of success. For years, for decades, the Bonn government had urged and paid the authorities in Warsaw, Moscow and Bucharest (not to mention in East Berlin) to let their Germans go. And now, suddenly, they came, not just in their tens of thousands but in their hundreds of thousands. The total number of out-settlers from the Soviet Union and Eastern Europe soared from just over 40,000 in 1986 to nearly 80,000 in 1987, over 200,000 in 1988, a staggering 377,055 in 1989 and nearly 400,000 in 1990. The main reasons for this growth were twofold: a fundamentally altered emigration policy of the Soviet Union under Gorbachev, embodied in a new decree of January 1987; and the virtually free-for-all travel policy of the Polish government, combined with an economic situation that was a powerful incentive to take up the 'German option'.

Here, surely, was a great success for German Ostpolitik. Was not this precisely what Chancellor Kohl had demanded, with renewed emphasis, in his government declaration of 1983, referring to those concerned not merely as 'people of German origin' but simply as 'Germans'? Yet the result of this great flood of Germans 'coming home' was not an outpouring of national welcome and public delight but, on the contrary, a growing public resentment and resistance, reflected in election successes for the new party of the far right: the *Republikaner*. The *Republikaner* were a curious phenomenon: an extreme right-wing, populist nationalist party one of whose main sources of electoral support was resentment against newly arrived German nationals.

In vain did politicians from the President and Chancellor down argue that many of these Germans had suffered long and hard just for being Germans. In vain did they recall that a ruined Germany had after the war welcomed and integrated many times this number of Germans from the East. In vain did ministers and economists point out that these mainly young, often well-qualified, highly-motivated people would be a net economic gain to a country whose own native-born German population was shrinking and ageing. What disgruntled voters in the big cities like Berlin or Frankfurt or the poorer parts of rural Bavaria saw was housing, jobs, and extra social security payments going to newcomers, even in preference to the locals.

To understand this reaction one must understand that this large increase in the number of out-settlers came at the same time, and partly for the same reasons, as a large increase in the number of Germans moving from East to West Germany, and of other East Europeans (for in the terms of Yalta Europe, the East Germans and the Germans in the East were also 'East Europeans') who came to visit, to stay illegally, or to seek political asylum. Here it is important to note that if in article 116 of its constitution, and the subsequent interpretation of that article in law and government practice, the Federal Republic had a remarkably generous definition of Germanity, then in article 16 of its constitution, and the subsequent interpretation of that article in law and government practice, the Federal Republic had a remarkably generous definition of asylum.

Mindful of the way in which Germans persecuted by the Nazis had been granted asylum in Scandinavia, America, Britain and other free countries, the drafters of the Basic Law said simply, sweepingly: 'Persons persecuted on political grounds shall enjoy the right of asylum.' In practice, even people with the barest claim to have been persecuted in Eastern Europe were not actually sent back. In the second half of the 1980s, the number of asylum-seekers from Eastern Europe, and particularly from Poland, soared, while, with the gradual *de facto* softening of the regime at home, the grounds on which they claimed asylum became ever thinner. Already in 1987, some eighty-five per cent of all those applying for asylum in the whole European Community were doing so in the Federal Republic. The total number of asylum-seekers topped the 100,000 mark in 1988, while at the end of that year some 200,000 Poles were registered as staying 'not just temporarily' in West Germany.

The cause for popular resentment was thus by no means only the Germans from the East, but rather a whole great influx of strangers of all shades and backgrounds. Even the Berliner who moved from one end of the Friedrichstrasse to the other was not immune to this resentment, and the tension between the so-called *Ossis* and *Wessis* – roughly, Easties and Westies – would become acute after the complete opening of the German-German frontier. But beyond this, opinion polls revealed a rough continuum of resentment from the (least resented) Germans from the GDR, through Germans from Romania or Russia, to Germans (or 'Germans') from Poland, to Poles, to the people known until the early 1990s as 'Yugoslavs', and thence to the (most despised) Gipsies, Africans and other lesser breeds without the D-mark. As one wit observed, the hostility was directed against everything beginning with A: *Asylanten, Ausländer, Aussiedler* (that is, asylum-seekers, foreigners, out-settlers).

Ironically, it was the Federal Republic's own interpretation of its own nationality and asylum laws which helped to create this continuum, especially by its treatment of that dubious middle ground represented above all by the inhabitants of Upper Silesia. For between the Silesian who suddenly rediscovered a German past, in order to secure his family a decent standard of living, and the Silesian who sought asylum as a Pole, in order to secure his family a decent standard of living, there was, in truth, scant difference. They were both, as the popular joke had it, less *Volksdeutsche* than *Volkswagendeutsche*. But then, could not that equally well be said of most ordinary West Germans? And why not?

As a result of this unexpected and disconcerting development, the position of the German minorities became, like so many other aspects of German Ostpolitik, simultaneously an issue of domestic and of foreign policy. In domestic policy, a major debate began about the right of asylum. In foreign policy, the Kohl government began to give new emphasis and urgency to the second possible line of policy towards the Germans in the East: that of helping them to stay rather than helping them to leave. Beside the individual human right – to leave – the Bonn government increasingly placed the group rights of minorities.

People qualified as Germans under article 116 of the Basic Law should, it was argued in Bonn, be able to live as Germans in whatever state they now found themselves. They should have German-language teaching, cultural life, journals, church services etc, and equal opportunities. The unique culture of Central Europe had been made by the tense yet seminal co-existence of Slavs, Germans and Jews. The Jews could never be brought back, but the Germans might still play their part. This was thus, at its best, neither an illiberal nor an unattractive vision. But so long as the states of Eastern Europe remained communist, it remained just that: a vision.

Hungary was the exception that proved the rule. Here, in a state with a small German minority, relatively unburdened historic ties with Germany, and increasingly warm relations with Bonn, János Kádár's regime recognised the advantages that could accrue from an exemplary treatment of its Germans. On the first visit by a President of the Federal Republic, in 1986, Richard von Weizsäcker was entertained by schoolgirls from the so-called Swabians of the Danube, dancing folk-dances in colourful folk-costumes, singing folk-songs and reciting folk-poems. It was, said the President, 'an occasion that moves the heart'. The exemplary folk-treatment did not only move the heart-strings of the Federal President. It also moved the purse-strings of the Federal Government. In giving an untied DM 1 billion credit to the Hungarian government in 1987, Bonn made it very plain that this was partly in recognition of the good treatment of the German minority. On a visit to Hungary in 1988, the Christian Democrats' foreign affairs spokesman, Volker Rühe, went so far as to say that 'the treatment of minorities plays a dominant role in my present conversations with the Hungarian leadership and the Association of Hungary Germans'.

What is more, politicians and policymakers in Bonn made no secret of the fact that this credit was to be understood as a signal to other states in the Soviet bloc: if Poland, Czechoslovakia, Romania or even the Soviet

Union conferred such rights on their Germans, they too could expect such rewards. Put very crudely, Bonn, having for years paid to get 'our compatriots' out of Eastern Europe and into West Germany, was now ready to pay to keep them (voluntarily) in Eastern Europe and out of West Germany. In a somewhat unguarded comment in a radio interview in August 1988, Chancellor Kohl, asked about the Bonn-Warsaw negotiations, replied: 'Both sides must move here. The Poles want economic support, we think of our compatriots ... who live there.'

The theme was high on the agenda of German-Polish negotiations in the late 1980s, and in the round of German-Soviet negotiations in 1988-89. During Gorbachev's visit to Bonn in 1989, Kohl raised with him the subject of a possible separate republic for the Germans in the Soviet Union, either on the Volga, where many of them had originally been, or elsewhere. In both the Soviet and German press there was discussion of the suggestion, first raised by a leading German banker, of turning the Kaliningrad – that is, Königsberg – enclave into some sort of a special economic zone or autonomous region, with a major role for the Germans. Yet none of these discussions bore major fruit before the revolutions of 1989, while in Romania the position of the German (as of all other) minorities actually worsened in the last years of Ceauşescu.

The main effective thrust of West German policy right up to 1989 therefore continued to be in helping the Germans to leave rather than in helping them to stay. In sum, nearly a million people came to the Federal Republic as 'out-settlers' from the Soviet Union and Eastern Europe in the years 1950 to 1969, and more than 1.3 million in the years 1970 to 1989. This policy thus brought inestimable benefits to hundreds of thousands of individual human beings, who gained freedom and life-chances, albeit at the price of uprooting. There were also significant potential long-term benefits for the ageing West German population. The young out-settlers would, in time, help to pay their pensions.

Yet there were multiple ironies here. A general objective of Ostpolitik was to restore a traditional German presence in Central and Eastern Europe, in a constructive, peaceful, liberal form. But one effect, one 'success' of this Ostpolitik, was to deplete the remaining, permanent, settled German presence in the region. The slow death of centuries-old German communities in Transylvania or the Banat was, by any standards, a further Central European tragedy. It was the continuation of Potsdam by other means. Obviously the primary responsibility lay with the communist regimes in Bucharest, Warsaw or Moscow. Perhaps Bonn had no alternative. But the plain fact is that Bonn directly contributed to – and in part simply paid for – this depletion of the remaining German communities. What is more, the domestic impact of this deeply ambiguous foreign policy 'success' was to fuel popular resentments, bring votes to a new far-right party, and even increase criticism of the Ostpolitik.

Carrots and sticks

'Foreign trade,' said the architect of West Germany's *Wirtschaftswunder*, Ludwig Erhard, 'is quite simply the core and premiss of our economic and social order.' The Federal Republic was (and is) dependent on foreign trade to an extraordinary degree. In the 1980s, at least one third of its gross domestic product was derived from exports. About one in every five jobs depended directly on foreign trade. The Federal Republic was (and is) a 'trading state'.

Long before 1945, Walter Rathenau had adapted Napoleon's famous remark to Goethe that 'politics is our fate'. 'The economy', said Rathenau, 'is our fate.' The new phase of intensive industrial development after 1945 greatly increased Germany's overall dependence on foreign trade. But this was also exacerbated by the post-1945 truncation of Germany's territory. Whereas previously the country had obtained many of its raw materials and energy supplies from its own eastern territories – Silesian coal, for example – the diminished state(s) had now to import them, and to export more to pay for those imports.

For most of the post-war period there was in fact an obvious complementarity between the supply and demand profiles of West Germany and Eastern Europe. Not only was West Germany able to supply the manufactured goods and technology that Eastern Europe increasingly sought. West Germany was also able to take more of the primary goods that the Soviet Union and Eastern Europe had to offer in return: whether natural gas, basic chemicals, gherkins or geese.

This complementarity was not lost on Soviet leaders. Indeed they were inclined, on occasion, to build upon it grand hopes – and threats. 'You forget,' Khrushchev told the French Foreign Minister Christian Pineau, 'that [Germany's] economy is much less complementary with yours than with that of the USSR. When you begin to compete with German industry, it will turn towards the USSR where it will be able to find an appropriate area for expansion. That will be the time of a new Rapallo. Then you will be sorry that you didn't listen to us.' And the German ambassador to Moscow at the beginning of Brandt's Ostpolitik records Kosygin saying to him in 1971: 'We have all the raw materials in the world, you have the know-how. Let's get together, and we'll be autarkic.' As we have seen, Brezhnev also harboured visions of grandiose German-Soviet economic co-operation.

Though German leaders obviously took a far more sober view of what was possible, and knew that the balance of Germany's economic self-interest lay overwhelmingly in the West, they nonetheless had both an economic and a political interest in expanding trade with the East. In the circumstances it would have been a mark of extreme abnormality if West

Germany had not had a substantial trade with its neighbours to the east and south-east. In the late 1940s and early 1950s that was the deeply abnormal position. West Germany's trade with Eastern Europe grew strongly in the 1960s, and then, as we have seen, even more rapidly through the 1970s (see Table II), with the increase mainly being accounted for by the growth of German-Soviet trade. German politicians described this as a piece of 'normalisation', but what full 'normality' would be it was extraordinarily hard to say.

Throughout the 1970s and 1980s, the Federal Republic's trade with the Soviet Union and Eastern Europe, excluding the GDR, was never more than seven and a half per cent of the country's total foreign trade. If one included trade with the GDR, the figure reached a peak of more than nine per cent in 1975. However, while the actual volume of eastern trade continued to expand, the *proportion* of West Germany's total trade done with the European members of Comecon actually declined over the next decade. West German policymakers never tired of repeating that the Federal Republic's eastern trade was less than its trade with Switzerland. The repetition was made, however, with slightly different emphasis to different audiences. To worried Western allies, and especially to Americans, the statement was one of reassurance: don't worry, it said in effect, our trade is so small that there is no danger of our becoming dependent on the East. To their own businessmen, and to Soviet and East European partners, the statement was rather: look how ridiculously small this is, we must increase it!

Speaking to the Economic Association of the Iron-, Tin- and Metal-Processing Industry at the height of the debate about the ratification of the Eastern treaties in 1972, Walter Scheel declared that the figure for 1971 was 'not much, in the light of the importance of a neighbouring economic area with some 350 million inhabitants. It is only 3.8 per cent of our total foreign trade . . . Before the war it was twelve per cent for the German Reich.' Fifteen years later, addressing the World Economic Forum in Davos, his successor Hans-Dietrich Genscher formulated the same proposition in rather more cosmopolitan terms. 'At present, economic exchange between East and West is at an extraordinarily low level, if one considers the potential on both sides. For the Federal Republic, for example, the largest trading partner of Comecon, eastern trade is only four per cent of total foreign trade.' And then he made the by now almost ritual observation: 'to Switzerland alone we export one and a half times as much as to all the European Comecon countries put together'.

Scheel's comparison with the pre-war Reich would immediately spring to mind – and especially to East European minds – when discussing the return of a major German economic presence in the East. It was, however, impossible to make with any precision. In 1938 the German Reich did twelve per cent of its trade with just six countries of south-eastern Europe.

But this was a result of the distinctly abnormal German economic expansion after the depression. In 1929 the figure was only 4.5 per cent. So perhaps we should rather go back to before the First World War? But then trade with nearly half of post-1945 Poland would have counted as domestic trade, inside the frontiers of Germany!

In trade, as in other aspects of Germany's eastward relations, there simply was no 'normal' status quo ante, no historical moment to which one could reasonably aspire to 'get back'. Nor was there any generally accepted definition of 'normality' in relations between planned and market economies. Moreover, if one was making a comparison with the position of Germany before the war, one would surely have to include East Germany's trade with the Soviet Union and Eastern Europe. But that was measured in different and strictly in-comparable units of account. Only after the collapse of communism in Eastern Europe and the reunification of Germany would it become possible to make such comparisons properly again.

In the circumstances of 'Yalta' Europe, the real comparison was with the eastern trade of other Western states. What one can say with confidence is that by the mid-1980s West Germany had more trade with the Soviet Union and Eastern Europe than any other Western power: three times more than the United States or Japan in 1985, and nearly four times more if one included trade with the GDR. What was true of trade was also true of the other main aspects of economic relations. West Germany's banks lent more money, its firms transferred more technology. And when joint ventures became possible, Germany was again in the lead.

West Germany was not very dependent on this trade, but it was relatively more dependent on it than any other Western state – with the signal exceptions of Austria and Finland. Specific branches of West German industry, moreover, had a much higher direct dependence on eastern trade. In the mid-1970s as much as twenty per cent of the exports of the iron and steel industry went east. The leaders of these industries, and the banks that supported them while also lending directly to the east, had a significant voice in Bonn. They were an important lobby. Estimates of the number of jobs directly dependent on this trade varied from 100,000 to 300,000. As a result of successive pipeline deals, by 1989 West Germany depended on the Soviet Union for thirty per cent of its natural gas – some five per cent of its imported energy supplies. If the original interest in developing eastern trade was mainly political, the effect of this politically-driven expansion was nonetheless to increase the real economic interest as well.

As the comments by successive Foreign Ministers indicate, there was also a vague, unquantifiable sense that there should be a larger eastern market there in the future, as there had been in the past. It has been well observed that the discussion of Central Europe among European intellectuals in the early 1980s hovered between nostalgia and utopia. Yet even German businessmen had their nostalgias and utopias, even trade had its poetry. The leading German banker involved in eastern trade, F. Wilhelm Christians of the Deutsche Bank, paints in his memoirs a glowing vision of the special role that Germans could play in modernising the Russian/Soviet economy. He compares it with the relations of the dynamic ethnic German Ivan Stolz to the permanently recumbent Russian Oblomov, in Goncharov's famous novel.

'For centuries,' declared Walter Scheel, to the assembled masters of the Iron-, Tin- and Metal-Processing Industry in 1972, 'the German businessman in the East has realised our natural role as the mediator between the products and needs of West and Central Europe on the one side and of the Balkans and Eastern Europe on the other'. Referring to the Mannesmann pipes being supplied to the Soviet Union, he declared: 'I myself find it especially satisfying that these pipes are once again fulfilling the leading and connecting function given them by nature.'

Yet any real economic, political, or, so to speak, anticipatory West German dependency on eastern trade fades into insignificance beside the growing real dependency of Eastern Europe on West Germany. Throughout the period under review, virtually all the European members of Comecon looked increasingly to the West for trade, technology, finance and know-how, and their leading partner in the West was the Federal Republic. As indicated in the 1969 Budapest Appeal of the Warsaw Pact, this was an important original motive for their opening to the West, and specifically to West Germany.

By the mid-1980s, the Federal Republic accounted for between a quarter and one third of the western trade of all the East European states except Romania (for which the figure was lower) and the GDR (for which the real figure was still higher). An extreme case of dependency was Hungary. By the end of the 1980s, some forty per cent of its gross domestic product was created by exports. Because of the different units of exchange in the eastern and western markets it was impossible to say precisely what proportion of this trading state's total exports was taken by West Germany, but a quarter of all Hungary's exports to OECD countries went to the Federal Republic, which accounted for no less than half her total trade with the EC. According to the statistics, West Germany was second only to the Soviet Union as a trading partner. Qualitatively, it was second to none. By the end of 1989 about a third of the country's joint ventures were with German companies and another third with Austrian ones. Such figures are an important background to understanding the crucial foreign policy decisions of Hungary's still ostensibly socialist political leadership in 1989.

At the other extreme was the Soviet Union. In 1989 it was only dependent on trade for some eight per cent of its Gross Domestic Product, and trade with the West accounted for less than a quarter of its total foreign trade. Nonetheless, already in the late 1970s, more than a quarter of all the Western high technology supplied to the Soviet Union came from West Germany. By 1989 some eighteen per cent of its Western trade was with West Germany (and almost exactly the same proportion of its trade inside Comecon was with East Germany). German banks held the largest single portion of its hard currency debt, much of it in loans guaranteed by the Bonn government. As Gorbachev made crystal clear on his visit to West Germany in June 1989, once the Soviet Union embarked on economic perestroika, it was looking to West Germany above all for trade, technology and know-how in the vast enterprise of modernisation.

In sum, all the European states which had, or had had, a Soviet-type centrally planned economy faced a common general dilemma of growing relative economic backwardness. Western Europe was pulling further ahead. Both the revolution of high technology already engulfing the far West and Far East, and the progress towards a single West European market in 1992, threatened to widen the gap still farther and faster. In confronting this dilemma, they all, collectively, had to recast their relationship to the West in general and the European Community in particular. But of the individual states in the EC, they all looked in the first place to West Germany.

This growing dependency, and even greater expectation, once again recalled a central problem of Western policy towards Eastern Europe and the Soviet Union. From the very beginning, from even before the Federal Republic had any diplomatic relations with the East, it had been thought, in Bonn as in Washington, that the economic power of the West would be a major, perhaps *the* major instrument of achieving Western political goals in the East. From the very beginning, the question of how to use that economic power had been hotly disputed in the West. Increasingly, the line of hottest dispute tended to run between Bonn and Washington, with Paris, London and Rome taking up intermediate positions.

Of course this is to simplify a very complicated story. German leaders had not invariably been opposed to economic sanctions, nor were American leaders always averse to offering economic incentives. In 1963 it was Konrad Adenauer who embraced the idea of a grain embargo against the Soviet Union. As he told de Gaulle, the West should say to Moscow: 'If you want grain, show your goodwill and get rid of the Berlin Wall!' Such a grain embargo would, however, have hit the American economy harder than the German one. What actually happened in 1962/63 was an embargo on the export of large-diameter steel pipes to the Soviet Union, which hit the German economy harder than the American. The Federal Republic only reluctantly went along with this American-led embargo – but to the Americans' surprise, the British were even more recalcitrant. Moreover, although the phrase 'change through trade' – *Wandel durch Handel* – sounds particularly euphonious in German, some of its earliest advocates were actually American liberals.

Even in the 1970s, the most far-reaching statement of the case for 'change through trade' came not from a German but from a French-American of Polish-Jewish origin, Samuel Pisar. His influential book of 1970, *Coexistence and Commerce*, was enthusiastically hailed by Valéry Giscard d'Estaing as 'the bible on East-West economic relations'. At the same moment the veteran German practitioner of eastern trade, Otto Wolff von Amerongen, was warning against the 'romantics of eastern trade', and painting a much more sober picture of what might seriously be expected. It is true that some West German politicians – including Franz Josef Strauss – displayed what was almost a vulgar Marxism in their belief that the economic base would alter the political superstructure. But a naive faith in the automatic, transformative qualities of economic exchange and imported Western technology could be found on both sides of the Atlantic, and at both ends of the political spectrum.

American businessmen sometimes found themselves closer to the position of the German government than to that of their own on these issues. While still a businessman at the Bechtel corporation, George Shultz railed against what he called 'light-switch diplomacy': that is, the idea that business ties could be turned on and off at will for political purposes. Conversely, parts of the German defence establishment may sometimes have been closer to the Pentagon than to their own political leaders in their concern about the transfer of militarily usable technology to the Warsaw Pact. Any generalisation about American-German differences is, moreover, made doubly difficult by the fact that whereas there was one, largely consensual, German approach, there were many different American ones – successively and even simultaneously.

The Nixon-Kissinger team's cautious advocacy of trade liberalisation and economic inducements to the Soviet Union, broadly linked to Moscow's conduct in foreign policy, was itself soon curbed and distorted by the narrower restraints and linkages imposed by Congress through the Jackson-Vanik amendment (see page 238). With these still remaining in force, the Carter administration attempted a more closely calibrated 'economic diplomacy' of leverage and linkage, as advocated by Zbigniew Brzezinski and Samuel P Huntington. Here there was to be a direct linkage not only to the foreign policy but also to the domestic political conduct of the Soviet and East European regimes, and particularly to their record of respect or disrespect for the human rights of their more independent-minded citizens. One part of the Reagan administration then advocated an even harder-nosed punitive linkage, while another part – represented most visibly by the defence specialist Richard Perle – returned to a notion of economic warfare against the Soviet Union which was closer to the early

1950s than it was to the early 1970s. Each of those approaches was, however, directly affected and changed by Soviet actions on the one hand, and, perhaps even more, by the policies and reactions of the United States' West European allies on the other.

For all these caveats and complexities, the fact remains that there was, from the late 1970s until the late 1980s, a major argument within the Western alliance about the proper place and uses of economic instruments in Ostpolitik, and Bonn and Washington were the two main poles of that argument. The argument began, in a minor key, with a small set of sanctions – strictly speaking, vetting procedures on specified US exports to the Soviet Union – imposed by the Carter administration in 1978, with an explicit linkage to the treatment of prominent Soviet dissidents such as Alexander Ginzburg and Anatoly (Natan) Shcharansky. Of these measures the Schmidt government certainly did not approve, but nor was it directly affected by them. That could not be said of the second, much more significant round of sanctions, including both a (short-lived) grain embargo and a (partially observed) boycott of the 1980 Moscow Olympics, imposed – and demanded of West European allies – in response to the Soviet invasion of Afghanistan.

The largest crisis came, however, in 1982. Following General Jaruzelski's declaration of a 'state of war' in Poland, the Reagan administration imposed sanctions first on Poland and then on the Soviet Union, which it held responsible for the repression in Poland. The United States then tried to persuade its West European allies to join in, and specifically to stop a German-led consortium from going ahead with what had been billed as the 'deal of the century' – a massive pipeline system to supply Western Europe, and above all West Germany, with natural gas from the Siberian gas field of Urengoi. When the allies in general, and the Germans in particular, refused to be persuaded, the Reagan administration took the extraordinary step of banning US subsidiaries in Europe, and even European companies using US technology under licence, from exporting the necessary compressors and other parts to the Soviet Union. This was to burn a bridge too far, and, faced with a chorus of outrage in which Margaret Thatcher joined almost as vociferously as Helmut Schmidt, the Reagan administration was forced to retreat. Whereas in 1962 the United States had successfully leaned on West Germany to comply with its embargo, in 1982 it no longer could. Yet the controversy left a bitter after-taste, and American-German differences over economic relations with the East continued to smoulder through the decade.

Like all arguments within the Western alliance, this one was ostensibly about means not ends. We all want the same thing, was the polite assumption, the disagreement is only about how best to achieve it. The maverick West German commentator Josef Joffe would have none of this. 'With equal insistence,' he writes, 'Americans and Europeans claimed superior wisdom in their opposing analyses. The din of mutual recrimination merely helped to obscure the obvious: that an irreducible difference of interests lay at the roots of all their disputes. It was these interests that coloured their perceptions, not their perceptions that brought on the clash of American and European interests.'

The point is well taken, and an important corrective to official pieties. Yet the line between interests and perceptions is far from clear, particularly in the German case. Exports and jobs clearly were a hard interest of the Federal Republic. By Bonn's own definition, the benefits to be secured for the German minorities in Eastern Europe and the German majority in the GDR, by direct or indirect economic incentives, were also a basic national interest. If Germans suggested that there was a deeper harmony between the development of economic and political ties, between *Osthandel* and Ostpolitik, this also reflected German experience. Talks about trade were the first kind of talks that West Germany had directly, bilaterally, with the Soviet Union. Trading ties were the first sort of ties that West Germany developed with the East. Trade Missions were the first diplomatic representations the Federal Republic had in Eastern Europe. The flag followed trade. Then the establishment of full diplomatic relations at the beginning of the 1970s was followed by a sharp increase in the level of trade. Trade followed the flag.

In every case, the potential economic benefit to be gained from a closer relationship with West Germany was a crucial motive for the Soviet Union and East European states. Moreover, as several East European states got into deep difficulty about repaying the hard-currency loans originally granted to facilitate the expansion of East-West trade, so the capacity of the Bonn government to offer further government-guaranteed credits, or simply debt relief, became a very direct negotiating lever. It was a basic interest of the Federal Republic not to be constrained in playing its strongest cards.

From this point on, however, interests begin to shade into perceptions. Trade had a 'tension-reducing role,' wrote Otto Wolff von Amerongen. It was the lifeline along which political relations could be restored when they were otherwise in trouble. 'The Europeans have been trading with the Russians for centuries,' observed Helmut Schmidt. 'They believe trading with a close neighbour is politically and psychologically a good thing even if the volume of trade is small.' (For 'Europeans' read Germans).

When Franz Josef Strauss went to Moscow in 1987 he declared: 'Mars must leave and Mercury take the stage'. Now as the historian Harold James points out, Mercury has been a uniquely important god in the German pantheon since the early nineteenth century. Economic success in general, and export success in particular, have long been central pillars of national identity. And after all, Mercury, the god of commerce, is a peaceful god. Who could not prefer him to Mars, the god of war? Yet at the same time, the plain fact is that West Germany was, to use the crude vocabulary of the stockmarket, long in Mercury but still short (and uniquely constrained) in Mars, whereas the United States was uniquely long in Mars, but relatively much shorter (and arguably declining) in Mercury. If the central focus of East-West relations shifted from the security to the economic field, the unique importance of the superpower relationship would be diminished and the relative importance of the old-new economic power, Germany, would increase. Interest and perception were therefore hard to disentangle.

In a carefully worded treatment of this subject written in 1987, Jürgen Ruhfus, then the top-ranking West German diplomat, averred: 'In the West, East-West economic relations . . . are also considered to be of major political significance. Trade with the East is seen as a contribution to the long-term building of confidence between the blocs and to the stabilisation and reinforcement of East-West relations altogether. This should strengthen the part of the double strategy of the Atlantic Alliance directed at détente, dialogue, the interweaving (*Verflechtung*) of interests and partial interdependence.' No automatic change or convergence was to be expected. But economic co-operation had already encouraged 'reform beginnings' in Eastern Europe. Moreover, 'in the long-term the goal is to replace the condition of non-war [secured] by deterrence with a peace based on trust and co-operative security structures.' But if you had offered that as an unsigned statement, how many people in Washington, or, for that matter in London or Paris, would have agreed it was a definition of the West's common goals?

Yet in Washington, too, interests were mixed with perceptions. There was, for example, the hard interest of a military superpower in seeing that its main opponent did not gain militarily usable technological advantages. There was, on the other hand, the relative lack of positive economic interest, for eastern trade remained of strictly marginal importance to the US economy. But there was also the (albeit fitful) perception that a primary goal of Western policy should be to encourage greater respect for human rights and liberalisation in Eastern Europe and the Soviet Union, and that Western economic power should be applied directly to achieving that goal.

Of course West German policymakers also wished for political change and greater respect for human rights in Eastern Europe and the Soviet Union. But they had so many other reasons – state interests, national interests, perceptions of European and Western interests – for continuing with the development of economic ties that they were not prepared to consider cutting those ties on purely political or 'human rights' grounds. Even if there was no progress, indeed even if there was actual regress in those fields, economic co-operation had still to be pursued in the interests of the West German economy, the Germans in the East, stability, confidence-building, reconciliation, peace, and the web of interdependence that Bonn hoped to spin between East and West. In this last respect, the development of economic ties was not merely a means to an end. It was an end in itself.

The argument was thus neither just a difference of perceptions, nor simply a clash of interests. It had elements of both. In the second half of the 1980s the argument subsided, for two main reasons. Firstly, both American and West German policymakers made strenuous efforts to resolve it: although Jürgen Ruhfus's attempt to summarise the common position in 1987 actually reveals how far apart they still were in basic concepts and assumptions. The second, more important reason was that the changes introduced by Mikhail Gorbachev in the Soviet Union gradually transformed the overall agenda of East-West economic relations.

Even here, there were predictable differences of emphasis, with the West German Foreign Minister, Hans-Dietrich Genscher, being the first major advocate in the West of 'helping Gorbachev to succeed' by a broad offer of economic co-operation. Even now there were continued German-American differences on how far and how fast the West should respond to Soviet and East European appeals to trim the CoCom list of items that should not be exported to the East. Yet with the end of communism, first in Eastern Europe then in the Soviet Union, the terms of the argument were transformed out of recognition. In the new argument, about how best to assist the transition from planned to market economies, and who would foot how much of the bill, the German Mercury played a role second to none. To pursue that argument would, however, go beyond the bounds of this chapter.

Does the now finished history of East-West economic relations – in the context of 'Yalta' – allow us to make any more definite statements about the controversies that boiled or simmered for so long? Can we say, with benefit of hindsight, that one side of the argument about sanctions, eastern trade, credits and technology transfer was more right than the other? Are there any conclusions one can draw about what David Baldwin has called the 'economic statecraft' of the West? Here, as elsewhere, the difficulties of reaching any firm conculsions are still acute. As we have seen, there were often not just two but many sides to each argument. Quite different approaches were actually applied simultaneously – notably by the United States and the Federal Republic. Economic relations with the West were only part of a whole spectrum of factors affecting decisions and developments in the East.

The question of the efficacy of the strategic embargo on the export of military usable goods to the Warsaw Pact, and the extent to which it was undermined by illegal or third-country exports and the covert acquisition of know-how or technology by Eastern spies, we shall put aside here: not because it is uninteresting or unimportant, but because we do not have the specialised competence necessary to discuss it. The question of how far the Reagan administration's strategy (insofar as there was a strategy) of arms build-up as a form of economic warfare with the Soviet Union contributed to the change in Soviet foreign policy in the late 1980s has been considered in Chapter Four. The putative long-term positive contribution of economic ties and technological transfer to the opening of East European systems and societies, as part of an overall strategy of weaving (*Verflechtung*) between East and West in Europe, is considered in the next section.

What remains is the attempted use by Western governments of economic instruments to achieve changes in the foreign or domestic policies of Eastern states, in the short to medium term. 'The Americans,' Pierre Hassner once remarked, 'believe in sticks, the Germans believe in carrots and the French believe in words.' When all caveats have been entered, his *bon mot* contains a large kernel of truth. Bonn governments tended, from a mixture of interests and perceptions, to advocate a medium- to long-term economic incentive linkage. Washington administrations inclined, from a different mixture of interests and perceptions, to advocate a short- to medium-term economic deterrent linkage. As we have suggested earlier, in their pure forms both variants were premissed on questionable hypotheses of behavioural psychology: the former treating communist rulers as rabbits, the latter, as donkeys.

Both were further hamstrung by three structural problems. First, in states with market economies, governments find it both in principle dubious and in practice difficult to direct the behaviour of bankers, investors, traders and industrialists. Second, in modern parliamentary democracies – especially in 'television democracies' – governments cannot make and unmake such linkages at will. On this point the magisterial remarks of the American diplomatist George Kennan are germane. 'In the harsh realities of international life,' Kennan writes,

a government influences another government through the dialectical interaction, in its own conduct, of measures favourable to the interests of the other government and measures that affect its interests adversely. Let us call these, for want of better description, favours and injury, respectively. Both are, at one point or another, necessary ingredients of any policy . . . But if these instruments of diplomacy are to be of any value, then whoever conducts policy must be in a position to manipulate them currently, fluidly and at will, as the situation may require . . . A favour which, to the certain knowledge of the other party, cannot be retracted, comes soon to be taken for granted and ceases to be regarded as a favour. An injury or hardship which, to the similar knowledge of the other party, cannot be removed, ceases to have any punitive effect . . .

Kennan wrote this with reference to a Congressional move to prevent the extension of Most Favored Nation status to Yugoslavia in 1962. But it could be applied to both American and German policies in the 1970s and 1980s. Kissinger argued, with some force, that the Jackson-Vanik amendment defeated its own purpose, because the prospect of its lifting became so remote that the Soviet Union ceased to respond to it. At the other extreme, with the tripartisan consensus on Deutschlandpolitik in the 1980s, West German financial transfers to the GDR came close to being favours that could not be retracted and therefore ceased to work as favours. In the one case the stick almost ceased to be a stick; in the other, the carrot almost ceased to be a carrot.

Thirdly, as we have seen, even the most powerful of free-trading liberal democracies could not simply compel other free-trading liberal democracies to behave as it thought fit. Indeed, in the West German view the impossibility of getting everyone to join in sanctions was one major reason why they never would 'work'. The readiness of Canadian and Argentinian producers to step into the breach left by the American grain embargo against the Soviet Union gave some force to this argument. Yet by themselves refusing to join in sanctions against the Soviet Union in 1982, West German policymakers made this a self-fulfilling prophecy.

Sanctions against the Soviet Union were thus never fully or consistently applied. In terms of the proclaimed goals, the record of the three main rounds of sanctions in American-Soviet relations could be construed as negative in the short term. If one considered the position in, say, 1985, then one could say: the Soviet dissidents have not been freed (or only in direct exchanges), the Red Army has not got out of Afghanistan, and Solidarity has not been restored in Poland. So the sanctions 'did not work'. But as Philip Hanson has argued, it is wrong to assess each 'sanctions episode' in isolation. One must also consider the cumulative effect. And the fact is that by the end of the 1980s the Soviet dissidents had been freed, the Red Army had got out of Afghanistan and Solidarity had been restored in Poland. Clearly, here as elsewhere, it is impermissible to say simply *post hoc ergo propter hoc*. Many other influences can be identified, including that of German-led incentive détente. Even with benefit of hindsight the causal reckoning remains highly speculative.

So far as direct sanctions against Poland are concerned, the story is also complex. But it would be quite wrong to suggest that support for sanctions was confined to government and newspaper offices in Washington DC. In the martial law period, many, probably most, Solidarity leaders and activists welcomed the Western economic sanctions against their own country. As late as November 1984 Adam Michnik, the opposition leader, told the author, for the record: '. . . it seems to me I have to thank the sanctions policy, among other things, for the fact that we can talk here today, that I'm sitting right here in my apartment and not in the prison·on Rakowiecka Street. For this, my colleagues and I would like to thank all those who have helped us.' Of course, the Solidarity leadership then encouraged the gradual lifting of sanctions, when the time was judged right.

Looking back from 1989, Neal Ascherson, a highly experienced writer on Polish affairs, and very far from being a cold warrior of the ideological right, commented:

> . . . Poland provided one of the rare examples in which economic sanctions took spectacular and rapid effect. . . . There was a great bluster about how capitalist blackmail wouldn't deter Poles from doing what they thought right. However, one sweeping amnesty was soon followed by a second; the overwhelming need to obtain renewed Western economic assistance has nudged the Polish regime forward into one democratic concession after another, and that mechanism – long after formal sanctions have ended – functions to this day.

In other words, these 'sticks' were effective, but only because there was a realistic prospect of them turning into 'carrots' which the regime desperately needed.

Ascherson's verdict is supported by the researches of Zbigniew Pelczynski, who has attempted to reconstruct the Polish authorities' process of decision-making in the political opening of the late 1980s. Having talked at length to many of the key decision-makers, he concludes that the hard linkage made by the United States played a crucial part in propelling those decision-makers down the path to the Round Table. So in this case the balance of evidence is that sanctions, flexibly applied, actually did 'work', although greatly helped, of course, by many other factors beyond the West's control.

It is also interesting to ask the opposite question: not 'did the sticks work?' but 'did the carrots work?' An attempt has already been made to address this question so far as the GDR is concerned. The other two countries to which an advocate of 'change through trade' would have pointed in the 1970s were Poland under Gierek and Hungary under Kádár. Here generous Western engagement in the development of economic relations was, it was suggested, helping to open up the regime, to make the communist powerholders themselves more modern, Western, pragmatic, liberal. Once again, there were half-articulated assumptions of behavioural psychology. Trade would soften political hostilities: you were less likely to hate someone with whom you were regularly doing business. Seeing capitalism at first hand, the communist rulers would discover its attractions.

Now at the level of individual biography, some of this may have been true. Individual Polish or Hungarian powerholders were convinced, seduced or simply corrupted by the developing economic ties with the West. (In the case of the Gierek team in Poland one might add: 'and how!'.) But this was not what happened at the level of the economic and political system. Western trade, credits, and technology transfer were overwhelmingly channelled through organs under the central control of the party-state. They were used less to facilitate economic reform than as a substitute for such reform. As a result of this systemic misapplication, the Western 'carrots', far from setting these states on the path of sustained growth, with political modernisation following economic modernisation, instead helped them down the road to economic crisis.

Although Western loans were less badly used in Kádár's Hungary than in Gierek's Poland, in the Hungarian case too, albeit a few years later and somewhat less dramatically than in Poland, the soaring hard-currency debt contributed to an economic crisis which then became a political crisis. In effect, the carrots became sticks. Opponents of incentive détente never tired of repeating Lenin's quip that the capitalists would sell the Soviet Union the rope with which it could hang them. But what happened in this case was rather that the West sold Gierck and Kádár the rope with which they hanged themselves. Yet this was not what the sellers had intended.

By 1988, Poland had a net hard-currency debt of more than $35 billion. Hungary had more than $18 billion – that is, nearly $2,000 a head. For Gierek's and Kádár's successors, the hard-currency debt had become a kind of permanent Western sanction. To be sure, the 'linkage' was ostensibly economic. The pure economists of the IMF and World Bank would come in; on purely economic grounds they would grant a Western certificate of approval for the purely economic measures that the Polish or Hungarian governments proposed to take. But politics and economics in communist systems were more closely connected than Siamese twins. You could not operate on one without seriously affecting the other.

Thus in order to implement the 'purely' economic measures advocated by the IMF or World Bank, the Polish and Hungarian regimes felt impelled also to institute political reforms. This Western economic pressure therefore contributed to the retreat of the party not only from the economy but also from social control, and ultimately from the state itself. To be sure, it was only one among many causes: but a major one, nonetheless. Furthermore, although the criteria applied by the IMF and World Bank remained purely economic, those political changes marvellously increased the willingness of Western governments to approve IMF agreements, stand-by loans and the rest. (In the case of Poland, the political linkage in the 1980s was, of course, also explicit.)

The history of 'carrots and sticks' is thus rich in ironies. For both Poland and Hungary, the carrots of the 1970s became the sticks of the 1980s. For Poland after 1981, the sticks of sanctions were also carrots in disguise. Arguably, for the reasons already mentioned, neither the United States nor the Federal Republic achieved on their own that flexibility in the combined use of favours and injuries which George Kennan identified as the prerequisite for successful economic statecraft. Crudely put, the

Americans remained too hooked on sticks, while the Germans became too partial to offering carrots.

Insofar as this aspect of Western Ostpolitik contributed to the achievement of the desired results it was rather through the combination, as much by accident as by design, of the two contrasting approaches, in the overall policy of the West. Yet, to the very end, representatives of each approach fiercely denied the wisdom of the other; and, after the end, claimed that history had proved them right.

Weaving

It was not only economic ties that the Federal Republic consistently endeavoured to forge with the Soviet Union and Eastern Europe. The Bonn government declared itself interested in developing almost every possible sort of tie: political, social, cultural, touristic, sporting, academic, technological, scientific, environmental, road or rail, animal, vegetable or mineral. The stated object was to create a whole *Netz* or *Geflecht* – a net, network, mesh or web – of ties between Eastern and Western Europe. This idea of *Verflechtung* or *Vernetzung* – interlacing, networking, weaving – was another leitmotif of German Ostpolitik in the 1970s and 1980s.

The most tireless advocate and inexhaustible practitioner of *Verflechtung* was Hans-Dietrich Genscher. If the simile were not generally felt to be a little insulting, one might compare the veteran Foreign Minister to a spider, ceaselessly spinning his web across the face of Europe, today in Prague, tomorrow in Moscow, at the weekend in Paris. But the idea was by no means his alone. President Richard von Weizsäcker was an eloquent advocate of what he called 'system-opening co-operation'. A typical report from an East European visit by the Federal Chancellor consisted largely in a listing of new ties, new forms of 'co-operation', that the two sides had agreed to establish or at least to explore. Although this or that detail might occasionally give rise to party-political controversy, the general idea was part of the tripartisan consensus on Ostpolitik.

Like other elements of German Ostpolitik, this concept had both common Western and specific German roots. As early as August 1957, John F. Kennedy was advocating the development of trading, technical and humanitarian ties with Poland, and 'an increase of people-to-people contacts, of cultural, scientific, and educational exchanges representing every aspect of life in the two countries'. American ideas of 'peaceful engagement' and 'bridge-building', of moving 'from confrontation to co-operation', were essential background to the vision that Willy Brandt unfolded in the early 1960s.

Indeed, his first general statement of that vision was made in America – at Harvard in October 1962. 'We need,' Brandt said there, to seek forms which can overlay and penetrate (*durchdringen*) the blocs of today. We need as many points of contact and as much meaningful communication as possible. We have no need to fear the exchange of academics and students, of information, ideas and services. What should be decisive for us is that these are sensible enterprises in responsible forms. We should welcome common projects between East and West. So I am in favour of as many meaningful ties as can be achieved, also with the communist East.

Yet while speaking in Harvard Willy Brandt was still the Governing Mayor of Berlin. Not merely at the back but at the very front of his mind were the immediate problems of alleviating the unprecedented, unique and absolute division of his city. It would clearly be wrong to suggest that his large and vague vision was merely a magnified projection, on to the clouds, so to speak, of what he and his circle now saw as the immediate necessities in Berlin. But it would be even more wrong to suppose that what they started to do in Berlin (and then in Germany, and then in Europe . . .) was merely the local application of general Western and especially American ideas. It is worth noting that the idea of weaving was advanced with special emphasis by politicians who had at some point been Governing Mayors of Berlin: a list that includes not only Willy Brandt but also Richard von Weizsäcker and Brandt's successor as leader of the SPD, Hans-Jochen Vogel.

In advancing this overall approach, West German politicians and policymakers argued that they were implementing the 'détente half' of the Nato double strategy agreed in the 1967 Harmel report. But the framework in which the implementation was pursued was that of the so-called 'Helsinki process', which followed the signing in Helsinki in 1975 of the Final Act of the Conference on Security and Co-operation in Europe. The 'Helsinki process' had the unique advantage of including both the Soviet Union and the United States, both East and West European states, both East and West Germany. It was also particularly well-suited to West Germany's favoured foreign-policy style – discreet, multilateral, consensus-seeking and patiently attritional. Indeed, that characteristic West German policy style and the Helsinki process to some extent evolved together, each influencing the other. If Harmel was the Bible of the West German approach to East-West relations, then the Helsinki Final Act became its prayer book, and the successive Helsinki review documents its Corpus Juris Canonici.

Yet like the Bible, the prayer-book, and even canon law, 'Helsinki' was susceptible to very different interpretations. From the outset, there was not one but many ideas of Helsinki. There was Helsinki as the confirmation of 'Yalta' and Helsinki as the negation of 'Yalta'. There was the Helsinki of the persecuted and the Helsinki of the persecutors. There was Brezhnev's idea of Helsinki and Yuri Orlov's idea of Helsinki; Gustáv

Husák's idea and Charter 77's; Gierek's and KOR's. There was Erich Honecker's idea of Helsinki, and there was the idea that prompted tens of thousands of ordinary East Germans, following the publication of the Helsinki Final Act in *Neues Deutschland*, to apply to emigrate on the basis of its ceremonious and solemn undertakings. The differences in conception and interpretation were not only within the East and between East and West; they were also within the West.

Henry Kissinger, for example, agreed to the long-standing Soviet wish for a European security conference essentially as a diplomatic concession in return for Soviet agreement to proceed with Mutual Balanced Forced Reduction talks and the Quadripartite Agreement on Berlin. His then aide, Helmut Sonnenfeldt, boasted in 1975: 'We sold it for the German-Soviet treaty, we sold it for the Berlin agreement, and we sold it again for the opening of the MBFR.' Kissinger famously did not consider human rights to be an appropriate subject for discussions between states. In the initial phase of negotiating the Helsinki Final Act there was therefore a curious role-reversal, with Kissinger acting in the old European *Realpolitik* spirit of Metternich, while West European leaders acted more in the spirit of Woodrow Wilson. (This could not, however, fairly be said of the lower-level American diplomats directly involved in the Helsinki negotiations.)

Kissinger's attitude changed somewhat in the last months before the signature of the Helsinki Final Act. Following America's defeat in Vietnam, and facing growing domestic criticism of what had been called 'détente', he actually played a significant part in securing Soviet acceptance of the commitments to improve human contacts, information flows and cultural exchange in the so-called 'Basket 3' of Helsinki. With the arrival of the Carter administration, human rights came to the very top of the agenda of American foreign policy, partly in an attempt to rediscover the United States' sense of historic purpose after the trauma of Vietnam. This directly affected American Helsinki policy.

The change in emphasis was greatly assisted by pressure from the representatives of the substantial East European minorities inside the United States, and by both Congressional and independent initiatives to monitor implementation of the Helsinki accords. In this respect, Americans responded faster than West Europeans to the courageous initiatives of independent Soviet and East European citizens – the persecuted Helsinki monitors in their own countries. By the end of the 1970s, for most American politicians and policymakers 'Helsinki' had come to mean essentially 'human rights'. American newspapers referred to the 'Helsinki Human Rights Declaration', although human rights are mentioned as such only in one of the ten principles at the beginning of the Final Act. This understanding of Helsinki was clearly reflected in the American approach to the Helsinki review conferences in Belgrade, Madrid and Vienna.

At the other extreme there was the Soviet idea of Helsinki. Robert

Legvold has aptly observed that Soviet leaders saw Helsinki as a 'medium for healing Europe's economic division while sealing its political division'. Not only the territorial but also the political status quo would finally be 'recognised', with all the ambiguities of 'recognition' that we have already explored in West Germany's relationship to East Germany. Not only the 'Yalta' frontiers but also the permanence of Soviet domination and Soviet-type regimes – everything that Soviet writers summed up in the innocuous-sounding phrase 'post-war realities' – would be accepted by the West. At the same time, Soviet leaders were deeply interested in what came to be the second of the three 'baskets' of Helsinki: the section headed 'Co-operation in the field of economics, of science and technology and of the environment'. This was, as the historian Vojtech Mastny succinctly puts it, 'the favourite Soviet basket'. They were, to be sure, prepared to consider limited and selective 'Co-operation in humanitarian and other fields', as the third basket was headed. But charges about their lack of respect for the human rights of their own citizens were to be rejected as that 'interference in the internal affairs' of another state, which the signatories also solemnly renounced in the introductory list of principles.

This basic Soviet position changed very significantly after Gorbachev came to power in 1985. But in the first decade of the Helsinki process the lines between the Soviet idea of Helsinki and the American idea of Helsinki were starkly drawn. Now plainly the democratic oppositions in Eastern Europe were closer to the American than to the Soviet idea of Helsinki. That the party-states of Eastern Europe were closer to the Soviet than to the American position is also plain. This latter point does, however, require some qualification.

Like the Soviet ruling nomenklatura, the East European ruling nomen-klaturas were alarmed at those parts of the Helsinki process which threatened their domestic power monopoly. Like the Soviet Union, in fact even more so, they were interested in all those parts of 'basket two' that seemed to offer the possibility of modernising their economies and strengthening their states, while not undermining their own domestic political positions. Yet at the same time, the leaders of at least some East European states saw an opportunity to use the incremental multilateralism of the Helsinki process to increase their state's own international room for manoeuvre, and cautiously to test the limits of their autonomy from Moscow. This intention did not, however, go *pari passu* with domestic liberalisation: it was true of Kádár's Hungary and Gierek's Poland, but it was also true of Honecker's still comprehensively illiberal GDR and of Ceauşescu's increasingly repressive Romania.

Where did the Federal Republic fit into this complex picture? What was the West German idea of Helsinki? To attempt a fair characterisation of the German position one would have, for a start, to collate the whole vast forest of official West German statements on the Helsinki process, and compare them systematically with, say, American or French statements. One would then have to look into the countless stages of consultation that preceded and accompanied all Helsinki meetings, for many differences were already ground down by this intra-(West) European and intra-Western *engrenage* before they even reached paper. The first would be a mammoth, the second a virtually impossible task.

As we have noticed, the Federal Republic was particularly interested in, and became outstandingly adept at, *not* clearly articulating distinctive national positions, but rather feeding its own special German concerns and priorities into a common approach. It did this, first and foremost, in Western Europe, above all though European Political Co-operation, which really came to life in the Helsinki negotiations. It did this in the West, through Nato and through the 'Bonn Group' of the three Western Allies and West Germany. And it did this in a wider Europe, through working with the neutral and non-aligned countries, which played an unusually important part in the actual diplomacy of the Helsinki process, and through discreet, often tacit understandings with some East European states, including, on occasion, East Germany. The German use of Helsinki was altogether a classic and highly successful example of that 'attempt to cover (*abdecken*) our actions multilaterally' which Helmut Schmidt prescribed in his confidential Marbella paper of 1977. This was one of the essential ingredients of what would later become known as Genscherism.

The multilateral, multi-level, multi-stage nature of the Helsinki process, and the German approach to it, thus make firm generalisation very difficult. A few tentative statements may nonetheless be made.

A memorandum written for Chancellor Schmidt (probably in 1975) noted: 'The Federal Government had no original interest of its own in the CSCE.' Its first negotiating goal was therefore, as the memorandum put it, 'damage prevention'. The Soviet Union must not be allowed to turn this into a substitute peace treaty, binding in international law; nor to use it to close the door to the future possibility of German unification; nor to exclude Berlin. The most distinctive contributions of German diplomacy in the early stages of the Helsinki negotiations concerned these essentially defensive goals, all of which were achieved with the help of her Western allies.

The preamble to the Final Act declared it to apply to the participating states and 'throughout Europe' – a diplomatic phrase which specifically meant 'in West Berlin'. As we have seen, Henry Kissinger negotiated on Germany's behalf the crucial sentence allowing for the possibility of a 'peaceful change' of frontiers. This was placed in the list of principles before the affirmation of the inviolability of frontiers, and augmented by the commitment to the self-determination of peoples. It was these paragraphs, not those on human rights and fundamental freedoms, that Hans-Dietrich Genscher singled out for special mention when commending the Helsinki Final Act to the Bundestag in the summer of 1975.

Yet following intensive internal discussion, the Bonn government also decided earlier than most that this Soviet initiative might be turned to the West's advantage. By 1973, the head of the Foreign Ministry planning staff and leader of the German delegation to the Helsinki preparatory talks, Guido Brunner, could already write in very positive terms about the conference developing 'common rules of the game for peaceful co-opera-tion and competition'. He went on to emphasise what would be a dominant theme in Bonn's approach to Helsinki. 'We intend,' he wrote, 'to establish contacts between people, contacts between professional groups, contacts from society to society, as autonomous factors in the process of detente.' And this theme of human contacts would be stressed again and again by German politicians and policymakers. This was something that Genscher did dwell on at length in commending the Final Act to the Bundestag. Détente, he said, using a formulation now common to the main Western participants, was a process which must directly benefit the people. The Final Act provided for a 'net of co-operation' and the increase of contacts. The subject of 'human alleviations', he went on, was now finally 'on the European agenda'. Progress, however, would be a matter of 'small steps'.

For anyone who had followed the evolution of West German policy towards the GDR over the previous decade, the code-words delivered a clear message. Here was the projection of Deutschlandpolitik onto a wider, European stage. The approach that had been adopted first in Berlin and then in Germany was now to be attempted 'throughout Europe' – which also meant, specifically, in Berlin! Of course the German approach had been combined with and modified by the attitudes and priorities of its negotiating partners. But the emphasis remained distinctive.

From the mid-1970s the United States saw the positive meaning and dynamic potential of Helsinki above all in its provisions for human rights. For the Federal Republic the positive meaning and dynamic potential lay above all in its provisions for co-operation and human contacts. Human contacts and human rights are closely related things. But they are not the same thing. American representatives would explicitly berate the Soviet Union and other East European states for their violations of human rights, pointing publicly to individual cases of persecuted dissidents, Christians and, not least, Helsinki monitors. German representatives tended to believe that this was misplaced energy, perhaps even counter-productive. 'Quiet diplomacy', Willy Brandt and others argued, actually did more for the persecuted individuals than American-style 'megaphone diplomacy'. Moreover, it was argued that by concentrating on these few spectacular cases one could block the path to more modest improvements – 'human alleviations' – for far more individual people. To increase contacts of all possible kinds between East and West in Europe, to knit the divided continent back together again by weaving and webbing: here was the real and larger meaning of Helsinki.

This West German approach was, in the short term at least, more congenial to East European rulers than it was to the small groups of human rights activists who pinned their colours to the Helsinki mast. While the 'quiet diplomacy' of Willy Brandt and others was of course appreciated, most persecuted human rights activists saw it as no alternative to, let alone a substitute for, the invaluable help of being loudly, publicly and individually mentioned by Western leaders, both in multilateral fora and in their bilateral dealings with the East. In Helsinki policy, as in other fields, the German-American difference was most acute in the months after the declaration of martial law in Poland, with the United States advocating a very hard Western line at the Madrid review conference, even at the risk of jeopardising it, while the Federal Republic advocated a softer line, emphasising the co-operative rather than the confrontational aspects of the Helsinki process.

The Federal Republic was also the major Western power which showed most demonstrative interest in pursuing the 'co-operation in the field of economics, of science and technology, and of the environment', mapped out in basket two. In these fields, the Federal Republic was the Western leader. And consciously so. 'Decisive is first of all basket two, co-operation,' wrote Richard von Weizsäcker in 1983. 'If we succeed in building up co-operation step by step in the fields of science, technology, nutrition, environment, transport, business, energy and development policy, then in the end arms control and even freedom of movement will move into the realm of the possible.' And 'to us Germans falls the task of making basket two a central focus of East-West relations.' Not accidentally, the first major Helsinki follow-on meeting to be held in Germany was on the subject of economic co-operation.

At the same time West Germany, like other Western states, hoped that all the multilateral and bilateral contacts permitted by the Helsinki process would enable East European rulers quietly to establish somewhat more autonomy from Moscow, while engaging more closely in all-European affairs. Helmut Schmidt sometimes presented himself, in Warsaw and Budapest, as the spokesman of the smaller and middle-sized states in Europe. In the 1980s, West Germany used these contacts, in a modest and cautious way, to push ahead the arms control and disarmament sides of the Helsinki process in ways which were not always wholly desired by the Soviet Union, but also, on occasion, by the United States. On these security and disarmament issues there was also some tacit co-operation with East Germany, sanctified by that famous mantra about 'only peace going out from German soil'.

While the cumulative, attritional effect on Soviet and East European leaders of all the countless rounds of talks involved in the Helsinki process should not be understated, it was only following the advent of 'new thinking' in Soviet foreign policy that a major step forward was taken from the provisions – so often honoured only in the breach – of the 1975 Final Act. Instead of hiding behind the 'interference in internal affairs' clause, the Soviet Union both curbed its own most obvious human rights abuses and engaged in a direct and spirited dialogue about respect for human rights in East and West. The Vienna review conference was finally wound up in January 1989, with a concluding document which established procedures for regular inquiry by member states into precisely those 'internal affairs' of other states, and with detailed provisions on such matters as freedom of movement, freedom of religion, freedom of information, the rights of national minorities and those of independent Helsinki monitors. For the West, this was certainly the greatest step forward since 1975.

Here, as in all the main Helsinki negotiations, there was a significant though complex linkage between the security and the human rights/contacts sides of the process – that is, in the jargon of Helsinki, between baskets one and three. This linkage evolved over time. As we have seen, at the outset Kissinger 'sold' the Conference for, among other things, the talks on Mutual Balanced Force Reductions (MBFR). While the MBFR talks got nowhere, the Helsinki talks proceeded with a series of broad trade-offs between the Soviet desire for recognition of frontiers and security in basket one and economic advantages from basket two, and the desire of the West – with varying national emphases – for advances above all in basket three. At the end of the Madrid follow-up meeting, the West secured modest improvements in the human rights field while agreeing to a Conference on Confidence- and Security-Building Measures and Disarmament in Europe held in Stockholm between 1984 and 1986. Yet this disarmament conference was also wanted by many European states – not least West Germany – and, with the change in Soviet foreign policy, its outcome was generally held to be highly acceptable to the West.

By the late 1980s, it was the Soviet Union which was looking for rapid progress in security talks, above all in the field of conventional arms reductions, while the West held out for more concessions at the Helsinki review conference in Vienna. This linkage was clearly spelled out at the time by the leader of the American delegation to the Vienna conference. The wheel had come full circle. Whereas in 1972, the United States would 'sell' the Helsinki conference in return for talks on conventional arms reductions, in 1988 the United States would 'sell' talks on conventional arms reductions in return for concessions at the Helsinki review conference in Vienna. The new round of conventional arms talks actually opened, also in Vienna, in March 1989, just a few weeks after the ceremonial conclusion of the Helsinki review conference.

It is, for the reasons already given, very difficult to establish what precisely was the German contribution to this outcome. The German Foreign Minister tried to push the Vienna review conference to an earlier conclusion in 1988, at a point when the Soviet (and some East European) delegations were still not prepared to concede some of the key detailed human rights provisions on which the American and British delegations were insisting, with active or tacit support from other Western, neutral, non-aligned, and even East Central European delegations. A senior American representative commented that while he spent his time talking about human rights, his German counterpart talked about town-twinning. This reinforces an impression one has from immersion in the relevant material, and from conversations with many policymakers, but it would be wrong to offer any firm conclusions without more detailed research.

There was, however, another remarkable document agreed in 1989 which perhaps gave a clearer idea of the German approach. This was the Joint Declaration signed by Helmut Kohl and Mikhail Gorbachev during the latter's visit to the Federal Republic in June 1989. The Bonn Declaration was a sort of bilateral Helsinki – although since the essence of Helsinki was multilateralism that may be a contradiction in terms. We have seen already its significance for the development of German-Soviet relations, and the novel statements it made about the right to self-determination. What should be noted here is the great emphasis that it placed on co-operation and, in a word, weaving.

Thus among the 'building elements' of a new 'Europe of peace and co-operation' it mentioned: a 'thick' dialogue on all themes, 'traditional as well as new', including regular meetings at the highest political level; 'the realisation of human rights and the advancement of the exchange of people and ideas' including 'town-twinning, transport and communication links, cultural contacts, tourist and sporting traffic, the encouragement of language teaching and also a benevolent treatment of humanitarian questions including family reunification and travel abroad'; the building of contacts between youth; comprehensive economic co-operation 'to mutual advantage, including new forms of co-operation'; 'the step-by-step construction of all-European co-operation in different areas, especially in transport, energy, health care, information and communication'; and 'intensive ecological co-operation'.

West Germany had come a long way from Brandt's Harvard speech in 1962. For here was a veritable weaver's charter – and signed by the Soviet leader.

What, then, was this network of contacts and co-operation supposed to achieve? What was the point of it all? Once again, there was a set of specific national grounds and a set of general ones. As Hans-Dietrich Genscher observed already in 1975, 'no one can have a greater interest than us Germans in the Conference achieving its goal, namely to improve the contacts between the states and people in Europe . . . I believe that no one would neglect their national duty more than us, were he to hesitate to use even the smallest chance for a development that could eventually ease the lot of the divided nation.' The divided nation could only be sewn back together again if the Europe around it was being sewn back together again. The closer the ties between Eastern and Western Europe as a whole, the closer could be the ties between Eastern and Western Germany. German-German, even Berlin-Berlin, contacts and 'co-operation' had to be embedded in European (including American)–European (including Soviet) contacts and co-operation. The basic thought was already there in Chancellor Kiesinger's speech on 17 June 1967.

All Western countries had a certain economic interest in expanded economic ties with the Soviet Union and Eastern Europe, but the truncated 'trading state' had a special interest in those ties. The vague but important goal of 'reconciliation' was another special national reason for wanting to develop ties – some of which, such as cultural or youth exchanges, were thought to contribute directly to 'reconciliation'. Rather as the physiotherapist will try to build up the muscles around an injured ligament, so West Germany – having some horribly torn ligaments with the East – tried to build up the muscles around them.

The idea of developing all-European ties in order to facilitate the growth of all-German ties was itself a multilateral version of what we have called the permissive function. But there were also more direct, bilateral versions. Even if no direct linkage was made, the development of a generous web of economic, technological, educational and other ties was thought likely to encourage Soviet and East European leaders to be slightly more 'co-operative' on those special German interests: the situation of the Germans in the GDR and the rest of Eastern Europe. For while this web of ties might politely be described as 'to mutual advantage', it was clear that in, say, science, technology, industry, or education West Germany would give more than it got. These ties were thus, in part, incentives: carrots from the second basket, in the hope of concessions on specifically German interests in basket three. But rather than talk of carrots it might be more accurate to talk of load-bearing structures. Having a special load in East-West European relations, the Federal Republic was especially interested in creating a strong framework: one that would bear the additional load and be resistant to shocks.

Now clearly these special functions overlapped. They also shaded into general considerations, such as would be discussed in other Western states. Naturally West German policymakers preferred the general Western or European formulation of this conception to the specific national one. In these formulations, too, several different ideas came glued together. 'The comprehensive extension of economic, technological and cultural co-operation,' said Hans-Dietrich Genscher in 1989, '. . . the networking of mutual interests, can make the détente process irreversible. We must create a web (*Verflechtung*) of interests and co-operations (*sic*) which no longer allows any country to get out of this association (*Verbund*) without severely damaging their own most vital interests. We need mutual dependencies in the good sense of the word.' The very difficulty of translating this off-the-cuff interview answer into English illustrates how specific the thinking was.

Earlier, in 1987, the Foreign Minister expressed it thus: 'through deepened co-operation, lying in the interests of both sides, an irreversible, system-opening process must be shaped. It must take account of mutual dependency but also of the indivisible responsibility for the survival of humanity. It must finally be an irreversible, inevitable process of co-operation.' 'Our policy,' he said in another speech in the same year, 'is today in harmony with the striving of Europeans, who can overcome the division of the continent by co-operation.'

It is perhaps helpful to try and separate out some of the ideas that came glued together in such portmanteau formulations. Firstly, there was the relatively simple idea that if you wanted to reduce the division of Europe you had to reduce the division of Europe. The division of Europe was not just a matter of political systems. It was also an economic, technological, scientific, educational and infrastructural division. As Genscher observed in a speech in 1985: 'We do not want a technological division of Europe. We want to hold open for our eastern neighbours the option of technological connection through co-operation.' Or as the then Governing Mayor of Berlin, Eberhard Diepgen, put it in 1988: 'Every jointly erected desulphurisation plant, every exchange of goods and services, every East-West traffic connection is to some extent a trust-building and division-reducing measure.'

Yet this was also the *reductio ad absurdum* of the idea. For it is plainly absurd to suggest that every exchange of goods and services between East and West was a 'trust-building and division-reducing measure'. Did the Siemens computers in the Polish Interior Ministry, or the American handcuffs with which the KGB held Vladimir Bukovsky, help to reduce the division of Europe? If so, how? Did the supply of Soviet or East European spies in the form of exchange scholars increase trust? If so, whose trust in whom? The examples are extreme. But they illustrate an important point. For there was indeed a tendency in German Ostpolitik to argue that all forms of tie and co-operation would help, in the long-run, to reduce the division. Yet in practice there were forms of tie and co-operation that reinforced the (political) division and reduced trust. It might reasonably be argued that these were unavoidable side-costs: if you supply a thousand computers it is hard to avoid one of them going to the secret police. The overall balance remained positive. But that argument had to be made concretely, and from case to case.

A second notion bundled up in the *Verflechtung* portmanteau was that of common problems, challenges or interests. We are all threatened by nuclear war or accident. Acid rain knows no frontiers. The pollutants put into the river in one country damage another. Drugs and disease endanger us all. We have only one world. This theme was announced by Genscher as early as 1971. 'We all have only one alternative,' he declared, 'namely to defuse the dangerous world-political tensions by together attempting to solve the great tasks of humanity in the last third of the twentieth century.' But it became a dominant motif only in the second half of the 1980s, with the emergence in the West of powerful Green and anti-nuclear movements, alarming reports of acid rain, dying forests and the greenhouse effect, the Chernobyl disaster, and Soviet 'new thinking' in foreign policy. Thus the Bonn Declaration began: 'The Federal Republic of Germany and the Union of Soviet Socialist Republics agree that on the eve of the third millennium humanity faces historic challenges. Problems that are of vital importance to all can only be resolved by all states and peoples together.'

Now at one level this was clearly true. Industrial and technological development meant that people in one part of the world were more directly affected by what people did in another part of the world. Chernobyl was one example of this; global warming another. There were (and are) new common problems. But it does not necessarily follow that there are common solutions. Pollution is a good example. Taken as a whole, Eastern Europe in the 1980s had less industrial production yet as bad or worse industrial pollution than Western Europe. Why? Because of the economic system which caused such wasteful, careless industrial practice, and because of the political system which did not allow popular discontent about life-threatening pollution to be translated into the appropriate corrective political-economic action.

To be sure, there were technical similarities between pollution in East and West: sulphur dioxide (East) was very similar to sulphur dioxide (West). To be sure, one might argue, as the Greens did argue, that the root of the problem in West as well as East was the common worship of economic growth. But the acuteness of the pollution problem in the Soviet Union and Eastern Europe was in large measure a result of the prevailing political-economic system. To take 'co-operative' steps, 'irrespective of system differences', was thus to treat the symptoms not the causes: a necessary, but by no means a sufficient, response.

The Chernobyl disaster well illustrated this distinction. The Chernobyl disaster was an accident. But it was not an accident that it happened in the Soviet Union, rather than in, say, West Germany. The West German response was, in effect, to say: 'we will help you to build safer nuclear power stations. In fact, if you like, we will build them for you' — common and self-interest happily coinciding. Now everyone, in East and West, would clearly breathe more easily if, given that the Soviet Union was determined to go on building nuclear power stations, those nuclear power stations were to be built by — or at least, with the advice of — West Germans. But this was not a common solution to a common problem. It was a Western panacea for a Soviet problem.

There is also the question of whether the growth in the prominence of such 'common problems' in East-West, and especially in (West) German-Soviet dialogue, was proportionate to the actual growth in the urgency of those common problems, or rather reflected a desire — essentially for other reasons — to find common ground. This would, after all, be nothing new. When John F Kennedy wished to signal his readiness to establish a better relationship with the Soviet Union, he said, in June 1963: '. . . let us also direct attention to our common interests . . . For, in the final analysis, our most basic common link is that we all inhabit this small planet. We all breathe the same air. We all cherish our children's future. And we are all mortal.' A remarkable discovery.

When two states wish to establish better relations they often reach for the highest common platitude. If there had been no 'common problems' for West Germany and the Soviet Union, it might have been necessary to invent them. Indeed it was curious to observe how hardened *Realpolitiker* on both sides suddenly developed a vibrant, tender concern for trees and plants, for 'all things bright and beautiful, all creatures great and small'. This is, of course, not to deny the reality or importance of these problems. It is merely to point out that their discovery and sudden prominence served a more traditional, instrumental function as well.

A third, related notion to be disentangled from the portmanteau is that of the desirability of interdependence. The argument from 'common problems' said, in effect: 'In the contemporary world we are increasingly interdependent, and our responses must therefore be multilateral and co-operative across the East-West divide.' But the Ostpolitik argument for *Verflechtung* went a stage further. It said not only that we are interdependent, but that we *should* be interdependent. This is a less obvious thing to say. Most states in modern history have wanted to be more independent, not less so. This remained true of the great majority of states in the world, in Africa, Asia or Latin America. Western Europe was a rare, partial exception, but even in Western Europe there were not so many French or British politicians who would have regarded increasing interdependence as a primary foreign policy goal. As for Eastern Europe, the central experience of this region in modern history was, precisely, dependency. For many, perhaps most people in Eastern Europe a primary meaning of 'freedom' continued to be the recovery of 'independence' for a nation in a state. The prospect of entering into new kinds of dependency — albeit 'mutual dependency' — before even sloughing off the old dependency (on the Soviet Union) was not instantly appealing.

So what was the case for interdependence? Insofar as any clear answer was offered to this question (and that is not very far) the underlying thought seems to be that the web of mutual dependencies would prevent any European state from striking at another, as they had done so often in the past. The *Verflechtung*, to recall Genscher's formulation, should no longer 'allow any country to get out ... without severely damaging their own most vital interests'. The model was the (West) European Community, and especially the Franco-German 'reconciliation', supposedly secured by precisely such a web of mutual dependencies. It was also linked to the notion of building trust and confidence between states. So in this respect, co-operation was primarily a means to achieving greater security between states in East and West, rather than to achieving change inside the states of Eastern Europe or the Soviet Union. There was more than an echo here of the Kissingerite notion of the 'Gulliverisation' of the Soviet Union. Interdependence was to be a pacifier.

Several caveats may be entered about this notion of interdependence as guarantee of international harmony. The first concerns the balance of dependence. The Franco-German interdependence functioned so well precisely because there was — in the Europe of 'Yalta' — a rough balance of mutual dependencies, political, economic and military, between the two countries. But there is no historical law that states this must be so. History offers far more examples of unequal dependencies: for example, the dependency of East Central Europe on Germany and/or Russia. Such unequal dependencies cannot be said to have diminished the likelihood of conflict between the states involved. Lenin's question — who, whom? — must therefore be applied to interdependence too: who becomes dependent on whom?

Secondly, there is the problem of third parties. If states A and B are 'interdependent' this may mean they are less likely to come into conflict with each other, but does it follow that state B is less likely to show aggression against state C? Only to the extent that state A chooses to make that a condition of its relationship with state B. Thus, for example, the Soviet invasion of Afghanistan did not directly threaten any Soviet-German interdependencies. It was a matter of choice — a calculation of interest — whether the Federal Republic responded by adjusting its own relationship to the Soviet Union. There was nothing 'inevitable', to recall Genscher's term, about that. In fact the Federal Republic's own perceived dependency on Moscow inclined it to react less strongly to Soviet aggression against a third party.

Now one German argument against imposing sanctions on the Soviet Union was that the Soviet Union was so relatively little dependent on economic ties with the West that it would not renounce what it saw as vital interests in order to preserve those ties. In other words, there was too little interdependence to pacify. There is some force in this argument. It is reasonable to suggest that interdependence must achieve, as it were, a critical mass, before it will affect the political behaviour of states. The necessary critical mass was, however, likely to be larger in the case of a Leninist party-state, because of the primacy of politics in such states. But how then might such a critical mass of interdependence be achieved? Was it possible to achieve such a critical mass without changing one or other system?

West Germany's own experience of trade, and more generally of economic, scientific and technical co-operation with the East, suggests that there are intrinsic limits to the number of ties that can be developed between two such different systems: between centrally planned and market economies, but also, more broadly, between dictatorships and democracies, between closed and open societies. Here was the problem. In order to affect the external conduct of the states in question, interdependence had to achieve a critical mass. In order to achieve that critical mass, however, there had to be change in the internal systems of the relevant states — of one system, or the other, or both.

West German politicians and policymakers did not fail to identify this problem. But here, too, they had an answer. To be sure, they said, an (unspecified) degree of systemic change is a precondition for achieving the peace-securing level of interdependence. But increasing interdependence is itself a means to promote systemic change! The favoured formula for this further golden harmony was 'system-opening co-operation'. Already in 1970 the influential policy intellectual, Klaus Ritter, had coined the phrase 'system-opening co-existence' as a response to the Soviet formula of 'peaceful co-existence'.

In June 1987 Ritter's friend and wartime comrade, Richard von Weizsäcker, now Federal President, took up and popularised the phrase, in the post-Helsinki form of 'system-opening co-operation'. The purely military aspect of East-West relations had been overemphasised, he argued, during a speech to mark the fortieth anniversary of the Marshall Plan, delivered, like Willy Brandt's a quarter-century before, at Harvard University. 'We must,' he said, 'find other "currencies" of relations with each other than simply military power.' And rather as Brandt and Bahr had taken as their exemplar the American John F Kennedy, so now von Weizsäcker summoned up the spirits of James Fulbright and George Marshall. In a subsequent speech at an Aspen Institute conference in Berlin — paying tribute to another American European, Shepard Stone — he repeated his plea for 'system-opening co-operation' adding: 'under the sign of perestroika'. Economic, scientific, technological, educational, environmental co-operation would, von Weizsäcker argued, not merely in itself reduce the economic, scientific and technological division of Europe, help to solve 'common problems', and increase the desirable 'interdependence'. It would also prove to be 'system-opening'.

What did this mean? One may safely assume that the 'system' referred to was primarily the Eastern system(s). The Gorbachev leadership, von Weizsäcker said in his Berlin speech, 'knows that it's a matter of reforming their system, not ours'. (Although there was some implication that the Western system needed a little 'opening' too: 'We too have our mistakes, we know the weaknesses of our virtues, we need to learn.') But what, in the context of the Soviet or Soviet-type system, was meant by 'opening'? Was this a polite euphemism for fundamental transformation, or did it just mean the same system made slightly more open — and if so, open for whom to do what? Again — as with the long-term definition of the 'European peace order' — the answers were vague and various.

Thus, in an intra-Western discussion devoted to precisely this subject, the then political director of the Foreign Ministry, Hermann von Richthofen, remarked: 'Through our policy we don't want to change the structures on the other side, just as we would not approve of an Eastern policy that aims to change the structures on our side . . .' 'For me,' said a German businessman in the same discussion, 'system-opening means above all people getting to know each other and the exchange of ideas and ways of thinking'. Soviet managers should be trained in West Germany, said the Federal President's press spokesman, 'that is then system-opening co-operation, because a Soviet manager who has been trained here will as a result later behave differently than he did before'.

The argument about the causal relationship between co-operation on the one side and systemic change (or 'opening') on the other was thus elusive and fragmentary. Sometimes the underlying thought seemed to be a modified version of convergence: the theory, most cautiously and precisely articulated by Raymond Aron, that advanced industrial societies would tend to become more like each other. 'I am inclined to believe,' Aron wrote, 'that advanced industrialisation, in Europe at least, favours an individualist rather than a collectivist civilisation . . . in the future perhaps Europe in this respect will extend as far as the Urals.' To encourage advanced industrialisation, by economic and technical modernisation, would therefore *ipso facto* encourage socio-political change.

At other times, the underlying thought seemed closer to that of subversion by example. The backwardness of the Soviet Union, said von Weizsäcker in Harvard, 'is the result of a closed system without participation (*Mitbestimmung*) and without incentives for the population, without free information . . . If there is now the chance of an opening, is that our risk?' By implication, to expose the Soviet population to Western habits, ideas, living standards was the risk of Soviet rulers. Again, the basic thought can be found already with Kennedy and Brandt in the early 1960s.

The new element linking these two notions was the nature of the latest phase of economic modernisation: the 'revolution of high technology', and, above all, information technology. The rapid, free flow of information, by computer, fax or satellite television, would be at once indispensable for economic modernisation and incompatible with the previously existing (or 'real existing') Soviet-type system, at whose very heart was the state's information monopoly — or, as Solzhenitsyn would put it, the Lie. The supposed magic of information technology would thus unite, as in a Hegelian synthesis, the two apparently opposed extremes of convergence and subversion.

Would an economic modernisation of the Soviet Union help the West? Hans-Dietrich Genscher rhetorically asked, in a spirited defence of developing Soviet-German economic ties in 1987. And he answered:

> whoever recognises the social developments which result from the new techno-
> logies in our free societies, towards more personal responsibility and smaller
> units, and whoever recognises that an opening of the Soviet Union quite
> automatically makes it necessary for it to move in this direction; they will also
> recognise that a Soviet Union which goes down the path of modernisation will
> in the end be a different one from that of today, a more open one, not a
> democracy in our sense, but a more open one compared with the Soviet Union
> of today.

Yet the claim for the system-opening effect of co-operation was not only made about the future. It was also made, albeit cautiously, about the past. 'The Conference on Security and Co-operation in Europe has, through its agreements in basket two, decisively contributed to the strengthening and deepening of East-West economic relations,' Richard von Weizsäcker observed in a further speech, in Hamburg in 1989. 'It has facilitated an economic, social and political change in Eastern Europe, one would like almost to say, it has made it in the long term unavoidable.' One might like almost to say this, but if one were to say it, then one would have to explain precisely how. Precisely what in economic, technical, scientific and environmental co-operation ('basket two') changed exactly what in Eastern polities?

'This attempt to cover the divided Europe again with a net of contacts, trade, exchange and co-operation, strengthens the reform forces in Eastern Europe,' said Horst Ehmke in a debate in January 1982, discussing the nature of Solidarity in Poland and the implications of martial law. Not that détente was the cause of reform movements. 'But the policy of détente, with its exchange and its contacts, has immensely increased the room for manoeuvre of this reform movement.' And again, 'détente policy naturally contributes indirectly to the setting free of ideas, forces, also productive forces, in Eastern Europe, which seek a new political expression'.

These hedged and fuzzy claims will be examined a little more closely later on. In particular we shall have to look at the balance between fostering an overall process which might indirectly encourage reforms, or 'system-opening', and, on the other hand, the direct encouragement (or discouragement) of people directly demanding respect for human rights and democracy. But before doing that it is worth briefly considering what sort of a web the Federal Republic did actually manage to spin with (around? over?) its Eastern neighbours in the twenty years from 1969 to 1989. How did the actual West German 'net' compare in quantity and quality with those of France, Britain, Italy or the United States?

The short answer is 'it was the thickest'. Starting from a position far behind its Western partners in everything except trade, the Federal Republic had by 1989, through the intensity and consistency of its efforts, built a more dense network of ties with all East European countries (not to mention East Germany) and even with the Soviet Union, than any other Western country. As we have seen, in all forms of economic tie, and not just in traditional Eastern trade, the Federal Republic far outstripped its main Western partners (see pages 244 f and Tables II and III).

In political relations, too, the sheer number of official visits and exchanges was unique. This included not just government ministers, officials and diplomats, but also senior and junior figures from all the main political parties, and from provincial as well as federal politics. There was not only a unique intensity of political contacts, but also a remarkable continuity on the West German side. In most East-West political contacts it was the Western partner who was constantly changing. In the case of West Germany it was almost the other way round. East European Foreign Ministers came and went, but the West German Foreign Minister remained the same. The same politicians, officials, commentators pursued the same business year in, year out. The only respect in which this political network was weak by comparison with, say, the American or British one, was in contacts with independent and oppositional political groups.

In cultural ties, the picture was more mixed. The Federal Republic gave a high priority to what in English would be called 'cultural diplomacy', in American sometimes also 'public diplomacy', and in German was described as *auswärtige Kulturpolitik* — that is 'external cultural policy'. The priority was emphasised by a new set of guide-lines in 1970, which also gave a more liberal and cosmopolitan definition of cultural policy, and remained so throughout the 1970s and 1980s, under the special care of a series of Free Democrat Ministers of State in the Foreign Ministry, but also under close parliamentary supervision. As much as one third of the budget of the Foreign Ministry went on cultural diplomacy, a proportion higher even than that of the traditional master of cultural diplomacy, France, and far higher than in the foreign affairs budgets of the United States or Britain. Roughly half this generous budget for external cultural policy was devoted to the teaching and promotion of the German language, called, in good German, *Sprachpolitik*.

Within this overall picture, Eastern Europe occupied a very special place. Cultural diplomacy in Eastern Europe was to serve as an important part of that overall Ostpolitik strategy of weaving a load-bearing web of ties. German culture, German scholarship, German enterprise had traditionally played a unique and even a leading role in much of the region now called Eastern Europe. But the last venture in the Ostpolitik of the German Reich, launched under the banner of *Kultur*, had delivered a terrible blow to the influence of the very culture in the name of which it claimed to act. The revulsion against everything German after 1945 was then swiftly reinforced by communist state policies in the conditions of the Cold War, and by the presence of a second German state which claimed alone to represent everything that was good, true and beautiful in German culture.

German, once the second language of many countries in the region (with French as that of the others), lost its place first to the officially imposed Russian and then to the unofficially triumphant English. French also lost out, but France fought a fierce semantic rearguard action, through well-endowed cultural institutes, often with a tradition dating back to before the war. The West German radio station broadcasting to the East — *Deutsche Welle* — achieved neither the audiences nor the impact of the BBC, Radio Free Europe or Voice of America.

These special difficulties remained remarkably persistent. If popular revulsion against all things German was gradually replaced, partly under the influence of the new Ostpolitik, by a more positive image of the new Germany, this did not necessarily endear the idea of expanding German cultural influence to the communist leaderships. In several East European states, the questions of German culture and language were also inextricably intertwined with the thorny issue of the German minorities. Last but not least, there was the dogged obstructionism of the GDR. Not the Goethe Institutes of West Germany but the Herder Institutes of East Germany should represent German culture in the East.

As a result, although the Federal Republic did negotiate framework cultural agreements with all East European states (except East Germany) in the 1970s, the responsible Foreign Ministry official, Barthold C Witte — himself, not accidentally, a Free Democrat — describes the years from 1975 to 1985 as a 'decade of stagnation' in West Germany's cultural relations with the East. He notes that official academic exchange with the Soviet Union, for example, remained at the ridiculous level of fifteen scholarships a year. Witte regards the Budapest Cultural Forum of 1985, the first major Helsinki follow-up meeting in this field, as the beginning of a breakthrough. But even in Hungary it was only in 1988 that West Germany was able to open an official cultural institute, and even then it was not formally called a Goethe Institute, due to the Hungarian authorities' residual concern about official East German sensibilities. (A Goethe Institute had, however, been established in maverick Romania in 1979, although it operated under increasing difficulties in the late Ceauşescu years.)

As late as mid-1989, the official map of German cultural establishments abroad shows an eloquent blank to Germany's east. So also with the statistics on German language-teaching — with the notable exception of the Soviet Union where, in another example of Russia's more sovereign approach to matters German, more than nine million schoolchildren officially learned German.

For most of Eastern Europe, in this as in other respects, 1989 marked the real breakthrough. Now official German cultural institutes were swiftly established in all the countries, and there was a veritable explosion of interest in learning German. While the objects of this cultural diplomacy continued to be stated in liberal and cosmopolitan terms, there were very clearly, as in British, French or American cultural diplomacy, goals of competitive national interest as well. German, wrote Barthold Witte in 1991, now had a chance to remain — by which he surely meant, to become again — a *lingua franca* in Central and Eastern Europe, although now 'beside English'. Elsewhere Witte would bluntly observe: 'Those who speak and understand German are also more likely to buy German . . .'

The special difficulties of official cultural diplomacy up to 1989 had, however, to some extent been circumvented by the very active programmes of what in English would be called 'quangos' (quasi-non-governmental organisations) such as the German Academic Exchange Service or the Alexander von Humboldt Foundation, which were largely or wholly financed from the public purse; by those of the party foundations, also partly financed from the public purse; and by those of major private foundations such as the Volkswagen Foundation, the Krupp Foundation, or the Robert Bosch Foundation, with its pioneering German-Polish projects.

Altogether, these public, semi-public and private West German institutions, including many individual universities, academies, cultural festivals and the like, managed to establish numerous links and to bring a large and increasing number of East European scholars, artists, intellectuals and students to work, study or perform in the Federal Republic, and sent a smaller (but also increasing) number to do the same in the other direction. By comparison with exchanges between West European nations, these remained very small, but the overall growth since the 1960s was impressive. Not a few members of the new governing élites of Central and Eastern Europe after 1989 had spent time in Germany on one or other of these programmes.

What was true at the level of the intelligentsia was even more true at the popular level: in both directions. No Western country sent more tourists into the East. But, in pursuit of its own special idea of Helsinki, the Helsinki of human contacts, the Federal Republic also let in far more ordinary, individual East Europeans than any other Western country. In 1988, the West German embassies in East Central Europe (taken here as Poland, Hungary and Czechoslovakia) issued a total of more than 1.3 million visas.

'It is important,' Kennedy had said at the Free University of West Berlin in 1963, 'that the people on the quiet streets in the East be kept in touch with Western society.' In the 1980s, few Western societies were more open to 'the people on the quiet streets' than West Germany. This brought benefits to the Federal Republic: for no one who actually visited West Germany could any more believe the Communist propaganda about an imperialist 'revanchist' German menace. But it also brought costs.

Many of these visitors worked illegally, to gain precious hard currency. A minority also sought political asylum, or simply remained in the country illegally. Due to the exceptionally liberal asylum clause in West Germany's Basic Law — and the generous interpretation of that clause — very few of them were actually sent back. If the generous interpretation of the nationality clause of the Basic Law meant that many East Europeans who were only dubiously Germans were accepted as such, the generous interpretation of the asylum clause meant that many East Europeans who were not even pretending to be Germans, but merely wanted to live in a free, prosperous country which happened to be called Germany, were allowed to do so. One way or the other, hundreds of thousands of East Europeans benefited directly from this policy of deliberate openness — and millions more benefited indirectly, through the hard curency, goods, and not least, experience that their relatives and friends sent or brought home.

Yet the numbers cannot tell the whole story. Beside the question of quantity there is the question of quality. And the quality of this web was uneven. We have mentioned already the weakness of the political ties to independent or opposition groups. In technology, in economics, and in the cultural and human exchanges, the interdependence was unequal. Genscher's offer of the 'technological connection' had a double-edge for East Europeans: the double-edge of recreating an historic dependency. Most East Europeans came to West Germany to learn or earn. Most Germans went East to spend or to teach. Most Germans in the East were holidaymakers, investors or employers. Most East Europeans in West Germany were impecunious shoppers, poorly paid *Gastarbeiter*, or, at best, poor relations. The small privileged crust of intellectuals, artists, and scholars was the exception which proved the rule.

This was not, of course, the West Germans' fault. They were not — or only in a very indirect, historical sense — responsible for the relative economic backwardness of Eastern Europe. They could not, as it were, help being rich. And ordinary men and women could hardly be expected to decline cheap labour or cheap pleasures out of some vague, elevated sense of moral or historical responsibility. Moreover, from the individual

East Europeans' point of view it was far better to earn a little hard currency — albeit on terms which for a West European would be considered exploitation — than to earn none. For the children at home, father's work as a window-cleaner in Dortmund, not his studies on Husserl at Warsaw University, made the difference between bearable austerity and sheer deprivation.

This was a lesser evil. But it was also a very long way from those elevated visions of mutually enriching European spiritual exchange to be found in the politicians' speeches. On the ground, the new 'interdependence' looked all too much like an old dependence. If East Europeans had become less dependent on the East they had become more dependent on the West. And if the East meant for them, as it had meant of old, Russia, the West increasingly meant, as it had meant of old, Germany. The phrase young Poles used for 'going to work in the West' was *na saksy*, a nineteenth-century slang phrase (containing the root 'Saxony') to describe the seasonal labour which, then as now, had been done primarily in Germany.

It must be stressed again that this situation was not of the Federal Republic's making and did not reflect its aims. But it was a reality which the Germans, as much as their eastern neighbours, would have to confront in the 1990s.

Stability before liberty

In October 1989 the prestigious Peace Prize of the German Book Trade was awarded to the Czech writer and opposition leader Václav Havel. Havel was prevented by the highest Czechoslovak authorities from travelling to Frankfurt to receive the prize. However, he sent an acceptance speech, which was read on his behalf at the ceremony in the Paulskirche in Frankfurt — where the assembly of German liberals and patriots had met in the revolution of 1848. President von Weizsäcker and Chancellor Kohl sat in the front row. Between them there was a symbolic empty seat. Havel's speech, entitled 'A Word about the Word', was a reflection both on the exceptional importance that words assume in a totalitarian system, and, beyond that, on the pitfalls, double-edges and multiple meanings of all the most important words: 'socialism', 'freedom', 'peace'.

'Your country,' Havel wrote at one point in his address,

has made a great contribution to modern European history: the first wave of détente, its well-known Ostpolitik. But even that word managed at times to be well and truly ambiguous. It signified, of course, the first glimmer of hope for a Europe without Cold War and iron curtain; yet at the same time — alas — it more than once signified the renunciation of freedom, and hence of a basic condition for any real peace. I still recall how at the beginning of the 1970s some of my West German friends and colleagues avoided me for fear that any sort of contact with me — someone out of favour with the authorities here — might needlessly provoke those authorities and thus threaten the fragile foundations of the nascent détente.

How was it possible that one of Czechoslovakia's most distinguished independent spokesmen could counterpose — albeit cautiously, personally, and in the past tense — the word 'Ostpolitik' to the word 'freedom'? Surely the highest representatives of the Federal Republic were sitting in the front row of the Paulskirche in Frankfurt to prove the opposite? To understand this one has to go back twenty years, to 1969, and notice again the ambiguities of another big word: 'normalisation'.

As we have seen, 'normalisation' was a key-term for the social-liberal architects of Ostpolitik in the early 1970s. For them it meant the restoration of a more 'normal' relationship of the Federal Republic with the Soviet Union and East European states, starting with the elementary 'normality' of diplomatic recognition. But 'normalisation' was also a key-word in Czechoslovakia at that time, and what it meant there was the attempt to return a European society, initially by the use of force, to Soviet norms. 'Normalisation' was what followed the Soviet invasion in August 1968. It was the crushing of the Prague Spring, the slow strangling of hard-won liberties, expulsions, sackings, censorship, repression.

These two kinds of 'normalisation' did not merely exist side-by-side. They were causally related. The Soviet invasion of Czechoslovakia was not the end of détente. It was not even, as the French Prime Minister Michel Debré memorably remarked, 'a traffic accident on the road to détente'. Rather it was the toll-gate on the highway to détente. 'That the Soviets found their way back to a more flexible diplomacy just at this time [i.e. early 1969],' writes Richard Löwenthal, 'was certainly in part a result of the fact that after the violent suppression of Czech reform communism they felt themselves more secure in their own sphere of influence: "Change through rapprochement" was no more to be feared.' 'Normalisation' à la Husák was thus a precondition for 'normalisation' à la Brandt.

Given this fateful connection, it became all the more important to ask what the effect might be in the other direction: that is, how East-West 'normalisation' might affect 'normalisation' inside the East. Would it facilitate 'normalisation' in the Brezhnev-Husák sense of a return, through repression, intimidation and *Gleichschaltung*, to Soviet norms? Or would it rather, albeit in the longer term, encourage a return to European, Western norms?

It must be said that this question — so crucial to the people of Czechoslovakia — was not high on the agenda of German Ostpolitik in the 1970s. West German politicians and policymakers were so preoccupied

with addressing their own 'constitutive double conflict' with the East —
the general Western and the special national — that they had little time to
address the East Europeans' constitutive double conflict: that of states with
the imperial centre, and of societies with (party-) states. The latter conflict
was, indeed, barely recognised as such in the approach of social-liberal
Ostpolitik.

In the speeches and writings of Helmut Schmidt, for example, the term
'East Europeans' seemed to apply almost exclusively to East European
states, and those states were — a further highly questionable assumption
— assumed to be represented by their communist rulers. So far as East
Central Europe (apart from the GDR) is concerned, it is hard to disagree
with the Polish writer Jacek Maziarski when he comments: 'of all the
Western states, it is probably the Federal Republic of Germany which
most weakly perceived the traps created by the disharmony between social
aspirations and the policy of the official authorities . . .'

To the extent that West German policy did recognise the tension
between party-state and society, it was argued that improvements could
only be achieved *with* the authorities and not against them. Even 'human
rights' it was said, could only be achieved with, not against the powers-
that-be. These insights were born of one triumph of Soviet-backed force,
the building of the Berlin Wall, and reinforced by another — the invasion
of Czechoslovakia. To the limited extent that German Ostpolitik did have
any notion of promoting domestic socio-political change in East Central
Europe — that is, tackling the internal aspect of the division of Europe —
it focussed on change in the party-state.

Insofar as there was any underlying concept, it remained that nostrum
of behavioural psychology, originally articulated by Egon Bahr under the
vague slogan 'change through rapprochement'; more precisely described
by Josef Joffe as 'relaxation through reassurance'; and analysed earlier
under the heading 'liberalisation through stabilisation'. With hindsight, we
can see that it did not work like that: neither in East Germany nor
anywhere else. But this is not just a matter of hindsight. For in Poland
and Czechoslovakia there were already independent intellectuals in the
1970s who were saying that it would not work; and suggesting an
alternative. One of them was called Václav Havel.

These independent East Central European intellectuals drew precisely
the opposite conclusion to the West German social-liberal Ostpolitiker
from the crushing of the Prague Spring. In the past some of them had
believed — believed passionately — in so-called 'revisionism', in change
from above following the growing progressive enlightenment of the
leaders, in the possibility of Communism reforming itself voluntarily into
democratic socialism. Indeed, as the Hungarian philosopher and social
critic János Kis wrote, from the mid-1950s until the late 1960s the 'general
idea of evolution in Eastern Europe was that of reforms generated from

above and supported from below'. But this hope was crushed in 1968, under the Soviet tanks in Prague and the police batons in Warsaw. Those events reinforced the West German Ostpolitiker in their belief that change, or at least 'human alleviations', could only be achieved by dealing with the communist powers-that-be, in the hope of eventually starting the 'virtuous circle' of relaxation and reassurance, liberalisation through stabilisation.

But these independent East Central European intellectuals concluded: We have concentrated too much on the powers-that-be. These events have shown that they alone cannot bring lasting, meaningful change, even if (which is to be doubted) they really want change that will inevitably result in their loss of power and privilege. Let us instead work from the bottom up. Let us draw on 'the power of the powerless' — to use Havel's phrase of 1978. Let us concentrate on people organising themselves deliberately outside the structures of the party-state, in multifarious independent social groupings, working together and 'living in truth'. The operative goal will not be the reform of the party-state but the reconstitution of civil society. Yet of course, if the strategy is at all successful, the party-state will be compelled to adapt to these *faits accomplis*, if only by grudgingly accepting an incremental *de facto* reduction in the areas of its total control. But what is *de facto* today may eventually become *de jure* too. The *pays réel* will finally shape the *pays légal*.

This strategy of 'social self-organisation' was prefigured by Leszek Kołakowski's *Theses on Hope and Hopelessness* — published just six months after the Warsaw Treaty was signed. It was further developed by the veteran opposition leader, Jacek Kuroń, and by Adam Michnik, in his essay on 'the New Evolutionism', and guided the work not only of the Polish Workers' Defence Committee, KOR, founded in 1976, and in 1977 significantly renamed the Social Self-defence Committee-'KOR', but also of other opposition groups. Similar ideas were developed in Czechoslovakia — for example by Václav Benda in his 1978 essay 'The Parallel Polis' — and underpinned the work of Charter 77. The Solidarity movement in Poland was a piece of social self-organisation on a massive and unprecedented scale.

'Social self-organisation' was considered not only as a means to an end, but also as an end in itself. These autonomous social groupings and movements would, it was hoped, give the added push of 'pressure from below' to compel the ruling nomenklatura into making reforms. But even if those reforms did not come, the existence of these ligatures of autonomous association would be good in itself. For the totalitarian aspiration of a Soviet-type state was precisely to break all such autonomous ties: to rule over an atomised society. The essential bedrock of a liberal, democratic, Western, European state, by contrast, was a strong civil society, rich in intermediate layers of free and frank association. Every restored fragment of civil society was thus in itself a blow against 'normalisation' in the

Soviet sense, and for 'normalisation' in the sense of a return to Western, European norms.

Now it may justly be observed that the web of co-operation, communication and exchange — in a word, *Verflechtung* — that German Ostpolitik set out to spin did, in practice, facilitate the growth of these fragments of civil society. This is surely so. But if one looks at what West German Ostpolitiker said and did in the 1970s, then it is clear that this was not a primary intention. Building up civil society against the party-state was not what they thought they were doing. Not even in East Germany.

To be sure, here, unlike in the rest of East Central Europe, a distinction was made between helping 'the people' (*die Menschen*) and dealing with the party-state. But the notion of *die Menschen* is subtly but importantly different from that of civil society. For *die Menschen* means individual people, whereas civil society means people in free, self-conscious groups. The former exist in all societies, the latter are the ligaments of free societies. It was much easier for a Soviet-type party-state to accept 'humanitarian improvements' for individual people, even for hundreds of thousands of individual people, so long as they remained individual. Indeed, that was the Soviet understanding of Helsinki 'basket three'. *Die Menschen* may get humanitarian improvements; only civil societies secure human rights. The latter is a far more ambitious, more fundamental goal.

There was a curious asymmetry here. On the one side, a few seemingly powerless intellectuals said: Whatever the party-state wants, we will recreate civil society! We will win back human rights! On the other side, one of the most powerful and successful democratic states in Europe said: if we speak very gently to the party-state, and offer it bags of 'co-operation', perhaps we can win some humane improvements. The apparently powerless had a seemingly unfounded presumption of strength. The apparently powerful had almost as curious a presumption of weakness.

In part this presumption was explicable by the special German concerns that have been described above. In many respects, West Germany was the asking party in its relationship even with Poland or Czechoslovakia, let alone with the Soviet Union, in the 1970s. It had other fish to fry. Perhaps another part of the explanation for these very modest goals lies in the real experience of weakness after 13 August 1961. To some extent the Federal Republic in its whole relationship with Eastern Europe in the 1970s was a magnified projection of the West Berlin city government in its relationship with East Germany in the 1960s: Be thankful for every small mercy, since the other side has all the cards. 'Small steps are better than none.' Reassurance is the only hope of relaxation; stabilisation, of liberalisation.

In sum, therefore, it is not true to say that German Ostpolitik in the 1970s had no concept of fostering desirable socio-political change inside Eastern Europe. It had one, but it was a long-term strategy of deliberate indirection, based on the hope of modifying the behaviour of communist rulers by example, trust, co-operation and incentives. The dialectical principle developed by Brandt and Bahr in the 1960s stated that one must recognise the status quo in order to overcome it. A strong meaning of 'recognition' and a political definition of 'status quo' led to the more specific dialectical prescription that one must strengthen the party-state in order to weaken it. Since outspoken intellectuals and the would-be democratic opposition unsettled rather than reassured the communist rulers, and even seemed capable of 'destabilising' these states — so powerful are a few unfettered words! — this led logically to a third dialectical principle: one must ignore the democrats in order to support democracy.

The West would best serve the cause of liberty by not demanding it. Václav Havel might not appreciate this, but in the long run what those German visitors were doing was in his own best interest. Ultimately, it was better for him that they should not meet him. They knew best what was good for him.

This logic was, to say the least, patronising. But until the end of the 1970s it affected — and offended — only a small minority in East Central Europe, albeit a distinguished one. Their 'representativeness' could seriously be questioned. An argument could be made that the majority in the countries affected benefited more from Bonn's exclusive dealings with the powers-that-were. At the birth of Solidarity in Poland in August 1980, however, the clash of — what? analyses? aspirations? interests? — took on entirely new dimensions. For it now became a central issue in East-West relations.

The Polish revolution of 1980-81 both challenged the theory and threatened the practice of German Ostpolitik in a particularly acute form. The Soviet invasion of Afghanistan, the growing dispute about the deployment of new medium-range nuclear missiles in East and West, and the more general confrontation between the Soviet Union and the United States, all this already threatened to jeopardise the overall 'framework conditions' thought to be required for the successful pursuit of West German détente policy in general, and German-German relations in particular. Now the Polish crisis could be the last straw.

The Bonn government had done what it could to prevent the consequences of the Soviet invasion of Afghanistan — and of the American reaction to it — from adversely affecting its Ostpolitik. Because détente within Europe had to be indivisible, so violations of détente outside Europe had to be, so far as possible, minimised or disregarded. (A 'stabilisation' and 'normalisation' in Afghanistan was thus rather to be desired.) But détente could not survive another Afghanistan. And a Soviet invasion of Poland would be far worse than Afghanistan.

At the same time, Solidarity was, by its very nature, a frontal challenge to the concept of political change in Eastern Europe which, to the extent that there was any such concept, continued to underpin the social-liberal Ostpolitik. For Solidarity was a massive demonstration of the gulf between society and state, and the realisation — on an extraordinary scale — of the democratic opposition's vision of a self-organising society. Instead of reforms voluntarily conceded from above, in conditions of 'stability', there were concessions wrested by a (peaceful and self-limiting) revolution from below. Solidarity put liberty before stability: analytically as well as politically and morally. Instead of liberalisation through stabilisation it proposed stabilisation through liberalisation — with an inevitable period of transitional instabilities, and, of course, economic dislocation. And Solidarity was anything but dialectical. It said: if you want to change the status quo you must change the status quo; if you want to weaken the party dictatorship you must weaken the party dictatorship; if you want democracy you must demand democracy.

Throughout the sixteen months of Solidarity's overground existence (September 1980–December 1981) there was a deep ambivalence in the responses of West German politicians and policymakers. On the one hand, they proudly observed that without détente Solidarity would not have been possible. Marion Gräfin Dönhoff described Solidarity as a 'result' of détente. Like all assertions about causal connections between Western policies and Eastern politics, this proposition requires close and careful examination.

Thus it is, for example, plausible to argue that the Western credits made to the Gierek regime as part of Western détente policy contributed to the birth of Solidarity. But, as we have seen, they did so in ways that were not intended by those that made (or, strictly speaking, guaranteed) them. The credits, and associated increase of trade and technological transfers, were meant to facilitate a process of modernising through economic reform. In fact, they were used as a substitute for reform. They led first to a short-lived direct satisfaction of consumer desires through Western imports, and then to the downward spiral of an economy staggering under both the accumulated burden of a largely unreformed plan economy and the specific legacy of mismanagement and soaring hard currency debt from the détente period. This, and the consequent sharp disappointment of artificially raised consumer expectations, can with some confidence be identified as a cause of the crisis from which Solidarity emerged.

Somewhat more speculatively, one can argue that the sharp increase in the number of Poles travelling to the West, and particularly to West Germany, contributed to the popular discontent which fed into Solidarity. The annual tally of journeys made by Poles to the West passed the half million mark in 1977, with a grand total of some four million visits to the West in the course of the 1970s. Having seen the West at first hand, people were all the more sharply aware of the shortcomings of their own system — and not just, as many Westerners condescendingly assumed, in the area of consumer supplies. At the same time, they could no longer give any credence to the horror stories dished up by communist propaganda about life in the West. Specifically, they could no longer be frightened into support for the communist authorities by dark threats of German revanchism, and altogether by the German bogey which had served the communist regime so well for so many years. To remove the sense of a German threat, and replace it so far as possible by the attractions of the West German model, was a conscious purpose of Ostpolitik, and one which had already borne some fruit by 1980. Opinion polls on this issue are more than usually unreliable, but one independent survey indicated that in 1980 only 10.7 per cent of those asked saw a threat to Poland's independence from the Federal Republic, compared with 49.6 per cent who saw such a threat from the Soviet Union.

It can also be argued that the Helsinki Final Act provided an international charter to which the democratic opposition in Poland could appeal, while the Helsinki review process was an institutional goad to the Gierek regime to respect its provisions. The usefulness of Helsinki in this respect was recognised by Polish activists. But the bold claim that 'without Helsinki Solidarity would not have happened' must be qualified in three respects. Firstly, the causes of Solidarity are to be found above all inside Poland. When key participants come to write their memoirs, they make only passing reference to international influences in general, and Helsinki in particular.

Secondly, Helsinki was only one among many international treaties, charters or documents with which the opposition — in Poland and elsewhere — formally buttressed its claims. In opposition documents, it was often the human rights conventions of the UN that were first adduced. In the twenty-one demands of the Gdańsk strike, which gave birth to Solidarity, the specific reference was to 'convention 87 of the International Labour Organisation (ILO) . . . ratified by the Polish People's Republic'. And the influence of the human rights demands made by another international organisation, the Roman Catholic Church, can hardly be overstated. In terms of direct, demonstrable influence on the Polish people, Vatican II, as applied to Poland by the Polish Pope, was more important than the Helsinki Final Act.

Thirdly, insofar as it was the specific détente instrument of Helsinki which had a direct, positive influence on the evolution of the democratic opposition in Poland, it was above all Helsinki in the interpretation given it by the United States from 1977 on. As we have seen, it was the United States under Carter which made the direct linkage between human rights and new credits, a linkage which clearly influenced Gierek's tolerance of the fledgling democratic opposition. It was governmental, congressional, labour and human rights organisations from the United States which provided the most support, political, symbolic, moral and, not least, financial, to the predecessors of Solidarity — and then to Solidarity itself. While this story is of course a complex one, with notable exceptions, it is generally true to say that, as Havel indicated in his Frankfurt speech, West Germany was at the other extreme in this respect.

The approach of most leading practitioners of German Ostpolitik was characterised not merely by what are known in German as *Berührungsängste* (contact fears), but, as we have seen, by a conscious and deliberate avoidance of such potentially destabilising contacts. Klaus Reiff, a Social Democratic journalist who served as press attaché in the German embassy in Warsaw in the early 1980s, recalls that when Hans-Dietrich Genscher visited Warsaw in March 1981, talks with Solidarity were not on his programme. When Reiff tried merely to introduce a Solidarity journalist to him during a press briefing, the German Foreign Minister reacted with extreme irritation. And this at a time when Solidarity was a fully legal organisation, recognised as a 'partner' even by the communist authorities! The evidence on such issues is inevitably anecdotal: but there is no doubt in which direction the anecdotal evidence points.

One other aspect of Helsinki and the policy of interweaving was a deliberate effort to increase the free flow of information both between East and West and within the East. If one looks at the direct contribution of the increased flow of information to the Solidarity revolution, then it is probably true that the large presence of Western media (specifically sanctioned by Helsinki) and even, marginally, improved information technology, did help the birth and growth of the Solidarity movement. But much the most important direct contribution was made by purveyors of information which both organisationally and technologically preceded détente: the telephone, telex and television inside Poland, and Western radio stations from outside. The Polish-language services of Radio France Internationale, the BBC, Voice of America, and, second to none, Radio Free Europe, known to most Poles colloquially — and aptly — just as 'Free Europe' (*Wolna Europa*), were crucial in the spread of information inside Poland throughout the whole period under review.

Yet Radio Free Europe was an institution more closely identified with the Cold War than with détente. Willy Brandt's notes of his talks in Warsaw in December 1970 record a revealing exchange with the then party leader, Władysław Gomułka. Brandt records Gomułka asking: 'what would a German court say if we sued Radio Free Europe?' Brandt summarises his own response thus 'Reference to overall development [?], relations with USA, possible changes through passing of time.' This does not sound like a very vigorous defence of RFE. And then Gomułka: 'But you give the licence.'

The connections between détente and Solidarity are thus by no means clear or linear. Among the putative Western causes, some were not specifically 'détente' causes at all. One has to ask which version of détente, which Helsinki, contributed to the rise of Solidarity. The Eastern results of détente policies were often quite different from those intended. Arguably this was true of Solidarity altogether. For this kind of rapid, unstable, revolutionary movement for change from below was clearly not envisaged by the makers of Ostpolitik, who had hoped to contribute to a reduction, not a sharpening, of the tension between rulers and ruled in Eastern Europe. In a dialectical twist not anticipated by the dialecticians of détente, the policy of reducing tensions (*Entspannungspolitik*) had itself produced tensions (*Spannungen*). To be sure, the reduction of tensions and the growth of ties between East and West may have contributed to the restraint both of the Polish and of the Soviet regime in their response to the popular revolt. But the increase in tensions inside the East would now increase tensions between East and West. As one Western specialist pithily observed: détente was bad for détente.

Precisely because they saw this, the same West German politicians and policymakers who said 'without détente, no Solidarity', at the same time argued that this was the wrong way to go. The Poles organised in Solidarity were trying to go too far too fast. Only gradual change, controlled from above — as in Hungary — was feasible. This romantic Polish adventure would end in tears. And those tears would then also be German tears, because a Soviet invasion of Poland would finally bring down the house of détente in Europe, and jeopardise the small humane improvements that had so painstakingly been negotiated for the Germans in the East: for *die Menschen*. A judgment about the internal possibilities in Poland was thus mixed with a profound fear of the external repercussions for Germany.

It must be emphasised that the official, public position of the Bonn government in these sixteen months differed little from those of its major Western partners. Their positions were, indeed, very carefully co-ordinated in Nato, European Political Co-operation and bilateral consultations. Bonn, like Washington, Paris and London, emphasised the imperative of non-interference in Polish internal affairs, thus turning one of Moscow's favourite Helsinki formulae against the Soviet Union. Directly and indirectly it underlined how catastrophic would be the effects of a Soviet intervention. Maintaining a dialogue with the authorities and the Church, it also did more than most Western powers to ease the Polish government's immediate financial crisis. By Schmidt's own account, this financial help amounted to some half billion DM in the twelve months to October 1981. But significant differences of emphasis were apparent. Where American policymakers tended to laud the political gains in Poland, German policymakers tended to note the economic cost. Where the former stressed the opportunity, the latter stressed the risk.

The differences became acute with the declaration of martial law on 13 December 1981. This could not have come at a worse time for Chancellor

Schmidt, who found himself on the last day of his summit meeting with Erich Honecker in East Germany — a meeting that had already been postponed on account of the Polish crisis. Asked by a journalist for his first reaction to the declaration of the 'state of war' in Poland, Schmidt said: 'Herr Honecker was as dismayed as I, that *this has now proved necessary*. I very much hope that the Polish nation will succeed in solving their problems. They have already lasted a long time. And the economic and financial capacities of other states to help Poland are certainly not unlimited' (my italics). Klaus Bölling, who was with him at the time, suggests that Schmidt himself soon understood 'that it was a mistake to portray the Poles indirectly as an interference factor for German-German relations.' And five days later the Chancellor declared to the Bundestag: 'I stand with all my heart on the side of the [Polish] workers.'

Although the 'internal' military solution had been on the cards for some time — and some part of the Reagan administration had known about it more definitely from a high-level Polish defector — the major Western powers had not agreed a co-ordinated response to this contingency. As a result, the crisis of the Soviet bloc became a crisis of the Western Alliance. An internal East German assessment of the Schmidt-Honecker summit meeting, drafted for the Politburo at the end of December 1981, noted that Schmidt's attitude 'has contributed to the fact that so far there has been no unified front of the USA, Western Europe and Japan towards the PR [People's Republic of] Poland, the USSR and the socialist community; and this despite the repeated and intensified efforts of the USA . . . ' According to the East German assessment, the Schmidt-Honecker summit had thus 'given the Military Council of People's Poland a breathing-space which is not to be underestimated'.

The Reagan administration held the Soviet Union directly responsible for martial law in Poland, and therefore imposed sanctions on Moscow as well as on Warsaw. The Schmidt government insisted that this was still an internal Polish solution, and therefore refused to impose sanctions on Moscow, while also agreeing to receive in Bonn the Polish deputy prime minister, Mieczysław F Rakowski. Two arguments must be distinguished here: the narrow argument about sanctions and the broader argument about political change. The narrow argument has been considered above. It is the broader argument that concerns us here.

This issue of the proper response to martial law provoked a storm of political and publicistic argument both in and around West Germany. It is impossible to summarise all the arguments pro and contra, because they were so diverse, so fragmentary and so laden with emotion. But the main lines are roughly as follows. Leading Social Democrats and, to a lesser extent, Free Democrats, were criticised because they seemed almost to condone Jaruzelski's coup. They were charged with being chillingly indifferent to the cause of liberty — and especially to the plight of Polish

290 · *In Europe's Name*

social democrats fighting for the cause of liberty — in Central and Eastern Europe, by contrast with their enthusiasm — and active support for — those fighting for liberty in, say, Central and Southern America. Herbert Wehner, to take an extreme example, travelled to Warsaw in February 1982, there actually to embrace General Jaruzelski, while at the same time circulating to his parliamentary colleagues an appeal from the Bolivian 'consulate in resistance' in West Germany.

Leading Social Democrats were further accused of condoning repression in Poland out of a selfish concern for specifically national interests in the continuation of Ostpolitik in general, and Deutschlandpolitik in particular. They were thus charged with indifference to liberty, hypocrisy and national selfishness. Such criticism came not only from the United States and from the Christian Democratic opposition in Bonn, but also from French and Italian socialists, and finally, when at last they could speak, from Poles who had actually been locked up on 13 December 1981.

The case for the social-liberal line was also made in several different ways, and quite as emotionally as that against it. It was argued that the Polish state of war was a lesser evil. Helmut Schmidt recalls that he felt 'great relief' that it was not a direct Soviet intervention. (Schmidt's first response to martial law and Adenauer's first response to the building of the Berlin Wall had this in common. In each case the West German leader had feared a worse Soviet action, so his first reaction was of relief as much as outrage.) It was suggested that because of Germany's historical record in Poland, Germans could not be so outspoken in their denunciation of what Poles did to Poles. Schmidt himself cited the imperative of 'reconciliation' as a decisive motive for his own restraint. There was the related argument that external criticism — especially from Germany — would only strengthen the hand of the oppressors. There was also the argument that the food parcels which Germans sent in millions helped the Poles more than sanctions. Beyond this, three main reasons were given for, as Theo Sommer put it in *Die Zeit*, 'wishing success' to Jaruzelski's 'perfectly executed military coup'.

Firstly, the 'destabilisation' in Poland had threatened to upset the whole precarious equilibrium between East and West, possibly even spilling over into neighbouring countries. As Germans had renounced their claim to national unity, for the sake of peace, so the Poles would have to renounce their claim to freedom — in the name of 'the highest priority . . . keeping the peace', as Egon Bahr put it. Preserving world peace, wrote Bahr, was 'even more important than Poland'. So the state of war in Poland was needed to preserve the state of peace in the world.

Secondly, there was the familiar argument that 'stability' was a precondition for internal reform. Only when Poland's rulers felt themselves secure, could they again relax. The Polish leadership's goal, Bahr averred, was 'stability with a moderate continuation of the reform course'. What

Poland needed, said the vice-chairman of the Social Democrats, Hans-Jür-gen Wischnewski, was rather 'the Hungarian model'.

The third reason was: yes, we have to think of our own German interests too, and especially of the interests of the people in East Germany and West Berlin. 'In the GDR,' wrote Klaus Bölling, then Permanent Representative of the Federal Republic in East Berlin,

> people not only understood Schmidt's reticence [in relation to Poland], they were also grateful for the fact that he was among the minority in the West who thought ahead. The citizens in the GDR could easily imagine that after a bloodbath in Poland a long period of the peace of the graveyard would come in Eastern Europe and the GDR, that we, the Germans in both states, might perhaps have to wait a whole decade before we could talk to one another again.

One of the best West German journalistic observers of the GDR put the underlying compulsion very plainly: 'Bonn depends on the Soviet Union, so far as these 19 million compatriots are concerned.' (19 million being 17 million in the GDR plus 2 million in West Berlin.)

These three main reasons were all expressed in terms of one key-word: stability. As we have seen already in the discussion of Deutschlandpolitik, that word was used in several, different but conflated senses. Here we had stability as world peace; stability as precondition for reform; and stability as the permissive function for Deutschlandpolitik. Now anyone who followed the German political discussion in the early 1980s could be in no doubt that many West Germans believed that world peace was endangered. The high-point of Solidarity in Poland was also the high-point of the peace movement in Germany. And anyone who talked to German policy-makers at this time would have little doubt that they believed the 'Hungarian way' (or, indeed, the GDR way) was a better path to liberalisation in Eastern Europe. The genuineness of these opinions need not be doubted. But they were just that: opinions. Opinions differ.

Since the West had made it perfectly clear (since 1961, at the very latest) that it would not intervene militarily in Eastern Europe even if the Soviet Union did, 'world peace' was not directly threatened by developments in Poland. To be sure, these would increase tensions between the nuclear-armed superpowers. Yet it was the repression of Solidarity, not the 'instability' associated with its toleration, that most sharply increased those tensions. As for the judgement about the best path to internal liberalisa-tion: many people disagreed. Above all, most Poles disagreed. Did the Poles not know what was good for the Poles? These two claims thus turn out, on a little closer examination, to be highly questionable, analytically as well as morally.

There remains the third reason: national interest. This everyone could see: internees in Poland as well as policymakers in Paris, London and

Washington. Some at that time said that the first and second arguments were merely decorative wrapping for the third, that of hard national interest. But that was too simple a view. The problem lay deeper. So intrinsic and habitual was the conflation of European and, indeed, global interests with national interests in the language of Ostpolitik that many of its own advocates were scarcely capable of distinguishing the one from the other.

Take, for example, the argument that as the Germans had renounced their claim to unity in the interests of peace, so the Poles must renounce their claim to freedom in the higher interest of peace. If one looks at the history of German Ostpolitik in the 1960s and 1970s it is perfectly clear that the (West) Germans had not renounced their claim to unity. They had not done so at the formal-legal level. The Preamble to the Basic Law remained sacrosanct, and was reinforced by the Letter on German Unity. They had not done so at the political-operational level. The whole Deutschlandpolitik was an attempt to keep the nation and the people together, pending more favourable external circumstances. Much of Ostpolitik was an attempt to create those more favourable external circumstances. It was those favourable conditions, finally, which Solidarity was seen to threaten. The real logic of the third argument (stability as permissive function) was thus the opposite of the ostensible logic (or morality) of this first one. The real logic was rather: the Poles must curb their claim to freedom in order that the Germans might continue to pursue their claim to unity.

Polish and German interests therefore conflicted. This was hardly new. So long as there had been nations in Europe their interests had conflicted, especially those of neighbours, and nowhere more so than in Central Europe. This did not suddenly cease to be the case after 1945, although in Western Europe those conflicts were now mediated without the use of force.

The singular feature of this crisis was not the clash of Polish and German national interests. It was rather the reluctance to admit — or perhaps inability to see — that it was national interests that were clashing. This reluctance — or inability — took two forms. On the one hand, the German national interest (stability as permissive function) was conflated with a general human interest (stability as world peace), a European interest (stability as precondition for détente), and even an alleged Polish interest (stability as condition for reform). Political, analytical and moral arguments were rolled into one. On the other hand, Solidarity's claim to represent the Polish national interest was questioned. After all, Jaruzelski said he had imposed martial law in the national interest.

There was a genuine difficulty here. When all three main parties in the democratically elected Bundestag agreed that a continuation of the Deutschlandpolitik — as outlined above — was in the national interest, then it clearly was in the national interest. Nations define their own interests. But in Poland in 1981 there was fundamental disagreement between the main political forces about what was in the national interest. Who was right? Who was representative? Even the most sympathetic Social Democrats felt that at this moment General Jaruzelski and Deputy Prime Minister Rakowski could not simply be assumed to represent the Polish nation. So they called in aid . . . the Catholic Church. 'I shall very much follow the judgement of the Catholic Church and the Vatican,' said the Social Democrats' vice-chairman, Hans-Jürgen Wischnewski.

The disagreement about who 'spoke for Poland' and what was ultimately in the Polish 'national interest' could not, by definition, be finally 'resolved' one way or the other: although the fact that in 1981 Solidarity had ten million members, and the fact that in 1989 the Solidarity list won an overwhelming majority in free parliamentary elections, may be taken as important indicators. The point is simply to illustrate the difficulty — and the conflict.

Now it may be objected that this case was extreme. Indeed it was. The truth is also to be found by studying the extremes. One must, however, keep this extreme in perspective. Measured by the standard of conflict-free, harmonious co-operation that German Ostpolitik set itself, it was very grave. Measured by the pre-1945 standard of conflict between European nation-states, and above all by the pre-1945 standard of conflict between Germans and Poles, it was extraordinarily mild. It was, after all, essentially a matter of words. In actual deeds, the only substantial difference was over economic sanctions, and in that argument the country most outspoken in support of Solidarity — France — was on the side of the Federal Republic.

Words mattered — especially, as Havel reminded his audience in the Paulskirche in Frankfurt, in would-be totalitarian states, and most especially when such states were attempting 'normalisation'. Words were therefore important instruments of Western policy, not to be taken lightly. Yet even the muted and contorted assertions we have discussed were far from being unchallenged inside the West German body politic. Rather they were the subject of acute and agonised controversy.

In his response to Chancellor Schmidt in the Bundestag debate on 18 December 1981, the then opposition leader Helmut Kohl said:

When a freely-founded union, a union movement that enjoys the broad sympathy of the country, is repressed by brutal terror, when tens of thousands, many tens of thousands, are put in concentration camps — let us use this term which God knows also through German guilt has become the word for such things — , when people are murdered and shot for their convictions — then, Mr Federal Chancellor, one must justify why one behaves this way rather than that . . . Surely you don't seriously believe that any Polish citizen would think we were intervening in the internal affairs of the proud Poles, if we protest today against the injustice that is taking place there. They are waiting for the word of sympathy from us.

It would, however, be quite wrong to reduce this to a party-political difference. The main line of policy in this period was set by the Social Democrat, Helmut Schmidt, and he maintained it for the remaining few months of his Chancellorship. One strand of this broader line was then developed, indeed, taken to an extreme, by the foreign policy leadership of the Social Democrats in opposition (see Chapter Six). But the Foreign Minister in the new Kohl government as in the old Schmidt one was the Free Democrat, Hans-Dietrich Genscher. There was a profound continuity of policy through the change of government, reflecting much deeper, underlying national interests and perceptions. When Franz Josef Strauss visited Poland in the summer of 1983, his verdict on the Jaruzelski regime was of almost social-liberal politeness.

'Normalisation' à la Husák inside Czechoslovakia had been a precondition for 'normalisation' à la Brandt in West Germany's relations with the Soviet Union, Eastern Europe, and, especially, East Germany. Now 'normalisation' à la Jaruzelski in Poland was seen as a condition for the further 'normalisation' of West Germany's relations with the Soviet Union, Eastern Europe, and, above all, East Germany. To be sure, it was hoped that Jaruzelski's 'normalisation', or 'stabilisation', would be as civilised as possible, and would lead on to 'reform', but this was not the first reason for desiring it. In the spectrum of Western policies, and within the frameworks of Western policy co-ordination, the Federal Republic was the major power that showed most understanding of, and sympathy for, Jaruzelski's position and policies. As a German diplomat closely involved at that time observes, the Federal government led the way in the restoration of trade, in arguing for an early IMF membership for Poland (un-linked to political conditions), and in pushing for what he calls, in a characteristic phrase, 'the renormalisation of political contacts'.

If this policy did not bear more fruit for Polish-German inter-state relations in the mid-1980s, it was not for want of trying by the Bonn government. In the autumn of 1984 a planned visit by Hans-Dietrich Genscher was called off at twelve hours' notice. The reasons for the cancellation were instructive. On the one hand, Genscher had proposed to lay a wreath at the grave of the Solidarity priest, Father Jerzy Popiełuszko, murdered by secret police officers just a few weeks earlier. Following the precedent set by the British Foreign Office minister, Malcolm Rifkind, this was a clear symbolic gesture of recognition for Solidarity, agreed as part of a larger Western, and particularly West European, approach. On the other hand, he proposed to lay a wreath at the grave of a German soldier killed in one of the World Wars. The Polish authorities objected to both proposed gestures with almost equal vehemence.

The Foreign Minister's official visit did not then take place until January 1988. This initiated a round of very difficult negotiations, plagued by old-new conflicts about the frontier question, reparations, credits, and the position of the German minority. These difficulties stretched out the negotiations so long that, despite a real interest in an earlier date on the part of the Bonn government, Chancellor Kohl's first official visit took place only in November 1989. It was therefore more by good luck than by design that his partner for this meeting was the non-communist, Catholic, former Solidarity adviser, Tadeusz Mazowiecki, rather than the former communist, stalwart opponent of Solidarity, and co-architect of martial law, Mieczysław F Rakowski.

Poland was the most vivid, but by no means the sole example of these priorities. Equally serious efforts were made to improve ('normalise'?) relations with Husák's Czechoslovakia, despite the internal policy of the regime. With Hungary, it was easier to argue that support for government policy was also support for 'reform' and 'liberalisation'. Yet even here there was a considerable difference between the judgements made by West German — but not, of course, only West German — policymakers about the policies and intentions of those in power, and the judgements made by the small democratic opposition in the country itself, by independent intellectuals, and then by the majority of the people in free elections.

One notable example was the Bonn government's guarantee for a DM 1 billion loan to the Hungarian government, given on the occasion of a visit to Bonn by the then Prime Minister, the communist Károly Grósz, in October 1987. This loan helped ease an acute debt-service crisis for the Hungarian government. The Bonn government portrayed this as a contribution to further 'reform'. Not only Hungarian dissidents, not just respected reform economists, but even Grósz's successor as Prime Minister, Miklós Németh, would beg to differ. 'We spent two thirds of it on interest,' Németh subsequently noted, 'and the remainder importing consumer goods to ease the impression of economic crisis.' To import consumer goods to ease the impression of economic crisis was a political soft option which delayed the necessary economic (and political) reform rather than contributing to it.

The loan guarantee could, however, clearly be justified in terms of German national goals. In return, the Federal Republic was able to open a cultural institute (a Goethe Institute by another name), despite the fierce objections of the GDR, and the Hungarian government promised to treat the country's small German minority even better than it did already. As we have seen, this was also intended as a signal to other Soviet bloc states. What is more, this clearly contributed to that gradual change in the attitude of the Hungarian leadership which culminated in the crucial opening of the Hungarian-Austrian frontier for East Germans in September 1989. The direct contribution to desirable economic and political change inside Hungary was, however, at best minimal and at worst negative.

If one looks beyond governments to ask who in the West helped sustain the democratic opposition groups in Hungary and Czechoslovakia, and the broad Solidarity and post-Solidarity opposition movement in Poland, through the 1980s, the record is also complex — not least because such sustenance was necessarily discreet, and even conspiratorial, as well as coming from the most diverse sources. Often disproportionate amounts of help came from relatively marginal groups and eccentric individuals, by no means necessarily in the largest countries of the West. But of the major Western states, America was in the first place, and West Germany was still, in this particular respect, in the last.

This was true of those meetings of Western visitors with opposition leaders, so important in the symbolic politics of East Central Europe. Here the Americans and, to a lesser extent, the British led, others followed. (When the Christian Democrats' foreign policy spokesman Volker Rühe wanted to meet with opposition leaders in Hungary in 1988, the German embassy had to ask the American embassy for the right addresses.) It was true of the publicly proclaimed support for the democratic oppositions, their cause and their values, in the speeches and statements of Western politicians. In these two respects, as we shall see, the Social Democrats in opposition were not more bold than the Christian and Free Democrats in power, but actually more timid — indeed, programmatically so.

It was true of support for the Helsinki human rights monitors from Helsinki committees in the West. (The West German committee was established only in 1984 and remained largely decorative.) Last but by no means least, it was true also of finance. For obvious reasons, the financing of opposition activities in Eastern Europe was veiled in secrecy, disinformation and (not least) confusion. But the currency of that finance was dollars. No West European country had anything to compare with the American National Endowment for Democracy. While German companies and banks led the field in trade, credits, joint ventures, technology, while German foundations were second to none in financing official academic and cultural exchanges, they were nowhere when it came to supporting genuinely independent, let alone explicitly oppositional, activities. It is hard to say how far these would have survived without the dollars poured in, partly through Western Europe, by American foundations. One single American, George Soros, with his extraordinary network of foundations devoted to promoting the Popperian idea of an open society, probably put more money into sustaining the democratic opposition in Eastern Europe than all German sources together. And as Eduard Shevardnadze would later observe: 'you cannot have democracy without an opposition — an opposition that can take power in a democratic way'.

All this is not an indictment. As we have seen, Western Europe in general, and West Germany in particular, made a larger contribution in other ways. West Germany had special interests and special dependencies. But individual Germans and other West Europeans may ask themselves why they did not do more; why, four decades after the end of the war in Europe, so much that was crucial to overcoming the division of Europe was still done from America and by Americans, whether officially, semi-officially or unofficially. At the very least, it is a matter of historical justice to give credit where credit is due. Among the major Western countries, the largest part of the credit for the direct sustenance of those who actually led the revolutions of 1989 belongs to the United States of America.

Towards the end of the decade, leading German policymakers did begin to question, or at least to redefine, the 'stability commandment'. In 1988 Chancellery Minister Wolfgang Schäuble wrote of the need for 'a new stability' in the GDR. Speaking more generally of Soviet and East European reforms, the CDU's foreign policy spokesman, Volker Rühe, observed in November 1988 that stability could only be achieved through change, not vice versa.

Finally, even Hans-Dietrich Genscher declared in a speech to mark the opening of an office of the Free Democrats' party foundation, the Friedrich Naumann Foundation, in Budapest on 9 June 1989, that 'the process of reform demands the insight in East and West that frequently instabilities must be allowed for, to permit change towards a stability of higher value. A new stability, resting on democracy, freedom and justice, on openness and plurality in politics, the economy, culture and society.' Genscher went on, repeating a phrase that he had used so many times before: 'We do not want a destabilisation of our eastern neighbours'. This time, however, he added: 'we want them, through the rule of law, pluralism and co-determination (*Mitbestimmung*), to win, instead of forced stability, stability on the basis of trust . . .' But in that case, what kind of stability had he been talking about for the last fifteen years?

Writing at this same moment, in early summer 1989, the distinguished historian Hans-Peter Schwarz, himself a Christian Democrat, made the following very pertinent observation:

Not only Social Democrats have allowed themselves to be persuaded by the nomenklatura in Prague, Warsaw, Moscow and East Berlin, that peace in Europe is only secure when the inner order of these countries remains basically unchanged. To be sure, one declares reforms and liberalisation to be desirable, but one is neither courageous nor principled enough to recognise, and — albeit quietly — to work towards that fundamental change of system which must be

the long-term goal — if only because the population in these countries
increasingly want it.

One might perhaps argue about who persuaded whom that European
peace depended on the continuation of the communist system in East
Central Europe, external 'stabilisation' on internal 'stabilisation', 'normalisation' on 'normalisation': for German policymakers surely persuaded
themselves as much as they were persuaded, and in some cases supplied
this argument to Soviet and East European leaders rather than receiving it
from them. One might marginally question the word 'increasingly': for it
was not exactly for lack of wanting a fundamentally different system that
the people of Poland or Czechoslovakia or Hungary or East Germany had
not had it for forty years. But the basic point is very well taken.

'There are more things in heaven and earth, Horatio, than are dreamt
of in your philosophy.' Like the unfinished Polish revolution of 1980-81,
the revolutions of 1989 — including that in East Germany — were not
dreamt of in the philosophy of Ostpolitik. These revolutions were dreamt
of in the philosophy of that banned and persecuted writer who in October
1989 was prevented by the highest Czechoslovak authorities from travelling to Frankfurt to receive the Peace Prize of the German Book Trade,
and in December 1989 became, himself, the highest Czechoslovak authority.

Reconciliation

Historic events are often fixed in our minds by one symbolic image, and
in the late twentieth century that image is usually a photograph. The
German invasion of Poland is those soldiers jovially lifting the frontier
barrier. The Warsaw ghetto is that one terrified little boy being forced out
of the cellars at gunpoint, with his hands in the air. The Hungarian
revolution of 1956 is the boots from the toppled statue of Stalin. Prague
1968 is a tank in Wenceslaus Square. And German Ostpolitik? For many
people around the world, Ostpolitik is Willy Brandt falling to his knees
before the monument to the heroes of the Warsaw ghetto.

No one who has read the record of German Ostpolitik, watched and
listened to its makers, can doubt for one moment that a genuine motive
and goal of that policy was reconciliation. Making good past damage.
Healing wounds. This was obviously, archetypically, true of Willy Brandt.
But it was no less true, indeed at a deeper level it was perhaps even more
true, of those like Helmut Schmidt and Richard von Weizsäcker who had
actually fought on the eastern front. In a real sense, this was the mission
of a generation. Helmut Kohl, although enjoying what he called 'the
blessing of a late birth' — that is, being too young to have fought in the

war — often stated his wish to achieve with Poland the kind of historic reconciliation that Adenauer had achieved with France.

The work of reconciliation with the East had not been pioneered by the politicians. In the so-called Tübingen Memorandum of 1962, a group of prominent Protestants declared themselves, for moral as much as political reasons, in favour of recognising the Oder-Neisse line. Richard von Weizsäcker recalls this as the moment at which he himself first became deeply engaged in discussions of Ostpolitik. The (then still all-German) organisation of the Protestant Church in Germany planted a further landmark with its 1965 report on 'the situation of the expellees and the relationship of the German nation to its eastern neighbours', as did the country's Catholic bishops with their response to a powerful letter from the Polish bishops in the same year.

'In spite of everything,' wrote the Polish bishops, 'in spite of this situation burdened almost hopelessly by the past, or rather just because of this situation . . . we cry out to you: let us try to forget! No polemics, no more Cold War . . .' And in a famous phrase, which earned them a torrent of abuse from the communist regime, the Polish bishops concluded: 'We forgive and ask for forgiveness.' 'We, too, ask to forget, yes, we ask to forgive,' replied the German bishops. Many individual writers, historians, young Christians in the so-called *Aktion Sühnezeichen*, young Social Democrats with their pioneering trips to Eastern Europe: all had prepared the way. But with Willy Brandt, those intellectual and moral impulses were taken up into the policy of the Federal government.

In this, he enjoyed the support of many of the country's best-known intellectuals, and perhaps most symbolically of Günter Grass, the great memorialist of German-Polish Danzig. At his own request, Grass actually accompanied the Chancellor to Warsaw in December 1970. In a letter written immediately afterwards, he thanked Willy Brandt for the privilege of being with him, and — in a striking and curious formulation — 'for the immediate gain of this journey: being allowed to be moved (*betroffen sein zu dürfen*)'.

'We must,' Brandt said in his television address from Warsaw, '. . . recognise morality as a political force.' A resonant formula, but, like all invocations of morality, not easy to translate into the practical policy of states. The problems of so doing were illustrated by the imprecise and shifting terms in which the makers of Ostpolitik defined this goal. The two German words for reconciliation — *Versöhnung* and *Aussöhnung* — are heavy with both emotional and religious overtones, containing in their root the word *Sühne*, meaning expiation, penance, atonement, and evoking the image, if not of 'God and sinners reconciled', then at least of two individual human beings falling tearfully into each others' arms. Yet German policymakers also used, in various combinations, and seemingly almost interchangeably, such terms as *Verständigung* (literally 'understanding' or 'coming to an understanding'), *gute Nachbarschaft* (good-neighbourliness), *friedliche Kooperation*, *friedliche Zusammenarbeit* (both meaning peaceful co-operation), *Ausgleich* (which implies a settle-ment based on the reconciliation or balancing of conflicting interests), *Entspannung* (for reconciliation might also be defined as the relaxation of historic tensions), and *Frieden* or *Friede* (peace), itself a term laden with emotional and religious overtones.

'We want to be a nation (*Volk*) of good neighbours', said Willy Brandt in his Government declaration in 1969. 'The social-liberal coalition,' said Helmut Schmidt in his farewell state of the nation address, 'has, with its treaty- and reconciliation-policy towards the eastern neighbours, created the second pillar, the necessary addition [to Adenauer's Western ties] for peaceful neighbourliness in all directions.'

The sentiments are admirable. The general message is clear. But the specific application was fraught with difficulties. For a start, there was the lapse of time: a quarter of a century between, as it were, the quarrel and the reconciliation. Of course one might argue that this passage of time was necessary for it to be possible at all. How could a German-Polish reconciliation, including a recognition of the Oder-Neisse line, possibly have been made in, say, 1950, when nearly one in every five citizens of the new Federal Republic had just fled or been expelled from the East? 'Time heals all wounds.' Yet clichés can mislead. For time also seals in old gunshot, which festers under the skin. It nurtures old grievances while repressing old guilt.

Were the psychological conditions for a reconciliation with Poland, Czechoslovakia or the Soviet Union actually so much worse in the 1950s than in the 1970s? To be sure, there was then the immediacy of bitter resentment among millions of expellees. Yet there was also the freshness of memory and the immediacy of shame. Freya von Moltke, widow of the German resistance hero Helmuth James von Moltke, recalls:

We lived until 1945 in Kreisau, Kreis Schweidnitz, Silesia. Then we had to leave. That was not easy. But we knew already that the land would in future belong to the Poles . . . What I want to report is this: my husband, Helmuth James von Moltke, an active opponent of the Nazis for ages, and who lost his life in that struggle in January 1945 — he was condemned to death and executed — already foresaw in the middle of the war that the Germans would lose Silesia. 'The only question is, whether Silesia will go to Poland or the Czechoslovak Republic. For that we have to thank Hitler!' he said. It is very important for peace in Europe that the Germans have no illusions. That Silesia now belongs to the Poles is a direct result of Hitler's war and Hitler's rule of terror. One can not blame it on the allies. The blame is Hitler's.

And if that is put aside as the judgement of one highly untypical

German, consider the testimony of an anonymous German woman from
Landeshut (now Kamienna Gora) in Lower Silesia. Writing in 1951, she
recalls a day in 1946 when she was hauled off by the new Polish police to
dig up the half-decomposed corpses of concentration camp victims. She
describes in harrowing detail this appalling work; how she cried with
horror and could not even wipe away the tears; and then suddenly she
says: 'so stop crying, be brave and thus help in the work of atonement
(*Sühneleistung*) for the crimes that had been done in our nation (*in unserem
Volk*)'.

Of course there is no way of knowing whether the noble spirit of the
Kreisau Moltkes, and the moving spirit of that one anonymous woman,
personally mistreated, driven out of her homeland, yet still, in 1951, as it
were mentally standing up for the work of atonement — whether those
spirits might have made a reconciliation with Poland or Czechoslovakia
subjectively possible for West Germany in the 1950s. For the Sovietisation
of Eastern Europe and the Cold War made it objectively impossible.

What one can say, however, is that when the work of official reconciliation finally began twenty years later, it was now closely intertwined
with the goals of perceived national interest on the one hand, and with
domestic party-political controversy on the other. In agreeing large reparations payments to Israel in the early 1950s, Konrad Adenauer was
restoring German 'honour', to use his own language, and seeking a
'purification of the soul'. He certainly expected — rightly — that this
would also work to the general advantage of the Federal Republic in the
world, but it was unthinkable that there should be any direct *quid pro quo*.
While the moral and emotional elements were clearly important in
the reconciliation with France in the late 1950s and early 1960s, the
national interest — of both sides — was more plainly to the fore. In the
relationship with Poland, as it developed in the late 1960s and early 1970s,
the motif of reconciliation was from the outset entangled with the pursuit
of other, direct German interests, in a context of domestic political
controversy.

Here, for example, is Willy Brandt in his 1971 state of the nation
address: 'In the relationship with Poland, too, we have in mind the
German interest in the broadest sense, when we do what we can so that
the German name can no longer be used as a symbol of injustice and
horror, but rather counts as a sign for the hope of reconciliation and
peaceful co-operation. That this hope is not in vain may also be seen by
the number of Germans who will come to the Federal Republic over the
next months.' Thus at home even Willy Brandt could equate 'reconciliation' with German emigration. We have seen already the same fateful
entanglement in the 1975 package of agreements with Poland. Was it cash
for Germans or a down-payment on forgiveness? And right through the
1980s the three elements — money, reconciliation, direct German interests

— were continually muddled up together in all official German-Polish dealings, and further confused by the domestic political context.

In an 'open letter to all Germans who wish to work for German-Polish reconciliation', written in 1982, the Polish critic Jan Józef Lipski observed that it would be 'favourable for a future reconciliation and friendship' if 'each should make the reckoning with their own guilt, and rather with their own than with the other's'. A familiar observation, you might think. 'Why beholdest thou the mote that is in thy brother's eye, but considerest not the beam that is in thine own eye?' as St Matthew had put it a few years earlier. Reconciliation consists in people saying 'I'm sorry for what I did' not 'I'm sorry for what *you* did'. But what might be feasible for individual human beings in relation to each other — although difficult enough even for them — was far more difficult for political leaders in the Federal Republic. They had to consider not only the unreconciled or unrepentant element in their electorate, but also the much larger number of Germans who considered that they were themselves in some sense victims of Hitler's (and Stalin's) crimes.

So again and again in official statements by the highest representatives of the Federal Republic, throughout the 1970s and 1980s, one finds the reference to Polish or Soviet or Czech suffering at German hands swiftly followed by the statement that of course the Germans suffered too. Thus, in a July 1989 declaration, Chancellor Kohl recalled that in the last war 'terrible things' (*Fürchterliches*) were done in the name of Germany and by German hands, especially to the Polish people. We neither wish nor may forget this,' he went on, 'but just as little may we forget that later bad things (*Schlimmes*) were done to Germans by Poles.'

President von Weizsäcker was widely regarded as more sensitive and adept in these matters, and his speech on the fortieth anniversary of the end of the war in Europe was a masterpiece of facing up to the German past in the spirit suggested by Lipski, and before him by the gospels. Yet even Richard von Weizsäcker did not entirely avoid the trope. In a message to the Polish President, General Jaruzelski, on the fiftieth anniversary of the German attack on Poland, the Federal President began by spelling out the terrible sufferings of Poland at German hands: 'The consequences of war and war crimes which the whole Polish nation has to bear are without parallel. But we Germans too,' he continued, 'were heavily marked by the war. We found that injustice and suffering struck back against our own nation, in whose name they had occurred. The heavy human losses, the destruction of Dresden and many other towns was followed by the expulsion of millions of Germans from their native homeland and, with the division of Europe, the division of our own nation and capital. Terrible wounds have been struck against each other . . .'

The President's and the Chancellor's words were chosen with painful care. Germans did *Fürchterliches* to Poles; Poles did only *Schlimmes* to

Germans. Injustice and suffering 'struck back'. Yet one is still moved to question. What had the Poles to do with the destruction of Dresden? Who suffered more from the division of Europe — the Germans or the Poles? Did the record of German-Polish relations really justify the symmetrical assertion 'terrible wounds have been struck against each other'? The point here is not to argue about any particular formulation. The point is that once the politician attempts to make such a summary historical reckoning — your suffering, our suffering, our guilt, your guilt — he is already lost. As the West German *Historikerstreit* (historians' dispute) around precisely such issues amply demonstrated, even independent scholars have difficulty in detaching comparative historical judgment from moral relativisation and hence at least implicit apologetics.

But a Federal President or Chancellor was in a far worse position than the independent scholar. He was compelled to simplify. He had to think all the time of preserving domestic political consensus as well: of, so to speak, internal reconciliation. And then — for even Federal Presidents are human — he too would have the personal need to be reconciled with his country's and his own past. Thus even with such a sensitive, thoughtful and liberal speaker as Richard von Weizsäcker, one did not ultimately know whether what was being sought was the reconciliation of Germans with Poles, of Germans with Germans, or of the speaker with himself. All three at once? But each reconciliation had slightly different requirements. As elsewhere in German Ostpolitik, so here in miniature, the attempt to pursue several divergent goals simultaneously — almost literally 'in the same breath' — resulted in dissonance rather than the longed-for harmony.

There was a further problem with the whole enterprise of, so to speak, governmental reconciliation. This was that governments had to deal with governments — which, in the case of the Soviet Union and Eastern Europe inevitably meant with communist rulers. But these communist rulers were not elected representatives of their peoples. Indeed they were generally in more or less acute conflict with the aspirations of their own peoples. If one sought reconciliation with these rulers, this did not necessarily help reconciliation with their subjects.

The most sensitive case in this respect was, once again, Poland. The problem of pursuing reconciliation with rulers to whom their own people did not wish to be reconciled was illustrated at the very outset. Brandt made the Warsaw Treaty with Gomułka — and within weeks the Polish people deposed that same Gomułka. Schmidt then pursued reconciliation with Gierek. His affection for, and grave misjudgement of, Edward Gierek are amply documented. He would, he said, 'take him straight into the cabinet'. When he sent Gierek a telegram congratulating him on the election of a Polish Pope, one might already detect a certain confusion. But when, on the evening before martial law was declared in Poland, we find

Schmidt asking Erich Honecker to use his good offices with the Polish authorities on behalf not of Solidarity but of Edward Gierek, then the confusion would have seemed to most Poles to go beyond a joke.

In defending his government's refusal to join in American-led sanctions against Poland and the Soviet Union, following the imposition of martial law, Schmidt directly confronts this issue. His 'specifically German motive' for not joining in these sanctions was, he writes in his memoirs, precisely the deep-seated desire for reconciliation. 'Reconciliation was a decisive motive for Willy Brandt's — and later my — Ostpolitik.' This meant dealing with the governments.

> 'Whoever as a German wanted to come to an understanding with Poland had to make treaties with the actual government in Warsaw — whether with Gomułka, Gierek, Kania or Jaruzelski. Any West German attempt to drive wedges between the Polish people and its (sic) government, to say friendly words to the former but to refuse help to the latter, was not only bound to fail; it would also supply the communist propagandists in Warsaw with arguments against the alleged 'German revanchism'.

Furthermore, sanctions would hurt the man in the street, not the rulers. Therefore he encouraged ordinary West Germans to send food parcels instead.

One cannot doubt the sincerity of his argument. The millions of food parcels sent by ordinary West Germans, with extraordinary speed, efficiency and generosity, were widely appreciated in Poland as gestures of humanitarian aid. As we have seen, Schmidt himself had declared in the Bundestag that he stood 'with all his heart' on the side of the Polish workers. Yet that was not the message that got through to the Polish workers and Solidarity activists in the internment camps. Quite the reverse. From the reported statements of leading West German politicians — and particularly of leading Social Democrats –, and from summaries of German commentaries, they got the impression rather of a sigh of relief. At least the Russians had not invaded. General Jaruzelski was probably a patriot. The German-German détente could continue. *L'ordre règne à Varsovie.*

A Catholic intellectual deeply committed to the Polish-German dialogue, Kazimierz Wóycicki, recalls his own experience in an internment camp at this time. High up in the corner of his cell was a loudspeaker, which could not be turned off. It spewed out official accounts of Western reactions to martial law in Poland. These praised especially the West German reactions: their good sense, their understanding of Polish realities, of the patriot Jaruzelski. 'We did not believe it,' writes Wóycicki,

> for we had other ways of keeping ourselves informed. In one of the cells there

was, as a hidden treasure, a transistor radio on which we could pick up more than just the official propaganda. But here was the confirmation. The Warsaw newspapers lied, but not entirely. In Germany people felt sorry for the Poles (this sympathy was later expressed in the large-scale sending of parcels) but in political circles one was of the opinion that reason was on the side of Jaruzelski; there would be no Soviet intervention, *so German Ostpolitik was saved.*

'We sat in the cell,' Wóycicki continues,

we were not radicals or professional revolutionaries but simple workers from Piaseczno and Ursus, farmers from the neighbourhood of Warsaw, also a few professors and journalists, and we discussed *at whose expense this German Ostpolitik was to be saved.* When you are in prison you have a lot of time and talk a lot. One of us, a young guy from the Ursus tractor factory, said: 'If they don't understand what our freedom is then they don't understand what their freedom is, and if they don't understand that, then they haven't changed, these *Hitlerowcy.*' We explained to him that one might have all sorts of objections to West German policy, but this last remark was stupid. So far as I can remember he was finally persuaded by the argument that if he described what was after all a democratic government in Bonn like this, he would be playing the tune of communist propaganda. (Emphasis added.)

Here is a circle of tragic irony. Helmut Schmidt believes that Germans should be reticent in their reaction to martial law, out of sense of historical responsibility for Hitlerite crimes, and in order not to furnish arguments for communist propaganda. The result: a simple worker in a prison cell feels the Germans haven't changed, and is only persuaded not to say this out loud by the reflection that this would furnish arguments for communist propaganda.

The misunderstanding was thus very deep. Among the factors that contributed to it on the German side was the previous failure to distinguish sharply enough between state and society in Eastern Europe; a general conviction (building out from the Bahr hypothesis about East Germany) that lasting change would come only 'from above'; and the mistaken belief that one could be friends with everyone, that is, in this case, with the gaoler and the prisoner. There was also one other element, which could not precisely be classed as a misunderstanding. For as the Polish prisoners rightly perceived, there was another 'special German motive' for welcoming the 'internal solution' in Poland. This was the belief that if the Soviets invaded 'everything would be *kaputt*' — where 'everything' meant the continuation of the German Ostpolitik, and especially of the policy towards the GDR, so painstakingly developed over so many years.

The dismay among those on the side of Solidarity in Poland extended also to the very symbol of German-Polish reconciliation: Willy Brandt. 'I must admit,' Adam Michnik wrote in 1984, 'that it made me angry that Willy Brandt had so quickly forgotten how bitter is the taste of that prison food, on which in his youth the German Social Democrats had been fed.' And he ended his article with an appeal to Willy Brandt to come to Poland, not just to shake the hands of 'our Generals and Party Secretaries' but to see the condition of political prisoners, to lay flowers on the memorial to the miners killed in December 1981. Willy Brandt did come to Poland in December 1985, to mark the fifteenth anniversary of the Warsaw Treaty. He shook the hands of the Generals and Party Secretaries. He spoke of reconciliation, peace, normalisation, stability. But he visited no prisons (in one of which he would have found Adam Michnik). He laid no flowers on the murdered workers' graves — nor on that of the martyred Father Popiełuszko. He declined an invitation to meet his fellow Nobel Peace Prize winner, Lech Wałęsa, in Solidarity's capital, Gdańsk.

The final irony of this focus on the Communist rulers was that it was they who were actually least interested in a reconciliation. They clung to the 'German bogey' as almost their last chance of winning popular support. It is, to be sure, far too simple to equate the internal divide — authorities/society — directly with attitudes to Germany. There were those in power who genuinely sought reconciliation and those in opposition who did not. As Primate Glemp demonstrated in his own person, the Church, too, contained elements of both. But as a rule, independent, Catholic and oppositional circles were far ahead of official circles in the quest for a genuine, lasting reconciliation.

It was the Polish Catholic bishops with their courageous message of 1965 — 'We forgive you and ask for your forgiveness' — who had paved the way, and been furiously attacked for it by the communist state. It was a Solidarity intellectual, Jan Józef Lipski, who wrote one of the most generous texts on the subject in 1981, and was again rewarded with a torrent of official abuse. West German historians exercised heroic patience in trying to come to terms with utterly unyielding communist-nationalist historians peddling the party line. Meanwhile, almost unnoticed in West Germany, there were independent scholars who offered far more common ground.

In an emotional message for a 'Day of Solidarity with Poland' on American television in January 1982, Helmut Schmidt declared: 'Germans and Poles have found their way to one another again, after a long history full of suffering. This belongs — like the reconciliation between Germany and France — among the great moral changes in Europe since the Second World War.' This noble statement contained, alas, a large measure of wishful thinking, about both the present and the past. For what did it mean to say that Germans and Poles had found their way to one another again? When were they together before? This implied a rose-tinted view of the German-Polish past worthy of the most nostalgic-utopian literary invocation of Central Europe. The 'normal, good-neighbourly' relations which West Germany had developed with France since the war were quite abnormal in European history: they were unprecedented. If Germany managed to do the same with Poland it would also be a first.

Nor did popular sentiments — of Poles about Germans and of Germans about Poles — entirely bear out this romantic contention, especially if one included among 'Germans' the population of the GDR. To be sure, many thousands of individual people on both sides had left the disputes of their leaders far behind. 'People are often ahead of politics,' as Richard von Weizsäcker wrote in his letter to General Jaruzelski on 1 September 1989, 'and level the path.' Introducing his new government to the Polish parliament later that same month, Poland's first non-communist Prime Minister for more than forty years, Tadeusz Mazowiecki, said almost exactly the same thing: 'We need a breakthrough in our relations with the Federal Republic of Germany. The societies of both countries have already gone much further than their governments.'

For all the complexities and contortions of the Bonn government's 'reconciliation policy', it must certainly be credited not only with permitting but with very substantially encouraging this popular rapprochement: in cultural, scholarly, youth exchanges, in tourism, in the large numbers of East Europeans allowed to visit and often to work in the Federal Republic, in everything that we have described as weaving. If in 1969 it was still possible for communist governments to win support by agitating against 'German revanchism', by 1989 such propaganda was almost entirely ineffective. Yet if the two peoples no longer saw each other as enemies, they were still far from seeing each other as friends. And not just in the older generation.

In a 1981 survey of Warsaw schoolchildren, fifty-six per cent of those asked said they did not like the Germans. Only the Russians, with sixty-five per cent, were more disliked. A majority of Poles and Germans asked in a major survey in 1991 expressed the view that a 'reconciliation was possible'. But this and other surveys also revealed that the two peoples still held a fairly low opinion of each other, by comparison with the view that each separately took of, say, the French or the Americans. Many incidents and conversations, especially in Berlin and the former GDR, revealed a high level of tension between Poles and Germans.

There was thus still a vast distance to travel before one could begin to talk of a (historically abnormal) normality such as prevailed between France and Germany. Some reasons for this have been indicated on both the West German and the Polish sides. The undemocratic nature of the Polish regime had also directly affected the attitudes of the younger generation, through the classroom. As one independent Polish writer put it, young Poles were brought up to believe that patriotism meant hatred of the Germans. In addition there was, even among those in outright opposition to the communist regime in Poland, the phenomenon that we have elsewhere described as the nationalism of the victim. Characteristic of the nationalism of the victim is a reluctance to acknowledge in just measure the sufferings of other peoples, and an inability to admit that the victim can also victimise. This naturally persists so long as the nation continues to be in some sense a victim: which post-Yalta Poland might reasonably consider itself to be.

It is also no accident that anti-Polish sentiments were more rife in the unfree than in the free part of Germany; indeed that national and ethnic resentments were altogether more acute in the unfree than in the free part of Europe. So in this respect, too, the internal aspect of the division of Europe was quite as important as the external aspect. By removing the credibility of the 'German bogey' the Federal Republic helped to facilitate internal change in Poland after 1970. But that internal change was then the *sine qua non* for a further, deeper rapprochement. Only the election in 1989 of a Solidarity prime minister, himself long committed to the work of Polish reconciliation with other nations, at last made that possible.

Shortly after Mazowiecki's election, Chancellor Kohl paid his long-delayed official visit to Poland. This visit was organised as a celebration of reconciliation, in a way that would have been impossible even a few months before. As Adenauer and de Gaulle had met for a High Mass in the cathedral of Rheims, so now the Polish and the German heads of government, Catholics both, would meet for an open-air Mass at the symbolic site of Kreisau — once an island of German resistance to Hitler, now Polish, as Helmuth James von Moltke had foreseen, but soon to be a joint Polish-German centre. After a sermon delivered partly in Polish, partly in German, by the Bishop of Opole (Oppeln), the two leaders would embrace in sign of peace.

Helmut Kohl's carefully prepared symbolic act did not achieve the historic radiation of Brandt's single, bleak, lone gesture. The Chancellor's trip was interrupted by his flying return to Berlin after the opening of the Berlin Wall, and marred by an ill-conceived plan to visit the St Anne Mountain in Silesia, the scene of bitter fighting between Germans and Poles after the First World War. For all that, it was a step forward. A state visit by Richard von Weizsäcker in the early summer of 1990 — the first time in 990 years that a German head of state visited Poland at the Poles' invitation! — reinforced the painful progress. Although negotiations about the frontier and the 'good neighbour' treaties remained fraught and long drawn-out, when both were finally signed and ready for ratification in 1991, Hans-Dietrich Genscher averred that they would break the vicious circle of injustice and new injustice 'once and for all'.

That bold claim reflected understandable but also double-edged sentiments. On the one hand, it expressed satisfaction that a long-pursued, high moral goal of West German policy could finally be said to have been achieved. After the reconciliation with Israel and France, here was the reconciliation with Poland. On the other hand, it signalled a hope that from now on Germans and Poles could talk less about this dark past and more about a brighter future, in peace, harmony and a united Europe. Intoning what was now officially the 'European anthem', Beethoven's choral setting of Schiller's Ode to Joy, they could sing:

> *Unser Schuldbuch sei vernichtet!*
> *Ausgesöhnt die ganze Welt!*

Let our book of guilt be destroyed — and the whole world reconciled!

The accepted pious wisdom was that to be reconciled did not mean in any way to forget that past. Quite the contrary. But when making up after a quarrel we say 'let's forgive and forget'. Forgiving and forgetting are, in real life, more intimately related than is quite comfortable for intellectuals, and especially for historians, to admit. As we have noticed, the Polish bishops in their letter of 1965 explicitly linked the offer to forgive with the offer to forget, a point taken up with what might almost be mistaken for eagerness in the German bishops' respc ise.

The statement 'reconciliation sealed' — mission accomplished! — thus also contains an element of what Franz Josef Strauss once memorably described as Germany 'stepping out . . . from under the shadow of the Third Reich'. This, as liberal historians hasten to point out, is a risky step, because it carries the temptation of artificially shortening the shadow by, so to speak, pruning the history tree that casts the shadow. Yet perhaps in the mid-1990s, half a century after 1945, it would be morally permissible and politically sensible for leaders to talk somewhat less about the bitter past, and somewhat more about a better future? Perhaps at last the conditions had been created in which the past could begin to be past?

Against this hope, some notes of caution must be entered. The record of the two decades following Brandt's great symbolic gesture shows clearly the limits of what politics can achieve in the relations between peoples. Politics and true human reconciliation have quite different time-scales. A British prime minister famously observed that a week is a long time in politics. But in the work of reconciliation, twenty years is a short time. The true unit of measurement is the generation. Moreover, except in very exceptional circumstances — such as arguably did prevail between West Germany and Eastern Europe in the Europe of 'Yalta' — it is doubtful whether reconciliation as such is a credible explicit goal for the foreign policy of a state.

States may create the conditions in which reconciliation can occur. Politicians can give an example. As President von Weizsäcker and then, even more strikingly, President Havel of Czechoslovakia and President Göncz of Hungary demonstrated, there can be such a thing as moral leadership. But at the end of the day, peoples can only be reconciled if the individual people who make up those peoples wish so to be. The ripening of that wish is a very long process. It takes generations.

It is a process, moreover, rooted in freedom. As we have seen, the condition of unfreedom, whether in East Germany, Poland or elsewhere in Eastern Europe, both directly and indirectly hampered and distorted the process. The observation made by one commentator on the occasion of Chancellor Kohl's visit to Poland in November 1989, that reconciliation was 'only just beginning', might seem unduly depressing to those in the free part of Germany who had spent decades working to advance that goal. But it contained more than a grain of hard truth. It has famously been said that no free people can rule over another. One might also say that only free peoples can be truly reconciled.

Moreover, freedom is a necessary but not a sufficient condition. In those reconciliations that may be described as successful there has also been a rough equality, or at least a crude balance of mutual interest, between the partners. This is archetypally true of the Franco–German case. Not only were both states democracies. They also had economies at roughly the same level. Neither people had strong material reasons to look at the other with pronounced contempt or deep envy. Co-operation would be to mutual advantage. And in the 1950s and 1960s each state had a major political interest in the rapprochement. German economic power and political support would underpin France's aspiration to grandeur and a leading role in Europe. French forgiveness, blessing and political support would make a major contribution to Germany's recovery of its self-esteem and a respected place in the world. Together they could shape the European Community. One may argue, according to taste, as to whether reconciliation was the moral and emotional foundation and this the political and economic superstructure built upon it, or vice versa, but either way they were complementary.

In Germany's relations with Poland and Czechoslovakia this has never been so. In the case of the Soviet Union one could argue that in the 'Yalta' period there was a very crude equality or balance of mutual interest. Germany and Russia had indeed, to recall von Weizsäcker's phrase, inflicted terrible wounds upon each other. Each now wanted big things from the other. They could, as it were, say 'quits' and start cutting deals. But after the events of 1989-91, and the end of the Soviet Union, this ceased to be true for Russia as well.

Now all of Germany's neighbours to her east were poor and weak. Economically, the Oder-Neisse line threatened to become a North-South divide on the East-West axis, with all the potential for envy, resentment, tension and contempt that that implied. For Germany, the long-term promise of eastern markets was tempered by the immediate cost of assistance and opening western markets to eastern goods. Politically,

Poland, Czechoslovakia or the states of the former Soviet Union, could offer the new Germany the promise of stability and the threat of instability. But the promised political good was not as substantial as that offered by France in the 1950s and 1960s, while the threatened political bad, though more substantial, was still less so than the threat so coherently and consistently presented by the old Soviet Union.

Thus if one condition for reconciliation, freedom, was present at the beginning of the 1990s in a way it had not been throughout the 'Yalta' period, two others, rough economic equality and political mutuality, were not. To say that 'reconciliation was only just beginning' was plainly an overstatement; but scarcely more so than to say that reconciliation had been finally sealed. The truth lay, as so often, in-between. Some of the conditions for reconciliation had been created, partly as a direct result of the deliberate efforts of German Ostpolitik, partly as a consequence of developments to which it was only a contributory cause. Other, equally important, conditions had yet to be created. The chance to create those conditions lay partly, but again only partly, in the hands of the politicians and citizens of the Federal Republic.

VI

A Second Ostpolitik

Social Democrats in the 1980s

Thus far we have discussed the Ostpolitik of the Federal Republic of Germany. We have concentrated on what persons and parties in power actually did and said in the name of the government and the state. Our subject has been the policy of a state, not the views of groups or individuals. Yet we have found that in this area of policy, and above all when examining German-German relations, it is extremely difficult to draw a clear line between government policy and the wider penumbra of published and public opinion, of opposition parties, the media, academe and intellectuals. All were in some measure actors in Ostpolitik.

To analyse their parts systematically, however, requires other methods. Sweeping generalisations about 'the left', 'the right', 'the intellectuals', and, of course, 'the Germans', supported by selective quotation from a few allegedly typical authors, have their place on the op-ed pages and in the *feuilleton* sections of our leading national and international newspapers. There they contribute to the vigour of political debate, the sharpening of wits and the gaiety of nations. But a serious study of published opinion requires detailed literary criticism, for each individual author is a special case. Nothing is easier and more tempting than to quote a few striking results from public opinion surveys to underpin an argument. But the proper study of public opinion is a specialised craft.

The subject of this chapter — the Ostpolitik of the Social Democrats in opposition, from the autumn of 1982 to the autumn of 1989 — lies somewhere in between the hard reality of government policy and the more elusive realities of published and public opinion. The policy of a party in opposition can never be pinned down as firmly as that of a party in government, because it does not need to be definite, and, indeed, may benefit precisely from being indefinite. Politicians in power have to make real choices, keep promises or break them. Even their words are deeds. Politicians in opposition can — and regularly do — promise more than they can deliver and offer all things to all men. Moreover, except in the immediate discipline of an election campaign, the scope for internal diversity and discord is large. This is particularly true of a party in a federal state, and especially in an area of policy which many leading members of the party consider to be peculiarly theirs. Thus there are times when, and subjects on which, an opposition party does not have anything deserving the name of 'policy'. Even when it does, this policy is not comparable with the policy of a government.

All these reservations apply to the Ostpolitik of the Social Democrats in opposition. Yet for a number of reasons, a study of Ostpolitik cannot ignore it. Firstly, Ostpolitik was very closely identified with the Social Democrats, not just in West German politics but also in both states in Germany and abroad. 'Ostpolitik?' people from Moscow to Milwaukee would say, 'you mean Willy Brandt . . .' Secondly, Brandt, Bahr and their younger colleagues not only developed but actively pursued in their years in opposition what they called a 'second phase of Ostpolitik', a 'second phase of détente policy', or, more casually, a 'second Ostpolitik'.

This consisted not just of speeches and programmes, but of extensive talks with the leaders and ruling communist parties of the Soviet Union and Eastern Europe, resulting in joint communiqués, common papers and even draft treaties. Conceptually, this 'second Ostpolitik' built on and extended certain lines of their own first Ostpolitik, and thus also casts light back on to the earlier period. In operative terms, Brandt's meetings with Gorbachev or the Social Democrats' dialogue with the ruling Socialist Unity Party of East Germany in the 1980s had a real impact on the relations of the Federal Republic with the East.

The beginnings of this second Ostpolitik must be traced back to the last years of the social-liberal coalition, with the coming of what some called the 'second Cold War' and the great debate about 'peace' following Nato's double-track resolution of December 1979. Karsten Voigt, one of the Social Democrats' parliamentary spokesmen on foreign affairs, called for a 'second phase of Ostpolitik' as early as January 1980. Its first distinguishing feature was the focus on security policy. As we have seen, in the first phase of Social Democratic Ostpolitik Willy Brandt and his colleagues had, for a mixture of tactical and strategic reasons, deliberately refrained from making any of those initiatives on security policy which Egon Bahr, for one, considered theoretically desirable and even essential for the long-term realisation of the strategic goals of Ostpolitik.

After the election victory in 1972, Brandt and Bahr had hoped to push ahead first and foremost with conventional force reductions in the centre of Europe. But the talks that came to be known as MBFR got nowhere, while Chancellor Schmidt pursued his own, distinctive security policy based firmly on nuclear deterrence through the Nato alliance and classical precepts of the balance of power. Now, as differences with the Soviet

314 · *In Europe's Name*

Union over precisely these issues seemed to be leading rapidly to the end of détente, the time had come to make good what Horst Ehmke would call the 'crucial deficit' of the first phase of Ostpolitik. With an echo of Clausewitz, Bahr would later characterise this second phase as 'the continuation of Ostpolitik in the military field'. Security, he would write, 'is the key to everything'.

The development of these new ideas was carried forward by a younger generation inside the party, with figures such as Karsten Voigt, Oskar Lafontaine, Andreas von Bülow and Hermann Scheer playing a prominent part. It was also clearly influenced by the growth of a large extra-parliamentary peace and ecological movement in West Germany. Here were hundreds of thousands of young people with voices that made headlines and votes that might be cast for the Social Democrats — or not, as the case might be. Yet the sharpest and arguably still the most potent formulation of the new security policy, or security Ostpolitik, came from an old man in a hurry.

Egon Bahr cast, or re-cast, his new-old ideas in his work for the Palme Commission in 1980–81. By his own account, it was in May 1981 that he first 'ventured' to formulate the view that 'security can now only be achieved in common. No longer against each other but only with each other shall we be secure.' This bold notion of 'common security' between East and West, to be achieved by means such as nuclear-weapon free zones, then became the leitmotif of the Palme Commission report, finally published in May 1982.

At about the same time, the Social Democrats — or at least, a very large number of them — parted company with their own Chancellor on the Nato missile issue, at the Munich party conference in April 1982. (Recalling the famous cartoon of Bismarck, on his resignation, as a pilot leaving the ship, wits observed that here the ship was leaving the pilot.) In attempting to defend his policy, Schmidt spoke in Munich of the need for a 'security partnership' with the Soviet Union, a term which he himself appears to have coined in 1978. Preserving a facade of unity, Egon Bahr, now appointed to chair a working group on 'New Strategies', respectfully referred to the Chancellor's formula of 'security partnership'. But a specialist close to Bahr clearly spells out the fundamental difference between 'security partnership' à la Schmidt and 'common security' à la Bahr. The former was a formula for arms control and arms reductions on the basis of deterrence. The latter was intended to replace deterrence, as Bahr himself wrote in a Festschrift for the Protestant peace philosopher (and brother of the President) Carl-Friedrich von Weizsäcker.

Like Bahr's own Conception C in his planning staff paper of 1968, the new notion of 'common security' clearly envisaged going beyond Nato and Warsaw Pact to a new European security system, called, of course, a 'European peace order'. Indeed, the new ideas on European security developed by leading Social Democrats in the 'peace debate' of the early 1980s contained substantial elements of earlier Social Democratic plans for European security from the 1950s — before the party's Godesberg programme and full acceptance of Adenauer's Western ties — , and more than a smidgen of the ideas of collective security popular on the left in the 1920s and 1930s. However, the superpowers' massive nuclear arsenals and split-second computer decisions gave a new apocalyptic backdrop, which some Protestant theologians would happily embroider.

By the time the Social Democrats were finally catapulted into opposition, in October 1982, their new thinking in this area was thus already far advanced. As not infrequently in the history of political parties (not just, though perhaps especially, those of the left, and by no means only in West Germany) the return to opposition — experienced at once as defeat and liberation — produced an explosion of critical debate and a quest for new ideas, with individual politicians jostling for position and competing for 'profile'. In such periods of ferment, the writings — or at least, the slogans — of political intellectuals are also more likely to be taken up, and so it was here.

This mixed crop was then sifted and ground through the mills of the party, to produce statements by the leadership, conference resolutions, and, for the 1983 and 1987 elections, two documents entitled 'government programme'. These documents were, of course, compromises between different tendencies inside the party, and between what party leaders themselves wanted and what they thought voters would vote for. While these programmatic papers were described as 'party policy' they contained commitments which would have been hard or impossible to reconcile in the real responsibility of government. Finally, there were the actual talks and dealings which leading figures in the party, more or less formally licensed by its leadership, conducted with political actors in Eastern Europe and the Soviet Union, and the documents that emerged from those encounters.

It is this last aspect which was most unusual, and most directly concerns us here. But before concentrating on this actual 'second Ostpolitik', a few words should be said about the prior and accompanying policy debate. The most reams of recycled paper were devoted to security issues. The basic idea of 'common security' was elaborated in the working group on 'new strategies'. The chairman of the party's commission on security policy, Andreas von Bülow, gave his name to a working paper (the so-called 'Bülow paper') which envisaged superpower disengagement from Central Europe by the year 2000, with a territorial militia left to defend West Germany from bunkers and woodland hideouts. Much thought was given to recasting conventional forces so they had a 'structural non-offensive capacity', thus giving 'defensive defence', as opposed to defence based on plans of attack. Two other members of the group profiled themselves with their own books: Hermann Scheer, with a volume entitled *Liberation from the Bomb*, and one of the party's rising stars, Oskar Lafontaine, with a little book revealingly entitled *Fear of the Friends*. The friends in this context meant above all the Americans.

The critical distance, to put it mildly, from the policies of the United States and its military presence in West Germany, found its positive counterpart in the neo-Gaullist concept of the *Selbstbehauptung Europas* — Europe's standing up for itself — or the 'Europeanisation of Europe'. The latter phrase appears to have been coined, or at least brought into wider circulation, by the commentator Peter Bender, who, like Egon Bahr, played an influential part in the formulation of the second as of the first Ostpolitik. In these writings there was a more or less explicit assumption that the past and present roots of Europe's (and, above all, Germany's) current problems lay in the hegemonial position and aspirations of both superpowers. Unless Europe stood up for itself, wrote Hermann Scheer, the European states would be pushed back to the status of 'relative vassals of the superpowers'.

It was in this general context that the slogan of Central Europe — *Mitteleuropa* — was taken up in the Social Democratic discussion. Initially revived by Czech, Hungarian and Polish intellectuals, in the debate about freedom in Eastern Europe rather than that about peace in Western Europe, the term was treated with understandable caution in Germany. If Brandt had initially thought that the word Ostpolitik was poisoned by pre-1945 German usage, then how much more so was the word *Mitteleuropa*, popularised by Friedrich Naumann in his book of 1915. The pioneer of the West German rediscovery of Central Europe as a cultural-historical concept, Karl Schlögel, was careful to disavow the political instrumentalisation of the concept, 'the proclamation of *Mitteleuropa* as goal'.

Peter Bender had fewer reservations. 'The renaissance of *Mitteleuropa*,' he wrote, 'is first a protest against the division of the continent, against the hegemony of Americans and Russians, against the totalitarianism of ideologies.' 'In the desire for détente,' he went on, speaking at a Social Democratic symposium on *Mitteleuropa* in early 1987, 'we have more in common with Belgrade and Stockholm, also with Warsaw and East Berlin, than we do with Paris and London'. Europe, he concluded 'was divided from the margins in; if it grows together again, then from the centre out'. (Some might argue that Europe was actually divided from the centre out: that is, starting with Hitler in Berlin.) Even more explicit and uninhibited was the then executive secretary of the SPD, Peter Glotz, himself born in the German part of Czechoslovakia before the war. 'We must win back *Mitteleuropa*,' he wrote, 'first as a concept, then as a reality.' 'Let us use the concept of *Mitteleuropa*,' he argued elsewhere, 'as an instrument in a second phase of détente policy.'

Going into detail, Glotz suggested a chemical-weapon-free zone embracing the Federal Republic, the GDR and Czechoslovakia; a nuclear-weapon-free corridor comprising the two German states; energy-sharing arrangements among Austria, Czechoslovakia and others; new kinds of tourist agreements; a more intensive *Wandel durch Handel* (change through trade), hindered as little as possible, he added, by 'Dick Perle's CoCom-ideology'; and even a modest Central European UNESCO for the systematic preservation of churches, market squares and houses, and for the restoration of communications inside this 'family of small nations'. (Was Germany small?.) The latter part of this agenda recalls the familiar Ostpolitik leitmotif of weaving.

Some of this would certainly have been acceptable and even attractive to some of those who were reviving the concept of Central Europe across the iron curtain, in Prague, Warsaw and Budapest. Yet a profound tension remained. For the immediate political thrust of the East European revival of the concept was clearly to get further away from the East — meaning above all the Soviet Union — and closer to the West. The political thrust of this German Social Democratic revival of the concept of *Mitteleuropa* was to pull away from the West — or at least, from the Western Alliance and the United States.

Now Social Democrats would immediately say that to distance themselves from what they saw as the mistaken security policy of the United States did not mean pulling away from the West *tout court*. Yet as the hard security discussion shaded into a larger geopolitical one, so the geopolitical shaded into an even more fundamental debate: about values. At just this time the chairman of the party's Commission on Basic Values, Erhard Eppler, was leading an extensive exercise to rewrite the party's basic programme, for after a quarter-century the Godesberg programme was felt to be in need of fundamental revision. Much of this revision concerned issues not directly connected with East-West relations: the position of women, for example, or the growing dangers to the eco-system which, in the view of Eppler and many other Social Democrats, required a fundamental reassessment of our attitude to economic growth. But over all this hung one commandment which was very directly related to Ostpolitik.

That commandment read: nothing is more important than peace. All other values and aspirations had to be subordinated to this. When Karl Kaiser criticised the seeming blindness of many of his fellow Social Democrats to violations of human rights in Eastern Europe, by contrast with their extreme alertness to such violations in, say, Central America, Egon Bahr charged Kaiser with 'lifting ideology on to the same level as peace'. The Social Democrats' new thinking demanded a 'de-ideologisation' of East-West relations, a notion eagerly taken up in Soviet new thinking. This demand was itself, of course, highly ideological. The ideology of de-ideologisation maintained that all the traditional differences of principles and values between West and East — for example, about human rights, the rule of law, freedom — must be subordinated to the requirements of the thing called peace. The authorised version of the new mantra, incorporated into the Social Democrats' 'government programme 1987–1990', ran: 'Peace is not everything, but without peace everything is nothing.' The word 'freedom' is not prominent in Social Democratic documents of this period.

This comprehensive relativisation of traditional Western values in the name of the supreme requirement of peace was, as we have noticed already, particularly apparent in relations with the GDR. The notion of the German-German 'community of responsibility' seems to have originated from the Social Democratic side. It was Social Democratic politicians and publicists who popularised the notion of a 'Peace of Augsburg' or 'Peace of Westphalia' between the two states in Germany, thus implying that the differences between Communism and democracy were little greater than those between Catholicism and Protestantism — just two versions of one faith. And it was, as we shall see, Social Democrats who went furthest in attempting to realise this singular peace.

Needless to say, none of this was undisputed inside the party. But if one looks at the official foreign policy resolutions of successive party conferences, and the two self-styled 'government programmes' of 1983 and 1987, then it is very clear that the trend was towards the increasing acceptance of this loose bundle of goals, mottoes, values and specific proposals. In the 'government programme' of 1983, after chapters on 'social peace' and 'peace with nature', the chapter on foreign policy was headed 'we want peace'. 'Humankind', it modestly began, 'wants peace. The highest goal of our whole policy is the preservation of peace. The SPD,' it went on, 'has never led Germany into a war.' (Had the Christian or Free Democrats?). It then reaffirmed the central importance of the Atlantic Alliance, although stressing the need for the Federal Republic to represent its own special interests within the alliance. ('In the German interest' was one of the party's 1983 election slogans.) The chapter went on to demand negotiations 'with the goal of a security partnership'.

If this still bore the clear imprint of Helmut Schmidt, the Cologne party conference in November 1983 saw the overwhelming rejection of the deployment of Cruise and Pershing II missiles, for which the conservative-liberal majority in the Bundestag was about to vote, and a ringing endorsement of the 'new strategies' proposed by the working group under Egon Bahr's chairmanship. By the 1986 Nuremberg conference, the new thinking was firmly established as party policy. 'The peoples in the East-West conflict will either survive together or perish together,' declared the main resolution on security policy. (That, while the Germans survived together, the people of Afghanistan were perishing separately was a detail too small to impinge on such a grandiose principle.) Consequently, 'the

Europeans in East and West can only survive in a security partnership'. (How they had survived for forty years without one remained mysterious.)

The need of the moment was to 'shape a security partnership in a second phase of détente policy', and for this the two German states had a special responsibility. 'Where the two German states give an example for the road to security partnership,' the resolution added, 'they are not treading a German special path (*Sonderweg*).' The long-term aim, as already affirmed at the 1984 Essen party conference, was 'to create, on the basis of a security partnership of the existing alliances, a European peace order which overcomes these blocs'.

In the 'government programme 1987–1990', prepared for the 1987 federal election with Johannes Rau as candidate for Chancellor, the chapter on foreign policy was headed 'securing peace'. Now, it said, the time had come to 'break the madness of the recently accelerated arms race and begin a second phase of détente policy'. This should include four elements: nuclear and chemical-weapon disarmament in Europe, the stabilisation of conventional forces at a lower level, increased economic ties between Eastern and Western Europe, and the promotion of cultural exchange to enhance the cultural identity of Europe. The aim was a European peace order 'which reaches over and eventually overcomes the power blocs'. The 'community of responsibility' between the two German states had a special part to play in developing this.

The programme went on to make a strong commitment to the further development of the European Community, which, among other things, 'should become a strong second pillar of the Atlantic bridge'. Within the Atlantic alliance, this chapter reiterated, the Federal Republic should be able to realise its own security interests, 'also our interest in common security'. Under the rubric of 'common security' it envisaged the revocation of the 1983 Bundestag resolution on the deployment of Cruise and Pershing II missiles, a chemical-weapon-free zone in Europe, and abrogation of the Kohl government's agreement with the United States on SDI. The Social Democrats' commitment to fight worldwide against violations of human rights was expressed in the concluding section. This, however, was devoted to the Third World.

Shadow policy

The Social Democrats' operative 'second Ostpolitik' consisted in high-level talks, the formation of joint working-groups and the drafting of common documents with the ruling communist parties of the East. This network had a basic geometry which both resembled and shadowed that of governmental Ostpolitik. The most important but not the most intensive contacts were those with the Communist Party of the Soviet Union. The

Moscow connection legitimised and facilitated the most intensive and special ties, with the ruling communist party in the GDR — the self-styled Socialist Unity Party of Germany. Relations with the Polish United Workers' Party, the Hungarian Socialist Workers' Party and the Communist Party of Czechoslovakia, played a secondary, supporting role — as did Bonn's relations with Warsaw, Budapest and Prague in governmental Ostpolitik.

The working groups with the Czechoslovak party, on ecological and subsequently on disarmament questions, with the Hungarian party, concentrating on the economic aspects of East-West relations, and with the Polish party, on 'confidence-building', produced ceremonious joint statements and communiqués, but without notable effect either in the countries concerned or in West Germany. That with the Soviet party produced vague joint proposals for redirecting the economic gains of disarmament to the benefit of the Third World. More important than this formal part, however, were the summit talks, notably between Brandt and Gorbachev, but also at a slightly lower level.

Reporting on one such set of talks to their East German comrades, the Soviet party leadership noted in October 1984 that 'many arguments that had previously been presented by us to the representatives of the SPD have now been taken over by them. This was especially apparent in the remarks of E. Bahr and K. Voigt'. Yet this complacent Soviet commentary can not simply be taken at face value. A cunning judo-player may seem to be yielding when in fact he is preparing to throw his opponent. Bahr, Voigt and others would maintain that after 1985 it was Soviet representatives who took over many of their ideas on security policy.

While Bahr's book of 1988, *Towards European Peace*, was sub-titled 'an answer to Gorbachev', it argued that Gorbachev had himself adopted many of the Palme Commission's recommendations. So, in a further triumph of Machiavellism, Bahr was actually answering himself! Although this claim was clearly exaggerated, it was not wholly without foundation. Social Democratic new thinking came before Soviet new thinking, and influenced it as well as being influenced by it.

Most intensive and most controversial were the contacts with the East German Socialist Unity Party. To older generations on both sides, this would have been like a true believer supping not just with the devil but — worse still — with heretics. Ever since the great schism in the German left, Communists and Social Democrats had been bitterly opposed. In the early 1930s the Communists described the Social Democrats as 'social fascists'. So deep was the enmity that even in Hitler's jails a Communist would tap furious polemics through the wall to the Social Democrat in the neighbouring cell. Many leftists from the generation of Willy Brandt and Erich Honecker held this fatal split to have been partly responsible for Hitler's triumph.

Yet if anything the old divide between Communists and Social Democrats had been made still deeper by the post-war, Stalinist attempt to overcome it. For the Socialist Unity Party of Germany (SED) was the product of the forced amalgamation, in 1946, of the Social Democrats in the Soviet occupation zone into a party of the Leninist-Stalinist type. Much of the Western, democratic identity of the West German Social Democrats, from Kurt Schumacher and Ernst Reuter to the younger Willy Brandt, had been forged in the furnace of opposition not just to Communism in general, but to this party in particular.

When Brandt launched a new phase of relations with the GDR, as Chancellor, the Social Democrats felt it necessary to pass a so-called 'demarcation resolution' defining their fundamental, irreconcilable differences with communism. The resolution was drafted by Richard Löwenthal, who had himself as a young man tried to bridge the differences between Communists and Social Democrats in order to fight Fascism. It was then amended by leading members of the party.

For its part, in the 1960s and early 1970s the Socialist Unity Party was if anything even more frightened of the influence of West German Social Democracy in the GDR than it was of that of the blackest reactionaries. The attempt to organise just an 'exchange of speakers' between the two parties in 1966, as part of the Social Democrats' vanguard role in Ostpolitik, had failed when the East German side cried off. Large areas of the GDR were traditional Social Democratic strongholds. The vision of democratic socialism had considerable appeal among the East German intelligentsia. In the 1970s, the most popular politician in East Germany was widely held to be Willy Brandt — and the reports of the Stasi's Central Evaluation and Information Group give some credence to this view.

Herbert Wehner, who had himself been a senior communist functionary in the 1930s, began his private message to Erich Honecker in December 1973 with the emphatic statement: 'In my view SED (Socialist Unity Party of Germany) and SPD (Social Democratic Party of Germany) are mutually exclusive.' (Wehner deliberately spelled out the full names of both parties.) Honecker agreed. Yet there was also, as we have noticed already in the particular case of Honecker and Wehner, a complex and profound fascination of each side with the other, as between brothers who have quarrelled or, indeed, between true believers and heretics. A close and sympathetic observer from a much younger generation talks in this connection of a 'love-hate relationship'.

Interestingly, the East German record of a conversation in 1979 between Honecker and Ponomaryev, the Soviet Central Committee Secretary responsible for relations with socialist countries, shows the East German leader gingerly raising the question of contacts with Social Democratic parties. After noting that Brandt had earlier proposed to establish inter-party relations, and that 'now Ehmke and Bahr pose the same question',

Honecker averred that 'we don't want to establish relations with the SPD. The SPD has a hostile attitude to the GDR.' The time, he indicated, was not ripe. Ponomaryev replied that this was a matter for the East German party but, he added, the Soviet Union wouldn't mind if they didn't! Summing up, Honecker observed: 'we have relations with the SPD government and Schmidt telephones me more often than is necessary. The question of inter-party relations is something quite different.'

In fact, until 1982 there was little need for special direct relations between the two parties, since the Social Democrats were in government in Bonn while the communists commanded the government in East Berlin. As we have seen, Honecker also used direct and informal channels of communication. He and Schmidt telephoned and corresponded. The lawyer Wolfgang Vogel carried private messages to Herbert Wehner, whom Honecker also met privately in East Germany.

But when the Social Democrats fell from power, a new situation arose. Already on 2 November 1982, the East German Politburo minutes record a formal resolution: 'The request of the chairman of the board (*Parteivorstand*) of the SPD, Willy Brandt, to establish party-to-party relations between the SPD and the SED will be granted.' The director of the Central Committee's Academy of Social Sciences, Otto Reinhold, was charged with establishing the links. When he became leader of the Social Democratic parliamentary party in 1983, Hans-Jochen Vogel took over from Herbert Wehner the more or less regular contacts with Erich Honecker. In Vogel's case this took the form of an annual meeting with Honecker, in East Berlin or in the Hubertusstock hunting lodge. At their second such meeting, in March 1984, the two leaders agreed to set up a joint working-group on the subject of a chemical-weapon-free zone.

The SPD delegation, led by Karsten Voigt and including Egon Bahr and Hermann Scheer, and the SED delegation, led by Hermann Axen, the Central Committee Secretary for international relations, met six times and in June 1985 produced a remarkable document. Formally approved, as the Joint Communiqué noted, by the Presidium of the SPD and by the Politburo of the SED, it was headed 'Framework for an Agreement on the Formation of a Chemical-Weapon-Free Zone in Europe'. Replete with preamble, diplomatic terminology and notes, this was nothing less than a draft treaty for a chemical-weapon-free zone in, as it put it, *Mitteleuropa*. At a minimum, the zone was to include the Federal Republic, the GDR, and the Czechoslovak Socialist Republic. (But only in April 1988 were the two German parties formally joined in this initiative by the Communist Party of Czechoslovakia.) The working-group, said the Joint Communiqué, had felt itself inspired by the commitment expressed in Article 5 of the Basic Treaty (negotiator: E. Bahr), and by a sense of responsibility that (once again) 'no war should go out from German soil, that from German soil peace must go out'. The agreement provided 'a framework for government negotiations; it will encourage and advance, although it cannot supplant, inter-governmental negotiations'.

Following a cordial summit meeting between Brandt and Honecker in September 1985, the working-group was authorised to explore the subject of a nuclear-weapon-free-corridor in Europe, 'in accordance with the proposal of the Palme Commission'. These talks bore fruit in a set of 'basic principles', jointly presented in October 1986, for a corridor extending 150 kilometres each side of the iron curtain from the Baltic to Austria. Although not a draft treaty, this 'contribution from the centre of Europe' indicated, according to the Joint Communiqué, 'what can be achieved as the result of government negotiations'. Commenting on the results, Egon Bahr noted that, as with chemical weapons, the two sides had been discussing weapons which were not 'in German possession'. Nonetheless, the view of the SED was 'on account of its leading role in the GDR even more important than that of the oppositional SPD'. Moreover, one could assume that the East German side had consulted with Moscow.

East German sources confirm that this was very much the case. Manfred Uschner, a key member of the East German delegation, recalls that 'questions from the SPD negotiators were usually passed on directly to Moscow, and one often waited long and impatiently for the answer'. He himself would generally fly first to Moscow before proceeding (via Prague) to Bonn. The records of the Politburo and Central Committee also contain evidence of this very close consultation. Such progress in the SPD–SED talks was only possible because it accorded with the new thinking on Soviet foreign policy under Gorbachev.

The paper on a nuclear-free corridor therefore clearly had Moscow's approval. Whether it had Washington's was very much less clear. In his commentary, Bahr nonetheless went out of his way to argue that the proposal was entirely compatible with and indeed complementary to what had been agreed multilaterally at the Stockholm Conference on disarmament, and with the position recently taken by Ronald Reagan at his Reykjavik summit meeting with Mikhail Gorbachev. As with Kennedy back in 1963, the unexpected intervention of an American president came like a gift from heaven. Western and especially American détente license could again be claimed for German détente designs.

This series of talks on security issues was continued with the production in July 1988 of a joint proposal for a 'zone of trust and security' in what was now described as *Zentraleuropa*. Once again, East Berlin checked every detail with Moscow. Thus, for example, a document in the files of Hermann Axen's Central Committee department for international relations gives the Soviet answers to Egon Bahr's questions at a meeting of the joint working-group in January 1988. Commenting on the draft German–German statement on the trust zone, the Soviet response says: 'In point two there is mention of "decisive power centres". The mention of centres should be dropped.' This peremptory instruction nicely illustrates the point that Moscow was, indeed, the decisive power centre.

Before the trust zone proposals, however, the results of a quite different joint working-group were presented to the public. After nearly two years of discussions about possible exchanges between SPD and SED 'social scientists', a joint working-group composed of delegations from the Commission on Basic Values of the SPD, chaired by Erhard Eppler, and from the Academy of Social Sciences of the Central Committee of the SED, chaired by Otto Reinhold, was established in the summer of 1984. The diplomatic protocol was thus delicately pitched one degree below full, direct party-to-party talks. At a guest-house on the Scharmützelsee, outside East Berlin, the 'social scientists' began their arduous deliberations.

As the fortieth anniversary of the forced merger of the Social Democrats into the SED in 1946 approached, Willy Brandt lent his unique authority to this dialogue, in a statement rather portentously entitled 'six theses on the relations between social democrats and communists'. Reaffirming his view that 'the securing of peace is more important than the quarrel about theories', he went on to quote Kurt Schumacher to the effect that 'one can make the case for democratic socialism in different ways, and certainly a Marxist case also has its place in social democracy'. The SED, for its part, timed its party congress to coincide with the anniversary of the merger, which it celebrated as overcoming the fateful, historic division of the German left. For the first time, a representative of the SPD was an official observer at this congress. The SED 'social scientist', Otto Reinhold, writing in the party's authoritative ideological monthly *Horizont* on the occasion of the congress, made a small but significant revision. The Social Democrats, he suggested, were no longer to be identified as 'anti-communists'. They were now merely 'non-communists'.

In August 1987, on the eve of Honecker's visit to Bonn, Eppler and Reinhold finally presented their common paper. Entitled 'The Ideological Argument and Common Security', this was published not only in the West German press but also in the East German party daily, *Neues Deutschland*. It was a contorted text. The first section, entitled 'Securing peace through common security', began with the by now familiar assertion that 'our world-historically new position is that humankind can now only survive together or perish together'. It then spelled out principles which, it said, now underlay the concepts of both common security and peaceful co-existence (i.e. the Soviet concept).

The second section, entitled 'peaceful competition of the social systems', argued that this competition should be judged according to which system made the most effective contribution to the solution of 'the overarching problems of humankind' and which offered 'the most favourable social conditions for the unfolding of *Humanität*'. Above all, it said, what was at issue was the contribution of each social system to securing peace, to overcoming the ecological dangers and to the development of the third world. The conditions required for this included 'social control of scientific-technical progress' and 'the development of living democracy, the realisation and further development of human rights in their mutual interdependence of social, political and personal (individual) rights'.

The next part, on 'the need for a culture of political argument and dialogue', began with the ceremonious statement 'we, German communists and social democrats, agree that peace in our time cannot be achieved by arming against each other but can only be agreed and organised with each other'. After observing that both social democrats and communists felt themselving to be continuing the humanistic tradition of Europe, it went on to lay out, in alternating paragraphs, what Social Democrats and 'Marxist-Leninists' regarded as their basic values. The former began with the clear statement that 'the social democrats understand themselves as part of Western democracy', and stressed the importance of a division of powers, human rights and pluralism.

The paper then outlined 'approaches' and 'ground rules' for this 'culture of political argument'. 'No side can deny the other the right to exist', it said. The hope had to be that both sides were 'capable of reform' (*reformfähig*). Both sides had 'to consider each other capable of peace' (*friedensfähig*). And again, both systems 'must concede to each other the capacity to develop and the capacity to reform'. Before criticising, each side should try 'first to think into the logic of the other'. The ideological argument should not lead to an intervention in the internal affairs of other states, but even sharp criticism should not be rejected as 'interference in internal affairs'.

'Open discussion of the competition of the systems, their successes and failures, advantages and disadvantages, must be possible inside each system,' it said. 'That this discussion is promoted and has practical results is even a precondition for this true competition.' A 'comprehensive informedness' of citizens was also of increasing importance, and this required the circulation of 'periodically and not periodically appearing newspapers' (*sic*) in line with the Helsinki Final Act. Also of growing importance was the network of visits and cultural exchanges 'across the system-frontiers'. In the cause of securing peace, concluded the paper, the competition between the systems must be carried forward within mutually agreed rules and a 'culture of political argument'.

Unsurprisingly, this paper itself provoked lively political argument on both sides of the German-German frontier. Its critics in the West charged that Eppler and his colleagues had gone too far in conceding legitimacy to Communism in general and the SED in particular, while relativising the Western values still firmly upheld in the SPD's 'demarcation resolution' sixteen years before. Gesine Schwan, one of the best qualified Social

Democratic critics of the party's second Ostpolitik, argued that the paper's central concept of 'peace-capability' was itself radically flawed, because it ignored the vital dimension of internal peace. In the same way, she wrote, one could describe the Bismarckian Reich at the time when it persecuted Social Democrats as 'capable of peace', for after all, it prosecuted no external war. Was it really the Social Democratic view, she asked, that a dictatorship is just as 'capable of peace' as a democracy? Did the SPD really have to certify the communist one-party dictatorship a 'right to exist' because the Soviet Union had atomic bombs?

The paper was defended by its authors and supporters among the Social Democrats on two lines. Firstly, as in the earlier new thinking within the party, they suggested that the nuclear and environmental challenges had indeed changed and relativised the traditional priorities and values expressed in the Bad Godesberg programme. Reform was needed on both sides. 'If it really happens that one system is victor in the competition,' wrote Eppler in 1988, '. . . it will not be the system of today'. As for democracy, it could take many forms: 'there is, in the Third World for example, one-party rule which becomes tolerable because democracy occurs inside the party, that is, free discussion between intra-party trends and groups'. (One might ask: tolerable for whom?).

The second line of defence was different, and somewhat in tension with the first. This was to argue that the Social Democrats had in fact been spokespersons for Western democracy and Western values in this dialogue, and that the paper — even more than the Helsinki Final Act — provided a basis on which would-be democratic socialists or social democrats inside the SED, and even would-be democrats outside the Party, could justify their criticisms and demands. Here, after all, the Party leadership had subscribed to the necessity of 'open discussion . . . *inside* each system' (my italics). Even a critic like Gesine Schwan pointed to the positive opportunity in this passage. It appears to have been one of the reasons why Richard Löwenthal, the main author of the 1971 'demarcation resolution', also felt able to support the joint paper.

Now this argument is not without foundation. The joint paper produced a rare argument in the Politburo, with one member, Alfred Neumann, sharply attacking it. The SED's veteran ideologist, Kurt Hager, soon publicly qualified the paper's claims about the 'peace-capability' of imperialism. 'There were, if you like, social democrats inside the Party,' Kurt Hager told the author in a retrospective conversation in 1992, and he mentioned particularly the main SED author of the paper, Rolf Reissig. Reissig himself made a similar retrospective claim. Among some intellectuals inside the Party it almost certainly did help to activate (or reactivate) the democratic socialist or social democratic yeast. There are, however, sharply contrasting testimonies on how far this was actually reflected in open discussion inside the Party at the time.

A September 1987 report by the Stasi's central evaluation group on popular reactions to the paper dwelled at length on the extent to which Party members and 'progressive citizens' were unsettled and confused by what it said. The Stasi report emphasised rather the critical than the supportive voices. Thus the critics reportedly said that it would now be more difficult to maintain the 'defence-readiness' of the younger generation. Also 'the discussion on the competition of the systems, the comparison of their successes and failures, would set the GDR difficult tasks, in light of the difficult economic situation and in particular of difficulties with consumer supplies . . .' The Stasi went on to report that leading figures in the Liberal Democratic Party (one of the 'front' or 'bloc' parties in the East German system) took this as an occasion to hope for fundamental changes in the information policy of the GDR. Finally, 'hostile-negative persons' saw in the paper a positive chance for developing their activities.

This source has of course to be treated critically. It was the Stasi's business to identify and emphasise developments that were, from the viewpoint of state security, worrying rather than reassuring. Moreover, Mielke himself was hardly an enthusiastic supporter of the SPD-SED dialogue. Nonetheless, this contemporary testimony clearly buttresses the argument made for the unsettling and stimulating impact of the paper inside the GDR. It was also welcomed by leading figures in the Protestant Church. In general, the period following the publication of the joint paper was one of growing criticism from below in the GDR.

Yet once again we must beware of our old friend *post hoc, ergo propter hoc*. As we have seen, there were other, far larger and more immediate causes of that mounting criticism. In such subsequent central Stasi reports as the author has thus far been able to examine, the joint paper does not recur as a major cause of, or even pretext for, such criticism. Moreover, the period following the publication of the joint paper actually saw a sharp increase in the repression of criticism outside the Party, starting with the search of the 'environmental library' in the Zion Church and continuing with the arrest of independent demonstrators on the Luxemburg-Liebknecht march. The people whom the party-state thus attempted to gag were exercising peaceful criticism precisely in the terms of the 'culture of political argument' advocated by the common paper, and, indeed, sometimes with reference to it.

This glaring contradiction, combined with the criticism in West Germany, prompted a discussion within the parliamentary leadership of the Social Democrats. A small group had already been licensed to make cautious, informal contacts not only with the Protestant Church in the GDR (which was relatively unproblematic for the SED) but also with Church-protected peace activists. However, this activity was extremely low-key and fragmentary, and its leading protagonist, Gert Weisskirchen, himself says that the Social Democratic leadership continued to concentrate almost exclusively on contacts with the leaders of the East German party-state.

The talks on both security policy and ideological issues continued, although the latter were more difficult and tense than before. Erhard Eppler, in particular, seems to have been genuinely affronted by the failure of the SED to take seriously its own solemn commitment to internal dialogue. A balance of the dialogue with the SED drawn up by the Social Democrats' Commission on Basic Values in March 1989 contained, after some liberal self-criticism of unemployment and the erosion of social rights in West Germany, a sharp attack on the repressive policy of the GDR. 'Those who refuse internal dialogue,' it concluded, 'also endanger the external dialogue.' Eppler's counterpart, Otto Reinhold, found this criticism 'singular'.

Delivering the traditional 17 June speech in the Bundestag, Eppler then surprised many of his listeners with a dark warning about the future of the GDR. There was, he said, such a thing as a 'GDR-consciousness, a sometimes almost defiant feeling of belonging to this smaller, poorer German state'. If he was not mistaken, he said, this feeling had been stronger two years before (when the joint paper was published, in the summer of 1987) than it was now, in the summer of 1989. But there was probably, he averred, still a majority in the GDR which hoped 'not for the end but for the reform of their state. If, however,' he went on, 'the leadership of the SED continues to practice that blind self-satisfaction which we have seen in recent months, then in two years' time this majority could have become a minority.' As for the joint paper's concept of the right to exist, he wished now to add: 'neither side can stop the other from condemning itself to ruin'. Whether Eppler accurately characterised a change in the feelings of the GDR's citizens about their state may be doubted; but he certainly expressed a change in his own. Such plain public speaking about the internal condition of the GDR had not been heard from a leading Social Democrat for many a long moon.

Yet not all shared his public pessimism about the leadership of the SED. Receiving a delegation headed by Egon Krenz in Saarbrücken just ten days before, Oskar Lafontaine, the Social Democrats' next candidate for Chancellor, told his guests: 'We are pushing for the opening of official relations between the German Bundestag and the People's Chamber of the GDR. In this connection talks on youth policy and agriculture will be held. Erich Honecker and Hans-Jochen Vogel have agreed a working-group on environmental protection.' 'Let us use détente (*Entspannung*),' he declared, 'to get closer to each other. This,' he observed philosophically, 'is a dialectical process: the closer we get, the more relaxed (*entspannter*) we become.'

However, relaxing was what East Germany's leaders could not do, as the developments which had begun in Poland and Hungary now spread to the

GDR in the form of the emigration wave via Hungary, and increased opposition at home. The Social Democrats' reaction was extremely confused, some maintaining that caution and 'stability' were now more important than ever, others demanding a change in party policy.

Particularly noteworthy was the response of leading Social Democrats to an independent initiative to found a Social Democratic Party in East Germany. Walter Momper, then Governing Mayor of Berlin, was dismissive. 'Nothing can be changed by small groups founding parties in the GDR,' he said. 'What is important is that the pressure for reform in the population of the GDR and in parts of the SED finally gets through into the top of the state-party. For the SED has real power in the GDR, and will keep it for the foreseeable future.'

Then, in early September, the SPD leadership was shocked by a parliamentary broadside from the Christian Democrats' general secretary, Volker Rühe. Recalling Bahr's famous formula of *Wandel durch Annäherung* (change through rapprochement), Rühe accused the Social Democrats of attempting to achieve *Wandel durch Anbiederung* (roughly: change through sycophancy). Revealingly, it seems to have been this West German party-political attack more than anything that actually happened in East Germany, let alone Eastern Europe, which impelled the Social Democrats to change their line.

Soon the Social Democrat Norbert Gansel was advocating *Wandel durch Abstand* — change through keeping-our-distance. A planned visit by a Social Democratic parliamentary delegation to East Berlin was cancelled by the SED, after Horst Ehmke let it be known that he would demand reforms and meet privately with Bärbel Bohley, the best-known leader of the newly-founded New Forum opposition movement. The Social Democratic party leadership then announced that it was revising its policy. From now on, contacts with the Church and opposition groups would take priority over those with the SED.

As the demonstrations in East Germany grew, so did the Social Democrats' disarray. Of particular historical interest was the contrast between the two great veterans of Ostpolitik. As always following the intellectual logic of the chosen policy to an outspoken conclusion, Egon Bahr called for a stabilisation of the GDR, with reforms leading to a third way. What was needed was 'a different GDR'. The people of the GDR, he said, would not let their state be taken from them. As late as 8 October, he made a cautious defence of Erich Honecker, pointing to everything that had been achieved in German-German relations in his time. Honecker had, said Bahr, allowed 'homeopathic changes in his state', thus recalling an image from the Tutzing speech a quarter-century before. 'There have been, if you like, reforms.' And, just ten days before the East German leader was deposed, Bahr said 'there's a principle that applies in every system: you don't change horses in the middle of the stream'.

Willy Brandt also urged caution and restraint. But with his more intuitive sense of politics, he seems to have grasped earlier than his old intellectual *alter ego* the direction in which history was heading — towards that reunification of which Bahr even more than Brandt had dreamed all those years before. Already in the spring of 1989, Brandt was scenting the possibility, not of a *re*unification but of a *new* unification (*Neuvereinigung*), although he said he would not live to experience it. Following Gorbachev's visit to Bonn in June, he declared in the Bundestag that the time was approaching when 'that which arbitrarily divides the people (*die Menschen*), not least the people of one people (*Volk*), will have to be dismantled'.

By mid-September Brandt was writing, in the tabloid *Bild*, that, while it was an open question 'how and how far and in what form the people in both present states would come together', nonetheless 'what then, after all, belongs together, cannot for ever be kept apart'. It was then Brandt who, returning from a visit to Gorbachev, discreetly let it be known that Honecker's days were numbered. It was Brandt who found the right words to respond to the opening of the Berlin Wall: 'now what belongs together is growing together'. And it was around the grand old man and his famous phrase that the disoriented Social Democrats rallied at their party conference in Berlin in December 1989.

After the event

With elections to be fought, ranks were closed. But the history of the second Ostpolitik could not simply be forgotten. As past compromises and collaboration became a major theme not just in East German but in all-German politics, so the subject was constantly revived — often by Christian Democrats, themselves embarrassed by the past of the East German CDU that they had taken over, but also by former opposition activists and, not least, by Social Democrats from the East. The criticism focussed as much on what the Social Democrats had not said as on what they had said, as much on whom they had not talked to as on whom they had talked to.

A first line of defence was to say that leading Social Democrats had after all had discreet contacts with Church and opposition figures in East Germany and throughout Eastern Europe. Had not Willy Brandt met with Tadeusz Mazowiecki in 1985, and Hans-Jochen Vogel with Solidarity advisers in 1987? And what of Gert Weisskirchen's contacts with Church peace and opposition groups in the GDR?

This defence was not sustainable. For those same Solidarity leaders and advisers would testify that, so far as recognition and dialogue was concerned, West German politicians had in general been close to the rear of the Western pack, and the Social Democrats had been at the very back of the very rear. Precisely because of the moral and symbolic capital which the Social Democrats had built up with Willy Brandt, his visit in 1985 had been experienced as a slap in the face.

As for East Germany, Erich Mielke reported to the Politburo in September 1989 that from 1 August 1988 to 1 August 1989 SPD functionaries had thirty-seven contacts with Church figures in the GDR. But, even more than in the Polish case, contacts with the Church could by no means simply be equated with contacts with the opposition, as the case of Manfred Stolpe was to show. To be sure, the opposition in the GDR was much smaller and less easily identified than Solidarity in Poland. But Gerd Poppe of the long-established Initiative for Peace and Human Rights can recall no contacts with anyone who could be considered an official representative of the Social Democrats, except perhaps in the margins of a Church meeting. To be sure, nor did the Free or Christian Democrats make such contacts with any greater regularity. But they could at least argue that they had the governmental responsibility of keeping good relations with the East German authorities. As Egon Bahr himself observed: the Social Democrats, in opposition, might have risked more.

The second Ostpolitik of the Social Democrats consisted in an intensive dialogue with the ruling communist parties. Why? Egon Bahr, gave a first, simple answer: these were the contacts they already had. To continue them at the highest level, for Social Democratic leaders to be received by Gorbachev and Honecker, was also, in the 1980s, to gain credibility at home. The Social Democrats could say to the electors: You see, we are the people who can deal with the East. Ostpolitik is our speciality. Beyond this, many in the party itself pointed to the 'governmental' or 'statist' tradition in German Social Democracy, which, they suggested, gained the upper hand in these seven years. Bahr, in particular, was characterised as the Metternich of the left.

Yet there was also the hypothesis of behavioural psychology which, we have argued, underlay the concept of *Wandel durch Annäherung*, and subsequent relations with the GDR. Power lay with the powerholders, so change could only come from them. Cold War and confrontation had only hardened their posture. Détente should relax it. Only contacts, dialogue and reassurance would move them to reform. And it was no accident that the internal goal of the second Ostpolitik was defined precisely with that word: reform. 'As the external dimension of détente is called peace,' said Horst Ehmke, 'so the inner dimension is called reform.' Karsten Voigt pinned his hopes on reformers from the younger generation — his own generation! — within the SED. All these contacts were therefore meant to promote reform from above.

Finally, it was argued that this dialogue with the ruling Party expanded its tolerance of criticism, and the room for manoeuvre of Church and opposition groups. Quiet diplomacy did more than megaphone diplomacy or cheap gestures. To meet with those groups directly might have jeopardised the party talks. But, as Egon Bahr argued to Bärbel Bohley, on a television programme after unification: 'by our not having publicly demanded freedom of movement for the opposition, that became attainable'.

Particularly in the light of this last argument, it is important to enquire not only why the leaders of the Social Democrats chose the leaders of the SED as their partners, but also how they dealt with them. Part, but only part, of the answer is to be found in the published record discussed above. But what of the dealings out of the limelight, the private talks, the 'quiet diplomacy' to help the opposition? Here there is an obvious problem of sources. What is available at the time of writing is some reminiscences by participants in the talks, some remarkable original documents from the SED archives, but only a few from the SPD side. As more documents become available from these and other sources, we should get a more rounded picture.

One must stress once again that the original documents from the East German Party archives clearly have to be treated critically. Through most of the internal Party reports there is a tendency to tell superiors what they want to hear, and sometimes outright sycophancy. As in the case of the relations of churchmen and women inside the GDR with the party-state authorities, so also with the relations of West German politicians to those authorities, all generalisations are suspect and all collective judgements unjust. The policy of the SPD, like the policy of the Federation of the Protestant Churches in the GDR, can fairly be described, analyzed and judged from the formal documents and official statements of its elected leaders. But in the direct confrontation with the representatives of a dictatorship, each man and woman stands alone. Each therefore has a basic right to be judged on his or her own particular record, not on anyone else's.

Having said this, it must be admitted that some of what one finds in the files is even more peculiar than one might expect from the published record. Here we have, for example, the record of a conversation between Egon Bahr and Erich Honecker on 5 September 1986, at a time when German-German relations were fraught with the problem of thousands of East Asian asylum-seekers whom the GDR allowed to fly into East Germany and then to take the local train (*S-Bahn*) into West Berlin, where they became West Germany's problem. Bahr said, according to this East German record: 'It is clear that with this problem the GDR wins influence over the FRG as never before, above all for the first time to this extent over the domestic politics of the FRG. This could be very important if it would serve the cause of understanding.'

Of course, Bahr went on, he understood that the GDR had to deal with the present coalition government in Bonn, but — and here the record turns to direct quotation –

> the question arises: is there a chance of achieving a solution . . . which would also be favourable in relation to the election results on 25.1.1987. On instructions from W. Brandt I would like to say: we want to state quite authoritatively that if the SPD came to power the government of the FRG would fully respect the citizenship of the GDR, and thus this subject would be buried.

Even allowing for the possibility of a tendentious record, it seems quite clear that Bahr was not only (in consultation with Wolfgang Schäuble) looking for a solution to the asylum problem, but also looking for an electoral boost for the SPD.

To this end, he was boldly dangling — as was his wont — the fine-sounding (yet in fact still vague) prospect of a concession on one of Honecker's key 'Gera demands' in return. In reply, Honecker claimed that in 1985–86 he had not accepted the invitation to visit West Germany 'because I did not want to appear as election-helper of the CDU. We did not want the SPD to get, as we were told, six per cent fewer votes.' But why, Honecker went on, this being so, had Hans-Jochen Vogel made such critical remarks at the Nuremberg party conference about the GDR's conduct on the asylum question?

Following more detailed correspondence between Bahr and Axen, with Bahr proposing a joint communiqué signed by Honecker and the Social Democrats' candidate for Chancellor, Johannes Rau, it was proposed that Rau would make a separate statement in Bonn, announcing that the GDR would solve this problem following the talks with the SPD. The official notice to the Permanent Representative of the Federal Republic should be postponed to give Rau time to make his announcement first. A characteristic orderly annotation in Honecker's hand — 'Agreed, EH, 17. 9. 86' — sealed the decision.

Near the end of the file is the transcript of an interview with Bahr on West German evening television news the next day.

> Question: You're an old fox . . . wasn't this after all at this moment a bonbon for the SPD? Bahr: Well first of all we are of course pleased, there's no question about that. I will also tell you (name of interviewer) quite openly and honestly that I thought to myself yesterday evening, *Mensch*, what could one do if one were in government, on the basis of the experiences and on the basis of the credit which one has won, given that this was possible as an opposition.

The passage is underlined and marked with a large exclamation mark in pink felt-tip.

This theme of domestic party politics played across the German-

German border, linked to the Social Democrats' proclaimed readiness to make further concessions in German-German relations, and laced with flattery, runs through the files. In a conversation with Hermann Axen in April 1987, the SPD's leader in Schleswig-Holstein Björn Engholm is recorded as saying that 'the policy of the GDR deserved the label historic. It filled him, B. Engholm, with pride, that the SPD had helped to co-formulate this policy.' And further: 'The SPD would most emphatically press for the respecting of the citizenship of the GDR, for the regulation of the Elbe frontier along the middle of the river, and for the abolition of the so-called Registration Unit in Salzgitter' (that is, three of the four Gera demands).

In a conversation with Axen in the Central Committee building later that month, Bahr is recorded as saying that Wolfgang Schäuble had informed him about his talks with the GDR, that he welcomed the positive development of relations between the states, 'however it was the SPD's view, and especially also that of H.-J. Vogel, that one should not make things too easy for the CDU/CSU. The time had come "finally to haul them across the table on the central questions of security".' Yet Bahr was not only concerned about the Christian Democrats. 'E. Bahr requested that all visits of SPD politicians in the GDR should again be brought more firmly under control . . . One should distinguish clearly between private journeys and polit-tourism.'

Responding in this confidential spirit, 'H. Axen drew E. Bahr's attention internally (*sic*) to the fact that one had noted with dismay that of all the prominent interlocutors from the Bundestag parties of the FRG only H.-J. Vogel had raised questions about the frontier-regime and E. Honecker's possible participation in West Berlin [i.e. in the 750th anniversary celebrations.]' (Here was a criticism that, in retrospect, the Social Democrats' leader might read as high praise!) 'Also tactless,' Axen continued, 'was that Vogel posed with visitors from the GDR in front of a picture of the Wall.' In the light of his remarks at the Nuremberg party conference, the question arose whether Vogel did not thus 'support the progaganda of the Stahlhelm-fraction. He [Axen] asked for this to be brought home to H.-J. Vogel in relation to his forthcoming visit to the GDR.' According to this record, 'E. Bahr, who was most embarrassed and concerned, said H. Axen was right, and promised to talk with Vogel accordingly.'

Now was Vogel more 'tactful' as a result? At this point we have a valuable check on the East German records, because Hans-Jochen Vogel made available to the author the Social Democrats' own records of his annual conversations with Honecker, written by his note-taker, Dieter Schröder. These suggest a series of sober, business-like meetings, which followed a well-defined pattern. After long discussion of the international situation, focussing primarily on the great issues of war and peace, and the joint disarmament initiatives of the two parties, Vogel would turn to bilateral issues. After making encouraging noises about the development of economic relations, and perhaps referring to environmental problems, he would raise concrete issues of contacts between the two states — for example a request for a new frontier crossing — and then 'humanitarian questions', including cases of 'family reunification', emigration requests, and the wish of those who had left the GDR years before to be allowed back for a visit. Details of specific difficult cases would be handed over: seventeen pages of them at their last meeting, in May 1989.

Now obviously the line on security policy presented by Vogel was different from that of the Bonn government — although in the record of the 1983 meeting we actually find him, *mirabile dictu*, making a cautious defence of Ronald Reagan. And to be sure, there are moments when he, too, makes party-political points against Kohl. But in large measure he pursues, solidly and cautiously, the basic strategy of Bonn's GDR policy, as developed by the centre-left and continued by the centre-right governments. Putting to one side all the basic systemic differences, soft-pedalling the larger issues of human rights, he seeks to achieve concrete 'improvements for people'. One may criticise the strategy, but his personal conduct of it does not — on the evidence of these documents — merit reproach. He was no more sycophantic, to recall Rühe's term, than most Christian and Free Democrats were in their contacts with Honecker.

The record of their conversation in May 1987 shows that Vogel and Honecker quite openly, albeit in a conciliatory tone, continued the disagreement about the 750th anniversary celebrations, to which Axen had referred in talking to Bahr. 'Dr. Vogel replied,' it says at one point, '[that] Honecker would surely know what he [Vogel] thought about the Wall.' And near the end of the talk, Vogel objected to an East German Foreign Ministry warning to West German journalists. No one, he said, had objected to the East German media's reporting of the riots in Kreuzberg — that is, in West Berlin.

Now the East German record of this same conversation does not include that little barb. On the other hand, it does include more detail on what Honecker said in reply. It also suggests a slightly more confidential tone between the two men than one might gather from the West German record. But for the most part, the two records are very close. A comparison of the East and West German records of their meeting in 1988 also reveals no dramatic differences or distortions. However, here too it seems that the East German note-taker did somewhat downplay the more critical parts of what Vogel had to say. Thus there is in the West German record a passage about how he himself had learned in his dealings with young people in the student revolt of 1968 how, for example, in the Munich borough of Schwabing, 'the administration slipped unprepared into such situations'. Young people, in his experience, were best won over by dialogue. 'He had therefore observed the events of January 1988 very closely.' The reference was of course to the suppression of the alternative Luxemburg-Liebknecht demonstration, and subsequent reprisals.

Now the West German version of Vogel's immediately following comments is: 'The Social Democrats did not want any destabilisation of the GDR. But, based on the joint [i.e. ideology] paper, one must ask questions.' The East German version reads: 'So far as the events of 17 January in Berlin were concerned he [Vogel] wanted to say that nothing was less desired than to talk up a destabilisation, but on account of the joint paper it had been asked what the SPD's attitude was.' There is a small but far from insignificant difference here, because the point of Vogel's slightly oblique remarks was of course to ask what the SED's attitude was. Honecker replied indignantly that the disruption of the (official) demonstration was an outrage, for until 1933 this march had never been disturbed. But Vogel could rest assured about the young people of East Germany, who 'at the moment were above all preparing for the fortieth anniversary of the foundation of the GDR'!

These documents show how each individual politician must be judged on his or her own conduct. The differences, in style, to stay the least, were clearly great. They also show how cautiously the East German records must be treated, and how important it is to have the West German ones as well. However, the comparison does not suggest that the East German records are unusable. At the very least, they are to the truth as smoke is to fire.

Returning to the documents in the East German Party archive, we find the record of a meeting that Oskar Lafontaine, Klaus von Dohnanyi and Klaus Wedemaier had with the East German leader, on the occasion of the East German state celebrations to mark the 750th anniversary of Berlin. According to this record, Dohnanyi, after saying that Hamburg would have been delighted to do what Franz Josef Strauss had done in Munich — that is, to give Honecker the full honours due to a visiting head of state — pointed to the desirability of the SPD returning to power in the Bundestag elections of 1990. Honecker, for his part, said that talk of reunification raised fears also among West Germany's Western allies. 'For the beginning of 1988 he had an invitation to France . . . This too showed that the French would rather have two German states.'

Honecker's fellow Saarländer, Oskar Lafontaine, observed that 'in the FRG it has become the general consensus that the dual statehood is a reality which no one can ignore. Just as much desired, however, were fundamental improvements for the people (*die Menschen*). He therefore wanted to request that in 1988 they should discuss together what in the view of the GDR leadership was feasible and what not.' Honecker agreed, and said this should be pursued with Axen. Later, Lafontaine suggested that 'a stabilisation on one side must be coupled with a maximum liberalisation in the relations between the two German states'.

Some two months later, Lafontaine was visited in Saarbrücken by a Central Committee department head, Günter Rettner, who raised the issue of a critical statement Lafontaine had made about the police search at the Zion Church. 'Personally, Comrade Rettner continued, O. Lafontaine was in the process of losing credibility in the GDR. Visibly dismayed,' continues the note, 'O. Lafontaine replied that it had never been his intention to discredit the policy of E. Honecker. He had profound confidence in E. Honecker.' His statement about the Zion Church events, 'had been made in the first place for domestic political reasons. He had not considered the effects in the GDR.' Precisely because he was known to have such good relations with Honecker and the SED, people expected a commentary from him 'when people in the GDR have difficulties on account of their views'. When Rettner objected to this interpretation, Lafontaine replied that 'for domestic political reasons he could not wholly abstain in the face of developments deserving criticism. However, one would have to weigh more carefully in future when and where one did it. A timely hint from Berlin could be very helpful in this connection. O. Lafontaine said that he was always ready to come to Berlin to talk with Erich Honecker about this.'

Receiving Rettner again five months later, Lafontaine was worried that — according to Rettner's report — the SPD would have a problem if it

left it to the conservatives to support forces critical of the system in the socialist states. . . . In the party presidium there was agreement that support for forces in the socialist states which exercised criticism was for the SPD first of all a domestic political issue. At the same time there was full agreement that in their appearances in the GDR the Social Democrats must avoid everything that would mean a strengthening of those forces.

This last, very plain statement, is underlined in black, presumably by Axen.

In the same file there is a short memorandum which relates closely to this theme. Dated 8 July 1988, and entitled 'note on a confidential [piece of] information from K.D. Voigt', it refers to a lunchtime conversation the previous day between Voigt and two members of the SED delegation who were in Bonn for the joint press conference to announce the joint document on a 'zone of trust and security in Central Europe'. According to this note, Voigt informed his luncheon guests that he had been told that two leading opposition figures from the GDR, Wolfgang Templin and Bärbel Bohley, who had been allowed out on fixed-term visas, 'intended, on 6. 8. 1988, in collaboration with the media and secret services of the FRG, to test the promise of the GDR to allow them to return after expiry of the exit-permission'.

'In his [Voigt's] personal opinion,' the note continued, 'the happiest solution would be first to let them enter and then to pick them up and expel them during or on account of relevant activities. They themselves and the services behind them hoped and reckoned that the security organs of the GDR would prevent their entry. It was intended to use this against the co-operation on security policy of the SED and SPD. Only for this reason was K.D. Voigt informing Comrade Uschner and Comrade Wagner about it.' Unsurprisingly, the interpetation of this unsigned note is hotly disputed by those involved.

In August 1988, Lafontaine had his eagerly sought personal summit with Erich Honecker. 'The question was,' Lafontaine said, according to the East German record, 'what shall we do in Deutschlandpolitik if we come to power: A concept for that eventuality was desirable, something that went beyond the concepts used up till now. O. Lafontaine suggested coming to an understanding about this with the SED and mentioned as a concrete example the problem of low-level [military] flights, which exercised many people particularly in the FRG.'

A year later, in August 1989, there was a tense exchange of messages with Egon Bahr about the arrangements for publishing yet another joint paper, this time on 'structural non-offensive capability'. Somehow the time did not seem quite right for a glowing presentation of these results, and the Politburo agreed to go ahead with publishing the document, but without a press conference. On 24 August an urgent message came to Axen from the GDR's Permanent Representation in Bonn. Bahr wished to meet with Honecker or Axen: 'He is afraid relations between both states could get out of control'. As indeed they could.

Perhaps fittingly, the very last document in this file is a copy, courtesy of the Stasi, of the proposal, signed by Martin Gutzeit and Markus Meckel, to form an 'initiative group with the goal of creating a social democratic party in the GDR'.

Now it must be stressed yet again that these documents have to be handled with care. One reason for quoting from them at length is precisely to give the reader a chance to savour their peculiar language and to judge how far they 'ring true'. Each document has to be placed in context. More will, we hope, become available. As the Vogel-Honecker papers show, only the release of the SPD's own records will allow a full and fair account. The people concerned will have to add their own commentaries. One should avoid the temptations both of tabloid sensationalism and of retrospective hypocrisy. As we have already seen, scholars and journalists also frequently indulged in flattery and dissimulation in order to obtain information from communist powerholders, and often in competition with each other.

Yet when all this is said, these documents still raise serious questions about the conduct of at least some representatives of one of Europe's great democratic parties. Looking back in 1992, Erich Honecker described his conversations with the Social Democrats as 'comradely' (*kameradschaft-*

lich). Yet what the available records suggest is less a closet comradeship of the left than an unprincipled party-political opportunism. Or was it Machiavellism? For if the object was, with the cunning sometimes called dialectical, to embrace the opponent in order to suffocate him, or to move him to 'reform', or to preserve that peace without which 'everything was nothing', then perhaps the end justified the means? Could not Bahr, or Voigt or Lafontaine say, adapting Bertolt Brecht 'we who hoped for uprightness could not ourselves be upright'? What, finally, is wrong with sycophancy and appeasement, if it works?

To this there are two responses. First, Brecht was not expressing the morality which is supposed to underpin Western democracy, whether Social, Christian or Free. This insists that there are some means that no end justifies, some minimum standards of dignity, some moral limits which should never be overstepped. The question then becomes: did this or that individual politician overstep that line?

Secondly, even if one puts aside the moral issue, the policy did not work. The only definite, concrete success one can confidently point to is the release (usually to the West) of many individual men and women from the GDR whose names were on the lists handed over by Social Democrats. According to a note prepared for Hans-Jochen Vogel in 1990, of some 4,320 cases raised since 1983 by the Social Democrats' office for 'humanitarian help/GDR', 2,128 were resolved before the opening of the Wall. (Whether some of these would not have been released anyway through the usual unusual channels is another question.) One cannot seriously maintain that world peace was preserved by the dialogue between the SPD and the SED. As for reform, we have seen in an earlier chapter that it did not happen. To be sure, the dialogue helped to promote discussion and even dissent within the SED. But was that of any decisive importance?

In a retrospective statement on the fifth anniversary of the joint paper on ideology, the Basic Values Commission of the (now themselves re-united) Social Democrats argued that it was: 'There is much to be said for the arguments of Rolf Reissig and Manfred Uschner that the uncertainty which the paper caused in the SED contributed to breaking the dogmatic self-confidence of the state-party' so that it lacked the resolve to use force against protesters. And again 'a bloodbath would probably have been unavoidable if in 1989 there had only been a movement against the SED and not also inside the state-party.'

Like all counter-factual arguments, this cannot be proved or disproved. But persuasive it is not. There is no evidence that 'reformers' were in any key decision-making posts at the critical moments, whereas the old guard certainly were. Moreover, in 1989 all the very different communist parties of Eastern Europe conceded without violence, with the single, unique exception of Romania. Thus, for example, the Communist Party of Czechoslovakia, purged of reformers after 1968 and unaffected by any dialogue with Western social democrats, surrendered power to an entirely extra-party movement more swiftly, peacefully and completely than the SED. If history had happened otherwise, the reform debate inside the SED might have been significant. In normal weather conditions, woodworm do weaken a fence. But if an avalanche sweeps away the fence, the woodworm's work makes little difference.

There were, in the event, two basic mistakes in the second Ostpolitik. The first was to believe that, as Bahr put it, 'security is the key to everything'. To be sure, the new thinking on security policy was a very important part of the first phase of new thinking in Soviet foreign policy, and the Social Democrats may rightly claim some credit for influencing it. To be sure, the nuclear disarmament agreements between the superpowers, and the conventional disarmament talks between all concerned, were an important precondition for the ending of the Cold War — although one should note that, to recall Bender's image, Europe was actually disarmed from the margins in, not from the centre out. Yet, as Havel and others had argued, it was political change, both from below and from above, in the Soviet Union and in Eastern Europe, that cut the path to the dissolution of the blocs, not vice versa.

When Bahr was asked early in 1990 'you expected everything from the government and little from the people?' he replied, with the clarity which was his hallmark, 'that's right. I thought: if we first provide for security, then social and political changes will follow over there. It happened precisely the other way round.' And two years later he observed:

> My real mistake was, as I see now, that in the last thirty-five years I have believed: since the heart of the matter is the security question, the power question, one must make sure that wars are no longer possible. Then politics and everything else will follow. Including German unity, including the overcoming of the East-West division in Europe. That was wrong. Politics have overtaken the security question.

The second basic mistake concerned politics. This was the belief that political change in Eastern Europe could only come from those who already held power, through reform from above — and the concomitant neglect of the individuals, groups and movements working for change from below. We have argued that, in the extreme form adopted by German Social Democrats in the early 1960s ('liberalisation through stabilisation'), this belief was always flawed. Nonetheless, in the 1960s it was a working hypothesis shared by many in Eastern Europe, and the opposition groups outside the Party scarcely existed. However, after the 1970s had demonstrated the limits of reform from above and the sixteen months of Solidarity in Poland had shown the possibilities of social self-organisation from below, it should no longer have been credible.

Yet it was a concept — or at least a word — that the key figures in the formulation of the second Ostpolitik clung to well into the autumn of 1989. Bahr's final defence of Honecker's GDR — 'there have been, if you like, reforms' — delivered on Sunday, 8 October 1989, just a day before the breakthrough of the Leipzig demonstration on Monday, 9 October, was the rather desperate *reductio ad absurdum* of this notion. For if what happened in the GDR in the 1980s was already reform, then how on earth should we describe what had happened in Hungary over the same period? The word was stretched to breaking-point, and then popped like a balloon.

The forlorn hope of reform in Eastern Europe, the idea that '89 could be '68 *bis*, was one which Social Democrats shared with Gorbachev. The illusions of the Prague Spring, long buried in East Central Europe, had a second life in Moscow — and in Bonn. As we have suggested already, these Russian illusions were, in the event, helpful illusions for the peoples of Eastern Europe. Inasmuch as the Social Democrats of the 1980s by their own illusions reinforced Gorbachev in his, while at the same time helping to reassure Erich Honecker that he did not really need to reform, one may argue that their second Ostpolitik also contributed to overcoming the division of Europe. But this was hardly the route intended.

These two basic mistakes are now matters of historical record. Theoretically it might have happened as the Social Democrats' second Ostpolitik anticipated and intended. In practice it did not. The whole issue of whom the Social Democrats did (or did not) deal with, and how, is also now a historical question — albeit still a live one. But the broader issue of the redefinition of values, concepts and priorities is not in the same sense a historical one.

At its Berlin party conference in December 1989, the party duly adopted the new basic programme over which Erhard Eppler and his colleagues had laboured so profoundly. Although hastily revised at a few points, the Berlin programme — still valid at the time of writing — contained much of the new thinking of the 1980s. 'We work for a world in which all peoples live in common security,' it said. 'Humankind can only survive together or perish together.' 'From German soil peace must go out.' A by now familiar litany. Of course, in its more than fifty pages this successor to the Bad Godesberg programme of 1959 made countless other commitments as well: also to freedom and human rights. But the contrast with the few, simple, old-fashioned principles which the peoples of Eastern Europe raised on their banners at this time was striking.

As we have noticed, the Social Democrats emphasised in the mid-1980s that what they were pursuing was not a new version of what has been called the German *Sonderweg*, or special historical path. And indeed it was not, if only because this particular path led nowhere. Yet German historians have also identified a more limited form of historical peculiarity: not a *Sonderweg* but a *Sonderbewusstsein*, a special consciousness. Taken all in all, and comparing the vocabulary and policies of the German Social Democrats with those of other West European parties of the left, there are at least traces of such a special consciousness, some of them still to be found in the Berlin programme of 1989.

One element of this special consciousness was the relativisation of what Social Democrats of an older generation had come, through bitter experience, to regard as basic values of the West. This relativisation did not result only from the specific version of détente known as Ostpolitik, but that was certainly one important cause. As Richard Löwenthal wrote in 1984, there was, 'in a large part of the young generation, a loss of the understanding that the conflict with the Soviet Union is not only a conflict between two great powers and their associates, but also a conflict between freedom and tyranny'.

The contemporaries of these West Germans on the other side of the 'Yalta' divide may indeed have been less alert to the new global challenges, to the problems of the Third World and the environment, or to feminist concerns. But this they had not forgotten. One of the founding fathers of the new Social Democratic party in the GDR, Martin Gutzeit, recalls meeting a representative of the West German Social Democrats in the summer of 1989. Gutzeit said to him: 'all we ask is that you should seek for us the same rights and freedoms that you yourselves enjoy'. And referring to the record of the SPD in the 1980s he said simply: 'how could you be so unprincipled?' 'Unprincipled?' a West German Social Democrat might reply. 'But look at the documents of our Commission on Basic Values. Look at our Berlin programme. There you will find tens, no, hundreds of principles. In fact, we have more principles than anyone else!' But perhaps these are two ways of saying the same thing.

VII

German Unification

Does the story of German unification belong to the history of Ostpolitik? Yes and no. No, because what followed the opening of the Berlin Wall on 9 November 1989 was fundamentally different from anything that West Germany had done, dealt with, envisaged or planned in its Ostpolitik. This unification was not the gradual coming closer of the people in the two states, not even the 'growing together' of which Brandt spoke, but a hurtling and hurling together, sanctioned by great-power negotiations. In many respects, what happened in the 329 days between the opening of the Wall and the 'day of German unity' was closer to Adenauer's hopes of the early 1950s than it was to Brandt's of the early 1970s. In this sense the Ostpolitik that began after the building of the Berlin Wall ended with the opening of the Berlin Wall. On the other hand, yes, it does belong, because unification came after Ostpolitik, many elements or legacies of Ostpolitik played an important part in the unification process, and Ostpolitik will now always be viewed through the prism of unification.

Yet it is clearly impossible to do justice to this story here. More happened in ten months than usually does in ten years. The whole map of Europe was — or began to be — redrawn. Even the basic headings are disputed. Was what happened in East Germany a revolution or merely *die Wende* (the turn)? When the two German states became one was that unification or reunification? New analyses are pouring from the presses. Many key witnesses have not yet given their accounts. Most documents are unavailable. Further years of research would be needed to collect the evidence, and more hundreds of pages to present it properly. And it may be that, as Peter Pulzer has suggested, the autumn of 1989 is one of those intense, pivotal historical moments — in this (and one hopes only in this) comparable to the summer of 1914 — the interpretation of which will forever be disputed.

What follows can be little more than a highly selective sketch, based on published sources, supplemented by personal observation, and concentrating on the external and especially the Eastern sides of the story. The next chapter then contains more analytical reflections on the contribution of German Ostpolitik to German unification, as compared with that of other putative causes.

Refolution and revolution

The word reunification, writes Michael Wolffsohn, should be spelt *H-u-n-g-a-r-y*; or at least, that is how it begins. By this he means that Hungary's decisions, first to dismantle what was literally an iron curtain along its frontier with Austria, beginning in May 1989, and then specifically to let East German refugees out to the West, starting on 11 September, were the immediate external causes of the collapse of the Honecker regime in East Germany. Such a claim is of course highly contestable. Some would maintain that, for a start, it was unification not reunification, and this should be spelt *G-o-r-b-a-c-h-e-v*. They would point to the whole background of perestroika, glasnost and the more permissive Soviet policy towards Eastern Europe, and then to the specific push to the Honecker regime that was delivered by Gorbachev's famous comment 'who comes too late is punished by life', and perhaps also by more direct and conspiratorial means.

Another spelling popular among German politicians after unification was *H-e-l-s-i-n-k-i*, while in America and Britain the alternative *N-a-t-o* was often preferred. Others again would write *E-u-r-o-p-e*, meaning primarily the (West) European Community which called itself that, or even *c-a-p-i-t-a-l-i-s-m*. Some in East Germany would still write *L-e-i-p-z-i-g*, referring to the great popular demonstrations in that city in the autumn of 1989. A few, mainly in Poland, would even suggest *S-o-l-i-d-a-r-i-t-y*, arguing that the Polish Solidarity movement had led the way both in the attempted, peaceful, self-limiting revolution of 1980–81 and in the negotiated transition from communism at the Round Table of early 1989. In any case, what is clearly wrong is to suggest, as Chancellor Kohl's former government spokesman Hans ('Johnny') Klein seems to in the title of his genial book on this subject, that 'It began in the Caucasus'. If 'it' means unification, then the crucial agreement between Kohl and Gorbachev in Moscow in mid-July 1990, consolidated at an obscure Caucasian hamlet, was not the beginning but almost the end of the historic process.

Without making any such apodictic claim about the 'real beginning', it is clearly true to say that in the summer of 1989 Hungary and Poland were making the running in Central Europe. Both were in the midst of what we have called a 'refolution', that is, a mixture of reform and revolution, with more of a revolutionary push from below in Poland and more of preemptive reform from above in Hungary. In August 1989, Poland became the first East European country to elect a non-communist prime minister,

Tadeusz Mazowiecki. Moscow's actual acceptance of this step was as important as any general declaratory statements about non-interference and free choice. However, Wolffsohn is right to suggest that the decisions of Hungary's still nominally socialist government had a greater direct impact on East Germany. The dismantling of the iron curtain encouraged a growing number of East German escapes, and attempts to get out by taking refuge in the West German embassies in Budapest, Prague and Warsaw. The formal opening of the Hungarian frontier for East Germans in mid-September turned the stream into a flood.

As we have seen, until the summer of 1989 emigration and opposition in the GDR were still more contradictory than they were complementary. To use Albert Hirschman's terms, 'exit' and 'voice' were both alternatives to 'loyalty', but they were alternative alternatives. The old quip that 'emigration is the German form of revolution' was actually a bitter one, implying as it did that Germans were not really capable of revolution. However, in the autumn of 1989, the quantity of emigration gave a new quality to the internal opposition. Now swelling crowds began to chant 'we're staying here'. Even if Gorbachev was mainly thinking of his own experience in the Soviet Union when he said 'who comes too late . . .', what mattered was not how the remark was meant but how it was understood.

The ninth of October, when security forces faced a massive crowd in Leipzig, but stepped back from a Tiananmen massacre, was the first crucial breakthrough in what many in East and West Germany would refer to at the time as a German revolution. The second crucial breakthrough came exactly a month later, on 9 November, when a mixture of common sense and bungling by the state's new communist leaders turned a planned opening of the German-German frontier and Berlin Wall into one of post-war Europe's most extraordinary and magical scenes. There followed, very swiftly, what German historians have called 'the turn within the turn'.

In East Germany's 'October Revolution', led by opposition groups drawn mainly from the intelligentsia, the chant had been 'we are the people' and the aim a truly democratic German Democratic Republic. In and after the 'November Revolution', the increasingly broad and popular protest turned the chant to 'we are one people', and the aim became, in the long unsung words of East Germany's own national anthem, 'Germany, united fatherland'. This change happened spontaneously, not at the instigation of Helmut Kohl or any other West German politician. But of course the response — and promises — of Kohl and others did subsequently encourage it.

When Kohl telephoned Erich Honecker's successor Egon Krenz on 26 October 1989 he was clearly still reckoning with the continued existence of the other German state, albeit with far-reaching reforms encouraged —

but also ultimately constrained — by the Kremlin. According to a transcript, he wished Krenz 'success' in the difficult task ahead of him and said the Bonn government was interested in 'a calm, sensible development'. In other words, the perspective for change was still within the horizons of Ostpolitik. When, just three and a half months later, Kohl coldly received in Bonn the Prime Minister of the GDR, Hans Modrow, one of Moscow's (and Bonn's) long-sought and cherished East German 'reformers', he did not even need to wish him failure. Modrow had already failed. Meanwhile, Kohl and Genscher had just got the go-ahead from Gorbachev to proceed with the internal unification of Germany, with no direct Soviet involvement. (The external aspects, concerning alliances, security arrangements and the like, were a different matter.) The cabinet in Bonn had formed a committee called 'German Unity', and decided to take the DM to East Germany.

The process of arriving at these decisions was more confused than it appears with hindsight. An important step was obviously Chancellor Kohl's '10 point programme' of 28 November, which sketched a path through the 'treaty community' already proposed by Prime Minister Modrow (and very much in the spirit of the earlier West German policy towards the GDR), through 'confederative structures' (of which East German leaders had also spoken in the past), to the final, but also the most distant point — full state unity. This programme was partly a response to developments inside East Germany, partly prompted by the questions of a Soviet emissary, and partly designed to improve the Christian Democrats' standing in the opinion polls and to regain the initiative in West German politics — all in all, a quite characteristic Bonn mixture. The real and very emotional breakthrough for the Chancellor was his visit to Dresden just before Christmas, where he was greeted by huge, patriotic crowds literally packing the rooftops and crying out for unity.

This cry from the people in East Germany, the continued flood of emigration and what can only be described as the collapse of the East German state were the three major factors which impelled the Bonn government to move from a measured 'calm and sensible development' to a headlong dash to unity. The East German Round Table(s), established following the Polish and Hungarian precedents, co-existed for a time with the Modrow government, in what Trotsky would have called 'dual power'. But by the end of January, it was rather dual impotence. Modrow was obliged to admit this collapse to Gorbachev in Moscow, and returned proclaiming his own commitment to 'Germany, united fatherland'. (Just three weeks earlier, Modrow had declared that unification was not on the agenda — one of many, many turns within the turn.)

Meanwhile, nearly 350,000 East Germans had gone west in 1989, and they were now leaving at the rate of 2,000 or more a day. The level of haemorrhage which in 1961 had led to the building of the Berlin Wall would now decisively hasten unification. To this challenge there seemed to be only two responses: to divide completely or to unite completely. *Tertium non datur!*

Yet while most West Germans might in principle dearly love their compatriots in the East they also dearly wished them to stay there — for their own good, of course. On the very evening of the opening of the Berlin Wall, the Free Democrat Wolfgang Mischnick concluded his welcoming speech in the Bundestag with a plangent plea to the East Germans to stay at home: *Bleibt daheim!* This from a man who had himself fled from East Germany forty-one years before, and enjoyed a successful career in the West. Whatever the degree of personal commitment which individual West Germans may or may not have had to the cause of unity, the single most important argument used to convince West German voters of the necessity of economic and monetary union was: if we don't take the DM to the people, the people will come to the DM.

The further steps to internal unification, intricate and fascinating as they are, cannot be our subject here. Vitally important was the resounding election victory won by the Christian Democrats and their allied parties in the 18 March elections in East Germany: a vote for rapid unification which cleared the way for a straight accession to the Federal Republic under article 23 of its Basic Law. With the introduction of the DM in the German economic and monetary union on 1 July 1990, the GDR effectively ceased to be a sovereign state. The details of the encyclopaedic Unification Treaty, negotiated by Wolfgang Schäuble, are more relevant to an understanding of what happened afterwards than to that of what went before.

Peace, agreement and Realpolitik

The story of external unification is much closer to our theme. As we have seen, it had been a consensual (though not wholly undisputed) maxim of West German policy up to 1989 that German unity could only be achieved by peaceful means and with the understanding/agreement/support of Germany's neighbours. After 1990 it became a commonplace of German politics to laud the fact that German unity had been achieved peacefully (in contrast to 1871) and with the understanding/agreement/support of her neighbours. But it did rather depend which neighbour one was talking about, which word one chose, and what meaning one gave to it.

All expressed their *understanding* and general approval at the Helsinki summit in Paris in November 1990; that is, after the event. Formal approval had obviously to be given by all the Federal Republic's EC partners to the arrangements for the European Community's incorporation of the former East Germany. *Agreement*, in a narrower and stronger sense, was given by just four non-German states, the Soviet Union, the United States, France and Britain, with the first being obviously the most important, the second very important, the last two somewhat less so. Of course linkages were also made to the interests of other states, notably Poland. Of course everyone in sight was wooed, reassured, sometimes informed and even occasionally consulted. But for all the polite words, probably only the Soviet Union and the United States had the power to stop it. As for *support*, in the autumn of 1989 the Bonn government's first tentative moves towards unification were actively supported by just one state: the United States. France and Britain became supportive only somewhat later, in the first half of 1990. Poland, as Bronisław Geremek frankly told a domestic readership, could not stop the unification of Germany and therefore had to get to like it.

The formula agreed in mid-February for negotiating the external aspects of unification was '2 + 4'. But of the two German states, the Eastern one was always a fraction of the Western one, and a rapidly disappearing fraction at that. France and Britain were a somewhat larger and more constant fraction of the American one. But the most important negotiations were between Bonn, Moscow and Washington — the Big Three at the end of the Cold War. Genscher would subsequently characterise the true mathematics of '2 + 4' to the author as 'perhaps two and a half', meaning that the central deal was between Bonn and Moscow, but with Washington playing a very important supporting role. Co-ordination between Bonn and Washington was exceptionally close and successful in this period, as was policy co-ordination inside the American government. Much remains to be told of the American side of this story, but some essentials are clear.

The American Ambassador to Bonn, Vernon Walters, and the American foreign policy planner, Francis Fukuyama, both guessed sooner than any leading German politician that unification really was back on the agenda. The Bush administration, having decided early in 1989 that the Federal Republic was to be its West European 'partner in leadership', backed Kohl unambiguously at the end of 1989. Even more important, it made this clear in direct talks with the Soviet Union. There were several possible ways of charting the path 'from Yalta to Malta', and it was by no means a foregone conclusion that Washington would chart it the same way as Bonn.

The American diplomatic team under James Baker was instrumental in winning French and above all Soviet agreement to the '2 + 4' formula, rather than a '4 + 0' peace conference of the victor powers of 1945 (Adenauer's nightmare called Potsdam!) or even a '4 + 2'. In close co-operation with Britain, it forged a common Western position on Nato membership for a united Germany, which was its own — and Britain's — central *sine qua non*. Yet at the same time, by pressing forward with summit, arms control and disarmament talks with the Soviet Union it gave Moscow an incentive which only the other nuclear superpower could offer. In the spring and early summer it brokered with Moscow the specific guarantees about united Germany's military and security position which enabled Gorbachev to accept Nato membership.

What American policymakers somewhat biblically described as the Nine Assurances were discussed by Baker with Shevardnadze in Moscow in mid-May, and then by Bush and Gorbachev at the Washington summit. The United States self-evidently took a leading role in the radical redefinition of Nato's role at the London summit, and in formulating the encouraging (if still vague) message delivered to the Soviet Union by the Houston summit of the Group of Seven leading industrial nations. These three summits formed the psychological take-off ramp for the Kohl-Gorbachev meeting in mid-July. Together, they contrived to suggest that the prize at which Gorbachev and Shevardnadze's whole foreign policy had been directed — a new co-operative relationship with the West which would permit the modernisation of the Soviet Union — was now within Moscow's reach. Just one more concession, and they could be there!

In the event, this was to prove yet another Gorbachevian illusion. But it was an extremely important, perhaps even a decisive illusion for the achievement of Soviet agreement to a united Germany within the Western alliance in the summer of 1990. Finally, the United States helped the Federal Republic through the last hoops at the 2 + 4 meeting in Moscow in mid-September, which saw the signature of the Treaty on the Final Settlement with Respect to Germany — the '2 + 4 Treaty', which was for the external unification what the Unification Treaty was for the internal.

In looking at the evolution of the Soviet position we have all the usual problems of incomplete sources and retrospective rationalisation. The story of the public positions taken by the Soviet leadership is that of a dramatic retreat. The Soviet leadership would 'see to it that no harm comes to the GDR', Gorbachev told his Central Committee in December 1989. It was 'quite impossible' that a united Germany should be in Nato, he said on West German television in March 1990. And so on. Of course these public statements cannot simply be taken at face value, since they were diplomatic bargaining positions and also intended for domestic political consumption. Private thinking was ahead of public speaking, although probably not so far ahead as some would fondly imagine with hindsight.

Three sets of factors seem to have determined the rapid evolution of the Soviet position. Firstly, there was the internal collapse of the GDR and the rapid emergence of non-communist states elsewhere in Eastern Europe. These developments meant that the near-impossibility of holding on to the outer empire became apparent to all but the most square-headed conservative and bull-necked marshal.

Secondly, there were developments inside the inner empire of the Soviet Union itself. With his acquisition of the powers of an executive president in March and his hard-fought but successful defence of his policies — including those towards Eastern Europe and Germany — at the 28th Party congress in July, Gorbachev briefly established matchless supremacy over the only partly reformed structures of the Soviet party-state. Yet at the same time economic crisis and nationality conflicts were shaking the very foundations of those structures, while in Russia itself his arch-rival Boris Yeltsin returned to power. Gorbachev as it were secured his command of the oil rig USSR, but the oil rig was itself being rocked by a gathering storm.

This in turn made the third factor, the active policies of the West, all the more important. Return to 'the civilised world' was the long-term goal of Soviet westernisers in foreign policy. But by now the West, and above all West Germany, was also the Soviet leader's last hope of help in an immediate crisis. As we have seen, here were Bonn's strongest cards even before the unification process began. During unification they were played as trumps.

Much from the German side is also still to be revealed, and we await the memoirs of Kohl, Genscher and others. Yet the published day-by-day account of Kohl's chief foreign policy adviser, Horst Teltschik, gives a vivid impression of the German-Soviet waltz danced inside the American-German-Soviet threesome (itself inside the '2 + 4' reel, which in turn was inside the multiple bilateral and multilateral, EC, Nato, Warsaw Pact, G7, G24 and Helsinki *mêlée*). Thus, for example, Teltschik reveals that, as East Germany imploded in early January 1990, a message came to the Chancellery from Shevardnadze. The message recalled Kohl's offer of help to Gorbachev during their conversations in Bonn in June 1989 — an offer made in response to Gorbachev's own account of his economic difficulties, following Kohl's weighty plea for German unity (see page 117f). Shevardnadze asked: did the offer still stand?

Within hours, Kohl was discussing with his Agriculture Minister arrangements for a huge delivery of meat. The Soviet Ambassador said that these supplies were needed to remedy some temporary bottlenecks — a familiar refrain! Naturally the Soviet Union wished to pay for them, but a 'friendship price' would be welcome. Less than three weeks later, the package was agreed: 52,000 tonnes of canned beef, 50,000 tonnes of pork, 20,000 tonnes of butter, 15,000 tonnes of milk powder, 5,000 tonnes of cheese, at a 'friendship price' subsidised by the Federal Government to the tune of DM 220 million. A mere bagatelle compared with what would follow.

Now it would of course be quite absurd to suggest that German unity was bought for 52,000 tonnes of beef. But this was an important and very specific signal that the prospect of Germany being Gorbachev's greatest helper in his embattled attempt to modernise the Soviet Union was made not less but more real by the possibility of German unification. This was of course a prospect which the Federal Republic had already skilfully painted in the years 1987 to 1989, and in a larger sense ever since 1969.

At the German-Soviet summit meeting in Moscow in mid-February, the first of the two external breakthroughs in the unification process, Kohl elaborated *fortissimo* on a theme that he had already played *basso profondo* at his meeting with Gorbachev in Bonn eight months earlier. By Teltschik's account, he now told Gorbachev that Germany and the Soviet Union should shape the last decade of the twentieth century together. Gorbachev, in return, said the Germans had the right to decide whether they wanted to live in one state. According to Teltschik's Russian counterpart at these talks, Anatoly Chernyaev, Gorbachev said: 'On the point of departure there is agreement — the Germans should make their choice themselves. And they should know that this is our position.' When Kohl asked, 'You mean to say that the question of unity is the choice of the Germans themselves?', Gorbachev replied, 'yes . . . given the realities'. The path to internal unification was open.

In April, the theme of German-Soviet co-operation was further developed, in theory and practice. Following a suggestion made by Boris Meissner, the Kohl government proposed to Moscow that they should already start negotiating a bilateral co-operation and 'friendship' treaty for the period after unification. This was a shrewd psychological move. According to Teltschik, the Soviet Ambassador to Bonn, Yuli Kvitsinsky, reacted almost euphorically. His dream since he came to Germany, he said, had been to build something 'in the Bismarckian spirit' between Germany and the Soviet Union. Two weeks later, Shevardnadze directly confirmed to Kohl the Soviet Union's delight at the proposal. At the same time, he asked for a loan.

Just ten days later, Teltschik was off on a secret mission to Moscow, with two leading German bankers in the plane. The Soviet side spoke frankly about their hard-currency debt, revealing that the Federal Republic was by a clear head their biggest creditor (with Japan in second place, and, rather surprisingly, Italy in third). After discussing the possible loan and the bilateral treaty, Teltschik recalled the suggestion once made by Gorbachev that he should meet with Kohl in the Soviet leader's Caucasian homeland. While James Baker discussed with Shevardnadze possible security guarantees and military limitations for a united Germany in Nato, Kohl organised an immediate, untied, government-guaranteed loan of DM 5 billion. Writing to Gorbachev with the good news, he emphasised that this was to be seen as part of an overall solution to the questions that still remained open in connection with German unification. A hefty *quid*, but for a much larger *quo*.

Once again, it would clearly be absurd to suggest that Soviet assent to united Germany's membership of Nato was bought for DM 5 billion. This was but one of many Western signals, and Western policy but one of many factors. Like the beef, it was nonetheless an important and well-timed move. Talking to Kohl in Moscow in mid-July, at the beginning of the summit that would end in the Caucasus, the Soviet leader himself said that the five billion credit was a 'chess move' made at the right moment. He valued it highly. Despite the suffering of the war, Gorbachev said, according to the edited and then retranslated Russian record which he himself released for publication in 1993, 'we must turn to Europe, and go down the path of co-operation with the great German nation'. However, it should not be forgotten that 'some accuse us of selling for German Marks the victory that was bought at such a high price, with such great sacrifices'.

After exchanging 'non-paper' drafts for the German-Soviet friendship treaty prepared by Anatoly Chernyaev and Horst Teltschik respectively — and, according to the Russian record, Kohl stressed that he had involved neither his Foreign nor his Finance Ministry in its preparation! —, the two leaders got to the point. And already there in Moscow, Gorbachev made the key concession that united Germany could be a member of Nato, although with special conditions and reservations, especially so long as Soviet troops remained 'on the former territory of the GDR', as he himself put it. But, Gorbachev went on, according to the Russian record: 'The sovereignty of united Germany will thereby in no way be put in doubt.'

The security conditions, agreed with the help of vodka and cardigans in the Caucasian hamlet of Arkhyz, were then extraordinarily favourable for West Germany, and for the West as a whole. Soviet troops would withdraw from East Germany within four years. While 'Nato structures' would not be extended to that territory, articles 5 and 6 of the Nato treaty would immediately apply and Bundeswehr units not integrated into Nato could be stationed there straight after unification. In return, Germany would limit its armed forces to 370,000, and at the moment of unification would solemnly reaffirm the renunciation of atomic, biological and chemical weapons already made by the old Federal Republic.

Now whenever Germany and the Soviet Union seemed to be getting close, the spectre of Rapallo would invariably be raised somewhere in the West. It was therefore not surprising that, picking up the name of the nearest big town, Stavropol, the relentlessly punning *Economist* would christen this meeting 'Stavrapallo'. The comparison with Rapallo helped to highlight the fundamental differences, for this was not an arrangement made against the Western powers, nor even in substance behind their backs. Yet this was also a very long way from the new, post-national, multilateral style of international relations which the Federal Republic publicly preached, and which went by the name of 'Helsinki'. In style and content this was a great-power deal. As Gorbachev himself remarked at the concluding press conference: 'We [have] acted in the spirit of the well-known German expression *Realpolitik*.'

Indeed, in some ways the whole negotiation of German unification recalled the meeting that had been held in another scenic Soviet location, in the Crimea, forty-five years before. Here was, so to speak, a Yalta to undo Yalta. It was, to be sure, diplomacy in peace not war. It was diplomacy transformed by the new technologies of communication. But it was still élite, great-power diplomacy, the few deciding about the many. While thousands of diplomats, officials and experts were involved in the whole process, Stephen Szabo, who has made a close study of the diplomacy of unification, concludes that the most important decisions and deals were made by eleven men in three capitals. And even President Bush and James Baker were apparently surprised and just a little piqued by the German-Soviet deal in the Caucasus. The Federal Republic's closest and most important West European allies, France and Britain, were neither present nor intimately involved in the crucial negotiations. In this sense Britain now experienced what France had always most bitterly resented about Yalta — not being there.

As for the neighbour most directly affected in both cases: then as now, Polish politicians might repeat the old cry *nic o nas bez nas* ('nothing about us without us'), but then as now the strong would decide about the weak. As we have seen, Chancellor Kohl had long recognised that Germany would have to concede the Polish frontiers established after Yalta and Potsdam as the price for German unification — although he would deliberately prevaricate until all but the most dunderheaded expellee could see that this was so (see page 230). Here was one thing on which all Germany's neighbours and partners agreed.

Yet at the same time, the Federal Republic made quite sure that Poland would not be a full participant in the 2 + 4 negotiations. According to the published, edited and re-translated Russian version (which must clearly be treated with great caution), Kohl told Gorbachev in Moscow in mid-July that he did not quite understand why 'the Poles' were hesitating about his offer of negotiating a frontier treaty after unification, followed by a general political treaty. 'But,' he continued, according to this version, 'when Germany then concludes its treaty with the Soviet Union they will immediately wrinkle their noses, make a great rumpus and remember history. We should try to think how that can be avoided, how one can bring the Poles to reason.'

At the insistence of other participants in the 2 + 4 negotiations, the Polish Foreign Minister was invited to the meeting in Paris which dealt with the frontier issue, the day after the Caucasus summit. Teltschik has an extraordinary vignette of Genscher talking to Shevardnadze about the next day's 2 + 4 meeting, during a helicopter trip to the town of Mineralniye Vody (that is: Mineral Waters) for the concluding press conference of the Caucasus visit. 'Genscher is mainly concerned,' noted Teltschik, 'to get Shevardnadze's support against Poland.'

Now the word 'against' in this sentence refers to diplomatic tactics, not to fundamental content. As we have recorded above, in substance Genscher was clearly for the final recognition of the Polish western frontier. So this conversation was to earlier German-Soviet ones (Rapallo, Ribbentrop-Molotov) as mineral water is to vodka. But in the politics of unification, as in the whole preceding Ostpolitik, Bonn put Moscow first and Warsaw second. The frontier treaty with Poland was not signed until after German unification. It was not actually ratified by the Bundestag until a year later, in a package with a bilateral 'good neighbour' treaty in which the Bonn government entrenched its interest in the German minority in Poland.

What was true of Poland was even more true of a little country like Lithuania, at this time struggling to regain the independence it had lost in 1939/40, as the result of a German-Soviet pact. When President Bush told Chancellor Kohl that he would find it difficult to sell to Congress a large package of economic aid to the Soviet Union, because of Moscow's attitude to Lithuania, Kohl replied that the Lithuanians had his 'sympathy', but they could not be allowed to determine the policy of the West. Up to and even beyond the Soviet ratification of the 2 + 4 Treaty, the Federal Republic was among the least supportive of all Western states in relation to Lithuania's struggle for independence. As Bonn itself raced headlong to realise the Germans' 'right to self-determination', it sagely advised the Lithuanians to take things very slowly.

Now there were powerful arguments for this attitude from the point of view of German interests, even of Western interests altogether. Germany was by no means alone in its concern about Lithuania's stance. But it is clearly not the case that the national interests of all other European states and peoples, as they themselves defined those interests — and who else should define them? — were all equally respected in the process of unification. This was *Realpolitik* in a highly civilised form, with the telephone and the cheque book instead of blood and iron; but it was *Realpolitik* all the same.

The last treaty work.

The veteran Soviet expert on Germany and head of the Central Committee's international department, Valentin Falin, would later describe the concessions made by Gorbachev in the Caucasus as the emotional decisions of an exhausted man. Shevardnadze's contribution he characterised witheringly as 'Georgian games'. The clear implication was that true Russian professionals — such as Falin — would have struck a harder deal.

Perhaps mindful of such criticism, Gorbachev haggled hard on the telephone with Kohl in early September, securing a round DM 12 billion plus a further DM 3 billion credit, to cover the costs of the Soviet troops in the (now hard-currency) territory of the former GDR and their relocation to the Soviet Union. This removed the last major obstacle to the conclusion of no fewer than four German-Soviet treaties, which had been negotiated in an extraordinary diplomatic sprint. The 2 + 4 Treaty could now be signed in Moscow, with a last-minute British objection brushed aside into an addendum.

Noting in the preamble 'the historic changes in Europe, which make it possible to overcome the division of the continent', the treaty gave united Germany 'full sovereignty over its internal and external affairs'. Thirty-five years after Adenauer celebrated the Federal Republic's day of sovereignty, the day of sovereignty had come.

The very next day, in Moscow, Genscher and Shevardnadze initialled their bilateral 'Treaty on good-neighbourliness, partnership and friendship'. A patchwork quilt of fragments from German-Soviet agreements and declarations over the twenty years since the Moscow Treaty, hastily sewn together with golden thread by Genscher's chief negotiator, Dieter Kastrup, this contained some remarkable statements. 'The Federal Republic of Germany and the Union of Soviet Socialist Republics,' said its preamble, 'wishing finally to have done with the past . . .' (Francis Fukuyama had recently declared the end of history, but perhaps only Germans and Russians could commit themselves in a treaty to have done with the past.) Yet, picking up a formula from the Bonn Declaration of June 1989, the preamble also said that the Federal Republic and the Soviet Union were 'determined to follow on from the good traditions of their centuries-long history'.

There followed a familiar catalogue of areas of co-operation and good intentions. This included, for example, the assertion that the two sides 'will never and under no circumstances be the first to use armed force against each other or against other states. They call upon all other states to join in this commitment to non-aggression.' Taken literally, this meant that Germany was joining the Soviet Union in calling upon, say, the United States not to use armed force against, say, Iraq. But of course it was not meant to be taken literally. It was meant to secure Soviet agreement to German unification. This was Machiavelli dressed as Luther.

On the third of October 1990, Germany celebrated, with fireworks, flags and champagne, what would henceforth replace the 17 June as the 'day of unity'. But two more detailed agreements remained to be signed: that on 'several transitional measures', meaning the agreed payments for the removal of Soviet troops, and that specifying the precise terms on which the Soviet troops would remain and withdraw by the end of 1994. On 9 November, the first anniversary of the opening of the Berlin Wall, Kohl and Gorbachev formally signed in Bonn the friendship treaty that Genscher and Shevardnadze had initialled in Moscow and yet another treaty — 'on the development of a comprehensive co-operation in the fields of economics, industry, science and technology'. Gorbachev concluded his speech with the modest words: 'Let the Soviet-German treaty signed for twenty years be transformed into the treatise "To Eternal Peace".' Kant as cant.

With this, the latest and in the event the last German-Soviet treaty work was complete. It was the most complex in form, the simplest in content. Yet the cautious diplomats said it was still not wholly secure. Ratification of the 2 + 4 Treaty by the Western signatories was a foregone conclusion. The complex arrangements with the EC had already been agreed. The frontier treaty with Poland would be signed by Genscher in Warsaw a week later. The blessing from the Helsinki summit in Paris was easy. But something could still go wrong in Moscow. Thus Genscher would argue that German unification was only definitely achieved when the Soviet Ambassador handed over the Soviet ratification document for the 2 + 4 Treaty, in the Foreign Ministry in Bonn on 15 March 1991. Only then was Germany finally united, again; or was it rather, anew?

In July 1987, Gorbachev had said to Weizsäcker that German unification might perhaps come 'in a hundred years'; generously reducing the period, on Weizsäcker's intervention, to a round fifty. In January 1989, Erich Honecker had declared that the Berlin Wall might survive for fifty or a hundred years, if the grounds for its existence were not removed. The hundred had happened in one.

Yet was Germany really united? Asked for his hopes on 'the day of unity', the writer Reiner Kunze, one of many free spirits driven out of Honecker's GDR, said he hoped that after this day the Germans would prepare themselves for it. The deep truth in that deceptively simple remark was to become apparent to everyone over the next two years. Economically, socially, culturally and pyschologically, the Germans were still very far from united. Nonetheless, Germany, the state, was united in a way that Europe, for example, was not. What is more, united Germany was, whether it liked it or not, once again a major power in the centre of a still disunited Europe.

VIII

Findings

German and European

An old truth: the more you know, the less you know. Politicians and commentators in happy possession of a little knowledge can make the most confident pronouncements about the certain future effects of a given policy on another country. After making a detailed study of what actually happened, one hesitates to make any positive statements at all. This applies not only to the tangled skein of cause and effect. It applies even to intentions.

If we return to the issue of the relationship between the German and the European questions, raised in Chapter One, then our first general finding is that German Ostpolitik was above all a German answer to the German question. However, from the 1960s onwards German politicians — not all German politicians, but politicians in all parties — concluded not only that this required seeking German answers to the European question, but also that these German answers must be built into a larger European answer to the European question. The way forward led not through reunification to détente but through détente to reunification. Bonn would work towards a European peace order, in which the Germans could achieve unity in free self-determination. West European integration or 'European Union' would be a contribution to the larger European unification. This in turn might be described as a European answer to the German question — indeed even, one German historian suggested, the most constructive answer to the German question since the Thirty Years' War.

Throughout, almost every aspect of Bonn's policy towards Europe (West) and Europe as a whole had (at least) two sides. The multilateral also facilitated the unilateral. The renunciation of sovereignty was also about the recovery of sovereignty. The transfer of power also served the (re)acquisition of power.

From Adenauer to Kohl, West German Chancellors asked the West and especially Western Europe to place golden handcuffs upon Germany. Both the Atlantic Alliance and the European Community were to save Europe from itself — that is, from reverting to the bad old ways of warring nation states —, to protect all of Western Europe from the Soviet Union and to protect the rest of Western Europe against Germany. But they were also to protect Germany against itself. However, it was precisely this German readiness to transfer or share power and give up sovereignty which helped to convince West Germany's neighbours that the Germans could be trusted with restored sovereignty. In a feat worthy of Houdini, it was by laying on the golden handcuffs that Germany set itself free.

Similarly with the East. In talking of and working for all-European solutions, the Bonn government was also thinking of and working for all-German ones. In being so comprehensively and demonstratively peaceful, co-operative and 'European', West Germany built up what Genscher called *Vertrauenskapital* — literally trust-capital — in West and East. These reserves of trust, as much as the reserves of DM — and the capital of trust was also partly trust in German capital — were heavily and successfully drawn upon to achieve German unification. When Genscher said 'the more European our foreign policy is the more national it is' he summarised the apparent paradox — and a real ambiguity.

There are strong echoes of Stresemann here. If one is looking for parallels in the earlier history of German foreign policy, then the admixture of the Adenauerian and Bismarckian traditions that Waldemar Besson identified in 1970 actually came out in the 1980s closest to Stresemann — a model whom both Kohl and Genscher would happily acknowledge. As with Stresemann, there was the attempt to achieve national and revisionist goals through the patient but active rehabilitation of Germany in the international community, peaceful negotiation, harmonising Europeanism and all-round reconciliation — with, nonetheless, important qualitative differences between the western and the eastern Locarnos. As with Stresemann, there was the mixture, so difficult to analyse, of genuine Europeanism and genuine nationalism, of more or less affected Europeanism for foreign audiences but also of more or less affected nationalism for domestic audiences — such as Germans from lost territories to the east.

Yet such comparisons are useful also for the differences they point up, starting with the fact that the Bonn government succeeded where Stresemann failed. The year of 1990 saw a triumph of peaceful, moderate German revisionism of which Stresemann could only dream. The Federal Republic, having in two great steps, the Western and the Eastern treaty works, regained its (relative) freedom of action as a state in Europe, West then East, had expanded its connections, attraction, good reputation and power to the point where it could seize an extraordinary (and unexpected) historic opportunity to achieve the maximum possible revision of the post-war ('Yalta') map of Europe to Germany's advantage. But this was a triumph within — and made possible by — a profoundly different domestic context.

The basic structures out of which West German foreign policy was made, the democratic polity, the modern, centrist character of stable parties of both left and right, the legal system, the economy, the social structure (with the remnants of the old agrarian, aristocratic élites from east of the Elbe now supporting neo-Stresemannesque policies from the leader columns of *Die Zeit* and the boardrooms of thoroughly modern banks), the subordinate and democratic character of the military (those model 'citizens in uniform'), the attitudes of writers, scholars, intellectuals, public opinion — all were quite different from those of Stresemann's day.

The question of the relationship between the German and the European can also be posed slightly differently, and more generally, in the terms of an ongoing debate about the nature of contemporary international relations. On the one side are those (sometimes loosely called Realists) who see these as still fundamentally about the immanently competitive relations between states, each struggling to maintain and increase its own power, in a great game that would in its innermost essentials be familiar to Metternich, to Machiavelli, to the Athenians of Thucydides' Melian debate. By no means only war belongs to this great game, but public and private diplomacy, economic statecraft, summitry, secret understandings and public alliances, including supposedly permanent ones, called Ententes, Empires, Treaty Organisations, Axes, Commonwealths or Communities.

On the other side there are those who emphasise the fundamentally new elements in post-1945 international relations, not only but perhaps especially in Europe: the degree of 'complex interdependence', the special attributes of the nuclear age in strategy, the global village in communications, the single world economy and ecology. All these, they argue, make today's international relations, Alliances and Communities qualitatively different from those analysed by historians from Thucydides to Lewis Namier.

Not only a large part of German scholarship but much of official German foreign policy consciously presented itself in the 1970s and 1980s as belonging to the latter school. Bonn's was the very model of a modern foreign policy: post-national, multilateral, acronymic, economistic, supremely peaceful in all respects, preaching interdependence in all directions, seeking friends everywhere, seeing enemies nowhere — only 'enemy-images' (*Feindbilder*) that had to be 'dismantled'. In this rhetorical world there were no conflicts, only 'irritations'; power was a dirty word, to be replaced by 'responsibility'; and national interests were always to be discreetly covered, like Victorian piano legs, by curtains marked 'Europe', 'peace', 'co-operation', 'stability', 'normality' or even 'humanity'.

Of course one should beware of caricature. As we have seen, there were notable exceptions in German scholarship and commentary, while German policymakers were themselves quite capable of thinking and even talking in terms of power and national interest, especially to domestic audiences and even more in internal discussions and private communications. In fact, we have found that the reality of German foreign policy in general, and German Ostpolitik in particular, was a great deal more national, power-oriented and, so to speak, hard-nosed and old-fashioned, than its public presentation.

German Ostpolitik gave a special twist to an analysts' term, by proclaiming 'interdependence' as a goal of foreign policy. Yet preaching interdependence helped to achieve full *in*dependence for the Germans who preached it, while contributing to a new (or new-old) dependence for many of those to whom interdependence was preached.

Now such a conclusion will naturally prompt the criticism that this merely reflects the general views of the author. The author, it will be said, has found what he set out to prove: his conclusion is actually his starting point. But this must be disputed in three very important respects. Firstly, these really are findings, not just opinions. We have carefully presented a mass of detailed evidence, drawing on sources often of unusually high quality, to show what German policymakers did actually say at the highest level, among themselves and to their key Eastern partners. Secondly, this is not what the author set out to find. This book started as a search for answers to the European question, as posed in the Prologue. Closer examination suggested that German answers would be the most important. Only still closer examination revealed the full extent to which these German answers were actually, first and last, answers to the German question.

Thirdly, and most importantly, it is by no means contended here that the German use of 'Europe' was merely instrumental. In fact, the sudden, unexpected achievement of German unification may not only reveal but also obscure what German policymakers themselves thought they were trying to do. As we have seen, German Ostpolitik was designed to clear away some heavy burdens of the past, to increase the Federal Republic's freedom of action, and to create European conditions in which the Germans in the two states could come closer together again, and eventually reunite. Inasmuch as one can talk of a basic 'logic' of a policy, irrespective of the understanding of the people practising it at a given moment, this remained the 'logic' of German Ostpolitik. But from the outset there was a wide range of different motives among policymakers. As different people came to the helm, and as things in Germany and Europe developed over the 1970s and 1980s, so different priorities, different intentionalities, different visions of a European peace order, would overlay that original and arguably always underlying logic.

Thus there is, for example, no doubt that Helmut Kohl was genuinely committed to a vision of European Union in the (then) boundaries of the European Community. In the early to mid-1980s his foreign policy was more concretely directed towards this goal than to that of German unification. If in the event he achieved German rather than (West) European unity, this does not mean that his commitment to the latter was any less genuine. It simply means that it did not happen.

In the 1980s, Willy Brandt may genuinely have thought as often and cared as deeply about the two parts of Europe, East and West, indeed about the two parts of the world, North and South, as he did about the two parts of Germany and Berlin. When Helmut Schmidt says that the idea of a European peace order had seemed to him, down the years, the most important thing, we have no good reason to doubt that to him it thus seemed. (One merely has to ask what he meant by it.) For Hans-Dietrich Genscher, pursuing the best possible relations with the largest possible number of states while maintaining the highest possible domestic profile may indeed at times have become almost an end in itself, rather than a means to an end which seemed so remote. And so on down the ranks, with many people at all levels sincerely committed to some vision of a larger European project.

Moreover, when German and European interests were so habitually conflated it would be wrong to assume that a clear private distinction was made between them. Between the national-instrumental usage at the one end and the selfless-visionary usage at the other there was a large area of quite genuine and quite characteristic higher confusion. The point about much German speaking and thinking about Europe was precisely that it was not clear. When, for example, in the early 1980s German interests clashed with Polish interests, many German policymakers and commentators honestly found it difficult to see (let alone to admit) that it was actually national interests that were conflicting. Beside the real difficulty in defining the national interests of an unfree country, such as Poland then was, there was a real confusion between German, European and indeed all-human interests, a confusion much assisted by the elastic and multi-layered concept of 'stability'.

However, in the decades of Ostpolitik the profound unclarities and latent tensions within and between the very diverse forms of German Europeanism produced no major controversy in Germany for three main reasons. Firstly, there undoubtedly was in most of the wartime and immediate post-war generations in German politics a deeply felt revulsion against the preceding perversion of German nationalism, and a correspondingly strong commitment to expand supra-national co-operation and integration in Western Europe; although this went hand-in-hand, or back-to-back, with an equally strong desire to restore Germany's freedom of action as an (at least) half-nation-state.

Secondly, in these decades West European integration did not reach the stage at which it threatened the real core essentials of state power and national sovereignty — such as, for example, the DM. Thirdly, and most importantly, even those who had little genuine commitment to a supranational European project, however defined, could see that, in the circumstances of Yalta Europe, Germany could only achieve her national goals by being demonstratively, emphatically European. As Genscher said: the more European, the more national.

These conditions are interesting not only for historical reasons but also because in the second half of the 1990s all three might no longer apply.

Ostpolitik and the end

What caused what? A simple question which, as we have repeatedly observed, is extraordinarily difficult to answer when looking at East-West relations in the era of hot peace. It is even more difficult to answer when looking at the end (to say 'outcome' is already to prejudge the issue) because German unification came not, as German politicians had hoped, in the course of a gradual transformation of the European scene, but in a revolutionary transformation of the world scene. For the events of 1989 to 1991, from the first snip at the barbed wire along the Austro-Hungarian frontier to the collapse of the Soviet Union, clearly do mark a caesura not just in European but in world history.

The specific causal effect that may tentatively be attributed to German policy is hard to discern between the internal Eastern causes and the effects of the policies of other major Western states. And all of this is bound up in the mystery of truly great events. While compelling reasons may be adduced for the collapse of communism, the reasons why it collapsed then — and not a decade earlier, or later — are much more difficult to pin down. Reference to the old Tocquevillian saw that the most dangerous moment for an autocracy is when it starts to try to reform itself is no doubt helpful. But this is a set of historical events so rich that, like the French Revolution, it offers ample stuff for almost every kind of historical explanation; even Marxist ones.

Some may point to changes in supposedly objective balances of military, economic and political power, what Soviet analysts used to call the 'correlation of forces'. Here the objective, infrastructural shift in the balance of (above all) economic power between the West and the East in general, West Germany and the Soviet Union in particular, was, they might argue, now working through into the formal realities of political superstructure. This is, however, an interpretation that would have been disputed by that well-known Marxist analyst of international relations, Leonid Brezhnev. In one of his confidential letters to Helmut Schmidt,

Brezhnev wrote that 'for all the importance of economics . . . the primacy in international affairs remains, as is well known, with politics'.

Others, mindful of Brezhnev's insight, would point to the significance of individual personalities — and the importance of the particularly good understanding between Kohl, Gorbachev and Bush, Shevardnadze, Baker and Genscher, cannot be ignored. Others again would invoke the *Weltgeist*, God, Time, Life, or, as the veteran Soviet pro-consul in Germany, Vladimir Semyonov, put it in conversation with the author, 'His Majesty History'. Yet others, less philosophically inclined, would point to the role played by Lady Luck — and that often neglected historical agent must certainly be credited with a part in the proceedings. For example, Germany was simply lucky that in the summer of 1990 Gorbachev had reached just the right combination of strength (inside the Soviet party-state) and weakness (all around it). He was weak enough to feel he had to concede German unification within the Western Alliance but still strong enough to push this through at home. Had he been a little stronger, he might not have conceded the deal of the century. Had be been a little weaker, he might no longer have been there to make any deal.

Gorbachev himself, on signing the German-Soviet friendship treaty in Bonn, paid fulsome tribute to the personal contribution of Helmut Kohl, but also to that of the 'Ostpolitik' (German in the original) which he associated with the names of Willy Brandt and Hans-Dietrich Genscher. However, elsewhere he paid equally fulsome tribute to 'my friend Ronald Reagan' and to Pope John Paul II, thus producing, in sum, a truly catholic endorsement of almost every major strain of Western policy.

Naturally enough, German politicians placed slightly different emphases among themselves: Christian Democrats drew a straight line from Konrad Adenauer via Helmut Kohl to unification, Social Democrats drew a great arch from the Willy Brandt of 1970 to the Willy Brandt of 1990, Free Democrats celebrated the triumph of Genscherism — and all ignored the many twists and turns on the way. In outward discourse, they joined in paying tribute to Gorbachev, first and foremost, to the Hungarians, to the Americans and the Western Alliance, to the EC, to the French, to the British, to the Poles, to Uncle Tom Cobley and all.

The most frequent and consensual explanation was, however, 'Helsinki'. President von Weizsäcker referred often to the success of what he called simply *Helsinkipolitik*. The Helsinki process, he averred, had become in Eastern Europe a 'human rights motor'. CSCE, said Genscher, '— that had to lead to German unification'. Thus, characteristically, both chose the most general, multilateral and harmonising form of explanation. In fact, these formulations are less a contribution to the historical explanation of Ostpolitik than a continuation of Ostpolitik in the shape of historical explanation.

As we have seen, Helsinki actually covered a multitude of approaches.

It was a very useful, original and flexible diplomatic form, which could be filled with very different contents. Weizsäcker's version is misleading in at least two respects. Firstly, while human rights activists in Eastern Europe paid generous tribute to 'the favourable atmosphere created by Helsinki' (in the words of a Charter 77 message to the Vienna review conference), his description of Helsinki as a 'human rights *motor*' is an historically indefensible overstatement. Men and women had fought for human rights in Eastern Europe long before Helsinki, and would have done so if Helsinki had never happened. To suggest that Helsinki was the 'motor' that drove Jan Patočka or Andrei Sakharov is like suggesting that the Atlantic Charter was the 'motor' that drove Dietrich Bonhoeffer. Secondly, insofar as a specific linkage was made in Western policy between the Helsinki process and the position of those fighting most actively for respect for human rights in Eastern Europe, it was American rather than German policy that made that linkage. As for Genscher's claim, this is the fallacy of historical inevitability; retrospective determinism in a particularly crass form.

Difficult though it is to establish clear connections between cause and effect, a little more clarity and precision is possible.

German Ostpolitik was a systematic combination of policy towards the Soviet Union, East Germany and the rest of Eastern Europe. While developments in all three areas remained important throughout the events of 1989 to 1991, those in Eastern Europe were most important in the spring, summer and early autumn of 1989, those in East Germany were critical from October 1989 to early 1990, while thereafter it was above all a matter of relations with the Soviet Union.

Broadly speaking, German Ostpolitik made the most direct and substantial contribution to the ultimate success in the area of relations with the Soviet Union, and the overall system of East-West relations. It made a still more direct but much more ambivalent, indeed deeply paradoxical contribution in relations with East Germany. The least substantial and direct contribution was in the area which was always its lowest priority, the rest of Eastern Europe.

The Federal Republic succeeded in what Weizsäcker called 'our most important task': to establish a good relationship with the 'Eastern leading power' while at the same time retaining the protection and support of the leading Western power. The achievement of all that wooing, reassurance, trade and 'honest interpreting', all those treaties, earnest speeches, nocturnal exchanges of war memories, joint economic projects and credits, is clearly reflected in an internal memorandum drafted by the Bogomolov institute in Moscow for one of Gorbachev's key foreign-policy advisers, Georgi Shakhnazarov, in January 1990. 'In principle,' said this memorandum, 'the reunification of Germany does not contradict the interests of the

Soviet Union. A military threat from that side is not very likely, if one considers the radical fracture in the consciousness of the German nation that occurred with the national catastrophe of the past war. In the economic sphere, the Soviet Union can obtain tremendous gains from co-operation and interaction with Germany.'

Here are the two crucial points. Forty-five years after the end of the war, Germany (West) had convinced key Soviet policymakers that it was no longer a threat, and that it was the Soviet Union's most promising and important economic partner in the West. Of course other causes were at work here. In considering the perception of threat we really do have to look at the factor 'time itself'. Gorbachev and Kohl were the first Soviet and German leaders since 1945 not to have experienced the war as adults. On the economic side, the underlying cause was of course the divergent performance of the two systems, Western and Eastern, mixed market and planned. But the contribution of conscious German policy is nonetheless very significant.

There has been some debate about the economic components of power. At least since Ranke, and in the latest version from Paul Kennedy, a great power has been identified by its military might. The economic power of a Germany or Japan is, it has been suggested, qualified and constrained by the multiple dependencies of a trading state. And Leonid Brezhnev's contribution to this scholarly debate should certainly be a caution against any simplistic economic determinism. Nonetheless, West Germany's economic power — that is, at the cutting edge, its *financial* power — demonstrably contributed to the achievement of its goals in German-Soviet relations.

From 1969/70 to 1989/90 the bankers and industrialists preceded or accompanied the diplomats and politicians on the way to Moscow, underpinning and facilitating their work. West Germany, as a prime mover of West European economic integration and a key player in the economy of the developed world, was able to wave the key not just to future economic co-operation with itself, but also to that with the EC and to some extent even with the G7 — as it 'honestly interpreted' Gorbachev's good intentions in the spirit of Genscher's Davos speech. Food supplies and hard currency played a very direct part in the actual diplomacy of German unification.

In the specific circumstances of Europe in the 1980s, where the 'Yalta' dividing line was also one between hard and soft currencies, and many of the soft-currency states had got themselves in debt to hard-currency states, a little hard currency went a long way. This applied even more, in different ways, to relations with Poland, Hungary and the GDR. The power transmission between the economic and the political was quite direct, and the gearing very high. There are circumstances in which a country's riches may not easily be usable for its political ends. But here they definitely were. The DM was indeed the currency of German power.

What of the other, even harder currency of power, arms? Was the success achieved in spite or because of the Federal Republic's continued commitment to the defence as well as the détente track of Nato's Harmel strategy? There are two issues here. The first is the general one of the relative contribution of defence and détente, of a policy of strength and proposals for co-operative security — at the extreme, of SDI or SI — to the revision of Soviet policy in the second half of the 1980s. We have found that evidence can be adduced for both sides, and suggested that the most likely answer is, maddeningly, 'at once neither and both'.

The second issue, however, is the Federal Republic's need to keep the trust of the West. For this, its continued commitment to Nato as a military alliance, including the deployments of the 1980s, was crucial. As Willy Brandt suggested, the term Ostpolitik was to some extent a misnomer, inasmuch as the continuation of Westpolitik was a fundamental premiss and *sine qua non* of this policy. German foreign policy was unavoidably a balancing act between preserving the desirable and changing the undesirable aspects of the status quo, between winning the trust of the East and retaining that of the West, a matter therefore of squaring several circles, reconciling the irreconcilable, of many-sidedness verging on the chameleon-like, of *sowohl-als-auch*.

Some of those most directly involved in the conception and development of Ostpolitik, such as Egon Bahr, pushed for more rapid and generous Western disarmament than Washington (or London) could happily bear. They hoped to yield to Soviet wishes only — judo again! — the better to realise their own. This eastward tilt or gamble was averted twice. First it was averted by Helmut Schmidt becoming Chancellor, thus preventing Bahr from trying out the second part of his 'concept'. Then it was averted by Schmidt ceasing to be Chancellor, thus preventing the Social Democrats from taking another such chance, sustained by an emotional, theological and national tide of protest for 'peace'.

Whether these experiments would have facilitated or delayed the revision of Soviet foreign policy is a hypothetical question, but in the author's judgement Andrei Gromyko might well have accounted them a great success for his own line — and therefore a good reason for continuing with it. Almost certainly, however, they would have rapidly depleted West Germany's 'capital of trust' in the West. While one can never finally know 'what would have happened if', this was a gamble well avoided. As the story of 1989/90 again clearly showed, Bonn needed the trust of both Washington and Moscow to achieve its goals.

In all this, Bonn was successful in the most straightforward and satisfying way. Not only did it achieve all (and even more than) it set out to achieve. It did so more or less in the ways it set out to. What of the other two sides of the Bonn-Moscow-Berlin triangle? The original idea of Brandt and Bahr's Ostpolitik was, after all, to work through Moscow to get back to Berlin, so that Germans could get closer to Germans again. It is hard to overstate the degree to which German-German relations, including those in and around Berlin, were and remained the epicentre, the alpha and omega, of German Ostpolitik.

Now here, too, the end of the story could be considered a remarkable success, going beyond even the highest original expectations. Yet the German-German path to this end was in many respects radically different from that intended or expected. It was hedged with ironies and paved with unconscious as well as conscious paradoxes. We have already presented our interim conclusions to this central chapter, of Ostpolitik and of this book (see p. 203f). A few of the main points should briefly be recapitulated here. By going through Moscow, Bonn got to Berlin. In this sense, the original paradox of only being able to change the status quo by first recognising the status quo proved right. However, the second paradox in the stategy of *Wandel durch Annäherung*, that of liberalisation through stabilisation, proved wrong, while the supplementary, that one could best help dissidents in the GDR by not helping them, was definitely a paradox too far.

The idea of liberalisation through stabilisation, with its behaviourist core of relaxation through reassurance, was always flawed. The West could never provide enough reassurance to make communist rulers relax, because the internal tensions came from the very nature of their regimes and not merely from the external tensions of the Cold War. Somewhere in this theory there was still the idea that a socialist third way, evolving out of reformed communism, could be as attractive as the already reformed capitalism of Western Europe. The theoretical possibility can never finally be disproved. But it has certainly not happened anywhere. And as the reformed capitalism of West Germany became ever more attractive (particularly when seen on television or a short visit) while the unreformed communism of East Germany became ever less attractive, so GDR policy in the original Social Democratic version drove ever deeper into an irresoluble contradiction.

Even if the Federal Republic had, for example, denied its own citizenship to East Germans and recognised the full sovereignty of the East German state in every conceivable way, this would still not have made that state acceptable to its own people. To achieve this end, the only thing would have been to make West Germany poorer, greyer, and altogether less attractive than East Germany. A glimmering of this absurd notion comes through the suggestion made in 1988 by the then Bishop of East Berlin that West Germany might 'try to reduce the temptation a bit'.

At the same time, the lesson of experience in other socialist states, indeed in dictatorships throughout history, was that a degree of tension, opposition, conflict, social pressure from below, was a necessary (though not, of course, a sufficient) condition for desirable change. This was the lesson that some of the best political thinkers in East Central Europe,

Kołakowski and Mischnik, Havel and Kis, had already drawn from the crushing of the Prague Spring. 'Revisionism', change by reforms from above, led by an enlightened Party, would never be enough. In this sense, the Social Democrats were a decade behind the times. They built the hope of revisionism into the heart of their strategy just at the time when the revisionists in Eastern Europe were abandoning it.

Instead of liberalisation through stabilisation, what happened in the GDR was stabilisation without liberalisation. The Federal Republic contributed to this with DM and recognition. Of course the interim benefits for West Berlin, visiting West Germans, and many thousands of individual East Germans — the famous *Menschen* — should by no means be underrated. The 'improvements for people' were great. Perhaps this also contributed to the 'keeping together of the people', although that is more debatable. However, one has to set against these specific alleviations for individual people the disadvantages that flowed from the stabilisation of an unreformed communist state for everyone who lived in it.

Many of the monies paid by West Germany were, in effect, ransom. The main objection to paying ransom was best expressed by Rudyard Kipling:

> That if once you have paid him the Danegeld
> You never get rid of the Dane.

In this case, however, they did ultimately get rid of the Dane. Bonn contributed to his departure in one partly intended and two unintended ways. The partly intended way was to increase contacts between the people in the two states, so the East Germans could see which was better and want to get still closer to it. To some extent this did happen, particularly with the growth of travel from East to West in the late 1980s. But arguably, given the chance, East Germans would always have wanted that anyway.

Curiously enough, one of the two unintended ways was actually the Danegeld itself. Far from helping to encourage a reform of the East German economy, this enabled the GDR to continue without significant reform, economic or political. Precisely that lack of reform, however, made the collapse, when it came, more precipitate and total. The growing direct financial dependency on West Germany was probably not a primary concern for Honecker, but it was for important decision-makers close to him, and contributed very directly to the rapid resignation of those who came after him.

The other main currency of German-German relations, recognition, also worked in an unintended way. Flattered and reassured, Honecker did not, as intended, relax his grip on his subjects in the GDR. In fact, he tightened it. But he did relax his grip on reality. West German illusions about East Germany reinforced his own, thus contributing to hubris, followed by nemesis. Hence our ultimate paradox of West German policy towards the GDR: they got it right because they got it wrong!

However, the successful leap from stabilisation without liberalisation to liberation through destabilisation was only possible because of external circumstances. West Germany had contributed to these directly, consciously and successfully in the development of German-Soviet relations within the overall system of East-West relations. Perhaps those Social Democrats and others who had illusions about the stability and reformability of the GDR also contributed a little to Gorbachev's illusions about the reformability of socialism in Eastern Europe: the illusions of '68 that were so unintentionally helpful in '89. But the other great unexpected cause was the radical yet peaceful push for change from the rest of Eastern Europe, starting in Poland and Hungary.

What was the role of Ostpolitik here? Two major intended effects were to remove the German bogey and to replace it with the attractive image of *Modell Deutschland*, the economic and social Model Germany. In removing, or at least radically diminishing, the fear of a revanchist Germany, the Bonn republic also removed one of the very few effective arguments that East European communist rulers had for securing the support of their own peoples. The policy of reconciliation, however contorted, did achieve this. Willy Brandt in Warsaw will forever remain its great symbol.

As for the attraction: already in the 1950s, first Schumacher and then Adenauer had developed what came to be called the magnet theory. A free, prosperous West Germany — and Adenauer added, in a free, prosperous, uniting Western Europe — would exert an irresistible magnetic pull on the peoples of Eastern Europe. However, what Adenauer thought would happen in years actually took decades — decades in which many other things happened as well.

Not only was the Soviet Union brought to the point where it could be persuaded to let Eastern Europe go — a necessary condition that Adenauer of course also acknowledged. The relative magnetism of Western Europe vis-à-vis Eastern Europe also increased steadily. And the iron curtain was made more permeable, thus allowing the magnet to exert its attractive force. This last was the specific contribution of détente in general, and Ostpolitik in particular. With its strategy of 'weaving', its Helsinki of human contacts, its open door policy for visitors from the East, West Germany did more than any other Western state to bring the full attractions of the West home to 'the people on the quiet streets', to recall John F Kennedy's phrase.

To many East Europeans in 1989, the Federal Republic was the model of a 'normal' Western Europe to which they hoped to 'return'. Such a perception of West Germany had been quite unthinkable in 1950, and still very hard to imagine in 1970. This great change was the combined legacy of Adenauer and Brandt, of West Germany's domestic and foreign, western and eastern policies. Hannah Arendt famously espied in Eichmann the 'banality of evil'. To say that what East Europeans saw in the new West Germany was the banality of good would no doubt be an exaggeration. Yet the West German example of slightly boring, prosperous, civilised, bourgeois — even petit bourgeois — democracy certainly had elements of both banality and good.

In this sense, West Germany made a major indirect contribution to the social and, as it were, psychological preconditions of the revolution of 1989. However, the direct contribution of German Ostpolitik was much smaller, and more ambiguous. As we have seen, relations with East European states had an essentially supporting role in the overall system of Ostpolitik. Following the imperative of synchronisation, they were meant to facilitate, or at least not to disrupt, Bonn's key relationships with Moscow and East Berlin. A little exemplary reform, as seen in Budapest, was a good thing, to encourage the others. But too many demands for freedom, as in the Prague Spring or the Polish August, would upset the whole diplomatic system of Ostpolitik. Soviet-style 'normalisation' in Czechoslovakia was actually a toll-gate on the road to East-West 'normalisation' à la Bahr and Brandt — however much they might personally dislike it.

In his 1989 memoirs, written before the great events of that year, Brandt wrote: 'Whether Warsaw or Prague or whatever other centre in Central and Eastern Europe: Federal German policy could hardly remove much of the burden from those responsible there, but it has not added anything to those burdens.' In one sense this is wrong, because by simply unfolding the magnetic power of its own attractions the Federal Republic did add greatly to East European rulers' problems. But so far as Bonn's intentions were concerned it is clearly right. The question is, however, whether this was something to be proud of. It is an interesting experiment to insert into Brandt's sentence, say, Santiago (under Pinochet) in place of Warsaw (under Jaruzelski), San Salvador instead of Prague, Central and South America instead of Central and Eastern Europe — and then see how it reads.

As we have seen, Bonn's policy was almost exclusively focussed on the powerholders, and ever solicitous not to 'destabilise' their states. The cases of Poland and Hungary do, however, contrast. Bonn's good relations with the reform communist powerholders in Budapest, strengthened by economic leverage through trade and the hard currency debt, contributed directly to the historical breakthrough in 1989. The then Hungarian Foreign Minister, Gyula Horn, records how, after a sleepless night in August 1989 worrying about the number of East German refugees building up in Hungary, he talked to his Prime Minister, Miklós Németh, tired after a sleepless night worrying about the country's economic problems, and especially its hard-currency debt. They decided to fly secretly to Bonn to discuss both problems: the money and the Germans.

According to Németh's recollection of the dramatic meeting in Schloss Gymnich, when the Foreign Minister had indicated to Kohl and Genscher that Hungary would probably open the frontier for the East Germans, Kohl's first response was: what can we give you in return? By Németh's account, it was actually the Hungarians who suggested that a decent interval should elapse before they got — as they did in October — DM 1 billion in new state-guaranteed credits. 'Do you realise,' Horn records the Hungarian Interior Minister commenting on the decision to open the frontier, 'that of the two German states we are choosing the West German one?' No, Horn replied, 'we are choosing *Europe*'!

The Polish case is quite different. Essentially, the Bonn government saw in the Polish revolution of 1980–81 a threat, not an opportunity. German policymakers knew it endangered the whole overall system of German Ostpolitik, and they thought it was the wrong way to go about overcoming Yalta anyway. The reaction to the imposition of martial law was therefore deeply ambivalent. As after the Soviet invasion of Czechoslovakia, a Soviet-style 'normalisation' in another East European country seemed to be necessary for the continued 'normalisation' of West Germany's relations with Moscow and East Berlin. To recall Havel's 1989 Frankfurt speech, for a long painful moment the word 'Ostpolitik' seemed again to signify 'renunciation of freedom' — other people's freedom. In a combination of higher confusion, hypocrisy and self-deception, German policymakers declared the need for 'stability' in the name of 'Europe' and 'world peace'.

In the event, this proved not just morally dubious but also politically short-sighted. For Solidarity made a major contribution to the end of Communism in Eastern Europe, and hence also to German unification. Napoleon said that all empires die of indigestion, and the Poles gave the Soviet empire its biggest stomach-ache. (By comparison, East Germany was positively eupeptic.) In 1989, the Polish Round Table and the subsequent elections led Eastern Europe down the road from refolution to revolution. German policy was focussed on the possibilities of change from the centre of the empire and from above. Poland showed the possibilities of change from the periphery and from below. Neither alone was sufficient. It needed both to achieve the desired result.

'The Germans,' write Jacques Rupnik and Dominique Moïsi, 'did not realise that Solidarity was the first hole in the Berlin Wall.' Really one should say that Solidarity was the second hole. The first was Ostpolitik.

German model

In the 1980s, Ostpolitik was sometimes presented as a model for East-West relations as a whole. This or that aspect of German-Soviet or German-

Hungarian relations, or German Helsinki policy, might, senior politicians would remark with quiet pride, have an 'exemplary' or 'model' character. For a time, German-German relations were also presented as exemplary. In 1984, in a short leading article in *Die Zeit* entitled 'German model', Marion Gräfin Dönhoff quoted two remarks about the necessity for calm negotiations, one from Genscher, the other from Erich Honecker. 'If only,' she concluded, 'the superpowers would show so much insight!' As one analyst has noted, the Federal Republic inclined sometimes to speak like a moralising schoolteacher to a recalcitrant world. So beside Model Germany in domestic policy there was now the German model in foreign policy.

We have found that there was indeed a German model, but its wider applicability is much more questionable. An old Soviet bloc quip defined socialism as the profound and scientific answer to problems that did not even exist in capitalism. A great deal of German Ostpolitik was the answer to problems that did not even exist for other Western states. While it presented itself as the very model of a modern foreign policy, it was actually a mixture of old and new elements: some very new, such as the emphasis on information technology in 'system-opening co-operation' or the desirability of interdependence; some very old, such as the hard *Realpolitik* of German-Soviet deals and the support for minorities defined according to what was ultimately a *völkisch* definition of German nationality. The mixture of old and new elements characterised the whole international environment in which the Federal Republic operated, but, as so often, Germany had both extremes.

Many aspects of this policy contributed, directly or indirectly, to the final achievement of Germany's main foreign-policy goals. However, others also contributed much to this success. Gorbachev did so, by doing something quite different from what he set out to do. He was the greatest 'hero of retreat', to use Hans Magnus Enzensberger's fine phrase. Hungary helped, as an adroit small country changing sides at just the right moment. But neither could count as 'models'. More interesting are two models which West German policy makers often criticised at the time, but which actually helped Germany to succeed. These are the Polish model of dealing with communism from the inside and the American model of dealing with communism from the outside.

In the early 1980s, German policymakers suggested that the Polish model was not good even for Poland. 1989 showed that the Polish model could be good not just for Poland but also for Germany. German politicians thought attempted revolution would never work: look at 1953, 1956, 1968 . . . Anyway, it risked bloodshed and war, than which nothing could be worse. Polish antipoliticians said: even defeats can turn out in the end to be victories, 'for freedom's battle once begun . . .' Different lessons were drawn from the experience of the Second World War. Günter Gaus expressed horror at the very thought of *sterben für Danzig*. Bronisław Geremek wrote: '*on peut mourir pour Dantzig*'.

The 'German realism' of which Brandt spoke in 1973 was, in many ways, realistic. But it underestimated the value of sacrifice, the deeper realism of idealists, even of dreamers such as Dienstbier and Havel. Realistic about the power of the powerholders, it overlooked the power of the powerless. 1989 was not dreamt of in its philosophy.

The history of Ostpolitik raised fundamental issues of values and priorities. In 1954, the Christian Democrat Eugen Gerstenmaier established a famous order of priorities for West Germany: first, freedom; second, peace; third, unity. The Federal Republic stuck to and enhanced freedom in its domestic affairs. No state was more emphatic in its advocacy of peace. Both the adherence to freedom at home and the advocacy of peace abroad helped Germany to achieve unity.

Brandt could say with justified pride that his greatest satisfaction was to see the words 'Germany' and 'peace' taken together. If German leaders had been warmongers in the 1930s, they were veritable peacemongers in the 1970s and 1980s. So much so, in fact, that some detected the old German inclination to swing from one extreme to another. The Marquise von O. And this 'peace' they advocated was a many-layered thing. In the closely related concept of 'stability', and in the very phrase 'European peace order', it also contained the notion of order. Now order, too, is an important value in international relations. But there were moments when West Germany's neighbours would still be tempted to exclaim, like Clawdia Chauchat to poor Hans Castorp in *The Magic Mountain*: '*Vous aimez l'ordre mieux que la liberté, toute l'Europe le sait*'.

In foreign, as opposed to domestic policy, the identification of 'Germany' with the word 'freedom' was much less complete than that with 'peace'. It is, however, very important to stress that this was not just a matter of values and aspirations. West Germany was constrained from being an outspoken advocate of freedom and respect for human rights in Eastern Europe by its geopolitical position at the divided centre, and especially by Berlin's position as the divided centre of the divided centre. Shortly after unification, Horst Teltschik observed that Germany was no longer 'vulnerable to blackmail'. He thus pithily expressed a basic truth about German Ostpolitik.

This was the policy of a state vulnerable to blackmail, by Moscow and East Berlin. Getting on with the powers-that-were in Moscow and East Berlin required caution, restraint, soft speaking, stealth. We have argued that a somewhat more outspoken policy would have been possible, even within these constraints. Particularly in German-German relations, and especially among Social Democrats, there was too much self-censorship, underpinned by a far-reaching relativism and much muddled and wishful thinking. Certainly there was no model for other Western states in the regular payment of ransom for hostages, or in the cross-frontier party politics. Nonetheless, the constraints were real, and a realistic policy had to reckon with them.

All the more reason, however, to be grateful to those in the East who would stand up for human rights — even at the risk of their own lives —, and for those in the West who would support them, and could afford to, because they were not vulnerable to blackmail. This brings us to the American model. Obviously, we are dealing in sweeping generalisations here, for the differences between (and even within) American administrations were much greater than those between (and within) German ones. Yet certain features remained fairly constant.

We have argued that the German debt to the United States does not merely lie on the defence side of the Harmel double-track. It was not just a matter of protection, of successful containment of Soviet power, and even, perhaps, of a policy of military strength. It also lies on the détente side, in the policies of peaceful engagement developed in dialogue between North America and Western Europe. With its policies of 'differentiation' in Eastern Europe, its readiness to use sanctions as well as economic incentives, its offensive public advocacy (since Carter) of human rights, and public and private support of those in the East fighting for them, Washington differed from Bonn. There were arguments, conflicts.

Now our conclusion here is by no means simply that on these points Washington was right and Bonn wrong. The truth is much more complicated. What was right for Washington was not necessarily right for Bonn, and vice versa. Left to itself, Washington might have placed too much emphasis on the sticks, Bonn would have relied too exclusively on the carrots. It was the combination of these approaches, partly intentional and co-ordinated but also partly unintended and conflictual, which produced the necessary mixture of incentive and deterrent, punishment and reward.

Beside the carrots and sticks there were the words. Ostpolitik had a major impact on the language of German politics. Sometimes, in the Bonn republic's little closed circuit of party politics and media, words were mistaken for deeds. Politics was sometimes reduced to phrase-making, or, since this was Germany, concept-coining. Many was the young aspiring politician who cheerfully followed the advice of Mephistopheles (dressed as Faust):

> *Im ganzen: haltet Euch an Worte!*
> *Dann geht Ihr durch die sichre Pforte*
> *Zum Tempel der Gewissheit ein.*

[In general: hold on tight to words!/Then through the sheltered gate you'll enter/The temple known as certainty. (Author's translation)]

If one looks more closely at the usage of such concepts as 'security partnership', 'system-opening co-operation', or the many variations played on Bahr's original *Wandel durch Annäherung*, one often finds that the politicians really did not know what they were talking about. They were just making phrases, to gain profile. Yet words, public and private, were also deeds, especially in a period and an area where the guns did not speak. As Havel noted, this was particularly true in relations with regimes that remained at least partly logocratic. Solzhenitsyn's 'one word of truth', and the Pope's, were worth many divisions in the battle against newspeak.

Plain speaking was not Bonn's forte. Waffle was. In vintage Brandt, the inspirational vagueness contained more than a little real wisdom. For no one knew better how much we do not know, how full history is of surprises, good and bad. But the archetypal Bonn waffler was Genscher. There is a fine study to be written of the language of Genscher's speeches, those endless coats of many shades of grey, those layered wedding-cakes of blancmange, those monuments of *sowohl-als-auch*. Yet this vague, harmonising use of language actually did serve Germany's purposes well in this period. For, as we have seen, the Federal Republic had to square many circles, bridge many gaps, above all those between its Eastern and Western ties, and the Genscher compound helped to do just that. It was this getting on with all sides, not the specific advocacy of taking Gorbachev at his word, that was the real essence of Genscherism.

Ostpolitik had the defects of its qualities. Konrad Adenauer's parting admonition to his party in 1966 was to remember that patience was the strongest weapon of a defeated people. West German policy was very patient, consistent, predictable, quietly chiselling away and waiting for the big chance. But at times the consistency hardened into rigidity, the patience became loss of imagination.

Waldemar Besson once wrote that the story of the evolution of a foreign policy is that of experiences becoming maxims. But in the history of Ostpolitik we also see how hypotheses can become burdens. The hypothesis of relaxation through reassurance is the best example. It was original to advance this hypothesis in the 1960s. It was reasonable to try it out in the 1970s, even though some in East Central Europe had already identified its fundamental flaws. But it was foolish to cling to it in the 1980s, ignoring the different course that history was actually taking. As Bahr later acknowledged, in putting disarmament before democratisation, the SPD's second Ostpolitik got things back to front.

The so-called policy intellectuals and the political scientists had a particular responsibility here. For many of them, having become so involved in supporting the policy of their state, trimmed reality to fit theory rather than adjusting theory to fit — and producing hypotheses for — the new reality. More critical independence would better have served the making of policy. Politicians have to work with half-truths and terrible simplifications; intellectuals have a duty not to. A wider penumbra of published opinion also contributed to German misjudgements, above all of the other Germany. Understandably enough, the strain of partition produced its own particular neuroses and hysteria.

Taken all in all, the record of Ostpolitik was thus a mixed one. How could it be otherwise? Some aspects were indeed exemplary and worthy of imitation — the open door policy, for example, the 'weaving' and the Helsinki of human contacts. Others were not. Some strands led directly, in the intended fashion, to the desired result; others led to the intended goal, but by quite unintended and curious paths; yet others led nowhere; a few led into dark alleys, down which it would have been better not to have gone.

Brandt, with his love of northern understatement, might have said this was 'not the worst' chapter in the history of German foreign policy. Given the rather low standards set through much of that history, this seems too little. One can go further: this was one of the better chapters in the history of German foreign policy. It was not by any means simply a policy conducted by Europeans for Europe. But nor was it just the policy of Germans for Germany. At its best, it was the work — Brandt again finds the right words — 'of German patriots in European responsibility'. That description could be applied to most of the leading actors, to Schröder, Kiesinger, Scheel, Bahr, Schmidt, Genscher, Weizsäcker, Kohl, each in their very different way. Close up, you see the smallness and the faults; in Brandt too. Yet in Willy Brandt, as in Konrad Adenauer, Germany has a historical figure at least touched with greatness. This matters. It is important for a country to have such figures.

Was it good for Germany, good for Europe? Here we come to the limits of writing contemporary history. For, alas, it really is too soon to say. As the judgement of Bismarck's achievement changed in the light of what happened in Germany and Europe after 1890, so would that of the Federal Republic's achievement change — for better or for worse — in the light of what happened in Germany and Europe after 1990.

Whether it had been in the German interest, would be for the Germans to decide. What of the European interest? The Germans had made a major contribution to getting the Red Army out of the centre of Europe. Hundreds of millions of Europeans were now free in ways they had not been for half a century or more. This was an incalculable gain. To recall George Bush's invocation of 'Europe whole and free', most of Europe was now more or less free. However, it was very far from whole. To talk of the 'reunification of Europe' was always misleading, because Europe had never properly been united before. Germany had been united, and was now again. Europe had not been, and still had yet to be. The one central Yalta divide was finished. But many smaller divides remained and others re-emerged, with a vengeance. Looking at the former Yugoslavia or the former Soviet Union, the phrase 'European peace order' did not exactly seem to sum up Europe at the end of Ostpolitik.

Beyond this, 'the European interest' had of course to be disaggregated. Russia had lost an empire — but was that loss or gain? Would the Soviet Westernizers' gamble pay off, and Russia now reap the full benefits of full co-operation with a West to which Germany was to be the door? Would the United States find in united Germany its looked-for 'partner in leadership', ready to share the burdens, not just in Europe and not only with the cheque-book?

Of course in many ways all West European countries gained from the end of the Cold War, and all welcomed it. But in some respects Britain and France, at least, lost as well as gained. When Douglas Hurd said in 1989 that the Yalta system was one 'under which we've lived quite happily for forty years', he was speaking more truth than perhaps he knew. The Cold War had preserved Britain in a great-power prominence which its underlying economic strength would no longer sustain. France was somewhat better placed, because of the special relationship it had built up with Germany. But in terms of power, France also lost, as its nuclear *force de frappe* no longer counter-balanced the German monetary one, and the European Community's centre of gravity began to move eastwards.

As for the countries of the former Eastern Europe, they won the greatest new chances, and faced the greatest new risks. They were free, but weak; liberated, but unsafe; newly independent, but also in a new dependency.

For everyone involved, the judgement of the past would depend upon the development of the future. That in turn depended on many things, but not least on the behaviour of Germany.

Epilogue

European Answers?

Consequences

In 1965, Konrad Adenauer chose to introduce his memoirs with a wry account of a conversation with an historian. This unnamed 'Professor of Modern History at a German University' was asked by Adenauer how he imagined things would develop. He replied that this was not his task. Historians were not prophets. Adenauer said he had a different view of the historian's task. Historians should at least attempt to recognise in what direction history might be heading. They should point to probable developments, 'and perhaps warn'.

In the more than quarter-century since Adenauer wrote those lines, a few historians but far more political scientists, policy intellectuals and specialists in International Relations, Sovietology and Security Studies have taken up the challenge. On the whole, and with a few notable exceptions, their forecasts, predictions or models have not fared well in the light of what happened in Europe in the years 1989 to 1991. By 1993, German intellectual life had experienced a *Historikerstreit*, about the treatment of the Nazi past, and a *Literaturstreit*, about writers and East Germany, but perhaps it still awaited its *Politologenstreit*. For the end of Soviet communism and of the Cold War posed the largest questions to those disciplines, or branches of disciplines, that made some claim to quasi-scientific prediction.

Most historians make no such methodological claims. Some would agree with E.H.Carr that they should at least have in their bones the question 'whither?' as well as the question 'why?' Others would dispute even that. Yet in his wry way, Adenauer identified a real problem. It surely is reasonable and right for politicians to ask historians to make informed personal guesses — so long as everyone clearly recognises that they are just that: personal guesses. These guesses are related to the history they write, but separable from it. The history may be good but the guesses bad — or even vice versa. At the very least, we can try to identify the new questions to which politicians then have to offer answers. However, what follows is quite deliberately written in the past tense, because these are the guesses and questions of early 1993, when this book went to press. They can be overtaken by events in a way that the historical analysis cannot be. For the one thing historians can confidently predict is surprises.

There is also the question of the relevant past. For the most recent is by no means always the most relevant past. Indeed, the history of Europe before 1939, before 1914, even before 1890, may well provide more analogies or clues for understanding the state of Europe after 1990 than does that of the immediately preceding period. After 1989 it was not just the Europe of Yalta but the Europe of Versailles that began to collapse. To understand the condition of, say, Bosnia-Herzegovina in 1993, Bismarck's Congress of Berlin in 1878 was as relevant as Genscher's (CSCE) Congress of Berlin in 1991. Old books had to be brought out of the stacks, as the new ones were put down there.

Not just Ostpolitik but the whole history of East-West relations in the Cold War belonged to this abruptly closed period. Perhaps the only direct lessons pertained to relations with the last surviving communist states, and above all with China. Here, for all the differences in culture and history, one met again many familiar issues: the degree of necessary recognition, the proper balance between human contacts and human rights, between economic and military carrots and sticks. Here again one found self-styled realists who argued that real change could only come from above, from the centre, from the present powerholders, and that what happened in Tiananmen Square in June 1989, at the very moment of East Central European refolution, showed the folly of insurrection. But here again we could reply that change can also come from below and from the periphery, that people have something to do with their own destiny, and that, in the memorably simple words of the poet James Fenton,

> They'll come again
> To Tiananmen.

Curiously enough, the Western state for which these direct lessons of Ostpolitik might therefore be most immediately relevant in the 1990s was not Germany but Britain. For Britain was directly responsible for the hostage city of Hong Kong. Many of the tensions and dilemmas which West Germany had faced with the hostage city, West Berlin, were now faced by Britain. In one respect, Britain's position was decisively worse than that of the Federal Republic had been. Whereas international law (and British, French and American troops) had upheld the West German position on West Berlin, respect for international law (and a desire to be decently rid of the problem) would have Britain withdraw in 1997. In another respect, however, it was better, because Communism's Wheel of History had now been reversed throughout Europe, and economically in China too.

Germany had no such direct dependencies in the Far East. Yet when its new Foreign Minister, Klaus Kinkel, visited China in the autumn of 1992, he raised human rights issues only discreetly, in his private talks; proclaimed his goal as the 'long overdue normalisation' of relations; described the Chinese Prime Minister partly responsible for the Tiananmen massacre, Li Peng, as 'completely normal and open'; and declared in Peking that 'relations are now normal'. This could have been Moscow or Warsaw twenty years before. Like the Bourbons, the German Foreign Ministry seemed to have forgotten nothing and learned nothing.

What, though, of the new Germany in the new Europe? Despite the vast changes, the history of Ostpolitik was relevant here in at least two respects. Firstly, the combination of West- and Ostpolitik constituted a foreign-policy tradition, although still a short one. The immediate successor generation in German politics, represented in early 1993 by Klaus Kinkel at the Foreign Ministry and Volker Rühe at the Defence Ministry, emphasised continuity. Secondly, the next generation after them had actually grown up in the years of Ostpolitik, and for many it had been formative. The time-lag in politics is often long — Adenauer's political world-view was formed before 1914, or at the latest in the 1920s, Kohl's in the 1940s and 1950s. So in the 2010s and 2020s Germany might have leaders whose truly formative experiences were in the 1970s and 1980s. Even if their delayed response consisted in a rejection of the way things were then said and done, it would still be important to know what they were rejecting.

Yet the situation in which Germany found itself had obviously changed drastically, and the European question was posed anew. After the end of Yalta, every state in Europe had to ask itself again: What sort of power are we? What do we want to be? What are our national interests? What are our priorities? But nowhere were the questions more difficult than for Germany.

What sort of power was united Germany? While neighbours and partners played with ill-defined terms like 'supremacy', 'hegemony', 'domination' or just 'leadership', the range of German self-definitions was immense. At one extreme, Chancellery Minister Rudolf Seiters spoke in November 1990 of the new Germany being 'equipped not with more power but with more responsibility'. A truly ridiculous statement, since every child in Europe could see that Germany had more power. An elephant does not win trust by pretending to be a dove. It merely invites doubt about its sanity — or its honesty. At the other extreme, a Green member of the Bundestag described Germany as a new superpower. In between, there were a hundred variations. Even before unification, one historian had described the Federal Republic as a 'world power against its will'. After unification, another historian described Germany as a new great power. But a political scientist said the Federal Republic should see itself as not as a *Mittelmacht*, let alone as the *Zentralmacht* of Europe, but as a *mittlere Macht*. Fine distinctions.

If they did not know exactly what sort of power Germany was, surely they at least knew where it was? Well, not exactly. Suddenly Hans-Dietrich Genscher spoke of 'we in West *and Central* Europe' (my emphasis). A television newscaster spoke of 'the new Central European *Ordnungsmacht* Germany'. A leading contemporary historian said Germany was now a Central European country. Another analyst suggested that Germany was still 'the East of the West and the West of the East'. In an interview on Austrian television, Chancellor Kohl summoned up the old self-image of Germany as a bridge between East and West, but added 'a bridge as part of the Western world'. So: a bridge all on one bank? Meanwhile, a publisher of the *Frankfurter Allgemeine Zeitung*, who single-handedly did more than any politician to change Bonn's policy towards the former Yugoslavia, could be read on the front page of that newspaper fulminating against the allegedly pro-Serbian policy of what he called 'the Western powers'. By this he meant France, Britain and the United States. But was not Germany a Western power?

The answers were confused. But so was the reality. Nearly two hundred years after Napoleon commented that becoming rather than being seemed to be Germany's natural condition, Germany was still in the condition of becoming. Its frontiers, and therefore its physical shape and size, were now clear. But it did not even have a capital. In a great symbolic decision, the Bundestag voted in June 1991 for Berlin to be Germany's capital and seat of government. But the move from Bonn to Berlin was likely to take many years. Above all, however, the results of the inner unification had yet to be seen. How would the accession of more than sixteen million people with sixty years' experience of two dictatorships, and now experiencing the traumatic impact of a sudden and uniquely sweeping transition, affect the liberal institutions and open society of the old Federal Republic? What would be the economic result?

Here the predictions of the economists, another group of specialists at hand to answer the politicians' questions (and, incidentally, another good candidate for a little professional *Streit*), differed greatly. Yet this was of course a crucial variable, for two reasons. Firstly, because it can plausibly be argued that while the fate of liberal democracy is everywhere closely tied to a certain level (and distribution) of prosperity, this is particularly true in the case of Germany. Certainly democracy in West Germany was consolidated during and after the so-called economic miracle, and had not yet faced the test of real economic hardship. Now, it just might face such a test.

Secondly, the power of united Germany was still above all economic, and, at the cutting edge, financial. We have seen that in its relations with the East, the Federal Republic had effectively used economic power to realise its political goals, albeit sometimes achieving the desired results in unintended ways. After the end of the Soviet empire, its potential to do this was still larger. But in the West, too, whether it liked it or not, it had extraordinary weight.

This was not just a matter of the sheer size of the economy, with a Gross National Product in 1992 roughly one and a half times that of Britain, a good third larger than that of France or Italy — although only half that of Japan and barely a third that of the United States. It was also a matter of the quality of its products, the trade surplus, the savings rate, and the reputation of the currency built up over forty years. While Chancellery Minister Seiters said that Germany had no more power, a word — no, even a silence — from the Bundesbank on interest or exchange rates would directly affect the conduct of domestic policy in many other countries. Here it was not a matter of Germany pursuing any foreign-policy goals, but simply of Germany pursuing its own domestic economic agenda, and above all, the Bundesbank's legal obligation to preserve the stability of the German currency. Even for Germany's neighbours and partners to the west, interdependence thus contained a good measure of dependence.

Helmut Schmidt's reflections on the connections between economic and foreign policy were now more relevant than ever (as he himself did not fail to remind his compatriots). Clearly the future size and quality of Germany's economic power would depend on developments in the world economy, which it could only partly influence (for example, through its contribution to the EC's stance in the GATT negotiations), and on those in Europe, which it could influence more than any other single state. But in the 1990s it would also depend on how it coped with the huge costs of unification, as well as the inherited burdens of what might almost be described as the overdeveloped social market economy of the old Federal Republic (high labour costs, subsidies, perhaps a certain clannish complacency). Germany's budget deficits were projected to be around DM 100 billion a year until 1995. Its total public debt in 1993 was estimated at DM 1,500 billion. A rich country.

Yet beside the economic dimension, the other dimensions of German power should not be ignored. Even with the 2 + 4 Treaty limit on its numbers, and even with financial cuts that might bring the numbers down even further, Germany would have some of the largest armed forces in Europe. In 1992, only those of Russia and Turkey (and possibly, depending what one counted, Ukraine) were numerically larger, but German forces obviously had better technology and better training. Whether they were better at fighting no one could say until they did some, but certainly German forces had been very good at it in the past.

Now whether and, if so, under what auspices, they should actually fight was still a subject of fierce discussion in German politics in early 1993. Both the Gulf War, to which the Federal Republic contributed more than

$6,500 million in cash and kind (but no troops) and the crisis in the former Yugoslovia had sharpened this emotional debate. However, even if the self-imposed constraints were removed, so that German soldiers could risk their lives (and not just German politicians their words) in other parts of the world, as American, British and French soldiers had never ceased to do since 1945; even then, Germany would not be in the same league as Russia, America, France and Britain. For in 1990 Germany had, under most solemn treaty, reaffirmed its renunciation of atomic, biological and chemical weapons.

Now if Germany were to behave as most powers have done over the centuries, one would expect it sooner or later to gain the military cutting-edge to complement (and defend) the economic one: albeit at first in a larger multilateral context (almost certainly containing the adjective European), and quite likely not as the fulfilment of a deliberate policy but rather as a response to an acute and unexpected challenge. But would it so behave? Or had Germany, Europe, international relations in an interdependent world, said good-bye to all that? Perhaps by the year 2000 there would no longer be a fully sovereign, independent German nation-state to face that decision, but rather a Federal (or at least Confederal) Republic of Europe? The Federal Republic of (United) Germany, 1990–2000, hail and farewell?

Before addressing this central German-European question we should mention one other dimension of German power. This third dimension is even more difficult to define than the economic and the military ones, but scarcely less important. It has to do with the overall attractiveness — the magnetism, to recall Schumacher and Adenauer's simile — of a particular society, culture and way of life. This is a dimension of power which Britain had in the late nineteenth century and early twentieth century, which America had in superabundance in the mid-twentieth century, and which, as we have seen, Model Germany developed strongly in the 1970s and 1980s. This attraction is closely related to a country's relative prosperity, but by no means simply a function of it. Other features — individual opportunity, tolerance, culture, security, space, freedom, tradition, beauty — all contribute to the magnetism.

As the Federal Republic discovered at the beginning of the 1990s, such magnetism can bring great problems — above all, immigration. Yet it remains a tremendous asset. As the example of the United States shows, restrictions on immigration do not in themselves necessarily reduce the attraction. They may even increase it. But how people are treated once they are in the country will, of course, very much affect the quality of the attraction. Under the strain of unification, a minority of Germans at the beginning of the 1990s were doing their best to reduce the attraction — with nationalist slogans, racial abuse and fire-bombs. Whether they succeeded would depend on the reaction of the majority.

Yet whatever the evolution of these three dimensions of German power in the 1990s, the united country would remain an awkward size in an awkward place. Germany now had precisely that 'critical size' to which Chancellor Kiesinger had referred back in 1967: 'too big to play no role in the balance of forces . . . too small to keep the forces around it in balance by itself'. Or, in the even pithier formulation of Henry Kissinger: too big for Europe, too small for the world. As for the place: to say that it had returned to the famous old *Mittellage* in the centre of Europe was an over-simplification, ignoring the genuinely new elements in Germany's geopolitical situation, reflected in shorthand by the acronyms EC, Nato and perhaps also OECD. But certainly the new Federal Republic was much closer to the challenges of the nineteenth-century *Mittellage* than the old Federal Republic had been.

The foreign policy of the old Federal Republic had gradually increased its room for manoeuvre and effective sovereignty, but always from a very tightly constrained situation as the divided centre of a divided continent. Now, united Germany had a formidable room for manoeuvre in the centre (though not necessarily *as* the centre) of a still disunited continent. The answers to the European and German questions, new and old, depended more than they had for at least half a century on what the Germans themselves wanted to do.

European Germany, German Europe

What did Germany want to do, indeed — to be? The answers given by most of its political and intellectual leaders at the beginning of the 1990s could be summarised in two words: normal and European. Both raised as many questions as they answered.

'Germany has again become a normal state', said Horst Teltschik a few days after unification, quoting with approval an observation of the British journalist David Marsh. Yet two years later Klaus Kinkel would speak of the need for the 'normalisation' of German foreign policy, notably in committing its troops abroad, and for 'the normalisation of our situation as a nation'. In the debate about Berlin it was argued that to have a large, historic, metropolitan capital was an essential part of being a normal country. The main comparison here was with Paris, London, Rome or Madrid — that is, with the 'normality' of other large historic European nation-states.

As we have seen, the words 'normal', 'normality' and 'normalisation' had a rich and chequered history in German politics since 1945. 'Normalisation' was a key-word of social-liberal Ostpolitik, where it meant establishing full diplomatic and other relations with communist states, at least one of which was simultaneously undergoing Soviet-type 'normalisation'.

In the 1980s, some West German politicians and intellectuals even argued that relations between the two German states were becoming 'normal'. After unification, 'normalisation' became a key-word of the centre-right, and was criticised as such by intellectuals of the centre-left who had enthusiastically embraced the earlier usage.

To say that Germany had become more normal since unification was common sense. Anyone who thought that it was normal to live with a wall through Berlin was not quite normal. It was more normal to take a bus from the Alexanderplatz to Bahnhof Zoo. Altogether, it was more normal for a nation that had once been united in a single state again to live in one. Hans-Peter Schwarz argued that the partition had been the single most important cause of the collective neuroses of the old Federal Republic, including, of course, the endless debates about German identity. It would be premature to suggest that with unification those debates would softly and suddenly vanish away. Nietzsche's famous dictum that what charac-terises the Germans is that the question 'what is German?' never dies out among them had yet to be disproved. But one could reasonably hope that the debates would become less tortured and obsessive.

Beyond this, however, the critics of the new usage did have a point. To talk seriously of normality and normalisation, you must first specify your norms. And here the comparison with France or Britain would only get you so far. Should one, for example, regard the British gutter press as part of a desirable normality? Should one, more seriously, consider it as normal to have a party of the nationalist, populist right getting around fifteen per cent of the popular vote, as Le Pen's National Front had in France? Could and should Germany really aspire to the foreign policy 'normality' of two of Europe's oldest and most centralised states, with the traditions and reactions of former great powers?

Here we come to the second German answer: Europe. 'Germany is our fatherland, Europe is our future', said Chancellor Kohl in his government programme for the years 1991–94. The aim was 'the political unification of Europe'. 'The *Staatsräson* of a united Germany', said one of his close advisers, 'is its integration in Europe'. In a symbolic act of profound significance, the same article 23 of the Basic Law under which German unification had been achieved was amended in December 1992 so that the Federal Republic, instead of being open for 'other parts of Germany' to join, was now committed to 'the realisation of a united Europe' through the 'European Union'. The European Union, that is, of the existing European Community of twelve member states, as envisaged in the Maastricht Treaty of December 1991.

Maastricht, said President von Weizsäcker, offered Germany 'the chance of being delivered (*erlöst*) from the *Mittellage*'. The twenty-first century, he averred, could become a 'European century', no less. The Bundeswehr's most senior officer, General Naumann, said he looked forward to the day when German soldiers could swear their oath of loyalty on the European flag.

Willy Brandt told the first sitting of the all-German Bundestag that 'German and European belong together, now and hopefully for ever'. The true fulfilment of his political life would be 'to see the day when Europe will have become one'. The dreams of the oldest Bundestag member were apparently shared — no, exceeded — by the youngest. In December 1990, some of the newest members of the Bundestag were asked by a weekly newspaper 'Nation 2000: what does that mean to you?' They answered: 'hope for a liberal, multicultural and tolerant society in united Europe' (25-year-old Free Democrat); 'peaceful Europe in which the East-West conflict is finally overcome and a European Germany' (31-year-old Christian Democrat); 'the future belongs to Europe and the regions!' (35, Social Democrat); 'united Europe of free fatherlands' (33, CSU); 'Germany reconciled with itself and its neighbours — part of the *Staatenbund* Europe' (26, CDU); 'Europe . . . What matters is the internal market, European Union and our responsibility towards the Third World' (35, CDU); or, in a word, 'Europe' (Social Democrat, aged 24!).

Yet it was not just these 'Bonn freshers' who gave such answers. So did seasoned veterans of Ostpolitik. In summer 1991, Egon Bahr — yes, Egon Bahr! — professed to see 'no single national, German foreign policy goal'. 'The foreign policy interests of this larger Germany,' he said, 'are European . . .' And children attending the Chancellor's traditional summer party were informed by Hans-Dietrich Genscher, through an article in the specially printed *Kanzler-Kinderfest-Zeitung*, that the larger Germany 'does not want more power but has more responsibility. We do not aspire to a German Europe but want to live in a European Germany.' This last formula was borrowed from Thomas Mann, and intoned many times like a blessing or a prayer at the birth of united Germany.

Let it not be thought that this was simply what Germany's leaders were telling the children — and the neighbours. It was, by and large, also what they were telling themselves. This was at once the reassuring and the slightly worrying thing. If they also had a clear foreign policy agenda based on fairly well-defined national interests, as the Federal Republic had had in the 1970s and 1980s, that would be fine. As Henry Kissinger observed, the nice thing about dealing with Egon Bahr in the 1970s was that he *did* have a hidden agenda. A little concealment of enlightened national interest behind European or internationalist rhetoric is — dare one say it? — quite normal. You only have to look at France. For more than thirty years the European Community had been built on compromises between such interests, though facilitated, of course — let us not be facile Realists! — by a real desire to learn from the tragedies of European history, cross-border regional experiences, new trans-national challenges, and so on.

Mann's formula, as redeployed by Genscher, is a good starting-point for identifying some of the problems with this German European vision. What does it mean to say 'a European Germany'? Here we must again confront the difference between the prescriptive and the descriptive use of the noun 'Europe' and the adjective 'European'. When Mann coined the phrase, talking to students in Hamburg in 1953, he was using the term 'European' prescriptively. The new Germany should be European, in contrast to Hitler's Germany, which was not, but had instead aimed for a German Europe. But what if we use the term descriptively?

Contemplating the way in which Central Europe had descended into barbarism in the years before 1945, the Germanist J. P. Stern wrote that the heart of Europe had become the heart of darkness. And then he quoted from the novel of that title by the Polish-British writer Joseph Conrad: 'No, they were not inhuman. Well, you know, that was the worst of it — this suspicion of their not being inhuman.' Of the university-educated mass murderers of the Third Reich one has to say: 'No, they were not un-European. Well, you know, that was the worst of it . . .'

Thomas Mann himself had earlier, in 1945, rejected the simplistic distinction between a 'good' and a 'bad' Germany. 'The evil Germany,' he wrote, 'that is the good gone awry, the good in misfortune, in guilt and fall'. And the history of Germany contains, in the most concentrated form, the highest and the lowest of European history. So if we use the term 'European' descriptively, we have to say that, alas, Nazi Germany was also a European Germany. Moreover, the actual words 'Europe' and 'European' have been relentlessly abused throughout European history. *Nation Europa* was the title of a Nazi periodical.

None of this disqualifies the attempt now to use the term 'European' prescriptively. But it does qualify it. 'There are a number of things,' wrote William Hazlitt, 'the idea of which is a clear gain to the mind. Let people, for instance, rail at friendship, genius, freedom, as long as they will — the very names of these despised qualities are better than anything else that could be sustituted for them, and embalm even the most venomed satire against them. It is no small consideration that the mind is capable even of feigning such things.' Is Europe such an idea? There are many, not least, indeed perhaps above all, in Central Europe, who hold with Milan Kundera that Europe is indeed a value in itself. On the other hand there are those (now more often met in London than in Berlin) who would say with Bismarck: '*qui parle Europe a tort. Notion géographique*'.

There is a tenable position in between. This is to say that Europe is less than a value in itself — it cannot and should not be put on the same plane as freedom, truth or justice — but more than merely a geographical notion. Like 'France', like 'England', yes, like 'Germany', we can choose to make it stand for certain things which are found in its past and present, even though many other things are found there as well. But if we do this, we have then to spell out what those things are, the ones we want and those we do not. Thomas Mann, for example, told an Oxford audience in 1949 that he first found his European Germany in Schopenhauer, Nietzsche and Wagner. Is that what was meant in 1992? Just to say 'a European Germany' is to say everything, and therefore nothing.

And 'not a German Europe'? Recalling Mann's remarks, we understand that the new Germany did not want to try and conquer Europe as Hitler did. Now admittedly, at the time of German unification wild Irish and Spanish references to a future 'Fourth Reich' might seem to have invited such reassurances; but did this really need saying? If, however, we take not a 1945 but a 1992 interpretation of 'German Europe', then it was in some respects actually the declared policy of the Federal Republic to seek a German Europe.

The revised article 23 of the Basic Law committed the Federal Republic to seek a European Union 'which is bound to democratic, legal (*rechtstaatliche*), social and federal principles and that of subsidiarity, and secures a protection of basic rights essentially comparable to that of this Basic Law'. 'At the end of this decade, this century,' said Chancellor Kohl, 'the countries of the European Community will have a common currency — a currency which must be just as strong and stable as the German Mark'. The federalism the Federal Government advocated for Europe was German-style, decentralised federalism rather than the centralising federalism of the 'Euro-super-state' so much feared in Britain.

Now these things might be good in themselves. It might indeed be a very good thing to have basic rights protected by a Basic Law. It might be a very good thing to have a currency as strong and stable as the DM. German-style federalism had much to commend it. Europe might very well want to adopt (and adapt) large parts of the Federal German model. But these were German things, and it would be obfuscation to pretend otherwise. (Of course, the French also wanted, in many respects, a French Europe, the Italians an Italian Europe, and so on.)

Where Bismarck had said 'we must put Germany in the saddle', Theo Sommer of *Die Zeit* declared: 'we must put Europe in the saddle'. But who was 'we' in this sentence? The royal we? The Germans? The elites of the main West European powers? And what if the old girl did not, after all, want to go for the ride? Would Sommer have us — whoever 'we' are — adopt the original method of Zeus, and, turning into a bull, carry her off to bed in Crete (or Brussels)? And who is she anyway? Which Europe are we talking about? And why only Europe?

Why Europe? Which Europe?

All the main choices before German foreign policy in the 1990s could be analysed around these two questions. Firstly: Why Europe? If we regard

Europe as a community of values, or of liberal democracies committed to mutual support and defence, the question immediately arises: why not 'the West'? Aren't the values of the West actually easier to define than those of Europe? How far was it actually Europe — specifically, the European Community — that had brought Western Europe peace, co-operation, security and prosperity for forty years, and how far the West — that is, concretely, the Western Alliance, the OECD, the Bretton Woods institutions and so on? How far could Europe now really manage on its own?

Beyond this, there was of course the even larger question: why not the world? This was not just an existential question, about the very survival of life of the planet, or a moral question, about human misery in the Third World, but also a hard political one, about what the miserable of the earth might do to the enclaves of relative peace and prosperity. However, since that was a question that applied equally to all developed countries, we shall frankly duck it here.

Another answer to the question 'why Europe?' was: economic self-interest. Certainly, Germany had done extremely well out of the EC, with its growing trade surpluses far outweighing the cost of its large direct budgetary contribution. Chancellor Kohl declared that the EC had overcome the old European habits of national *sacro egoismo*. But anyone trying to negotiate with the EC on trade matters soon found that economic *sacro egoismo* was very much alive and kicking. Indeed, in many ways the EC did not transcend but rather aggregated the sacred egoisms of nations, regions and, indeed, specific industries and special interests.

Yet the long-term economic self-interest of the trading state Germany clearly also required keeping open existing markets in the wider world — at the very least, in the OECD world — and opening up new ones, particularly in the east. Furthermore, it was by no means self-evident that the German economic interest would best be served by giving up control of its own currency, since even a Euro-Mark was most unlikely to be as strong and stable as the DM had been.

The most characteristic, but also the most singular answer was the political one given by West German Chancellors from Adenauer to Kohl. The European Community was needed to save Germany from itself. This argument continued to be made after unification. One of Germany's most distinguished former diplomats said in 1992 that the aim of German foreign policy must be to prevent German hegemony. In the immediate post-war period, Europe had seen a Western 'double containment': of the Soviet Union and of Germany. As Lord Ismay famously remarked, Nato was designed to keep the Americans in, the Russians out and the Germans down. Was Europe now to see German self-containment?

Genuine and even admirable though this Adenauerian argument had been, could it really be the main sustaining political rationale for German commitment to European integration fifty years after Hitler? Could

Germany's new leaders really say to people born in 1970: 'you know, we have to do this because we really cannot trust ourselves'? 'Why shouldn't we?' those young people would quite reasonably reply. Moreover, until 1990 this rationale always had two sides. In laying on the golden handcuffs, Germany had also been working to set itself free. Having surrendered sovereignty in order to regain it, had it now regained sovereignty in order to surrender it?

There was, however, a further argument that applied specifically to Germany after the end of Yalta. This was that it simply could not cope on its own with the new challenges from the east. Big though it was, these were far bigger. And they were quite literally at Germany's front door: just sixty kilometres from Berlin. Helmut Kohl saw the project of European Union as putting a European roof over Germany. But a roof that just reaches but does not overlap your east wall would not even keep the drizzle out, let alone hail and snow.

This brings us to the second question: Which Europe? After trying to prevent or at least to slow down the unification of Germany at the end of 1989, François Mitterrand was reassured by Helmut Kohl's emphatic commitment to push ahead with the further political and economic integration of the existing EC of twelve member states. This Franco-German understanding was the single most important driving force behind the inter-governmental conferences on what was loosely called European political and monetary union, and hence of the Maastricht treaty. At a meeting with Kohl in April 1990, Mitterrand expanded on his vision of three circles — a geometric image familiar to historians from its earlier and quite different usage, scribbled by Churchill for Adenauer on the back of a menu in 1953.

Whereas Churchill's three circles — the United States, Britain and the Commonwealth, United Europe — were polycentric but intersecting, as in a Venn diagram, Mitterrand's circles were concentric. In the innermost circle were France and Germany. In the next circle was the rest of the existing EC. In the third circle was continental Europe. This was what one might call the Little European idea. It came from the (or at least a) main stream of the original European Communities as they developed from the early 1950s, and even more from the time of the Elysée Treaty between France and Germany in 1963. It also built on older foundations, ranging from post-war social Catholic ideology right back to Charlemagne. It was a vision of Europe close to Helmut Kohl's heart. Indeed, Kohl once described Mainz as being in the middle of Europe.

Until 1989, this Little European project was pretty much what was meant in Bonn by the term *Europapolitik*. There was *Europapolitik* to the West and Ostpolitik to the East. The *pars pro toto* use of the term 'Europe' was always questionable, and questioned, but the realities called in shorthand 'Yalta' made the political option defensible.

Little Europe, it could be argued, was to be the magnetic core for a larger Europe.

But could this position be maintained after 1990? If one takes Mitterrand's second circle, then the existing EC of twelve Western and Southern European states was now a very peculiar shape, its outline explicable only by reference to the iron curtain. On grounds of history, culture, economic development, political institutions, the rule of law, civil society — in fact, on every possible domestic ground for membership — there was no reason why Austria should not belong if Portugal did, while for Greece to be in and Sweden out was clearly nonsense.

Yet if one argued from pre-Yalta history, culture, tradition, and the aspiration to West European liberal and democratic norms, then one had to go further. Almost every argument that was made in the 1970s for admitting the fledgling democracies Spain, Portugal and Greece into the EC could be made in the 1990s for, at the very least, Poland, Hungary and the Czech Republic. If the arbitrariness and 'abnormality' of the Yalta divide had been seen most vividly in the divided city of Berlin, then the arbitrariness of this new dividing line could be seen in the divided towns along the River Oder. Was Görlitz in Europe but Zgorzelec (part of the same town until 1945) not in Europe? Had the Oder suddenly become the Bosporus?

However, we cannot stop there. For if one looked at the eastern and south-eastern frontiers of these East Central European states, then very similar arguments could be made, on grounds of history, culture, traditions and aspirations. If the Czech lands, why not Slovakia? If Hungary, why not Romania? If Poland, why not Lithuania? And what of Ukraine? And then the largest question of all: Russia. Certainly there were deep historical fault-lines here, not least between the lands of western and eastern Christianity. Yet the fact is that Europe does not have a single clear eastern end. It merely fades away. (Fortunate are the continents defined by seas.) To be sure, the practical steps to be taken before, say, Romania or Ukraine could seriously be considered for membership of the EC were so numerous and daunting as to make these, politically speaking, questions for the next century.

Mitterrand's definition of the third circle, 'continental Europe', contained a further, still larger problem. Even if one assumed that with the Channel tunnel Britain had physically rejoined the continent, after a short absence of some 5,000 years, there remained the issue of America. In the Helsinki process, North America — that is, the United States and Canada was explicitly included. When Mitterrand launched his ill-conceived and ill-fated scheme of a 'European Confederation' — a consolation prize for the countries in his third circle —, the participants at what was billed as the founding meeting sat beneath a large map which showed Europe stretching almost to the Kurile islands in the east, but stopping abruptly just to the west of Spain. De Gaulle would have nodded in approval.

Yet for the Federal Republic, the relationship with the United States, though much resented by significant sections of German intellectual and political opinion, had all along been of vital importance. Adenauer, for all his great reconciliation with de Gaulle, had seen this with crystal clarity. And this was not just true of West Germany's position in the West. We have seen in this book how not merely American defence and support in the West, but also active American policies in the East, contributed to the realisation of the goals of German Ostpolitik. Had all that changed now? The American had done his work, the American could go?

Of course, German politicians and diplomats saw all these questions. But, understandably enough, their first inclination was to respond with the old Genscherist *sowohl-als-auch* prose which really had served the Federal Republic rather well for the last quarter-century. France was the most important partner, but so was America. Deepening the EC was the top priority, but so was widening it. Russia was item number one in the East, but so was Poland. And so on. Josef Joffe summed it up in the words of Yogi Berra: if you see a fork in the road, take it. Now up to a point this is what large, powerful countries with a lot of neighbours, partners and petitioners always have to do. But if they are to achieve anything they also have to set priorities. And to set priorities you have first to decide what is most important to you, in other words, what is your national interest. Germany was now too independent, too sovereign, too powerful, to enjoy the luxury of not making choices.

Kohl identified two great tasks on the path to 'the Europe of the future': to deepen the (existing) EC into a European Union, and, secondly, 'the final overcoming of the division of the continent between East and West'. It was far from clear that these two things were compatible. Even if they were, there was a priority choice between them. Looking both west and east there were further big priority choices. Policymakers and policy intellectuals would often discuss these in terms of the relationship between the plethora of multilateral institutions, piling up the acronyms like children's spelling bricks and calling the result a new European architecture. Another way of looking at it would be to chart the real allocation of resources. But one can put it most simply in terms of choices between countries.

Germany could put France first. If France and Germany then did something that could loosely be called uniting, this would be new. If Belgium, the Netherlands and Luxemburg joined in, the result might perhaps be called, with a little poetic licence, a Federal or Confederal Republic of North-Western Europe. But it would not be Europe. Nor was it clear that such a (very) Little Europe would any longer necessarily be the magnetic core of further European integration that many of its German advocates envisaged: *Kleineuropa* as *Kerneuropa*. A process that had seemed to work almost like a successful physics experiment, in the very special, insulated, low-temperature laboratory conditions of divided 'Yalta' Europe, might not work at all in the harsh open air of the new Europe. Or it might work quite differently there. Far from finally overcoming the bad old European habits of forming competing alliances and coalitions, it might actually contribute to their re-emergence.

Thus the pursuit of the Little European strategy might well be at the cost of Germany's relationships with Britain, with other countries in the existing EC, and with those still outside it. America seemed to support moves towards a larger (West) European partner. But that support was by no means guaranteed, particularly if the Gaullist inheritance and an aggregation of French, German and Benelux protectionist reflexes fed into the international economic and security policies of such a *soi-disant* European Union. There might very well, therefore, be an even harder priority choice for Germany — between France and America.

As for the lands to Germany's east, the list of choices was almost endless. But if the most important potential priority conflict to the west was between France and America, the most important one to the east was between Poland and Russia. Traditionally, Germany had given priority to Russia. This old priority was, as we have seen, revived in Ostpolitik — Moscow first! — but for compelling reasons of national interest. Now, however, there was a real choice. Russia was no longer the superpower reaching into the centre of Europe, although it still had the weapons of one. It was not even the neighbour's neighbour. Namier's rule of odd and even numbers (see page 217) might actually now dictate 'friendship' with Ukraine rather than Russia. However, if it wanted to, Germany could even break with tradition and put its neighbour Poland first.

There were arguments for and against each of these priorities. But the one thing Germany could not do was everything. If it tried to do everything it would achieve nothing.

Beyond Ostpolitik

Now obviously Germany did not do nothing. The country was absorbed and obsessed by the costs and strains of its own internal unification, itself a unique version of the 'great transition test' facing all former communist countries. Yet it still had an active policy towards what were loosely described as its neighbours (actually, there were only two) in what was now carefully called 'Central, Eastern, and South-Eastern Europe'. Was this an 'Ostpolitik mark-two', as the *Economist* jauntily remarked? *Should* Germany have a new 'new Ostpolitik'? A second, or, in the case of the Social Democrats, a third Ostpolitik? Or perhaps: a new

'European Ostpolitik', meaning a common Ostpolitik of the European Community?

Our answer may perhaps initially surprise some readers. It is: no! Not an *Ost*politik, that is. The *Ost* in Ostpolitik was a bloc of communist states dominated by the Soviet Union. That bloc no longer existed. Where previously Western states, and especially West Germany, had to deal with the bloc as a bloc whether they wanted to or not — although even then, some 'differentiation' was possible — now they could not deal with the East as a bloc even if they wanted to. Moreover, many of those formerly East European states and peoples were now doing their level best to join — or, as they put it, with varying degrees of historical plausibility, to return to — Europe. And not just to Europe, but to something they called the West, or indeed to what many Russians called simply the world. In most respects, they had a very long way to go. But not in all. Some things — values and ideals, for example — cannot be eradicated by a mere system or partition. If you were to take a teacher from the class of '68 in Frankfurt and a teacher from the class of '68 in Kraków, and soberly compare their values and ideals, you might well conclude that the person to the east was actually closer to the West.

The very word Ostpolitik therefore implies the continued existence of an East. So does the old self-image of Germany as bridge, for it makes no sense to have a bridge between West and West. Yet the passionate aspiration of at least the larger part of the political and intellectual élites of Germany's immediate eastern neighbours was precisely to be — they would say 'again' — part of the West, part of a truly Western Europe. And was not here the real key to that security, that European normality, which Germany's leaders themselves so evidently sought? If Germany wanted to be a normal, European and Western country, like France or Britain, then it had, like France or Britain, to have normal, European and Western neighbours to its east. To say this is, of course, already to suggest a certain priority.

Now in the case of those immediate eastern neighbours, the prospects of achieving this Western, European 'normality' were simply inseparable from the conduct and development, not just external but also internal, of the (currently West and South) European Community. Perhaps the greatest single flaw of the Maastricht treaty was that it had nothing to say about the rest of Europe knocking at Europe's doors. Ostpolitik and Europapolitik, to recall the Bonn terms, could no longer be thought apart. Europe was still very far from being one, but there could now at least be one Europapolitik.

What did Germany actually do to its east, in the first two years after its own 'day of unity'? To tell the story in any detail would distort the proportions of this book. In any case, unlike the history of Ostpolitik told above, this is a story without an end. There are areas and periods in which the only safe form of commentary is the hourly radio broadcast. But a few points may nonetheless be singled out.

Until the Soviet ambassador to Bonn handed over the Soviet ratification document on the 2 + 4 Treaty in March 1991, the Bonn government's overwhelming concern was to keep the Soviet Union together and co-operative. Even after ratification, the Soviet troops still had to be got out of what was now eastern (rather than East) Germany. The Baltic republics continued to be told to go slow. This changed with the failed Soviet coup in August 1991. Immediately thereafter, Germany recognised — or, strictly speaking, restored diplomatic relations with — what were now again described as the Baltic states. Kohl called this 'a moving moment'. At the same time, he looked forward, publicly at least, to a 'renewed Soviet Union', which should take its place next to what the Bonn government insisted on calling the 'reform states' of the former Eastern Europe. Instead, the Soviet Union broke up.

The Federal Republic rightly claimed that it contributed the largest share of Western financial transfers to the former Soviet Union, although if one looked closely at the dramatic headline figures produced by the German government one found that these included all the very large payments for German unification, exports from the former GDR paid for in transferable roubles, export credit guarantees and even private donations. In terms of direct grants and aid, the American contribution was at least comparable.

In December 1992, Kohl agreed with Yeltsin that Soviet troops would withdraw by the end of August 1994, four months before the deadline in the 1990 treaty. Former Foreign Minister Hans-Dietrich Genscher called for a new comprehensive *Russlandpolitik* of the West, and specifically of the EC. What this would be was still wholly unclear, not least because nobody knew what Russia would be. Even less clear was whether Germany, the EC, or anybody in the West had what, in time, might be almost as important: a *Ukrainepolitik*.

What of the other large multi-national communist state, Yugoslavia? In the immediate aftermath of German unification, the general Western hope of keeping together the so-called federal republic of Yugoslavia accorded both with Bonn's general wish for stability (order/peace) and with its specific concern not to countenance any bad example of republican self-determination which might 'destabilise' the Soviet Union. But this also changed in the summer of 1991. After Slovenia and Croatia declared their independence, in the face of Serbian aggression, Hans-Dietrich Genscher, then still Foreign Minister, found himself confronted with a growing barrage of moral outrage and criticism from the media and politicians of all parties in Bonn. He then ran out ahead of his critics, and declared that Slovenia and Croatia should be recognised as sovereign states. It must be done; he insisted on it; how could he — for whom human rights and self-determination were sacred — ever be thought to have thought anything else?

German diplomacy then devoted its considerable skills, and new muscle, to securing a 'European' (that is, EC) initiative for recognition. The task was intricate. To give just one small example: according to a credible source, Genscher at one point put heavy pressure on Bulgaria not (yet) to recognise Macedonia, although this was actually a very bold and construct-ive move by Bulgaria — in fact, almost the Bulgarian equivalent of Germany's recognition of the Oder-Neisse line. Why did Genscher do this? Could it possibly be something to do with Greece, so often the joker in the EC pack, and now, in a fashion more often loosely identified with 'Eastern Europe', furiously opposing the recognition of Macedonia? Could it, just possibly, be a deal: Germany would not (yet) support the recognition of Macedonia if Greece did not oppose the recognition of Slovenia and Croatia? Oh, brave new world!

For all this diplomatic finesse, Germany was still unable to persuade its main West European partners of the wisdom of the step. It therefore bounced them into it, by declaring that it would go ahead with the recognition itself anyway, and before Christmas. Having then secured a reluctant resolution of all the EC member states to extend recognition on 15 January 1992, provided certain conditions were met, it proceeded to do so itself, before Christmas, declaring that the conditions had already been satisfied.

There are at least four different issues here. The first is how this was done, which was extremely European in the descriptive, historical sense, but not inordinately European in the prescriptive, futuristic sense. The second is why it was done. One can safely say that most of the Germans who supported this step did so with the very best of intentions, which had nothing in common with Hitler's wartime alliance with Croatia. On the contrary. Milošević's Serbia had been presented to them as the new Nazi Germany and this time they wanted to be on the right side. (One result was that the Federal Republic was presented by Milošević to the Serbs as the new Nazi Germany.) What one could not say, however, is that this sudden turn in German policy was the result of any sober calculation of national interest. It was a hasty over-reaction, following public and especially published opinion rather than leading it. Of course, it was by no means only in Bonn that this was liable to happen. It was one of the structural problems of making foreign policy in a television democracy.

The third issue is the consequences of the decision in the former Yugoslavia. Did it ameliorate the situation, by sending a clear warning to the military-political leadership in Belgrade, or did it exacerbate it, as many American, British and French policymakers feared it would? The real problem with recognition was not Croatia and Slovenia in themselves, but the remaining republic of Bosnia-Herzegovina. Here a nightmare developed to which the principle of self-determination could provide no easy cure — and may even have been part of the disease. The fourth issue is: who faced the consequences? Above all, of course, the bereaved, maimed, brutalised and dispossessed men, women and children of the former Yugoslavia. Yet Germany faced the consequences indirectly, by taking in some 250,000 refugees from the former Yugoslavia in 1992, compared with just 4,000 taken by Britain and just over 1,000 taken by France. The usually humane and generous reception given to these people was something of which Germany could be proud.

But what of tackling causes rather than results? In 1990–91, German diplomacy had hoped that new conflicts in the rest of Europe could be restrained by a strengthened CSCE. The Helsinki process was seen as a golden bridge between the European Community and the long-sought European peace order. Unfortunately, the CSCE 'crisis mechanism' inaugurated at Genscher's Congress of Berlin proved even more powerless to prevent mayhem in Bosnia than the solution found at Bismarck's Congress of Berlin. Instead, the West had to resort to methods which would have been more familiar to Bismarck. Multilateral diplomacy, the cheque-book and the telephone were not enough.

Under joint United Nations and EC auspices, soldiers from France, Britain and many smaller European nations tried to help 'make peace'. The United States initially said this was Europe's business, and a test of the EC's much-vaunted new common foreign and security policy. Yet, willy-nilly, America once again found itself playing a major role. In early 1993, German soldiers were still notable by their absence, although the political parties in Bonn were edging towards the removal of the constitutional impediments to their deployment under UN auspices. Meanwhile, Britain and France sent the soldiers, Germany took the refugees. To describe this as a European division of labour would no doubt be too harmonious an interpretation.

To raise these issues in this cursory way is not to offer any comprehensive or final judgements. It is merely to help concentrate minds on questions. In the former Eastern Europe, by contrast with the former Yugoslavia and the former Soviet Union, the picture was more encouraging. To be sure, there were no simple lines between black and white. To call Romania in 1992 a democracy would be a romanesque — not to say, a baroque — use of the word. In Czechoslovakia, which had generally been regarded as the most Western of the former East European countries, there erupted a quite bitter nationality conflict which resulted in a peaceful separation into two different states: the Czech Republic and Slovakia. In the domestic politics of Poland and Hungary there were, in high and even in the highest places, strong elements not just of the European (prescriptive) but also of the European (descriptive) — the latter being described by the former as nationalist, populist, chauvinist, xenophobic and so on.

Nonetheless, there was some real progress here, and Germany played a notably constructive part. Together with the United States, Germany was instrumental in bringing the East Central European states into a new Nato Co-operation Council, although the fact that all the other post-Soviet states were brought in at the same time rather diminished the attraction. Quiet bilateral co-operation in the security field went further and was more promising. As (West) Germany had itself been welcomed into the Council of Europe, just a few years after being liberated from a dictatorship, so now Germany was able to join other established Western democracies in welcoming the new democracies into that often neglected institution of democratic Europe.

Meanwhile, Germany played a leading role in the negotiation of the so-called 'Europe Agreements' signed between the European Community and the 'Visegrád three' — Hungary, Poland and (then still) Czechoslovakia. In most of the crucial economic sectors where these countries could immediately hope to export more goods to the EC (agriculture, coal, steel, textiles), these agreements were in fact still protectionist, perfectly illustrating the way in which the EC could, at its worst, function as the aggregation of national, regional and sectoral *sacro egoismo*. But here the responsibility lay much more with France and the weaker economies of the south than it did with Germany.

Nonetheless, the treaties set the goal of creating a free-trade relationship in ten years, and this was interpreted in Germany as suggesting a possible time-scale for the opening of negotiations for full membership of the European Community. Moreover, in the bilateral treaties which Germany negotiated with Poland, Hungary and Czechoslovakia, the Federal Republic also committed itself to supporting those countries' progress towards eventual membership of the EC. Similar treaties with Bulgaria and Romania mentioned progress towards the EC, but not membership. Altogether, these bilateral treaties signalled the Federal Republic's desire to place its relations with its eastern neighbours on a new footing; building, of course, on the achievements of Ostpolitik.

Not just on paper but in practice, not just in trade but in assistance for building new democratic, legal and educational institutions, Germany was in the front line — whether through direct action by the Federal Government, by the federal states, by individual towns, by the wealthy party foundations, by other 'quangos' (quasi non-governmental organisations), by the churches, by private foundations or simply by individual initiative. Moreover, insofar as any Western model was applicable to post-communist Europe it would be Model Germany: not just because it was the closest but also because it was a social market economy, a legal system and a liberal democracy built on the ruins of a totalitarian system and designed specifically to prevent the return of totalitarianism. Who would have thought forty or even twenty years before that it would be to Germany that Hungarians, Czechs and Poles would turn first when it came to drafting the constitutions of liberty? This was an extraordinary and heartening novelty.

Recalling a leitmotif of Ostpolitik, one could almost imagine a huge sign hovering over Central and Eastern Europe with the inscription: 'Weaving in progress'. German language-teaching was one of the region's great growth industries. In line with a central tenet of weaving, the Federal Republic also led the way in abolishing visa requirements for Poles as well as Hungarians, Czechs and Slovaks. The millions of visitors, and travellers in transit, provoked not a little hostility, above all in the former East Germany. Yet on balance this bold step was remarkably successful. In early 1992, a Polish quality newspaper could write that never in the twentieth century had Polish-German relations been as good.

Nonetheless, there were still (or again) problems. While the Polish frontier issue was closed by treaty, that of reparations for Poles deported to work in the Third Reich continued to rumble on. The negotiation of the bilateral treaty with Czechoslovakia proved unexpectedly tense, because of continued differences over the date from which the Munich Agreement of 1938 should be deemed invalid (*ex tunc* or *ex nunc?*) and because of demands raised by the organisation of the Sudeten German expellees.

While President Havel had handsomely apologised for the post-war expulsions, and demonstratively made his first visit as President to Germany (even before visiting Slovakia), the Sudeten German leaders stubbornly insisted on the right to resettle in the Sudetenland as German citizens and on compensation for the German property expropriated after the war. At one point they even demanded a halt to the programme of privatisation of state property in Czechoslovakia until this issue had been resolved. Through their influence in the CSU they plagued the progress of the treaty right up to its final ratification in the Bundesrat, where the state of Bavaria still opposed it. And then, with the separation of the Czech lands and Slovakia, they tried to reopen the whole issue yet again.

Elsewhere, there was still the problem of the remaining German minorities. In Romania, the centuries-old German communities had been almost extinguished by emigration to Germany. But there remained up to a million Germans 'in the sense of the Basic Law' (see page 234f) in Poland, and over two million in the former Soviet Union. The German government, working mainly through the department of the Interior Ministry responsible for 'out-settlers', now concentrated on trying to ensure that, as Chancellor Kohl put it, they would 'see a future in the ancestral *Heimat*'.

The numbers of out-settlers from Poland actually fell dramatically, from more than 133,000 in 1990 to less than 18,000 in 1992. Partly this was because the rules for the admission of out-settlers had been tightened in summer 1990. Partly, it was because the general prospects for anyone remaining in Poland had improved. (Polish emigration from Poland had also been high in the 1980s.) But it was also because the democratic Polish government had recognised the cultural rights of the German minority, and the German government was pumping money into their towns and villages. To have a German passport but stay in Silesia could now be an attractive option.

However, the number of out-settlers from the former Soviet Union rose rather than fell, in spite of German-Russian, German-Ukrainian and even German-Kazakh agreements to provide better facilities for Germans in old and new areas of settlement. As a result, the Federal Republic still took a total of just over 230,000 out-settlers in 1992. From the point of view of the ordinary German voter, this was only part of a much larger overall challenge. Immigration had replaced the Red Army as the new threat from the east, and become a (sometimes all too literally) burning issue in German domestic politics. The reaction of the sheltered consumer society of the old Federal Republic to immigration, and even more that of the traumatised society of the former GDR, ranged from the nervous to the hysterical. 'The boat is full', headlines proclaimed, although as Hans Magnus Enzensberger pointed out, the people who were actually at sea in a leaking lifeboat were the refugees.

Nonetheless, the total numbers were very large. In addition to the 230,000 ethnic German out-settlers, there were in 1992 more than 250,000 refugees, nearly 440,000 people using and abusing Germany's exceptionally liberal right of asylum to stay in the country as 'asylum-seekers', and, according to the Interior Minister, some 310,000 people who had 'illegally entered' the country. There was a considerable overlap between these figures, especially since Sunday's illegal immigrant or refugee often became Monday's asylum-seeker. But the total was equivalent to more than one per cent of Germany's existing population, in one year. As usual, Germany looked for a 'European solution' of its problem. But when that was not forthcoming it produced its own attempt, presented as paving the way for a European solution.

After tortuous negotiations between the main parties, agreement was reached to limit the right of asylum so it did not apply to people from countries where there was no longer political persecution. Bogus asylum-seekers who came to Germany through 'secure third countries' would be returned to them. Poland and the Czech Republic were now classified as 'secure third countries'. The burden was therefore to be passed back to Germany's immediate eastern neighbours, although Bonn was ready to pay something for the service — and to help them improve the walls and fences on their own eastern frontiers. To describe this as European burden-sharing would again be a too harmonious interpretation.

This whole complex of issues — minorities, out-settlers, asylum-seekers, immigration and the treatment of foreigners — raised further questions. One of them could hardly be more fundamental. It was: Who is a German? The answer given by the old Federal Republic had not been solely *völkisch*. But in the interpretation of article 116 of the Basic Law there had undoubtedly still been what Johannes Gross has called 'the *völkisch* worm'. The problems this caused were compounded by an exceptionally liberal asylum law but also by a quite illiberal law on the acquisition of citizenship for foreigners living in Germany. The result was a mess.

Foreigners could secure long-term residence in Germany by pretending to be persecuted at home, when they clearly were not. Meanwhile, a young Turkish man who had been born and lived his whole life in Germany, attended German schools and spoke fluent German, could not become a German citizen unless he renounced Turkish citizenship. Yet at the same time, Germany was handing out German citizenship to thousands of Polish citizens, according to criteria such as descent, 'inclination to Germanity', and ancestors in the *Wehrmacht* (see page 236).

The matter should not be made simpler than it was. Many people really had suffered, in Poland and even more in the Soviet Union, just for being Germans. France had felt a responsibility to its *pieds noirs*, Britain to its Falklanders. Simply to abandon the Germans in the East would not necessarily be a noble thing. But the question 'who is a German?' was too important to be left for ever as a hostage of history. Would the Germans leave the primary emphasis on the *Volk*, the tribe, the *ethnos*, or would they shift the emphasis to a more modern, liberal version of citizenship, as they had in most other fields? 'That only those of German origin can be true Germans,' wrote Johannes Gross, 'is a barbaric superstition.' And the East Berlin theologian, Richard Schröder, sharpened the debate by defining a desirable normality as one in which there would be full acceptance of *black Germans*. To put it another way: Did Germany want to stop at being a 'normal European nation-state', or would it try to become a, historically speaking, somewhat less normal state-nation?

Now this was, of course, a question for all European countries. But it was a question particularly for Germany, and Germany would have first to answer for itself. Europe would not do the job for it, even if, in the longer term, the EC were to develop a real European citizenship. And this was not just a matter of self-definition, in Germany's condition of stillbecoming. It also concerned the example that Germany would give to the countries to its east. The provisions for the German minorities sought by the German government, and written in to the bilateral treaties, were presented as being in line with multilateral agreements, with CSCE and European norms. This was no doubt true. But it was also true that one powerful nation-state was making bilateral arrangements to support, culturally, economically and legally, a minority of its own nationals (by its own definition) inside other states. The degree of support and protection accorded them depended on the will and power of the protector-state. It was mainly done through a department of the German *Interior* Ministry.

Hans-Dietrich Genscher said the foreign policy of united Germany should be a 'policy of the good example'. But was this really such a good example? If Germany acted like this, then why should not Hungary, in relation to the large Hungarian minorities in Slovakia, Transylvania and the former Yugoslavia? And Poland in relation to the Polish minority in Lithuania? And Russia for the huge new Russian minorities in other states of the former Soviet Union? And then, what of Croatia? What, even, of Serbia? The German minorities had suffered in the past. But so had most other minorities. To be sure, unlike Serbia (and, in smaller measure, Croatia and Russia), Germany was not using force, the threat of force, or even the hint of a threat of force. But was this model of the protector-state the cure or part of the disease?

In Poland, German officials, and the more enlightened representatives of the expellee organisations through which some of the public funds were channelled, exerted themselves to see that the subsidies benefited Poles as well as Germans and to respect local sensibilities. But some of the local Germans were not so restrained. Here as elsewhere, old-fashioned nationalism had been stoked rather than dampened by oppression. And in this the locals were sometimes encouraged by unrepentant expellees and marginal nationalists from Germany itself. Genuine irredentism was still very unlikely, not least because the German minority (unlike, say, the Hungarian minority in Slovakia) was not contiguous to the fatherland, but concentrated in the area around Opole (Oppeln). Local friction was likely.

Hartmut Koschyk, a Christian Democrat member of the Bundestag working for a genuinely constructive peaceful engagement of the expellees in the area, wrote that 'European normality must be seen as the ultimate goal.' A familiar invocation! But he went on: 'a normality that was practised as a matter of course in Central Europe — which is more than just an idea — for centuries'. If one considers soberly, without nostalgia or wishful thinking, what the normality of Central Europe had really been over at least the previous century and a half, this was not a very encouraging perspective.

All this was of course bound up with the further question of the German economic presence in the region. Despite much loose talk of 'hegemony', 'supremacy' or 'domination', this presence was still difficult to quantify at the end of 1992, both because trade patterns had not fully settled down after the end of East Germany, Comecon and the Soviet Union, and because investment patterns had not yet built up. For what they are worth, the trade patterns for three countries in 1991 and 1992 are given in Table IV. At the end of 1992, German investment was said to account for more than eighty per cent of total foreign investment in the Czech Republic. Rather surprisingly, there was significantly more American than

German investment in Hungary, while in Poland the German share was estimated at about one third. But the total figures for investment were still so small that these proportions could quickly change.

That in the Czech Republic, for example, was substantially affected by one big investment, of Volkswagen in the Skoda car factory. The fact that Skoda went to Volkswagen rather than to Renault was, however, widely interpreted as a sign of things to come. Even with the huge drain of public monies and private capital to eastern Germany, Germany was still a far larger and more active presence than any other West European country. It seemed to be a reasonable guess that German investment would sooner or later pull further ahead, when the former GDR began to be less of a drain on German resources.

This naturally produced fears as well as hopes. The Polish writer Andrzej Szczypiorski commented that whereas previously the Poles had been afraid of the Germans coming with guns now they were afraid of them coming with cheque-books. Yet one has to say that the one thing worse than the Germans coming with their cheque-books would be for the Germans not to come with their cheque-books. These post-communist countries wanted some version of a market economy; that is, of capitalism. Capitalism requires capital. Capital is what they did not have. Therefore, as so often before in the history of the region, the capital had to come from outside. Germany was next door and had a lot of capital.

Under the strain of unification, Germany was actually a net importer of capital in 1992, but within a few years this would almost certainly change for the better. Yet why should this capital then flow to the former Eastern Europe rather than to other European areas with low wages but better communications and guaranteed market access, such as Spain or Portugal? And if it were to go east, why not to the Far East? Beside physical proximity, the main competitive advantage that the former Eastern Europe had to offer would be very cheap skilled and unskilled labour. An unkind word for seizing this advantage would be 'exploitation'. Yet it was not realistic to expect capital to behave philanthropically in a highly competitive world where even Western Europe would have its work cut out to keep up with the Far East. So if there was no way to avoid this dilemma, it would be necessary to confront it.

'Nothing might do greater harm to German-Slav relationships,' wrote Elizabeth Wiskemann in 1956, 'than for Poles and Czechs to feel that, no sooner are they free of the communist yoke than they must go into German economic harness.' A prophecy come true? Wiskemann continued: 'It would call for exquisite tact for this impression to be avoided: the very same German who worked very well with the French or Italian or Benelux representatives in the West might find it traditionally too difficult to keep his manners as good in the East.' Wiskemann, writing just a decade after Hitler, was being ironical, even sarcastic. But might we not now repeat her sentence quite calmly and seriously? Was it not, precisely, exquisite tact that was called for of the Germans in this region in the 1990s?

Here we must dwell for a moment on Wiskemann's word 'traditionally'. In the new bilateral treaties there was talk in the preambles of continuing the 'good traditions . . . in the centuries-old history of Germany and Poland', of 'fruitful traditions' with Bulgaria, 'the tradition of fruitful relations' with Romania, 'centuries-old fruitful traditions' with Czechoslovakia and even 'traditional friendship developed over centuries' with Hungary. But did most Germans have any inkling of Germany's history and traditions in the east? In the Third Reich, German studies of the lands to Germany's east were poisoned by Nazism. The poisoned chalice was carried forward by some of the same scholars after 1945. Then there was a sharp break, and 'the East' — now in the ahistorical 'Yalta' definition — became the territory of political science, security studies, policy intellectuals, journalists and professional policymakers. With some notable scholarly exceptions, the history and traditions of the German presence east of the Oder and Neisse rivers, and south-east of the Erz mountains, were left for expellees to brood on. As has often been observed, for most younger West Germans Majorca was closer than Leipzig and California more familiar than Silesia. They lived with their backs to the Wall — and more protected by it than was quite comfortable to admit.

Now all this had changed. Unification opened the window to the east. But what would people see? How would it be presented to them? What were those 'good traditions' to be carried forward? Were there any? One of Germany's most influential and enterprising publishers, Wolf Jobst Siedler, announced a lavish scholarly ten-volume series entitled 'German History in the East of Europe'. It should, he said, describe the world of 'the German-settled or German-permeated East Central and Eastern Europe' — a world 'sunk in the cataracts of history and finally, guiltily gambled away'. A timely undertaking.

Yet this same distinguished publisher could be found, in a book he published in 1991 entitled *Germany, what now?* (as in Fallada's *Little man, what now?*), talking expansively of Germany as 'again the hegemonial power of the whole of Central-Eastern Europe'. Germany, he said, would be for Czechoslovakia, Hungary and partly for Poland 'the leading power' (*Führungsmacht*). Germany might possibly, he suggested, 'be regaining her traditional role in Eastern Europe'. 'Bohemia and Moravia,' he observed, 'are a part of Europe, of the German world, I would almost have said.' Germany could not avoid a 'supremacy'. It would have to take over a 'key role' for Hungary, Czechoslovakia and above all for Poland. 'Of course we don't want to drive out the Poles, but I do indeed believe that one day Pomerania and Silesia and Bohemia-Moravia will orient themselves again towards Germany.'

The historian Arnulf Baring, under whose name the book appeared, was more sceptical. He thought the Germans were more likely to duck the challenge, and erect new walls to protect their modest, bourgeois idyll. If they did take up the challenge, however, he doubted their capacity to do it 'cautiously and yet energetically, tactfully and yet purposefully'. Yet even he, in trying to find the terms in which to present this task to his compatriots, found himself talking about 'a colonisation task, a new *Ostkolonisation*', and about the formerly German territories immediately to the east (i.e. Pomerania and Silesia) as 'these, if you like, common territories'. Now one understands and applauds the intention: to provoke realistic discussion of issues that were urgently in need of it. But such formulations themselves illustrate the difficulty of finding the 'good traditions'. Exquisite tact this was not. Imagine a British historian talking of a British 'colonisation task' in Ireland!

At this point one has to say something slightly shocking. In 1991, many people, in Germany and elsewhere, hoped and believed that at least the territorial questions for the Germans were resolved for good and all. But even of that one could not be certain. All over the former Eastern Europe, the former Soviet Union, the former Yugoslavia, territorial questions were coming open again. It has been said that half the frontiers in Europe are newer than those of Africa, and some already proved to be less durable. For Germany, one territorial question already on the agenda was that of the Kaliningrad region, now a highly militarised Russian exclave between Lithuania and Poland, but formerly Kant's city of Königsberg and a part of East Prussia.

As early as 1988, the banker Friedrich Wilhelm Christians had suggested turning this area into a special economic zone: a 'Baltic region K'. As the perestroika of the Soviet Union turned to the collapse of the Soviet Union, the proposal was seriously discussed in the Russian press. It was by no means impossible that Russia would at some stage in the 1990s be prepared to, in effect, sell the area for hard currency and the promise of more Western 'co-operation'.

How would the Germans react to such an offer? At a conference in mid-1992, an Israeli journalist posed this question, and answered himself: They would say 'yes, but in a European framework'. Some three months later the historian Michael Stürmer, who had been present at this conference, contributed a leading article to the *Frankfurter Allgemeine Zeitung*. It was entitled 'A Task called Königsberg'. After describing the miserable and threatening condition of the Russian military region, he endorsed the idea of a free-trade zone, although not the suggestion (which had been supported by Christians) that the ethnic Germans from the former Soviet Union should be resettled there.

'The German interest,' wrote Stürmer, 'does not only come from the past and history. It must above all be directed to making the Baltic coasts a zone of stability and prosperity.' However, Germany could not alone make such proposals: 'The European Community must be given precedence, in thought and action'. An overall concept of the EC 'should within the foreseeable future bring Königsberg into the EC's internal market. Russia would thus get partial membership and so also an advantageous special status vis-à-vis the European Community.' Whatever was to be done, he wrote, 'it can only be done with Russia'. Although there was mention of the interests of all the Baltic basin states, the words 'Lithuania' and 'Poland' did not appear.

Now this delightful combination of Euro-planning and neo-Bismarckian *Russlandpolitik* should not, of course, be taken as representing official German policy, although Professor Stürmer was the head of the country's leading government-funded foreign policy think-tank. But the question of Königsberg would not go away. In fact, the better things went in Russia the more likely it was to be posed. If things went badly, the Russian military would simply hold on to their desirable base. A more western-oriented, civilian government would be more likely to open talks about it.

It is important to stress that the demilitarisation of the Kaliningrad area might also be in the interests of Poland and Lithuania. However a free-trade zone, as part of a re-emerging Hanseatic league, would be for them a mixed blessing, since it would almost certainly attract investment — above all, German investment — which might otherwise go to Gdańsk or Klaipeda. The precise legal status of the area would obviously be the subject of delicate negotiations. Writing in *Die Zeit*, Marion Gräfin Dönhoff suggested a four-power condominium, the powers being Russia, Poland, Lithuania and — since some might still object to Germany — Sweden! After the four-power city of Berlin, the four-power city of Königsberg? But even if formal sovereignty remained with Russia, a heavy economic commitment would involve Germany very directly at an extraordinarily sensitive point.

What of the territories immediately to Germany's east? Reflecting in his memoirs on the arrogation to Poland, at Stalin's insistence, of the large part of Silesia between the eastern and western Neisse rivers, Churchill wrote: 'One day the Germans would want their territory back, and the Poles would not be able to stop them'. This was a brutally harsh statement which nonetheless accurately reflected what had generally happened in Central and Eastern Europe over the centuries. If strong states were next to weak states which had territory they coveted, and to which they could construct some historical claim, they sooner or later took it. That was, after all, how Prussia had got Silesia in the first place. Of course, there was now a quite different Germany in a quite different Europe. But the co-operation between strong and weak states, in historically disputed territories, with remaining national minorities, would still be a very delicate affair. And Poland was not just economically but also politically a weak state.

One did not need to share Günter Grass's nightmare vision of a Germany economically subordinating 'a good chunk of Silesia, a little slice of Pomerania', in order to foresee tensions here. The German border town of Görlitz advertised itself in the *Financial Times* as the 'Centre of Lower Silesia'. Exquisite tact? German policymakers were particularly keen on co-operation in what were described as 'Euroregions', spanning the borders between Germany, the Czech Republic and Poland, or, in regional terms, between Bavaria, Saxony and Bohemia, Saxony, Brandenburg and Lower Silesia, Mecklenburg-Vorpommern and Pomerania. Here, to Germany's east, as previously to Germany's west, frontiers should be opened and gradually deprived of their importance. They should unite people rather than dividing them. But, as Siedler's remarks suggest, regionalism could mean something rather different in East Central Europe than it did between old-established states of roughly comparable strength in Western Europe.

As we have noticed throughout this book, the history of Ostpolitik abounded in paradoxes, both deliberate and unintentional. In crafting a new Europapolitik, German policymakers might need to consider a further paradox. In the former Eastern Europe, the path to going beyond the state-nation might lead through first consolidating the state-nation. It would be nice to think otherwise, but no better guarantor of human and civil rights had yet been found in Europe than the established, constitutional, liberal and democratic state-nation. That the EC, or the CSCE, or the UN, could substitute for the state in that regard remained still a hope, but not a reality.

Let it again be stressed that none of this is for a moment to doubt German policymakers' good intentions. Indeed, if there was a problem with the formulation of German foreign policy in the first years after unification it was not that there were any bad intentions but that there were too many good ones. What we have tried to do here is simply — following Adenauer's exhortation — to identify a few questions that might soon arise, 'and perhaps [to] warn'. It is hard to overstate the difficulty and sensitivity of the challenges that Germany still faced to its east. The great work of reconciliation would take at least another generation. It would require an honest and unsentimental reading of history, respect for the different achievements even of poor neighbours, and great sensitivity.

Sitting on a bench in front of the Strahov monastery in Prague, a German editor asked an elderly Czech whether the Germans should come back again. 'To be sure,' he replied, 'but you would have to bring the Jews with you.' Central Europe would never again be what it once was. But it could in some ways actually be better: hardly in high culture, but politically, economically and socially. This would require extraordinary commitment from Germany, but also exceptional self-restraint. After forty-five years of steadily working to widen the bounds of German power, the Germans would now have to aquire the new habit of not fully exerting the power they had. More dramatically still: they had the particular task of helping the consolidation of other democratic state-nations in territories where Germans had until quite recently lived and ruled.

Possibilities

Shortly before his death in the autumn of 1992, Willy Brandt wrote a valedictory message in almost Old Testament style. 'Our time,' he wrote, 'like hardly any before, is full of possibilities — for good and ill. Nothing comes of itself. And little lasts. So — reflect on your strength, and on the fact that every period demands its own answers . . .' As the grand old man of Ostpolitik penned his delphic parting words, the range of possibilities in Europe was indeed vast.

It was possible that, in the early twenty-first century, at least part of the former Eastern Europe would be an area of secure, liberal, democratic states, co-operating with neighbours and partners in a larger European Community and Western Alliance. It was possible that Polish, Hungarian and Czech citizens would have rights, freedoms and life-chances comparable to those enjoyed by Spanish, Portuguese and Greek citizens in the 1980s. It was possible that tolerance, pluralism, democracy and the virtues of ever closer co-operation would spread from west to east, so that Germany would at last find itself between West and West — and therefore indeed, to recall Weizsäcker's phrase, 'delivered from the *Mittellage*'. This would not be the final 'unification' or 'healing' of Europe, of which people had dreamed in the early 1980s, in Prague, in Berlin, even in Oxford. But it would be a great step closer to it.

It was also possible that intolerance, tribalism and the forces of disintegration would spread from east to west, threatening even the substance of what had already been achieved in the European Community. In Brecht's words, 'the womb is fertile still, from which that crawled': and the womb was of course not capitalism, as Brecht had claimed to think, but Europe — and human nature. The examples of the former Yugoslavia and parts of the former Soviet Union showed what could happen. And they were not far away. 'Easter holidaymakers in civil war' proclaimed a horrified headline in an Austrian tabloid newspaper. Germany was already shaken.

Altogether, Central Europe was the area in which this new European question was posed most sharply. The peoples of East Central Europe had the first and best chance of gaining from the former, optimistic variant. Those of West Central Europe, the Germans and the Austrians, stood in most immediate danger of suffering from the latter. Perhaps one should again call this not the European question but the Central European question. But once again, the Central European question bid fair to be the central European one.

Germany, specifically, had what the historian Fritz Stern has called its 'second chance'. At the end of the nineteenth century, Germany was the emergent major power in the centre of Europe, a powerhouse of economic and scientific modernity. It had a chance to use this power peacefully and constructively. It spectacularly failed so to do. Now, at the end of the twentieth century, it was again a major power in the centre of Europe. For all the new quality of institutionalised co-operation and permanent communication between allies and partners in the European Community, the Western Alliance, and altogether in the Western world, it was Germany that had this second chance and Germany that faced these particular challenges. Burden-sharing would only go so far, because other Western states had other vital interests, other special problems, other priorities. Britain and America had to look to their own battered economies and tattered social fabric. France, Italy and Spain had also to look south, across the Mediterranean to North Africa. To say that Germany's problems were also Europe's did not mean that Europe would solve them.

Could Germany do it? Could it not only preserve but also help to spread the achievements that had made it a magnet and a model? In another twenty years could another Willy Brandt have the satisfaction of seeing the word Germany become a synonym not just for peace but also for freedom? Some said that Germany lacked the 'internationalist élite' for the task. Yet it did not want for highly educated, well-travelled, idealistic men and women. True, what they had experienced before was little preparation for what they faced now. They were somewhat like the pilot of a barge on the Rhine who suddenly finds himself in charge of an oil-tanker on a high sea. But to some extent that had also been true of America's élites in 1945. And the American half-century had not been Europe's worst (for those in the West, that is).

There were perhaps a few very general lessons they could take with them from that half-century, and more particularly from the quarter-century of Ostpolitik. Firstly, they would need to define anew their own national interest. It would be useful if they did not try to define other people's. Making unilateral, national definitions of the European interest was a habit as old as the nation-states in Europe. But it was a bad habit. Unless and until there was a directly-elected all-European parliament and government, a fair definition of European interest could only be reached as a series of compromises between national interests. Moreover, if they did not define their own national interest consciously and clearly, it would be made up as they went along, in reaction to external challenges and to the pressures of public and published opinion in a television democracy.

They would need to watch out for those abstract nouns ('stability', 'normalisation'), and to remember not to take Mephistopheles' advice.

Hypotheses would, however, be useful. But the history of Ostpolitik also shows how hypotheses can become burdens. So they would need to keep revising the hypotheses against reality. In trying to build a new Europe, they would need always to remember the West — in trade, in defence, above all, in values. Those values could not always be borne aloft at full mast. It would sometimes be necessary to be a 'cunning idealist', to borrow Golo Mann's description of Adenauer. But if they were again to play down, conceal or relativise those values, they would have to be quite sure they knew to what purpose and with what effect. The history of Ostpolitik shows just how little one can ever be certain of the effects. When in doubt, they might therefore remember Mark Twain's advice: If you don't know what to do, do the right thing.

They would still have to beware the tendency to emotional overreaction. If Kleist and Thomas Mann were not sufficient authorities on this point, they might take it from Boris Becker. 'I have the impression,' said the young tennis star, 'that with success — and this nation has great success — many Germans have a certain tendency to flip their top.' They would do well not to overestimate what Germany could achieve, with the best will in the world. One of Germany's most gifted young political scientists declared in an inaugural lecture in 1991 that the 'European tasks' of 'the Germans in their second nation-state' would include above all 'the task of keeping the national and European consciousness of all countries of the continent in harmony'. When Britain was the most powerful country in the world it could barely maintain the balance of power on the continent of Europe, yet now Germany, troubled, burdened, medium-heavyweight Germany, was to hold the balance of consciousness?

Finally, they could not expect to be thanked for what they were doing. If they thought neighbours and partners were being ungrateful (which they would be), they could do worse than to remember what many Germans had said about America over the previous half-century.

This was not much to be getting on with. But who said history teaches any plain lessons? These younger Germans could still count on help from their friends. However, like it or not, it was they who would face the main challenge, and the main chance.

'And,' the ghost of Adenauer might still insist, 'your best guess?' The earlier history of German foreign policy did not give grounds for excessive optimism. Even the largely constructive period of that history described and analysed in this book had some worrying features. Taking all in all, the favourable variant that we have imagined for Germany and Europe at the beginning of the twenty-first century did not seem probable. But it was still possible. There are worse combinations than that of scepticism and hope.

Abbreviations

Wherever possible, we have tried to avoid the use of abbreviations in the main text. The exceptions — such as EC, Nato and GDR — have virtually become words in their own right. The following abbreviations have been used when it seemed unavoidable, especially in direct quotations from documents, and throughout the Notes.

ACDP   *Archiv für Christlich-Demokratische Politik*

AdDL   *Archiv des Deutschen Liberalismus*

AdsD   *Archiv der sozialen Demokratie*

APZ   *Aus Politik und Zeitgeschichte.* A supplement to the weekly *Das Parlament.*

BBC   British Broadcasting Corporation

BPA   *Bundespresseamt,* formally the *Presse- und Informationsamt der Bundesregierung.* This abbreviation refers mainly to transcripts prepared by the federal press office.

CC   Central Committee. As used in Soviet, East German and other Soviet bloc documents.

CDU   *Christlich-Demokratische Union.* Christian Democratic Union. A party of the Federal Republic of Germany. Usually referred to in the main text, together with the Bavarian CSU, as 'Christian Democrats'.

CMEA   Council for Mutual Economic Assistance. Usually referred to in the main text as 'Comecon'.

CoCom   Co-ordinating Committee for Multilateral Export Controls

Comecon   Council for Mutual Economic Assistance. The CMEA.

CPSU   Communist Party of the Soviet Union

CSCE   Conference on Security and Co-operation in Europe. Often referred to in the main text as 'Helsinki'.

CSU   *Christlich-Soziale Union*. Christian Social Union. A party of Bavaria and the Federal Republic of Germany. Usually referred to in the main text, together with the CDU, as 'Christian Democrats'.

DA   *Deutschland Archiv*

DM   *Deutsche Mark*. German Mark. The D-Mark.

EA   *Europa-Archiv*

EC   European Community. Originally, and still in some formal usage, the European Communities.

EDC   European Defence Community

EEC   European Economic Community

EKD   *Evangelische Kirche in Deutschland*. The Protestant Church in Germany. In 1969–90 there was a separate church organisation in East Germany, the Federation of Protestant Churches in the GDR. In this period, the EKD was therefore, in effect, the Protestant Church in West Germany.

EPC   European Political Co-operation

FAZ   *Frankfurter Allgemeine Zeitung*

FDJ   *Freie Deutsche Jugend*. Free German Youth. The mass youth organisation of the GDR.

FDP   *Freie Demokratische Partei*. Free Democratic Party. A party of the Federal Republic of Germany. Usually referred to in the main text as 'Free Democrats'.

FRG   Federal Republic of Germany. The abbreviation was used systematically by the East German and Soviet authorities, to put the FRG on the same level as the GDR. It was as carefully avoided by the West German authorities.

G7   The Group of Seven

GATT   General Agreement on Tariffs and Trade

GDR   German Democratic Republic

HVA   *Hauptverwaltung Aufklärung*. The espionage section of the MfS.

HZ   *Historische Zeitschrift*

IMF   International Monetary Fund

INF	Intermediate-range Nuclear Forces
KoKo	*Bereich Kommerzielle Koordinierung*. The GDR's 'Commercial Co-ordination' agency, for dealings in hard currency.
KOR	*Komitet Obrony Robotników*. Workers' Defence Committee.
LDPD	*Liberaldemokratische Partei Deutschlands*. The so-called Liberal Democratic Party of Germany was one of the 'bloc' parties in the GDR.
MBFR	Mutual and Balanced Force Reduction talks
MFN	Most Favored Nation. A status granted by the United States of America.
MfS	*Ministerium für Staatssicherheit*. The Ministry for State Security of the GDR. The 'Stasi'.
Nato	North Atlantic Treaty Organisation
ND	*Neues Deutschland*
NG	*Neue Gesellschaft*. Since 1985: *Neue Gesellschaft/Frankfurter Hefte*.
OECD	Organisation for Economic Co-operation and Development
RFE	Radio Free Europe
SALT	Strategic Arms Limitation Talks, and subsequently treaties.
SDI	Strategic Defense Initiative. Also known as 'star wars'.
SED	*Sozialistische Einheitspartei Deutschlands*. Socialist Unity Party of Germany. The ruling communist party of the GDR, founded by a forced merger of KPD and SPD in the Soviet zone of occupation.
SI	Socialist International
SPD	*Sozialdemokratische Partei Deutschlands*. Social Democratic Party of Germany. A party which predates the Federal Republic of Germany, but references to 'Social Democrats' in the main text are usually to the SPD in the Federal Republic.
START	Strategic Arms Reduction Talks, and subsequently treaty.
SZ	*Süddeutsche Zeitung*
TAZ	*Die Tageszeitung*
USSR	Union of Soviet Socialist Republics

VfZ	*Vierteljahrshefte für Zeitgeschichte*
WEU	Western European Union
ZAIG	*Zentrale Auswertungs- und Informationsgruppe*. The Central Evaluation and Information Group of the MfS.
ZPA	*Zentrales Parteiarchiv*. The Central Party Archive of the SED.

Unpublished Sources

Some of the most interesting, though least reliable, unpublished sources are people's memories, unpacked in conversation. Conversations with the author in connection with this book are cited in the Notes by name, place and date, thus: Helmut Kohl, Bonn, 1 October 1991; Erich Honecker, Berlin-Moabit, 27 November 1992, and so forth.

Obviously these memories, and those in published memoirs, often do not tally with papers produced at the time. Many of these are still unavailable. However, some important documents have already been published, while the following archival collections have been both accessible and useful. Only the main holdings consulted are listed. Abbreviations used in the Notes are given in brackets. Note that reference numbers are those in 1992. Particularly in the case of the East German records, they are quite likely to change.

Archiv für Christlich-Demokratische Politik (ACDP)
　Werner Marx papers (I–356)
　Alois Mertes papers (I–403)

Archiv des Deutschen Liberalismus (AdDL)
　Akten des Bundesvorsitzenden Walter Scheel
　Akten des Bundesvorsitzenden Hans-Dietrich Genscher (Bundesvorsitzender Genscher)
　Wolfgang Schollwer, *Tagebücher*, 1966–1970 (Schollwer *Tagebuch*)

Archiv der sozialen Demokratie (AdsD)
　Egon Bahr papers (Dep EB)
　　– Individual documents
　Depositum Willy Brandt (Dep WB)
　　– *Beruflicher Werdegang und politisches Wirken in Berlin, 1947–1966* (Rbm)
　　– *Bundesminister des Auswärtigen, 1966–1969* (BA)
　　– *Bundeskanzler und Bundesregierung, 1969–1974* (BK)
　　– *Publizistische Tätigkeit* (Publ)
　Helmut Schmidt papers (HS)
　　– *Person und Werk*
　　– *Gespräche*
　　– *Reisen*
　　– *Schriftwechsel*
　　– *Reden als Bundeskanzler*
　　– *Sacharchiv*
　Files are continuously numbered through the whole collection

Der Bundesbeauftragte für die Unterlagen des Staatssicherheitsdienstes der ehemaligen Deutschen Demokratischen Republik (The *Gauck-Behörde*)

Reports of the *Zentrale Auswertungs- und Informationsgruppe* (ZAIG)

Individual documents

Documents from the *Gauck-Behörde* are cited as MfS-and then the reference number, which is sometimes new and sometimes still the original.

Zentrales Parteiarchiv (ZPA)

Politburo internal archive, minutes and working papers (JIV 2/2, JIV 2/2A etc)

Central Committee records (IV 2/1)

Büro Axen (IV 2/2.035)

Büro Hager (IV B 2/2.024)

Büro Herrmann (IV 2/2.037)

Documents collected in the preparation of Baring, *Machtwechsel* (Baring Papers)

Short Titles

The following published works are cited in the Notes in a short title form. For ease of reference, documentary series and collections, memoirs, monographs and tracts are listed here in a single alphabetical sequence of short titles, together with full publication details. This is not a full bibliography. Guidance to further reading on individual subjects can be found in the Notes.

Apel, *Abstieg*: Hans Apel, *Der Abstieg. Politisches Tagebuch, 1978–1988* (Stuttgart: Deutsche Verlags-Anstalt, 1991)

Arndt, *Verträge*: Claus Arndt, *Die Verträge von Moskau und Warschau. Politische, verfassungsrechtliche und völkerrechtliche Aspekte* (2nd edition, Bonn: Verlag Neue Gesellschaft, 1982)

Aussiedler 1: Wilhelm Arnold, ed., *Die Aussiedler in der Bundesrepublik Deutschland. Forschungen der AWR Deutsche Sektion 1. Ergebnisbericht. Herkunft, Ausreise, Aufnahme* (Vienna: Wilhelm Braumüller, 1980 = Association for the Study of the World Refugee Problem, Treatises on Refugee Problems, Vol. XII/1)

Aussiedler 2: Hans Harmsen, ed., *Die Aussiedler in der Bundesrepublik Deutschland. Forschungen der AWR Deutsche Sektion. 2. Ergebnisbericht. Anpassung, Umstellung, Eingliederung* (Vienna: Wilhelm Braumüller, 1983 = Association for the Study of the World Refugee Problem, Treatises on Refugee Problems, Vol. XII/2).

Bahr, *Sicherheit*: Egon Bahr, *Sicherheit für und vor Deutschland. Vom Wandel durch Annäherung zur Europäischen Sicherheitsgemeinschaft* (Munich: Hanser, 1991)

Bahr, *Zum europäischen Frieden*: Egon Bahr, *Zum europäischen Frieden. Eine Antwort auf Gorbatschow* (Berlin: Corso bei Siedler, 1988)

Baring, *Anfang*: Arnulf Baring, *Im Anfang war Adenauer. Die Entstehung der Kanzlerdemokratie* (Munich: Deutscher Taschenbuch Verlag, 1971)

Baring, *Deutschland*: Arnulf Baring, *Deutschland, was nun? Ein Gespräch mit Dirk Rumberg und Wolf Jobst Siedler* (Berlin: Siedler, 1991)

Baring, *Grössenwahn*: Arnulf Baring, *Unser neuer Grössenwahn. Deutschland zwischen Ost und West* (Stuttgart: Deutsche Verlags-Anstalt, 1988)

Baring, *Machtwechsel*: Arnulf Baring, in Zusammenarbeit mit Manfred Görtemaker, *Machtwechsel. Die Ära Brandt-Scheel* (Stuttgart: Deutsche Verlags-Anstalt, 1982)

Bark & Gress, *Democracy and its Discontents*: Dennis L Bark & David R Gress, *Democracy and its Discontents, 1963–1988* (Oxford: Blackwell, 1989 = A History of West Germany Vol. 2)

Bender, *Neue Ostpolitik*: Peter Bender, *Neue Ostpolitik. Vom Mauerbau zum Moskauer Vertrag* (Munich: Deutscher Taschenbuch Verlag, 1986)

Benz & Graml, *Aspekte*: Benz, Wolfgang & Graml, Hermann, eds, *Aspekte der deutschen Aussenpolitik im 20. Jahrhundert. Aufsätze Hans Rothfels zum Gedächtnis* (Stuttgart: Deutsche Verlags-Anstalt, 1976)

Benz, *Vertreibung*: Wolfgang Benz, ed., *Die Vertreibung der Deutschen aus dem Osten. Ursachen, Ereignisse, Folgen* (Frankfurt: Fischer, 1985)

Bergedorfer Gesprächskreis: The privately circulated stenographic records of the series of high-level conferences organised by the Körber-Stiftung (Hamburg-Bergedorf), are cited here by the number and date of the conference. Thus *Bergerdorfer Gesprächskreis 97* (15–16 October 1992), is the record of the 97th conference, which took place on those days.

Bergsdorf, *Sprache*: Wolfgang Bergsdorf, *Herrschaft und Sprache. Studie zur politischen Terminologie der Bundesrepublik Deutschland* (Pfullingen: Neske, 1983)

Beschloss & Talbott, *Highest Levels*: Michael R Beschloss & Strobe Talbott, *At The Highest Levels. The Inside Story of the End of the Cold War* (New York: Little, Brown, 1993)

Besson, *Aussenpolitik*: Waldemar Besson, *Die Aussenpolitik der Bundesrepublik Deutschland. Erfahrungen und Massstäbe* (Munich: Piper, 1970)

Besuch: *Der Besuch von Generalsekretär Honecker in der Bundesrepublik Deutschland. Dokumentation zum Arbeitsbesuch des Generalsekretärs der SED und Staatsratsvorsitzenden der DDR, Erich Honecker, in der Bundesrepublik Deutschland im September 1987* (Bonn: Bundesministerium für innerdeutsche Beziehungen, 1988)

Bingen, *Bonn-Warschau*: Dieter Bingen, *Bonn-Warschau 1949–1988. Von der kontroversen Grenzfrage zur gemeinsamen europäischen Perspektive?* (Köln: Berichte des Bundesinstituts für ostwissenschaftliche und internationale Studien, 13–1988)

Birrenbach, *Sondermissionen*: Kurt Birrenbach, *Meine Sondermissionen. Rückblick auf zwei Jahrzehnte bundesdeutscher Aussenpolitik* (Düsseldorf: Econ, 1984)

Bismarck, *Reden*: Lothar Gall, ed., *Bismarck. Die grossen Reden* (Berlin: Severin & Siedler, 1981)

Böll, *Verantwortlich*: Heinrich Böll, Freimut Duve, Klaus Stäck, eds., *Verantwortlich für Polen?* (Reinbek: Rowohlt, 1982)

Bölling, *Die fernen Nachbarn*: Klaus Bölling, *Die fernen Nachbarn. Erfahrungen in der DDR* (Hamburg: Stern-Buch, 1983)

Brandt, *Erinnerungen*: Willy Brandt, *Erinnerungen* (Frankfurt: Propyläen, 1989)

Brandt, *People and Politics*: Willy Brandt, *People and Politics. The Years 1960–1975* (Boston: Little, Brown, 1978). A slightly abridged and edited version of the German original, *Begegnungen und Einsichten. Die Jahre 1960–1975* (Hamburg: Hoffmann & Campe, 1976).

Brandt, *Zusammen*: Willy Brandt, ". . . *was zusammengehört" Reden zu Deutschland* (Bonn: Dietz, 1990)

Broszat, *Polenpolitik*: Martin Broszat, *Zweihundert Jahre deutsche Polenpolitik* (Frankfurt: Suhrkamp, 1972)

Bruns, *DDR-Politik*: Wilhelm Bruns, *Von der Deutschlandpolitik zur DDR-Politik? Prämissen. Probleme. Perspektive* (Opladen: Leske & Budrich, 1989)

Bulletin: The *Bulletin* of the Federal Government's Press and Information Office (*Presse- und Informationsamt der Bundesregierung*), which reproduces a wide range of official speeches, lectures and statements, is here cited simply as *Bulletin*, with date and page reference.

Bundestag Drucksachen/Bundestag Plenarprotokolle: The reports of the West German parliamant (*Verhandlungen des Deutschen Bundestages*) are published in two series: the Plenary Protocols (*Plenarprotokolle*), which give a Hansard-like, stenographic record of the main parliamentary proceedings, and the Printed Matter (*Drucksachen*), which contains committee records, draft motions, reports and so forth. A reference to *Bundestag Plenarprotokolle* is a reference to the former, main series. These stenographic records are identified by electoral period (*Wahlperiode*), sitting (*Sitzung*), and date. We have slightly simplified the reference system, so that, for example, *Verhandlungen des Deutschen Bundestages. Plenarprotokolle.* — 6. Wahlperiode. — 59. Sitzung. Bonn, Mittwoch, den 17. Juni 1970, S.3269, becomes *Bundestag Plenarprotokolle*, 6/59, p.3269 (17 June 1970). *Drucksachen* are identified by electoral period and number: e.g. 10/914 means 10th electoral period/914th printed item.

Burleigh, *Ostforschung*: Michael Burleigh, *Germany Turns Eastwards. A Study of Ostforschung in the Third Reich* (Cambridge: Cambridge University Press, 1988)

Christians, *Wege*: F. Wilhelm Christians, *Wege nach Russland. Bankier im Spannungsfeld zwischen Ost und West* (Hamburg: Hoffmann & Campe, 1989)

Clemens, *Reluctant Realists*: Clay Clemens, *Reluctant Realists. The Christian Democrats and West German Ostpolitik* (Durham, NC: Duke University Press, 1989)

Cramer, *Bahr*: Dettmar Cramer, *Gefragt. Egon Bahr* (Bornheim: Dangmar Zirngibl-Verlag, 1975)

Davy, *Détente*: Richard Davy, ed., *European Détente. A Reappraisal* (London: Sage for the Royal Institute of International Affairs, 1992)

DDR-Reisebarometer: *DDR-Reisebarometer '88* (Munich: Infratest Kommunikationsforschung, 1989)

DDR Handbuch: Hartmut Zimmermann, ed., *DDR Handbuch* (3rd revised edition, Köln: Verlag Wissenschaft und Politik, 1985)

Deutschland 1989: The extraordinary twenty-five volumes of photocopies of media coverage of the events in Germany in 1989, produced in 1992 by the indefatigable archivists of the *Zentrales Dokumentationssystem* of the *Presse- und Informationsamt der Bundesregierung*, are cited here by short title and volume number.

Dokumente: *Dokumente zur Deutschlandpolitik*. Volumes of this magisterial documentation, published under the auspices of the *Bundesministerium für innerdeutsche Beziehungen* are cited by Series and Volume number. Thus *Dokumente*, IV/7, is Series IV, Volume 7. Series IV covers the period from 10 November 1958 to 30 November 1966, Series V from 1 December 1966 onward.

Dralle, *Deutsche*: Lothar Dralle, *Die Deutschen in Ostmittel-und Osteuropa. Ein Jahrtausend europäischer Geschichte* (Darmstadt: Wissenschaftliche Buchgesellschaft, 1991)

Ehmke, *Zwanzig Jahre*: Horst Ehmke, Karlheinz Koppe, Herbert Wehner, eds., *Zwanzig Jahre Ostpolitik. Bilanz und Perspektiven* (Bonn: Verlag Neue Gesellschaft, 1986)

Freedman, *Europe Transformed*: Lawrence Freedman, ed., *Europe Transformed. Documents on the End of the Cold War* (New York: St Martin's Press, 1990)

Fricke, *Opposition*: Karl Wilhelm Fricke, *Opposition und Widerstand in der DDR. Ein politischer Report* (Köln: Verlag Wissenschaft und Politik, 1984)

Fritsch-Bournazel, *Europa*: Renata Fritsch-Bournazel, *Europa und die deutsche Einheit* (Stuttgart: Bonn Aktuell, 1990)

Funke, *Demokratie und Diktatur*: Manfred Funke *et al.*, eds, *Demokratie und Diktatur. Geist und Gestalt politischer Herrschaft in Deutschland und Europa* (Bonn: Bundeszentrale für politische Bildung, 1987 = *Schriftenreihe der Bundeszentrale für politische Bildung*, Vol. 250

Garthoff, *Détente*: Raymond L Garthoff, *Détente and Confrontation* (Washington DC: Brookings Institution, 1985)

Garton Ash, *DDR*: Timothy Garton Ash, '*Und willst Du nicht mein Bruder sein . . .*' *Die DDR heute* (Reinbek: Rowohlt, 1981)

Garton Ash, *Solidarity*: Timothy Garton Ash, *The Polish Revolution. Solidarity* (2nd, revised edition, London: Granta Books, 1991)

Garton Ash, *Uses*: Timothy Garton Ash, *The Uses of Adversity. Essays on the Fate of Central Europe* (2nd, revised edition, London: Granta Books, 1991)

Garton Ash, *We*: Timothy Garton Ash, *We the People. The Revolution of '89 Witnessed in Warsaw, Budapest, Berlin & Prague* (London: Granta Books, 1991)

Gaus, *Deutschland*: Günter Gaus, *Wo Deutschland liegt. Eine Ortsbestimmung* (Hamburg: Hoffmann & Campe, 1983)

Geissel, *Unterhändler*: Ludwig Geissel, *Unterhändler der Menschlichkeit. Erinnerungen. Mit einem Begleitwort von Manfred Stolpe* (Stuttgart: Quell, 1991)

Genscher, *Unterwegs*: Hans-Dietrich Genscher, *Unterwegs zur Einheit. Reden und Dokumente aus bewegter Zeit* (Berlin: Siedler, 1991)

Gipfelgespräche: Michail Gorbatschow, *Gipfelgespräche. Geheime Protokolle aus meiner Amtszeit* (Berlin: Rowohlt, 1993)

Gorbachev, *Haus Europa*: Michail Gorbatschow, *Das gemeinsame Haus Europa und die Zukunft der Deutschen. Mit Beiträgen sowjetischer Wissenschaftler und Politiker* (Revised edition, Düsseldorf: Econ, 1990)

Gordon, *Eroding Empire*: Lincoln Gordon, ed., *Eroding Empire* (Washington DC: Brookings, 1987)

Grenville, *Treaties*: JAS Grenville and Bernard Wasserstein, *The Major International Treaties Since 1945. A History and Guide with Texts* (London: Methuen, 1987)

Grewe, *Rückblenden*: Wilhelm G Grewe, *Rückblenden. 1976–1951* (Frankfurt: Propyläen, 1979)

Griffith, *Ostpolitik*: William E Griffith, *The Ostpolitik of the Federal Republic of Germany* (Cambridge, Mass.: MIT Press, 1978)

Gromyko, *Memories*: Andrei Gromyko, *Memories* (London: Hutchinson, 1989). Translated and edited by Harold Shukman

Grosser, *Unification*: Dieter Grosser, ed., *German Unification. The Unexpected Challenge* (Oxford: Berg, 1992 = German Historical Perspectives, Vol. VII)

Haberl & Hecker, *Unfertige Nachbarschaften*: Othmar Nikola Haberl & Hans Hecker, eds, *Unfertige Nachbarschaften. Die Staaten Osteuropas und die Bundesrepublik Deutschland* (Essen: Reimar Hobbing, 1989)

Hacke, *Wege und Irrwege*: Christian Hacke, *Die Ost- und Deutschlandpolitik der CDU/CSU. Wege und Irrwege der Opposition seit 1969* (Köln: Verlag Wissenschaft und Politik, 1975)

Haftendorn, *Aussenpolitik*: Helga Haftendorn, Lothar Wilker, Claudia Wörmann, *Die Aussenpolitik der Bundesrepublik Deutschland* (Berlin: Wissenschaftlicher Autoren-Verlag, 1982)

Haftendorn, *Sicherheit*: Helga Haftendorn, *Sicherheit und Stabilität. Aussenbeziehungen der Bundesrepublik zwischen Ölkrise und Nato-Doppelbeschluss* (Munich: Deutscher Taschenbuch Verlag, 1986)

Haftendorn, *Verwaltete Aussenpolitik*: Helga Haftendorn & ors, eds, *Verwaltete Aussenpolitik. Sicherheits- und Entspannungspolitische Entscheidungsprozesse in Bonn* (Köln: Verlag Wissenschaft und Politik, 1978)

Hanrieder, *Germany, America, Europe*: Wolfram F Hanrieder, *Germany, America, Europe. Forty Years of German Foreign Policy* (New Haven: Yale University Press, 1989)

Hanson, *Western Economic Statecraft*: Philip Hanson, *Western Economic Statecraft in East-West Relations* (London: Routledge & Kegan Paul, 1988)

Heep, *Schmidt und Amerika*: Barbara D Heep, *Helmut Schmidt und Amerika. Eine schwierige Partnerschaft* (Bonn: Bouvier, 1990)

Hildebrand, *Von Erhard zur Grossen Koalition*: Klaus Hildebrand, *Von Erhard zur Grossen Koalition 1963–1969* (Stuttgart: Deutsche Verlags-Anstalt, 1984 = *Geschichte der Bundesrepublik Deutschland*, Vol 4)

Holzer, *Solidarität*: Jerzy Holzer, *"Solidarität" Die Geschichte einer freien Gewerkschaft in Polen* (Munich: Beck, 1985). Edited by Hans Henning Hahn.

Horn, *Erinnerungen*: Gyula Horn, *Freiheit, die ich meine. Erinnerungen des ungarischen Aussenministers, der den eisernen Vorhang öffnete* (Hamburg: Hoffmann & Campe, 1991)

Innerdeutsche Beziehungen: *Innerdeutsche Beziehungen. Die Entwicklung der Beziehungen zwischen der Bundesrepublik Deutschland und der Deutschen Demokratischen Republik 1980–1986. Eine Dokumentation* (Bonn: Bundesministerium für innerdeutsche Beziehungen, 1986)

Jacobsen, *Bonn-Warschau*: Hans-Adolf Jacobsen & Mieczysław Tomala, eds, *Bonn-Warschau, 1945–1991. Die deutsch-polnischen Beziehungen* (Köln: Verlag Wissenschaft und Politik, 1992)

Jacobsen, *Bundesrepublik-Volksrepublik*: Hans-Adolf Jacobsen, *Bundesrepublik Deutschland. Volksrepublik Polen. Bilanz der Beziehungen. Probleme und Perspektiven ihrer Normalisierung* (Frankfurt: Alfred Metzner, 1979)

Jacobsen, *Nachbarn*: Hans-Adolf Jacobsen, ed., *Misstrauische Nachbarn. Deutsche Ostpolitik 1919/1970. Dokumentation und Analyse* (Düsseldorf: Droste, 1970)

Jentleson, *Pipeline Politics*: Bruce W. Jentleson, *Pipeline Politics. The Complex Political Economy of East-West Trade* (Ithaca, NY: Cornell University Press, 1986)

Jesse & Mitter, *Einheit*: Eckhard Jesse & Armin Mitter, *Die Gestaltung der deutschen Einheit. Geschichte — Politik — Gesellschaft* (Bonn: Bundeszentrale für politische Bildung, 1992)

Kaiser, *Vereinigung*: Karl Kaiser, *Deutschlands Vereinigung. Die internationalen Aspekte. Mit den wichtigen Dokumenten* (Bergisch-Gladbach: Bastei-Lübbe, 1991)

Kissinger, *White House Years*: Henry Kissinger, *The White House Years* (London: Weidenfeld & Nicolson, 1979)

Kissinger, *Years of Upheaval*: Henry Kissinger, *Years of Upheaval* (London: Weidenfeld & Nicolson, 1982)

Koch, *Brandt*: Peter Koch, *Willy Brandt. Eine politische Biographie* (Bergisch Gladbach: Bastei Lübbe, 1989)

Kovrig, *Walls and Bridges*: Bennett Kovrig, *Of Walls and Bridges. The United States and Eastern Europe* (New York: New York University Press, 1991)

Kreile, *Osthandel*: Michael Kreile, *Osthandel und Ostpolitik* (Baden-Baden: Nomos, 1978)

KSZE Dokumentation: *Sicherheit und Zusammenarbeit in Europa. Dokumente zum KSZE-Prozess, einschliesslich der KVAE* (7th revised edition, Bonn: Auswärtiges Amt, 1990)

KSZE Dokumentation 1990/91: *Sicherheit und Zusammenarbeit in Europa. Dokumentation zum KSZE-Prozess 1990/91* (Bonn: Auswärtiges Amt, 1991)

Kuwaczka, *Entspannung von Unten*: Waldemar Kuwaczka, *Entspannung von Unten. Möglichkeiten und Grenzen des Deutsch-Polnischen Dialogs* (Stuttgart: Burg Verlag, 1988)

Lehmann, *Oder-Neisse*: Hans Georg Lehmann, *Der Oder-Neisse-Konflikt* (Munich: Beck, 1979)

Lehmann, *Öffnung*: Hans Georg Lehmann, *Öffnung nach Osten. Die Ostreisen Helmut Schmidts und die Entstehung der Ost- und Entspannungspolitik* (Bonn: Neue Gesellschaft, 1984)

Liesner, *Aussiedler*: Ernst Liesner, *Aussiedler. Die Voraussetzungen für die Anerkennung als Vertriebener. Arbeitshandbuch für Behörden, Gerichte und Verbände* (Herford: Maximilian-Verlag, 1988)

Link, *Ära Brandt*: Karl Dietrich Bracher, Wolfgang Jäger, Werner Link, *Republik im Wandel 1969–1974. Die Ära Brandt* (Stuttgart: Deutsche Verlags-Anstalt, 1986 = *Geschichte der Bundesrepublik Deutschland*, Vol. 5/I). Chapters on foreign policy by Werner Link.

Link, *Ära Schmidt*: Wolfgang Jäger, Werner Link, *Republik im Wandel 1974–1982. Die Ära Schmidt* (Stuttgart: Deutsche Verlags-Anstalt, 1987 = *Geschichte der Bundesrepublik Deutschland*, Vol. 5/II). Chapters on foreign policy by Werner Link.

Löwenthal, *Vom kalten Krieg*: Richard Löwenthal, *Vom kalten Krieg zur Ostpolitik* (Stuttgart: Seewald, 1974). Originally published as a chapter in Richard Löwenthal and Hans-Peter Schwarz, eds, *Die zweite Republik* (Stuttgart: Seewald, 1974)

Lutz, *Bahr*: Dieter S. Lutz, ed., *Das Undenkbare denken. Festschrift für Egon Bahr zum siebzigsten Geburtstag* (Baden-Baden: Nomos, 1992)

Maresca, *Helsinki*: John J. Maresca, *To Helsinki. The Conference on Security and Cooperation in Europe, 1973–1975* (New edition, Durham: Duke University Press, 1987)

Mastny, *Helsinki I*: Vojtech Mastny, *Helsinki, Human Rights and European Security. Analysis and Documentation* (Durham NC: Duke University Press, 1986)

Mastny, *Helsinki II*: Vojtech Mastny, *The Helsinki Process and the Reintegration of Europe, 1986–1991. Analysis and Documentation* (London: Pinter, 1992)

Mastny & Zielonka: Vojtech Mastny & Jan Zielonka, eds, *Human Rights and Security. Europe on the Eve of a New Era* (Boulder: Westview Press, 1991)

Materialien: *Materialien zum Bericht zur Lage der Nation im geteilten Deutschland 1987* (Bonn: Bundesministerium für innerdeutsche Beziehungen, 1987)

Meissner, *Deutsche Ostpolitik*: Boris Meissner, ed., *Die deutsche Ostpolitik 1961–1970. Kontinuität und Wandel. Eine Dokumentation* (Köln: Verlag Wissenschaft und Politik, 1970)

Meissner, *Moskau-Bonn*: Boris Meissner, ed., *Moskau-Bonn. Die Beziehungen zwischen der Sowjetunion und der Bundesrepublik Deutschland 1955–1973. Dokumentation* (Köln: Verlag Wissenschaft und Politik, 1975 = *Dokumente zur Aussenpolitik*, Vol. III/1 & 2)

Meuschel, *Legitimation*: Sigrid Meuschel, *Legitimation und Parteiherrschaft. Zum Paradox von Stabilität und Revolution in der DDR, 1945–1989* (Frankfurt: Suhrkamp, 1992)

Mittag, *Preis*: Günter Mittag, *Um jeden Preis. Im Spannungsfeld zweier Systeme* (Berlin: Aufbau, 1991)

Mitter & Wolle, *Lageberichte*: Armin Mitter & Stefan Wolle, eds, *'Ich liebe Euch doch alle!' Befehle und Lageberichte des MfS. January-November 1989* (Berlin: BasisDruck Verlagsgesellschaft, 1990)

Moreton, *Germany*: Edwina Moreton, ed., *Germany between East and West* (Cambridge: Cambridge University Press, 1987)

Morsey & Repgen, *Adenauer Studien III*: Rudolf Morsey & Konrad Repgen, eds, *Adenauer Studien. Bd. III. Untersuchungen und Dokumente zur Ostpolitik und Biographie* (Mainz: Matthias-Grünewald-Verlag, 1974)

Moseleit, *Zweite Phase*: Klaus Moseleit, *Die "Zweite" Phase der Entspannungspolitik der SPD, 1983–1989. Eine Analyse ihrer Entstehungsgeschichte, Entwicklung und der konzeptionellen Ansätze. Mit einem Vorwort von Willy Brandt* (Frankfurt: Peter Lang, 1991 = European University Studies, Series XXXI, Vol. 180)

Oberdorfer, *Turn*: Don Oberdorfer, *The Turn. How the Cold War came to an end. The United States and the Soviet Union, 1983–1990* (London: Jonathan Cape, 1992)

Pravda, *End*: Alex Pravda, ed., *The End of the Outer Empire. Soviet-East European Relations in Transition, 1985–90* (London: Sage for the Royal Institute of International Affairs, 1992)

Przybylski, *Tatort 1*: Peter Przybylski, *Tatort Politbüro. Die Akte Honecker* (Berlin: Rowohlt, 1991)

Przybylski, *Tatort 2*: Peter Przybylski, *Tatort Politbüro. Band 2. Honecker, Mittag und Schalck-Golodkowski* (Berlin: Rowohlt, 1992)

Rehlinger, *Freikauf*: Ludwig A Rehlinger, *Freikauf. Die Geschäfte der DDR mit politisch Verfolgten 1963–1989* (Berlin: Ullstein, 1991)

Reissmüller, *Vergessene Hälfte*: Johann-Georg Reissmüller, *Die vergessene Hälfte. Osteuropa und wir* (Munich: Langen Müller, 1986)

Schevardnadse, *Zukunft*: Eduard Schevardnadse, *Die Zukunft gehört der Freiheit* (Berlin: Rowohlt, 1991)

Schmid, *Entscheidung*: Günther Schmid, *Entscheidung in Bonn. Die Entstehung der Ost- und Deutschlandpolitik 1969/70* (Köln: Verlag Wissenschaft und Politik, 1979)

Schmid, *Politik*: Günther Schmid, *Politik des Ausverkaufs? Die Deutschlandpolitik der Regierung Brandt/Scheel* (Munich: tuduv, *1975*)

Schmidt, *Menschen und Mächte*: Helmut Schmidt, *Menschen und Mächte* (Berlin: Siedler, 1987)

Schmidt, *Nachbarn*: Helmut Schmidt, *Die Deutschen und ihre Nachbarn. Menschen und Mächte II* (Berlin: Siedler, 1990)

Schröder, *Bahr*: Karsten Schröder, *Egon Bahr* (Rastatt: Verlag Arthur Moewig, 1988)

Schulz-Vobach, *Die Deutschen im Osten*: Klaus-Dieter Schulz-Vobach, *Die Deutschen im Osten. Vom Balkan bis Sibirien* (Hamburg: Hoffmann & Campe, 1989)

Schwarz, *Adenauer I*: Hans-Peter Schwarz, *Adenauer. Der Aufstieg: 1876–1952* (Stuttgart: Deutsche Verlags-Anstalt, 1986)

Schwarz, *Adenauer II*: Hans-Peter Schwarz, *Adenauer. Der Staatsmann: 1952–1967* (Stuttgart: Deutsche Verlags-Anstalt, 1991)

Schwarz, *Gezähmten Deutschen*: Hans-Peter Schwarz, *Die gezähmten Deutschen. Von der Machtbesessenheit zur Machtvergessenheit* (Stuttgart: Deutsche Verlags-Anstalt, 1985)

Schweigler, *Grundlagen*: Gebhard Schweigler, *Grundlagen der aussenpolitischen Orientierung der Bundesrepublik Deutschland. Rahmenbedingungen, Motive, Einstellungen* (Baden-Baden: Nomos, 1985)

Siebenmorgen, *Gezeitenwechsel*: Peter Siebenmorgen, *Gezeitenwechsel. Aufbruch zur Entspannungspolitik* (Bonn: Bouvier, 1990)

Spangenberg, *Mitteleuropa*: Dietrich Spangenberg, ed., *Die blockierte Vergangenheit. Nachdenken über Mitteleuropa* (Berlin: Argon, 1987)

Stares, *New Germany*: Paul B Stares, ed., *The New Germany and the New Europe* (Washington DC: Brookings, 1992)

Stent, *Embargo to Ostpolitik*: Angela Stent, *From Embargo to Ostpolitik. The Political Economy of West German-Soviet Relations 1955–1980* (Cambridge: Cambridge University Press, 1981)

Stern, *Brandt*: Carola Stern, *Willy Brandt* (Hamburg: Rowohlt, 1988)

Stökl, *Osteuropa*: Günther Stökl, *Osteuropa und die Deutschen* (3rd revised edition, Stuttgart: S. Hirzel Verlag, 1982)

Strauss, *Erinnerungen*: Franz Josef Strauss, *Die Erinnerungen* (Berlin: Siedler, 1989)

Szabo, *Diplomacy*: Stephen F Szabo, *The Diplomacy of German Unification* (New York: St Martin's Press, 1992)

Teltschik, *329 Tage*: Horst Teltschik, *329 Tage. Innenansichten der Einigung* (Berlin: Siedler, 1991)

Texte: *Texte zur Deutschlandpolitik.* Published, like the *Dokumente zur Deutschlandpolitik*, under the auspices of the *Bundesministerium für innerdeutsche Beziehungen*, the *Texte* are also cited by series and volume number. Series I covers the period 13 December 1966–20 June 1973; Series II, 22 June 1973–1 October 1982; Series III, 13 October 1982–31 December 1990.

Umbruch: *Umbruch in Europa. Die Ereignisse im 2. Halbjahr 1989. Eine Dokumentation* (Bonn: Auswärtiges Amt, 1990)

Uschner, *Ostpolitik*: Manfred Uschner, *Die Ostpolitik der SPD. Sieg und Niederlage einer Strategie* (Berlin: Dietz, 1991)

Van Oudenaren, *Détente*: John Van Oudenaren, *Détente in Europe. The Soviet Union and the West since 1953* (Durham NC: Duke University Press, 1991)

Verträge: *Dokumentation zur Ostpolitik der Bundesregierung. Verträge und Vereinbarungen* (11th edition, Bonn: Presse- und Informationsamt der Bundesregierung, 1986)

Vierzig Jahre: Auswärtiges Amt, *40 Jahre Aussenpolitik der Bundesrepublik Deutschland. Eine Dokumentation* (Stuttgart: Bonn Aktuell, 1989)

Volle & Wagner, *KSZE*: Hermann Volle & Wolfgang Wagner, eds, *KSZE. Konferenz über Sicherheit und Zusammenarbeit in Europa in Beiträgen und Dokumenten aus dem Europa-Archiv* (Bonn: Verlag für Internationale Politik, 1976)

Weber, *DDR* (1988): Hermann Weber, *Die DDR 1945–1986* (Munich: Oldenbourg, 1988 = *Oldenbourg-Grundriss der Geschichte* Vol. 20)

Weber, *DDR* (1991): Hermann Weber, *DDR. Grundriss der Geschichte. 1945–1990* (new edition, Hannover: Fackelträger, 1976)

Weber, *Links*: Hermann Weber, *Das Prinzip Links. Beiträge zur Diskussion des demokratischen Sozialismus in Deutschland, 1848–1990. Eine Dokumentation* (Berlin: Ch. Links, 1991)

Weizsäcker, *Deutsche Geschichte*: Richard von Weizsäcker, *Die deutsche Geschichte geht weiter* (Berlin: Siedler, 1983)

Wiskemann, *Eastern Neighbours*: Elizabeth Wiskemann, *Germany's Eastern Neighbours. Problems Relating to the Oder-Neisse Line and the Czech Frontier Regions* (London: Oxford University Press for the Royal Institute of International Affairs, 1956)

Witte, *Kulturpolitik*: Barthold C Witte, *Dialog über Grenzen. Beiträge zur auswärtigen Kulturpolitik* (Pfullingen: Neske, 1988)

Wörmann, *Osthandel*: Claudia Wörmann, *Der Osthandel der Bundesrepublik*

Deutschland. Politische Rahmenbedingungen und ökonomische Bedeutung (Frankfurt: Campus, 1982)

Wörmann, *Problem*: Claudia Wörmann, *Osthandel als Problem der Atlantischen Allianz. Erfahrungen aus dem Erdgas-Röhren-Geschäft mit der UdSSR* (Bonn: Forschungsinstitut der Deutschen Gesellschaft für Auswärtige Politik, 1986 = *Arbeitspapiere zur internationalen Politik*, 38)

Zahlenspiegel: Zahlenspiegel. *Bundesrepublik Deutschland/Deutsche Demokratische Republik: Ein Vergleich* (3rd revised edition, Bonn: Bundesministerium für innerdeutsche Beziehungen, 1988)

Zehn Jahre: *Zehn Jahre Deutschlandpolitik. Die Entwicklungen der Beziehungen zwischen der Bundesrepublik Deutschland und der Deutschen Demokratischen Republik 1969–1979. Bericht und Dokumentation* (Bonn: Bundesministerium für innerdeutsche Beziehungen, 1980)

Zernack, *Osteuropa*: Klaus Zernack, *Osteuropa. Eine Einführung in seine Geschichte* (Munich: Beck, 1977)

Zündorf, *Ostverträge*: Benno Zündorf, *Die Ostverträge. Die Verträge von Moskau, Warschau, Prag, das Berlin-Abkommen und die Verträge mit der DDR* (Munich: Beck, 1979). Benno Zündorf is a pseudonym for Antonius Eitel.

Notes

Prologue: European Question

...**West Central Europe**... The distinction between East Central and West Central Europe was made by, among others, Oskar Halecki in Chapter VII of his *The Limits and Divisions of European History* (London: Sheed & Ward, 1950). East Central Europe was, he argued, 'inhabited by a great variety of ethnic and linguistic groups in contradistinction to the homogeneously German West-Central Europe', ibid., p. 127. But see also critical remarks by Philip Longworth in *The Slavonic and East European Review*, Vol. 65, No. 3, July 1987, pp. 422–29, the excellent discussion in Zernack, *Osteuropa*, Werner Conze, *Ostmitteleuropa. Von der Spätantike bis zum 18. Jahrhundert* (Munich: Beck, 1992), edited by Klaus Zernack, and Winfried Eberhard & ors, eds, *Westmitteleuropa-Ostmitteleuropa. Festschrift für Ferdinand Seibt* (Munich: Oldenbourg, 1992).

In the context of 'Yalta' Europe, we have used the term West Central Europe to refer mainly to West Germany and Austria; East Central Europe refers mainly to Poland, Hungary and Czechoslovakia. East Germany was obviously a special case.

The terms Eastern and Western Europe, East European and West European, are used in the sense of the 'Yalta' political shorthand, as discussed in this Prologue. The Epilogue considers the cacophony of usages after 1989.

...**arguing that it had brought peace and stability**... An attitude that provoked the following observation from the distinguished British historian of Central and Eastern Europe, Hugh Seton-Watson, in one of the last texts he wrote. Having asserted that the peoples of 'the eastern half of Europe' would not reconcile themselves to the division of Europe, he continued: 'My last sentence probably suffices to damn me in many minds as a "cold warrior". But all that I have done is to state in simple words the basic fact of which forty years of study have convinced me. Yet such has been the impact of propaganda, counter-propaganda, and disinformation that in the minds of hundreds of thousands of enlightened Western men and women, firmly devoted to freedom in their own countries, the present division of Europe has acquired a sanctity which they will fanatically justify; and to say that this division is permanently unacceptable for more than a hundred million Europeans, and will not last, is seen by them as tantamount to preaching nuclear war.' The eleventh Martin Wight lecture, Royal Institute of International Affairs, reprinted as 'What is Europe, Where is Europe?'

in *Encounter*, July/August 1985, this quotation on p. 14, and in George Schöplin & Nancy Wood, eds, *In Search of Central Europe* (Oxford: Polity Press, 1989), pp. 30–46, quotation on p. 41.

'The peace of Europe . . .' This was Günter Gaus, a leading political commentator close to the Social Democrats, and appointed by the Brandt government to be West Germany's first Permanent Representative in the GDR. See Gaus, *Deutschland* p. 283. At a seminar at the Free University in Berlin on 4 February 1987, Gaus said simply: 'the Yalta system is the guarantee of peace in Europe' (author's notes).

More diplomatic versions . . . a lucid analytical presentation of the argument was A W de Porte's *Europe between the Superpowers. The Enduring Balance* (2nd edition, New Haven: Yale University Press, 1986). The first edition was completed in 1978. The jacket of the second edition observes that the author contributed a new Preface 'noting how recent developments have confirmed the book's thesis that the Atlantic alliance system and the division of Europe between East and West are likely to survive indefinitely'.

'under which we've lived quite happily . . .' The *Independent*, 22 December 1989 (interview with the author).

'We deplore the division . . .' quoted in *The Times*, 4 May 1985, p. 5.

. . . a 'Prague Appeal' . . . Charter 77 document 5/1985, reprinted in the journal *East European Reporter* (London), Vol. 1, No. 1, Spring 1985, pp. 27–28.

'the goal of Europeans . . .' quoted in *KOS* (Warsaw), No. 14 (144), 18 September 1988.

Even before he became Party leader . . . Gorbachev seems first to have used the image in his remarks to a group of parliamentarians during his visit to Britain in December 1984, three months before he became Party leader. See the text in *Pravda*, 19 December 1984, English in *Current Digest of the Soviet Press*, Vol. XXXVI, No. 51, esp. p. 4. I owe this reference to a typescript by Ernst Kux on Gorbachev and the Common European Home.

. . . used by Brezhnev . . . 'Whatever divides us, Europe remains our common home,' *Bulletin*, 26 November 1981, p. 966. Writing in *Osteuropa*, 8/1991, p. 352, Fred Oldenburg attributes the coinage to Andrei Alexandrov-Agentov, a leading foreign policy aide to Brezhnev and to Gorbachev in his first years in office.

'This metaphor,' Gorbachev writes in his book *Perestroika*, 'came to my mind in one of my discussions. Although seemingly I voiced it in passing, in my mind I had been looking for such a formula for a long time.' *Perestroika. New Thinking for Our Country and the World* (London: Collins, 1987) p. 194. Clearly great minds think alike.

This Declaration stated . . . see *Bulletin*, 15 June 1989, p. 542.

. . . the Russian text . . . see *Pravda*, 14 June 1989.

Soviet commentators . . . see for example the interesting commentary by V. Zhurkin in *Pravda*, 17 May 1989, which offered the following definition of the common European home: 'It is a new system of security and co-operation growing out of the all-European process and extending it, a system based on gradually eliminating the military-political and economic division of Europe and replacing it with effective and mutually beneficial forms of co-existence among states with different social systems . . .' Quoted from *Current Digest of the Soviet Press*, vol. XLI, No. 22, 1989, p. 15. Zhurkin was the head of a newly formed Institute of Europe, which itself symbolised this new approach. Vitaly Zhurkin, Moscow, 7 February 1992.

. . . 'a relic of the Cold War' . . . this comment came from Vyacheslav Dashitchev, a maverick but, as it proved, vanguard Soviet specialist on Germany, as early as June 1988. See the report in *FAZ*, 8 June 1988, p. 1, and summary of the ensuing controversy in the *Monatsbericht* of the Bundesanstalt für gesamtdeutsche Fragen for June 1988.

. . . different 'social systems' . . . even Dashitchev could aver in an interview in *Der Spiegel*, 27/1988, that socialism had established deep roots in Eastern Europe. See also the commentary by Zhurkin quoted above.

. . . 'I know that many in the West . . .' Russian text in *Pravda*, 7 July 1989, pp. 1–2. English in *Current Digest of the Soviet Press*, Vol. XLI, No. 27, 1989, p. 6.

. . . 'Let Europe be whole and free.' . . . this and following quotations are from the text reprinted in Freedman, *Europe Transformed*, pp. 289–94.

. . . he went on to underline this message . . . see the authoritative account by the former Deputy Assistant Secretary of State responsible for relations with the Soviet Union and Eastern Europe, Thomas W Simons, *The End of the Cold War?* (New York: St Martin's Press, 1990), p. 155 f. Simons suggests that there was basic agreement between the two Presidents on the need to end the division of Europe. See also Oberdorfer, *Turn*.

In events which, taken together . . . see the account in Garton Ash, *We*, p. 20 and *passim*, and Ralf Dahrendorf, *Reflections on the Revolution in Europe* (London: Chatto & Windus, 1990), esp. p. 5 ff. François Furet, the distinguished historian of the French Revolution, has argued that the events of 1989 cannot be described as a 'revolution' in the same sense as the French Revolution of 1789 or the Russian Revolution of 1917, both because of the decisive importance of the external factor — Gorbachev and Soviet policy — and because no new ideas were brought to power by these revolutions. In this sense, intellectually, they could even be described as 'counter-revolution', since they aimed to sweep away all traces of the heritage of the Russian October revolution, and restore or imitate the existing liberal capitalist order. See his article in *Politische Studien*, No. 318/1991. Yet this was an extraordinarily swift and sweeping removal of an *ancien régime* in six countries, which changed the political map of Europe out of recognition, and paved the way for the end of Communism in the Soviet Union itself.

. . . faster and farther . . . It is extremely difficult to say what exactly Gorbachev and his closest associates hoped for or expected, particularly since they may not themselves have had a very clear idea at the time, and certainly see things slightly differently with hindsight. For more discussion on this very important point see p. 123 f.

... refused all siren calls ... see Schewardnadse, *Zukunft*, pp. 215–17. In English, Eduard Shevardnadze, *The Future belongs to Freedom*. (London: Sinclair-Stevenson, 1991)

'We now have the Frank Sinatra Doctrine ...' quoted by Michael Simmons in the *Guardian*, 26 October 1989, p. 8.

'No more let us falter!' ... see *Foreign Relations of the United States. The Conferences at Malta and Yalta* (Westport: Greenwood Press, 1976, reprint of 1st edition of 1955), p. 26.

'The post-war split ...' quoted from BBC, Summary of World Broadcasts, SU/0652, B/I, 3 January 1990.

... 'the iron curtain' ... Churchill's classic description of the 'iron curtain' in his 1946 Fulton speech had it running 'from Stettin in the Baltic to Trieste in the Adriatic ...', quoted in Martin Gilbert, *Never Despair* (London: Heinemann, 1988), p. 200. In practice, after the creation of East Germany, the Soviet split with Yugoslavia, and the Austrian State Treaty, the line ran from Pötenitz on the Baltic to Rezovo on the Black Sea.

... the European question ... two earlier usages of the term may be of interest here. AJP Taylor concluded the Introduction to his *The Struggle for Mastery in Europe. 1848–1914* (Oxford: Clarendon Press, 1954) with the observation (p. xxxvi) that following the First World War the traditional Balance of Power was not restored and 'Henceforward, what had been the centre of the world became merely "the European question".' In his *Pan-Europa*, Richard Coudenhove-Kalergi wrote: 'The European question is: "Can Europe, in its political and economic fragmentation, preserve its peace and autonomy against the growing extra-European world powers — or is it compelled to organise itself into a state-federation (*Staatenbund*) to save its existence?"', Richard N. Coudenhove-Kalergi, *Pan-Europa* (Vienna: Pan-Europa-Verlag, 1923), p. IX.

Mitterrand ... 'sortir de Yalta' ... see *Le Monde*, 2 January 1982. See also his elegantly non-committal comments in François Mitterrand, *Réflexions sur la Politique Extérieure de la France* (Paris: Fayard, 1986), pp. 68–70.

When Zbigniew Brzezinski ... Zbigniew Brzezinski, 'The Future of Yalta', *Foreign Affairs*, Vol. 63, No. 2, Winter 1984/85, pp. 279–302.

... usually in the forms 'post-Yalta' or 'anti-Yalta' ... See, for example, the first chapter of György Konrád's *Antipolitics* (London: Quartet, 1984), entitled 'Peace: Anti-Yalta'; Ferenc Fehér, 'Eastern Europe's Long Revolution Against Yalta', *East European Politics and Societies* (EEPS), Vol. 2, No. 1, Winter 1988, pp. 1–34; Barbara Toruńczyk, 'Kings and Spirits in the East European Tales' in *Cross Currents*, No. 7, esp. pp. 185, 187, 205; and the East European contributions in Initiative Ost-West-Dialog, ed., *Frieden im geteilten Europa 40 Jahre nach Jalta* (Dokumentation eines Diskussions-Forums in Berlin, Februar 1985). Many more examples can be found in Polish, Hungarian and Czech independent publications.

... **earlier political-military decisions** ... on this, see the author's review articles in the *New York Review of Books*, 7 May and 11 June 1987. A good starting point for this whole subject is now Robin Edmonds, *The Big Three. Churchill, Roosevelt and Stalin in Peace and War* (London: Hamish Hamilton, 1991). On the importance of Tehran see Keith Sainsbury, *The Turning Point* (Oxford: Oxford University Press, 1986).

... **Hajo Holborn** ... Hajo Holborn, *The Political Collapse of Europe* (New York: Knopf, 1951).

... **assertions about Western failures over Yalta** ... see the discussion in Theodore Draper, 'Neoconservative History', *New York Review of Books*, 16 January 1986, and the ensuing controversy.

... **Rolf Steininger's influential book** ... Rolf Steininger, *Eine vertane Chance. Die Stalin-Note vom 10. Marz und die Wiedervereinigung* (Bonn: Dietz, 1985), which is actually a paperback edition of the introduction to a larger documentation. This smaller volume went through three editions in five years. An English translation, with a selection of the most important documents, has been published as *The German Question. The Stalin Note of 1952 and the Problem of Reunification* (New York: Columbia University Press, 1990). For further reading on this controversy see Notes to p. 48.

... **'a Germany ... such as Stalin offered in 1952'** ... ibid., p. 128.

John Lewis Gaddis observed ... John Lewis Gaddis, *Strategies of Containment. A Critical Appraisal of Postwar American National Security Policy* (Oxford: Oxford University Press, 1982), p. 354.

... **Bernhard Friedmann** ... Friedmann's proposal was originally proffered as the basis for a discussion in the CDU/CSU parliamentary party about Deutschlandpolitik and security policy, see his *Thesenpapier. Die Wiedervereinigung der Deutschen als Sicherheitskonzept* (Typescript, dated 16 May 1987) and the attached covering letter to the parliamentary leader of the CDU/CSU, Alfred Dregger, of the same date, where he suggests that the paper was written at Dregger's request. Friedmann subsequently developed his ideas into a book, pregnantly entitled 'Unity instead of Missiles': *Einheit statt Raketen* (Herford: BusseSeewald, 1987), which also reprints the original memorandum on pp. 145–52. In his Introduction he makes it clear that the catalyst for his proposal was the Reagan-Gorbachev summit meeting in Reykjavik in October 1986, with its dramatic suggestion of total nuclear disarmament. What he makes less clear is the significance of the proposal in the internal debate about Deutschlandpolitik and security policy inside the CDU and CSU, with himself belonging to a conservative nationalist minority tendency led by the original addressee, Alfred Dregger, and irreverently described — by its opponents — as the 'Stahlhelm fraction'.

... **Wilhelm Grewe** ... reader's letter entitled 'Alte Hüte in wölkiger Drapierung', *FAZ*, 5 June 1987.

... **the way in which the division was completed, sealed and acknowledged** ... a useful, if not wholly persuasive account is given by Wilfried Loth, *The Division of the World* (London: Routledge, 1988).

'The United States and its allies . . .' quoted in a report by John M. Goshko in the *International Herald Tribune*, 9 September 1985. In a speech about US policy to Central and Eastern Europe delivered to the Austrian Association for Foreign Policy and International Relations in Vienna on 21 September 1983 the then Vice-President George Bush went so far as to call it 'this fictitious division'.

. . . the Treaty of Trianon . . . It will be recalled that the 1920 Treaty of Trianon, part of the post-war peace settlement whose main architects were Woodrow Wilson, Clemenceau and Lloyd George, stripped Hungary of more than two-thirds of its pre-1914 territory, including the Slovakia in what then became Czechoslovakia; Transylvania, which went to Romania; and Croatia, to what then became Yugoslavia.

. . . many attempts have been made . . . on this see Zernack, *Osteuropa*.

. . . those of Charlemagne's empire . . . see the map in William Wallace, *The Transformation of Western Europe* (London: Royal Institute of International Affairs, 1990), p. 16.

. . . economic historians have argued . . . see, for example, the important essay by Jenő Szűcs, 'Three Historical Regions of Europe', reprinted in John Keane, ed., *Civil Society and the State. New European Perspectives* (London: Verso, 1988), pp. 291–332. But see also Péter Hanák, 'Central Europe: A Historical Region in Modern Times' in George Schöpflin and Nancy Wood, eds, *In Search of Central Europe* (Oxford: Polity Press, 1989), pp. 57–70, and the detailed discussion in Daniel Chirot, ed., *The Origins of Backwardness in Eastern Europe. Economics and Politics from the Middle Ages until the early Twentieth Century* (Berkeley: University of California Press, 1989). Piotr Wandycz, *The Price of Freedom. A History of East Central Europe from the Middle Ages to the Present* (London: Routledge, 1992), argues persuasively that it makes most sense to think in terms of 'centre' and 'periphery' rather than developed West and backward East.

. . . running far to the east of the Yalta line . . . see the map in William Wallace, *The Transformation of Western Europe* (London: Royal Institute of International Affairs, 1990), p. 18.

. . . lines . . . finally agreed . . . See Tony Sharp, *The Wartime Alliance and the Zonal Division of Germany* (Oxford: Clarendon Press, 1975), p. 203. For a description of the lines dividing Berlin and Germany, as they appeared in the 1980s, see Garton Ash, *DDR*, Chapter 2; Anthony Bailey, *Along the Edge of the Forest. An Iron Curtain Journey* (New York: Random House, 1983); *Die innerdeutsche Grenze* (Bonn: Bundesministerium für innerdeutsche Beziehungen, 1987).

According to Western specialists . . . quoted in Adam Bromke, *Eastern Europe in the Aftermath of Solidarity* (New York: Columbia University Press, 1985), p. 22.

When Czech, Hungarian and Polish intellectuals . . . see Garton Ash, *Uses*, especially the essay entitled 'Does Central Europe Exist?'; George Schöpflin & Nancy Wood, eds, *In Search of Central Europe* (Oxford: Polity Press, 1989); and the special issue of *Daedalus*, Winter 1990, entitled 'Eastern Europe . . . Central

Europe . . . Europe', republished as Stephen Graubard, ed., *Eastern Europe . . . Central Europe . . . Europe* (Boulder: Westview Press, 1991).

. . . the Trabant and *soljanka* . . . for future generations one should perhaps record that the Trabant was a tiny motor-car produced in the GDR, with a noxious two-stroke engine, while *soljanka* was an East German version of a Ukrainian peasant soup.

. . . a matter of the hottest dispute . . . The development of the dispute was also the development of a dialogue between parts of the West European peace movement and parts of the democratic opposition in Eastern Europe. This could be followed in the journals, occasional papers and pamphlets of such groups as European Nuclear Disarmament (END), the Dutch Inter-Church Peace Council (IKV), and the West Berlin-based Network for East-West Dialogue. The East European side of the debate is well-documented in such journals as *L'Alternative* (Paris, 1979–85) — subsequently relaunched as *La Nouvelle Alternative* — and the *East European Reporter* (London, 1985–   ).

. . . more need for change in Eastern than in Western Europe . . . A fairly characteristic and grudging admission of this asymmetry, from one of the most eloquent exponents of the 'symmetry' thesis, came in EP Thompson's 1984 essay on 'The Two Sides of Yalta'. 'The Soviet and American presences in Europe have of course been of a different order,' he wrote. 'If we leave aside the case of Greece (1945–50) the United States' presence has not imposed regimes of its choice by military force. But while operating in a different mode and under different constraints, it has been an immensely powerful and distorting presence nonetheless.' Quoted from EP Thompson, *The Heavy Dancers* (London: Merlin Press, 1985), p. 175.

Needless to say, the overwhelming emphasis in his own extensive and rich pamphleteering work, and in the statements of the European Nuclear Disarmament (END) movement, was on the symmetry rather than the asymmetry. Thus END's response to the imposition of martial law in Poland in December 1981 was a statement of protest reprinted in the movement's journal with an interpretative gloss saying that 'along with Italy (1948), Hungary (1956), Greece (1967), Czechoslovakia (1968), Turkey (1980), it [i.e. the coup in Poland] demonstrates the limits of independent political development for European countries within the framework of military blocs'. See *END Bulletin*, No. 8, Spring 1982, p. 8. Thompson himself described the effects of the original Cold War as follows: 'Those who worked for freedom in the East were suspected or exposed as agents of Western imperialism. Those who worked for peace in the West were suspected or exposed as pro-Soviet "fellow-travellers" or dupes of the Kremlin. In this way the rival ideologies of the Cold War disarmed those, on both sides, who might have put Europe back together', quoted from his lecture 'Beyond the Cold War', reprinted in *Zero Option* (London: Merlin Press, 1982), p. 160.

The original END appeal of April 1980 declared that 'The powers of the military and of internal security forces are enlarged, limitations are placed upon free exchanges of ideas and between persons, and civil rights of independent-minded individuals are threatened, in the West as well as the East. We do not wish to apportion guilt between the political and military leaders of East and

West. Guilt lies squarely upon both parties', quoted from E. P. Thompson & Dan Smith eds, *Protest and Survive* (London: Penguin, 1980), p. 224

Petra Kelly, one of the best known figures among the West German Greens, applied the argument specifically to Germany: 'To people who advise us to "Go East, if you don't like it here," we say East German principles apply in our country too. There is minimal provision for the poor and less and less of an opportunity to speak out. The system is the same; the differences are only of degree', quoted from Petra Kelly, *Fighting for Hope* (Boston, Mass.: South End Press, 1984), p. 14.

... the position of West European states vis-à-vis the United States ...
Again, the clearest and most eloquent statements in English came from E P Thompson, see the three books mentioned above, and the collection of essays by Thompson and others entitled *Exterminism and Cold War* (London: Verso, 1982). One might also mentioned the extraordinary remark of the playwright Harold Pinter, speaking in 1988: 'It seems to me that we [i.e. Britain] are as much a satellite of the USA as Czechoslovakia was (sic) of Russia.' Quoted in the *Independent*, 18 October 1988.

... the more independent East European states became from the Soviet Union ... An emphatic statement of this view could be found in Peter Bender's stimulating and influential book, *Das Ende des ideologischen Zeitalters. Die Europäisierung Europas* (Berlin: Severin & Siedler, 1981). Bender wrote: Eastern Europe cannot emancipate itself from the Soviet Union unless Western Europe emancipates itself from the USA—like the forces so also the losses must remain in balance' (p. 260). Of course the basic idea can be traced back to the disengagement proposals of the 1950s, and even more directly to de Gaulle's proposals of the mid-1960s, see the concise summary by Pierre Hassner in Gordon, *Eroding Empire*, p. 196.

... 'in the second half of the 1980s ...' 'Europa muss sich selbst behaupten,' in *Die Zeit*, 28 November 1986.

Independent intellectuals and opposition activists in Eastern Europe, by contrast, ... The most eloquent and thoughtful exposition of the position summarised in these two paragraphs is that of Václav Havel in his 1985 essay 'The Anatomy of a Reticence', published as a pamphlet by the Charta 77 Foundation, Stockholm, as the first in their series 'Voices from Czechoslovakia', and reprinted in Jan Vladislav, ed., *Václav Havel or Living in Truth* (London: Faber, 1987), pp. 164–95. Among many other contributions to this debate see, for example, the response of the Hungarian philosopher and leading opposition activist János Kis to Charter 77's 'Prague Appeal' [see note below], reprinted in the *East European Reporter*, Vol. 1, No. 4, Winter 1986, pp. 52–56; the Polish contributions to Initiative Ost-West Dialog, ed., *Frieden im geteilten Europa 40 Jahre nach Jalta* (Dokumentation eines Diskussions-Forums in Berlin, Februar 1985); the Czechoslovak essays collected in Jan Kavan and Zdena Tomin, eds, *Voices from Prague. Czechoslovakia, Human Rights and the Peace Movement* (London: END & Palach Press, 1983); and the article by the Yugoslav philosopher Mihailo Marković 'On peace and human rights' in *END Journal* No. 12, Oct-Nov 1984.

... these East Europeans said: Europe has not been at peace since 1945 ... The classic statement is the 'Prague Appeal' of Charter 77, launched in March 1985. Charter 77 Document No. 5/85, reprinted in the *East European Reporter*, Vol. 1, No. 1, Spring 1985, pp. 27–28. There also the formulation 'a state of non-war'.

'Without internal peace ...' Jan Vladislav, ed., *Václav Havel or Living in Truth* (London: Faber, 1987), p. 187.

... the contrasting positions ... A serious attempt to map out common ground, under the general motto of 'détente from below', was the memorandum 'Giving real life to the Helsinki Accords', co-ordinated and published by the European Network for East-West Dialogue in November 1986, and reprinted in the *East European Reporter*, Vol. 2, No. 2, pp. 52–60.

Chapter I: German Answers

... a long line of German historians ... a few are mentioned by Harold James in his *A German Identity 1770–1990* (London: Weidenfeld & Nicolson, 1989), p. 211. See also Renata Fritsch-Bournazel, *Confronting the German Question. Germans on the East-West Divide* (Oxford: Berg, 1988), esp. p. 76 f. The book was originally published in German under the title *Das Land in der Mitte. Die Deutschen im europäischen Kräftefeld.* (Munich: iudicium Verlag, 1986). A representative and influential contemporary statement of the argument can be found in the work of the conservative historian Michael Stürmer, see for example his *Dissonanzen des Fortschritts. Essays über Geschichte und Politik in Deutschland* (Munich: Piper, 1986). Andreas Hillgruber, in his *Zweierlei Untergang. Die Zerschlagung des Deutschen Reiches und das Ende des europäischen Judentums* (Berlin: Siedler, 1986), a book which played some part in the German 'historians' debate' (*Historikerstreit*) of the late 1980s, refers at one point (p. 25) to 'the events [i.e. the Second World War], that would bring the German Reich *and thus the European centre* to an end ...' (my italics). An academically partisan but stimulating discussion of the 'centre' as a historical category is given by Immanuel Geiss in *Zeitschrift für Geschichtswissenschaft*, 10/1991, pp. 979–94.

... Polish historians ... see Norman Davies, *God's Playground. A History of Poland*, Volume 1 (Oxford: Clarendon Press, 1981), p. 23 ff and references.

... 'the heart of Europe' ... Renata Fritsch-Bournazel traces the use of this metaphor for Germany back to Madame de Staël's famous book of 1810, see Fritsch-Bournazel, *Europa*, p. 171. As we shall see (below, p. 75), in his negotiations with Gromyko, Egon Bahr referred to Berlin as the heart of Europe. Norman Davies traces the use of this metaphor for Warsaw back to the poet Juliusz Słowacki, as well as using it himself for Poland, see his *Heart of Europe. A Short History of Poland* (Oxford: Clarendon Press, 1984). For a spontaneous popular identification of Prague as the heart of Europe see Garton Ash, *We*, p. 123.

... no other country ... except, of course, Austria until the State Treaty of 1955.

... Germany was the divided centre ... a point succinctly recalled in Weizsäcker, *Deutsche Geschichte*, p. 12.

... 'found in the West only ...' Jiři Dienstbier, *Träumen von Europa* (Berlin: Rowohlt, 1991), p. 13.

... the Soviet Union's diplomatic note ... see Meissner, *Moskau-Bonn*, pp. 71–73.

... Adenauer took up the word ... ibid., pp. 85–88, the quotation on p. 87.

An important Bundestag resolution ... *Bundestag Drucksachen* 3/2740, also quoted in Meissner, *Deutsche Ostpolitik*, p. 17.

... 'nothing but the attempt ...' *Bundestag Plenarprotokolle*, 6/53, p. 2685 (27 May 1970), also reprinted in *Texte* I/5, p.171 ff. For a powerful critique of this usage, see the contribution by Karl Theodor Freiherr von und zu Guttenberg, also reprinted in *Texte* I/5, esp. p. 197.

The term was then used ... Thus Article I of the August 1970 treaty with the Soviet Union proclaims the parties' common desire to advance the 'normalisation of the situation in Europe' (*Verträge*, p. 13). The December 1970 treaty with the People's Republic of Poland is formally entitled a 'Treaty ... on the bases of a normalisation of mutual relations' and Article III (1) reads: 'The Federal Republic of Germany and the People's Republic of Poland will undertake further steps towards the full normalisation and comprehensive development of their mutual relations, whose firm basis is this Treaty' (*Verträge*, pp. 21–22. My italics.) The December 1972 Basic Treaty with the GDR speaks in Article 1 of developing 'normal good-neighbourly relations' and in Article 7 of 'the normalisation of ... relations' (*Zehn Jahre*, p. 206). The treaty of December 1973 with Czechoslovakia speaks only of 'good-neighbourly relations' (*Verträge*, p. 50). English texts in Grenville, *Treaties*, pp. 192–200.

... they wanted to change, not the frontiers in Europe ... The point being, of course, that official East European propaganda had as tirelessly claimed that the Federal Republic — or certain 'revanchist' circles within the Federal Republic — *did* want to restore the 1937 frontiers of the German Reich.

... in Helmut Schmidt's 1978 state of the nation address ... what we have referred to throughout as the 'state of the nation' address was proposed by an all-Party resolution of 1967 (see *Texte* I/4, p. 149) and formally instituted by Chancellor Kiesinger in 1968 under the title 'Report on the state of the nation in divided Germany' — 'Bericht über die Lage der Nation im geteilten Deutschland', see *Bundestag Plenarprotokolle*, 5/158, p. 8168 (11 March 1968). In the last years of Schmidt's Chancellorship, the annual address was simply entitled 'Report on the state of the nation' — 'Bericht zur Lage der Nation', see, for example, *Bundestag Plenarprotokolle*, 8/208, p. 16615 (20 March 1980), 9/31, p. 1541 (9 April 1981), 9/111, p. 6745 (9 September 1982). When he came to power, Chancellor Kohl made a great point of this dropping of the explicit reference to 'divided Germany', suggesting that the emphasis of the addresses under Schmidt had shifted to a discussion of the political situation inside the Federal Republic.

'We Germans will not reconcile ourselves to the division of our fatherland,' he roundly declared, *Bundestag Plenarprotokolle*, 10/16, p. 987 (23 June 1983). But a look back through Chancellor Schmidt's 'state of the nation' addresses hardly bears out the contention that he was, in substance, neglecting the issue of the German and European divisions.

'gradually a situation of matter-of-course normality . . .' *Bundestag Plenarprotokolle*, 8/78, p. 6115 (9 March 1978). Emphasis in the original. Wolfgang Schäuble, a key political appointee responsible for Deutschlandpolitik under Chancellor Kohl from 1984 to 1989, himself pointed to the difficulty of determining what 'normality' between the two German states would be, in a lecture in 1986: see 'Deutsche Einheit und menschliche Erleichterungen', in *Bulletin*, 29 April 1986, pp. 379–87, also reprinted in *Innerdeutsche Beziehungen*, pp. 246–53.

It seems to have appeared for the first time . . . this is according to Meissner, *Moskau-Bonn*, p. 27, footnote 50, and text of the declaration on pp. 283–85.

. . . used fitfully, but with growing frequency . . . see, for example, the conclusion of a speech by the Christian Democrat Kopf, welcoming the Jaksch report and resolution in June 1961: 'As a goal we see the creation of a European peace order which includes all the countries of Europe and in which the free united Germany also cheerfully and responsibly takes its place'. *Bundestag Plenarprotokolle*, 3/162, p. 9367 (14 June 1961). In June 1962 Foreign Minister Schröder declared that 'our goal is a just new European order, based on peaceful agreements . . .', quoted in Jacobsen, *Nachbarn*, p. 348. The Federal Government's so-called 'peace note' of March 1966 used an almost identical formulation: 'a just European order, based on peaceful agreements', ibid., p. 385.

. . . in the first government declaration of the 'Grand Coalition' . . . see *Bundestag Plenarprotokolle*, 5/8, p. 3663 (13 December 1966).

. . . used repeatedly . . . see the entries under 'Europäische Friedensordnung' in the index volume to *Texte I*. One version of Brandt's vision of a 'European peace order, that is, an order which really overcomes the Cold War and the political tensions', is given in an interview of July 1967, reprinted in Haftendorn, *Aussenpolitik*, pp. 326–28. But the formulations were vague and varied.

. . . in Nato's 1967 Harmel report . . . this talks variously of a 'peaceful order in Europe', a 'final and stable settlement in Europe' (both in paragraph 8, concentrating on the division of Germany and Europe) and, in paragraph 12, of 'policies designed to achieve a just and stable order in Europe, to overcome the division of Germany and to foster European security', see *Texts of Final Communiqués issued by Ministerial Sessions of the North Atlantic Council, the Defence Planning Committee, and the Nuclear Planning Group* (Brussels: Nato Information Service, 1975), pp. 198–202. German text in EA, 23/1968, pp. D75–77. An important article on the background to the Harmel report is that by Helga Haftendorn in *VfZ*, 40/2, 1992, pp. 169–221.

Helmut Schmidt expresses . . . Schmidt, *Menschen und Mächte*, p. 11

. . . a high level of conceptual imprecision . . . Siebenmorgen, *Gezeitenwechsel*,

p. 327, suggests that Willy Brandt's conceptual imprecision was deliberate and tactical, enabling him not be pinned down by critics or opponents to any precise definition, such as the earlier usage of a 'European security system' had seemed to demand. Bender, *Neue Ostpolitik*, p. 163, suggests that Brandt's conceptual imprecision was deliberate but philosophical, reflecting a genuine humility before the openness of history. Could it not be both?

The objective of the new Ostpolitik, said Scheel in 1970 . . . both quotations are from *Bundestag Plenarprotokolle*, 6/59, pp. 3269–70 (17 June 1970). He restated this goal, retrospectively, in the journal *Liberal*, 30. Jg., Heft 1, February 1988, p. 39.

'The development is inexorably . . .' Rede des Bundesministers des Auswärtigen Hans-Dietrich Genscher aus Anlass der Verleihung des 'Thomas-Dehler-Medaille' am Sonnabend, dem 03. Januar 1987. Der Bundesminister des Auswärtigen, Mitteilung für die Presse Nr. 1005/87, p. 63. An almost identical formulation is to be found in his 11 June 1988 speech to a conference of the Institute for East-West Security Studies at Potsdam. Der Bundesminister des Auswärtigen, Mitteilung für die Presse Nr. 1140/88, p. 15. This speech is reprinted in Genscher, *Unterwegs*, pp. 151–69.

. . . 'last week influential politicians . . .' Marion Gräfin Dönhoff, 'Ein Dach für ganz Europa,' in *Die Zeit*, 1 April 1988.

. . . 'the necessary structure of international law' . . . Egon Bahr, *Zum europäischen Frieden*, p. 90.

. . . could be achieved by the end of the century . . . ibid., p. 84.

. . . 'would be equivalent to European peace' . . . ibid., p. 92.

. . . 'the western principles of the Helsinki Final Act . . .' ibid., p. 92. What 'binding' quality these principles would acquire, and how or why, is not explained.

. . . 'to be historically resolved' . . . ibid., p. 31.

. . . 'could be very exciting' . . . ibid., p. 34.

. . . 'guaranteed peaceful competition . . .' ibid., p. 83.

. . . 'culture of dispute' . . . ibid., p. 99.

. . . 'growing co-operation in unchanged political structures' . . . ibid., p. 42. One should note that the nationally-minded CDU parliamentarian, Bernhard Friedmann, came up with a not altogether dissimilar vision: that of the two German states increasingly co-operating on 'questions of ecology, energy, technology and so forth' while retaining 'wholly different social systems'. Friedmann was less circumspect than Bahr, and talked of a 'Confederation' in which, amongst other things, the Federal Republic and the GDR would conduct a 'more or less common foreign policy'. See Bernhard Friedmann, *Einheit statt Raketen* (Herford: BusseSeewald, 1987), p. 137.

. . . 'everything that one says must be true . . .' Interview in Bayerischer Rundfunk, 19 May 1973.

Social Democrats in government had firmly and consistently maintained
... A classic forum for such statements was the American journal *Foreign Affairs*.
See, for example, Willy Brandt, 'German policy toward the East,' in *Foreign
Affairs*, Spring 1968, pp. 476–86, and Helmut Schmidt, 'A policy of reliable
partnership,' in *Foreign Affairs*, Spring 1981, pp. 743–55.

... 'And therein lies the real problem ...' *Bundestag Plenarprotokolle*, 10/59,
p. 4164 (15 March 1984).

... 'the basic freedoms are realised ...' *Bundestag Plenarprotokolle*, 11/33,
p. 2160 (15 October 1987).

... 'The clear articulation of our own goals ...' Wolfgang Schäuble, 'Die
deutsche Frage im europäischen und weltpolitischen Rahmen,' EA, 12/1986,
p. 342 (based on the text of a lecture to the Swedish Institute for International
Relations on 15 May 1986). Schäuble was Chancellery Minister from 1984 to
1989, when he became Interior Minister.

... 'To be sure, it verbally subordinates ...' ibid., p. 342.

... 'Peace begins with respect ...' Kohl used this formula in his televised
keynote speech during Erich Honecker's visit to Bonn in September 1987: see the
Bulletin, 10 September 1987, p. 706. He repeated an almost identical formula in
his state of the nation address the same year: see *Bundestag Plenarprotokolle*,
11/33, p. 2163 (15 October 1987).

Chancellor Kohl echoed Chancellor Schmidt ... For Kohl see his 1983 state
of the nation address in *Bundestag Plenarprotokolle*, 10/16, p. 988 (23 June 1983).
For Schmidt see his 1980 state of the nation address in *Bundestag Plenarprotokolle*,
8/208, p. 16623 (20 March 1980).

... Genscher said simply: 'the division of Germany is the division of our
European continent'. Rede des Bundesministers des Auswärtigen Hans-Dietrich
Genscher aus Anlass der Verleihung des 'Thomas-Dehler-Medaille' am Sonnabend, dem 03. Januar 1987. Der Bundesminister des Auswärtigen, Mitteilung
für die Presse Nr. 1005/87, p. 10.

... 'above all a matter for the Germans' ... quoted from his 1985 speech on
'The Germans and their Identity', reprinted in Richard von Weizsäcker, *Von
Deutschland aus. Reden des Bundespräsidenten* (Munich: Deutscher Taschenbuch
Verlag, 1987), p. 56. An English edition is *A Voice from Germany. Speeches by
Richard von Weizsäcker*, translated by Karin von Abrams (London: Weidenfeld &
Nicolson, 1986), this passage on p. 78.

'To overcome the division of Germany is simultaneously ...' Wolfgang
Schäuble, 'Die deutsche Frage im europäischen und weltpolitischen Rahmen', EA,
12/1986, p. 344.

... always and simultaneously 'European peace policy' ... This particular
formula seems to have been coined, and was most often repeated by Hans-Dietrich
Genscher. As early as January 1971, while still Interior Minister, he declared in a
speech in New York: 'The Ostpolitik of the Federal Government is thus in its

substance and its goals at once Deutschlandpolitik and European peace policy', *Bulletin*, 15 January 1971, p. 27. For typical later usages see, for example, his remarks in *Bundestag Plenarprotokolle*, 11/33, p. 2193 (15 October 1987), and his 11 June 1988 speech to a conference of the Institute for East-West Security Studies at Potsdam, Der Bundesminister des Auswärtigen, Mitteilung für die Presse Nr. 1140/88, p. 3. This speech is also reprinted in Genscher, *Unterwegs*, pp. 151–69.

... no contradiction between West European integration and Ostpolitik ... An argument made forcefully by Walter Scheel in the original debates about the Eastern treaties and restated most emphatically by Helmut Kohl in the late 1980s. 'We should,' he told his party's foreign policy congress in April 1988, 'avoid a phoney debate about the question of whether and to what extent our Germany-political (*deutschlandpolitische*) goals can be brought into harmony with the policy of European integration.' See the typescript of the speech, pp. 7 ff. In his 1984 state of the nation address Kohl declared that 'for us, Europapolitik [i.e. the policies related to West European integration] and Deutschlandpolitik are like two sides of the same coin'. *Bundestag Plenarprotokolle*, 10/59, p. 4163 (15 March 1984).

'... the identity of our interests with the interests of Europe.' *Bundestag Plenarprotokolle*, 6/23, p. 915 (15 January 1970).

'I have always found ...' dictated by Bismarck on 9 November 1876, see Johannes Lepsius & ors, eds, *Die Grosse Politik der Europäischen Kabinette 1871–1914* (Vol. 2, Berlin: Deutsche Verlagsgesellschaft für Politik und Geschichte, 1922), No. 256, p. 88.

... how often and how eloquently Hitler spoke of Europe ... with consummate mendacity, of course, and only in the pre-war years. Thus in the subject index to Max Domarus, *Hitler: Reden und Proklamationen* (Wiesbaden: R Löwit, 4 Vols, 1973) there are twenty-two references to 'Europe' for the period 1932–38, but only one reference for the period 1939–45. Europe had done its work. Europe could go. For peace, respect and equal rights for neighbours, see, for example, Domarus, *op. cit.*, pp. 193, 273. Perhaps the high-point of Hitler's 'European' humbug is his speech to the Reichstag on 7 March 1936, with its eloquent references to German-French reconciliation, 'European co-operation', and the need for a peaceful solution of Europe's problems — all in fact justifying the remilitarisation of the Rhineland. See Domarus, *op. cit.*, pp. 583–97. For his private, wartime talk of 'Europe' in quite a different vein — although still repeating some of the same leitmotifs — see Henry Picker, *Hitlers Tischgespräche im Führerhauptquartier* (Seewald, Stuttgart, 1976), and in English, *Hitler's Table Talk* (London: Weidenfeld & Nicolson, 1953).

... wrote his biographer Alan Bullock ... *Hitler. A Study in Tyranny* (London: Penguin, 1962), p. 335.

... Willy Brandt, Helmut Kohl and Hans-Dietrich Genscher ... For Brandt, see his very interesting 10 May 1968 speech at the Stresemann-Gedenkfeier in Mainz, reprinted as the introduction to Arnold Harttung, ed., *Gustav Stresemann. Schriften* (Berlin: Berlin-Verlag, 1976), esp. pp. XI, XIII–XV, where he explicitly compares his own proposed new policy with that of Stresemann. He also made the comparison in his December 1971 Nobel Peace Prize lecture, see *Texte* I/9, pp. 309–10. For Kohl, see, for example, his 2 May 1984 Adenauer Memorial Lecture in Oxford, where he presents Locarno as the first great attempt at — and missed opportunity for — that Western integration of Germany which Adenauer finally achieved. German text in *Bulletin*, 9 May 1984, p. 433; English text published as *German Foreign Policy Today* (London: St Antony's College/Konrad Adenauer Foundation, 1984). For Genscher, see Helmut R. Schulze & Richard Kiessler, *Hans-Dietrich Genscher. Ein deutscher Aussenminister* (Munich: Bertelsmann, 1990), p. 29.

. . . a means to the achievement of national ends . . . For contrasting judgements on the vexed, and perhaps falsely posed question of whether or in what sense Stresemann was 'a good European' see Gordon A. Craig, *Germany 1866–1945* (Oxford: Clarendon Press, 1978), pp. 511–24 (with further references); Griffith, *Ostpolitik*, pp. 6–15 (and further references on pp. 239–41); A. J. Nicholls, *Weimar and the Rise of Hitler* (London: Macmillan, 1968), pp. 120–22; Golo Mann, *The History of Germany Since 1789* (London: Peregrine Books, 1987), pp. 636–37; Sebastian Haffner, *Von Bismarck zu Hitler* (Munich: Kindler, 1987), pp. 193–95. Two hostile but vivid assessments by contemporary observers may be found in F. W. Foerster, *Europe and the German Question* (London: Allen & Unwin, 1941), pp. 305–06, and Claud Cockburn, *Cockburn Sums Up* (London: Quartet Books, 1981) p. 36. Now see also the biography by Kurt Koszyk, *Gustav Stresemann. Der Kaisertreue Demokrat* (Köln: Kiepenheuer & Witsch, 1989). Jonathan Wright of Christ Church, Oxford, is preparing a major biography of Stresemann which will also address this question.

. . . Konrad Adenauer . . . on all that follows see the superb two-volume biography by Hans-Peter Schwarz, cited below as Schwarz, *Adenauer I* and *Adenauer II*.

'The only opportunity left to Germany . . .' Michael Stürmer, 'The evolution of the contemporary German question,' in Moreton, *Germany*, pp. 23–4. See also the discussion on p. 48 f and notes.

. . . two sides . . . see, for example, Schwarz, *Adenauer I*, p. 850 ff, *Adenauer II*, pp. 146–48, 285–6, 367, 384, 893. Schwarz emphasises that Adenauer was extremely flexible in his thinking about how 'Europe' might be built, and that, by contrast with Walter Hallstein, he inclined to the inter-governmental rather than the supranational model of EC development. Altogether, the second aspect, that of regaining sovereignty, powers and freedom of manoeuvre for the Federal Republic, seen as the core of the nation-state Germany, comes through most strongly from the portrait Schwarz paints. Adenauer once observed that there were Hyper-Europeans, Europeans and Anti-Europeans. He himself, he said, was a European. Quoted in Schwarz, *Adenauer II*, p. 753.

. . . he sometimes doubted . . . see Baring, *Anfang*, pp. 101–03, Schwarz, *Adenauer II*, p. 152. See also the note by the then Permanent Under-Secretary of the Foreign Office, Sir Ivone Kirkpatrick, of a conversation with the German ambassador to London on 16 December 1955. Noting Adenauer's fear of the

Western allies making a deal with the Soviet Union, perhaps involving a united but demilitarised Germany, he goes on, recording the German ambassador's account of the Chancellor's remarks: 'The bald reason was that Dr Adenauer had no confidence in the German people.' The document is reprinted in Josef Foschepoth, *Adenauer und die deutsche Frage* (Göttingen: Vandenhoeck & Ruprecht, 1988), pp. 000.

... the first step ... Adenauer celebrated this at the time as the 'foundation-stone for the building of a European *Bund*', Schwarz, *Adenauer I*, p. 850. But it is clear that he attached at least as much importance to the security dimension, and the plans for a European Defence Community.

... the plan for a European Defence Community ... see Baring, *Anfang*, *passim*, Schwarz, *Adenauer II*, pp. 121–40, and Edward Fursdon, *The European Defence Community. A History* (London: Macmillan, 1980).

... a special, unique commitment ... on this see Olaf Mager, *Die Stationierung der britischen Rheinarmee. Grossbritanniens EVG-Alternative* (Baden-Baden: Nomos, 1980).

... the ties with the United States ... see Schwarz, *Adenauer II*, p. 728 and *passim*. For a vigorous, polemical re-statement of this view see Baring, *Grössenwahn*.

... the striving to become subject rather than object ... Two interesting German usages of the subject/object terminology: '... the Cold War offered the Germans, more particularly those in the West, the opportunity to change their role from object to subject'. Michael Stürmer in Moreton, *Germany*, p. 23. And in the lecture already quoted Wolfgang Schäuble observes 'Without Germany there is no Europe, and without Europe the Germans would only be an object of world policy (*Objekt der Weltpolitik*)', *Bulletin*, 29 April 1986, p. 383.

... 'a more self-reliant German policy' ... the word both Brandt and Scheel used is *selbstständig* which means literally 'self-standing', but with the clear implication, in this context, of greater autonomy. In his seminal 'Government declaration' of 28 October 1969, Brandt spoke of the common interests of the Federal Republic and the United States of America being 'strong enough to sustain a more self-reliant (*selbständigere*) German policy in a more active partnership', *Bundestag Plenarprotokolle*, 6/5, p. 31 (28 October 1969). In a debate early in 1970 Scheel referred to 'the desire for a greater self-reliance (*Selbstständigkeit*) of German policy', *Bundestag Plenarprotokolle*, 6/53, p. 2685 (27 May 1970).

... West Germany had more ties than any ... a point well emphasised by Helga Haftendorn in her contribution to Ekkehart Krippendorff & Volker Rittberger, eds, *The Foreign Policy of West Germany. Formation and Contents* (London: Sage, 1980).

... with the 'understanding', 'agreement' or 'support' ... for a political-theological debate about the precise wording see the note on p. 446. For what actually happened, see Chapter VII.

... 'without the assent of the East European peoples'. *Bundestag Plenarprotokolle*, 8/154, p. 12257 (17 May 1979).

'... there was hardly a government in Europe ...' Schmidt, *Menschen und Mächte*, p. 41. At a seminar organised by the author at St Antony's College, Oxford, on 3 May 1988, the veteran British diplomat Sir Frank Roberts put it quite charmingly. By the mid-1960s, he observed, Germany's Western allies felt the commitment to reunification had become 'a bit of a nuisance'.

... perfect understanding of the fears ... see, for example, *Bundestag Plenarprotokolle*, 8/154, p. 12264 (17 May 1979).

... policymakers in Washington ... on this, see now the work of Hermann-Josef Rupieper, *Der besetzte Verbündete. Die amerikanische Deutschlandpolitik 1949–1955* (Opladen: Westdeutscher Verlag, 1991).

... in American State Department discussions ... see, for example, the note of a discussion on 1 April 1952, in *Foreign Relations of the United States. 1952–1954* Volume VII (Washington: US Government Printing Office, 1986), pp. 194–99.

... France, although sporadically interested in overcoming the division of Europe ... see the masterly short survey by Pierre Hassner in Gordon, *Eroding Empire*, pp. 188–231.

... 'The trench that divides my country ...' Notes for a conversation with de Gaulle in Paris, 15 December 1966, in AdsD: Dep WB, BA 17. Brandt gives an account of the conversation in *People and Politics*, pp. 130–35 and *Erinnerungen*, pp. 251–53.

'Our chance lies in the fact ...' Wolfgang Schäuble, 'Die deutsche Frage im europäischen und weltpolitischen Rahmen', in EA, 12/1986, p. 345.

... the phrase 'unifying Europe' ... see, for example, remarks by Helmut Kohl in *Bundestag Plenarprotokolle* 11/125, p. 9130 (16 February 1989).

... what Strauss then described as the chimera of a Greater Europe ... *Bundestag Plenarprotokolle*, 6/53, p. 2713 (27 May 1970).

'The unity of the Germans ...' *Bundestag Plenarprotokolle*, 6/22, p. 843 (14 January 1970).

... a formula from the late 1960s ... Renata Fritsch-Bournazel traces this formula to a 1968 lecture by Klaus Bloemer, then adviser to Franz Josef Strauss on foreign affairs. See Renata Fritsch-Bournazel, *Confronting the German Question* (Oxford: Berg, 1988), p. 131 [German original: *Das Land in der Mitte. Die Deutschen im europäischen Kräftefeld*, Munich: iudicium Verlag, 1986]. The whole theme of the relationship between the German and the European questions is explored with characteristic brilliance by Pierre Hassner in his contribution to Werner Weidenfeld, ed., *Die Identität der Deutschen* (Munich: Hanser, 1983), pp. 294–323, with this formulation on p. 299.

'Do not do unto others. ...' George Bernard Shaw, *Maxims for Revolutionists*.

Chapter II: Ostpolitik

... **true of Willy Brandt** ... see above, p. 62.

... **eminently true of Hans-Dietrich Genscher** ... a serious political biography of Genscher remains to be written. Two journalistic portraits are Werner Filmer & Heribert Schwan, *Hans-Dietrich Genscher* (Düsseldorf: Econ, 1988) and Helmut R Schulze & Richard Kiessler, *Hans-Dietrich Genscher. Ein deutscher Aussenminister* (Munich: Bertelsmann, 1990). Two collections of his speeches are *Deutsche Aussenpolitik. Ausgewählte Reden und Aufsätze 1974–1985* (Stuttgart: Bonn Aktuell, 1985), and *Unterwegs*. These small selections do not, however, begin to give an idea of the sheer volume and diversity of the minister's publicly spoken words.

... **to delay the opening of the Brandenburg Gate** ... see Peter Siebenmorgen, 'Des Kanzlers Jubelplan' in *Die Zeit*, 19 April 1991. Siebenmorgen bases this report on the notes and recollections of the East German emissary Alexander Schalck-Golodkowski, but confirmed it also with West German sources.

... **nearly one fifth of the new state's population** ... Benz, *Vertreibung*, p. 8, quotes a figure of 16.5 per cent of the total population from the September 1950 census. This does not include those who fled from the Soviet Occupied Zone/GDR. *Aussiedler* 2, p. 3, quotes a *Statistisches Bundesamt* calculation according to which there were some 11.9 million refugees and expellees, of whom, in September 1950, 7.6 million were in West Germany (including West Berlin), 3.7 million in East Germany. Of course some who initially fled to East Germany subsequently fled again from East Germany.

... **claimed three million members** ... this in notes in preparation for a meeting of Willy Brandt with leaders of the Federation of Expellees on 17 February 1961, in AdsD: Dep WB, Rbm 63.

... **some two million members** ... the figure of 2.2 million members was claimed in the Federation of Expellees 1991 annual report, which also reported an increase in membership, due to the number of recent German migrants from Eastern Europe. See the report in FAZ, 1 July 1991.

... **Bavaria's 'fourth tribe'** ... Strauss, *Erinnerungen*, p. 66.

... **to pay close attention** ... see, for example, the accounts of Brandt's meetings with expellee leaders in AdsD: Dep WB, Rbm 63

... **the defection** ... **Herbert Hupka** ... see Baring, *Machtwechsel*, pp. 398–400.

... **a February 1984 joint resolution** ... The resolution was a compromise worked out in the Bundestag's Committee for Intra-German Relations between two proposals, one from the Christian and Free Democrats, one from the Social Democrats. The separate proposals were tabled on 22 June 1983, see *Bundestag Drucksachen* 10/187 and 10/192, the joint resolution presented on 24 January 1984, see *Bundestag Drucksachen* 10/914. For the debate on the joint resolution, see *Bundestag Plenarprotokolle* 10/53, pp. 3842–51 (9 February 1984).

... a security *Teilhaberschaft* ... Speech to the Aspen Institute's Berlin conference on 'Perspectives for the 21st Century', 25 October 1987, reprinted in Theo Sommer, ed., *Perspektiven. Europa im 21. Jahrhundert* (Berlin: Argon, 1989), pp. 107–18, this on p. 115.

... the precise terms ... see, for example, the distinction drawn between the Federal Republic's *Westbindungen* and *OstVERbindungen* by Werner Link, 'Die aussenpolitische Staatsräson der Bundesrepublik Deutschland' in Funke, *Demokratie und Diktatur*, pp. 400–16.

... many (though not all) of them had attacked ... An exception, notable also on account of his subsequent elevation, was Richard von Weizsäcker, see Baring, *Machtwechsel*, pp. 437 & 441.

... a government-guaranteed one billion DM loan ... see above, p. 155 and notes.

... few Western visitors were more fulsome ... 'I must say ... that I left with the most agreeable feelings,' 'one can only wish Gorbachev all the best,' East and West might stand 'on the eve of a new age', 'Mars must leave and Mercury take the stage.' see *Der Spiegel*, 1/1988.

'Divided Germany ...' see Herbert Wehner, *Wandel und Bewährung. Ausgewählte Reden und Schriften 1930–1980* (Frankfurt: Ullstein, 1986), pp. 232–48, this quotation on p. 248. The turn was subsequently confirmed by a major resolution on foreign policy at the November 1960 Hannover party congress. 'In the argument between East and West,' declared this resolution, 'the place of the Federal Republic is firmly on the side of the West, the Federal Republic is a reliable ally.' Quoted in Siebenmorgen, *Gezeitenwechsel*, p. 325.

... a long, complex, not to say confused process ... See Clemens, *Reluctant Realists*, Hacke, *Wege und Irrwege*, and the lecture by Alois Mertes, 'Kontinuität und Wandel in der deutschen Aussenpolitik', in *Bulletin*, 14 May 1983, pp. 437–44.

... the May 1972 'Joint Resolution' ... See Baring, *Machtwechsel*, pp. 427–47, with the text of the resolution on pp. 438–40; also in *Verträge*, pp. 66–67.

... an encyclopaedic resolution ... Even after five years of relatively successful government practice of Ostpolitik, and even with the right flank secured by the 'conversion' of Franz Josef Strauss, this theoretical codification produced some ructions inside the Christian Democratic Union.

The original 'discussion paper' produced by a party commission in February 1988, placed a fulsome description of the Federal Republic's commitments to, and hopes for, the Western Alliance and the European Community, before a discussion of Deutschlandpolitik. In the latter section, it declared that the 'core' of Deutschlandpolitik was 'the maintenance of national unity', but without explicitly mentioning the goal of reunification in one state. 'The goal of unity is only to be achieved by the Germans with the agreement (*Einverständnis*) of their neighbours to East and West,' it said. Some party members objected vehemently to the omission of any explicit reference to the goal of reunification, and to the implication that Germany's neighbours might have a veto over Germany's future.

The final resolution passed at the Wiesbaden party conference in June 1988 put the discussion of Deutschlandpolitik before that of the Western Alliance and Western Europe, declared that 'the core of the CDU's Deutschlandpolitik remains "to maintain national *and state* unity" (Preamble of the Basic Law)' [my italics], and observed that 'we need the understanding (*Verständnis*) and support (*Unterstützung*) of our neighbours for the realisation of our nation's right of self-determination'. The overwhelming majority of the long text remained a theoretical affirmation and elaboration of what the Kohl government had, in practice, already been doing for the previous five years.

. . . 'realistic' and 'illusion-free' détente . . . See, for example, the 1978 paper on CDU/CSU policy towards the Soviet Union, prepared by a commission under the chairmanship of Alois Mertes, and published in FAZ, 24 February 1978.

'Pacta sunt servanda' . . . Strauss used the phrase in an article in the *Bayernkurier* of 26 May 1972, just nine days after the Joint Resolution. 'The treaties with Moscow and Warsaw are unquestionably valid in international law,' he declared in the Bundestag on 24 January 1973. 'There is now no alternative to them: *pacta sunt servanda.*' *Bundestag Plenarprotokolle*, 7/8, p. 170.

. . . a significant change of rhetoric . . . an important commentary on this will be the planned new edition of Wolfgang Bergsdorf's illuminating *Herrschaft und Sprache. Studien zur politischen Terminologie der Bundesrepublik Deutschland* (Pfullingen: Neske, 1983), hereafter cited as Bergsdorf, *Sprache*. Having dissected the political terminology of federal governments from Konrad Adenauer to Helmut Schmidt, Bergsdorf went on to help mould the political terminology of the Federal Government under Helmut Kohl, as a senior political appointee at the Federal Press and Information Office and adviser to the Chancellor.

'there is no break in the continuity . . .' *Die Zeit*, 28 October 1988.

'Despite all the party-political disputes . . .' see *Bulletin*, 2 February 1988, this quotation on p. 130, from a lecture delivered at the Evangelical Academy in Tutzing on 20 January 1988, entitled 'Im Dienste der Menschen. Unsere Politik gegenüber unseren östlichen und südöstlichen Nachbarn'. It was, of course, at the Tutzing academy that Egon Bahr delivered his seminal lecture in 1963, see p. 65 f.

'there are no more differences between him and me' . . . *Die Zeit*, 7 October 1988. Strauss actually died between the delivery and the publication of this text, which therefore acquired the character almost of a political testament.

President von Weizsäcker declared . . . See *Bulletin*, 24 January 1989, p. 38.

All the major parties . . . agreed . . . this is not to count the Greens as a 'major party'.

. . . to describe it as *German* Ostpolitik . . . a 1971 study by Lawrence L. Whetten is even called, simply, *Germany's Ostpolitik*, although the sub-title is 'Relations between the Federal Republic and the Warsaw Pact Countries' (Oxford: Oxford University Press, 1971).

. . . much though the other German state might object . . . whereas the West

German state had an *Ostpolitik* but a *Westbindung*, the East German state had a *Westpolitik* but an *Ostbindung*. The GDR was 'for ever and irrevocably allied to the Union of Soviet Socialist Republics', said Article 6.2 of the 1974 constitution. As the bonds of the Soviet bloc loosened in the 1980s, however, the GDR did increasingly differentiate between its East European partners: for example, welcoming Hungary as an ally in defence of détente in 1984–5 (see pp. 168), but deploring her domestic reforms in 1989 (see remarks by Joachim Herrmann at a Central Committee meeting, ND, 23 June 1989), embracing Ceauşescu's Romania both on account of its relative independence in foreign policy *and* because of its internal political Stalinism. The GDR's East European policy under Honecker was thus almost an ironical perversion of the US policy of 'differentiation' (see p. 178 f). Whereas the US 'rewarded' East European states for relative foreign policy autonomy and/or relative domestic liberalism, the GDR 'rewarded' its fraternal allies for relative foreign policy autonomy and/or domestic *illiberalism*! Although relations between East European states increasingly came to resemble 'normal', or even pre-war relations between European states—witness the cold war between Hungary and Romania, or the frontier dispute about territorial waters between Poland and the GDR—it was still never plausible to talk of the GDR having a distinctive Ostpolitik.

... 'German foreign policy' ... thus the title of Hans-Dietrich Genscher's collected speeches: *Deutsche Aussenpolitik. Ausgewählte Reden und Aufsätze 1974–1985* (Stuttgart: Bonn Aktuell, 1985).

... 'the German Ostpolitik' ... thus also the title of Boris Meissner's documentation of 1970: *Die deutsche Ostpolitik* ...

... sanctified by *Duden* ... Duden. *Das grosse Wörterbuch der deutschen Sprache*, Vol. 5, 1980.

... the concept of 'national interest' ... see the lucid short book by Joseph Frankel, *National Interest* (London: Macmillan, 1970).

... meaning Bavaria, Baden-Württemberg ... thus, welcoming Erich Honecker to Munich in 1987, Franz Josef Strauss said 'Between the Federal Republic of German and the Free State of Bavaria on the one hand, and the German Democratic Republic on the other, a sober co-operation has developed since 1983 ..', quoted in EA, 19/1987, p. D 549. Similar tones could be heard during Strauss's visit to Moscow in December 1987, but also, for example, in Lothar Späth's reception of Gorbachev in Baden-Württemberg in June 1989. Several of the states nad their own missions in Brussels, and in Moscow.

... traditionally called *Staatsräson* ... Perhaps the most famous work on this subject was Friedrich Meinecke's *Die Idee der Staatsräson in der neueren Geschichte*.

... Virtually all ... it must be emphasised that the 'all' here refers to the Federal Republic's political and intellectual *élites*, not to a wider public. A public opinion poll in January 1984 asked 'When people talk about Germany, what does that mean to you?' 57 per cent of respondents said 'the Federal Republic' while only 27 per cent said 'Federal Republic and GDR'. Another poll, in July 1986, had 37 per cent of those asked averring that the 'German nation today' means the

Federal Republic, while 35 per cent said Federal Republic and GDR together. But interestingly the figure for those who said 'German nation' meant both Federal Republic and GDR had *risen* three per cent since November 1981, while the proportion of those who said only Federal Republic had *fallen* by six per cent in the same period. For these figures, and an authoritative discussion of them, see Gebhard Schweigler, 'Normalcy in Germany', paper for the Woodrow Wilson Center European Alumni Association conference in Dubrovnik, 1988, published in a revised German version as 'Normalität in Deutschland' in EA, 6/1989, pp. 173–82.

... Josef Joffe called it ... in his perceptive discussion of West German policy Joffe distinguishes between 'raison d'état' and 'raison de nation', see Josef Joffe, *The Limited Partnership. Europe, the United States and the Burdens of Alliance* (Cambridge, Mass.: Ballinger, 1987), pp. 22, 33.

... *Duden* ... Duden: *Das grosse Wörterbuch der deutschen Sprache*, Vol. 5, 1980.

... *Brockhaus-Wahrig* ... Brockhaus-Wahrig: *Deutsches Wörterbuch*, Vol. 4, 1982.

Langenscheidt's concise German-English dictionary ... *Handwörterbuch Englisch*, 1977.

... *Oxford English Dictionary* ... the second edition appeared in 1989, but the entry for Ostpolitik is that from the *Supplement* volume of 1982.

... 'will scarcely overlook...' the quotation comes from Terence Prittie, *Germany Divided* (London: Hutchinson, 1961), p. 155.

... 'Today's German Ostpolitik...' quoted from Henry Picker, *Hitlers Tischgespräche im Führerhauptquartier* (Stuttgart: Seewald, 1976), p. 165. See also the slightly different version in *Hitler's Table Talk* (London: Weidenfeld & Nicolson, 1953), p. 379. Of course in pre-1945 usage the term Ostpolitik was only one among a whole family of *Ost*-compounds: *Ostpreussen, Ostmark, Ostmarkenpolitik, Ostsiedlung, Ostkolonisation, Osthilfe, Ostfront, Ostwall, Ostraum* etc.

... in his 1971 Nobel Peace Prize speech ... see *Texte I/9*, pp. 312–13.

'Twenty five years ago yesterday...' *Deutschland-Union-Dienst* (Pressedienst der CDU und CSU), No. 170, 10 September 1980, p. 1.

... also a party-political statement ... yet an independent scholar agrees: 'The beginning of an Ostpolitik of the Federal Republic,' writes Lothar Wilker, 'can be dated precisely: to the opening of diplomatic relations with the Soviet Union, agreed in September 1955...' Haftendorn, *Aussenpolitik*, p. 316 (this section by Lothar Wilker).

... as Social and Free Democrats generally implied ... for a fine example of partisan aetiology, see Ehmke, *Zwanzig Jahre*, p. 11.

... the milestone at the 13 August 1961 ... thus Bender, *Neue Ostpolitik*. See below, 'The Road from Berlin', p. 58 f.

... with the formation of the Grand Coalition ... thus Ehmke, *Zwanzig Jahre*.

... the whole complex of the Eastern treaties ... see below, p. 67 f.

... the hope-filled crowds at Erfurt shouting 'Willy! Willy!' ... this on Brandt's first visit as Chancellor to the GDR, on 19 March 1970. See Brandt, *People and Politics*, pp. 370–72.

... Willy Brandt falling to his knees ... this on 7 December 1970, see ibid., p. 399, and Bender, *Neue Ostpolitik*, pp. 178–79.

... Ostpolitik may therefore also be described as détente policy ... this is implicit in the title of Richard Löwenthal's masterly study with its opposition of 'Ostpolitik' to 'Cold War': *Vom kalten Krieg zur Ostpolitik*. See also Siebenmorgen, *Gezeitenwechsel*, p. 6.

... so closely associated ... with the years 1969–1972 ... thus the Index to the *Bulletin* has references to 'Ostpolitik' only for these years. After 1972, references are by individual countries, or, from 1976 to 1980, under *Entspannungspolitik*.

... used already by Konrad Adenauer ... see Siebenmorgen, *Gezeitenwechsel*, p. 13 ff, Schwarz, *Adenauer II*, p. 19.

... Americans had made the French word into an English one ... but Leon Wieseltier has wittily suggested that détente is 'the French word for German goodwill towards Russia', *The New Republic*, 10 February 1982, quoted in Schweigler, *Grundlagen*, p. 141. This was not how it looked from Bonn in the mid-1960s, however, when détente seemed to be rather a French word for American (and French and British) goodwill towards Russia.

... the adjective 'realistic' ... see his Bundestag speech about the Helsinki conference on 25 July 1975, reprinted in Hans-Dietrich Genscher, *Deutsche Aussenpolitik. Ausgewählte Reden und Aufsätze 1974–1985* (Bonn: Bonn Aktuell, 1985), p. 77 ff.

... 'the failure of *Entspannungspolitik*' ... see, for example, Haftendorn, *Sicherheit*, p. 133 ff. The 'End of *Entspannung*' was discussed as early as 1976, when President Ford said he would no longer use the word 'détente'. In response, Helmut Schmidt resorted to the marvellously sophistical argument that 'the renunciation of the foreign word 'détente', which we have never used in German', would not affect the continuity of the American policy of *Entspannung* towards the Soviet Union! See *Bulletin*, 20 April 1976, pp. 429–36, this comment on p. 430.

... in a Joint Declaration at the end of Brezhnev's visit ... *Bulletin*, 9 May 1978, pp. 429–30.

... the Kohl-Genscher government's ... 'Programme of Renewal' ... according to Gebhard Schweigler, when the SPD criticised this omission, 'government representatives declared this was just an accident...', see Schweigler, *Grundlagen*, p. 151 note. For Brandt's criticism, see *Bundestag Plenarprotokolle*, 10/6, p. 274 (6 May 1983).

... in an official government documentation ... *Verträge*, p. 7.

In official Bonn usage ... see, for example, the *Bonner Almanach 1987/88*

(Bonn: Presse- und Informationsamt der Bundesregierung, 1987), which has fifteen pages on Deutschlandpolitik and one page on Ostpolitik.

... **Deutschlandpolitik meant** ... in the 1940s and 1950s, Deutschlandpolitik actually meant the policy of other countries (mainly the victor powers) *towards* Germany. In fact as late as 1976, *Duden* gave this as the only meaning of the term ('the policy of foreign states concerning Germany', *Das Grosse Wörterbuch der deutschen Sprache*, Vol. 2, 1976). *Brockhaus-Wahrig* is once again more canny: 'Policy which concerns the problems arising from the division of Germany', it says, without specifying whose policy (*Deutsches Wörterbuch*, Vol. 2, 1981). Deutschlandpolitik as a term for the policy of the Federal Government towards these problems — and primarily towards the GDR — seems to have become firmly accepted only with Chancellor Kiesinger's programmatic statements at the outset of the Grand Coalition in December 1966 and January 1967. The term Deutschlandpolitik, unlike the terms Ostpolitik or *Entspannungspolitik*, figures continuously in the index of the *Bulletin* since the end of 1966.

The great series of *Dokumente zur Deutschlandpolitik* documents Deutschlandpolitik in both senses: that of the wartime allies and subsequently victor powers, and that of the Federal Republic.

... **simply as** *DDR-Politik* ... see Bruns, *DDR-Politik*, especially pp. 11 & 123–4, where the coinage is attributed to Günter Gaus, and below, Chapter Four, *passim*.

... **a quarter of what was once Germany** ... in the December 1937 frontiers of the German Reich, the territories to the east of the Oder-Neisse line comprised roughly twenty-five per cent of the total land-area, but contained only some fifteen per cent of the population, see *Zahlenspiegel*, p. 4.

... **the policymaking process** ... on this see Haftendorn, *Aussenpolitik*, pp. 9–12; Joffe in Gordon, *Eroding Empire*, pp. 169–78; and more extensively, Haftendorn, *Verwaltete Aussenpolitik*.

... **the direct control of the Chancellery** ... on this, see below p. 130.

... **the Foreign Ministry** ... strictly speaking, of course, it is the Foreign Office: *Auswärtiges Amt*. But since British readers assume there is only one Foreign Office, we have used the term Foreign Ministry to avoid confusion.

... **informal East German emissaries** ... most notable among the East German emissaries were the lawyer Wolfgang Vogel and the financial operator Alexander Schalck-Golodkowski. On all this, see p. 130.

... **the direct responsibility of the Foreign Ministry** ... although the Economics Ministry was also responsible for East-West (including Intra-German) trade, and the Finance Ministry was, of course, closely involved in all issues that concerned public funds: e.g. credits and loan guarantees.

... **the role of the Chancellor and his advisers** ... the supremacy of the Chancellery in the crucial first phase of Ostpolitik is emphasised in Schmid, *Entscheidung*, esp. p. 181 ff, although this was a period in which the Foreign Minister was unusually weak, see Baring, *Machtwechsel*, esp. p. 269 ff.

... unofficial intermediaries and 'back channels' ... Thus Hans-Peter Schwarz records an extraordinary series of meetings in East Berlin between Adenauer's Finance Minister, Fritz Schäffer, and his former schoolmate, Vinzenz Müller, now chief of staff of the East German 'Garrisoned People's Police', as well as a message from the Polish leadership brought by the industrialist Berthold Beitz. To some extent, Adenauer's unconventional and wilful Ambassador in Moscow, Hans Kroll, could also be regarded as such a channel to Khrushchev. See Schwarz, *Adenauer II*, pp. 190–93, 686, and 699 ff. Günter Buchstab describes Kiesinger's personal soundings in his article in Karl Dietrich Bracher & ors, eds, *Staat und Parteien. Festschrift für Rudolf Morsey zum 65. Geburtstag* (Berlin: Duncker & Humboldt, 1992). Egon Bahr performed this function over many years for Willy Brandt, and set up his own direct lines both to Washington and to Moscow. His special Soviet channel was the journalist Valery Lednyev. Bahr also made his own top-level 'channels', for example to the Central Committee of the Soviet Communist Party, available to Chancellor Kohl's foreign policy adviser, Horst Teltschik. (Horst Teltschik, Bonn, 12 July 1991). Eugen Selbmann, foreign policy adviser to the Social Democrats' parliamentary fraction, played a role much more important than his formal position would suggest, in maintaining top-level, informal contacts with Party leaders in Warsaw, Budapest, Prague and Moscow, both for Willy Brandt and even more for Helmut Schmidt. His real importance was recognised by the presentation to him of a Festschrift with contributions from most of the leading figures in Social Democratic Ostpolitik, see Ehmke, *Zwanzig Jahre*, especially the tributes on pp. 385–90. Selbmann himself is, at the time of writing, working on a volume of analytical memoirs. (Eugen Selbmann, Bonn, 8 July 1991). Senior figures from the world of business also on occasion passed on messages or top-level background information directly to the Chancellor.

... [Foreign ministry] department ... formally the department for 'foreign policy questions which concern Berlin and Germany as a whole'. Günther van Well, head of this department from 1967 to 1971, and subsequently the top official in the foreign service, Ambassador to the UN and to Washington, recalls that it included such high-fliers as Gerold von Braunmühl, Otto von der Gablentz and Hans Otto Bräutigam, subsequently the Federal Republic's Permanent Representative in the GDR. Günther van Well, Bonn, 8 July 1991.

... 'so now we are setting you down ...' quoted in Schröder, *Bahr*, p. 148. There was a double irony in Duckwitz saying this, since he was himself personally close to the Chancellor (they were neighbours on the Venusberg in Bonn), took part in the daily 'situation meeting' at the Chancellery, and caused a minor row between the Chancellor and the Foreign Minister when, during the German-Polish negotiations in 1970, he took a personal letter from Brandt to Gomułka, of which Scheel had not been informed. After this affair, Scheel demanded that Duckwitz no longer be included in the daily 'situation meeting' in the Chancellery, and Duckwitz was retired in June 1970. See Baring, *Machtwechsel*, p. 285 f & 305 f, and Schmid, *Entscheidung*, pp. 112–14, & 187. That Duckwitz was not entirely happy with his departure in the middle of the German-Polish negotiations can be seen from his letters to Willy Brandt, including copies of distinctly aggrieved letters to his successor as State Secretary of the Foreign Ministry, in AdsD: Dep WB, BK4.

... a high degree of consistency and continuity ... this extended not only to the civil service and the politicians but even to the media commentators. On the relative inconsistency of the American and French political and policy-making processes, see the relevant chapters in Gordon, *Eroding Empire*. The British political and policymaking process secured a relatively high degree of consistency, but so far as Eastern Europe is concerned this was, until the early 1980s, rather the consistency of disinterest.

... increasingly a matter of working through multilateral institutions ... this is well described in Haftendorn, *Verwaltete Aussenpolitik*

... European Political Co-operation ... see the valuable book by Simon J Nutall, *European Political Co-operation* (Oxford: Clarendon Press, 1992)

... pursue different goals or interests through separate instruments ... but where in this matrix should one fit the competition between Western countries for Eastern trade? And where the attempts not just of West German but of British and French leaders to act as 'intermediaries' between Moscow and Washington? Were Mrs Thatcher 'going between' Reagan and Gorbachev in 1985, or Giscard d'Estaing seeking to mediate between Carter and Brezhnev in 1980, pursuing common or special interests? Both, to be sure.

... 'trading states' ... on this, see especially Richard N Rosecrance, *The Rise of the Trading State* (New York: Basic Books, 1986)

... 'an insatiable striving ...' Schwarz, *Gezähmten Deutschen*, pp. 28–35, this on p. 35

... which Ralf Dahrendorf has argued ... see Ralf Dahrendorf, *Society and Democracy in Germany* (New York: Norton, 1979), esp. p. 142 ff & 202–03.

Having by 1945 become enemies ... Hans-Peter Schwarz, remarks at a conference of the Woodrow Wilson Center European Alumni Association, Dubrovnik, 1988, and Schwarz, *Gezähmten Deutschen*, passim.

... 'an unmanly dream' ... see the entry for 'Friede' in Wilhelm Janssen & ors, *Geschichtliche Grundbegriffe* Vol. 2, (Stuttgart: Klett, 1975), pp. 543–91, this on pp. 579–80.

It has also been suggested ... for example by Johannes Gross, *Phönix in Asche* (Stuttgart: Deutsche Verlags-Anstalt, 1989), p. 21 ff. See also Ralf Dahrendorf, *Society and Democracy in Germany* (New York: Norton, 1979), p. 9.

... as the Christian Democrat Jakob Kaiser put it ... quoted in Besson, *Aussenpolitik*, p. 35.

... placed the division of Germany at the centre ... '... the central political issues in Europe, first and foremost the German question ...' (Par. 5), '... no final and stable settlement in Europe is possible without a solution of the German question which lies at the heart of present tensions in Europe' (Par. 8), Harmel report, quoted from *Texts of Final communiqués issued by Ministerial Sessions of the North Atlantic Council, the Defence Planning Committee, and the Nuclear Planning Group* (Brussels: Nato Information Service, 1975), pp. 198–202.

... between the interests of the (undemocratic) states and those of their societies ... British and American policy makers sometimes spoke in this connection of relations with 'peoples' and with 'governments' in Eastern Europe. But the term 'societies' (with no ethnic overtones) was more widely used by the democratic oppositions in Eastern Europe, while the governments were, at least until the very end of the decade, merely one arm of a party-state.

'The main characteristic of the "hot peace" ...' Pierre Hassner, *Europe in the Age of Negotiation* = The Washington Papers, Vol. 1, No. 8 (Beverly Hills: Sage, 1973), pp. 69–70. In an article in *Europa-Archiv* in the same year, Josef Joffe described this 'dialectic of social interaction' as one of two key problems for future Ostpolitik, see EA, 4/1973, pp. 111–24, reprinted in Haftendorn, *Aussenpolitik*, pp. 378–93. Hassner recalls having begun to use this formula in late 1969 or early 1970.

... substantial impact of a different policy ... France was a partial exception, see p. 136, but it is very doubtful if this had a substantial impact.

... as Reinhart Koselleck has pointed out ... 'Sprachwandel und Ereignisgeschichte', *Merkur*, August 1989, pp. 657–72.

... in personal encounters at summit meetings ... Thus Helmut Schmidt points out that often no proper record was kept of his summit encounters, for example, when he spoke English with Giscard d'Estaing. Helmut Schmidt, London, 3 June 1991.

... on the telephone ... Jochen Thies records the following from his time working in the Chancellery. With a change of superior, an official exclaimed: 'Thank heavens we won't need to write any more memos. Now it'll only be telephoning.' Jochen Thies, *Helmut Schmidts Rückzug von der Macht. Das Ende der Ära Schmidt aus nächster Nähe* (Stuttgart: Bonn Aktuell, 1988), p. 38.

... or on television ... given the supreme importance of this one medium in contemporary politics, future historians will surely need to spend as much time in front of video screens as in press archives. The Konrad Adenauer Foundation's archive (ACDP) has presciently laid down a collection of television news and current affairs programmes, starting in 1982.

... what Bergson called ... quoted in Dominique Moïsi & Jacques Rupnik, *Le Nouveau Continent. Plaidoyer pour une Europe renaissante* (Paris: Calmann-Lévy, 1991), p. 78.

... legal provisions ... the key provisions are, for the party archives, in the law of 13 March 1992 amending the existing *Bundesarchivgesetz* (see *Bundesgesetzblatt*, 1992, Teil 1, p. 506), and, for the Stasi files, in article 32 of the so-called *Stasi-Unterlagen-Gesetz* (see *Bundesgesetzblatt*, 1991, Teil 1, pp. 2272–87).

... the 'essential triangle' ... Pierre Hassner in Gordon, *Eroding Empire*, p. 194.

Chapter III: Bonn-Moscow-Berlin

'not just the East of the West...' Weizsäcker, *Deutsche Geschichte*, p. 12.

The history of these plans and attempts... See Hermann Graml, *Die Allierten und die Teilung Deutschlands. Konflikte und Entscheidungen 1941–1948* (Frankfurt: Fischer, 1985); Hans-Peter Schwarz, *Vom Reich zur Bundesrepublik. Deutschland im Widerstreit der aussenpolitischen Konzeptionen in den Jahren der Besatzungsherrschaft 1945–1949* (2nd edition., Stuttgart: Klett-Cotta, 1980); Theodor Eschenburg, *Jahre der Besatzung. 1945–1949* (Stuttgart: Deutsche Verlags-Anstalt, 1983 = *Geschichte der Bundesrepublik Deutschland* Bd. 1); Hans-Peter Schwarz, *Die Ära Adenauer. Gründer jahre der Republik 1949–1957* (Stuttgart: Deutsche Verlags-Anstalt, 1981 = *Geschichte der Bundesrepublik Deutschland* Bd. 2); Hans-Peter Schwarz, *Die Ära Adenauer 1957–1963. Epochenwechsel* (Stuttgart: Deutsche Verlags-Anstalt, 1983 = *Geschichte der Bundesrepublik Deutschland* Bd. 3); Josef Foschepoth, ed., *Kalter Krieg und deutsche Frage. Deutschland im Widerstreit der Mächte 1945–52* (Göttingen: Vandenhoeck & Ruprecht, 1985). See also, more recently, Hermann-Josef Rupieper, *Der besetzte Verbündete. Die amerikanische Deutschlandpolitik von 1949 bis 1955* (Opladen: Westdeutscher Verlag, 1991).

... the possible alternative... the best and most balanced short account of Adenauer's reaction is in Schwarz, *Adenauer I*, pp. 906–24. For an account of Adenauer's response by a close associate see Wilhelm G Grewe, *Rückblenden 1976–1951* (Frankfurt: Propyläen, 1979), and the same author's short article, 'Ein zählebiger Mythos. Stalins Note vom März 1952' in FAZ, 10 March 1982. Specifically on the Soviet proposals of 1952–53, see also the well-documented but tendentious book by Rolf Steininger, *Eine vertane Chance. Die Stalin-Note vom 10. März 1952 und die Wiedervereinigung* (Bonn: Dietz, 1985), originally published as the introduction to a collection of documents, and now translated into English as *The German Question. The Stalin Note of 1952 and the Problem of Reunification* (New York: Columbia University Press, 1990); Hans-Peter Schwarz, ed., *Die Legende von der verpassten Gelegenheit. Die Stalin-Note vom 10. März 1952* (Stuttgart: Belser, 1982 = Vol. 5 of *Rhöndorfer Gespräche*); Hermann Graml, 'Die Legende von der verpassten Gelegenheit. Zur sowjetischen Notenkampagne des Jahres 1952', VfZ, 3/1981, pp. 307–41; Hermann-Josef Rupieper, 'Zu den sowjetischen Deutschlandnoten 1952. Das Gespräch Stalin-Nenni', VfZ, 3/1985, pp. 547–57; Gerhard Wettig, 'Die sowjetische Deutschland-Note vom 10. März 1952', DA, 2/1982, pp. 130–48 and most recently his articles in DA, 2/1992, pp. 157–67 and DA, 9/1992, pp. 943–58. See also the still cogent discussion in Löwenthal, *Vom Kalten Krieg*, pp. 14–22.

'it's called Potsdam'... quoted in Schwarz, *Adenauer I*, p. 833.

... Churchill did in fact... see Anthony Glees, 'Churchill's Last Gambit' in *Encounter*, April 1985, pp. 27–35; Martin Gilbert, *Winston S. Churchill. Volume VIII: 'Never Despair' 1945–1965* (London: Heinemann, 1988), pp. 818 ff; Schwarz, *Adenauer II*, p. 73 f.

... **still significantly limited** ... for an interesting discussion of these limits see Ludolf Herbst, 'Wie souverän ist die Bundesrepublik?', in Wolfgang Benz, ed., *Sieben Fragen an die Bundesrepublik* (Munich: dtv, 1989), pp. 72–90.

... **'We are a free and independent state** ...' see Konrad Adenauer, *Erinnerungen 1953–1955* (Stuttgart: Deutsche Verlags-Anstalt, 1966), pp. 430–34. Text of the declaration also in *Vierzig Jahre*, p. 83.

... **the 'day of sovereignty'** ... see, for example, Chancellor Kohl in *Bundestag Plenarprotokolle* 11/33, p. 2160 (15 October 1987).

... **'the interests of peace and European security** ...' reprinted in Meissner, *Moskau-Bonn*, pp. 71–3. Hans-Peter Schwarz notes that Adenauer had received an informal signal that the Russians wanted to talk directly but responded that one should first wait until the Paris treaties came into force, see Schwarz, *Adenauer II*, p. 192.

... **tough and dramatic negotiations** ... a vivid account is given in Schwarz, *Adenauer II*, pp. 207–22, but see also Meissner, *Moskau-Bonn*, pp. 15 ff, Rainer Salzmann, 'Adenauers Moskaureise in sowjetischer Sicht', in Dieter Blumenwitz & ors., eds, *Konrad Adenauer und seine Zeit* (Stuttgart: Deutsche Verlags-Anstalt, 1976), Vol. 2, pp. 131–59, and, of course, Adenauer's own memoirs.

Adenauer certainly did not belong ... for Adenauer's attitudes and policies towards the East see, first and foremost, the two volumes of Schwarz, *Adenauer*. Still valuable is the pioneering study by Klaus Gotto, 'Adenauers Deutschland- und Ostpolitik 1954–1963' (hereafter: Gotto, 'Adenauer') in Morsey & Repgen, *Adenauer Studien III*. See also Dieter Blumenwitz & ors., eds, *Konrad Adenauer und seine Zeit* (2 Vols, Stuttgart: Deutsche Verlags-Anstalt, 1976) and the revisionist treatments in Josef Foschepoth, ed., *Adenauer und die deutsche Frage* (Göttingen: Vandenhoeck & Ruprecht, 1988). In English see Hans-Peter Schwarz, 'Adenauer and Russia' in *Adenauer at Oxford. The Konrad Adenauer Memorial Lectures 1978–82* (Oxford: St Antony's College & Konrad-Adenauer-Stiftung, 1983).

'Asia stands on the Elbe' quoted in Schwarz, *Adenauer I*, p. 466.

... ***The Russian Perpetuum Mobile*** ... Wilhelm G Grewe, *Rückblenden 1976– 1951* (Frankfurt: Propyläen, 1979), p. 635. The book mentioned was by one Dieter Friede. Grewe points out that Adenauer could be unduly if briefly influenced by the last book he had read. But since Adenauer subsequently also presented Friede's book to de Gaulle (see Schwarz, *Adenauer II*, p. 923) it must clearly have made a more lasting impression.

... **got on quite well with the representatives** ... Wilhelm G Grewe, Bonn, 6 July 1991. As Hans-Peter Schwarz notes, Adenauer concludes the account in his memoirs with the comment that, with all due scepticism, he had the feeling that one day they might be able to solve Germany's problems with the men in the Kremlin ... see Schwarz, *Adenauer II*, p. 961.

... **'this terrible power'** ... this in a conversation with Alois Mertes in 1964, recalled by Mertes in Dieter Blumenwitz & ors., eds, *Konrad Adenauer und seine*

Zeit (2 Vols, Stuttgart: Deutsche Verlags-Anstalt, 1976), pp. 673–79. Adenauer also commended to Mertes, as he had to Kennedy and de Gaulle, Dieter Friede's book *The Russian Perpetuum Mobile*.

. . . **holding hands with Bulganin** . . . It is interesting to find Adenauer using, to describe his gesture at the Bolshoi, the same literary device that Brandt uses to describe his gesture of kneeling before the ghetto rising memorial in Warsaw: that is, describing it through the words of an outside observer. See Konrad Adenauer, *Erinnerungen 1953–1955* (Stuttgart: Deutsche Verlags-Anstalt, 1966), pp. 529–30, and compare Brandt, *People and Politics*, p. 399.

. . . **'until now we were like the growing young man . . .'** quoted in Siebenmorgen, *Gezeitenwechsel*, p. 141.

. . . **two main tendencies discernible** . . . Meissner, *Moskau-Bonn*, pp. 47–8.

. . . **Moscow First** . . . a point made particularly clearly in Schwarz, *Adenauer II*, p. 420 and 456–7.

The basic vision from which he started . . . neatly summarised in Klaus Gotto, 'Der Realist als Visionär', in *Die Politische Meinung*, 249/1990, pp. 6–13. One should note, however, that the image of the magnet seems first to have been used by his Social Democratic arch-critic Kurt Schumacher. See Willy Albrecht, *Kurt Schumacher. Ein Leben für den demokratischen Sozialismus* (Bonn: Verlag Neue Gesellschaft, 1985), pp. 54, 126.

'The hour of great disillusionment . . .' Heinrich Krone, 'Aufzeichnungen zur Deutschland- und Ostpolitik 1954–1969' (hereafter: Krone, 'Aufzeichnungen'), in Morsey & Repgen, *Adenauer Studien III*, pp. 134–201, this on p. 162 (entry for 18 August 1961). According to Schwarz, *Adenauer II*, p. 363, between 1957 and 1961 Krone was the second most powerful man in the Federal Republic.

. . . **expected a stronger reaction from Konrad Adenauer** . . . Even the Christian Democrat Eugen Gerstenmaier was dismayed that Adenauer did not fly immediately to Berlin. See Eugen Gerstenmaier, *Streit und Friede hat seine Zeit. Ein Lebensbericht* (Frankfurt: Propyläen, 1981), pp. 451–52. By his own account, Adenauer felt that the Soviet action could have been much worse — for example, a direct challenge to the West's connections with West Berlin; that worse challenges might still be to come; and that the crucial thing was to keep 'strong nerves', calm, and, above all, the support of the Americans, for, as he told a group of trusted journalists in one of his regular 'teatime conversations' on 17 August 1961, 'Without the United States we simply can't stay alive, that's as clear as day.' For all that can be said rationally for this position, the coolness with which he — and his Foreign Minister — reacted to the building of the Berlin Wall was eloquent of the distance between Bonn and Berlin. See Konrad Adenauer, *Teegespräche 1959–61 Bearbeitet von Hanns-Jürgen Küsters* (Berlin: Siedler, 1984), pp. 538–54 (quotation about the Americans on p. 550), Schwarz, *Adenauer II*, pp. 659–66, and also the interesting discussion in Arnulf Baring, *Sehr Verehrter Herr Bundeskanzler! Heinrich von Brentano im Briefwechsel mit Konrad Adenauer 1949–64* (Hamburg: Hoffmann & Campe, 1974), pp. 330–37. See also, most recently, the article by Hanns-Jürgen Küsters, 'Konrad Adenauer und Willy

Brandt in der Berlin-Krise 1958–1963' in VfZ, 40/2, 1992, pp. 483–542, esp. p. 527 ff, and Peter Siebenmorgen, 'Konrad Adenauer und die Berliner Mauer' in Boris Meissner, ed., *Die Deutschlandfrage von der Berliner Mauer bis zum Rücktritt Adenauers* (forthcoming).

'Adenauer probably did not abandon ...' Andrei Gromyko, *Memories*, translated by Harold Shukman (London: Hutchinson, 1989), pp. 196–97.

... more rather than less committed ... Wilhelm G Grewe, in conversation with the author (Bonn, 6 July 1991), made the simple but illuminating suggestion that it is difficult — while retaining self-respect — to continue publicly to maintain over two decades a position in which you do not privately believe. And since, whatever his private views, Adenauer was plainly convinced that for domestic political reasons he had to maintain a demonstrative commitment to reunification of the Germany 'divided in three', it is not impossible that his private conviction gradually adjusted to his public stance. But plainly this cannot be more than a speculation.

... a source of continuing controversy ... for a useful statement of the 'revisionist' view, see Josef Foschepoth, ed., *Adenauer und die deutsche Frage* (Göttingen: Vandenhoeck & Ruprecht, 1988). Schwarz's biography shows that there is simply no simple answer.

In a 'word to the Soviet Union' ... *Bundestag Plenarprotokolle*, 4/39 p. 1639 (9 October 1962). He repeated this passage in his government declaration of February 1963, adding 'The Soviet Union has not responded to these words', see *Bundestag Plenarprotokolle*, 4/57, p. 257/6 (6 February 1963). For his informal expressions of the same sentiments earlier in 1962, see Siebenmorgen, *Gezeitenwechsel*, pp. 342–43.

... schemes for reaching some *modus vivendi* ... see the contributions by Klaus Gotto and the so-called 'Globke plans' in Morsey & Repgen, *Adenauer Studien III*, pp. 3–91, 202 ff, and Hans Globke, 'Überlegungen und Planungen in der Ostpolitik Adenauers', in Dieter Blumenwitz & ors., eds, *Konrad Adenauer und seine Zeit* (Stuttgart: Deutsche Verlags-Anstalt, 1976), Vol. 1, pp. 665–72.

... an 'Austrian solution' ... see Siebenmorgen, *Gezeitenwechsel*, pp. 146–51; Gotto, 'Adenauer', in Morsey & Repgen, *Adenauer Studien III*, pp. 34–40; Schwarz, *Adenauer II*, p. 425 ff. Schwarz also records that this was preceded already in 1955–56 by secret discussions between Adenauer's Finance Minister, Fritz Schäffer, and the East German General Vinzenz Müller, in which the idea of a confederation between the two German states was also discussed, see ibid., pp. 190–93, and 416–17.

... further tentative advances ... see Siebenmorgen, *Gezeitenwechsel*, pp. 331–46, Klaus Gotto in Morsey & Repgen, *Adenauer Studien III*, pp. 67 ff.

... 'for the rest of his life ...' Krone, 'Aufzeichnungen', in Morsey & Repgen, *Adenauer Studien III*, p. 164 (entry for 7 December 1961). However Klaus Gotto points out that Adenauer inclined to make such apodictic statements, sometimes saying the opposite a few days later; and that in the same period he at least once indicated another order of priorities. See his comments in Morsey & Repgen, *Adenauer Studien III*, p. 84 (n. 387) and p. 70 (n. 402).

. . . **The period between** . . . good introductory accounts in Hildebrand, *Von Erhard zur Grossen Koalition*, Bender, *Neue Ostpolitik*, and Griffith, *Ostpolitik*.

. . . **an important all-party Bundestag resolution** . . . reprinted in Meissner, *Deutsche Ostpolitik*, pp. 17–18, Jacobsen, *Nachbarn*, pp. 345–46.

. . . **based on a report** . . . *Bundestag Drucksachen*, 3/2740. It is interesting to note that this was paired with another resolution, based on another Jaksch report, on the situation of the German minorities in Eastern Europe, see Chapter Six.

Kennedy's 'strategy of peace' . . . Kennedy proclaimed his 'strategy of peace' in an eloquent commencement address (drafted by Ted Sorensen) at American University in Washington on 10 June 1963. See *Public Papers of the Presidents: John F. Kennedy* (Washington: US Government Printing Office, 1964), pp. 459–64 & 526–29. Note also the seminal article by Zbigniew Brzezinski and William E Griffith advocating 'Peaceful Engagement in Eastern Europe', *Foreign Affairs*, Summer 1961.

. . . **Johnson's 'bridge-building'** . . . Johnson's key-note statement on 'bridge-building' came in a speech at the dedication of the George C Marshall library in Lexington, Virginia, on 23 May 1964, see *Public Papers of the Presidents: Lyndon B Johnson* (Washington: US Government Printing Office, 1965), pp. 708–10.

. . . **de Gaulle's advocacy of what he called 'détente'** . . . on this, see Jean Lacouture, *De Gaulle. The Ruler, 1945–1970* (London: Harvill, 1991), Chapter 29.

. . . **the so-called 'Hallstein Doctrine'** . . . for an authoritative account of the origins of the so-called 'Hallstein Doctrine', by the man who was perhaps most responsible for it, see Wilhelm G Grewe, *Rückblenden 1951–76* (Frankfurt: Propyläen, 1979), pp. 251–62.

. . . **since the Federal Republic alone represented Germany** . . . this was known in German as the *Alleinvertretungsanspruch*, the 'claim to sole representation'.

. . . **trade missions** . . . in the light of Grewe's role in formulating the 'Hallstein Doctrine' it is interesting to note that this 'intermediate solution' had already been proposed by the same Wilhelm G Grewe in a memorandum to the Foreign Minister in January 1957, see ibid, pp. 263–65. The opening of trade missions was agreed with Poland, Hungary and Romania in 1963 and with Bulgaria in 1964; with Czechoslovakia only in 1967.

. . . **demonstratively to ostracise the GDR** . . . this was the policy advocated by one of the early advocates of 'peaceful engagement', Zbigniew Brzezinski, in his book of 1965, *Alternative to Partition*. 'In these years at least,' writes Hans-Peter Schwarz, 'the concepts of German foreign policy were developed less on the Rhine than on the Hudson and Charles rivers!', Hans-Peter Schwarz & Boris Meissner, eds, *Entspannungspolitik in Ost und West* (Köln: Carl Heymanns Verlag, 1979), p. 177. But challenged on this point by George Urban in 1981, Brzezinski himself said 'My suggestions in the mid-1960s for the isolation of East Germany were tactical. I wanted the Federal Republic to recognise the Oder-Neisse line and the new realities in Eastern Europe so that we could more effectively pursue a policy of "peaceful engagement" with Eastern Europe. I knew that I could not get the West Germans to do that *and* recognise East Germany at the same time. So the best way to induce West Germany to be interested in this approach was to say that Communist East Germany was an embarrassment to the Kremlin and in need of being isolated.' See 'A Long conversation with Dr Zbigniew Brzezinski, *Encounter*, May 1981, p. 25.

. . . 'peace note' of March 1966 . . . reprinted in Meissner, *Deutsche Ostpolitik*, pp. 120–24; Jacobsen, *Nachbarn*, pp. 383–89; *Vierzig Jahre*, pp. 171–75.

'Soviet Russia has entered the ranks . . .' quoted in Morsey & Repgen, *Adenauer Studien III*, p. 189 (n. 27), and see also the analysis by Klaus Gotto in his contribution to that volume. In his memoirs, Wilhelm G Grewe suggests that Adenauer may have been temporarily convinced by de Gaulle, against his own basic judgement. See Wilhelm G Grewe, *Rückblenden 1976–1951* (Frankfurt: Propyläen, 1979), pp. 633–37. A similar view is taken in Schwarz, *Adenauer II*, p. 923 ff.

. . . his first government declaration . . . on 13 December 1966, see *Bundestag Plenarprotokolle*, 5/80, pp. 3656–65. According to Schmid, *Politik*, p. 17, Kiesinger drafted this declaration himself.

. . . enshrined in Nato's Harmel report . . . see above, p. 17 and note.

. . . a secret mission . . . see the article by Günter Buchstab in Karl Dietrich Bracher & ors, eds, *Staat und Parteien. Festschrift für Rudolf Morsey zum 65. Geburtstag* (Berlin: Duncker & Humboldt, 1992).

'We all know . . .' *Bundestag Plenarprotokolle*, 5/115, p. 5667 (14 June 1967).

'Germany, a reunited Germany . . .' see *Bulletin*, 20 June 1967, pp. 541–43, this on p. 542. The speech is also reprinted in Meissner, *Deutsche Ostpolitik*, pp. 205–08.

. . . 'détente through reunification' . . . see Hildebrand, *Von Erhard zur Grossen Koalition*, pp. 83–98, but note his cautionary remarks about the degree to which Adenauer had already departed from the concept of 'détente through reunification' in his last years as Chancellor. This point is made still more forcefully in Siebenmorgen, *Gezeitenwechsel*, p. 378.

. . . a list of proposals . . . see *Bulletin*, 14 April 1967, p. 313, and above p. 127 f.

. . . 'a phenomenon' . . . *Bundestag Plenarprotokolle*, 5/126, p. 6360, also in *Texte* I/2, pp. 22–32, this on p. 28.

. . . Herbert Wehner . . . In the first volume of his memoirs, Helmut Schmidt writes: 'Wehner's ideas about Ostpolitik were already clear before Willy Brandt developed his . . . In the whole period of my Chancellorship I discussed my policy with Herbert Wehner every week, especially my Ostpolitik — and I could always rely on him.' Schmidt, *Menschen und Mächte*, p. 30. The judgement is clearly not a full and fair historical one, but it serves as a useful corrective. In the Brandt papers deposited in the AdsD there are numerous letters from Wehner, concerned primarily with East Germany, but also with Poland and Czechoslovakia. These demonstrate a profound interest in pursuing an Ostpolitik based on dealing with the communist 'powers that be' in Eastern Europe. They do not, however, immediately display an overall *conception* for the pursuit of Ostpolitik, particularly in relation to Moscow. A balanced judgement on this point must, however, await the opening of the Wehner papers, which are already partly deposited in the AdsD.

. . . by Helmut Schmidt . . . For an account of Schmidt's part in the early years of Ostpolitik, which, in turn, somewhat exaggerates Schmidt's role, see Lehmann, *Öffnung*.

. . . Ulrich Sahm . . . Ulrich Sahm, Bodenwerder, 27 September 1992.

. . . a somewhat neglected figure . . . and not just in the history of Ostpolitik. A useful recent book, by two of his former aides, is fittingly entitled 'The Forgotten Government': Reinhard Schmöckel & Bruno Kaiser, *Die vergessene Regierung. Die Grosse Koalition 1966 bis 1969 und ihre langfristigen Wirkungen* (Bonn: Bouvier, 1991).

. . . 'did not do badly . . .' letter of 9 October 1969 in AdsD: Dep WB, BA 13.

In January 1967 . . . for this and the following two paragraphs see Löwenthal, *Vom kalten Krieg*, pp. 72–74, Meissner, *Moskau-Bonn*, pp. 766–74, and Bender, *Neue Ostpolitik*, pp. 139–41.

. . . Moscow was prepared to do business . . . see Griffith, *Ostpolitik*, pp. 158–69, Löwenthal, *Vom kalten Krieg*, pp. 71–79, Meissner, *Moskau-Bonn*, pp. 766–74, Bender, *Neue Ostpolitik*, p. 137 ff.

In a lecture delivered in 1971 . . . Frank's lecture, delivered to the *Deutsche Gesellschaft für Osteuropakunde* on 13 October 1971, is printed in *Bulletin*, 14 October 1971, pp. 1573–79.

'Détente . . . is compelled' . . . quoted by Siebenmorgen, *Gezeitenwechsel*, p. 381, from a marginal comment by Egon Bahr on an article by Richard Löwenthal.

. . . and specifically for the Prague Spring . . . see H Gordon Skilling, *Czechoslovakia's Interrupted Revolution* (Princeton: Princeton University Press, 1976), esp. pp. 728 & 732–33.

. . . one of the main Soviet pretexts . . . see, for example, the leading article from *Pravda*, 22 August 1968, reprinted in Meissner, *Moskau-Bonn*, p. 1142.

. . . the reaction of West German leaders . . . see statements following 21 August 1968 in *Dokumente*, V/2, *Texte*, I/3, Meissner, *Deutsche Ostpolitik* and *Moskau-Bonn*. Specifically for Brandt and Bahr's reaction see Baring, *Machtwechsel*, p. 231 ff, Brandt, *Erinnerungen*, pp. 221–22, *People and Politics*, p. 217 ff.

. . . **the March 1969 Budapest Declaration** . . . see *Current Digest of the Soviet Press*, Vol. XXI, No. 11, pp. 11–12. While this 'reaffirmed' the proposals of the Warsaw Pact's 1966 Bucharest Declaration, it was much more conciliatory in tone, and did not make the satisfaction of Moscow's demands a precondition for the opening of talks. For the text of the Bucharest Declaration see *Current Digest of the Soviet Press*, Vol. XVIII, No. 27, pp. 3–7.

. . . **after the failure of the 1965 Kosygin economic reforms** . . . I owe this point to Mark Smith. See also Mikhail Heller and Aleksandr Nekrich, *Utopia in Power. The History of the Soviet Union from 1917 to the Present* (New York: Summit Books, 1986), pp. 629–41.

. . . **unsettled by** . . . **China** . . . this element is stressed by Griffith, *Ostpolitik*, pp. 162–67, and Arndt, *Verträge*, pp. 20–21. The Chinese 'threat' was dramatised by the Sino-Soviet border clash at Ussuri in March 1969. The Soviet Ambassador in Bonn was instructed to inform Chancellor Kiesinger directly of the Soviet Union's concern, see Meissner, *Moskau-Bonn*, p. 1166.

. . . **no longer made** *preconditions* . . . a point subsequently confirmed to Willy Brandt by the Soviet Ambassador, see Löwenthal, *Vom kalten Krieg*, p. 77.

. . . **including Franz Josef Strauss** . . . see the sharp observations in Bender, *Neue Ostpolitik*, pp. 122–23.

. . . **stuck to, indeed retreated to,** . . . this is well charted by Schmid, *Politik*, pp. 22–24. The difference, in tone as much as content, can be appreciated by comparing Kiesinger's state of the nation address on 17 June 1969 (see *Bundestag Plenarprotokolle* 5/239, pp. 13246–13254), with Willy Brandt's first government declaration just four months later, on 28 October 1969 (see *Bundestag Plenarprotokolle* 6/5, pp. 19–34). Ulrich Sahm (Bodenwerder, 27 September 1992) recalls that Foreign Ministry drafts of important notes and statements would come back from the Chancellery with all the daring, innovative passages struck out by Karl Theodor Freiherr von und zu Guttenberg or Karl Carstens.

. . . **Kiesinger had sarcastically described** . . . see *Texte*, I/3, pp. 24–25.

. . . **innovative proposals** . . . for the discussion initiated by the so-called Schollwer Papers see Baring, *Machtwechsel*, pp. 211–29, and Hildebrand, *Von Erhard zur Grossen Koalition*, pp. 342–47.

. . . **what moved and informed Willy Brandt** . . . beside Brandt's *People and Politics* and *Erinnerungen*, see also his earlier volume *Mein Weg nach Berlin* (Munich: Kindler, 1960), translated into English as *My Road to Berlin* (London: Peter Davies, 1960), and the collection of writings from his period in exile, *Draussen* (Munich: Kindler, 1966), translated into English as *In Exile* (London: Oswald Wolff, 1971), with a biographical introduction by Terence Prittie. The restrained, simple and moving memoirs of his wife of many years, Rut Brandt, *Freundesland. Erinnerungen* (Hamburg: Hoffmann & Campe, 1992), give extraordinary insights into his character, as well as some interesting incidental detail about his eastern contacts. Among numerous biographies, Stern, *Brandt*, is concise, lucid and sympathetic, Koch, *Brandt* is comprehensive and revealing, although tending to portray Brandt as a selfish and ambitious party politician, whereas Günter Hoffmann, *Willy Brandt. Porträt eines Aufklärers aus Deutschland*, (Reinbek: Rowohlt, 1988) verges on the hagiographical. There are also astute biographical observations in Baring, *Machtwechsel*. The best short biography in English is Barbara Marshall, *Willy Brandt* (London: Cardinal, 1990).

'We consider . . .' in AdsD: Dep WB, Rbm 30. Formally this was a message from the Berlin city government, the *Senat*.

'The barred walls . . .' in AdsD: Dep WB, Rbm 30.

'In my Wedding constituency . . .' Brandt, *Erinnerungen*, p. 11.

'Gentlemen,' Brandt told the Western Allied commanders . . . quoted from Koch, *Brandt*, p. 279, although Koch does not name his source for this version.

Kennedy, he gathered, . . . Brandt, *Erinnerungen*, p. 10. In fact, Kennedy did interrupt his yachting trip, to the extent of staying onshore in his lakeside bungalow! See the blow-by-blow account in Curtis Cate, *The Ides of August. The Berlin Wall Crisis of 1961* (London: Weidenfeld & Nicolson, 1978), pp. 331–33.

In a cool response . . . both letters are reprinted and expertly introduced by Diethelm Prowe, 'Der Brief Kennedys an Brandt vom 18. August 1961', in VfZ, 33/2 (1985), pp. 373–83. See also Prowe's more recent article, drawing on the American documents, in Hans J Reichhardt, ed., *Berlin in Geschichte und Gegenwart. Jahrbuch des Landesarchivs Berlin 1989* (Berlin: Siedler, 1989), pp 143–67.

'Was it this letter . . .' Brandt, *Erinnerungen*, p. 11. In a conversation with the author (Bonn, 2 October 1991), Willy Brandt recalled his own letter to Kennedy as being above all a gesture to show the dismayed Berliners that he was doing something decisive. He went on to reflect that in the months before the building of the Wall he and his close associates lived in a curious sort of schizophrenia: knowing that this was the American attitude, but also not wanting to know that this was the American attitude. It was thus a moment of truth in the sense of bringing home to them what they already knew.

'I said later . . .' Brandt, *People and Politics*, p. 20.

'I wondered then . . .' Ibid., pp. 290–30. In his 1989 memoirs, Brandt takes a side-swipe at Ronald Reagan for his claim that, had he been President in 1961, he would have had the Wall torn down. 'To be sure,' writes Brandt, 'Reagan publicly called on Gorbachev to get rid of the Wall. But in negotiations with the Russians he set other priorities and certainly did not put in question the division of Germany — *established in 1945 at Yalta.' Erinnerungen*, p. 55 (my italics).

. . . the historical Autobahn . . . a seminal treatment remains Diethelm Prowe, 'Die Anfänge der Brandtschen Ostpolitik in Berlin 1961–1963', (hereafter Prowe, 'Anfänge') in Benz & Graml, *Aspekte*, pp. 249–86.

. . . a tight circle of colleagues . . . beside Bahr it included Heinrich Albertz, himself later Governing Mayor of Berlin, Klaus Schütz, who succeeded

Albertz as Governing Mayor, and Dietrich Spangenberg, head of the Senate Chancellery from 1963. See Bender, *Neue Ostpolitik*, pp. 125–26, Siebenmorgen, *Gezeitenwechsel*, pp. 351–71, Prowe 'Anfänge' in Benz & Graml, *Aspekte*, pp. 251, 255, 265.

... **the first, strictly unofficial contact** ... Bender, *Neue Ostpolitik*, pp. 126–27. The meeting, in December 1961, was between Dietrich Spangenberg and the East German academic Hermann von Berg, who played an important 'middleman' role in German-German relations at this time. Twenty-five years later, in 1986, von Berg emigrated to the Federal Republic, and published a bitterly disillusioned book about the GDR: *Vorbeugende Untwerwerfung. Politik im realen Sozialismus* (Munich: Universitas, 1988). Curiously, he there (pp. 156–58) simply quotes Peter Bender's description of this first contact, without elaborating on it himself. In a conversation with the author (Berlin, 27 June 1991), von Berg explained that he was chosen for this task because, as a leader of the official student organisation in Leipzig in the 1950s, he had made some contacts with Social Democrat student leaders in the West. He recalled that he used to meet Spangenberg by the back entrance of the city hall, 'near the dustbins', so they would not be noticed. He reported to Willi Stoph.

In November 1961 there had been technical contacts on the issue of traffic and telecommunications contacts between the two halves of the divided city, see Prowe, 'Anfänge' in Benz & Graml, *Aspekte*, p. 259.

One of Brandt's Scandinavian connections, Carl Gustav Svingel, was also an important intermediary in these discreet, humanitarian dealings with the GDR. Willy Brandt, Bonn, 2 October 1991. See also the article in *Der Spiegel*, 13/1992, and further detail in Craig Whitney's biography of Wolfgang Vogel, *Spytrader. Germany's legendary spy broker and the darkest secrets of the Cold War* (New York: Times Books, 1993).

... **then tried to negotiate** ... see *Dokumente*, IV/7, pp. 1166–68.

'Since the total strangulation ...' *Dokumente*, IV/7, p. 1006. The increase in suicides is vividly documented in Dietfried Müller-Hegemann, *Die Berliner Mauerkrankheit. Zur Soziogenese psychischer Störungen* (Herford: Nicolaische Verlags-Buchhandlung, 1973)

... **Peter Fechter** ... see the official statements in *Dokumente*, IV/8, pp. 948–50, Brandt, *People and Politics*, p. 37, and Bender, *Neue Ostpolitik*, pp. 124–25.

... **through unconventional, even conspiratorial channels** ... notably through Dr Kurt Leopold of the Trust Office for Inter-Zonal Trade (the West German agency for trade between the two states), through the Protestant churches, and through personal contacts such as those between Spangenberg and von Berg. It seems fair to say that all these contacts had essentially the same basis: the Western side wanted the GDR to grant more elementary freedoms (above all, of movement) to at least a few of their own citizens; the GDR wanted hard currency and/or diplomatic recognition in return. In 1962 there was an attempt to negotiate the first 'Permit Agreement' as a direct *quid pro quo* for a hard currency credit being sought by the GDR: see Prowe, 'Anfänge' in Benz & Graml, *Aspekte*, pp. 262–63 and *Dokumente*, IV/9, p. XI.

`. . .` the first so-called 'Permit Agreement' . . . For the texts see *Dokumente*, IV/9, pp. 1023–38.

`. . .` no less than 790,000 West Berliners . . . see Brandt, *Erinnerungen*, p. 81.

`. . .` again and again return . . . see, for example, the reference in Brandt's 1971 Nobel Peace Prize lecture, *Texte*, I/9, p. 307; in his small book *Menschenrechte misshandelt und missbraucht* (Reinbek: Rowohlt, 1987), pp. 89–90; and, most strikingly, in his speech to the Berliners on the day after the opening of the Berlin Wall, see *Umbruch*, pp. 79–81, this on p. 80.

`. . .` this emotional moment . . . see, for example, the touching exchange between Dettmar Cramer and Egon Bahr in their conversation of 1975. Bahr recalls the experience of going across to East Berlin at that time, and seeing the many West Berliners:

    Cramer: I still remember, the cars six-deep down Unter den Linden
    Bahr: Fantastic!
    Cramer: . . . from the corner of Friedrichstrasse
    Bahr: Wonderful!
    Cramer: . . . up to the [old Prussian] Arsenal
    Bahr: Wonderful! That was really splendid. And one saw masses of people and the people's faces were happy.
    quoted from Cramer, *Bahr*, pp. 41–42.

'It was then . . . that the foundation-stone was laid . . .' 'Ein Fortschritt für die Menschen. Passierschein-Regelung war Grundstein für die Ost-Politik,' in *Sozialdemokratischer Pressedienst*, 42. Jg., No. 33, 17 February 1987, p. 5.

`. . .` 'an Ostpolitik of their own' . . . Krone, 'Aufzeichnungen' in Morsey & Repgen, *Adenauer Studien III*, p. 183 (entry for 31 December 1963).

'What you must do . . .' in AdsD: Dep WB, Rbm 39/40.

`. . .` the 1969 Bonn coalition was forged on the basis . . . see Baring, *Machtwechsel*, p. 199.

'Don't believe . . .' quoted from *Der Spiegel*, 13 March 1963, by Prowe, 'Anfänge' in Benz & Graml, *Aspekte*, p. 271, see also ibid. p. 285, and Baring, *Machtwechsel*, pp. 202–03.

'What most people don't know . . .' in AdsD: Dep WB, BK 3. However according to a report in *Der Spiegel* 18/1991, papers found since unification suggest that Borm may have worked for — or at least co-operated with — the East German State Security Service.

Two planned personal meetings with Khrushchev . . . Stern, *Brandt*, pp. 57–8, Brandt, *People and Politics*, pp. 101–03. Some detail on the preparation for the 1963 meeting is in AdsD: Dep WB, Rbm 73.

'The German side . . .' in AdsD: Dep WB, Rbm 72.

'Khrushchev wants a Western signature . . .' in AdsD: Dep WB, Rbm 72.

`. . .` meetings with . . . Abrassimov . . . Brandt's notes, and a long memorandum (in Swedish) by the host, the Swedish Consul-General Sven Backlund, are in AdsD: Dep WB, Rbm 74. See also the detailed accounts in Brandt, *People and Politics*, pp. 104–110, and Rut Brandt, *Freundesland. Erinnerungen* (Hamburg: Hoffmann & Campe, 1992), pp. 161–78.

'All this is very stupid.' in AdsD: Dep WB, Rbm 72.

. . . de Gaulle had envisaged . . . see Peter Bender, 'War der Weg zur deutschen Einheit vorhersehbar? Charles de Gaulle — Realist und Prophet' in DA, 3/1991, pp. 258–63.

In a series of meetings . . . see Chapter 5 of Brandt, *People and Politics*, entitled 'Conversations with de Gaulle'.

. . . 'alleviation and encouragement . . .' Note on meeting of 24 April 1963, in AdsD: Dep WB, Rbm 74.

'De Gaulle expressed himself very positively . . .' Note on meeting of 2 June 1965, in AdsD: Dep WB, Rbm 74.

. . . American backing for his practical policy . . . See Prowe, 'Anfänge' in Benz & Graml, *Aspekte*, pp. 272–73, Diethelm Prowe, 'Der Brief Kennedys an Brandt vom 18. August 1961', VfZ, 33/2 (1985), pp. 379–80, and the same author's more recent article in Hans J Reichhardt, ed., *Berlin in Geschichte und Gegenwart. Jahrbuch des Landesarchivs Berlin 1989* (Berlin: Siedler, 1989), pp. 143–67; Brandt, *Erinnerungen*, pp. 65–83; Siebenmorgen, *Gezeitenwechsel*, p. 364.

Encouraged by . . . Klaus Schütz . . . Stern, *Brandt*, p. 64. Egon Bahr, Bonn, 4 July 1991.

. . . a German Kennedy . . . see Prowe, 'Anfänge' in Benz & Graml, *Aspekte*, pp. 272–73, and rather sarcastically, Koch, *Brandt*, pp. 310–11. Following Kennedy's assassination, Brandt penned a short book entitled 'Encounters with Kennedy': *Begegnungen mit Kennedy* (Munich: Kindler, 1964).

. . . 'small steps are better than none' . . . this catchphrase, made memorable in German by a play on words — '*kleine Schritte sind besser als keine* — became one of the SPD's slogans during Willy Brandt's second attempt as Chancellor-candidate, in the 1965 federal election. Diethelm Prowe points to the government declaration of the new social-liberal coalition in Berlin, on 18 March 1963, as the first major programmatic declaration of this new approach: see Prowe, 'Anfänge' in Benz & Graml, *Aspekte*, p. 271.

. . . *Coexistence: The Need to Dare* . . . *Koexistenz — Zwang zum Wagnis* (Stuttgart: Deutsche Verlags-Anstalt, 1963). Extracts in *Dokumente*, IV/8, pp. 1151–55.

'Brandt likes to talk . . .' Krone, 'Aufzeichnungen', pp. 155–56 in Morsey & Repgen, *Adenauer Studien III*. On this, see also Bergsdorf, *Sprache*, p. 210 ff.

. . . in the drafts of his speeches and articles . . . which make a quite formidable holding in the Brandt papers.

. . . still needing to be persuaded . . . this point is made explicitly in a letter of

1 August 1963 from Heinrich Albertz to Willy Brandt, in AdsD: Dep WB, Rbm 38.

... **John F Kennedy suddenly proclaimed his 'strategy of peace'** ... for Kennedy's eloquent 10 June 1963 commencement address (drafted by Ted Sorensen) see *Public Papers of the Presidents: John F Kennedy* (Washington: US Government Printing Office, 1964), pp. 459–64.

... **'to redefine the whole ...'** see Arthur M Schlesinger, *A Thousand Days. John F Kennedy in the White House* (New York: Fawcett Premier, 1965), pp. 821–24. The phrase 'strategy of peace', and some of the ideas, can, however, already be found in a collection of Kennedy's pre-1960 speeches published as *The Strategy of Peace* (London: Hamish Hamilton, 1960).

... **'a gift from heaven'** ... Egon Bahr, Bonn, 4 July 1991.

... **at the Free University** ... on 26 June 1963, see *Public Papers of the Presidents: John F Kennedy* (Washington: US Government Printing Office, 1964), pp. 526–29.

... **'Ich bin ein Berliner'** ... According to Eugen Selbmann (Bonn, 8 July 1991) this famous phrase was actually suggested to Kennedy by the German Social Democrat Max Brauer. Willy Brandt (Bonn, 2 October 1991) had not heard this version of events, but recalled Ted Sorensen mentioning the phrase the night before, and rehearsing it with Kennedy on the morning before the speech. See also the handwritten note in AdsD: Dep WB, Rbm 74 and Willy Brandt, *Begegnungen mit Kennedy* (Munich: Kindler, 1964), pp. 191–215. The phonetic note is reproduced in the article by Diethelm Prowe in Hans J Reichhardt, ed., *Berlin in Geschichte und Gegenwart. Jahrbuch des Landesarchivs Berlin 1989* (Berlin: Siedler, 1989), p. 147.

... **the text of his talk** ... reprinted in *Dokumente*, IV/9, pp. 565–71. On the background to this and Bahr's own talk see Schröder, *Bahr*, p. 111 ff. Drafts in AdsD: Dep WB, Pub 159.

'the application of the strategy of peace ...' see *Dokumente*, IV/9, pp. 572–75, for this and following quotations. This famous speech is also reprinted in Meissner, *Deutsche Ostpolitik*, pp. 45–48, Jacobsen, *Nachbarn*, pp. 351–56, Haftendorn, *Aussenpolitik*, pp. 255–60, and Bahr, *Sicherheit*, pp. 11–17.

... **'a policy of transformation'** ... see *Dokumente*, IV/9, pp. 567–68.

'The German question ...' ibid., p. 570.

... **Wandel durch Annäherung** ... In a conversation with Hans Magnus Enzensberger in 1984, Bahr suggested that this formula had made such a career through the 'chance' that his deputy had chosen it as the headline for the circulated copy of his typescript. See *Kursbuch*, Nr. 77, 1984, pp. 97–110, this on p. 98. The same version is given in Schröder, *Bahr*, pp. 111–12, citing a conversation with Bahr. Yet in the passage quoted, Bahr himself offered this formula as the summation of his argument.

... **'common thoughts'** ... Brandt, *Erinnerungen*, p. 73. Brandt says he was slightly unhappy with the formula *Wandel durch Annäherung* — for 'it could nourish the illusion that we sought to come closer to the communist system' — but immediately adds a warm tribute to his 'most conceptually gifted' collaborator. And Bahr comments: 'on the substance, he [Brandt] completely agreed with me', quoted in Schröder, *Bahr*, p. 115.

. . . designed for a specific, transitional phase . . . see Bahr's own comments on the tenth anniversary of his Tutzing speech, published as 'Der Gewaltverzicht und die Allianzen' in *Aussenpolitik* 3/1973, p. 243 ff, and reprinted in Haftendorn, *Aussenpolitik*, pp. 354–67, this on p. 355; similar comments in the discussion on the tenth anniversary of this speech in *Die Zeit*, 15 July 1973, in Cramer, *Bahr*, pp. 43–44, and in Egon Bahr, *Was wird aus den Deutschen?* (Reinbek: Rowohlt, 1982), pp. 219–20.

. . . the courtly, almost exaggerated emphasis . . . the point is made by Brandt himself in the *Erinnerungen*, p. 75. And Peter Bender comments that while Bahr claimed to be applying Kennedy's stategy of peace 'his [Bahr's] thoughts had come earlier', Bender, *Neue Ostpolitik*, p. 126.

Friedrich Naumann said of Bismarck . . . see Baring, *Anfang*, p. 86 ff.

Arnulf Baring has argued . . . ibid.

. . . from Berlin out . . . Diethelm Prowe suggests that the members of Brandt's close circle, mostly not native Berliners, had been drawn to Berlin originally because they believed it was the best place from which to work against the division of Germany. He also makes the interesting comment that Governing Mayors of Berlin received an extraordinary education in foreign affairs, but perhaps at the expense of their grounding in domestic social and economic policy — precisely the strength, and the weakness, that would characterise Brandt's chancellorship. Prowe, 'Anfänge', in Benz & Graml, *Aspekte*, p. 251 and 286. In an article pleading that Berlin should be the capital of united Germany, Brandt himself wrote, in May 1991: 'I stand under suspicion of not having forgotten my time as Governing Mayor — and the preceding years at the side of Ernst Reuter, and the subsequent years with the Ostpolitik, inextricable from Berlin. I am happy to confirm this suspicion.' FAZ, 8 May 1991.

. . . his concept for negotiations . . . see Cramer, *Bahr*, esp. pp. 50–51, 58 ('the whole concept was to hand'), Schröder, *Bahr*, p. 137 ff, Bahr, *Sicherheit*, p. 42, Schmid, *Entscheidung*, esp. pp. 19–20, 225–26.

. . . other senior officials . . . themselves divided . . . Ulrich Sahm, Bodenwerder, 27 September 1992. One should, however, note that the 'Germany department' of the Foreign Ministry worked out its own guidelines and perspectives for negotiations, especially in respect of Berlin. According to the then head of that department, Günther van Well, they did not see the 'concept' worked out in Bahr's planning staff (Günther van Well, Bonn, 8 July 1991). For an example of the careful work of this department see the memorandum (drafted by Hans Otto Bräutigam) quoted in Baring, *Machtwechsel*, pp. 241–42.

. . . every available channel . . . thus the handwritten notes in AdsD: Dep WB,

BA 17–18, record direct encounters with, for example, Piotr Abrassimov, 'my Prague acquaintance W. T.', N. Polyanov of *Izvestia*, the Polish journalist Ryszard Wojna, and a representative of the Czechoslovak trade mission. See also Brandt, *People and Politics*, pp. 171–72, Brandt, *Erinnerungen*, pp. 174–77, and the partial summary of these more or less informal contacts in Schmid, *Entscheidung*, p. 20 f.

... confidential mediation by Italian communists ... the mediation here being particularly between SPD and SED, see the account by Heinz Timmermann, 'Im Vorfeld der neuen Ostpolitik', in *Osteuropa*, 6/71, pp. 388–99, Brandt, *People and Politics*, pp. 220–22, Brandt, *Erinnerungen*, p. 182. A key figure in these contacts was Brandt's close associate Leo Bauer, and more details can be found in AdsD: Dep WB, PV, Verbindungen zu Leo Bauer. See also Peter Brandt & ors, *Karrieren eines Aussenseiters. Leo Bauer zwischen Kommunismus und Sozialdemokratie 1912 bis 1972* (Bonn: Dietz, 1983).

... a discreet lunch in a journalist's flat in Vienna ... for an interesting account of this encounter between Egon Bahr and a Polish diplomat, in January 1968, and its consequences, see the article by Hansjakob Stehle (in whose flat the meeting took place) in *Die Zeit*, 7 December 1990, pp. 41–2.

... shared even by Chancellor Kiesinger ... This can be seen vividly in Brandt's correspondence with Kiesinger in the Brandt papers. On 30 June 1967, for example, Kiesinger wrote to Brandt to complain of an official memorandum of Bahr's conversations in Prague on 12 and 13 June, where it was stated that Bahr 'explained again the readiness of the new Federal Government to live with the GDR in peaceful co-existence'. In January 1969 there then errupted a controversy about Bahr's secret eastern contacts, and in particular about allegations that he had visited the Central Committee of the Socialist Unity Party in East Germany. On 16 January 1969 Brandt wrote to Kiesinger stating plainly that Bahr's contacts were 'on my instructions or with my approval'. On 18 April 1969, Kiesinger wrote with plaintive irritation to say that he gathered from the press that Bahr was going to Washington, and wondered what he would do there! All the above in AdsD: Dep WB, BA 13. In conversation with the conservative journalist Giselher Wirsing, Kiesinger described Egon Bahr as 'a really dangerous man', quoted in Hildebrand, *Von Erhard zur grossen Koalition*, p. 327.

... 'If one wants to maintain...' in an interview in December 1968, reproduced in *Dokumente*, V/2, pp. 1610–11.

... 'Reflections on the foreign policy' ... a copy of this document, datelined New York, 21 September 1969, was kindly made available to the author by Egon Bahr, from his collection now in the AdsD: Dep EB. Brandt was in New York for the annual meeting of the UN general assembly. Bahr confirms that this was the second of the two major working papers of the planning staff, to which he had several times subsequently referred, for example in Bahr, *Sicherheit*, p. 42. He also notes that the paper was prepared on the assumption that the Grand Coalition would probably continue.

That pessimistic assumption ... this was also the optimistic assumption of the East German side. Karl Seidel, Berlin, 30 September 1992.

A shorter version . . . A copy of this was kindly made available to the author by Werner Link. See also Link, *Ära Brandt*, pp. 163–64. A comparison with the longer paper shows this to be essentially an abridgement of it, trimmed for discussion with the Free Democrats.

'Scheel stated in the debate . . .' draft minute by Hans-Jürgen Wischnewski in AdsD: Dep WB, BK 61. The word 'largely' was inserted by Willy Brandt.

. . . a general treaty with the GDR . . . see Baring, *Machtwechsel*, pp. 226–29. Bahr recalls: 'Since thinking in the FDP — independently of us — went in a similar direction, we took only, one could almost say, minutes to agree the foreign policy part of the government declaration. So much were the vision and direction of our thinking in harmony.' Egon Bahr, *Was wird aus den Deutschen?* (Reinbek: Rowohlt, 1982), p. 222.

. . . drawn by Helmut Schmidt and his Social Democratic delegation . . . see the exhaustive account in Lehmann, *Öffnung*, pp. 71–112.

. . . the great common ground . . . 'The regulation of our relationship to the Soviet Union and the East European states including the GDR, was the real, indeed perhaps the only real basis for the social-liberal coalition at the outset', Baring, *Machtwechsel*, p. 199.

. . . a paper written by Bahr in October 1968 . . . a copy of the paper, headed 'Ostpolitik after the occupation of the CSSR', and dated 1 October 1968, was kindly made available to the author by Egon Bahr from AdsD: Dep EB. Baring, *Machtwechsel*, p. 231 records Bahr as 'remarking spontaneously to his associates' that the end of the Dubček era had not changed the overall conditions for Bonn's policy. In fact it clearly *strengthened* the case for dealing with Moscow first and foremost, see Löwenthal, *Vom kalten Krieg*, p. 78 f. It was not only Bahr and Brandt, however, who concluded that the invasion reinforced the argument for the new Ostpolitik. Asked about the consequences of the invasion in a television interview on 21 August 1968, Chancellor Kiesinger responded that he could only answer for the consequences of 'this event' on the Ostpolitik of the Federal Government: 'Here I can only say: we shall consistently pursue this Ostpolitik', see *Texte*, 1/3, p. 63 ff, this on p. 64. It must again be emphasised, however, that German leaders had special reasons to be restrained in their response — since Soviet propaganda had held them directly responsible for the Prague Spring —, and the same thing was said more strongly by American and French leaders. Thus de Gaulle's prime minister, Michel Debré, famously observed that this was 'a traffic accident on the road to détente', while de Gaulle himself remarked to his ambassador in Moscow: '*la Tchécoslovaquie, je m'en bats l'oeil*', both quoted by Pierre Hassner in Gordon, *Eroding Empire*, pp. 196–97.

. . . notably Ralf Dahrendorf . . . see Wolfgang Schollwer, 'Ost-West-Politik eines Europäers' in *Liberal*, 1/88, p. 45, and Schmid, *Entscheidung*, p. 293. Schollwer noted Dahrendorf's insistence on this point in his diary entry for 1 June 1970, AdDL: Schollwer *Tagebuch*.

The secrecy of the negotiations . . . while Gromyko was happy to regard his talks with Bahr as negotiations — which of course in reality they were —, Bahr, in accordance with his brief, insisted that this was only an 'exchange of views'. According to the recollection of Bahr and one of his aides, Antonius Eitel, Gromyko remarked, on once again being reminded of this fine distinction: 'I'll tell you what an "exchange of views" is. An "exchange of views" is when Falin comes to me with his views and goes away with mine.' (Antonius Eitel, Bonn, 1 July 1991. Egon Bahr, Bonn, 4 July 1991).

... the whole library of works ... In English, basic narrative and analysis can be found in Griffith, *Ostpolitik*, Chapter 5; Hanrieder, *Germany, America, Europe*, Chapter 7; Bark & Gress, *Democracy and its Discontents*, Part VIII. In German, the best general accounts are to be found in: Link, *Ära Brandt*, pp. 163 ff, and for the Moscow Treaty specifically pp. 179–90; Meissner, *Moskau-Bonn*, pp. 775–808, and the documents contained in the same volume; Löwenthal, *Vom kalten Krieg*, pp. 79–90; Baring, *Machtwechsel*; Bender, *Neue Ostpolitik*. Schmid, *Entscheidung* is a meticulous and perceptive study of the decision-making process in Bonn from Brandt's October 1969 government declaration to the August 1970 signature of the Moscow Treaty. Detailed accounts of the treaties by informed insiders are Zündorf, *Ostverträge* and Arndt, *Verträge*. Among memoirs and biographies one should mention, beside Brandt's two volumes and Baring's *Machtwechsel*, which is itself a kind of collective biography, the two works of Bonn's then ambassador to Moscow, who was at once personally resentful and substantively critical of Bahr's conduct of the negotiations: Helmut Allardt, *Moskauer Tagebuch. Beobachtungen, Notizen, Erlebnisse* (Düsseldorf: Econ Verlag, 1973) and *Politik vor und hinter den Kulissen. Erfahrungen eines Diplomaten zwischen Ost und West* (Düsseldorf: Econ Verlag, 1979). For Bahr's side of the argument see Schröder, *Bahr*, which also gives references to a number of important interviews with Bahr; the selection of his speeches and articles in Bahr, *Sicherheit*; and two revealing interview volumes: Cramer, *Bahr*, and Egon Bahr, *Was wird aus den Deutschen? Fragen und Antworten* (Reinbek: Rowohlt, 1982).

... three major sweeteners ... see Meissner, *Moskau-Bonn*, p. 775 ff.

it signed the nuclear non-proliferation treaty ... on 28 November 1969.

... a European security conference ... Mastny, *Helsinki I*, p. 3, notes that such a conference was first proposed by Molotov shortly after Stalin's death. It was, of course, also called for in the 1966 Bucharest Declaration and 1969 Budapest Declaration of the Warsaw Pact.

... the banker F Wilhelm Christians ... see his own account in his book *Wege nach Russland. Bankier im Spannungsfeld zwischen Ost und West* (Hamburg: Hoffmann & Campe, 1989), pp. 17–44, hereafter Christians, *Wege*.

... agreements were signed in Essen ... see Meissner, *Moskau-Bonn*, pp. 1209–10, and the excellent treatment in Wörmann, *Osthandel*, pp. 115–25. DM 494m of the DM 1.2bn credit was guaranteed by the Hermes AG — that is, in effect by the Federal Government. The rate of interest was a closely guarded secret, but contemporary estimates put it at 6.25 per cent.

... 'the existing real situation' ... the treaty says the two parties '*gehen dabei von der in diesem Raum bestehenden wirklichen Lage aus*', that is, 'proceed from the existing real situation in this region', see *Verträge*, p. 13. On the legal significance — or non-significance — of the formula see Arndt, *Verträge*, pp. 45–50. Zündorf, *Ostverträge*, p. 34, argues that the substitution of the word *wirklich* for the term *real*, used in earlier Warsaw Pact declarations, 'may perhaps mean a greater proximity to the inclusion of legitimate claims. They too can be *wirklich*. The term *real* by contrast was to be interpreted closer to the material.' The difference is hard to see with an untutored eye.

. . . 'including the Oder-Neisse line' . . . ibid., p. 14.

. . . **first by Bahr, then in the official negotiations by Walter Scheel** . . . the question of Bahr's negotiating ability — or lack of it –, and the significance — or insignificance — of the improvements subsequently achieved by Scheel, is discussed at length in the works listed above.

. . . **down to 'inviolable'** . . . see Griffith, *Ostpolitik*, p. 191 for German and Russian wording.

. . . **a reference in the preamble of the treaty** . . . see Zündorf, *Ostverträge*, pp. 54–55.

. . . **by Adenauer to Bulganin** . . . Meissner, *Moskau-Bonn*, p. 124. The Soviet side merely acknowledged receipt of this letter. Schwarz, *Adenauer II*, p. 219, nonetheless emphasises the importance of this letter for Adenauer's policy, and describes it as the 'letter on German unity', a description more usually applied to that of 1970.

. . . **'solving the main national problem** . . .' for the texts of the letters see Meissner, *Moskau-Bonn*, pp. 122–23. According to the versions there given, while Bulganin's letter talks of the 'national main problem of the whole German people', Adenauer's refers to 'the whole national main problem of the German people'. The formula had been used in the original Soviet note proposing talks about opening diplomatic relations, see above p. 49.

a 'letter on German unity' . . . reprinted in *Verträge*, p. 15, Meissner, *Moskau-Bonn*, pp. 1271–72, *Vierzig Jahre*, p. 226.

Twenty years later . . . see the letter from Ludwig Mertes in the FAZ, 7 August 1990, and the responses from Dr Claus Arndt and Professor Konrad Repgen (both 3 September), Rainer Barzel and Egon Bahr (both 20 September). In a telegram from Moscow dated 21 May 1970, Bahr reported that he had informally handed to Falin the draft of a letter on the right of self-determination. There follows the text of a somewhat longer and more complicated version of what became the Letter on German Unity. (Copy in possession of the author). Falin claims that he actually contributed to the formulation of the letter, Valentin Falin, Hamburg, 14 May 1992. This does not, however, necessarily contradict the claim made by Christian Democrats that they contributed to this initiative from the German side at an earlier stage.

. . . **diplomatic notes** . . . reprinted in *Verträge*, pp. 16–17, *Vierzig Jahre*, p. 227.

. . . **the Christian Democratic opposition insisted** . . . on the Christian Democratic side see, beside the works listed above, Clemens, *Reluctant Realists* and Hacke, *Wege und Irrwege*. The then Party leader, Rainer Barzel, gives his retrospective account in Rainer Barzel, *Im Streit und umstritten. Anmerkungen zu Konrad Adenauer, Ludwig Erhard und den Ostverträgen* (Frankfurt: Ullstein, 1986). A more concrete and detailed memoir is Birrenbach, *Sondermissionen*. A reasoned retrospective summary of the opposition's position was given by Alois Mertes in *Politik und Kultur*, 2/81, pp. 20–38, and in APZ, 18 December 1982, pp. 3–9. A notable contemporary critique was Karl Theodor Freiherr von und zu Guttenberg, *Die neue Ostpolitik. Wege und Irrwege* (Osnabrück: Verlag A Fromm, 1971), while the same author's posthumous *Fussnoten* (Stuttgart: Seewald, 1973) give some fascinating insights. A wealth of material on this subject can be found in the Marx and Mertes Papers in the ACDP.

... a **Common Resolution of the Bundestag** ... reprinted in *Verträge*, pp. 66–67, and *Vierzig Jahre*, pp. 260–62.

... the **Constitutional Court averred** ... the Constitutional Court delivered two main judgements relating to the Eastern treaties, on 31 July 1973 and 7 July 1975. Although the first of these formally referred to the Basic Treaty with the GDR, whereas the second referred explicitly to the Moscow and Warsaw treaties, it was the first — with its insistence on the continued legal existence of the German Reich — which was both juridically and politically most important. The full verdict can be found in *Zehn Jahre*, pp. 232–43, analytical commentary on all the verdicts (including a further minor one of 2 February 1980) in Arndt, *Verträge*, pp. 224–29.

'**Even if two states in Germany exist** ...' see Link, *Ära Brandt*, pp. 166–67.

... '**the constitutive political statement** ...' ibid. quoting from von Weizsäcker's contribution to Diertrich Rollmann, *Die CDU in der Opposition. Eine Selbstdarstellung* (Hamburg: Christian Wegner, 1970), p. 41 f.

.. the '**German signature**' ... see above p. 63.

'**When on 12 August 1970** ...' Bender, *Neue Ostpolitik*, p. 174.

... **resented even by the communist leadership of Poland** ... see Bender, *Neue Ostpolitik*, pp. 176–77, Schmid, *Entscheidung*, p. 115 ff, and 290 ff, and Mieczysław F Rakowski in Lutz, *Bahr*, p. 98. Brandt, in his *Erinnerungen*, pp. 211–12, gives a sensitive account of these Polish sensibilities. He makes the point — also made in many other commentaries — that the Bonn government attempted to take account of them by putting the recognition of the frontier in the first article of the Warsaw Treaty, before the renunciation-of-force clause, whereas in the Moscow Treaty the frontier-recognition was carefully put *after*, and made to follow from, the renunciation-of-force clause. He also reports that when he raised with Gomułka the suggestion that the Warsaw Treaty might be ratified before the Moscow Treaty — thus giving it symbolic priority — Gomułka urged him not to split the two, since any attempt to drive a wedge between Moscow and Warsaw was doomed to fail.

Leaked extracts from the German records ... These were published in the

FAZ and *Die Welt*, both on 18 April 1972. They are reprinted in Meissner, *Moskau-Bonn*, pp. 1473–80, together with the extremely sharp government response, which gives a vivid impression of the atmosphere at that time. The government did not basically deny that the extracts were genuine — indeed they were later to publish one of the fragments themselves (see above p. 74 and note) — but Chancellery Minister Horst Ehmke wrote to the opposition leader, Rainer Barzel, that 'the quotations are torn out of context, changing their sense. In part there are omissions inside individual sentences, in part additions, which are not taken from the records and apparently are meant to be explanatory. In certain cases the text is falsified.' The opposition's suspicions were deepened by the fact that the government did not allow even respected senior Christian Democrats to look through the records of the Moscow and Warsaw negotiations, a bipartisan consensus-building privilege which they claimed Adenauer had given to leading Social Democrats during the negotiation of the Western treaties. Instead, on 6 and 7 May 1972, Egon Bahr read aloud from the records of the Moscow negotiations to a senior Christian Democrat, Kurt Birrenbach, and State Secretary Paul Frank did the same from the records of the Warsaw negotiations. According to Birrenbach, Bahr read him the records for some twenty to twenty-four hours of the total ca. sixty hours of negotiations, with Birrenbach interrupting to ask him to go back or clarify. So far as the authenticity of the leaked extracts is concerned, Birrenbach summarises his impressions thus: 'The fragments published in the press were written by someone who had had direct access to the records. They were, so far as I found them again in the records, reproduced word-for-word. There was only one exception: one quotation was incomplete in an important point. The passages omitted were important, but not crucial for an overall judgement. But to this extent they diminished the value of the publication.' Birrenbach, *Sondermissionen*, pp. 402–04.

In conversation with the author, Egon Bahr said that he did not actually bother to read the records carefully until the opposition started asking for them, and then he was dismayed at what he found. In his judgement, Immo Stabreit, the diplomat at the German Embassy who actually wrote the records, was critical and even 'hostile' to his approach, and this hostility is reflected in the wording and tone of the records. He said, however, that the actual quotations are generally correct. (Egon Bahr, Bonn, 4 July 1991).

Although the leaked fragments must clearly be treated with care, Birrenbach's testimony, the very partial nature of the government denial, and, not least, everything else we know about Bahr's overall approach, all suggest that they give an important insight into the terms and atmosphere of the Bahr-Gromyko talks. A set of the protocols is apparently in AdsD: Dep EB, but Egon Bahr was not yet willing to let the author read them.

In addition to the records, there are the 'delegation reports' sent by telegram to Bonn from the Moscow embassy.

'We had to make sure . . .' This and the following quotations are from Meissner, *Moskau-Bonn*, p. 1476.

At the end of their preliminary talks . . . see Schmid, *Entscheidung*, p. 67.

. . . the 'Bahr paper' . . . this is conveniently printed next to the text of the

Moscow Treaty in Bender, *Neue Ostpolitik*, pp. 233–39. Also in Bahr, *Sicherheit*, pp. 36–39, where Bahr himself comments 'The ten points of the "Bahr paper" were the summation of the single whole of Ost-Politik until the green light for the European conference in Helsinki 1975.'

Its first four points became ... in the official cover-sheet to the 'Bahr paper' it is clearly stated that '1. Of the attached 10 points, points 1–4 are conceived as the subject of the real treaty negotiations.' Further: '2. A renunciation-of-force treaty to be concluded on the basis of numbers 1–4 will be complemented by a letter averring that the conclusion of the treaty does not signify that the Federal Government gives up its political goal to work towards self-determination for all Germans by peaceful means. During the exchange of views, the Soviet delegation declared that it might, in the right circumstances, accept such a letter without rebuttal.' Baring, *Machtwechsel*, p. 318 and copy of text from Baring Papers.

... **joint 'declarations of intent'** ... see Meissner, *Moskau-Bonn*, pp. 1280–81. There also an interview with Scheel, who says that while these declarations are not binding in international law, they 'form for the future, too, the basis of our behaviour, they have political significance'.

... **'Twenty-five years after** ...' Meissner, *Moskau-Bonn*, pp. 1272–73. An earlier draft has the weaker formulation 'with this treaty nothing is given away, which was not already lost in 1945'. AdsD: Dep WB, Publ 0285.

... **'accept[ed] the results of history'** quoted in Bender, *Neue Ostpolitik*, p. 165. The translation given in Brandt, *People and Politics*, p. 407, is 'accepts the consequences of history'.

... **'gambled away by a criminal regime** ...' see the text of his 7 December 1970 television address in *Texte*, I/6, pp. 263–65. Many drafts of this powerful speech are in AdsD: Dep WB, Publ. Responding to a letter of 7 December 1970 from Marion Gräfin Dönhoff, in which she said she had wept the day through, Willy Brandt replied, on 13 December 1970: 'So far as the "weeping" is concerned, it overcame me at my desk, as I was preparing the texts for Warsaw.' AdsD: Dep WB, BK4.

... **'If two states agree** ...' Meissner, *Moskau-Bonn*, p. 1416. Since this passage appeared — word-for-word — in the leaked fragments from the records of the Moscow negotiations (see above p. 72 and note) it rather strengthened the argument for the genuineness of the leaked fragments.

... **by German leaders as much** ... in an interview with *US News and World Report*, 29 December 1969, Brandt said: 'I must confess that I have stopped speaking about reunification'. But stopping speaking and stopping thinking are two slightly different things.

... **conceded too much** ... this impression was strengthened by publication of the so-called 'Gromyko paper', which two leading Christian Democrat opponents of the treaties, Werner Marx and Karl Theodor Freiherr von und zu Guttenberg, claimed had been tabled by Gromyko during his talks with Bahr on 6 March. This bore a remarkable resemblance to the final 'Bahr paper', although with some interesting minor differences. The 'Gromyko paper' spoke, for example, of the 'unalterability' of frontiers. (See Meissner, *Moskau-Bonn*, pp. 1222–23.) In a letter to Brandt ('Lieber W.B.') from Moscow, dated 1 August 1970 — that is, during Scheel's final negotiations — Egon Bahr wrote: 'A small quotation from the negotiations: Gromyko: "The opposition has talked of a Gromyko paper. You sitting round this table will surely not doubt that I am Gromyko, and I don't know this paper." ' AdsD: Dep WB, BK 2. But in the 'delegation report' telegram from Moscow dated 6 March 1970 (copy in the author's possession) there is reference to 'ten theses' handed over by Gromyko, in response to a paper handed over by Bahr the previous day. Insofar as the 'Gromyko paper' existed, it must probably be seen as one of several interim summations, following the more than three weeks of talks that he had already conducted with Bahr.

. . . the armchair Metternich . . . while Bahr had direct experience of East Germany, he had little direct experience of the Soviet Union and Eastern Europe, having only negotiated one agreement with Czechoslovakia, and briefly visited Romania. See Lehmann, *Öffnung*, p. 171, who contrasts him in this respect unfavourably with Schmidt, and reports the professional diplomats' sarcastic quip that 'Bahr speculates for Germany'.

. . . 'a notable success . . .' Meissner, *Moskau-Bonn*, p. 789.

. . . 'painful' concessions . . . Meissner, *Moskau-Bonn*, p. 1416.

. . . 'Consistently in favour . . .' Andrei Gromyko, *Memories*, translated by Harold Shukman (London: Hutchinson, 1989), p. 198.

As in a judo throw . . . see Bahr's own lapidary summary in Bahr, *Sicherheit*, p. 36.

Brandt's handwritten notes . . . in AdsD: Dep WB, BK 91. Brandt's reminiscences of these meetings are in *People and Politics*, Chapter 13, and *Erinnerungen*, pp. 195–210.

. . . he would later note . . . Brandt, *Erinnerungen*, p. 205. In conversation with the author (Bonn, 2 October 1991), Brandt observed that this wish to settle the reparations issue once and for all reflected his concern about public opinion in West Germany, for, he observed, support for the Ostpolitik was not really as broad and deep as it seemed in the 1972 election.

. . . the 'heart of Europe' . . . recollection of Antonius Eitel, Bonn, 1 July 1991.

. . . an explicit linkage . . . for the origins of this linkage see Schmid, *Entscheidung*, p. 62 ff and p. 92. On the 'cover sheet' to the 'Bahr paper' it was plainly noted: '3. It must be stated to the Soviet Union, in addition to the treaty to be concluded, that the Federal Government sees a satisfactory regulation of the situation in and around Berlin as an indispensable part of its détente policy, and will not put the treaty into force until such a satisfactory regulation has been achieved.' Copy from Baring Papers.

. . . notes scribbled for his response . . . in AdsD: Dep WB, BK 91. The reading of '*Ml-Eur*' as '*Mitteleuropa*' was given by Brandt himself in conversation with the author (Bonn, 2 October 1991).

This so-called *Berlin-Junktim* ... One of the Christian Democratic opposition's criticisms was that the Brandt government had signed the Moscow Treaty before getting a satisfactory agreement on Berlin — see, for example, the statements by former Foreign Minister Gerhard Schröder in *Texte I/6*, pp. 308–9 & 378–81. Once again, there is a large literature on just this one point. For two balanced and differentiated accounts, one moderately critical of the Government's conduct, the other moderately supportive, see Meissner, *Moskau-Bonn*, p. 787 ff, and Löwenthal, *Vom kalten Krieg*, p. 82 ff. Brandt and Bahr were certainly the last people to neglect the special interests of Berlin.

Immensely intricate and delicate negotiations ... a brilliant and vivid account is given in Kissinger, *White House Years*, pp. 801 f, 805 f, and 823–33. See also Brandt, *Erinnerungen*, pp. 229–31, Brandt, *People and Politics*, pp. 387–93, Bark & Gress, *Democracy and its Discontents*, pp. 190–99, Griffith, *Ostpolitik*, p. 196 ff, Bender, *Neue Ostpolitik*, pp. 186–90.

... the two Metternichs of détente ... Bahr and Kissinger had a healthy mutual suspicion and grudging mutual respect. Thus Kissinger, in his memoirs, describes Bahr as 'a German nationalist who wanted to exploit Germany's central position to bargain with both sides' but adds: 'as for his alleged deviousness, I tended to share Metternich's view that in a negotiation the perfectly straightforward person was the most difficult to deal with. I at any rate did not lack the self-confidence to confront Bahr's tactics.' Kissinger, *White House Years*, pp. 410–11. For his part, Bahr paid tribute to Kissinger's deviousness in an interview with Hans Magnus Enzensberger in *Kursbuch*, 77, September 1984, p. 99.
In conversation with the author, Egon Bahr averred that Kissinger's initial mistrust seemed to him to have been largely overcome by the time of the Moscow Treaty, and that they worked together closely and effectively thereafter, especially in the negotiation of the Quadripartite Agreement on Berlin. (Egon Bahr, Potsdam-Berlin, 29 June 1991). A conversation with Henry Kissinger on the same day suggested that perhaps some of the mistrust after all remained. But while describing Bahr as a left-nationalist, and arguing that he was perhaps excessively preoccupied with the Bonn-Moscow-Berlin triangle, Kissinger nonetheless acknowledged Bahr's analytical brilliance and strategic clarity. (Henry Kissinger, Berlin, 29 June 1991).

... the resulting Quadripartite Agreement ... English text in Grenville, *Treaties*, pp. 196–98, German text, with the important annexes, in *Verträge*, pp. 70–87.

... 'it is still difficult for me ...' quoted in Kissinger, *White House Years*, p. 830.

... 'three Zs' ... see Bender, *Neue Ostpolitik*, p. 187 f. For judgements on the agreement overall, compare Bark & Gress, *Democracy and its Discontents*, pp. 196–97, Meissner, *Moskau-Bonn*, pp. 794–95, Griffith, *Ostpolitik*, pp. 196–200, Kissinger, *White House Years*, pp. 830–31.

... 'ties' ... in one of those absurd diplomatic fandangles in which the post-war history of Berlin was replete, the French declined to have the German text of this agreement about Germany recognised as 'official'. As a result, there were two German texts, West and East. The West Germans, for example, translated 'ties' as *Bindungen* while the East Germans used the weaker *Verbindungen*, thus providing stuff for further endless legal-symbolic-theological disputation. See Brandt, *Erinnerungen*, pp. 230–31, and Kissinger, *White House Years*, p. 832.

'Tomorrow [i.e. 13 August 1970] . . .' Meissner, *Moskau-Bonn*, p. 1273.

. . . top of his personal agenda . . . see the handwritten notes in AdsD: Dep WB, BK 92, where the item 'DDR' comes second only to the complex 'ratification/Berlin'.

. . . 'regards the creation of *a modus vivendi* . . .' AdsD: Dep WB, BK 58. In the German he does not use any article, definite or indefinite, before 'central task', thus leaving it open to the reader to guess whether it is *a* or *the* central task of his policy! This omission of the article is a characteristic trick of Brandt's style, one of the small keys to its elevated vagueness.

. . . a message sent with Egon Bahr . . . in AdsD: Dep WB, BK 74.

. . . Bahr spent four hours . . . Schröder, *Bahr*, pp. 204–05.

. . . what direct effect . . . in his 1976 memoirs, Brandt notes that Brezhnev visited East Berlin in November 1971 'after I had been his guest in the Crimea. . . It is likely that he prompted the GDR leaders to take a few initiatives in the matter of intra-German agreements — at any rate, that had been my suggestion to him.' Brandt, *People and Politics*, p. 393.

A few of these documents . . . already accessible . . . notably in the Central Party Archive (ZPA) in East Berlin. At the time of writing, publication of such documents has mostly occurred in the form of more or less sensational 'revelations', generally of documents sold or leaked by people in high places, or with access to high places, in the former ruling apparatus of the GDR. This is the case, for example, with the bestselling Peter Przbylski, *Tatort Politbüro. Die Akte Honecker* (Berlin: Rowohlt, 1991), henceforth cited as Przybylski, *Tatort 1*. This is a selection of documents from the file of the state prosecutor's judicial investigation against Erich Honecker, after his downfall, documents copied, selected, and tendentiously introduced by the former press spokesman of the state prosecutor's office of the GDR. The dubious form of the publication does not seriously put in question the authenticity of the actual documents, although it does increase the risk of taking them out of their proper context. One must hope that a more disinterested, systematic and scholarly publication will follow.

. . . Honecker's own notes . . . typewritten notes dated 2.12.1969 and 15.5.1970. These come from a remarkable source, a synthetic-leather-bound volume of photocopied documents with, embossed in gilt on the front cover, the single word '*Dokumente*'. Almost all the documents in the volume concern relations between the East German and Soviet Party leaderships at critical junctures, in 1953, and then in 1969–71. The collection was apparently put together at the behest of Erich Honecker, and circulated to all members of the Politburo in February 1989, but the copies were then collected in. Kurt Hager recalled this curious sally in conversation with the author (Berlin, 8 May 1992) and interpreted it as part of Honecker's defence against any attempt to replace him. These documents should demonstrate that he had always had the closest ties with Moscow. Similarly Egon Krenz (Berlin, 29 September 1992). Copy 29 of the 'Dokumente' can be found in ZPA: JIV 2/2A/3196.

It should however be noted that these documents were prepared in this form for this particular purpose under Honecker's supervision. A collection of the manuscript originals on which the *'Dokumente'* are based is apparently in the Central Party Archive, but was not available to the author for examination. It is possible that amendments may therefore have been made, or simple errors of transcription.

Many of the documents in Pryzybylski, *Tatort 1*, are actually taken from this source, as he himself notes on pp. 101–14.

... Brezhnev and Honecker on 28 July 1970 ... this also comes from the 'Dokumente' (see note immediately above). For the convenience of readers, page references are given to the version printed in Przybylski, *Tatort 1*, pp. 280–88, but quotations have been checked against the copy in ZPA: JIV 2/2A/3196. However note again the possibility that some changes may have been made in preparing the documents for circulation to the Politburo in 1989.

'*I tell you quite openly* ...' Przybylski, *Tatort 1*, p. 281.

'This will not solve ...' ibid, p. 283.

'Brandt is under double pressure ...' ibid, p. 287.

'It ... must not come' ibid, p. 283.

... 'concentrate everything ...' ibid, p. 284.

... 'objectively one must pay him ...' this and the following quotation are from the record (*Niederschrift*) of the conversation between Honecker and Brezhnev in the Kremlin on 18 June 1974, now in ZPA: IV 2/2.035/55.

... recognise the status quo in order to overcome it ... Bahr had already come close to this dialectical formula in his Tutzing speech, see above p. 65. In a television discussion in September 1967, he observed that the Bonn government had accepted the status quo: 'When the Federal Government says renunciation-of-force. What else does that mean?' But he went on to say that the Government 'wants to start from the status quo, in order to overcome it'. See *Dokumente* V/1, pp. 1575–87, this on pp. 1579–80. In his Nobel Peace Prize lecture, Brandt returned to the achievement of the first permit agreement in Berlin and said: 'this was in a nutshell the application of the insight that there can be a new, only apparent paradox, which will have benign effects: to improve the situation through recognition of the situation as it is', see *Texte* I/6, p. 307.

... 'Alliances, us: Rome, loyal' ... in AdsD: Dep WB, BK 91.

... 'Basic principle: in loyalty to allies ...' in AdsD: Dep WB, BK 91.

In his Nobel Peace Prize lecture ... reprinted in *Texte* I/9, pp. 302–19, this on p. 313. He repeats the same point in his *Erinnerungen*, p. 187.

... **to West Germany's Western partners** ... for a wealth of detail on this, see Kurt Birrenbach's account of his trips to Western capitals to sound out reactions to the new Ostpolitik, in Birrenbach, *Sondermissionen.*

... **two working papers** ... this was attested several times by Bahr, for example in Bahr, *Sicherheit*, p. 42, and Egon Bahr, *Was wird aus den Deutschen?* (Reinbek: Rowohlt, 1982), pp. 221–22. In his interview with Hans Magnus Enzensberger in *Kursbuch*, 77, September 1984, p. 99, he notes that 'the paper' (presumably that on security) was also shown to Walter Scheel.

... **to 'analyse German interests** ...' this paper was first published, as a leak, in the weekly *Quick*, 27 September 1973, under the provocative title 'How Egon Bahr wants to neutralise Germany'. Bahr himself reprints it in Bahr, *Sicherheit*, pp. 42–52, commenting that 'the overcoming of the two blocs through a European security system, in order to achieve unity, remains a task, after unity has been achieved'. Egon Bahr kindly made available to the author a copy of the original paper, which is datelined Bonn, 27 June 1968.

... **from Conception A to Conception C** ... Conception B was an intermediate stage in which Nato and Warsaw Pact would be 'tied together' by common organs, eventually becoming an 'institutional roof (permanent European security conference) over the pacts ...' ibid.

... **Walter Hahn** ... see Walter F Hahn, 'West Germany's Ostpolitik. The Grand Design of Egon Bahr', in *Orbis*, Winter 1973, pp. 859–80. This is not only a vivid report but also a fine analysis. In a note to Willy Brandt dated 19 August 1968, Bahr reported on an evening discussion of the security paper *'bei Ducki'* (that is, Duckwitz). The consensus was, he wrote, that C was the really interesting part, on which more preparatory work needed to be done. This from AdsD: Dep EB.

... **what the Federal Republic's Western allies feared** ... for a measured account of such fears see Kissinger, *White House Years.* Kissinger's mistrust of the new German Ostpolitik is more sharply and critically recalled in Seymour M Hersh, *Kissinger: The Price of Power* (London: Faber, 1983), pp. 415–22.

... **'in foreign policy** ...' in AdsD: Dep WB, BK 68.

... **pressed hard but unsuccessfully** ... note that Article 5 of the Basic Treaty with the GDR made an emphatic commitment of both states to supporting both conventional and nuclear arms reductions in Europe. For the exact wording see *Zehn Jahre*, p. 206.

'We deflected the German initiative ...' Kissinger, *White House Years*, p. 534.

... **simply exhausted** ... Egon Bahr, Bonn, 4 July 1991.

... **motives and attitudes** ... this point is made by, among others, Schmid, *Politik*, p. 92 f and Schmid, *Entscheidung, passim*; Meissner, *Moskau-Bonn*, p. 777 ff; Wolfgang Schollwer in *Liberal*, 1/88, p. 46.

... **the support of Germany's Western partners** ... probably not untypical of British attitudes was Peter Carrington's comment to Kurt Birrenbach that he had 'put aside' his initial fears after seeing the commitment with which Helmut Schmidt, as Defence Minister, supported the development of Nato and the maintenance of close ties with the United States, see Birrenbach, *Sondermissionen*, pp. 377–78.

The existential argument ... this argument is made most clearly and forcefully in Baring, *Grössenwahn*.

... **urged most forcefully by Helmut Schmidt** ... see his book *Strategie des Gleichgewichts. Deutsche Friedenspolitik und die Weltmächte* (Stuttgart: Seewald, 1969), translated into English as *The Balance of Power. Germany's Peace Policy and the Superpowers* (London: Kimber, 1971).

... **a leitmotif of the new policy** ... see above p. 22 f. Brandt, *Erinnerungen*, pp. 185–95. Link, *Ära Brandt*, p. 224, notes that when Brandt arranged to meet Brezhnev at Oreanda in the Crimea in September 1971, 'the Western allies were merely informed, not consulted'.

'I think it is no exaggeration ...' in AdsD: Dep WB, BK 42

... **tactical for some** ... Thus Bahr's working paper of 21 September 1969 concludes by considering two possible German tactics inside the EEC, and comes down in favour of the more conciliatory one partly because the Federal Republic would need the 'good will' (in English in the original) of its closest European allies for its alliance policy and Ostpolitik. Copy from AdsD: Dep EB, in the author's possession.

... **its multilateral development** ... see, for example, an interview Brandt gave to the London *Times*, reprinted in *Bulletin*, 1 March 1973, pp. 225–30, esp. p. 229.

'After public opinion in our country ...' letter of 30 May 1973, in AdsD: Dep WB, BK 58.

... **Falin, said** ... note of 1 June 1973 by Carl-Werner Sanne, in AdsD: Dep WB, BK 58

'The Soviet side may not realise ...' letter of 30 December 1973, in AdsD: Dep WB, BK 58.

... **the two sets of talks as intimately linked** ... in a letter to Brezhnev dated 4 May 1973 he reported his full agreement with Nixon on the 'inner connection' between 'the subjects treated in Helsinki and in Vienna'. AdsD: Dep WB, BK 58. For a clear public statement see *Bulletin*, 14 July 1972, p. 1361.

... **a time-scale of five years** ... see his notes for his meeting with Brezhnev in Bonn, dated 18 May 1973, and those dated 20 May 1973, in AdsD: Dep WB, BK 94.

... **Waldemar Besson** ... Waldemar Besson, 'The Conflict of Traditions. The Historical Basis of German Foreign Policy', in Karl Kaiser & Roger Morgan, eds., *Britain and West Germany. Changing Societies and the Future of Foreign Policy* (Oxford: Oxford University Press, 1971), pp. 61–80.

Henry Kissinger ... Kissinger, *Years of Upheaval*, p. 147, see also Kissinger, *White House Years*, pp. 410–12.

'I have been fascinated...' Cramer, *Bahr*, p. 65.

...'the real mastery...' ibid., p. 66.

'one of the great statesmen...' reprinted in *Texte* I/6, pp. 351–2. For other indications of Brandt's ambivalent and qualified respect for Bismarck see Prowe, 'Anfänge' in Benz & Graml, *Aspekte*, p. 251, and the references in Brandt, *People and Politics*.

... the system demanded ... the next three paragraphs owe a significant debt to the very stimulating chapter by Josef Joffe in Gordon, *Eroding Empire*. He uses there the term 'synchronisation'; the distinction between 'horizontal' and 'vertical' synchronisation is, I believe, mine.

... a principle of synchronisation ... this was implicit already in the crucial statement in the 'Bahr paper' that the treaties with the Soviet Union, the GDR, Poland and Czechoslovakia formed 'a single whole' (see above, p. 73). Bahr spells out the imperative of horizontal synchronisation clearly in Cramer, *Bahr*, p. 70. For a clear public statement by Schmidt see *Bundestag Plenarprotokolle*, 7/218, p. 15085 (29 January 1976). The contrast with American 'differentiation' is made by Joffe in Gordon, *Eroding Empire*, pp. 162–64.

Similarly, but *a fortiori*,... this was clearly spelled out by Schmidt in his 1975 state of the nation address, to a chorus of 'very true!' from Herbert Wehner, see *Bundestag Plenarprotokolle*, 7/146, p. 10038 (30 January 1975).

... the first external preoccupation ... two excellent general treatments of German foreign policy in the Schmidt period are Haftendorn, *Sicherheit* and Link, *Ära Schmidt*.

'Never since...' This and following quotations are from the 10 April 1977 typescript version of the paper, which was originally written over the New Year holiday. Now in AdsD: HS 002.

... Hans Georg Lehmann ... see Lehmann, *Öffnung*, p. 201 and passim.

... a representative of this *Frontgeneration* ... this element emerges very clearly from Schmidt's own memoirs and statements. Franz Josef Strauss himself observed in his review of the first volume of the memoirs that this was a formative experience which he and Schmidt had in common, and which had a decisive influence on both their subsequent approaches to the Soviet Union, see *Die Zeit*, 7 October 1988. A brief account of Schmidt's war years can be found in Harald Steffahn, *Helmut Schmidt* (Reinbek: Rowohlt, 1990).

... methods and manners ... this is quite vividly apparent in the contrast between the organisation of the official papers of the Chancellery under Brandt and under Schmidt. The point was also made by Holger Börner in conversation with the author, Bonn, 11 July 1991. It is interesting to note that Schmidt enrolled in the Bundeswehr Reserve forces, in his old rank of first lieutenant, and in 1958 was promoted to Captain, see the brief account (with picture) in Harald Steffahn,

Helmut Schmidt (Reinbek: Rowohlt, 1990), pp. 69–70. Gromyko wrote sourly that 'although capable and strong-willed, he had not fully freed himself from the outlook of an officer in the German Wehrmacht', Andrei Gromyko, *Memories* (London: Hutchinson, 1989), p. 202.

'**We seek . . .**' Helmut Schmidt, *The Balance of Power. German Peace Policy and the Superpowers* (London: Kimber, 1971), p. 24. German edition: *Strategie des Gleichgewichts. Deutsche Friedenspolitik und die Weltmächte* (Stuttgart: Seewald, 1969).

. . . in his bilateral discussions with the United States . . . a thorough treatment of this aspect of his Chancellorship is Heep, *Schmidt und Amerika.*

. . . 'in the eyes of the world . . .' this and following quotations from the 10 April 1977 typescript version in AdsD: IIS 002.

. . . summit meetings . . . on this see Schmidt's own comments in his essay, 'Glanz und Elend der Gipfeldiplomatie—und ihre Notwendigkeit' in Helmut Schmidt and Walter Hesselbach, eds., *Kämpfer ohne Pathos. Festschrift für Hans Matthöfer zum 60. Geburtstag am 25. September 1985* (Bonn: Verlag Neue Gesellschaft, 1985), pp. 235–39. See also Dieter Rebentisch, 'Gipfeldemokratie und Weltökonomie', in *Archiv für Sozialgeschichte*, Vol. XXVIII, 1988, pp. 307–32.

. . . described as *Staatslenker* . . . see, for example, Schmidt, *Menschen und Mächte*, pp. 141, 459.

. . . 'the role of the Federal Republic . . .' this and following quotation from the protocol by the Foreign Ministry interpreter E Hartmann of the conversation between Schmidt and Brezhnev on 4 May 1978, with manuscript corrections in Schmidt's hand. Now in AdsD: HS 174.

. . . a good and even sentimental relationship . . . In a conversation with Mrs Thatcher on 18 November 1981, Schmidt said that Brezhnev 'reminded him of the Russian characters that we know from the great Russian novels . . . After six meetings, he [i.e. Schmidt] had developed a personal sympathy for him. His wish for peace is genuine. He is deeply afraid of a new war. He comes back again and again to his own wartime experiences.' This from a minute of the conversation by the then head of the foreign policy department in the Chancellery, Otto von der Gablentz, now in AdsD: HS 199. In his memoirs, Schmidt also characterises Brezhnev as a man such as Maxim Gorky and other Russian writers might have described, see Schmidt, *Menschen und Mächte*, p. 71.

. . . Schmidt responded . . . Schmidt's account is in *Menschen und Mächte*, pp. 19–20. See also Brandt's account in *People and Politics*, p. 364, where he writes that 'Brezhnev was deeply moved by the reminiscences of the then Finance and former Defence Minister'. Also in Brandt, *Erinnerungen*, pp. 201–2.

. . . 'when war reminiscences are exchanged . . .' Brandt, *Erinnerungen*, p. 201. The comment is related directly to his account of Schmidt's response to Brezhnev.

. . . genuine sorrow . . . Schmidt, *Menschen und Mächte*, p. 131.

... **better understood** ... ibid., p. 228. Schmidt repeated this in conversation with the author, London, 3 June 1991. The point is also picked up by Brandt, *Erinnerungen*, p. 359.

... **a conversation with** ... **Falin** ... minute of the conversation on 25 September 1974 by the then head of the foreign policy department in the Chancellery, Carl-Werner Sanne, now in AdsD: HS 130.

... **the GDR announced** ... see Link, *Ära Schmidt*, p. 293.

... **Berlin, which occupied a great deal of time** ... on this, see the useful summary in Avril Pittman, *From Ostpolitik to Reunification. West German-Soviet Political Relations since 1974* (Cambridge: Cambridge University Press, 1992), Chapter 3.

... **Gromyko spoke dismissively** ... following quotations are from the minute of a conversation between Schmidt and Gromyko on 16 September 1974, in preparation for the Chancellor's visit to Moscow. The note seems to have been written by the then head of the foreign policy department of the Chancellery, Carl-Werner Sanne, and is now in AdsD: HS 129.

.... **'strict observance and full application'** ... Brandt, *People and Politics*, p. 365.

.. **a personal letter** ... datelined Hamburg [not Bonn!], 5 April 1975. A copy of this letter was made available to me from AdsD: Dep EB, 409, by kind permission of Helmut Schmidt and Egon Bahr. The first copies of the whole correspondence with Brezhnev are presumably in Schmidt's private archive in Hamburg.

... **somewhat at odds with the Foreign Ministry** ... the tougher and more status-oriented line of the Foreign Ministry was authoritatively expressed by Günther van Well in an article entitled 'The participation of Berlin in international affairs. An urgent point on the East-West agenda', in EA, 20/1976, pp. 647–56.

... **the presence of Federal Government institutions** ... the siting of the Federal Office for Environmental Protection in West Berlin in 1974 had provoked strong Soviet protests.

... **openly and contemptuously dismissive** ... even in his memoirs he described the Carter human rights campaign as as 'mistake' and a 'threat to the détente process', Schmidt, *Menschen und Mächte*, pp. 222–23.

... **in a lecture in 1991** ... this was a lecture to members of the German Society for Foreign Policy (DGAP) in Bonn in September 1991, printed as 'Germany's role in the new Europe' in EA 21/1991, pp. 611–24, this on p. 624.

His book published in 1969 ... Published under this title in English in 1971. The original German title was *Strategie des Gleichgewichts. Deutsche Friedenspolitik und die Weltmächte* (Stuttgart: Seewald, 1969).

The foreign policy of a state ... attributed to Georges Pompidou by Michael

Stürmer in Peter R Weilemann, ed., *Aspects of the German Question* (Sankt Augustin: Konrad-Adenauer-Stiftung, 1985), p. 9.

... a key element in that Westpolitik of Brezhnev ... this is clearly brought out in the excellent discussion in Stent, *Embargo to Ostpolitik*. (See also the further discussion in Chapter Four, below.)

... jumped into a gleaming new Mercedes ... ibid., p. 192.

... in glowing terms ... ibid., p. 193. Brandt, *People and Politics*, p. 360 ff.

... 'the political motive ...' minute of a conversation between Schmidt and Gromyko on 16 September 1974, now in AdsD: HS 129.

... some economic motives ... see the balanced discussion in Stent, *Embargo to Ostpolitik*, Chapter 9. See also Chapter Five, below, pp. 244 f. In conversation with the Chancellor on 25 February 1974, the Soviet Ambassador, Valentin Falin, noted in passing that the Soviet Union would buy 10,000 lorries from the firm Klöckner-Humboldt-Deutz. This, he observed, was one third of the annual output of that firm! See the minute now in AdsD: HS 130.

... a clear complementarity ... this point was made frequently by both sides. Thus, in the aforementioned conversation with Gromyko in September 1974, Schmidt said: 'We proceeded on the assumption that the conditions and products of the two economies were complementary. The Federal Republic could supply investment goods and technology in large quantities to the Soviet Union ... The Soviet Union could supply us with raw materials and processed raw materials'. Note in AdsD: HS 129. In a personal letter from Brezhnev to Schmidt, dated 23 September 1974, the Soviet leader expressed his satisfaction 'that we agree to pay special attention to the economic theme during your stay in Moscow' — German version ('unofficial translation') now in AdsD: HS 130.

... some 300,000 jobs ... Stent, *Embargo to Ostpolitik*, p. 217.

... for advancing German national interests ... Schmidt, *Menschen und Mächte*, pp. 138–40. In Schmidt, *Nachbarn*, p. 448, he goes so far as to say that to the Bonn government eastern trade and eastern credits were 'of purely political interest'.

... 'the long-term securing ...' the memorandum, dated 17 October 1977, was signed by the then head of the Chancellery department for economic and financial policy, and is now in AdsD: HS 168.

... the barter deals frowned upon ... this was a major subject at the aforementioned brainstorming session, on 18 October 1977, see the minute now in AdsD: HS 168.

... Kaliningrad ... Kursk ... see Stent, *Embargo to Ostpolitik*, pp. 223–32.

... 'into the third millennium' ... this, in direct quotation marks, in the minute of the meeting on 18 October 1977, now in AdsD: HS 168.

... a very broadly framed agreement ... text in *Bulletin*, 9 May 1978, pp. 431–2.

... 'political act without parallel ...' quoted in Stent, *Embargo to Ostpolitik*, p. 206.

... 'It is not a historic accord.' ibid., p. 207.

The total volume ... this and further figures in this paragraph are taken from ibid., pp. 209–15.

... nearly thirty per cent ... Stent, *Embargo to Ostpolitik*, pp. 212–13, gives a figure of 28 per cent by 1990, which she says would represent five per cent of total energy supplies. Schmidt set a ceiling of 30 per cent, which he says would be six per cent of the Federal Republic's total energy imports, see Schmidt, *Menschen und Mächte*, p. 79. The actual figures for 1989 were 30 per cent of West Germany's natural gas supplies and 4.99 per cent of the total value of its energy imports. Figures from the Foreign Ministry.

... confidential personal letters ... the author has at the time of writing only been able to see a few letters from this remarkable correspondence, in copies from AdsD: Dep EB. Nonetheless, even from these the warming of tone is apparent.

... the already seriously ill Soviet leader ... Schmidt notes that he was dismayed by the obvious deterioration in Brezhnev's health, *Menschen und Mächte*, p. 98. Valentin Falin says that Brezhnev was 'mortally sick' from as early as 1975. Valentin Falin, Hamburg, 14 May 1992.

... a Joint Declaration ... *Bulletin*, 9 May 1978, pp. 429–31. As already noted, the word 'détente' here occurs seven times in two pages.

... a sharp polarisation ... this argument produced an immense and largely ephemeral literature. For those who wish to get a taste of the argument at a fairly high level one might recommend the sharply contrasting books of Robert Conquest, *Present Danger. Towards a Foreign Policy* (Oxford: Blackwell, 1979) and Fred Halliday, *The Making of the Second Cold War* (London: Verso, 1983).

... withering criticism ... see, for example, Schewardnadse, *Zukunft*, p. 109 f and the devastating passage on p. 116. For an early public expression, see the article by the Soviet policy intellectual and Foreign Ministry adviser, Vyacheslav Dashitschev, in *Literaturnaya Gazeta*, 18 May 1988. It is reprinted in Wolfgang Seiffert, *Die Deutschen und Gorbatschow. Chancen für einen Interessenausgleich* (Erlangen: Straube, 1989), pp. 211–25.

... influence in the Third World ... this is, of course, a highly complex and controversial subject. For a very measured discussion of this and the impact on Soviet-American relations, see Garthoff, *Détente*, esp. Chapter 19. For a more critical view, which was to become highly influential under the Reagan Administration, see the 11 November 1976 policy statement of the Committee on the Present Danger, reprinted in Charles Tyroler, ed., *Alerting America. The Papers of the Committee on the Present Danger* (Washington: Pergamon Brassey's, 1984), pp. 3–5. For accounts more sympathetic to the Soviet position see Fred Halliday, *The Making of the Second Cold War* (London: Verso, 1983), especially Chapter 4, and Jonathan Steele, *World Power. Soviet Foreign Policy under Brezhnev and Andropov* (London: Michael Joseph, 1983).

... 'in my view' ... Letter of 13 February 1976. Copy in AdsD: Dep EB, 409.

'Altogether ...' this in a luncheon speech on 5 May 1978, see *Bulletin*, 9 May 1978, p. 428.

... 'he liked to think ...' minute of their conversation on 16 September 1974, now in AdsD: HS 129.

Defence or Retaliation ... Verteidigung oder Vergeltung. Ein deutscher Beitrag zum strategischen Problem der Nato (Stuttgart: Seewald, 1961). English edition: *Defence or Retaliation. A German Contribution to the Consideration of Nato's Strategic Problem* (Edinburgh: Oliver and Boyd, 1962).

... a memorable speech to the Bundestag ... see *Bundestag Plenarprotokolle*, 3/87, pp. 4758–4767 (5 November 1959).

... 'Why?' ... Lehmann, *Öffnung*, p. 172

... the West German leader had serious concerns ... by some accounts, Schmidt was significantly influenced in this concern about the gap in the chain of deterrence by a group of American and European defence intellectuals headed by Albert Wohlstetter, see Garthoff, *Détente*, p. 855, and the article referred to there by Fred Kaplan in the *New York Times Magazine*, 9 December 1979. It is interesting to find that this claim was taken up by one of the leading Soviet specialists on the United States, Georgi Arbatov, see Georgi A. Arbatov, *Cold War or Détente? The Soviet Viewpoint* (London: Zed Books, 1983), p. 126. Schmidt himself makes favourable mention of Wohlstetter in *Menschen und Mächte*, p. 274 but in a letter to the author (13 November 1992) Schmidt denied that there was a specific influence with regard to the SS-20 build-up.

By his own account ... Schmidt, *Menschen und Mächte*, p. 64

In what was to become a famous speech ... the best account of this whole episode is in Haftendorn, *Sicherheit*, pp. 1–31, with the most important parts of the speech reprinted on pp. 195–212. English text in *Survival*, Vol. 20, No. 1, Jan-Feb 1978, pp. 2–10. It is remarkable how little of the speech was actually devoted to this subject. Schmidt's own brief account is in *Menschen und Mächte*, pp. 230–31. In a letter to the author (13 November 1992) he himself stressed that the speech itself was rather diplomatic and what he called 'the real burst-out' happened over dinner.

... Michael Howard, would describe ... conversation with the author.

... a transatlantic comedy of errors ... this is, of course, a slightly frivolous summary of an immensely complicated story, with intricate military and political arguments on both sides of the Atlantic. Good summary accounts are given by Garthoff, *Détente*, Chapter 25, Haftendorn, *Sicherheit*, Chapter 3, Link, *Ära Schmidt*, pp. 315–21, and Heep, *Schmidt und Amerika*, pp. 113–51. Writing in 1982, Zbigniew Brzezinski observed: 'I was personally never persuaded that we needed [the new weapons] for military reasons. I was persuaded reluctantly that we needed [them] to obtain European support for SALT. This was largely because Chancellor Schmidt made such a big deal out of the so-called Eurostrategic imbalance that was being generated by the Soviet deployment of the SS-20. To keep him in line we felt that some response in Europe on the intermediate level would be necessary.' Quoted in Strobe Talbott, *Deadly Gambits. The Reagan Administration and the Stalemate in Nuclear Arms Control* (London: Picador, 1985), p. 33

... **Guadeloupe** ... see Schmidt's account in *Menschen und Mächte*, pp. 231–32. However both Link, *Ära Schmidt*, p. 318 and Heep, *Schmidt und Amerika*, pp. 130–32, point out that, according to reports at the time and the memoirs of Carter and Brzezinski, Schmidt was more or less explicitly criticised by the American, French and British leaders for what they saw as his excessive fear of offending the Soviet Union by a new deployment.

... **set for 1983** ... Hans Apel, the then German Defence Minister, notes in his 'political diary' that one reason for this deadline was that the Pershing II and Cruise missiles would simply not be ready before 1983. See Apel, *Abstieg*, p.72.

... **'détente could not survive...'** text in Haftendorn, *Sicherheit*, pp. 232–3. For good summary accounts of American and German reactions see Garthoff, *Détente*, Chapters 26 and 27, and Heep, *Schmidt und Amerika*, pp. 153–92.

... **to visit Moscow** ... see Schmidt, *Menschen und Mächte*, pp. 108–25, Link, *Ära Schmidt*, p. 335 ff, Heep, *Schmidt und Amerika*, pp. 186–89.

... **a high-risk visit** ... but Link, *Ära Schmidt*, p. 335, points out that on 19 June 1980 Schmidt had been given an indication, by someone identified by Link only as a high-placed 'American personality not in the government', following a conversation with Ambassador Dobrynin in Washington, that the Chancellor could expect some 'success' on this trip.

... **to negotiate** ... thus letting fall the 'conditions' of prior ratification of SALT II, and a withdrawal of the Nato two-track decision. See report and quotations from leaked protocols of the meeting in *Die Welt*, 7 July 1980. The Soviet party leadership's report of this meeting sent to the East German party leadership can be found in ZPA: IV 2/2.035/65.

'The dialogue...' Klaus Bölling, *Die letzten 30 Tage des Kanzlers Helmut Schmidt. Ein Tagebuch* (Reinbek: Rowohlt, 1982), p. 116. In this quotation Bölling appears to be summarising, in indirect speech, the gist of what Schmidt himself said.

The Polish revolution ... on this see Garton Ash, *Solidarity*, and Jerzy Holzer, *'Solidarność 1980–81. Geneza i Historia* (Warsaw: Kraag, 1983), translated into German as *'Solidarität'. Die Geschichte einer freien Gewerkschaft in Polen* (Munich: Beck, 1985), edited by Hans Henning Hahn.

'If the Russians invade...' quoted by Josef Joffe in Gordon, *Eroding Empire*, p. 161. See *Der Spiegel*, 1/1982.

... **the Bonn government was not entirely clear** ... this is discussed in more detail in Chapter Five, pp. 288 ff.

... 'only a postman'... quoted from leaked protocols of the meeting in *Die Welt* of 7 July 1980.

... 'the one was talking Eskimo...' Helmut Schmidt to the author, London, 3 June 1991.

... 'honest broker'... this famous comment came in a speech to the Reichstag on 19 February 1878. It is interesting to note that the context was Bismarck insisting that Germany could *not* play the role of a mediator, let alone that of a 'referee', just the modest part of an honest broker... See Bismarck, *Reden*, pp. 140–67, this on p. 152.

... 'honest interpreters...' in a speech to the Federal Association of German Publishers on 10 November 1981, reprinted in *Bulletin*, 19 November 1981, pp. 921–28, this on p. 925. Asked about this image in a television discussion on the occasion of Brezhnev's visit to Bonn, Schmidt said that 'we are probably at the moment the best interpreters in both directions', see the transcript, BPA — DFS/26.11.81/20.15, p. 4. For further discussion of the interpreter image see Haftendorn, *Sicherheit*, p. 150, Joffe in Gordon, *Eroding Empire*, p. 184 f, and Avril Pittman, *From Ostpolitik to Reunification. West German-Soviet Political Relations since 1974* (Cambridge: Cambridge University Press, 1992), pp. 101–08.

... revived by Chancellor Kiesinger... in his initial government declaration, Kiesinger said: 'Germany was for centuries a bridge between Western and Eastern Europe. We would be happy to perform these tasks in our age too.' *Bundestag Plenarprotokolle*, 5/80, p. 3662 (13 December 1966).

... used by Schmidt himself... 'Our task is to perform the function of a bridge' he declared in a speech to the extraordinary party conference of the SPD in Cologne on 10 December 1978, quoted in Link, *Ära Schmidt*, p. 309.

... the proposed deployment... provoked... a recent book on this is Jeffrey Herf, *War by Other Means. Soviet Power, West German Resistance and the Battle of the Euromissiles.* (New York: Free Press, 1991).

... deep into Schmidt's own party... a vivid account, by someone very hostile to this development, is given in Apel, *Abstieg*.

... both overtly and covertly... Schmidt refers in passing to the covert actions, disinformation etc in *Menschen und Mächte*, p. 108. After the end of the GDR, more evidence emerged of how active the East German State Security Service had been in this connection. While it is important to establish the facts about this support, which was more important and substantial than many in the peace movement would have like to believe, it does not amount to an 'explanation' of it, any more than the overt and covert support given to Solidarity in Poland by the United States amounts to an 'explanation' of that movement.

... 'with God's and your help'... quoted from the report by Herbert Häber, head of the SED's Western Department, on his trip to West Germany, 16–22 February 1981, now in ZPA: JIV 2/10.02/12.

... encouraged the key foreign-policy decision-makers... Valentin Falin argues, retrospectively, that from as early as 1975, when Brezhnev became seriously ill, Soviet foreign policy was really made by what he calls a 'gang of four' consisting of Gromyko, Ustinov, Andropov and Suslov. Valentin Falin, Hamburg, 14 May 1992.

... the Social Democrats' party conference ... see *Parteitag der Sozialdemokratischen Partei Deutschlands. 19. bis 23. April 1982. München, Olympiahalle. Vol 1: Protokoll der Verhandlungen* (Bonn: Vorstand der SPD, 1982), especially the discussion on the report by Egon Bahr on 'peace and security policy', pp. 305–83. For more on this, see Chapter Six.

... this decision was put off ... according to Apel, *Abstieg*, p. 198, the decision to postpone was made already at the beginning of the year, due to the atmosphere in the regional party organisations.

... planning staff paper ... published in *Der Spiegel*, 20/1982, pp. 22–3. There also all the following quotations. According to *Der Spiegel*, the government spokesman, Klaus Bölling, confirmed the authenticity of the paper. The head of the planning staff and main author of the paper, Albrecht Müller, recalls that he had prepared similar planning papers for Schmidt in 1980 and 1981. The particular concern, he says, was the fraught relationship with the Free Democrats. The public opinion polls referred to included some specially commissioned by the government itself. Albrecht Müller, Bonn, 20 March 1992.

... Kant but also Cruise ... Schmidt paid considerable attention to the philosophical and ethical underpinnings of his political work, to what he called at the end of his valedictory speech to the Bundestag in 1986, 'the sober passion for practical reason'. See *Bundestag Plenarprotokolle* 10/228, p. 17685 (10 September 1986). This favourite phrase of his was then taken up as the title of a Festschrift in his honour, Manfred Lahnstein, ed., *Leidenschaft zur praktischen Vernunft* (Berlin: Siedler, 1989). Both Kant and Popper earn several mentions in his memoirs. There is some evidence that he suffered under his image of the *Macher*, the businessman-manager in politics. Thus in a rather touching note to the head of the Chancellery dated 7 January 1975, Schmidt suggests that he should deliver a speech to mark a noteworthy cultural or historical date, such as the 100th birthday of Albert Schweitzer or Thomas Mann. 'I could imagine,' he writes, 'that in this way the strongly economically coloured *Macher*-image could be complemented by a part of the components [i.e. of Helmut Schmidt] which are really present but lacking in the public awareness.' Now in AdsD: HS 1. Yet clearly his philosophical and ethical concerns went far deeper than just concern about the image. They were strongly held and vividly and personally expressed. See, for example, his response to the author in the protocol of the *Bergedorfer Gesprächskreis* 88 (6–7 September 1989), pp. 66–7.

... 'if an agreement cannot be reached ...' dinner speech on 23 November 1981, reprinted in *Bulletin*, 26 November 1981, pp. 963–66, this on p. 965.

... other, more direct causes ... for a partisan but vivid account of the break-up of the social-liberal coalition, see Klaus Bölling, *Die letzten 30 Tage des Kanzlers Helmut Schmidt. Ein Tagebuch* (Reinbek: Rowohlt, 1982). A more scholarly and critical account is given by Wolfgang Jäger in Wolfgang Jäger and Werner Link, *Republik im Wandel. 1974–1982. Die Ära Schmidt* [= Geschichte der *Bundesrepublik Deutschland* Vol 5/II] (Stuttgart: Deutsche Verlags-Anstalt, 1987), pp. 188–263.

... truly unprecedented movement in American-Soviet relations ... Oberdorfer, *Turn*, and Beschloss & Talbott, *Highest Levels*, are both excellent and accessible chronicles, displaying the best of American quality journalism. But see also Seweryn Bialer and Michael Mandelbaum, eds, *Gorbachev's Russia and American Foreign Policy* (Boulder: Westview Press, 1988), and the account of a policy maker closely involved, Thomas W Simons, *The End of the Cold War?* (New York: St Martin's Press, 1990).

'The Alliance,' said Kohl ... see *Bundestag Plenarprotokolle* 9/121, pp. 7213–7229 (13 October 1982), this on p. 7220. (See also Genscher's speech on pp. 7254–64.) The Government rather pointedly included the Social Democrats' heckling reaction in the version printed in *Bulletin*, 14 October 1982, this on p. 860.

... 'not only to keep ...' this from point (19) of the CDU-CSU coalition agreement on foreign, security, EC, Ostpolitik and Deutschlandpolitik issues, as circulated to CSU parliamentarians by the General Secretary of the CSU on 13 May 1983. Copy in the papers of Werner Marx, ACDP: I–356, 005/3.

Helmut Kohl, the Catholic from the Rhineland-Palatinate ... in the not very impressive literature on Helmut Kohl see the rather partisan biography by Werner Maser, *Helmut Kohl. Der Deutsche Kanzler* (Frankfurt: Ullstein, 1990); an interesting collection of critical articles, Reinhard Appel, ed., *Helmut Kohl im Spiegel seiner Macht* (Bonn: Bouvier, 1990); and the rather good essay by Peter Scholl-Latour in a volume of photographs by Konrad R Müller, *Helmut Kohl* (Bergisch Gladbach: Gustav Lübber Verlag, 1990). A good summary of Kohl's own views on German foreign policy is given in his 1984 Konrad Adenauer Memorial lecture (Oxford: St Antony's College, 1984).

The record of his meeting with Alexei Kosygin ... a copy of the twenty-one page record of the conversation on 30 September 1975 is in the Werner Marx papers, ACDP: I–356, 022/4. All following quotations are from that copy. Unfortunately this record does not cover the concluding forty-five minute one-to-one conversation.

... 'We wouldn't dream ...' this from the copy of Weizsäcker's five-page 'Note for the Moscow Visit', dated 18 September 1975, also in ACDP: I–356, 022/4.

... all the stages ... for a first attempt see Clemens, *Reluctant Realists*, and the same author's 1992 Alois Mertes Memorial Lecture on *CDU Deutschlandpolitik und Reunification, 1985–1989* (Washington: German Historical Institute, 1992).

... 'the object in East-West relations ...' quoted from the Free Democrats' protocol of the coalition talks on the evening of 22 March 1983, now in AdDL: Bundesvorsitzender Genscher, 13544.

... **the most solicitous attention** ... Note, for example, the despatch of no less a figure than the Economics Minister, Otto Graf Lambsdorff, to chair the meeting of the German-Soviet economic commission in Moscow in November 1983, just a week before the Bundestag vote on the deployment.

The confidential note on these talks ... The note is dated 14 July 1983. Following quotations are from the copy in the office papers of Hermann Axen, ZPA: IV 2/2.035/65.

... **the Bundestag's vote** ... The actual vote was on 22 November 1983. For the debate see *Bundestag Plenarprotokolle*, 10/35 & 36 (21 & 22 November 1983).

... **'limit the damage'** ... see the text in ND, 26/27 November 1983, also reprinted in *Texte* III/1, pp. 267–71.

... **'a coalition of reason'** ... see Ronald D Asmus, 'The Dialectics of Détente, and Discord. The Moscow-East Berlin-Bonn Triangle,' in *Orbis*, Winter 1985, pp. 743–74, and A James McAdams, 'The New Logic in Soviet-GDR Relations', in *Problems of Communism*, September–October 1988, pp. 47–60.

While Soviet negotiators walked out ... for a good contemporary documentation see Ronald D Asmus, *East Berlin and Moscow. The Documentation of a Dispute* (Munich: Radio Free Europe, 1985 = RFE Occasional Papers No. 1). It will, however, now be possible to write an account based on the East German and perhaps also on the Soviet archives.

... **joined in this by Hungary** ... ibid., especially pp. 9–10, 21 ff, 27 ff.

As Honecker himself recalled ... Erich Honecker, Berlin-Moabit, 27 November 1992.

... **a stormy meeting with the Soviet leadership** ... see p. 169. The East German record is in ZPA: JIV 2/2A/2678.

... **a public lesson, in the Bundestag** ... *Bundestag Plenarprotokolle* 10/81, pp. 5896–5902 (12 September 1984).

'The Soviet Union ...' ibid., p. 5903.

... **Moscow First** ... see his article in APZ, 16 February 1985, pp. 3–13, especially p. 11.

... **the obdurate Gromykos and Ustinovs** ... in conversation with the author, Valentin Falin argued that a 'gang of four' consisting of Gromyko, Ustinov, Andropov and Suslov, had been effectively making — and blocking — Soviet foreign policy since Brezhnev became seriously ill in the mid-1970s. Valentin Falin, Hamburg, 14 May 1992. In the meeting with Honecker and the East German leadership on 17 August 1984, Ustinov was particularly outspoken in his criticism.

... **Europe remained a subsidiary theatre** ... on Gorbachev's policy towards Europe see Neil Malcolm *Soviet Policy Perspectives on Western Europe* (London: Routledge, 1989). Anatoly Chernyaev specifically confirmed this in a lecture in

1992, printed in Gabriel Gorodetsky, ed., *Soviet Foreign Policy, 1917–1922. A Retrospective* (London: Frank Cass, forthcoming).

... **in the frontiers of 1937**... the bald statement 'The German Reich continues to exist in the frontiers of 1937' actually appears in point 20 of the spring 1983 coalition agreement of CDU and CSU. Quoted from the copy in the papers of Werner Marx, ACDP: I–356, 005/3.

... **not reflect the real convictions**... this was certainly Brandt's impression of Gorbachev from their first meeting, see his account in Brandt, *Erinnerungen*, p. 405 ff, esp. p. 407.

... **F Wilhelm Christians**... See his own account in Christians, *Wege*, pp. 136–47.

... **only after the Kohl–Genscher government**... In 1989, Horst Teltschik wrote that 'it [Soviet policy towards Germany] changed after Chancellor Helmut Kohl's re-election in January 1987', see his article in *Aussenpolitik* (English-language edition), 3/1989, pp. 201–14, this on p. 208.

... **letter to Gorbachev dated 30 January 1986**... a copy of this letter was passed by the Soviet to the East German Party leadership and is now in ZPA: IV 2/2.035/65.

... **the quantitative reduction**... the reference was of course to the very sharp downturn in the number of ethnic Germans allowed to emigrate, down from a high point of more than 9,000 in 1977 to just 460 in 1985.

Genscher recalls... Hans-Dietrich Genscher, Bonn, 23 June 1992.

... **a new page**... Genscher's speech in Moscow is reprinted in *Bulletin*, 24 July 1986, pp. 745–48. A very useful account of the development of German–Soviet relations from 1986 to mid-1989 is Fred Oldenburg, *Sowjetische Deutschland-Politik nach den Treffen von Moskau und Bonn 1988/89* (Köln: Bundesinstitut für ostwissenschaftliche und internationale Studien, 1989 = *Bericht des BIOst* 63/1989), hereafter Oldenburg, *Sowjetische Deutschland-Politik*.

... **'He [Gorbachev] is a modern communist leader...'** *Newsweek*, 27 October 1986. See also *Der Spiegel* 44/1986

... **the Politburo actually decided to freeze**... this emerges clearly from the record of a meeting between Hermann Axen and the Soviet Central Committee Secretaries Anatoly Dobrynin and Vadim Medvedev in Moscow on 27 July 1987, now in ZPA: IV 2/2.035/59, pp. 108–25. 'After Kohl's attacks,' Dobrynin is there recorded as reporting, 'the Politburo of the CPSU had passed a resolution to freeze all political contacts with the FRG for the time being',

... **a widely reported speech**... this now famous Davos speech, drafted by Konrad Seitz, is reprinted in Genscher, *Unterwegs*, pp. 137–50.

... **'worst case analysis'**... ibid., p. 146

... **'take Gorbachev seriously, take him at his word!'**... ibid., p. 150. In the ensuing discussion, some Foreign Ministry officials insisted that the correct translation of the German would be 'hold him to his word'. The German phrase says literally 'take him by his word' but the correct English translation is certainly 'take him at his word'!

... 'pacemaker' ... See, for example, an interview with Genscher in Deutschlandfunk, 12 September 1988 (BPA transcript).

... as much a rival ... the notes of the head of the Western Department of the SED, Herbert Häber, on a conversation with Weizsäcker on 4 March 1980, record the following: 'so far as Helmut Kohl is concerned, it had proved to be a mistake that he had come from Mainz to Bonn. He would never become Chancellor and did not possess the abilities for it. In the two main areas which really matter — economic and foreign policy — he had learned nothing.' ZPA: J IV 2/10.02/10.

'However,' as one of his hosts recorded him saying ... Note of 28 May 1984 by Herbert Häber on the meeting of Richard von Weizsäcker with Horst Sindermann and Herbert Häber in the Hubertusstock, now in ZPA: J IV 2/10.04/14.

... giving Gorbachev a marvellous pretext ... Oberdorfer, *Turn*, p. 230 records a senior Soviet official joking that for this reason Rust should be awarded the Order of Lenin. In a sense, this obviously disturbed young man also deserved the West German *Bundesverdienstkreuz*, for the political results of his madcap venture were clearly to West Germany's long-term advantage.

... 'for the time being, however ...' This is the official Soviet version of the talks, given in *Pravda*, 8 July 1987 and reprinted in Gorbachev, *Haus Europa*, pp. 103–06.

... history would decide ... ibid., p. 106. Note that this is the official published version. What Gorbachev actually said may therefore be slightly different, but neither the Soviet nor the German protocols of the conversation were accessible to the author at this writing. Gorbachev repeated this formula in his book *Perestroika*, see Mikhail Gorbachev, *Perestroika. New Thinking for Our Country and the World* (London: Collins Harvill, 1987), p. 200, and, for comparison of the Russian and German texts, Oldenburg, *Sowjetische Deutschland-Politik*, p. 45.

Weizsäcker recalls ... Richard von Weizsäcker, Bonn, 30 September 1991.

'Already in 1986' ... Schewardnadse, *Zukunft*, p. 233.

Asked about this by the author ... Eduard Shevardnadze, Moscow, 7 February 1992. I am grateful to Gabriel Gorodetsky for giving me the opportunity of this discussion in a small group.

Anatoly Chernyaev ... see his lecture printed in Gabriel Gorodetsky, ed., *Soviet Foreign Policy, 1917–1992. A Retrospective* (London: Frank Cass, forthcoming).

In a separate conversation ... Alexander Yakovlev, Oxford, 29 January 1992. I am grateful to my colleague Archie Brown for enabling me to join in this discussion in a small group at St Antony's College.

... **Vyacheslav Dashitschev** ... Vyacheslav Dashitschev, Berlin, 26 June 1991. See also his interview in *Der Spiegel* 4/1991, where he also mentions a subsequent presentation in the International Department of the Central Committee. This interview provoked a furious response from Valentin Falin (reader's letter, *Der Spiegel*, 20/1991) who claimed there, and repeated in conversation with the author (Hamburg, 14 May 1992), that he had no recollection of such a presentation, and that Dashitschev was not an adviser to Gorbachev. Dashitschev, head of the foreign policy department in the then Institute for the Economics of the World Socialist System (the 'Bogomolov Institute'), says that he was an adviser in the sense that some of his papers came back with marginal annotations by Gorbachev (letter to *Der Spiegel*, 34/1991, and in conversation with the author). Certainly by 1988 Dashitschev was going public, both inside the Soviet Union and in Germany, with extremely outspoken criticism of Soviet foreign policy in the Soviet years. See, for example, his well-known article in *Literaturnaya Gazeta*, 18 May 1988, reports of his remarks in FAZ, 8 June 1988, interview in *Der Spiegel*, 27/1988. In *International Affairs* (Moscow), 10/1992, p. 132 ff, Oleg Bogomolov retrospectively described this as the general line of his Institute since about 1986. See also remarks by Bogomolov himself in June 1988, quoted in Garton Ash, *Uses*, p. 221.

... **Honecker remembered** ... in Reinhold Andert & Wolfgang Herberg, *Der Sturz. Erich Honecker im Kreuzverhör* (Berlin: Aufbau, 1990), p. 21.

In a television interview ... on ARD, 10 October 1991.

Dashitschev himself says ... Vyacheslav Dashitschev, Berlin, 26 June 1991, and in *Der Spiegel* 4/1991, 34/1991

... **wrangling over** ... **German-Soviet agreements** ... Dieter Kastrup, Bonn, 18 March 1992. For detail on Berlin and the so-called 'PO Box solution' of 1986 — whereby Berlin participants in German-Soviet agreements were listed only with a PO Box address — see Oldenburg, *Sowjetische Deutschland-Politik*, pp. 29–35.

The East German record ... This extremely revealing document is in ZPA: IV 2/2. 035/59, pp. 108–25, from which the following quotations are drawn. The consultation was in preparation for Honecker's visit to Bonn. Its formal basis was an 'Analysis of the situation in the FRG — conclusions for a common policy' (now in ZPA: IV 2/2. 035/14) which had been prepared on the instructions of the East German Politburo, and sent to the Soviet leadership, with a covering letter from Honecker to Gorbachev, on 23 June 1987. Axen opined in a memorandum to Honecker on 29 July 1987 (now in ZPA: IV 2/2.035/59, pp. 153–55), enclosing the formal report on the visit and draft resolution for the Politburo (pp. 146–52), that the fact that the Soviet side had accepted the East German analysis and conclusions for a common policy of the 'socialist community' towards West Germany was 'undoubtedly a success for the policy of the SED'. He also noted a difference of emphasis between Dobrynin and Medvedev, with the latter having 'passages which contained the old, false reservations and misjudgements of the correlation of forces between the GDR and the FRG and the situation in the GDR and the FRG'. For further detail, see p. 170 f.

... 'with the most agreeable feelings ...' report and quotations in *Der Spiegel*, 1/1988.

... Shevardnadze visited Bonn ... see *Bulletin*, 21 January 1988, pp. 53–57, Oldenburg, *Sowjetische Deutschland-Politik*, pp. 9–10.

... sacrificing ... Pershing 1A missiles ... this story is well told in Michael Inacker's useful account of the security policy of the Kohl government in Reinhard Appel, ed., *Helmut Kohl im Spiegel seiner Macht* (Bonn: Bouvier, 1990), pp. 73–112, on this esp. pp. 89–98.

The Soviet information note ... one of the German texts of the note, dated 19 February 1988, is in ZPA: IV 2/2.035/65, pp. 209–16. Following quotations are all from this text.

'The CDU,' he said ... in a long interview in *Blätter für deutsche und internationale Politik* 11/1987, pp. 1392–1404, this on p. 1396.

... that Kohl at last visited Moscow ... for details of this visit see *Bulletin*, 1 November 1988, pp. 1265–76, Oldenburg, *Sowjetische Deutschland-Politik*, and extensive press reports in the second half of October.

'Now,' said Gorbachev ... *Bulletin*, 1 November 1988, p. 1265.

... the beginnings ... rapport ... Anatoly Chernyaev in Gabriel Gorodetsky, ed., *Soviet Foreign Policy, 1917–1992. A Retrospective* (London: Frank Cass, forthcoming).

... 'new chapter' ... *Bulletin*, 1 November 1988, p. 1271.

... the reception given to Gorbachev ... the following paragraph is based on my observations in Bonn at the time. For the main official documents and speeches of this visit see *Bulletin*, 15 June 1989, pp. 537–48; EA, 13/1989, pp. D371 ff; and, with more of Gorbachev's speeches, *Gorbatschow in Bonn. Die Zukunft der deutsch-sowjetischen Beziehungen. Reden und Dokumente vom Staatsbesuch* (Köln: Pahl-Rugenstein, 1989).

... 'Gorbasm' ... that is, in German, *Gorbasmus*. The coinage was attributed to Günter Diehl, see *Der Spiegel* 24/1989.

... 'A kiss for Annette ...' *Bild*, 13 June 1989.

... 'the object of desire' ... TAZ 13 June 1989.

'After a good sowing ...' from Kohl's speech on 12 June, *Bulletin*, 15 June 1989, p. 537.

... eleven agreements ... details from an information sheet of the *Presse- und Informationsamt der Bundesregierung*, 12 June 1989.

... similar connections ... reported in FAZ, 11 February 1989 (from which it appears that the 'hot line' was actually installed in the run-up to the visit).

'We are drawing the line ...' from Gorbachev's speech on 12 June, *Bulletin*, 15 June 1989, p. 541.

'This must be . . .' ibid.

This remarkable document . . . all following quotations from the text in *Bulletin*, 15 June 1989, pp. 542–544. Also in *Vierzig Jahre*, pp. 591–594.

. . . 'a catalyst for new relations . . .' in a speech on 13 June, *Bulletin*, 15 June 1989, p. 547.

. . . 'the growing young man' . . . see above p. 51 and notes.

. . . 'partners in leadership' . . . English text in Freedman, *Europe Transformed*, pp. 289–94, this on p. 289.

Connoisseurs pointed out . . . see Hannes Adomeit, 'Gorbachev and German Unification' in *Problems of Communism*, July–August 1990, pp. 1–23, this on p. 5. (This important article is hereafter cited as Adomeit, 'Gorbachev and German Unification'.) Oldenburg, *Sowjetische Deutschland-Politik*, p. 44, notes that the changed usage was subsequently adopted in the Soviet press.

. . . the only comparable bilateral document . . . the Soviet Foreign Ministry spokesman, Genady Gerassimov, compared it to the Delhi Declaration between the Soviet Union and India (author's notes). But India's position could hardly be compared with that of the most important West European state, on the front line of the East-West conflict.

'I must admit . . .' quoted in SZ, 14 June 1989.

'Differences in ideology . . .' See the full text in Grenville, *Treaties*, pp. 456–58. It is interesting to note that Egon Bahr, in praising the Bonn Declaration, also compared it to this one. See his speech in *Bundestag Plenarprotokolle*, 11/150, pp. 11202–204 (16 June 1989).

. . . already well on the way . . . on this, see Garton Ash, *We*.

. . . 'to promote free elections . . .' see the text of his Mainz speech reprinted in Freedman, *Europe Transformed*, pp. 289–94, this on p. 291, and extracts from his speech to the Polish parliament on pp. 333–35.

. . . 'an open wound' . . . this and following quotations from his speech on 12 June, *Bulletin*, 15 June 1989, p. 537–39.

. . . a major controversy with Washington . . . a clear and detailed account is given by Michael J Inacker in Reinhard Appel, ed., *Helmut Kohl im Spiegel seiner Macht* (Bonn: Bouvier, 1990), p. 92 ff.

'The shorter the range . . .' quoted in ibid., p. 93.

. . . 'the continental Europeans' . . . ibid., p. 103, and see also the commentary by Thomas Kielinger in *Rheinischer Merkur*, 28 April 1989.

. . . 'the opening of Eastern societies . . .' see the text reprinted in Freedman, *Europe Transformed*, pp. 295–303, this on p. 300.

He recalls, in particular . . . Helmut Kohl, Bonn, 1 October 1991. See also his account in *Die Welt am Sonntag*, 27 September 1992. Kohl referred back to this particular conversation in a crucial meeting with Gorbachev in Moscow on 15 July 1990, see Teltschik, *329 Tage*, p. 320, and publicly in an extraordinary televised telephone chat with Mikhail Gorbachev on the first anniversary of the unification of Germany, ARD 3 October 1991.

... 'the decisive moment'... Helmut Kohl, Bonn, 1 October 1991.

... 'Du'... 'Sie'... see the telegrams to Bush and Gorbachev reproduced in *Bulletin*, 5 November 1991, p. 969.

... a long track-record... see above p. 101 and the handwritten letter of thanks from Alois Mertes following Kohl's trip to Moscow in July 1983, ACDP: I–403, A–000.

Willy Brandt... poured gentle scorn... Brandt, *Erinnerungen*, pp. 354, 405.

... highlighted the influence... ibid., pp. 404, 407, and 426–36. See also, Mikhail Gorbachev, *Perestroika. New Thinking for Our country and the World* (London: Collins Harvill, 1987), p. 207.

... compelled the decisive turn... a very lucid and valuable treatment of this subject is Jonathan Haslam, *The Soviet Union and the Politics of Nuclear Weapons in Europe, 1969–1987* (London: Macmillan, 1989).

... via Georgi Arbatov to Gorbachev... Egon Bahr, Potsdam, 29 June 1991, Willy Brandt, Bonn, 2 October 1991.

... 'without Ostpolitik, no Gorbachev'... Willy Brandt, Bonn, 2 October 1991. Egon Bahr in SZ *Magazin*, 27 September 1991, p. 18.

... in an interview with *Die Zeit*... *Die Zeit*, 13 March 1992.

Schmidt, Kohl and Genscher all stressed... Helmut Schmidt, London, 3 June 1991; Helmut Kohl, Bonn, 1 October 1991; Hans-Dietrich Genscher, Bonn, 23 June 1992. For an interesting though slightly confused discussion of the relationship between INF and the revision of Soviet foreign policy, see the article by Thomas Risse-Kappen in *International Security*, 16/1, Summer 1991, pp. 162–88.

Yes, said ex-Chancellor Brandt... Willy Brandt, Bonn, 2 October 1991.

... perhaps Palme and SI pointed to a possible way out... Vitaly Zhurkin, Director of the Institute of Europe created in Moscow in 1988 and an active participant in the revision of Soviet foreign policy thinking, believes this was true particularly of the earlier years, ca. 1985–87, when the focus of discussion was on security issues. Vitaly Zhurkin, Moscow, 7 February 1992.

... alarmed and goaded the Gorbachev leadership... for Gorbachev's concern about the economic development of the EC, and a security dimension of the Franco-German relationship, see Neil Malcolm, *Soviet Policy Perspectives on Western Europe* (London: Routledge, 1989).

'our firm anchoring in the West...' *Bulletin*, 1 November 1988, p. 1269.

... 'no destabilisation' ... author's notes of remarks by Hans Klein. See also reports in SZ and FAZ, 14 June 1989.

... 'a commensurate change on the Soviet side ...' Meissner, *Moskau–Bonn*, p. 824.

... ten ... i.e. since Brezhnev's growing incapacity ushered in a decade of growing inflexibility and 'stagnation' in Soviet foreign and domestic policy.

... some even as twenty ... i.e., since the fall of Khrushchev.

... by no means be underrated. ... Hannes Adomeit nonetheless surely goes too far in the other direction when he writes that 'the conceptual basis for the collapse of the GDR was supplemented by a practical precondition: the removal of the Berlin Wall'. Some supplement! See Adomeit, 'Gorbachev and Unification', p. 5.

... the main components of 'new thinking'. ... Among the many good treatments of this subject one might mention, Archie Brown, ed., *New Thinking in Soviet Politics* (London: Macmillan, 1992), Gerhard Wettig, *Changes in Soviet Policy Towards the West* (London: Pinter, 1991), Adomeit's excellent article, quoted here as 'Germany and Unification', and a characteristically precise and lucid article by Boris Meissner in *Aussenpolitik* (English-language edition), 2/1989, pp. 101–18.

... especially when it came to Germany ... see the revealing remark by Georgy Shakhnazarov, quoted in Beschloss & Talbott, *Highest Levels*, p. 82.

... what Severyn Bialer has called ... see his *The Soviet Paradox. External Expansion, Internal Decline* (New York: Knopf, 1986), p. 191.

... not least ... Uzbekistan ... the point is made by Oldenburg, *Sowjetische Deutschland-Politik*, p. 11.

... Soviet policy towards Eastern Europe ... an excellent introduction to this topic is Pravda, *End*, especially the editor's own introductory chapter.

... a short memorandum to the Politburo ... and communicated in general terms ... this was mentioned by Alexander Kaptov in his speech to the 19th Party Conference in June 1988, reprinted in *International Affairs* (Moscow), November 1988, pp. 28–32, this on p. 29. Its significance was confirmed to the author by Oleg Bogomolov, Moscow, 7 February 1992, and Nikolai Kolikov, Moscow, 10 February 1992. Kolikov, a consultant to the Central Committee department for relations with socialist countries, recalls that an earlier draft of this memorandum contained the key formulation 'more socialism, more democracy'. Subsequently it was changed to the more cautious 'more socialism — more democracy', thus implying that more socialism would lead to more democracy. From the East European side, Erich Honecker (Berlin-Moabit, 27 November 1992) and Egon Krenz (Berlin, 20 February 1990) both confirmed in conversation with the author that autumn 1986 was the moment at which the East German leadership understood that they had, as Krenz put it, a 'green light' to change — or not to change. Honecker recalled what he described as the 'meeting of General

Secretaries' in Moscow when Gorbachev explained that the Soviet Union did not have a monopoly of the truth — 'we'd known that for some time', Honecker commented tartly — and proposed a new relationship of 'partnership'. He recalled Zhivkov asking what exactly this meant, and receiving only a vague reply. It would clearly be very interesting to see a record of this meeting.

... practice lagged a long way behind ... a point made very forcibly to the author by Oleg Bogomolov (Moscow, 7 February 1992) and confirmed by numerous East European sources. Erich Honecker (Berlin-Moabit, 27 November 1992) said emphatically that at no point did the Soviet Union refrain from 'interfering' (*sich einmischen*) in the GDR. He described the consular officials of the Soviet Embassy in the provinces of the GDR as *Provinzgouverneure*.

... Gorbachev ... extremely cautious ... witness, for example, his non-response to a question on this subject from a Polish intellectual, Marcin Krol, during Gorbachev's visit to Warsaw in July 1988, see Garton Ash, *Uses*, p. 222.

... Gorbachev gave his assent ... see Pravda, *End*, pp. 24–25. Miklás Németh, Oxford, 22 January 1991.

... 'beyond containment' ... see Oberdorfer, *Turn*, p. 345 ff, Beschloss & Talbott, *Highest Levels*, p. 69 ff, and Thomas W Simons, *The End of the Cold War?* (New York: St Martin's Press, 1990), p. 154 ff.

'This isn't meant ...' quoted in Oberdorfer, *Turn*, p. 342.

... he also warned ... ibid., p. 360.

'Yes, we had in principle ...' quoted in Adomeit, 'Gorbachev and Unification', p. 22, citing *Pravda*, 5 July 1990. See also the translation in *Current Digest of the Soviet Press* XLII, No. 29, 1990, pp. 12–13.

... a report from the Soviet ambassador to Bonn ... Schevardnadse, *Zukunft*, p. 258.

... other Soviet specialists ... the best known of these is a memorandum by Dashitschev of April 1989, reprinted in *Der Spiegel* 6/1989. But this was only one of a number of memoranda prepared by, among others, the Bogomolov Institute, the Foreign Ministry and the Central Committee on Moscow's relations with Eastern Europe (copies in the possession of the author). *Die Welt*, 15 September 1989, reported a West German Federal Intelligence Service (BND) report of early August 1989 which in turn contained a report by Valentin Falin on dangerous instability in the GDR.

Sergei Tarasenko ... Moscow, 10 February 1992.

... 'would be the end of perestroika' ... quoted in Oberdorfer, *Turn*, p. 360.

... strongly influenced by the Prague Spring ... on this, see Pravda, *End*, p. 3, and Archie Brown, *The Gorbachev Factor in Soviet Politics* (forthcoming).

... 'nineteen years' ... quoted in William E Griffith, ed, *Central & Eastern Europe: The Opening Curtain?* (Boulder: Westview Press, 1989), p. 423.

... 'reveal the human face of socialism' ... this in a speech in Kiev in February 1989, quoted by Adomeit, 'Gorbachev and Unification', p. 3, citing *Pravda*, 24 February 1989. See also his note of 2 February 1989 'On Stalin', reprinted in *Gipfelgespräche*, pp. 258–63, this on p. 263.

... 'a particular significance ...' Horst Teltschik, 'Gorbachev's Reform Policy and the Outlook for East-West Relations', in *Aussenpolitik* (English-language edition) 3/1989, pp. 201–214, this on p. 212.

... the time-scale Teltschik imagined ... Horst Teltschik, Bonn, 12 July 1991.

Chapter IV: Germany and Germany

... all Ostpolitik was Deutschlandpolitik ... 'The new Ostpolitik,' writes a leading West German specialist, Werner Link, 'was at the same time and in its innermost intentions, Deutschlandpolitik', in Link, *Ära Brandt*, p. 214.

... the Brandt government re-named ... this was announced in the first Government declaration, see *Bundestag Plenarprotokolle*, 6/5, p. 21 (28 October 1969).

... 'German-German relations' ... a leading article in the FAZ, 13 August 1973, denounced this usage as a further concession to the GDR.

Egon Bahr memorably commented ... Quoted, by Bahr himself, in Schmid, *Politik*, p. 257, and Bender, *Neue Ostpolitik*, p. 195.

The Berlin Agreement of September 1951 ... see *Materialien*, p. 627, the article on 'Innerdeutscher Handel' in *DDR-Handbuch*, and further references given below.

Starting in 1963 ... see p. 142 f for further detail.

Chancellor Kiesinger's April 1967 declaration ... text in *Bundestag Plenarprotokolle*, 5/101, pp. 4686 ff (12 April 1967). There also Barzel's response.

... some heavy use of the Bonn-Moscow-Berlin triangle ... see Baring, *Machtwechsel*, pp. 475 ff, 490–91.

'The day of Erfurt ...' Brandt, *Erinnerungen*, p. 226.

... merely exchanged numbers ... Ulrich Sahm, Bodenwerder, 27 September 1992.

The Politburo briefing book ... attached as an appendix to the minutes of the Politburo meeting on 19 May 1970, now in ZPA: JIV 2/2/1283.

... forgot to remove his hat ... thus Karl Seidel, Berlin, 30 September 1992.

... that same official ... Karl Seidel again. He retells both stories in Lutz, *Bahr*, p. 101.

... drawing on the wealth of documents ... some at least of the East German records of the Kohl-Bahr negotiations are in ZPA: B2/20/433 and 434. Egon Bahr holds a set of the West German records in his papers deposited in the Archiv der sozialen Demokratie in Bonn. For two complimentary assessments see the contributions by Hans-Otto Bräutigam and Karl Seidel in Lutz, *Bahr*, pp. 81–88, 101–02.

... the '20 Points' ... text in *Zehn Jahre*, pp. 138–39.

... already agreed in Erfurt ... Brandt, *Erinnerungen*, p. 227. Ulrich Sahm, who was directly responsible for putting the phrase in as one of the 20 points, suggests that its origins go back much farther, even to the Potsdam agreement or the Atlantic Charter (Bodenwerder, 27 September 1992).

The treaty itself ... a comprehensive and learned insider's commentary is given by Bahr's legal adviser, Antonius Eitel, in Zündorf, *Ostverträge*, pp. 211–310. See also Baring, *Machtwechsel*, pp. 491–98, Bender, *Neue Ostpolitik*, pp. 192–95, Link, *Ära Brandt*, pp. 222–24, Brandt, *People and Politics*, pp. 394–96.

... 'without prejudice to the different views ...' text in *Zehn Jahre*, p. 205–16, together with the important accompanying letters, protocols and declarations, and the Federal Government's memorandum expounding the treaty. The following quotations are taken from those pages. English text of the main treaty in Grenville, *Treaties*, pp. 198–99.

In a statement to mark the initialling of the treaty ... see *Texte*, I/11, pp. 320–21. The same formula was used by Bahr in a statement at the actual initialling of the treaty, ibid., pp. 311–13.

... a letter accompanying the treaty ... see *Zehn Jahre*, p. 208.

... detailed provision for easier travel ... see *Zehn Jahre*, pp. 208–10.

'*Wandel durch Annäherung* ...' the lecture is reprinted in Bahr, *Sicherheit*, pp. 44–59, this on p. 45.

... 'the respective seats of government' ... the formula is in Article 8 of the Basic Treaty, see *Zehn Jahre*, p. 206.

... reported directly to the Chancellor ... the precise lines of reporting and command were laid down in memoranda dated 10 July 1974 from the head of the Chancellery, Manfred Schüler. AdsD: HS, 449.

... policy had to be co-ordinated ... see Gaus, *Deutschland*, p. 255 ff. In conversation with the author, Gaus recalled what he called a 'gang of four' chaired by the Chancellery minister and including the state secretaries from the Chancellery (Gaus himself, in a personal union!), the Foreign Ministry and the Intra-German Ministry. Günter Gaus, Hamburg, 14 May 1992. For a later period, one of the heads of the *Arbeitstab Deutschlandpolitik* in the Chancellery recalls a co-ordinating group of five, with the Chancellery Minister, the state secretaries from the Foreign Ministry, Intra-German Ministry and Economics Ministry, and the federal plenipotentiary for Berlin. Hermann von Richthofen, London, 3 March 1992.

After Brandt's re-election in 1972, there was a serious discussion inside the

Brandt Chancellery about dissolving the Intra-German Ministry altogether, and gathering the operative part of its work in a new 'Germany- and Berlin-political department' in the Chancellery. See the confidential memorandum from Horst Ehmke as head of the Chancellery dated 13 November 1972, memorandum from Egon Bahr dated 14 November 1972, and further memorandum from Ehmke dated 27 November 1972, all in AdsD: Dep WB, BK 68. Günter Gaus restates the argument that this would have been a better way to organise things in Gaus, *Deutschland*, p. 256. According to Gaus's recollection, this did not happen mainly for party-political and coalition reasons: the Intra-German Minister, Egon Franke, was a pillar of the right-wing SPD, Herbert Wehner did not wish to see his old ministry dissolved, and there were concerns about the FDP's response to such a reshuffling of cabinet-level responsibilities. Günter Gaus, Hamburg, 14 May 1992.

... **the man who took the key decisions** ... Honecker confirmed his own direct responsibility for foreign policy, and especially for relations with West Germany, in conversation with Helmut Schmidt during their summit meeting in December 1981, see Schmidt, *Nachbarn*, p. 71. In conversation with the author, the former Politburo member Günter Schabowski said that Honecker kept four key areas to himself: foreign policy, especially relations with the Federal Republic, internal security, the media, and 'cadre questions' (i.e. who should get what post). Günter Schabowski, Berlin, 29 June 1991.

... **'Working Group FRG'** ... this group was supposed to deal mainly with the economic aspects of relations with West Germany, but there were few German-German ties which did not have an economic aspect. (Information from Günter Mittag, Gerhard Schürer, Alexander Schalck-Golodkowski, Karl Seidel.) Its secretary was Alexander Schalck-Golodkowski. See also Mittag, *Preis*, p. 91 ff. Regrettably, the papers of this working group now deposited in the Central Party Archive had not been catalogued at the time of writing.

... **the Foreign Ministry's 'FRG Department'** ... thus the head of that department could say that he was 'his own boss'. Most of the Foreign Ministry, like most other ministries, was directly subordinated to the Central Committee apparatus. Karl Seidel, Berlin, 30 September 1992.

From 1976 ... **Schalck** ... Gaus's first negotiating contact with Schalck dates from 1976. Günter Gaus, Hamburg, 14 May 1992. The significance of the date is by now well-established, as Schalck's 'Commercial Co-ordination' agency was given wider responsibilities following the 9th party congress and a Politburo decision of 2 November 1976. See the appendix to the Politburo minutes in ZPA: JIV 2/2/1642. However, in testimony to the Bundestag special committee Schalck mentioned earlier contacts with Carl-Werner Sanne and Karl-Otto Pöhl, both important senior officials in the Bonn government in the early 1970s, see the transcript in *Die Zeit*, 4 October 1991. The central importance of Schalck as a negotiating partner for the Bonn government was confirmed to the author by, among others, Wolfgang Schäuble, Bonn, 17 March 1992, and Hermann von Richthofen, London, 3 March 1992. His standing as a key negotiator for the East German side was confirmed to the author by, among others, Günter Mittag,

Berlin, 28 June 1992, and the head of Honecker's personal office in the Council of State, Frank-Joachim Hermann, Berlin, 8 October 1991. In his testimony to the Bundestag special committee, Schäuble described Schalck as not merely a messenger but a plenipotentiary (*Bevollmächtigter*), see *Deutscher Bundestag. 12. Wahlperiode. I. Untersuchungsausschuss "Kommerzielle Koordinierung"* [hereafter cited as *Schalck-Ausschuss*], Protokoll Nr. 24, p. 28 f.

... a Bundestag special committee struggled ... Author's observation at the hearing with Schalck on 24 June 1992. See now the special committee's first two reports, *Bundestag Drucksachen*, 12/3462 and 12/3920. Günter Mittag insists that he was not empowered to give direct orders to Schalck, see Mittag, *Preis*, p. 92, but the evidence makes it clear that he (but not only he!) was.

... taking orders ... see p. 165 and notes.

... and especially ... Abrassimov ... a taste of Abrassimov's fierce criticism of the 1978 package of German–German agreements, negotiated by Gaus and Schalck on behalf of Schmidt and Honecker, can be had from the East German documents now in ZPA: IV 2/2.035/65.

Wolfgang Mischnick ... recalls ... Bonn, 17 March 1992.

Wolfgang Schäuble suggests ... see his testimony in *Schalck-Ausschuss*, Protokoll Nr. 24, p. 4 ff.

... Günter Gaus, subsequently described ... according to Bruns, *DDR-Politik*, p. 123, Gaus first publicly used this term in an important interview in *Der Spiegel*, 6/1977.

... much criticised in West Germany ... for a taste of the immediate reaction see *Der Spiegel*, 7/1977. Copies of this and the original interview and lead story are in the Schmidt papers, a small indication of the importance attached to it at the time.

... an 'inner' recognition ... Gaus, *Deutschland*, p. 274.

Yet can one thus separate it? ... Bruns, *DDR-Politik*, pleads for the analytical usefulness of the term, but also himself argues in a partisan, Gausian direction.

... somewhat in the tones of the Spanish inquisition ... see Jens Hacker, *Deutsche Irrtümer. Schönfärber und Helfershelfer der SED-Diktatur im Westen* (Berlin: Ullstein, 1992), *passim*.

... that reunification was the *Lebenslüge* ... Brandt appears first to have used this term, in passing, in a lecture delivered in Munich in 1984. See *Nachdenken über Deutschland* (Munich: Bertelsmann, 1988), pp. 177–190, this on p. 183. His more emphatic and deliberate use of it was, however, in a lecture in Berlin on 11 September 1988, reprinted in Wolf Jobst Siedler, ed., *Berliner Lektionen* (Berlin: Siedler, 1989), pp. 72–88. He repeated it shortly thereafter in a lecture to mark the fortieth anniversary of the Basic Law, at the Friedrich Ebert Stiftung in Bonn on 14 September 1988.

... came the somewhat strained reply ... in a letter from Brandt to the CSU

Chairman Theo Waigel, reprinted in *Frankfurter Rundschau*, 2 November 1990. Brandt traced the sense in which he used the word back to Ibsen.

. . . **not see German unity in his lifetime** . . . quoted by Angela Stent in *Foreign Policy* No. 81, Winter 1990/91, pp. 53–70, this on p. 60.

The few who did thus speak or write . . . See, for example, Wolfgang Venohr, *Die deutsche Einheit Kommt bestimmt* (Bergisch Gladbach: Gustav Lübbe Verlag). But in a book published in 1989, Venohr wrote: 'All the indications are that the GDR will still celebrate its fiftieth anniversary in October 1999,' although he did suggest that this would be 'hopefully as member-state of Democratic Confederation of Germany . . .' Wolfgang Venohr, *Die roten Preussen. Vom wundersamen Aufstieg der DDR in Deutschland* (Erlangen: Straube, 1989), p. 323.

. . . **whereas in the 1950s and 1960s** . . . see Schweigler, *Grundlagen*, p. 118, note 72

'The time seems to me to have come . . .' reprinted in *Zehn Jahre*, pp. 122–23. The original is in AdsD: Dep WB, BK 41.

. . . **'I must confess that I have stopped speaking . . .'** interview in *US News and World Report*, 29 December 1969.

. . . **German unity could only be achieved** . . . the thought was expressed to me — retrospectively — in precisely this paradoxical way by one of the key practitioners of policy towards the GDR, Hans Otto Bräutigam, who was deputy head of the Permanent Representation in East Berlin, then leader of the working group on Deutschlandpolitik in the Federal Chancellery under Helmut Schmidt, then the Federal Republic's Permanent Representative in East Berlin. Hans Otto Bräutigam, Potsdam, 25 June 1991.

. . . **hard-fought negotiations and agreements** . . . the basic agreement was made simultaneously with the initialling of the Basic Treaty, on 8 November 1972, see *Zehn Jahre*, pp. 203–05. But the role and possibilities of Western journalists remained a major bone of contention, with such incidents as the expulsion of the ARD correspondent Lothar Loewe and the closure of the *Spiegel* office counting as minor 'crises' in German-German relations.

. . . **France . . . a distinctive policy** . . . this was, at least, the clear impression of the East German leadership. See Honecker's remark quoted above, p. 336. Also Erich Honecker, Berlin-Moabit, 27 November 1992; Kurt Hager, Berlin, 8 May 1992; Karl Seidel, Berlin, 30 September 1992.

. . . **essentially supportive of Bonn's** . . . Jonathan Greenwald (US Embassy), East Berlin, 6 July 1989.

'The intra-German treaty policy . . .' *Bundestag Drucksachen* 10/914.

No one talked more movingly . . . yet this emphasis, like so much else in Deutschlandpolitik, owed a great deal to Herbert Wehner as well. See, for example, Baring, *Machtwechsel*, pp. 611–12.

... 'when considerable German payments-in-advance ...' *Bundestag Plenar-protokolle*, 6/22, p. 847 (14 January 1970).

... 'We are aware ...' *Bundestag Plenarprotokolle*, 11/33, p. 2161 (15 October 1987).

... negotiations with the East German authorities ... the most comprehensive and detailed summary accounts are contained in *Zehn Jahre* (for 1969–79) and *Innerdeutsche Beziehungen* (for 1980–86), while the last years (1987–89) are summarised in the annual reports (*Jahresberichte*) and other publications of the Ministry for Intra-German Relations.

... *Verklammerung* ... For the slogan of *Verklammerung* already in the FDP's 'Schollwer paper' in the mid-1960s see Hildebrand, *Von Erhard zur Grossen Koalition*, p. 342.

... fifteen of the seventeen agreements ... Bender, *Neue Ostpolitik*, p. 211.

... an agreement on cultural co-operation ... see *Innerdeutsche Beziehungen*, pp. 15 and 259–62. The main obstacle to the signature of such an agreement was the dispute about former Prussian state museum and library holdings, which, due to wartime evacuations, often ended up in the West when they had originally been in the East, or vice versa. As so often in German-German relations this dispute was not resolved but rather put aside, in this case with a 'common protocol declaration' which read: 'The different standpoints on the question of cultural property moved as a result of war are not affected. The partners to the agreement declare their readiness insofar as possible to seek solutions in the areas of cultural goods moved as a result of war.' This, in several cases, they actually proceeded to do.

... fifty-eight such agreements ... for an exhaustive study of these town–twinnings see Beatrice von Weizsäcker, *Verschwisterung im Bruderland. Städtepartnerschaften in Deutschland* (Bonn: Bouvier, 1990), these statistics on pp. 365–66. For a very interesting top-level East German assessment of the town–twinnings see the appendix to the minutes of the Politburo meeting on 6 September 1988 in ZPA: JIV 2/2/2292.

... 1969 ... just half a million ... *Zahlenspiegel*, p. 130.

... 1988 ... 40 million ... see *Texte*, III/6, p. 543.

... little more than one million visits ... this and following statistics in *Zahlenspiegel*, p. 124, supplemented by *DDR-Reisebarometer*. See Table VII.

... some 60,000 a year ... *Zahlenspiegel*, p. 124.

... the numbers who travelled by land to West Berlin ... *Zahlenspiegel*, p. 126.

... 1988 ... some one and a half million visits ... *DDR-Reisebarometer*, p. 17.

... phone calls ... *Zahlenspiegel*, p. 130.

... among them Hans-Dietrich Genscher ... for Genscher's flight see Werner

Filmer, Heribert Schwan, *Hans-Dietrich Genscher* (Düsseldorf: Econ Verlag, 1988), pp. 102–7.

. . . his heart remained in Halle . . . In a speech in Potsdam in June 1988 Genscher said: 'The GDR is the part of Germany in which, in Halle on the Saale, there stands the house of my birth, in which I grew up, in which I went to school, in which I studied at the Universities of Halle and Leipzig — here my father, my grandparents are buried — here I have my *Heimat*.' Genscher, *Unterwegs*, p. 153. In a 1985 eulogy for Alois Mertes, Genscher also described himself as 'a Protestant from the heart of our fatherland'. Der Bundesminister des Auswärtigen, Mitteilung für die Presse, Nr. 1074/85. In a speech of thanks on receiving the honorary citizenship of Halle, after unification, he remarked that his associates had sometimes got the impression that Halle was larger than Shanghai, FAZ, 10 June 1991.

. . . becoming easier for Poles and Czechs . . . According to figures in the *UN Statistical Yearbook* the number of Hungarians visiting Austria rose from just 9,000 in 1960 to 45,000 in 1970, and 126,000 in 1980. These are almost certainly underestimates, since they are based on registrations at places of overnight stay. To this period, one might note, belongs a minor sub-genre of East Central European literature: the account of the first visit to the West. See, for example, Zbigniew Herbert's marvellous *A Barbarian in the Garden* (Manchester: Carcanet, 1985).

. . . top operative priority . . . 'Our most important goal, Ladies and Gentlemen, remains the achievement of more freedom of movement in Germany,' Chancellor Kohl in his 1987 state of the nation address, *Bundestag Plenarprotokolle* 11/33, p. 2163 (15 October 1987).

It began with the Protestant Church . . . for this and the following see Geissel, *Unterhändler*, pp. 328–334 and *passim*. See also the important article by Armin Volze, 'Kirchliche Transferleistungen in die DDR', in DA, 1/1991, pp. 59–63 (hereafter Volze, 'Kirchliche Transferleistungen'), Rehlinger, *Freikauf*, pp. 14–15, the long investigative article by Thomas Kleine-Brockhoff and Oliver Schröm in *Die Zeit*, 28 August 1992, which draws on material from the Schalck investigations, but also Volze's critical commentary on it in DA, 1/1993 pp. 58–66. These sources, together with the figures in Figure X, supplant the earlier and necessarily speculative work of the French journalist Michel Meyer, *Freikauf. Menschenhandel in Deutschland* (Vienna: Paul Zsolnay, 1978). This is clearly the subject for an important book, although one that will be very difficult to write given the lack of written evidence and the often conflicting testimonies.

. . . an intervention by the publisher Axel Springer . . . Rainer Barzel, Bonn, 2 October 1991. Rehlinger, *Freikauf*, pp. 17–18. Springer was responding to a suggestion from the West Berlin lawyer Jürgen Stange, who in turn had got the hint from Wolfgang Vogel.

. . . Ludwig Rehlinger describes . . . in Rehlinger, *Freikauf*, p. 23 ff.

. . . in a large unmarked envelope . . . ibid., pp. 32–35. Jürgen Stange, Berlin, 9 October 1991.

In August 1964 the first 'regular' transports... Wolfgang Vogel, Berlin, 9 October 1991.

...**the East Berlin lawyer extraordinary**... a first attempt at a biography of this controversial figure was Jens Schmidthammer, *Rechtsanwalt Wolfgang Vogel. Mittler zwischen Ost und West* (Hamburg: Hoffmann & Campe, 1987). A biography by Craig Whitney, *Spy Trader. Germany's Legendary Spy Broker and the Darkest Secrets of the Cold War* (New York: Times Books, 1993), was made available to the author in typescript as this book was going to press. A fine example of American investigative journalism, it contains many new details.

...**a certain Heinz Volpert**... see Przybylski, *Tatort 2*, the special report in *Die Zeit*, 28 August 1992, Whitney's *Spy Trader*, and the reports of the Bundestag special committee.

...**a price on the head**... in an interview in *Der Spiegel*, 15/1990, Vogel claimed that the criterion was the length of sentence. But see Rehlinger, *Freikauf*, p. 28.

...**a detailed record of what it called 'B-Deals'**... see Volze, 'Kirchliche Transferleistungen', pp. 62–64. The East German side also referred to 'C-Deals', which were payments from the Roman Catholic Church. Alexander Schalck, Berlin, 1 July 1992.

...**Commercial Co-ordination** (*KoKo*...) An authoritative book on *KoKo*, drawing on the mass of documents collected by the Bundestag special committee, other documents in the Party, state and Stasi archives, and the testimonies of Schalck and other participants, remains to be written. The first two reports of the Bundestag special committee, *Bundestag Drucksachen*, 12/3462 and 12/3920, present much basic information. On three 'instant' Schalck books to appear on the market see the review by Armin Volze in DA, 6/1992, pp. 646–56. For the specific relationship with the Protestant church see Geissel, *Unterhändler*, p. 346 ff and *passim*.

The first delivery... the following two paragraphs are based on the work of Armin Volze, the special report in *Die Zeit*, 28 August 1992, reports by Wolfgang Stock in the FAZ, and the official records of the Bundestag special committee.

...**oil, copper, silver and industrial diamonds**... see the table in Volze, 'Kirchliche Transferleistungen', p. 63.

Jürgen Stange estimates that... Jürgen Stange, Berlin, 9 October 1991.

...**a letter**...**August 1972**... this letter, dated 1 August 1972, is in AdsD: HS, 347, a file of correspondence with the Minister for Intra-German Relations.

...**proposed to take this seriously**... Günter Gaus, Hamburg, 14 May 1992.

...**broke off the talks**... Rehlinger, *Freikauf*, p. 77.

According to Wolfgang Vogel... Wolfgang Vogel, Berlin, 9 October 1991.

... Wehner ... travelled to East Berlin ... for this at the time famous incident see Baring, *Machtwechsel*, pp. 608–14, Rehlinger, *Freikauf*, p. 77, and Wehner and Mischnick's statements reproduced in *Texte*, I/12, pp. 676–81. Wehner's fascinating correspondence with Brandt following this episode is in AdsD: Dep WB, BK 75, while Wehner's own collection of his interviews and speeches on the subject in the second half of 1973 fills a fat file in BK 76. Mischnick joined Wehner and Honecker somewhat later in the day, Wolfgang Mischnick, Bonn, 17 March 1992. Honecker's own account in Reinhold Andert & Wolfgang Herzberg, *Der Sturz. Erich Honecker im Kreuzverhör* (Berlin: Aufbau-Verlag, 1991), pp. 348–49, confirms the details.

'They will get serious . . .' letter of 24 June 1973 in AdsD: Dep WB, BK 75.

... a memorandum of a conversation ... the memorandum, dated 2 December 1973, is in AdsD: Dep WB, BK 75. The memorandum contains both Wehner's summary of this 'verbal report' and his own commentary upon it. It is clear from accompanying notes that Wehner actually sent this to Honecker, as well as to Brandt, who asked Horst Ehmke to discuss it with Egon Bahr and Günter Gaus. More remarkably, Honecker wrote a long reply, dated 2 February 1974, of which more below.

Talking to Leonid Brezhnev ... record (*Niederschrift*) of their conversation in Moscow on 18 June 1974, now in ZPA: IV 2/2.035/55.

... happy with us ... for one contrary example see Garton Ash, *DDR*, pp. 21–22.

... emotional relationship ... see also p. 321.

... neither Vogel nor Schalck will aver ... Wolfgang Vogel, Berlin, 9 October 1991, Alexander Schalck-Golodkowski, Rottach-Egern, 10 October 1991.

... set at DM 40,000 ... Wolfgang Vogel in *Der Spiegel*, 15/1990. There also the following details and quotation.

... DM 4,500 a head ... this figure from Wolfgang Vogel, Berlin, 9 October 1991.

... in sum ... the Rehlinger, *Freikauf*, p. 247. They tally with those given by Vogel in *Der Spiegel*, 15/1990. For the payments, the most precise figures are given by Volze, 'Kirchliche Transferleistungen', p. 64, who lists both the Church figure of DM 3,436,900 (cf. Geissel, *Unterhändler*, p. 470) and the federal budget figure of DM 3,464,900. Rehlinger gives a slightly higher figure of 'over 3.5 billion'. The uncontrolled nature of these transfers led to a scandal in the Ministry for Intra-German Relations, where the senior official responsible for these proceedings under the social-liberal coalition was convicted of having misappropriated large sums. For further detail, see the special report in *Die Zeit*, 28 August 1992. The lawyers also took a number of cases in which private individuals paid to 'buy free' people from the GDR.

... 'The government of the German Democratic Republic . . .' *Zehn Jahre*,

p. 188. See also the account of these negotiations in Baring, *Machtwechsel*, pp. 457–62.

. . . the formula 'urgent family matters' . . . it seems first to have been used in the second permit agreement of September 1964, see *Dokumente*, IV/10, pp. 987–90, and Egon Bahr's commentary, pp. 996–97.

. . . a directive according to which . . . *Zehn Jahre*, p. 199. The one word 'Westberlin' reflected the GDR's position that West Berlin was a separate unit, neither half a divided city nor an integral part of the Federal Republic, but a land unto itself . . .

. . . the GDR promising to take further steps . . . *Zehn Jahre*, p. 208.

. . . a set of detailed notes . . . ibid., pp. 208–10.

. . . a further directive of June 1973 . . . ibid., pp. 231–2.

. . . a new travel decree . . . on visits to 'non-socialist states and Berlin (West)' of 15 February 1982, replacing those of October 1972 and June 1973. Text in *Innerdeutsche Beziehungen*, p. 100.

. . . West German statistics . . . see Table VI and notes.

. . . the introduction in January 1989 . . . see reports in FAZ, 15 December 1988, and for the criticism, FAZ 20 February 1989 and 23 March 1989. Text of the decree in *Texte*, III/6, pp. 554–562.

. . . no less than eighty-four per cent . . . *DDR-Reisebarometer*, p. 94.

. . . 'the most important achievement . . .' *Bundestag Plenarprotokolle*, 11/33, p. 2159 (15 October 1987).

. . . a 'meeting about GDR issues' . . . the minute, signed by Carl-Werner Sanne, is in AdsD: HS 127. Part of the follow-up can be seen in the exchange of letters between Schmidt and Honecker in ZPA: JIV 2/2A/1815.

. . . with Schalck, Vogel . . . see, for example, Gaus, *Deutschland*, pp. 257–62, Bölling, *Die fernen Nachbarn*, Chapter V. For a conversation between Schmidt and Vogel, in preparation for the Chancellor's planned summit with Honecker in 1980, see the note of 16 July 1980 in AdsD: HS 322. Some of Gaus's reports on his talks with Schalck are in AdsD: HS 449. Many East German reports of these talks emerged in a fragmentary way through the work of the Bundestag special committee on Schalck, which sifted the holdings of the Central Party Archive in Berlin.

. . . Karl Seidel . . . the papers of Seidel's department would be an indispensable source for any serious treatment of this subject. But at the time of writing they were under lock and key in the archives taken over directly by the West German Foreign Ministry. Even the archivists themselves had only limited access to them.

. . . to be found in the Schmidt papers . . . notably the correspondence with the Permanent Representation in AdsD: HS 449. See also the illuminating discussion in Link, *Ära Schmidt*, p. 353 ff.

... when, for example, men and women took refuge ... a moving description of one such case was given by Klaus Bölling in a confidential letter to the Chancellor dated 26 February 1981, in AdsD: HS 449. For a fine account see Rehlinger, *Freikauf*, pp. 121–93.

... 'I. *Introduction*: 20 years ...' these notes, the outline for the speechwriters, are in AdsD: HS 2439. Schmidt actually used the terms near the end of the final version of his speech, adding 'Moderation, persistence and predictability are not exactly traditional virtues of the Germans. Instead we must make them German virtues, if we want to survive in our very special historical and very special geographical situation.' *Bundestag Plenarprotokolle* 9/31, pp. 1548–49 (9 April 1981).

... the 'Church in socialism' ... see references in note on p. 530.

... Stolpe ... On Stolpe, as on Schalck, there is already a vast literature. The case against Stolpe is well summarised in Ralf Georg Reuth, *IM "SEKRETÄR". Die "Gauck-Recherche" und die Dokumente zum "Fall Stolpe"* (2nd, revised edition, Frankfurt: Ullstein, 1992), which reprints many of the most important documents. Stolpe's own successive versions can be followed in Manfred Stolpe, *Den Menschen Hoffnung geben. Reden, Aufsätze und Interviews aus zwölf Jahren* (Berlin: Wichern Verlag, 1991), and Manfred Stolpe, *Schwieriger Aufbruch* (Berlin: Siedler, 1992). Among innumerable articles on the case one might single out that by Richard Schröder in *Die Zeit*, 9 October 1992.

'Stolpe was a détente politician ...' this in an open letter to Bärbel Bohley in FAZ, 13 February 1992.

... close to Stolpe's methods ... report on an interview by Peter Jochen Winters in FAZ, 3 February 1992.

When Günter Gaus first made contact ... this story from Günter Gaus, Hamburg, 14 May 1992.

... heartily relieved ... Hans Otto Bräutigam, Berlin, 28 June 1992.

... Strauss ... secret communications with Schalck ... copies of documents originally made available by the CSU were kindly placed at the author's disposal by Wolfgang Stock.

... Schäuble, tried to regularise ... see his own account in *Schalck-Ausschuss*, Protokoll Nr. 24., p. 13 ff.

... pending the necessary masterwork ... short accounts are given in *Materialien*, pp. 626–35, a section written by specialists from the Deutsches Institut für Wirtschaftsforschung, and Karl C Thalheim, *Die wirtschaftliche Entwicklung der beiden Staaten in Deutschland* (Opladen: Leske & Budrich, 1988), Chapter 10. The best starting-points in English are the chapter by Michael Kaser in Moreton, *Germany*, John Garland, 'FRG-GDR Economic Relations', in *East European Economies. Slow Growth in the 1980s* (Washington: US Government Printing Office, 1986 = Selected Papers submitted to the Joint Economic Committee, Congress of the United States), Vol. 3, pp. 169–206 (hereafter, Garland

'FRG-GDR'), and H-D Jacobsen, *Security Implications of Inner-German Economic Relations* (Washington DC: Wilson Center International Security Studies Program Working Paper No. 77, 1986). (After unification, Jacobsen was reportedly discovered to have been collaborating with the Stasi, which gives a certain piquancy to this last title.)

... 'intra-German trade'... on this see the article by Siegfried Kupper in *DDR-Handbuch*, Bruns, *DDR-Politik*, pp. 98–107, Siegfried Kupper's earlier book, *Der innerdeutsche Handel* (Köln: Markus, 1972), Doris Cornelsen & ors, *Die Bedeutung des innerdeutschen Handels* (Berlin: Duncker und Humboldt, 1984) and Reinhold Biskup, *Deutschlands offene Handelsgrenze. Die DDR als Nutzniesser des EWG-Protokolls über den innerdeutschen Handel* (Berlin: Ullstein, 1976).

... 'a part of internal German trade'... see *Treaties establishing the European Communities* (Luxemburg: Office for Official Publications of the European Communities, 1987), Vol. I, pp. 513–14. The precise wording of the first paragraph is: 'Since trade between the German territories subject to the Basic Law for the Federal Republic of Germany and the German territories in which the Basic Law does not apply is a part of German internal trade, the application of this Treaty in Germany requires no change in the treatment currently accorded this trade.' In a discussion to mark the twentieth anniversary of Bahr's Tutzing speech, Alois Mertes recalled Walter Hallstein telling him about the 'hard struggle' he had to get the above-mentioned Protocol on Intra-German Trade accepted by the Federal Republic's new partners in the EEC. See *Die Zeit*, 15 July 1983. The formula 'German territories in which the Basic Law does not apply' reflected the Bonn government's then non-recognition of the sovereignty of both the GDR and the Polish and Soviet states over former German territories to the East. Needless to say, the benefits of Intra-German Trade were only ever extended to the GDR, or what was then known as the Soviet Occupation Zone. The agency which dealt with Intra-German Trade was actually known as the 'Trust Office for Intra-Zonal Trade' until the end of 1981, when it was renamed the 'Trust Office for Industry and Trade.'

... a drizzle of discontent... see the balanced discussion in Garland, 'FRG-GDR', pp. 204–5.

... more than half its western trade... According to GDR official statistics, in 1984 only 30 per cent of the GDR's total Western trade was with the Federal Republic, but the statistics of its trading partners produce a figure of about 50 per cent (*Materialien*, p. 630). In his calculations for 1985, Lincoln Gordon concludes that trade with West Germany comprised 59.4 per cent of East Germany's trade with 'industrial countries' (Gordon, *Eroding Empire*, Table A–12). For a fine analysis of the amazingly diverse statistics see Raimund Dietz, 'Der Westhandel der DDR', in DA, 3/1985.

... 'Swing'... as a card... see Link, *Ära Schmidt*, pp. 358–59.

... even more cautiously... in 1980–81... see Schmidt, *Nachbarn*, pp. 70–71, Mittag, *Preis*, pp. 94–95.

In 1985, the Kohl government privately... see Schäuble's testimony in *Schalck-Ausschuss*, Protokoll Nr. 24, p. 12.

... public and private transfers... the best summary account is now given in three scrupulous articles by Armin Volze, 'Geld und Politik in den innerdeutschen Beziehungen 1970–1989', in DA, 3/1990 (hereafter Volze, 'Geld und Politik'), the already cited 'Kirchliche Transferleistungen' (DA, 1/1991, pp. 59–66), and 'Die Devisengeschäfte der DDR. Genex und Intershop', DA, 11/1991, pp. 1145–1159 (hereafter Volze, 'Devisengeschäfte'). A critical account is given by Jerzy Lisiecki, 'Financial and Material Transfers between East and West Germany', in *Soviet Studies*, Vol. 42, No. 3, July 1990, pp. 513–34. Some additional detail can be found in the *Materialien*, and in an earlier article by Armin Volze, 'Zu den Besonderheiten der innerdeutschen Wirtschaftsbeziehungen im Ost-West Verhältnis' in *Deutsche Studien*, No. 83, September 1983, pp. 184–99.

... some DM 2 billion... Volze, 'Geld und Politik', p. 386. The 'greeting money' was raised from DM 30 to DM 100 per head in 1987.

... a leading specialist estimates... ibid.

... some DM 2.2 billion... calculated from the table in Volze, 'Kirchliche Transferleistungen', p. 64.

... of the order of $1–$1.5 billion... see Jacek Rostowski's contribution to Stanisław Gomułka and Antony Polonsky, eds, *Polish Paradoxes* (London: Routledge, 1990), p. 219, with further detail from the author's original typescript.

... some DM 5 billion... Volze, 'Geld und Politik', p. 386.

... some DM 3.2 billion... calculated from the table in Volze, 'Kirchliche Transferleistungen', p. 64.

... by Willy Brandt to Piotr Abrassimov... 'In this connection [links with West Berlin] Abrassimov reacted extremely positively to a passing comment of mine that it would be sensible to negotiate a lump-sum payment for the use of the motorway etc.' — Brandt's handwritten notes of a conversation with Abrassimov, 18 June 1968, in AdsD: Dep WB, BA 18.

... a lump-sum payment for the transit and other 'road use' fees... see *Materialien*, Table 7–6, p. 796. Strictly speaking, the DM 575 million was DM 525 million for transit fees plus a further DM 50 million for 'road-use fees'. This did not include sums paid by other travellers in transit, or special 'road use fees' for lorries etc. The overall figure of DM 8.3 billion is given by Volze, 'Geld und Politik', p. 384.

... under an agreement signed in October 1988... see *Texte*, III/6, pp. 343–57. Formally speaking, this was an annual DM 860 million for transit plus DM 55 million for 'road use'. The GDR undertook to open a new frontier crossing and to use some of these DM to improve the transit routes. In the formal agreements, provision was made for a negotiation in 1999, to agree a rate for the first decade of the twenty-first century.

... the papers presented to the Politburo... for the meeting of 30 August

1988. In the draft 'informal verbal declaration', the GDR said it would 'continue the measures taken and alleviations which have led to an increase in the travel — and visit-traffic of citizens of the GDR to non-socialist foreign countries'. Now in ZPA: JIV 2/2/2291. As noted above, new regulations on visits to the West were introduced at the end of 1988.

. . . **more than DM 2.4 billion** . . . Volze, 'Geld und Politik', p. 385 says 'nearly' DM 2.4 billion, but if one adds payments from the Berlin and Bavarian governments for sewage disposal etc., the figure is slightly more.

. . . **that Bonn got 'value for money'** . . . this was emphatically confirmed by one former Permanent Representative, Klaus Bölling, in conversation with the author (Berlin, 26 June 1991).

. . . **West German investigators found** . . . see the report in *Handelsblatt*, 24 October 1990, p. 6. I am grateful to Jurek Lisiecki for drawing my attention to this detail.

. . . **initially negotiated** . . . for Strauss's own account, which includes his drafting the letter for the East German Finance Minister to send to the West German Finance Minister, see Strauss, *Erinnerungen*, pp. 470–74.

. . . **unusually favourable terms** . . . As befitted a Strauss initiative, the consortium of banks was led by the Bayerische Landesbank. Exceptionally, the guarantee covered 100 per cent of the loan and the banks had to pay nothing for the guarantee. The conservative-liberal government thus went further in helping the GDR than the social-liberal government ever had. See Bruns, *DDR-Politik*, pp. 164–67. On the second loan, the banks did have to pay the usual 'provision' for the guarantee. See *Materialien*, p. 634. The 'security' offered by the GDR was an undertaking to renounce the equivalent amount of the lump-sum payment on transit fees, if it failed to repay the loan.

. . . **that it would pay off in other fields** . . . a specific example is a letter from Gaus to Chancellor Schmidt dated 24 October 1978, in which, noting that the financial difference between Bonn and the GDR's proposals for a package of projects is DM 137.5 million, he then writes: 'My recommendation is that in the final version we should meet the GDR's demands in this area, because our prospects of their giving ground on other questions could thereby be decisively improved.' AdsD: HS 449

. . . **'the principle of a balance of give and take** . . .' Bölling, *Die fernen Nachbarn*, p. 93

. . . **'cash against hope'** . . . thus Rainer Barzel in *Bundestag Plenarprotokolle*, 9/118, p. 7169, 1 October 1982.

. . . **the Social Democrats could hardly resist retorting** . . . see the speech by Hans Apel, responding to Chancellor Kohl's 1985 state of the nation address, in *Bundestag Plenarprotokolle*, 10/122, p. 9017 (27 February 1985).

. . . **they would point** . . . these arguments were mustered by Wolfgang Schäuble in a clear defence of the policy, see the report by Karl Feldmeyer in FAZ, 17 August 1991.

... **a political signal** ... this was said in so many words by Chancellor Kohl in his 1984 state of the nation address, see the discussion in *Innerdeutsche Beziehungen*, p. 11.

... **Schalck's internal note** ... copy of report dated Berlin, 12.03.1984, from papers of the *Schalck-Ausschuss*. For Honecker's acceptance of such linkages in connection with the first billion credit, see Strauss, *Erinnerungen*, p. 473.

... **the hard currency balance of payments deficit** ... one of the first to point this up was Schalck himself, see the report in FAZ, 2 January 1990, referring to an interview with Schalck on ARD television. It has subsequently been extensively referred to, not only by Schalck but also, notably, by the head of the State Plan Commission, Gerhard Schürer, who also chaired the operative Balance of Payments Working Group. See also Mittag, *Preis*, pp. 82 ff, 287 ff, and the embittered memoirs of one of his associates, Carl-Heinz Janson, *Totengräber der DDR. Wie Günter Mittag den SED-Staat ruinierte* (Düsseldorf: Econ, 1991), p. 33 ff.

... **Schalck and others now testify** ... Alexander Schalck-Golodkowski, Berlin, 1 July 1992. Gerhard Schürer, Berlin, 7 October 1991.

Günter Mittag goes so far ... Günter Mittag, Berlin, 28 June 1992, and see Mittag, *Preis*, p. 82 ff.

Gerhard Schürer ... **suggests** ... Berlin, 7 October 1991 and 30 June 1992.

... **the key operational Balance of Payments Working Group** ... one must distinguish between the Politburo Balance of Payments Working Group, set up by the Politburo resolution of 2 November 1976 and chaired by Mittag, and the *operational* Balance of Payments Working Group, chaired by Schürer.

The internal statistics of the GDR in this field ... The most important series of statistics would appear to be that kept by the hard currency department of the Finance Ministry, under Deputy Minister Herta König, who was also a member of the Balance of Payments Working Group.

... **about 2 billion Valutamarks** ... Carl-Heinz Janson, *Totengräber der DRR. Wie Günter Mittag den SED-Staat ruinierte* (Düsseldorf: Econ, 1991), p. 65, gives a figure of 2.2 billion for 1970 and 25.3 billion for 1985. These figures were confirmed to the author by Gerhard Schürer (letter of 13 November 1992) on the basis of his own papers.

... **this 'plinth'** ... in German, *Sockel*. The term is used frequently by Mittag, *Preis*, and by those responsible in conversation with the author.

... **more consumer than producer** ... Schürer gives a figure of sixty per cent consumer to forty per cent producer goods for the early 1970s. Gerhard Schürer, Berlin, 7 October 1991. This general critique of Honecker's strategy is made in a number of memoirs and recollections. Mittag, *Preis*, blames it all on Honecker. Carl-Heinz Janson, *Totengräber der DDR. Wie Günter Mittag den SED-Staat* *ruinierte* (Düsseldorf: Econ, 1991) blames it all on Mittag. Most others blame it on both Honecker and Mittag. See, for example, the notes by Werner Krolikowski reprinted in Przybylski, *Tatort 1*, p. 321 ff. Schürer gives his account in a memoir entitled *Gewagt und Verloren. Die Planwirtschaft der DDR und ihr Untergang* (typescript, October 1991, copy in the author's possession).

. . . **constantly warning** . . . this was a point made to me by almost all the former members of the East German Politburo, with the signal exception of Erich Honecker, who flatly denied that Brezhnev had given any such warning.

. . . **'did not reach a dangerous level'** . . . report on Brezhnev's meeting with the Czechoslovak politburo in April 1981 in ZPA: IV 2/2.035/54.

. . . **also warned** . . . Günter Schabowski, *Der Absturz* (Berlin: Rowohlt, 1991), p. 121 f, credits Schürer with making a first protest in 1972, a version also given by Schürer himself. Werner Krolikowski also claims to have warned about the consequences at an early stage (see the documents in Przybylski, *Tatort 1*), a claim broadly confirmed by Schürer. See also Przybylski, *Tatort 2*, p. 49 ff. For Schürer's 1988 attempt see below.

Ludwig Geissel recalls . . . Geissel, *Unterhändler*, pp. 264–65.

. . . **an enclave of real-price, market-oriented economic activity** . . . an interpretation given by Schalck himself (Berlin, 1 July 1992), this is nonetheless plausible.

. . . **formally in 1972 and again in 1976** . . . that is, after the 8th and 9th party congresses. A rather vivid account of the irresistible rise of Alexander Schalck is given in Przybylski, *Tatort 2*.

. . . *de facto* **even more thereafter** . . . see, for example, the letter dated 23/24 April 1981 from Mittag to Honecker, reprinted in *Bundestag Drucksachen*, 12/3462, pp. 898–900, and all the evidence cited above about his crucial role as German-German intermediary.

Karl Seidel . . . Berlin, 30 September 1992.

. . . **Gerhard Schürer rightly points out** . . . Berlin, 30 June 1992.

. . . **'secured'** . . . **DM 50 billion** . . . thus Schalck many times, for example in testimony to the *Schalck-Ausschuss*, Bonn, 24 June 1992.

. . . **DM 27 billion** . . . **DM 23 billion** . . . Alexander Schalck-Golodkowski, Berlin, 1 July 1992.

. . . **casually mentioned** . . . ibid.

. . . **corresponds almost exactly** . . . The precise total from the ten years' transit and road-use lump-sum payments would have been DM 9.15 billion. Subtracting this from the round figure of DM 23 billion we get DM 13.85 billion. The total of the state-to-state transfers, as calculated by Armin Volze on the basis of the West German figures, is DM 13.9 billion.

. . . **of the order of 2 billion Valutamarks** . . . Gerhard Schürer, Berlin, 30 June 1992 and letter of 13 November 1992. One should also note that the so-called

Staatsdevisenreserve (state hard currency reserve), which was controlled by the Council of Ministers, was probably also fed directly from the hard currency visa and minimum compulsory exchange income from Western visitors.

... about 5 billion Valutamarks ... ibid. Of course these figures should be verified if and when the full, internal statistics are available. But Schürer's round figures give a good sense of the orders of magnitude.

... figures used by Schürer and others ... Carl-Heinz Janson, *Totengräber der DDR. Wie Günter Mittag den SED-Staat ruinierte* (Düsseldorf: Econ, 1991), p. 65, gives the figures as 30.0 billion for 1985 and 34.7 billion for 1987.

A memorandum ... memorandum of 30 October 1989, reprinted in DA, 10/1992, pp. 1112–20, this on p. 1116.

... the Bundesbank ... see its *Monatsbericht*, 7/1990. Further detail in this paragraph comes from Gerhard Schürer, and from the leading West German specialist, Armin Volze (letter of 11 January 1993).

... including arms and ammunition ... these raids on the strategic reserves had formally to be approved by the Politburo, see, for example, the appendices in ZPA: JIV 2/2A/2582.

... Schürer and Schalck would privately discuss ... Gerhard Schürer, Berlin, 7 October 1991. The first serious journalistic treatment of this story came in an article by Peter Siebenmorgen in *Die Zeit*, 3 May 1991. More details can be found in Hans-Hermann Hertle, *Vor dem Bankrott der DDR = Berliner Arbeitshefte und Berichte zur sozialwissenschaftlichen Forschung Nr. 63* (Berlin: Zentralinstitut für sozialwissenschaftliche Forschung, 1991), which contains both a transcript of a long interview with Schürer and copies of the actual documents submitted to Honecker and then to the Politburo.

... Mittag would claim, retrospectively ... Günter Mittag, Berlin, 28 June 1992, and Mittag, *Preis*, p. 97 ff. Mittag there credits Gerhard Beil with also thinking in terms of an eventual confederation. Gerhard Beil was unfortunately not prepared to talk to the author.

... slightly less alarming ... Günter Schabowski, Berlin, 29 June 1991. Egon Krenz, Berlin, 29 September 1992. Among other things, monies owed to the GDR were credited in full, even where there was effectively no chance of their being repaid.

'When you took over ...' quoted by Gerhard Schürer in his (at the time of writing, unpublished) memoirs, *Gewagt und Verloren. Die Planwirtschaft der DDR und ihr Untergang* (typescript, October 1991, copy in the author's possession).

Egon Krenz knew the true facts ... Egon Krenz, Berlin, 29 September 1992.

... Werner Krolikowski colourfully remarked ... the memorandum is reprinted in Przybylski, *Tatort 1*, pp. 321–339, this on p. 327.

... the above-mentioned Schürer memorandum ... DA, 10/1992, pp. 1112–20, this on p. 1116.

'Where has all the hard currency gone?' . . . Garton Ash, *We*, p. 70.

. . . understood little of economics . . . Gerhard Schürer, Berlin, 7 October 1991; Mittag, *Preis*; and see below, p. 198.

. . . to make quite sure . . . thus, explicitly, Strauss, *Erinnerungen*, p. 476. Also Wolfgang Schäuble, Bonn, 17 March 1992.

. . . Schäuble recalls . . . Wolfgang Schäuble, Bonn, 17 March 1992.

. . . Schalck recalls . . . Alexander Schalck-Golodkowski, Rottach-Egern, 10 October 1991.

. . . some of West Germany's economic experts . . . on the political-academic tensions behind the 1987 *Materialien* see the brief and distinctly partisan account in Jens Hacker, *Deutsche Irrtümer. Schönfärber und Helfershelfer der SED-Diktatur im Westen* (Berlin: Ullstein, 1992), pp. 442–49.

. . . the average East German cow . . . *Materialien*, p. 442.

. . . enough to cover the interest payments . . . ibid., p, 634. In the event, this almost certainly underestimated the debt service burden. The authors' guesstimate was based on the work of Armin Volze. In the light of Hacker's criticisms it should perhaps be noted that this passage comes in the part of the *Materialien* prepared by the Deutsches Institut für Wirtschaftsforschung.

. . . 'choreograph the West German grande bourgeoisie' . . . Günter Schabowski, Berlin, 29 June 1991.

Did not the World Bank say . . . quoted, with apparent relish, by Jonathan Steele, *Socialism with a German Face. The State that Came in From the Cold* (London: Jonathan Cape, 1977), p. 7. The GDR was said to have 'overtaken' Britain in 1974.

. . . James McAdams . . . 'Inter-German Détente. A New Balance', in *Foreign Affairs*, Fall 1986, pp. 136–53. This article developed the argument of his earlier book *East Germany and détente. Building Authority after the Wall* (Cambridge: Cambridge University Press, 1985). See also his delightfully titled article 'The GDR at Forty. The Perils of Success' in *German Politics and Society* (Harvard) Issue 17, Summer 1989. McAdams's notable book on German-German relations, *Germany Divided. From the Wall to Unification* (Princeton: Princeton University Press, 1993) appeared too late to be used in the preparation of this chapter.

. . . the subject of fierce debate . . . see the illuminating discussion in Bergsdorf, *Sprache*, p. 212 f.

. . . a more important distinction . . . this distinction was drawn with characteristic clarity by Ralf Dahrendorf, see *Bundestag Plenarprotokolle*, 6/23, p. 925 (15 January 1970).

. . . Christian Democratic opponents . . . see Clemens, *Reluctant Realists* and Hacke, *Wege und Irrwege* for more detail. In his last state of the nation address, in June 1969, Chancellor Kiesinger himself made this point quite forcefully. The people in East Germany did not support either the regime or the imposed constitution or even the very existence of a second German state, he said. 'A recognition by us or by others could not substitute for this lacking support.' See *Bundestag Plenarprotokolle*, 5/239, p. 13246 (17 June 1969), also in *Texte* I/3, p. 256 ff.

'We . . . are not prepared' . . . reprinted in *Texte* I/5, pp. 189–201, this on p. 193.

Social and Free Democrats replied . . . see the speeches by Brandt and others listed under 'Anerkennung' in the index to *Texte* I. See also the brief discussion in Brandt, *Erinnerungen*, p. 234 ff, Bender, *Neue Ostpolitik*, p. 160 ff, and for an eloquent publicistic statement of the case, Peter Bender, *Zehn Gründe für die Anerkennung der DDR* (Frankfurt: Fischer, 1968)

Willy Brandt quoted . . . see *Bundestag Plenarprotokolle*, 6/94, p. 5183 (29 January 1971) and Brandt, *Erinnerungen*, p. 235

. . . Erich Honecker proudly announced . . . personal observation by the author. He was still trumpeting this achievement in his defence speech before the West Berlin court in 1992, see DA, 1/1993, pp. 97–105, this on p. 97.

In a speech at Gera . . . for the demands, and their context, see Bruns, *DDR-Politik*, pp. 139–43, and, in English, A. James McAdams, *East Germany and Détente. Building Authority after the Wall* (Cambridge: Cambridge University Press, 1985), pp. 170–72.

Häber's records of his conversations . . . these are now in ZPA with the signatures (in 1992) JIV 2/10.02/10–14 and JIV 2/10.04/14–17.

. . . the delight expressed . . . this in Häber's reports in ZPA: JIV 2/10.02/13. The tendency to sycophancy is particularly apparent in Häber's reports — perhaps one reason why Honecker lifted him so unexpectedly into the Politburo?

. . . 'a fanatical Polish nationalist' . . . quoted from Häber's report of 27 June 1978 on a trip to West Germany, 19–24 June, now (1992) in ZPA: JIV 2/10.02/10.

. . . 'there was hardly an interlocutor . . .' from Häber's report on his trip of 2–8 March 1980, in ZPA: JIV 2/10.02/10.

. . . 'the difference between Carter and Reagan . . .' from Häber's report of 15 September 1980 on his trip of 5–14 September, in ZPA: JIV 2/10.02/10.

Herbert Wehner, among others, . . . see the correspondence in AdsD: Dep WB, BK 75. Another example in a letter of 19 May 1981 from Egon Franke to Chancellor Schmidt in AdsD: HS 347. See also the testimonial given by Schmidt, *Nachbarn*, p. 40,

. . . Hermann Axen, hurried off . . . Axens's notes on his conversations with Suslov, Ponomaryev and Zagladin on 23 and 24 January 1980 are now in ZPA: IV 2/2.035/57. There all the quotations in this paragraph.

The East German record . . . record (*Niederschrift*) of the meeting in Belgrade on 8 May 1980, in ZPA: IV 2/2.035/86.

... Bahr's hope ... see, for example, his statement on the signing of the treaty in *Texte* I/11, pp. 311–13.

... solemnly exchanged that code-phrase ... in his state of the nation address in March 1980, Chancellor Schmidt noted 'In December last year the Chairman of the Council of State, Erich Honecker, and I said in Berlin, independently of one another but in full agreement: war may never again go out from German soil.' See *Bundestag Plenarprotokolle*, 8/208, p. 16617 (20 March 1980).

'We have signed ...' quoted in Bölling, *Die fernen Nachbarn*, p. 135

'We don't want to show off ...' ibid., p. 140. Obviously there was a strong element of tactical flattery in this.

... a dark shadow ... see Schmidt, *Nachbarn*, p. 73 ff, Bölling, *Die fernen Nachbarn*, p. 152 ff.

... Walther Leisler Kiep ... this in a report of 8 February 1982 on a trip to West Germany, 1–6 February 1982, in ZPA: JIV 2/10.02/13.

... real concerns on the East German side ... Thus the Minister for State Security, Erich Mielke, gave a dark warning about the dangers of increased subversion, embargoes and sanctions in his speech to a 'central service conference' of the Stasi in Potsdam on 11 October 1982. MfS: GVS o008–12/82. On a memorandum from Herbert Häber reporting a lunch with Hans Otto Bräutigam on 5 October 1982, Honecker scribbled: 'Our position [?] is clear — Kohl's "accents" will be decisive for how relations develop. Elections 6 March. i.e. Kohl is transitional government?' ZPA: JIV 2/10.02/11. But Kohl was confirmed in office, and Honecker clearly did not like the initial 'accents', see the message he sent to Kohl via Häber and Bräutigam in April 1983, in ZPA: JIV 2/10.02/11.

... 'these days it is almost ...' this in a report of 17 October 1983 on trip to West Germany, 9–16 October 1983, in ZPA: JIV 2/10.02/13.

... 'As genuine advocates of peace ...' ND, 26/27 November 1983.

... other signals the Kohl government gave ... see, for example, the letter sent by Kohl to Honecker on 24 October 1983, in response to Honecker's letter of 5 October, ZPA: 2/2.035/87. Here Kohl has already picked up the phrase 'coalition of reason'. This was in response to a letter from Honecker, published in ND, 10 October 1983. Both letters are reproduced in *Texte*, III/1, pp. 242–44 and 255–59.

'The two states in Germany ...' in ZPA: IV 2/2.035/87. Kohl was responding to a letter from Honecker on 25 November 1983.

Two months later, Honecker replied ... letter of 17 February 1984 in ZPA: IV 2/2.035/87.

... in a guesthouse in the Lenin Hills ... both Helmut Kohl (Bonn, 1 October 1991) and Erich Honecker (Berlin-Moabit, 27 November 1992) recalled the importance of this first personal meeting.

...blamed this ... offensive commentaries ... see Ronald D Asmus, *East Berlin and Moscow. The Documentation of a Dispute* (Munich: Radio Free Europe, 1985), pp. 14, 76–77.

'the future of the Federal Republic ...' *Die Welt*, 21 August 1984.

As late as mid-August ... see the minutes of the Politburo meeting on 14 August 1984, which sanctioned an extensive briefing paper for the Party (*Informationen* 1984/6, Nr. 209) arguing in this direction, ZPA: JIV 2/2/2070. The *Pravda* article, of 2 August 1984, ostensibly attacking the *West* German position, is reprinted in *Texte* III/2, pp. 297–98. Honecker seems to have believed that he had Chernenko's sanction from their earlier conversation on 14 June 1984, see the record in ZPA: JIV 2/2A/2660. At a Politburo meeting on 17 August 1984 (ZPA: JIV 2/2/2071) those who were not accompanying Honecker agreed the text of his plea to be allowed to go, and the text (already in proof form) of his interview in ND, 18 August 1984.

A dramatic encounter ... see the record in ZPA: JIV 2/2A/2678.

...Honecker recounted proudly ... Erich Honecker, Berlin-Moabit, 27 November 1992.

Egon Krenz vividly recalls ... Berlin, 29 September 1992. The minutes of the meeting, on 20 August 1984, are in ZPA: JIV 2/2/2072.

...minutes for 28 August ... ZPA: JIV 2/2/2073

...the word 'peace' ... see the discussion in Bergsdorf, *Sprache*, p. 246 ff.

...a joint statement ... the declaration, dated 12 March 1985, is reprinted in *Innerdeutsche Beziehungen*, p. 212.

How can I explain to the Soviet people ... Egon Krenz, Berlin, 29 September 1992. At the time of writing, a documentation of the Honecker-Gorbachev meetings was promised by Daniel Küchenmeister, but not yet available. He gave a very preliminary account of his findings in DA, 1/1993, pp. 30–40.

...Hermann Axen to Moscow ... Axen's records of this 'consultation' on 27 July 1987 are in ZPA: IV 2/2.035/59.

...a long document ... the original text is in ZPA: IV 2/2.035/14. It was given to the Soviet leadership on 23 June. Another copy, from the papers of the East German trades union head, Harry Tisch, is usefully reproduced in Hans-Hermann Hertle, & ors, *Der Staatsbesuch. Honecker in Bonn: Dokumente zur deutsch-deutschen Konstellation des Jahres 1987* (Berlin: Freie Universität, 1991 = FU Informationen aus Lehre und Forschung, 2/1991).

'That sounded exactly ...' internal memorandum from Axen to Honecker, 29 July 1987, in ZPA: IV 2/2.035/59.

'The visit would be ...' quoted from the record (*Niederschrift*) of the meeting in ZPA: IV 2/2.035/59. Of course the GDR only became a member of the United Nations in 1973.

... merely informed ... Kurt Hager, Berlin, 8 May 1992. Egon Krenz, Berlin, 29 September 1992. The author had not, at the time of writing, been able to find the precise documentation of the 'information' to Moscow.

... Helmut Kohl ... very far from enthusiastic ... Wolfgang Schäuble, Bonn, 17 March 1992. Schäuble recalls Kohl saying 'this is a bad day'.

... virtually all the honours ... But not the full number of police outriders due in protocol to a head of state. In Bonn, Honecker got only seven. But, characteristically, Franz Josef Strauss gave him the full head of state's complement — fifteen — for his day in the capital of the Free State of Bavaria. See *Der Spiegel*, 1/1988, p. 22.

... two German leaders stood to attention side by side ... see, for example, the photographs on the front-page of the tabloid *Bild*, 8 September 1987, which, however, offered the headline: 'Two Flags, Two Anthems, One Fatherland'.

... keynote dinner speech ... most of the speeches and statements of the Honecker visit are usefully collected in a Ministry for Intra-German Relations booklet, *Der Besuch von Generalsekretär Honecker in der Bundesrepublik Deutschland* (Bonn, 1988), hereafter *Besuch*, this on p. 26 ff. The keynote speeches can also be found in *Bulletin*, 10 September 1987. All the following quotations from the speeches can be found there.

... reported on 9 September ... in MfS: Z4229.

... talking to the Free Democrat Otto Graf Lambsdorff ... record of a conversation on 4 February 1988 in ZPA: IV 2/2.035/83.

Their joint communiqué ... *Besuch*, p. 36 ff. It should be noted that the communiqué emphasised the different positions on arms control as 'Chancellor Kohl presented the concept agreed in the Atlantic Alliance ...' while 'General Secretary Honecker drew attention to the proposals of the member states of the Warsaw Treaty ...'

... offering hitherto unexposed charms ... of course there were other motives, including concerns about a weakening American commitment, defence costs, and a rethinking of French military strategy. See, for example, Pierre Lellouche, *L'Avenir de la Guerre* (Paris: Mazarine, 1985). Nonetheless, the concern about a possible German eastward or national-neutralist drift remained a dominant motive. An extreme but highly successful example was Alain Minc, *La Grande Illusion* (Paris: Bernard Grasset, 1989).

... point 9 ... see the neatly organised agenda issued in a briefing package for the Washington Summit. Reagan's speech in front of the Brandenburg Gate on 12 June 1987 is reprinted in *Texte* III/5, pp. 96–100.

Publicistic reaction ... see Karl Wilhelm Fricke, 'Der Besuch Erich Honeckers in der Bundesrepublik Deutschland', EA, 23/1987, pp. 683–90.

... presciently formulated by ... Pierre Hassner ... see his essay 'Zwei deutsche Staaten in Europa: Gibt es gemeinsame Interessen in der internationalen

Politik?' in Werner Weidenfeld, ed., *Die Identität der Deutschen* (Munich: Hanser, 1983), pp. 294–323, this on p. 301.

... **to influence its own alliance** ... in a prepared statement to open the first round of talks, Chancellor Kohl referred to the desirability of arms control measures on short-range nuclear forces, conventional arms and chemical weapons, and then said 'We expect that the GDR will make its influence felt in the framework of its alliance so that here too it soon comes to concrete steps.' *Bulletin*, 10 September 1987, p. 709.

... **the Federal Republic's role, influence and room for manoeuvre in Nato** ... on this, see Josef Joffe, *The Limited Partnership. Europe, the United States, and the Burdens of Alliance* (Cambridge: Ballinger, 1987) and David P. Calleo, *Beyond American Hegemony. The Future of the Western Alliance* (New York: Basic Books, 1987).

'It's a short step ...' *Frankfurter Rundschau*, 26 June 1982.

'Incidentally ... if your neighbour put up some new wallpaper ...' ND, 10 April 1987.

The basic lesson of the Cold War ... see Peter Bender, *Offensive Entspannung. Möglichkeit für Deutschland* (Köln: Kiepenheuer & Witsch, 1964), Bender, *Neue Ostpolitik*, p. 163.

'Increasing tension ...' for this and following quotations from the Tutzing speech see p. 65 f. and notes.

'This weakness ...' Peter Bender, *Offensive Entspannung. Möglichkeit für Deutschland* (Köln: Kiepenheuer & Witsch, 1964), p. 110.

'A material improvement ...' see p. 66 above and notes.

Josef Joffe has forcefully argued ... See his chapter in Gordon, *Eroding Empire*, pp. 129–87, especially pp. 15–51, 161–62, 178–80.

... **a 'virtuous circle'** ... ibid., p. 151.

... **with deliberate oversimplification** ... The complexity of the German origins of détente has already been indicated. For the complexity of the American origins of détente see, for example, Kovrig, *Walls and Bridges*, and John Lewis Gaddis, *Strategies of Containment. A Critical Appraisal of Postwar American National Security Policy* (Oxford: Oxford University Press, 1982).

... **the United States' policy of 'differentiation'** ... for 'differentiation' see, out of a large literature, Kovrig, *Walls and Bridges*, passim; Gordon, *Eroding Empire*, esp. pp. 73–74, and Charles Gati, *Hungary and the Soviet Bloc* (Durham NC: Duke University Press, 1986), Chapter 10.

... **rather childish simplifications** ... Hans-Peter Schwarz suggests that the correct distinction is rather between (American or German) *liberal* notions of détente, and (American or German) *conservative* notions of détente. Yet in the end, when it came to actual policy-making, did the conservative Kissinger have more in common with the conservative Strauss or with the liberals Carter and

Brzezinski? Conversely, when it came to actual policy-making, did the conservative Strauss have more in common with the conservative Kissinger or with the 'social-liberal' Schmidt and Genscher? See Hans-Peter Schwarz, 'Supermacht und Juniorpartner. Ansätze amerikanischer und westdeutscher Ostpolitik', in Hans-Peter Schwarz & Boris Meissner, eds., *Entspannungspolitik in Ost und West* (Köln: Heymann, 1979), p. 159 ff.

... 'only the *unconditional* recognition of the status quo ...' Italics mine. Peter Glotz, *Manifest für eine neue Europäische Linke* (Berlin: Siedler, 1985), p. 65. So also Günter Gaus: 'We must firmly hold fast to the fact that peace in Europe — enriched by a relative détente — remains bound for the foreseeable future to the unconditional recognition of the status quo, of the political property relations as they are', from a speech of 1981, reprinted in Günter Gaus, *Deutschland und die Nato. Drei Reden* (Hamburg: Rowohlt, 1984), p. 103.

... the distinction between state and system was relatively easy to make ... Which does not mean, however, that West German policymakers always managed to make it, see p. 280 ff.

... 'only thinkable ...' Prof. Otto Reinhold on Radio DDR II, 19 August 1989, quoted here from the BPA/DDR-Spiegel transcript, 22 August 1989.

'The more firmly entrenched the SED leadership ...' Wilhelm Bruns quoted in an article by Joachim Nawrocki in *Die Zeit*, 15 June 1979.

'Only a consolidation of the GDR ...' Michael Kreile, 'Ostpolitik Reconsidered', in Ekkehart Krippendorff & Volker Rittberger, eds, *The Foreign Policy of West Germany* (London: Sage, 1980), p. 140.

Bahr himself modified and qualified ... see above p. 67 f. and references.

Willy Brandt cautioned ... '... interests, power relations and social differences are neither dialectically to be resolved, nor should they be obscured', government declaration of 28 October 1969, *Bundestag Plenarprotokolle*, 6/5, p. 32. He quoted this passage again in his 1974 state of the nation address, see *Bundestag Plenarprotokolle*, 7/76, p. 4771 (24 January 1974).

Richard von Weizsäcker described ... Weizsäcker, *Deutsche Geschichte*, pp. 13–14.

Peter Bender, wrote ... see *Vorwärts*, 16 July 1988.

... 'not aimed at a destabilisation ...' EA, 12/1986, p. 346. In the same article Schäuble wrote: 'The Federal Government knows that steps forward in the intra-German relationship are only possible in homeopathic doses' (ibid., p. 343). Did he realise that he was using the exact metaphor — homeopathic doses — that Bahr had used in Tutzing in 1963?

'We have no intention of harming ...' see his article 'The Two States in Germany', *Aussenpolitik* (English edition), 3/1984, p. 241.

... as Eberhard Schulz well described it ... see Ehmke, *Zwanzig Jahre*, p. 219. Schulz uses the term *Stabilitätsgebot* here in the specific context of security, alliance and frontier issues, but it has a wider application. See also the revealing discussion by Peter Hardi, then of the Karl Marx University in Budapest, in EA, 13/1986, pp. 387–90. 'The most important security question for East European governments,' writes Hardi, 'is the preservation of social and political stability. This means a stable socialist society under the leadership of a communist party.'

... 'a serious domestic crisis' ... *Bundestag Plenarprotokolle*, 8/78, p. 6112 (9 March 1978).

... simply did not believe ... this was evident from conversations the author had with German policymakers at the time. Of course it will only be possible to document this more precisely when the West German official papers are opened, in 2011.

... 'unrealism' of the Poles ... see, for example, Bölling, *Die fernen Nachbarn*, p. 120. Although Bölling ascribes these views to thoughtful Germans in the GDR, they could be heard in Bonn almost as much as in East Berlin.

... seemed only to bear out ... See Schmidt's own recollection of his remarks to Mitterand in January 1982: 'Unfortunately Solidarność wanted to advance the process of change too quickly, which led to the recent reverse ...' Schmidt, *Nachbarn*, p. 259 ff, this on p. 264. For analysis of this general judgement see Garton Ash, *Solidarity*, p. 297 ff.

'It is in the liberal and socialist traditions ...' letter dated 20/22 August 1963 in AdsD: Dep WB, Rbm 38.

... Alois Mertes would later make ... in a discussion reprinted in *Politik und Kultur* 2/1981, p. 34.

Brandt at the window ... the photograph on which the gesture can be seen is in Koch, *Brandt*, also in *Die Zeit*, 9 March 1990.

'I was moved, but ...' Brandt, *People and Politics*, p. 372. Similarly, Brandt, *Erinnerungen*, p. 226.

'For freedom's battle ...' these lines from Byron's 'Giaour', well-known in Poland through the translation by Adam Mickiewicz, were scribbled on a piece of paper pinned to the wooden cross erected outside the Lenin Shipyard, during the strike that gave birth to Solidarity. But the unknown striker who made the dedication omitted the word 'bleeding'. See Garton Ash, *Solidarity*, p. 49.

In nineteenth-century Poland ... see the discussion in Norman Davies, *God's Playground. A History of Poland* (Oxford: Clarendon Press, 1981), especially Volume 2, Chapter 1.

In the twentieth century ... thus the title of a book by Adam Bromke, *Poland's Politics. Idealism vs. Realism* (Cambridge, Mass.: Harvard University Press, 1967).

... 'German realism' ... speech to the Bundestag on 11 May 1973, reprinted in *Texte* I/12, pp. 523–31, this on p. 526.

... 'Polish conditions such as ...' Gaus, *Deutschland*, pp. 270–71.

526 · *Notes to Page 184*

The Minister for Intra-German relations talked ... see the report in FAZ, 2 January 1989.

Hans Otto Bräutigam ... spoke ... lecture at St Antony's College, Oxford, 6 June 1988. An earlier, internal usage, where he talks of the 'stabilisation' of German-German relations, is to be found in his memorandum of 9 January 1979 on 'Germany-and Berlin-policy at the beginning of 1979' in AdsD: HS 01442.

... a reliable and forthcoming partner in negotiations ... in an interview immediately after his retirement as Permanent Representative, Günter Gaus argued explicitly 'that we need the GDR as a strong partner. We don't gain when the GDR is weak.' See his interview in NG 8/1982, pp. 712–21, this on p. 714. Bräutigam expressed a similar view, albeit somewhat more cautiously.

... nor the West German government should put too much pressure ... 'If we now forcefully urge the GDR to change itself, or else this or that won't work any more, that only strengthens the *Abgrenzung* [i.e. the defensive policy of the GDR against West German influence] and can completely halt the little there is of inner movement', Hans Otto Bräutigam in *Die Zeit*, 3/1989.

'I wanted to help to increase ...' Schmidt, *Nachbarn*, p. 67.

... the available East German records ... in 1991–92, the most important sources available for research on this topic were the minutes and working papers of the Politburo, some other holdings in the internal archive of the Politburo, and the papers of the office of Hermann Axen (Büro Axen). Also available for consultation were the papers of the offices of Kurt Hager and Joachim Herrmann. Those of Honecker's own office were not available for systematic research, while those of Egon Krenz's office were catalogued but then closed by the state prosecutors' office. Still unavailable were most of the papers of the so-called Western Department (subsequently Department for International Politics and Economics) and the curiously named Traffic Department, which actually dealt in the covert 'traffic' (including financial traffic) with organisations and parties in the West.

Perhaps the most important records *not* available, however, were the papers of the 'FRG Department' of the East German Foreign Ministry, which the West German Foreign Ministry took over at unification and then firmly closed. For it was the head of this department, Karl Seidel, who was generally the note-taker at the meetings of prominent West German visitors with the East German leader. A number of these records are to be found in the party archives, but all of them, in a matchless series from 1970 to 1990, were, by Seidel's own account, left neatly in his office cupboard when — the correct functionary to the last — he handed over the keys and departed in early 1990. Karl Seidel, Berlin, 30 September 1992.

Those of Seidel's protocols that we have thus far been able to examine are generally credible, on two grounds. Firstly, on account of the great detail, the generally authentic vocabulary, and the significant variations between the records of individual conversations. Secondly, on account of the personal credibility of Karl Seidel as a note-taker. Seidel took shorthand notes. Returning to his office, he dictated a full record as soon as possible to his secretary. He insists that, while he may have very slightly emphasised the praise and de-emphasised the criticism, both praise and criticism were mentioned if and when they came. (Karl Seidel, Berlin, 30 September 1992). The variations between, for example, the record of Honecker's conversation with Volker Rühe and those of his conversations with Oskar Lafontaine, bear out this contention. Moreover, Seidel is himself personally credible, as a no doubt limited but also calm and conscientious official. His West German partners would certainly confirm this. While all official papers, and especially the papers of a dictatorship, clearly have to be treated with care, these particular records cannot be disqualified with sweeping statements about 'documents that lie'.

. . . only a few . . . the most notable example we have come across so far is the conversation between Volker Rühe and Erich Honecker on 28 April 1988, of which the record is now in ZPA: IV 2/2.035/84. However, Karl Seidel recalls that Rühe was desperately keen to be received by Honecker, and remained polite and respectful in tone. Karl Seidel, Berlin, 30 September 1992. In a conversation in 1992, Erich Honecker could not recall his meeting with Volker Rühe (Erich Honecker, Berlin-Moabit, 27 November 1992).

. . . summarising his own conversation . . . this in an internal memorandum for Honecker dated 28 April 1988, in ZPA: IV 2/2.035/84.

. . . perhaps the most outspoken . . . however, the files on contacts with CDU politicians in the Party archives are relatively thin. For historians to be able to make a fair and balanced judgement, the Bonn government will need to open the files now controlled by its own Foreign Ministry.

Wolfgang Leonhard made a powerful critique . . . in NG 10/1982 (responding to the Gaus interview mentioned above), and reprinted in Wolfgang Leonhard, *Das kurze Leben der DDR. Berichte und Kommentare aus vier Jahrzehnten* (Stuttgart: Deutsche Verlags-Anstalt, 1990), pp. 174–78. This volume also contains his earlier analysis of the possible connection between Western economic help and lack of reforms, for example p. 164. A commentary by Ilse Spittmann in DA 8/1981, also deserves mention. It is reprinted in Ilse Spittmann, *Die DDR unter Honecker* (Köln: Verlag Wissenschaft und Politik, 1990), pp. 83–87.

. . . an even more swingeing critique . . . in DA, 7/1988, pp. 738–46.

. . . Hermann von Berg, Franz Loeser and Wolfgang Seiffert . . . see their co-authored *Die DRR auf dem Weg in das Jahr 2000* (Köln: Bund-Verlag, 1987), pp. 179–88. See also Hermann von Berg, *Vorbeugende Unterwerfung. Politik im realen Sozialismus* (Munich: Universitas, 1988), Wolfgang Seiffert, *Das ganze Deutschland. Perspektiven der Wiedervereinigung* (Munich: Piper, 1986), and brief critical articles by Hermann Rudolph, SZ, 16 January 1989, and Ernst-Otto Maetzke in FAZ, 4 February 1988 and 28 November 1988.

At least until 1988 . . . in a lecture in spring 1988, Wolfgang Schäuble talked of the need for a 'new stability' in the GDR, see EA, 14/1988, p. 417. In a note under the title 'correct pressure for reform' (*Richtiger Reformdruck*) in the FAZ, 9 August 1988, Ernst-Otto Maetzke noted that the Kohl government seemed inclined to step up the pressure for reform in the GDR. This slight shift was reflected also in the explicit criticism of political conditions inside the GDR with which Chancellor Kohl opened his state of the nation address for 1988, see *Bundestag Plenarprotokolle, Bundestag Plenarprotokolle*, 11/113, p. 8094 f (1 December 1988).

. . . Hans Otto Bräutigam . . . Potsdam, 25 June 1991.

. . . the politics of the GDR . . . since GDR-studies was a large scholarly field in West Germany, with hundreds of scholars and publications, any small selection is bound to be invidious and unsatisfactory. Probably the most useful single introduction to the subject, indicating most of the major problems and themes, is Weber, *DDR* (1991). The earlier edition, Weber, *DDR* (1988) is still useful, and has a very clear and extensive bibliography. The third edition of the *DDR-Handbuch*, edited by Hartmut Zimmermann, also contains invaluable articles on individual topics and a comprehensive bibliography. No other East European state could boast a Western chronicle to compare with the *Deutschland Archiv* (DA). In the notes for this section I have not attempted to indicate primary and secondary sources for the overall assessment, but only for specific assertions, quotations etc.

. . . the strategies by which it endeavoured . . . in the analysis of these strategies and their effects I have found particularly stimulating and useful the Habilitation thesis of Sigrid Meuschel, 'Legitimation und Parteiherrschaft. Zum Wandel der Legitimitätsansprüche der SED 1945–1989' (Free University, Berlin, November 1990) now published as *Legitimation und Parteiherrschaft. Zum Paradox von Stabilität und Revolution in der DDR 1945–1989* (Frankfurt: Suhrkamp, 1992), hereafter cited as Meuschel, *Legitimation*. She gives a useful short summary of some of her main points in Rainer Deppe & ors, eds, *Demokratischer Umbruch in Osteuropa* (Frankfurt: Suhrkamp, 1991), pp. 26–47.

. . . a 'hypertrophied function' . . . Markus Wolf at a press conference in Munich, 10 October 1991.

. . . in direct consultation . . . see the account in Günter Schabowski, *Der Absturz* (Berlin: Rowohlt, 1991), pp. 115–17.

. . . as attractive as by its nature . . . my attention was drawn to this fine piece of ideological casuistry by Honecker's former aide Frank-Joachim Hernmann, Berlin, 8 October 1991.

. . . the key-word *Geborgenheit* . . . see Weber, *DDR* (1988), pp. 97–98.

. . . an understanding of socialism . . . the point was made by, among others, Hans Modrow, as quoted in Volze 'Devisengeschäfte', p. 1144, citing the FAZ, 18 March 1990. Talking to the author in Moabit prison in late 1992, Honecker dilated at length on this aspect of his achievement. Erich Honecker, Berlin-Moabit, 27 November 1992.

. . . a consolidation of traditional, Soviet-type central planning . . . and a further nationalisation of small-scale private enterprise, see Anders Åslund, *Private Enterprise in Eastern Europe. The Non-Agricultural Private Sector in Poland and the GDR, 1945–83* (London: Macmillan, 1985), Chapter 3.

. . . one of the main substitutes for reform was — imports . . . this was the central burden of the charge made against Honecker by the former Politburo member, Werner Krolikowski, in a memorandum of 16 January 1990, reprinted in Przybylski, *Tatort 1*, pp. 321–39. Krolikowski claims that as early as 1973 he pointed out to Honecker the dangers of concentrating on consumer goods at the expense of capital investment, and warned against the soaring debts to the West. In the same place, pp. 340–56, are reprinted what are claimed to be notes by Krolikowski from the period 1980–83, showing that not only he but also Erich Mielke and Willi Stoph were afraid of the dangers of Honecker getting too close and too indebted to West Germany. But as Krolikowski himself notes, they did not stop him. The basic point about too many consumer imports was also made to Honecker at the time by Gerhard Schürer (see above, p. 516), and in retrospect by Mittag, Schabowski and many other former members of the Party leadership.

... 'peaceful co-existence' ... see, for example, the entries for 'Entspannungspolitik' and 'Friedliche Koexistenz' in the *Kleines Politisches Wörterbuch* (3rd edition, Berlin: Dietz, 1978).

... a series of top-level internal briefings ... these were delivered to meetings of the so-called *Kollegium* or to the 'central service conferences' of the Ministry.

... 'above all struggle'. ... this in 'Theses' for the *Kollegiumssitzung* on 29 September 1971, now in MFS: 4751. A handwritten annotation indicates that the meeting did not actually take place, but the text is nonetheless a good expression of Mielke's concerns.

... Erfurt should never be repeated ... see his 'Theses' for the *Kollegiumssitzung* on 29 May 1970 (MfS: 4739), which clearly convey his anger at what had happened in Erfurt eight days before.

... 'hard and complicated' ... this and the following quotations from a massive 111-page lecture delivered to the central service conference on 16 November 1972, MfS: 4770.

... the 1968 constitution ... see Bruns, *DDR-Politik*, p. 32.

... the words of the GDR's 'national anthem' ... see the entry for 'Nationalhymne' in *DDR Handbuch*, p. 939. The text was written by the poet Johannes R. Becher in 1949.

... the GDR ... a 'socialist nation' ... see the entry for 'Nation und nationale Frage' in *DDR Handbuch*, the extensive discussion in Meuschel, *Legitimation*, and Gerhard Naumann & Eckhard Trumpler, *Der Flop mit der DDR-Nation 1971* (Berlin: Dietz, 1991).

... 'a socialist German nation' ... ND, 10 April 1987.

Looking back from 1992 ... Erich Honecker, Berlin-Moabit, 27 November 1992.

... still 'German' ... quoted in *DDR-Handbuch*, from ND, 13 December 1974.

See also the entries for 'Nation' and 'Nationalität' in *Kleines Politisches Wörterbuch* (3rd edition, Berlin: Dietz, 1978).

... **to acknowledge its own indubitable Germanness** ... this is one of the main themes of Garton Ash, *DDR*. The rediscovery and reassessment of German history in the GDR was noted by Helmut Schmidt in his state of the nation address for 1981, *Bundestag Plenarprotokolle*, 9/31, p. 1541 (9 April 1981).

'Defence education' ... see the entry under 'Wehrerziehung' in *DDR-Handbuch*, and the discussion in Klaus Ehring/Martin Dallwitz [a pseudonym for Hubertus Knabe], *Schwerter zu Pflugscharen. Friedensbewegung in der DDR* (Hamburg: Rowohlt, 1982) and Wolgang Büscher & ors, *Friedensbewegung in der DDR. Texte 1978–1982* (Hattingen: Scandica Verlag, 1982 = edition transit, Vol. 2).

... **'perhaps my brother ...'** quoted in Garton Ash, *DDR*, p. 144 f.

... **relations with the Protestant Church** ... strictly speaking one should say Churches, because there were no less than eight different *Landeskirchen* in the GDR, often jealously guarding their particular traditions, although since 1969 joined in a Federation of Protestant Churches in the GDR. To avoid confusion, we have used the more usual English singular. Developments in the Church could best be followed in the excellent bi-monthly journal of the Berlin Arbeitsgemeinschaft für Kirchliche Publizistik, *Kirche im Sozialismus*. The best short introduction was Reinhard Henkys, *Gottes Volk im Sozialismus. Wie Christen in der DDR leben* (Berlin: Wichern-Verlag, 1983); a more extensive survey, Reinhard Henkys, ed., *Die Evangelischen Kirchen in der DDR* (Munich: Kaiser, 1982). A new study in English is Robert F Goeckel, *The Lutheran Church and the East German State. Political conflict and change under Ulbricht and Honecker* (Ithaca: Cornell University Press, 1990). A controversial analysis and detailed documentation of Church relations with the Stasi is Gerhard Besier & Stephan Wolf, eds, *'Pfarrer, Christen und Katholiken'. Das Ministerium für Staatssicherheit der ehemaligen DDR und die Kirchen* (2nd edition, Neukirchen-Vluyn: Neukirchener, 1992). Much of the following analysis is, however, based on the author's own personal enquiries, observations and conversations, in which he owes a very special debt of gratitude to Werner Krätschell.

... **Manfred Stolpe** ... for references, see above, p. 511.

... **'swords into ploughshares'**.... on the peace groups and initiatives more or less under Church auspices see Wolfgang Büsche, & ors, eds, *Friedensbewegung in der DDR. Texte 1978–82* (Hattingen: Scandica-Verlag, 1982 = edition transit Vol. 2), Klaus Ehring/Martin Dallwitz [pseudonym of Hubertus Knabe], *Schwerter zu Pflugscharen. Friedensbewegung in der DDR* (Hamburg: Rowohlt, 1982), and Chapter 14 in Fricke, *Opposition*. In English, see John Sandford, *The Sword and the Ploughshare. Autonomous Peace Initiatives in East Germany* (London: Merlin Press/END, 1983) and the relevant sections of Roger Woods, *Opposition in the GDR under Honecker, 1971–85* (London: Macmillan, 1986).

... **the authorities dealt decisively** ... by far the best single survey is Fricke, *Opposition*. In English, see Roger Woods, *Opposition in the GDR under Honecker, 1971–85* (London, Macmillan, 1986).

... **as one young Christian put it** ... Joachim Krätschell, Berlin, 6 July 1989.

... **most** ... **chose emigration** ... the authorities resorted to direct deportation in the case of the Jena peace activist, Roland Jahn, see the detailed and vivid report by Helmut Loelhoeffel in SZ, 9 June 1983. In 1988, Bärbel Bohley and others agreed to leave only temporarily, and on condition that they would be allowed to return.

... **that the 'Zone' was behind** ... *Dokumente*, IV/9, p. 573

... **'niche society'** ... see Gaus, *Deutschland*, p. 156 ff.

... **nothing that seriously deserved the name of reform** ... on the definition of reform see Garton Ash, *Uses*, p. 252 ff.

West German historians agreed ... on this see Weber, *DDR*, and compare such official histories as Zentral Institut für Geschichte der Akademie der Wissenschaften der DDR, ed., *Grundriss der deutschen Geschichte. Von den Anfängen der Geschichte des deutschen Volkes bis zur Gestaltung der entwickelten sozialistischen Gesellschaft in der Deutschen Demokratischen Republik* [!] (Berlin: VEB Deutscher Verlag der Wissenschaften, 1979), and, more concisely, Heinz Heitzer, *DDR. Geschichtlicher Überblick* (Berlin: Dietz, 1979).

'Important, important strong GDR' ... Ulrich Bürger, *Das sagen wir natürlich so nicht! Donnerstag-Argus bei Herrn Gegel* (Berlin: Dietz, 1990), p. 189 f. This book gives vivid insights into the arguments, and delusions, of the party leadership in the 1980s.

... **three former East German intellectuals suggested** ... Hermann von Berg, Franz Loeser and Wolfgang Seiffert in their co-authored *Die DRR auf dem Weg in das Jahr 2000* (Köln: Bund-Verlag, 1987), p. 186.

... **Ludwig Rehlinger has argued** ... Rehlinger, *Freikauf*, p. 110, and in conversation with the author, Bonn, 6 December 1990.

... **a circle of activists.** ... this group was kindly brought together by one of the leading activists of the Initiative for Peace and Human Rights, Gerd Poppe, in East Berlin.

... **'slice-by-slice'** ... Bärbel Bohley in FAZ, 25 January 1992. It appears that in the early 1988 crisis, following the Luxemburg/Liebknecht demonstration, the Federal Government did pay directly for the release of some dissenters to the West. Wolfgang Vogel, Berlin, 9 October 1991. Leslie Collitt and David Marsh reported in the *Financial Times*, 4 February 1988: '... East German supporters of the four released dissidents complained that Bonn was helping the East Berlin authorities to undermine the civil rights movement'. Other activists, including Bärbel Bohley herself, were, however, allowed out for six months, and subsequently returned to play an important part in the revolution of autumn 1989.

... **the one to two thousand members of the democratic oppositions** ... The democratic oppositions in Hungary and Czechoslovakia were probably nearer to one thousand than two until the late 1980s. Obviously it is impossible to give a precise 'membership', and there were many more sympathisers than activists.

Charter 77, for example, had 242 signatories at the outset, 617 by March 1977, 1,065 by June 1980, and 'more than 1,300' by the end of 1986, with the proviso that some of the earlier signatories subsequently emigrated, or ceased to be so active. See *A Decade of Dedication. Charter 77 1977–1987* (New York: Helsinki Watch, 1987), p. 7. For Poland this figure plainly applies only for the period up to August 1980.

... **between one and three thousand of East Germany's most active citizens** ... see Table VIII.

... **Gorbachev was indicating to East European rulers** ... see above, p. 123. Erich Honecker specifically recalled the meeting of East European leaders in autumn 1986 when Gorbachev delivered this general message, Erich Honecker, Berlin-Moabit, 27 November 1992. Egon Krenz confirmed in conversation with the author (Berlin, 20 February 1990) that this was certainly the message which Honecker chose to hear from Gorbachev in 1986.

Honecker's last gamble ... the following section is based on sources in the Party archive, a wide range of conversations with senior officials and Politburo members, including one with Honecker himself, and published sources. There is as yet no good life of the East German Party leader. Before his fall, Honecker gave his own version, courtesy of Robert Maxwell, in *Erich Honecker, From My Life* (Oxford: Pergamon Press, 1981). After his fall, he gave a series of long, self-justificatory, illusion-ridden, but nonetheless sometimes revealing interviews to Reinhold Andert and Wolfgang Herzberg, who published them as *Der Sturz. Erich Honecker im Kreuzverhör* (Berlin: Aufbau-Verlag, 1990). His successor Egon Krenz, wrote a highly critical, but also quite revealing review in *Der Spiegel* 6/1991, as well as giving his own first, hastily (ghost-)written account in Egon Krenz, *Wenn Mauern fallen. Die friedliche Revolution: Vorgeschichte-Ablauf-Auswirkungen* (Vienna: Neff, 1990). Another witness quick to the press was Krenz's fellow 'conspirator' in overthrowing Honecker, Günter Schabowski, see his *Der Absturz* (Berlin: Rowohlt, 1991) and *Das Politbüro. Ende eines Mythos* (Hamburg: Rowohlt, 1990). See also the documents and discussion in Przybylski, *Tatort 1* and *Tatort 2*, and Mittag, *Preis*. All witnesses confirm the supremacy of Honecker in decisions regarding relations with the West.

... **a church weekly was forbidden to reprint** ... see the commentary by Gisela Helwig in DA, 8/1988, p. 602. The weekly in question, *Die Kirche*, played a modest but important role in the development of Church-protected freedom of expression, comparable in some ways to that of the weekly *Tygodnik Powszechny* in Poland.

... **the Soviet journal *Sputnik* was banned** ... According to the GDR's Postal Ministry, *Sputnik* had no articles 'which served the strengthening of German-Soviet friendship, but instead distorting historical articles'. see FAZ, 21 November 1988. On the subsequent protests from Party members see *Der Spiegel*, 48/1988.

... **'socialism in the colours of the GDR'** ... he used this phrase at the 7th plenum of the Central Committee in December 1988, see ND 2 December 1988. Of course the colours of the GDR were the same as those of the Federal Republic.

... referred to in Politburo minutes ... see, for example, the minutes of the meeting on 3 May 1988, now in ZPA: JIV 2/2/2271.

Egon Krenz ... Berlin, 29 September 1992.

... even a penchant for taking risks ... thus, for example, Günter Schabowski, Berlin, 29 June 1991, and one of Honecker's personal assistants, Frank-Joachim Herrmann, Berlin, 8 October 1991.

... Erich Honecker himself ... Berlin-Moabit, 27 November 1992.

'The German Democratic Republic ...' EA, 19/1987, p. D549, quoting ND, 11 September 1987.

Gerhard Schürer recalls ... Gerhard Schürer, Berlin, 25 November 1992.

... talking to the author in 1992 ... Erich Honecker, Berlin-Moabit, 27 November 1992.

... 'only' about DM 30 billion ... Honecker added that even this was an overestimate, since it did not show the credits with such countries as Iran, Iraq, Syria etc, that were regularly shown in the figures given to the Politburo.

... 'the last all-German' ... He went on: 'Those who follow are GDR-Germans', quoted in *Der Spiegel*, 48/1985.

Honecker became 'more German' ... see his article in *Die Zeit*, 31/1987.

Old men remember ... Schmidt, *Nachbarn*, p. 26. This impression was confirmed by others who spoke to him at this time.

... of whom he would often speak ... this is confirmed by numerous sources. It is interesting to note that the role of Herbert Wehner was also singled out for special remark by the head of the Agitation department of the Central Committee, in his briefing for senior editors at the time of Honecker's visit to West Germany, see Ulrich Bürger, *Das sagen wir natürlich so nicht! Donnerstag-Argus bei Herrn Gegel* (Berlin: Dietz, 1990), p. 189.

... a remarkable text ... in AdsD: Dep WB, BK 75.

... in or near East Berlin ... Erich Honecker, Berlin-Moabit, 27 November 1992.

... 'his goal was still ...' in Reinhold Andert & Wolfgang Herzberg, *Der Sturz. Erich Honecker im Kreuzverhör* (Berlin: Aufbau-Verlag, 1990), p. 348. Honecker also made a special point of mentioning the part played by his regular contact with Herbert Wehner (also through Wolfgang Vogel) in a statement on his attitude to humanitarian questions in early 1990, reproduced in Przybylski, *Tatort 1*, pp. 363 66. He and Wehner, wrote Honecker, 'worked together in a comradely way'.

In 1992 he affirmed ... Erich Honecker, Berlin-Moabit, 27 November 1992.

... 'we are going the German way' ... quoted by Brigitte Seebacher-Brandt in Jesse & Mitter, *Einheit*, p. 36.

... the element of simple vanity ... Honecker's vanity is attested by many who worked with him. This was also stressed by Hans-Otto Bräutigam in a conversation with the author (Potsdam, 25 June 1991).

... *hubris* ... an interpretation also subscribed to by Helmut Schmidt in conversation with the author (London, 3 June 1991). Confirmed from close observation by Frank-Joachim Herrmann, Berlin, 8 October 1991.

... **the growing distance from everyday reality** ... first-hand evidence of his growing distance from reality is given in the books by Krenz and Schabowski.

... **refer to the happy expression** ... Wolfgang Vogel, Berlin, 9 October 1991

... **'that the majority of the population...'** Note of 6 February 1989 on a conversation in Berlin, 3 February 1989, in ZPA: IV 2/2.035/54. Talking to the author in November 1992, Honecker also stressed that the GDR was, as he put it, 'the only socialist country' where to the end everyone could go into a shop and buy sausage, butter etc. Erich Honecker, Berlin-Moabit, 27 November 1992.

... **'I would wish every one who rules over us...'** in *Der Spiegel*, 11/1987. Gabriele Eckart had earlier made a collection of long interviews, *So sehe ick die Sache. Protokolle aus der DDR* (Köln: Kiepenheuer & Witsch, 1984), which give a very good insight into the ground-floor reality of life in the GDR.

... **their reactions to some aspects of West German life** ... 'Sodom and Gomorrah!' was the not wholly untypical commentary of one East German friend on the obscene profusion of food and drink displayed in the famous top-floor delicatessen of West Berlin's *Kaufhaus des Westens*.

... **'one of the freest countries...'** quoted in Weber, *DDR* (1988), p. 103.

... **young East Berliners gathered** ... Their other chant was 'the Wall must go' (*Die Mauer muss weg*). These were the most serious public disorders in East Germany for a decade. See reports in *Washington Post*, 10 June 1987, FAZ, 10 June 1987, and *Der Spiegel*, 25/1987.

... **Honecker ... youth** ... for one example, see above p. 336.

Whereas in 1985 ... these results are quoted in Michael Brie/Dieter Klein, eds, *Zwischen den Zeiten. Ein Jahrhundert verabschiedet sich* (Hamburg: VSA-Verlag, 1992), p. 147.

Figures to the Politburo ... Item 3 on the minutes of the Politburo meeting on 19 April 1988, now in ZPA: JIV 2/2/2269. Interestingly, no less than 30,000 of these applications came from Dresden, in the so-called 'valley of the clueless', where people could not receive West German television.

Western estimates in 1988–89 ... *Der Spiegel*, 36/1988, declared, with characteristic omniscience, that 'a quarter of a million GDR citizens have filed applications to leave. Five to six million count as GDR-tired.' The *Frankfurter Rundschau*, 29 July 1988, spoke of an estimate in 'well-informed West Berlin circles' of 300–400,000 applications, but indicated that the *Tagesspiegel* had recently cited 'information from Bonn' to give a figure of 500,000 applications for a total of no less than 1.5 million people. Another organisation put the figure at

1.2 million in November 1988, see FAZ, 28 November 1988. When I asked the Permanent Representative of the Federal Republic to the GDR, Franz Bertele, for his guesstimate in July 1989, he indicated a similar range, but declined to name his own figure (Berlin, 6 July 1989). Rehlinger, *Freikauf*, p. 115, says that estimates of over one million came from 'the various services', by which he presumably means the West German intelligence services.

... **grew in strength and boldness** ... a good short account is given in the introduction to Hubertus Knabe, ed., *Aufbruch in eine andere DDR* (Reinbek: Rowohlt, 1990), p. 12 f.

... **'freedom is always** ...' see report and photograph in *Der Spiegel*, 5/1988.

... **more or less compelled to leave** ... here again the traditional 'heaven or hell' method was used. The balladeer Stephan Krawczyk and his wife Freya Klier, for example, said they did not leave the GDR 'voluntarily', but faced with the threat of heavy charges they did actually fill out applications to leave. See *Der Spiegel*, 6/1988. Speaking in an East Berlin church in April 1989, the former Party functionary Rolf Heinrich confirmed that he, too, after writing a book critical of the system, had been urged to file an application to leave. See report in FAZ, 13 April 1989.

... **20 Theses for a reformation of the GDR** ... these were not actually pinned to the church door, like Luther's 95 Theses, but were first presented to a synod in Halle by the Wittenberg theologian Friedrich Schorlemmer, see the report in DA, 8/1988, pp. 801–02.

... **the dissidence acquired — for the first time** ... this is also the judgement of Hubertus Knabe, who closely followed the evolution of this Church-based dissidence throughout the 1980s, see Hubertus Knabe, ed., *Aufbruch in eine andere DDR* (Reinbek: Rowohlt, 1990), p. 14.

... **to monitor local elections of May 1989** ... according to the official figures, there were 142,301 (1.15 per cent) votes against, compared with 14,683 (0.1 per cent) in 1984, and the turn-out was a mere 98.77 per cent, compared with 99.37 per cent in 1984. Opposition monitors reckoned that in, for example, the East Berlin borough of Friedrichshain, there were 6.93 per cent votes against, whereas the official result was 1.89 per cent. Opposition protests took the form of letters and petitions to the Council of State, and even laying charges on the suspicion of electoral fraud — a crime under Article 211 of the GDR's Penal Code! *Monatsbericht* of the *Gesamtdeutsches Institut*, May 1989, p. 1. Report in *Der Spiegel*, 20/1989.

... **a report to Honecker** ... the report, dated 1 June 1989, is printed in Mitter & Wolle, *Lageberichte*, pp. 46–71. It went to all the senior functionaries concerned with internal security.

... **'is it that tomorrow**. . .' ibid., p. 125.

... **'so far as the power question is concerned** ...' ibid., p. 127.

... **'refolutions'** ... on 'refolution' see Garton Ash *We*, p. 14 f.

. . . Willy Brandt once again at the window . . . see the report and photographs in *Die Zeit*, 9 March 1990.

. . . 'the final measure . . .' quoted by Klaus Gotto in *Die Politische Meinung* 249/1990, p. 12.

As Robert Leicht observed . . . in *Die Zeit*, 6 October 1989, quoted by Sigrid Meuschel in Rainer Deppe & ors, eds, *Demokratischer Umbruch in Osteuropa* (Frankfurt: Suhrkamp, 1991).

. . . in a conversation in June 1991 . . . Egon Bahr, Potsdam-Berlin, 29 June 1991. But at the end of this conversation, in a taxi driving from Potsdam to central Berlin, the East German taxi-driver, who had obviously listened closely to my critical questioning, turned to Egon Bahr and demonstratively thanked him 'for everything that you have done for us over the years'. With tributes like that, who needs to worry about the carping of historians?

. . . 'If our demands add up . . .' *Bergedorfer Gesprächskreis* 88 (6–7 September 1989), this on p. 62. One should note that it is the custom of the organisers to send the typescript of the stenographic record to individual participants to be checked and authorised before publication.

Until very late in the day. . . this distinction was, however, made by Horst Teltschik in a spontaneous response to the remarks by Egon Bahr quoted above. By putting in question the recognition of the GDR, said Teltschik, Bonn would block reforms there: 'But the population of the GDR can of course themselves put this state in question. If one day they really can exercise the right to self-deter-mination, it is quite possible that the majority of the people in the GDR will decide for an *Anschluss* to the Federal Republic. Then we cannot be against it. Just as we cannot be against it if the majority of the population of the GDR should decide that they wish to remain a second German state. I must add that I am profoundly convinced that if the population of the GDR could freely exercise their right of self-determination today, they would decide for *Anschluss*.' ibid., p. 63. A very sound judgement.

. . . might have saved the GDR . . . this is suggested by Sigrid Meuschel in the original (Free University, Berlin, 1990) version of her Habilitation thesis, p. 495, footnote 8. See also various contributions to Hubertus Knabe, ed., *Aufbruch in eine andere DDR* (Reinbek: Rowohlt, 1989). In an interview in October 1989, Egon Bahr spoke of a possible process 'at the end of which we will have another GDR, sustained by the overwhelming will of its own population,' *Der Spiegel*, 42/1989.

. . . which 1989 marked the end of . . . see Garton Ash, *We*, p. 151 f.

. . . eighty-four per cent . . . see above, p. 148 and note.

When the mayor of Bonn . . . see reports in FAZ, 28 January 1988, *Express*, 29 June 1988, and *Neue Zürcher Zeitung*, 30 June 1988. According to an 'Information' now in the files of the Büro Axen, and dated 28 January 1988, the then deputy head of West Germany's Permanent Representation observed that Mayor Daniels had clearly gone too far, confusing Potsdam with the marketplace in Bonn. ZPA: IV 2/2.035/88. However, it is not clear whether this was a private comment, obtained by secret police methods, or the report of an actual conversation with the diplomat. Even if it is the latter, it may be distorted. According to the report to the Politburo on Wolfgang Schäuble's visit to the GDR on 9–10 November 1988, the then Chancellery Minister brought a 'declaration' which enabled the Bonn-Potsdam relationship to be resumed. Although, the SED report says, 'the expectation will be expressed that in future no such disturbances of the relations between the two towns will be permitted'. ZPA: JIV 2/2/2303.

To substantiate this generalisation . . . One crude experiment made by the author was to ask the Central Documentation System of the Federal Government to put into its computerised media database the combination 'dictatorship-GDR' for the years 1987 and 1991. The pile of cuttings produced for 1991 was some five times as high as that for 1987! I am most grateful to Frau Anna Maria Kuppe for this as for numerous other researches.

'As a result . . .' the letter, dated 25 February 1970, is in AdsD: Dep WB, BK 6.

Out of the attempt at 'normalisation' . . . Martin Kriele, a Professor of Law who defended the Basic Treaty in the Constitutional Court for the Brandt government, and then became bitterly disillusioned with what he saw as the rampant relativism and self-censorship on human rights resulting from the social-liberal 'peace policy', offered a more general version of this explanation. Starting from the well-known legal concept of 'the normative force of the given' — i.e. that people accept as normal and right what they have been used to — he argued that there was something one could call 'the normative force of the Red Army'. As Soviet power seemed to be so overwhelming, and, in the 1960s and 1970s, to be waxing rather than waning against that of the United States, so some people in West Germany made an anticipatory adjustment of their own values and norms from a position close to that represented by the United States to a position closer to that represented by the Soviet Union. Might was taken for right. The clearest and most provocative statement of his argument is in *Kontinent* (German edition) 3/1983, pp. 6–17. For his earlier, more ambivalent discussion of the danger of relativisation and self-censorship on human rights see his *Die Menschenrechte zwischen Ost und West* (Köln: Verlag Wissenschaft und Politik, 1977). A later, more developed and outspoken argument is his *Die demokratische Weltrevolution. Warum sich die Freiheit durchsetzen wird* (Munich: Piper, 1987). Allowing for the provocative overstatement born of personal disillusionment, the argument nonetheless deserves to be noticed.

. . . different 'terms of business' . . . Bölling, *Die fernen Nachbarn*, p. 294.

. . . a 'Peace of Augsburg' . . . Gaus, *Deutschland*, p. 275, see also the reference on p. 282 to 'the believers of both confessions'.

. . . 'that time has passed by . . .' Bölling, *Die fernen Nachbarn*, p. 187 f.

. . . this particular history of the left . . . a first attempt to address this special history is Brigitte Seebacher-Brandt, *Die Linke und die Einheit* (Berlin: Siedler, 1991). Now see also Dieter Groh & Peter Brandt, *'Vaterlandslose Gesellen'. Sozialdemokratie und Nation, 1860–1990.* (Munich: Beck, 1992).

... a distinctive history of journalism ... A good case-study would be the book by journalists from *Die Zeit*: Theo Sommer, ed., *Reise ins andere Deutschland* (Reinbek: Rowohlt, 1986), an important example of the other hand working overtime. The papers of the Central Committee Secretary responsible for the press, Joachim Herrmann, ZPA: IV 2/2.037/58, contain remarkably detailed information on the preparations for, execution and subsequent evaluation of the visit. Here there is, for example, a letter sent by the chief editor of *Die Zeit*, Theo Sommer, to the head of the press department of the East German Foreign Ministry, Wolfgang Meyer. 'If I may say so,' Sommer writes, in a letter dated 31 January 1986, recalling his recent interview with Honecker, 'your Chairman of the Council of State does not need to take second place to Mr Gorbachev, so far as skilful dealing with Western journalists is concerned.' Sommer gave a retrospective justification of *Die Zeit*'s line in general, and this book in particular, in *Die Zeit*, 11 May 1990. But see also the honest and perceptive confessions of a former television correspondent in the GDR, Michael Schmitz, in *Die Zeit*, 14 February 1992.

... a special history of scholarship ... a sharp but perceptive first attempt at a critical analysis was made by Hartmut Jäckel in DA 10/1990, pp. 1557–65. An informative sketch and qualified defence of the GDR-studies of the 1970s and 1980s is given by Rüdiger Thomas in *Zeitschrift für Parlamentsfragen*, 1/1990, pp. 126–36. Critical remarks on the failure of West German contemporary historians to tackle the subject of the other German dictatorship at all are made by Wolfgang Schuller in FAZ, 18 March 1991.

A younger generation ... this argument is well and sympathetically described by Gert-Joachim Glaessner in Gert-Joachim Glaessner, ed., *Die DDR in der Ära Honecker. Politik, Kultur, Gesellschaft* (Opladen: Westdeutscher Verlag, 1988), pp. 111–19. The contributions to this Festschrift for Hartmut Zimmermann, one of the leading figures of the new, social-science orientation, give a good impression of its strengths and weaknesses. Christian Fenner makes some perceptive comments on the so-called *Immanenzansatz* in the *Jahrbuch Extremismus & Demokratie*, 3/1991, pp. 33–51.

Opening these schoolbooks ... all quotations from *Der Spiegel* 21/1990.

An associate of Adenauer's. ... Wilhelm G Grewe in conversation with the author, Bonn, 6 July 1991.

... that older Germany ... on this, see Garton Ash, *DDR*.

... in a curious novella ... Günter Gaus, *Wendewut* (Hamburg: Hoffmann 8 Campe, 1990). It must be said that the identity of the heroine, like much else in this book, is distinctly obscure.

... described himself ... Hans-Jürgen Schierbaum, Bonn, 16 March 1989.

... strange bonds developed ... see, for example, the account of the 'Leipzig circle' of those involved in negotiating the 'Church deals', in Geissel, *Unterhändler*, p. 350 and *passim*.

In a remarkable article ... in *Die Zeit*, 31 July 1987. But less than five years later, Schmidt wrote a short leading article in *Die Zeit*, 28 February 1992, in which he said that too much attention was being paid to the aged Erich Honecker. 'The fact that he was once the head of a dictatorship on German soil,' Schmidt wrote, 'should no longer suffice for this. He is now only a case — albeit an important one — for the German courts . . .' This little article was headed, 'Quite normal' — *Ganz normal.*

. . . 'the charge that the federal government . . .' Schmidt, *Nachbarn*, p. 53.

'The suffering of partition . . .' *Bundestag Plenarprotokolle*, 10/228, p. 17684 (10 September 1986).

. . . *Vergangenheitsbewältigung* . . . the comparison was of course made many times, see, for example, the contribution by Ludwig Elm in DA, 7/1991, pp. 737–43, and the excellent article by Richard Schröder in FAZ, 16 February 1993.

. . . **to be made on the West German side** . . . It is hard to agree with Richard von Weizsäcker when, in the course of an eloquent speech about coming to terms with the history of East Germany, he describes the continuation of the debate about 'the West-West chapter of the past' — that is, presumably, including all the controversies about Ostpolitik — as 'otiose'. See his speech on receiving the Heine Prize, reprinted in *Bulletin*, 17 December 1991, pp. 1165–70, this on p. 1169.

This West-West debate had, however, already begun in the media, with innumerable revelations, personal declarations and polemics. A useful way in to the debate is Cora Stephan, ed., *Wir Kollaborateure. Der Westen und die deutschen Vergangenheiten* (Reinbek: Rowohlt, 1992), with a sharp, polemical introduction by the author.

This debate was closely linked to that about the role of the Protestant Church, and not just in the case of Stolpe. In a newspaper interview shortly before unification the widely respected East Berlin Bishop Forck said, referring to the policy of his Church: 'We worked for much too long in the hope of achieving a better socialism, of changing the representatives of the state. We erred.' FAZ, 24 September 1990. Similar remarks were made by the former bishop of Magdeburg, Bishop Krusche, in a retrospective survey of the twenty-one years of the Federation of Protestant Churches in the GDR, see the report in FAZ, 25 February 1991.

'We erred', says the East German churchman, who faced at first hand the agonising dilemmas of living under a dictatorship. Meanwhile the West German politicians who faced those dilemmas only indirectly, from the comfort of secure freedom, shouted to each other across the party lines: '*You* erred!' 'No, you got it wrong!' 'But so did you!'

One cannot, of course, expect politicians to behave like priests. But between the moving self-criticism of the priest and the maddening *tu quoques* of the politicians, perhaps the historians may tell us how it really was — provided the politicians give them access to the sources. Particularly important in this connection is the so-called *Enquete Kommission* set up by the Bundestag to examine the history and legacy of what it now referred to as the 'SED dictatorship'. Point 7 of its terms of reference requires it to look at German-German relations. See *Bundestag Drucksachen*, 12/2597, reprinted in DA, 7/1992, pp. 782–84.

Chapter V: Beyond the Oder

. . . a seminal essay . . . Löwenthal, *Vom kalten Krieg*, pp. 2, 90.

. . . markedly easier . . . Thus Haberl and Hecker, *Unfertige Nachbarschaften*, pp. v, 3 ff, class the Federal Republic's relations with Hungary, Romania, Bulgaria and — they add, very questionably — Yugoslavia, as 'unburdened' relationships. But their own chapter on unadjacent Yugoslavia notes that the wartime conflict did place a considerable burden on post-war relations (pp. 133–51).

It has been suggested . . . ibid., p. 3 ff.

. . . 'the rule of odd and even . . .' Lewis Namier, *Vanished Supremacies. Essays on European History 1812–1918* (London: Hamish Hamilton, 1958), p. 170.

. . . without formal treaties . . . for the short Communiqués on the opening of diplomatic relations with Romania (31 January 1967), and Bulgaria and Hungary (both 21 December 1973), see *Verträge*, pp. 63–4.

. . . troubled historiography . . . one excellent recent book on this subject in English is Burleigh, *Ostforschung*, which concentrates mainly on the Third Reich period. Zernack, *Osteuropa* is a fine critical introduction to the discipline and problems of studying 'Eastern Europe' in German, with a bibliography up to the mid-1970s. There are important comments in Haberl and Hecker, *Unfertige Nachbarschaften*, which has a useful short bibliography including works published up to 1989. Stökl, *Osteuropa*, first published in 1967, is a magisterial introductory essay on a thousand years of German relations with Eastern Europe. The third edition (1982) includes a short essay on books published up to 1981. A very useful survey concentrating specifically on German settlement in East Central and Eastern Europe is Dralle, *Deutsche*.

Men and women of goodwill . . . a notable example on the Polish side is the seminal essay by Jan Józef Lipski, 'Two fatherlands, two patriotisms', in *Kontinent* (German-language edition), No., 22, 1982, pp. 3–48. Lipski points out, to give one small but telling example, that the Polish words for roof (*dach*), brick (*cegła*), bricklayer (*murarz*), printer (*drukarz*), painter (*malarz*) and woodcarver (*snycerz*), all come directly from the German (*Dach*, *Ziegel*, *Maurer*, *Drucker*, *Maler*, *Schnitzer*).

. . . the German-Polish relationship . . . there is no single book on 'Germans and Poles' to compare with the works of Wiskemann and Brügel on 'Czechs and Germans' (see below). Beside the general works mentioned above, Broszat, *Polenpolitik* remains an outstanding overview of German policy. A volume of essays by German and official Polish historians, very much in the spirit of 1970s détente, is Jacobsen, *Bundesrepublik-Volksrepublik*. Jacobsen, *Bonn-Warschau*, is an essential reference work, but the selection of documents clearly reflects the editors' 'détente from above' school. Both in the works edited by Jacobsen and in Haberl and Hecker, *Unfertige Nachbarschaften*, extensive reference is also made to the painful but interesting attempts of a German-Polish joint commission to work out recommendations for German and Polish school textbooks. Independent contributions from the Polish side are to be found in Kuwaczka, *Entspannung von*

Unten, and the special German-language edition of the Paris-based Polish quarterly *Kultura*, Autumn 1984, devoted to German-Polish relations.

... **Germans had ruled over Poles** ... Burleigh, *Ostforschung*, p. 3, rightly begins with this observation, arguing that this fact coloured German perceptions of the whole of Europe east of Germany.

'*Placet* ... quoted in Josef Homeyer, 'Deutsche und polnische Katholiken', *Die Politische Meinung*, January 1991, pp. 15–22, this on p. 15.

... **Czechs and Germans** ... there are several good works on this theme, with almost identical titles: Elizabeth Wiskemann, *Czechs and Germans* (2nd edition, London: Macmillan, 1967); J W Brügel, *Tschechen und Deutsche*, Vol. 1 (Munich: Nymphenburger Verlag, 1967), covering the period 1918–38, and published in an abridged but also revised English edition as *Czechoslovakia Before Munich* (Cambridge: Cambridge University Press, 1973); J W Brügel, *Tschechen und Deutsche* Vol. 2 (Munich: Nymphenburger Verlag, 1974), covering the period 1939–45; Ferdinand Seibt, *Deutschland und die Tschechen. Geschichte einer Nachbarschaft in der Mitte Europas* (Munich: List, 1974); Rudolf Hilf, *Deutsche und Tschechen. Bedeutung und Wandlungen einer Nachbarschaft in Mitteleuropa* (2nd edition, Opladen: Leske & Budrich, 1986); Jan Křen & ors, *Integration oder Ausgrenzung. Deutsche und Tschechen 1890–1945* (Bremen: Donnat & Temmen, 1986).

... **as Sebastian Haffner has written** ... see Sebastian Haffner, *Der Teufelspakt. Die Deutsch-russischen Beziehungen vom Ersten zum Zweiten Weltkrieg* (Zürich: Manesse, 1988), p. 5 and *passim*, and the review essay by Gordon A Craig, 'Dangerous Liaisons', in the *New York Review of Books*, 30 March 1989. On the pre-1945 relationship see also Walter Laqueur, *Russia and Germany. A Century of Conflict* (London: Weidenfeld & Nicolson, 1965).

... **to recall the spirit of Rapallo** ... with the exception of Germans on the pro-Soviet left, see, for example, Ulrike Horster-Philipps, ed., *Rapallo - Modell für Europa? Friedliche Koexistenz und internationale Sicherheit heute* (Köln: Pahl-Rugenstein, 1987). But see also an interview with Rudolf Bahro, 'Rapallo—why not?' in *Telos* 51, Spring 1982.

'**For the first time in their lives** ...' Norman Davies, *God's Playground. A History of Poland*, Vol. 2 (Oxford: Clarendon Press, 1981), p. 565.

'**One ought** ...' Golo Mann, *The History of Germany since 1789* (London: Penguin Books, 1974), p. 813.

... *Historikerstreit* ... the historians' debate already has its own extensive historiography. The early texts were collected in '*Historikerstreit*'. *Die Dokumentation der Kontroverse um die Einzigartigkeit der nationalsozialistischen Judenvernichtung* (Munich: Piper, 1987). The subject can be approached in English through the books by Charles S Maier, *The Unmasterable Past. History, Holocaust and German National Identity* (Cambridge, Mass.: Harvard University Press, 1988) and Richard J. Eraus, *In Hitler's Shadow. West German Historians and the Attempt to Escape from the Nazi Past* (London: Tauris, 1989), and the article by Geoff Eley in *Past & Present*, No. 121, November 1988, pp. 171–208.

German historians at once documented . . . see the massive *Dokumentation der Vertreibung der Deutschen aus Ost-Mitteleuropa* edited by Theodor Schieder and others, and originally published in 1954 under the auspices of the Bundesministerium für Vertriebene. Deutscher Taschenbuch Verlag (Munich) issued a paperpack reprint in 1984. This was a scholarly and careful work: the point, however, is the selection of subject matter for first attention.

. . . the prior horrors of German occupation . . . thus Martin Broszat's *Nationalsozialistische Polenpolitik* was published in 1961. It is interesting to note that both Broszat and another outstanding West German liberal historian who has written on German-Polish relations, Hans-Ulrich Wehler, started their academic careers by working on the documentation of the expulsions under Theodor Schieder.

. . . the Polish deportations . . . see the discussion in Kuwaczka, *Entspannung von Unten*, pp. 69–71, and the article published under the pseudonym Stefan Krupiński in 1986 in *Kontakt* 1/1986, reprinted in Kuwaczka, *Entspannung von Unten*, pp. 229–46. It is significant that a Polish historian felt obliged, as late as 1986, to publish this article under a pseudonym. See also the excellent treatment of the whole period in the work of another Polish historian, Włodzimierz Borodziej, *Od Poczdamu do Szklarskiej Poręby. Polska w stosunkach międzynarodowych 1945–47* (London: Aneks, 1990).

. . . by isolated, independent (indeed banned) Czech scholars . . . Although there were the beginnings of a discussion in the 1960s, a more sustained discussion began only in 1978 with the essay by 'Danubius' (pseudonym of the Slovak historian J Mlynárik), 'Tézy o vysídlení Československých Nemcov' in *Svědectví*, 5–7, 1978, pp. 105–34. The whole debate is now well documented in Bohumil Černý & ors, eds, *Češi, Němci, Odsun. Diskuse Nezávislých Historiků* (Prague: Academia, 1990). See also the chapter by Eva Schmidt-Hartmann in Benz, *Vertreibung*, pp. 143–57.

. . . as the historian Norman Davies has written . . . in the *Independent*, 29 December 1987.

. . . the Western allies wished to punish . . . for a good introductory survey see Hermann Graml, *Die Allierten und die Teilung Deutschlands. Konflikte und Entscheidungen 1941–1948* (Hamburg: Fischer, 1985), but see also the still magisterial survey in John Wheeler-Bennett and Anthony Nicholls, *The Semblance of Peace. The Political Settlement After The Second World War* (London: Macmillan, 1972).

. . . that some Polish leaders . . . see Sara Meiklejohn Terry, *Poland's Place in Europe. General Sikorski and the Origin of the Oder-Neisse Line 1939–43* (Princeton: Princeton University Press, 1983). But see also the balanced and authoritative treatment by Piotr Wandycz, *Polish Diplomacy 1911 45. Aims and Achievements* (London: Orbis Books, 1988), which also has a very useful bibliographical essay.

. . . Churchill . . . argued . . . 'I am sorry about the Western Neisse . . .' Churchill wrote to his successor Clement Attlee on 3 August 1945, 'this was certainly not the fault of the British Delegation', see *Documents on British Policy Overseas*, Series 1, Vol. 1 (London: HMSO, 1984), p. 1278. In a powerful speech to the

House of Commons on 16 August 1945, his first as Leader of the Opposition, Churchill said 'I must put on record my own opinion that the provisional Western frontier agreed upon for Poland . . . is not a good augury for the future map of Europe.' In this same speech, referring to the fate of the Germans east of the Oder-Neisse line, he said 'it is not impossible that a tragedy on a prodigious scale is unfolding itself behind the iron curtain which at the moment divides Europe in twain'. *Hansard*, 5th Series, Vol. 413, p. 83. In his memoirs he claims to have had in mind at Potsdam 'to have a show-down at the end of the Conference, and, if necessary, to have a public break rather than allow anything beyond the Oder and the Eastern Neisse to be ceded to Poland'. Winston S Churchill, *The Second World War. Vol. VI: Triumph and Tragedy* (London: Cassell, 1954), p. 582. David Cecil rightly comments that this 'is magnificent, but it is not history'. See his article, 'Potsdam and its Legends', in *International Affairs* (London), July 1970, pp. 455–65, this on p. 456. Earlier in the same volume, explaining the basis of his position, Churchill writes: 'For the future peace of Europe here was a wrong beside which Alsace-Lorraine and the Danzig Corridor were trifles. One day the Germans would want their territory back, and the Poles would not be able to stop them.' ibid., p. 561.

. . . **it was Stalin's unbending insistence** . . . see Vojtech Mastny's masterly study, *Russia's Road to the Cold War. Diplomacy, Warfare and the Politics of Communism* (New York: Columbia University Press, 1979), and R C Raack, 'Stalin Fixes the Oder-Neisse Line', *Journal of Contemporary History*, Vol. 25, 1990, pp. 467–88, which shows how Stalin worked through his Polish puppets. A rich flow of material on this whole subject may be expected as the Soviet and East European archives reveal their hidden treasures.

. . . **almost all** . . . by conceding the small stretches of territory between the Molotov-Ribbentrop and the Curzon lines, Stalin managed to confer legitimacy on his claim, for the 'Curzon line' was the proposal not of a Soviet or Nazi but of a British foreign minister.

In one move . . . this is also the interpretation of Broszat, *Polenpolitik*, p. 314 ff.

. . . **the Soviet Union then devoted** . . . although there was some initial hesitation even on the Soviet side, and the 16 August 1945 Soviet-Polish Treaty actually left the question of the final delineation of the frontier line through East Prussia open until 'the final regulation of territorial questions by the peace settlement', see Lehmann, *Oder-Neisse*, p. 52 and *passim*.

. . . **'the final delimitation** . . .' see the English text in Grenville, *Treaties*, p. 36.

'The Socialist Unity Party regrets . . . quoted by Bingen, *Bonn-Warschau*, p. 10. On this see also Lehmann, *Oder-Neisse*, pp. 120–22, and the interesting discussion in Włodzimierz Borodziej, *Od Poczdamu do Szklarskiej Poręby. Polska w stosunkach międzynarodowych 1945–1947* (London: Aneks, 1990), pp. 290–314

. . . **'the state frontier between Germany and Poland'** . . . see the text in Grenville, *Treaties*, pp. 187–88. The German wording can be found in Jacobsen, *Bonn-Warschau*, pp. 72–73 and Fritsch-Bournazel, *Europa*, pp. 144–46.

Polish Lwów moved to German Breslau ... see the vivid discussion in Norman Davies, *God's Playground. A History of Poland*, Vol 2. (Oxford: Clarendon Press, 1981), pp. 512–14.

... **the sealing of Yalta** ... see Maresca, *Helsinki*, pp. 110–11, 212, Gromyko, *Memories*, p. 187. In his speech on the signature of the Final Act, Brezhnev described the conference as 'a necessary summing-up of the political outcome of the Second World War', quoted in Mastny, *Helsinki I*, pp. 87–88.

... **'forever'** ... see Zdeněk Mlynář, *Night Frost in Prague* (London: C Hurst & Co., 1980), pp. 239–40.

... **to 'regard as inviolable...'** the text of the Final Act is conveniently reprinted in Maresca, *Helsinki*, pp. 248–305, this on p. 252.

... **a formula negotiated by Henry Kissinger** ... The remarkable story of how this formula was arrived at is told in Maresca, *Helsinki*, pp. 110–16.

... **'consider that their frontiers can be changed...'** ibid., p. 251.

... **'regard as inviolable now and in the future...'** *Verträge*, p. 14.

... **'have no territorial claims...'** ibid., pp. 14, 22, 52.

... **as we have seen** ... see above, p. 71 f, and further references in the notes to those pages.

... **the 'Letter on German Unity'** ... *Verträge.*, p. 15.

... **'rights and responsibilities for Germany as a whole...'** ibid., p. 16.

The Common Resolution ... ibid., pp. 66–7.

... **'so far as its territorial extent...'** full text of the crucial 1973 verdict in *Zehn Jahre*, pp. 232–43, this on p. 237. In taking this position the Constitutional Court was, however, reaffirming what had clearly been the intention and understanding of those who framed the Basic Law in 1949, see Lehmann, *Oder-Neisse*, pp. 145–47. One of the judges who delivered the 1973 verdict, Willi Geiger, emphasises the continuity of the Constitutional Court's position on this issue, pointing out that the Court, with a different membership, unconditionally reaffirmed it in a judgement in 1987. See Willi Geiger, 'Der Grundlagenvertrag und die Einheit Deutschlands', in Dieter Blumenwitz & Gottfried Zieger, eds, *40 Jahre Bundesrepublik Deutschland. Verantwortung für Deutschland* (Köln: Verlag Wissenschaft und Politik, 1989), pp. 53–64.

... **a suggestion by a leading German specialist** ... the specialist was Karl Kaiser, see the report in FAZ, 13 July 1989, the critical response by Wilhelm G Grewe in *Rheinischer Merkur*, 28 July 1989, Karl Kaiser's eloquent statement of his general argument in *Die Zeit*, 22 September 1989, and a further response by Wilhelm G Grewe in FAZ, 19 October 1989.

... **genuinely a territorial revisionist** ... see Schwarz, *Adenauer I*, pp. 945–96.

... **'Oder-Neisse, Eastern provinces...'** quoted by Hans-Jakob Stehle in Josef

Foschepoth, ed., *Adenauer und die deutsche Frage* (Göttingen: Vandenhoeck & Rupprecht, 1988), p. 85. His source is given as a note by the journalist Fritz Sänger on a conversation with Adenauer on 30 August 1955. The remark was quoted by Karl Kaiser in his article in *Die Zeit*, 22 September 1989, and I am grateful to his assistant Klaus Becher for pointing me to the source.

... by the late 1950s ... A plan for German unification worked out by Adenauer's close associate Felix von Eckardt in September 1956 already envisaged a plebiscite in which the Germans in East and West Germany would be asked if they would be willing to accept 'certain sacrifices in the drawing of the eastern frontier' in return for reunification (of East and West Germany), see Schwarz, *Adenauer II*, pp. 321–23. The diplomatic trade-off of frontier recognition for reunification was also suggested by Wilhelm Grewe in a lecture in New York in November 1959, see Grewe, *Rückblenden*, pp. 419–20.

... following Byrnes' Stuttgart speech ... see Lehmann, *Oder-Neisse*, pp. 70, 78 ff.

... Kennedy and Macmillan as well as de Gaulle ... see Schwarz, *Adenauer II*, pp. 551–52. De Gaulle made his position unmistakeably clear in a famous press conference on 25 March 1959. Schwarz rightly points out that if Adenauer was under pressure on this issue from the German expellees in the Federal Republic, American presidents — particularly Democratic presidents — were under countervailing pressure from Polish émigrés in the United States.

... a diplomatic card ... Schwarz, *Adenauer II*, p. 687. Wilhelm Grewe to the author, Bonn, 6 July 1991.

... 'it is difficult for Germany's neighbours ...' Elizabeth Wiskemann, *Germany's Eastern Neighbours. Problems relating to the Oder-Neisse Line and the Czech Frontier Regions* (London: Oxford University Press, 1956), p. 112, hereafter Wiskemann, *Eastern Neighbours*.

... as Egon Bahr's closest legal adviser ... Antonius Eitel, in conversation with the author, Bonn, 1 July 1991. Eitel is the pseudonymous author of Zündorf, *Ostverträge*.

Alois Mertes ... argued ... see, for example, his comments recorded in *Politik und Kultur* (Berlin), 2/1981, pp. 20–38, especially pp. 32–33, and letter to the FAZ, 12 October 1982.

... the necessary starting-point ... the clearest statement is in his Memorandum for the leader of the CDU/CSU parliamentary party dated 20 August 1980. That the Basic Law did not require this to be a target was authoritatively confirmed by one of the judges who made the controversial Constitutional Court ruling of 1973, Willi Geiger, in *Neue Juristische Wochenschrift*, Heft 41, 1983, pp. 2302–04.

... Wilhelm Grewe ... a particularly clear and concise statement in his letter to the FAZ, 2 December 1983.

... an interesting exchange of letters ... in ACDP: I-403, 038/2. The exchange was initiated by Mertes, who was then Minister of State in the Foreign Ministry, and prompted by the Soviet compaign against German 're- vanchism'.

... 'too much effort' ... letter of 13 July 1984, ibid.

The devil, replied Mertes ... letter of 18 July 1984, ibid.

... the frontiers of 1937 as a target ... even the Hupkas and Czajas would not say this explicitly in the 1970s and 1980s. But they fiercely insisted that the frontiers of 1937 were more than just a starting-point — see, for example, letter from Herbert Hupka to the FAZ, 30 July 1983 — and some of their followers were certainly less cautious. Thus, for example, a motion proposed by the Mainz-Bin- gen local group of the Federation of Expellees to that organisation's regional assembly (*Landesdelegiertentag*) on 7 March 1982 read as follows: 'The People's Republic of Poland has, in the last decades, proved itself in every respect incapable of administering the east German areas put under its control. The Federation of Expellees therefore calls on the victor powers to remove from Poland, even before peace treaty regulations, the administration of the German eastern territories as defined in the Potsdam resolutions.' It then went on to make a suggestion which curiously reflected the impact of Brandt's new Ostpolitik and the improvement in German-German relations: 'The Federation of Expellees,' so the draft resolution continued, 'further demands that in a first step to the unification of the divided German territories, the provinces currently under Polish administration should be subordinated and attached to the German Democratic Republic'! With the exception of this last sentence, the resolution was passed by the regional assembly, in Helmut Kohl's home territory, just before he became Chancellor — a vivid, if extreme, example of what he was up against. This curious document is in ACDP: 1403, 130/1.

... the 'Stuttgart Charter' ... see Jacobsen, *Nachbarn*, pp. 232–33.

... Willy Brandt himself observed ... in his contribution to Dieter Blumen- witz & ors, eds, *Konrad Adenauer und seine Zeit* (Stuttgart: Deutsche Verlags-An- stalt, 1976), Vol. 1, p. 107.

... a double integration ... On this there is a large literature. A brief account is given by Dennis L Bark and David R Gress, *From Shadow to Substance 1945–1963 = A History of West Germany, Vol 1*, (Oxford: Blackwell, 1989), pp. 305–10. See also the chapters by Bauer, Wiesemann and Schillinger in Benz, *Vertreibung*. A useful account of the state of research is given by Arnold Sywottek in APZ, 15 December 1989, pp. 38–46. On the party-political side the most vivid impression is given by the narrative in Schwarz's biography of Adenauer.

An author who knew Helmut Kohl well ... Peter Scholl-Latour in *Helmut Kohl. Fotografiert von Konrad R. Müller, mit einem Essay von Peter Scholl-Latour* (Bergisch-Gladbach: Gustav Lübbe Verlag, 1990), p. 32.

... Friedrich Zimmermann ... in a speech to the Bavarian regional association of the Federation of Expellees on 29 January 1983, billed as presenting the policy of the new government. Zimmermann maintained his position, against a formal protest from the Polish government, which the minister ascribed to 'obdurate communists', see *Die Welt* 11 February 1983.

. . . 'Silesia remains ours' . . . Kohl had already addressed at least one meeting of expellees, in September 1984, in line with his conscious policy of active dialogue with them, see his speech reprinted in *Bulletin*, 5 September 1984, pp. 873–79. The planned motto became known at the end of 1984, provoking a whirlwind of media intention. The chairman of the Silesian *Landsmannschaft* (that is, organisation of Germans from that region), Herbert Hupka, observed: 'I cannot wholly understand the excitement . . . — perhaps the language sounds too old-German, too Lutheran — nothing else is meant but that Silesia remains our homeland (*Heimat*), that Silesia remains our task, that we may and should not give up the claim to Silesia, historically, spiritually, culturally, morally and politically.' Interview on Bavarian Radio, 29 December 1984, quoted from BPA/KU I/2.1.85. Very reassuring. Matters were made still worse by a fantastic article in the Silesians' newspaper, *Der Schlesier* (25 January 1985), in which one Thomas Finke imagined West German troops sweeping forward to the Soviet frontier as a result of a 'New Ostpolitik' of the Federal Government, the goal of which was the destabilisation of the Soviet bloc. Only in Poland and Czechoslovakia, wrote Thomas Finke, in this charming fantasy, 'did parts of the armed forces put up resistance, which was, however, soon broken. The overwhelming majority of the population greeted the Germans as liberators.' Even Herbert Hupka felt compelled to distance himself from this article, pleading freedom of the press. After an icy public exchange of letters between Hupka and Kohl (the Chancellor's letter being printed in the *Bulletin*, 25 January 1985, pp. 69–70, a fairly unusual proceeding), and a clarifying statement in the Bundestag (also reprinted, unusually, in the *Bulletin*, 8 February 1985, pp. 121–23), the Silesians were prevailed upon to change the motto and the furore somewhat subsided.

In his speech . . . reprinted in *Bulletin*, 20 June 1985, pp. 577–83. There also the following quotations.

. . . a resolution of the Silesian association . . . the resolution dated from 2 March 1985, and was connected with the foregoing controversy.

'. . . and not put it in question' . . . my own notes of the meeting, which I attended, record 'boos and whistles' at this point. Kohl had earlier used an almost identical formulation, referring to 'the territories beyond Poland's western frontier', see *Bulletin*, 28 February 1985, p. 200.

. . . a banner . . . torn down . . . author's observation. See also my report in the *Spectator*, 22 June 1985.

. . . a 'political binding effect' . . . *Bundestag Plenarprotokolle*, 10/119, p. 8812 (6 February 1985). This statement, regarded at the time as an act of political courage, came following a visit by Volker Rühe to Poland, and at the height of the controversy about the Silesians' meeting. Karl Kaiser credits the Social Democrat jurist Claus Arndt with coining the concept, see Kaiser's article in *Die Zeit*, 22 September 1989.

. . . an independent opinion survey . . . this was one of the fascinating series of surveys by Polish sociologists called simply 'Poles', see Garton Ash, *Uses*, p. 239, note 29.

... **a minister from the Christian Social Union** ... this time the Finance Minister and Chairman of the CSU, Theo Waigel, once again at the Silesians' meeting, see reports in SZ and FAZ, both 3 July 1989. The FAZ's reporter noted that of some 100,000 people attending the whole festival, only some 5,000 bothered to come to hear Herr Waigel's speech. This was nonetheless rolled into the controversy about Karl Kaiser's comments (see above) to become the lead story in *Der Spiegel*, 29/1989.

... **'the Polish people should know** ...' see *Umbruch*, pp. 75–6. This was the wording of the resolution proposed by CDU/CSU and FDP, see *Bundestag Drucksachen* 11/5589. The particular force of it was the commitment expressed in the formulation 'us Germans', implying that this would hold for Germans in a unified state as well. However, reflecting the painful compromises to be made within the ranks of the Christian Democrats, this passage was prefaced with the phrase 'For the Federal Republic of Germany it holds that ...' On the argument inside the coalition see report in FAZ, 9 November 1989. The Greens proposed a much less qualified resolution, which said that the Oder-Neisse line as Poland's western frontier 'is inviolable for any German state authority', see *Bundestag Drucksachen*, 11/5591. The government resolution was supported by the Social Democrats. Four hundred votes were cast for the resolution, four against, and there were thirty-three abstentions.

'The Chancellor tried to calm my fears ...' *Rok 1989. Bronisław Geremek Opowiada, Jacek Żakowski Pyta* (Warsaw: Plejada, 1990), pp. 327–28.

... **did not mention the frontiers** ... see Kaiser, *Vereinigung*, p. 91.

... **the Chancellor** ... **surprised and appalled** ... see reports in FAZ, 3 March 1990, *Le Monde*, 4–5 March 1990, *Observer*, 4 March 1990. The result of this further flurry was another Bundestag resolution which paved the domestic political path for the agreement on the Oder-Neisse line in the '2 + 4' negotiations for German unity, and the final frontier treaty between united Germany and liberated Poland.

... **the other five (including Markus Meckel** ...) this was clearly the impression of the Poles involved (Jerzy Sułek, Berlin, 11 May 1992). See also p. 353 f.

... **the final ratification of the final frontier treaty** ... for the vote on 17 October 1991, see *Bundestag Plenarprotokolle*, 12/50, pp. 4098–99. At a meeting with Poland's first non-communist prime minister, Tadeusz Mazowiecki, in Frankfurt on the Oder in early November 1990, Kohl assured him that the frontier treaty could be signed already that month — a nice electoral gift to the presidential candidate Mazowiecki — and held out the prospect that it would be ratified, together with the 'neighbour' treaty, in February 1991. See report in FAZ, 9 November 1990 and *Bulletin*, 16 November 1990, pp. 1389–96, with text of the treaty signed on 14 November by foreign ministers Genscher and Skubiszewski. In fact, the negotiations on the second treaty lasted much longer, especially because of Bonn's insistence on detailing the rights of the German minority in Poland, see, for example, report in *Der Spiegel* 11/91. The texts on the signature of the 'neighbour' treaty in June 1991 are in *Bulletin*, 18 June 1991, pp. 541–56.

. . . a retrospective conversation with the author . . . Helmut Kohl, Bonn, 1 October 1991.

. . . precisely as it ran . . . A former head of the Bonn Foreign Ministry's legal department suggested in conversation with the author that Bonn might perhaps have tried for a slightly different interpretation of the Oder-Neisse line, closer to the original wording of the Potsdam Agreement. Since this suggested that the line run 'from the Baltic Sea immediately west of Swinamunde, and thence along the Oder river' it could be argued that the west bank of the Oder, including most of Stettin — now Szczecin — should have gone to Germany. The Görlitz Agreement, trying to square this vague provision with the line to the west of Szczecin that the Soviets had actually decided on, referred to 'the established and existing frontier running from the Baltic Sea along the line west of Swinoujscie and along the Odra river . . .'. (See Grenville, *Treaties*, pp. 36 & 188.) In fact there was a fierce border dispute between the GDR and Poland in the 1980s over the exact dividing line through the Szczecin harbour waters at the mouth of the Oder, after both sides had unilaterally extended their territorial waters to twelve miles. This dispute was only resolved, with a precise delineation of the line, in a treaty between the GDR and the People's Republic of Poland on 22 May 1989. See FAZ 24 May 1989. This line was then explicitly referred to in the treaty between united Germany and liberated Poland. One of the few lasting foreign policy acts of the GDR was thus to determine the exact line of the frontier between the Federal Republic and the Republic of Poland!

. . . the price which Germany simply had to pay . . . see the speech by Ottfried Hennig to the East Prussian *Landsmannschaft* (that is, organisation of the Germans from that region) in Bad Honnef on 8 September 1990. Hennig, a Parliamentary State Secretary in the Ministry for Intra-German Relations, there explains why he felt obliged to support the Chancellor on this point — because otherwise the reunification of East and West Germany would be impossible — but also felt obliged to resign his post as spokesman of the East Prussian organisation.

. . . the basic outlines of the problem . . . there is no satisfactory overall account of this issue. Beside the useful essays in Benz, *Vertreibung*, much essential information is given in the detailed research reports prepared for the German section of the Association for the Study of the World Refugee Problem, referred to here as *Aussiedler 1* and *Aussiedler 2*, and in the official publications of the Federal Ministry of the Interior. Most of the material on the remaining German minorities is to be found either in official publications or in newspaper and journal articles, but Schulz-Vobach, *Die Deutschen im Osten*, is a useful journalistic *tour d'horizon* reflecting the state of affairs in the mid- to late 1980s. Dralle, *Deutsche*, is good for the general background. Ingeborg Fleischauer & Benjamin Pinkus, *The*

Soviet Germans. Past and Present (London: Hurst, 1986), is invaluable on the history of the Germans in the Soviet Union up to the mid-1980s.

... **and their replacement by settlers** ... see the brief but vivid description in Broszat, *Polenpolitik*, p. 286 ff. More detail in Martin Broszat, *Nationalsozialistische Polenpolitik* (Stuttgart: Deutsche Verlags-Anstalt, 1961).

... **some four million** ... see the introduction by Hans Harmsen to *Aussiedler 2*, pp. 1–12, this on p. 3.

... *Germanissimi Germanorum* ... On this community see also August Ludwig Schlözer, *Kritische Sammlungen zur Geschichte der Deutschen in Siebenbürgen*, (Vienna: Bohlau, 1979), a reprint of the original edition of 1795–97, and the review article by William C Dowling, 'Germanissimi Germanorum. Romania's Vanishing German Culture' in *East European Politics and Societies*, Vol. 5, No. 2, pp. 341–55.

... **the remaining Germans within** ... **Poland** ... for an introduction to this fiendishly intricate and delicate subject see the chapter by Gerhard Reichling in *Aussiedler 1*, pp. 9–56, and articles by Gotthold Rhode in APZ, B11–12/88, pp. 3–20 and Hans-Werner Rautenberg in APZ, B50/88, pp. 14–27. Christian Th. Stoll, *Die Deutschen im polnischen Herrschaftsbereich nach 1945* (Vienna: Österreichische Landsmannschaft, 1989 = *Eckart-Schriften* Heft 98) is a tendentious book, which nonetheless contains useful information.

... **Upper Silesia** ... for the exceptionally complex history of this area see the introduction to Hugo Weczerka, ed., *Schlesien* (Stuttgart: Kröner, 1977 = *Handbuch der Historischen Stätten*), and Wiskemann, *Eastern Neighbours*, pp. 22–33.

... **now turning one way, now the other** ... Interestingly enough, Helmut Schmidt reports Edward Gierek saying precisely this to him in Helsinki in 1975: 'We Upper Silesians were Poles when the Poles were doing well and Germans when you were doing well!' See Schmidt, *Nachbarn*, p. 481.

... **the *Auslandsdeutsche*** ... very roughly 'Germans abroad'. On this see John Hiden, 'The Weimar Republic and the problem of the *Auslandsdeutsche*', in *Journal of Contemporary History*, 12/1977, pp. 273–89, and the same author's book, *The Baltic States and Weimar Ostpolitik* (Cambridge: Cambridge University Press, 1987), with bibliography.

... **German foreign ministry support** ... on this see Norbert Krekeler, *Revisionsanspruch und geheime Ostpolitik der Weimarer Republik. Die Subventionierung der deutschen Minderheit in Polen 1919–33* (Stuttgart: Deutsche Verlags-Anstalt, 1973). He summarises some of the main points in his chapter in Benz, *Vertreibung*.

... **the devil's grandmother** ... quoted by Rainer Salzmann in Dieter Blumenwitz & ors, eds, *Konrad Adenauer und seine Zeit*, Vol 2, (Stuttgart: Deutsche Verlags-Anstalt, 1976), p. 151. However in an article in *Die Zeit*, 1 January 1993, Karl-Heinz Jansen reports the conclusion of the historian Heinrich Meyer, on the basis of previously unpublished documents, that Adenauer might in fact have been able to get the prisoners-of-war home earlier. Another historical 'what would have happened if . . .'.

. . . **significant improvements for the ethnic Germans** . . . see the article by Barbara Dietz and Peter Hilkes in APZ, B50/1988, pp. 3–13, esp. p. 5.

. . . **a second, extremely difficult round of negotiations** . . . the best short account is given by Boris Meissner, who was very directly involved in them, see Meissner, *Moskau-Bonn*, pp. 27–30 and the documents indicated in the footnotes to those pages, with the actual agreement reprinted on pp. 370–72. The essential qualification for repatriation was to have possessed German citizenship on 21 June 1941.

The 1961 Bundestag initiative . . . **explicitly linked** . . . as one might expect from an initiative led by the Sudeten German Wenzel Jaksch. See the Jaksch report on the position of the Germans in the East, *Bundestag Drucksachen*, 3/2807, which was clearly linked to the more often quoted main 'Jaksch report', which is *Bundestag Drucksachen*, 3/2740.

. . . **a measure of their success** . . . see, for example, comments by the Interior Minister in *Bulletin*, 16 January 1979, p. 35, and by Chancellor Schmidt in *Bundestag Plenarprotokolle* 9/111, p. 6748 (9 September 1982).

. . . **the official translation** . . . *Basic Law of the Federal Republic of Germany* (Bonn: Press and Information Office of the Federal Government, 1977).

. . . **two key categories** . . . the following paragraph draws heavily on the authoritative commentary, Maunz-Dürig-Herzog, *Grundgesetz-Kommentar* (Munich: Beck, 1991). For this, as for many other legal references, I am grateful to Michael Mertes.

. . . **guidelines** . . . **Friedland reception camp** . . . the 1976 'Friedland guidelines' are reprinted in the 'working handbook' by a senior legal official: Liesner, *Aussiedler* pp. 66–77, but see also Liesner's introduction.

'A member of the German *Volk* . . .' ibid., p. 61.

. . . **'by his behaviour the consciousness and will . . .'** ibid., p. 79.

. . . **'their overall behaviour . . .'** ibid., p. 81.

. . . **'If the dominant influence . . .'** ibid., p. 84.

. . . **'immediately before the beginning . . .'** ibid., p. 82.

. . . **'they could not be expected . . .'** ibid., p. 85.

. . . **'the concept of German stock . . .'** ibid., p. 85.

. . . **at the Friedland reception camp** . . . A vivid description is given by Amity Shlaes in Chapter 1 of her *Germany. The Empire Within* (New York: Farrar Strauss, 1991). However, as will be clear from the above, she oversimplifies when she writes (p. 20) that 'In Germany blood is what counts, and the settlers are Germans because they are of German blood.'

... entering them in group three or four of the so-called *Volksliste* ... see, for example, Broszat, *Polenpolitik*, pp. 288–89. The *Volksliste* had four groups, of which the largest — and most problematic for West Germany — was Group 3. This contained persons described as Germans with 'ties to *Polentum*'. Some 1.7 million people were entered in this group alone between 1941 and 1944. Group 4, which contained only some 80,000, contained persons described as having 'gone up into *Polentum*' — that is, as an official of the Federal Interior Ministry nicely described it to me, 'Poles with blue eyes and blond hair'. Manfred Meissner, Bonn, 8 September 1989.

... generally depended on a certification of Germanity ... Manfred Meissner, Bonn, 25 March 1992. For the precise details, and exceptions, see Liesner, *Aussiedler*.

Question 15 of the questionnaire ... reprinted in Liesner, *Aussiedler*, p. 55. Those seeking recognition therefore sought evidence from such sources as the Berlin Document Center, the *Bundesarchiv*, and the so-called German Office for Informing the Next-of-kin of the Fallen of the former German Wehrmacht.

... roughly half ... Manfred Meissner, Bonn, 8 September 1989.

... more German ... in the sense of preserving national traditions, habits, even language lost in the commercialised, Americanised Federal Republic. This point was stressed in publications designed to win popular acceptance for the out-settlers, see for example the official free paper of the Federal Centre for Political Education, *PZ*, 56/1989, headlined '*Aussiedler ... Deutscher als wir ...*'.

... not a family past in the Polish resistance ... a first-hand observer told me of one applicant initially accepted, because he furnished evidence of having served in the *Wehrmacht*, but then definitively rejected, because it emerged that he had later fought with the Polish Army against the Germans.

... could be bought on the black market ... see reports in SZ, *Die Welt* and *Berliner Morgenpost* of 30 March 1988 and *Stuttgarter Zeitung* of 2 April 1988.

... the Gomułka regime did permit ... this included the founding, in April 1957, of a 'German Social-cultural Society'. See the valuable article by a leading West German historian of Poland, Gotthold Rhode, 'Die deutsch-polnischen Beziehungen von 1945 bis in die achtziger Jahre,' in APZ, B11–12/88, this on p. 14.

... not in Upper Silesia ... incredibly, a ban on the teaching of German in the voivodships of Opole and Katowice — that is, in Upper Silesia — was only lifted in September 1988. See the report by Stefan Dietrich in FAZ, 23 January 1989.

... the Polish authorities at first maintained ... for this and the following see Baring, *Machtwechsel*, pp. 482–87.

... a so-called 'Information' ... text in *Verträge*, pp. 27–29.

... unpublished 'Confidential Notes' ... see Baring, *Machtwechsel*, p. 484.

Following a long and emotional late-evening talk . . . see Link, *Ära Schmidt*, pp. 307–08, Bingen, *Bonn-Warschau*, pp. 26–29, Schmidt, *Nachbarn*, pp. 479 ff.

. . . a pension agreement . . . see *Verträge*, pp. 29–38. Bonn's main objective here was to ensure that Germans living in Poland who had payed their pension contributions to German pension funds in the *Reich* before 1945, would get a decent pension. But clearly the Polish side would not accept the direct payment by West Germany of pensions to people whose separate identity, as Germans, they anyway disputed. The compromise found was that West Germany would pay any Pole who came to live in the Federal Republic a regular state pension based on the years he had (notionally) contributed to a pension fund in Poland, and Poland would honour — at its regular state pension rates — the years for which people now living in Poland had previously paid into German pension funds. The results were threefold. First, a few tens of thousands of old people in the former German territories received a zloty pension which they might otherwise not have received. Secondly, the Gierek equipe pocketed a further DM 1.3 billion. Thirdly, any Pole coming to live permanently in the Federal Republic had a DM pension entitle-ment for the years he notionally contributed in Poland. Thus, for example, as the *Bild-Zeitung* hastened to point out, a Polish General (Leon Dubicki) who defected to West Germany shortly before martial law was declared in 1981 automatically received a pension larger than many ordinary West Germans. A detailed account of the agreements, looking particularly at their status in international law, is given by Dieter Blumenwitz in Dieter Blumenwitz and Gottfried Zieger, eds, *Menschen-rechte und wirtschaftliche Gegenleistungen. Aspekte ihrer völkerrectlichen Verknüpfun-gen* (Köln: Verlag Wissenschaft und Politik, 1987), pp. 9–28.

. . . a DM 1 billion loan . . . see *Verträge*, pp. 38–40.

. . . 'on the basis of investigations . . .' ibid., p. 41.

. . . led by Franz Josef Strauss . . . see Bingen, *Bonn-Warschau*, p. 28; Link, *Ära Schmidt*, pp. 307–08; and, for Strauss's own colourful account, Strauss, *Erinnerun-gen*, pp. 458–66.

. . . further, quite humiliating public assurances . . . see *Verträge*, pp. 46–49. The then spokesman of the (Bonn) Foreign Ministry described these assurances as 'on the borderline of what can be reconciled with the concept of sovereignty', quoted in Bingen, *Bonn-Warschau*, p. 28.

The Jackson-Vanik amendment . . . on this see the detailed discussion in Kissinger, *Years of Upheaval*, pp. 250–55, 986–95, & 1252–53 (with the final text of the amendment).

In the case of Romania . . . see Kovrig, *Walls and Bridges*, esp. pp. 182–86.

So also with Romania . . . the best short account is given in the article by Anneli Ute Gabanyi in APZ, B50/88, pp. 28–39.

. . . cash being carried to the border . . . Günther van Well, Bonn, 8 July 1991.

. . . for the next five years . . . in 1988, Genscher began negotiations about raising the payment and accelerating the emigration programme, since the position

554 · *Notes to Pages 238–241*

of the German minority was held to have become intolerable, see the report by Olaf Ihlau in SZ, 4 August 1988.

... **cash for Germans** ... thus Werner Link: 'West German capital for Polish exit-liberalisation for German and German-stock citizens!' Link, *Ära Schmidt*, p. 307. See also the chapters by Schweitzer and Sułek in Jacobsen, *Deutschland-Polen*.

... **a personal declaration of friendship** ... Schmidt's remarkable *faible* for Edward Gierek is well documented. Klaus Bölling records him saying he would 'take him straight into the cabinet', and, on the night before martial law was declared, asking Erich Honecker whether he could not intervene with the Polish authorities on behalf of — Edward Gierek! See Bölling, *Die fernen Nachbarn*, p. 157.

... **'to advance the conditions'** ... *Verträge*, p. 38.

... **DM 290.5 million in interest subsidies** ... Link, *Ära Schmidt*, p. 308.

Alois Mertes estimated ... this came in an eight-page letter to a parliamentary colleague, Carl Otto Lenz, dated 14 December 1983, and widely publicised. All the following quotations are from a copy of the original letter in the Mertes file in the ACDP press archive.

... **that liberal-conservative interpretation** ... see above, pp. 224 f. The independent Polish specialist on German affairs, Artur Hajnicz, points out that the leader of the Silesian expellees, Herbert Hupka, 'instantly protested against the letter, which he had thoroughly perused and the intention behind which he understood'. See *Aussenpolitik* (English-language edition), I/89, p. 35.

Primate Glemp preached a sermon ... extracts in FAZ, 18 August 1984. Glemp attempted to undo some of the damage in an interview in *Die Zeit*, 13 June 1985.

'What Germans, what injury?' ... For this attitude he was, however, criticised in the independent, underground press. See, for example, an article in *CDN. Głos Wolnego Robotnika*, No. 85, December 1984.

The main reasons ... Manfred Meissner, Federal Ministry of the Interior, Bonn, 8 September 1989.

... **with renewed emphasis** ... as noted by Johann Georg Reissmüller in the FAZ, 16 May 1983, reprinted in Reissmüller, *Vergessene Hälfte*, pp. 118–21.

... **a net economic gain** ... see the article by Klaus Leciejewski in *Das Parlament*, 25 August 1989, and the Institut der deutschen Wirtschaft study reported in FAZ, 23 September 1989.

... **'Persons persecuted ...'** this is the official translation in *The Basic Law of the Federal Republic of Germany* (Bonn: Press and Information Office of the Federal Government, 1977). The German is actually simply and stronger: '*Politisch Verfolgte geniessen Asylrecht*'.

In practice ... detail and the following figures from Jürgen Haberland, Federal Ministry of the Interior, Bonn, 15 March 1989.

... **some 200,000** ... this figure came from the Federal Republic's central register of foreigners. It did not include temporary visitors, those with dual citizenship, and, of course, those staying illegally.

... **a rough continuum of resentment** ... this emerges very clearly in the results of a survey in *Der Spiegel*, 16/1989.

... **less *Volksdeutsche* than *Volkswagendeutsche*** ... this is not, it must be emphasised, to deny the existence of a minority for whom the denial of cultural identity was a major motive for wishing to leave. See, for example, the article by Bronisław Tumilowicz in *Polityka*, 24 June 1989, and that by Hans Krump in *Die Welt*, 24 October 1987. But when Krump's article is subtitled 'More than a million Germans in Poland fight for their identity', it compounds the fateful confusion. There might be more than a million Germans *in the sense of the Basic Law* in Poland. What there certainly was not, however, was a million 'fighting for their identity'. On this see also Klaus Reiff, *Polen. Als deutscher Diplomat an der Weichsel* (Bonn: Dietz, 1990), p. 76 ff.

On the first visit by a President ... see Schulz-Vobach, *Die Deutschen im Osten*, p. 128 ff.

... **'the treatment of minorities...'** press statement of the CDU/CSU parliamentary party, 1 September 1988.

... **to be understood as a signal** ... Volker Rühe, Bonn, 14 October 1988.

... **'Both sides must move...'** quoted from BPA/KU I/08.08/88: Kohl, 0805–8/I.

... **a leading German banker** ... this was F Wilhelm Christians of the Deutsche Bank. See Christians's own account in SZ, 27 September 1989, and the article by Michel Tatu in *Le Monde*, 27 July 1990.

... **the young out-settlers** ... according to Federal Interior Ministry statistics, forty-three per cent of the out-settlers who came to the Federal Republic in 1988 were under twenty-five, while only four per cent were over sixty-five.

'Foreign trade...' Ludwig Erhard, 'Die geistigen Grundlagen gesunden Aussenhandels,' 1953, quoted in Haftendorn, *Aussenpolitik*, p. 403.

At least one third ... the *Bonner Almanach 1987/88* (Bonn: Presse- und Informationsamt der Bundesregierung, 1987), p. 88, gives a figure of thirty-two per cent for 1985. In his chapter in Susan Stern, ed., *Meet United Germany* (Frankfurt: FAZ, 1991), p. 187, Norbert Walter, chief economist of the Deutsche Bank, says 'over one third'. Jürgen Bellers points out in *Liberal* 1/1989, p. 5, that if one includes the half-finished goods that go into the exports one can arrive at a figure of nearly fifty per cent.

... **one in five** ... this estimate for 1974/75, see Kreile, *Osthandel*, p. 165.

... **a 'trading state'** ... see Richard Rosecrance, *The Rise of the Trading State* (New York: Basic Books, 1986).

'The economy is our fate'... quoted by Otto Wolff von Amerongen in Hans-Dietrich Genscher, ed., *Nach vorn gedacht... Perspektiven deutscher Aussenpolitik* (Bonn: Bonn Aktuell, 1987), p. 113. Walter Rathenau's remark might also be translated as 'business is our fate'.

'You forget...' quoted in Van Oudenaren, *Détente*, p.259.

'We have all the raw materials...' Helmut Allardt, *Politik vor und hinter den Kulissen. Erfahrungen eines Diplomaten zwischen Ost und West* (Düsseldorf: Econ Verlag, 1979), p. 251.

... never more than seven and a half per cent... the figures are usefully collated in Table 3 of Haberl & Hecker, *Unfertige Nachbarschaften*, p. 272.

... more than nine per cent... ibid.

... Walter Scheel declared... speech of 18 May 1972 quoted in Meissner, *Moskau-Bonn*, pp. 1507–13, this on p. 1510.

'At present, economic exchange...' this famous Davos speech was on 1 February 1987. Quoted from Der Bundesminister des Auswärtigen, Mitteilung für die Presse No. 1022/87, this quotation on p. 42. The speech is now reprinted in Genscher, *Unterwegs*, pp. 139–50. As will be clear from the table in Haberl & Hecker, *Unfertige Nachbarschaften*, p. 272, this remarkably low percentage figure was achieved by excluding the Federal Republic's trade with both Yugoslavia and East Germany. Including those two, the figure for 1986 was actually 6.7 per cent.

... the distinctly abnormal German expansion... see M C Kaser and E A Radice, eds., *The Economic History of Eastern Europe 1919–1975* (Oxford: Clarendon Press, 1985), p. 436.

... three times more than the United States... see Table A.3 in Gordon, *Eroding Empire*, pp. 332–33, and Table II below.

... more dependent on it than any other Western state... see Table A.3 in Gordon, *Eroding Empire*, pp.332–33.

... as much as twenty per cent... Kreile, *Osthandel*, p. 173.

... an important 'lobby'... see Chapter 3 in Kreile, *Osthandel*, and the chapter by Arno Burzig in Haberl & Hecker, *Unfertige Nachbarschaften*. Because of the 'pioneer function' of economic ties for Ostpolitik as a whole, individual figures like the head of the Ost-Ausschuss der deutschen Wirtschaft, Otto Wolff von Amerongen, and the Chairman of the Deutsche Bank, F Wilhelm Christians, had an importance even beyond the lobbying 'weight' of the interests they represented. See Christians, *Wege*, Wolffs memoirs, *Der Weg nach Osten. Vierzig Jahre Brückenbau für die deutsche Wirtschaft* (Munich: Droemer Knaur, 1992), which unfortunately appeared too late to be used in the preperation of this edition.

... the number of jobs... see Stent, *Embargo to Ostpolitik*, p. 217.

... thirty per cent... figures from the Foreign Ministry.

... to increase the real economic interest as well... This is also the conclusion of Wörmann, *Osthandel*, pp. 269–70.

... **paints in his memoirs** ... see Christians, *Wege*, esp. pp. 247–50.

'For centuries ...' see Meissner, *Moskau-Bonn*, p. 1510.

... **an important original motive** ... this point is stressed by Hanns-Dieter Jacobsen, Heinrich Machowski & Kalus Schröder, 'The Political and Economic Framework Conditions of East-West Relations', in *Aussenpolitik* (English-language edition), II/88, p. 139. See also the quotations in Wörmann, *Problem*, note 120, p. 215.

... **between a quarter and one third** ... see Table A-12 in Gordon, *Eroding Empire*. The figure given for Czechoslovakia is actually more than one third: 35.9 per cent.

... **some forty per cent** ... this estimate is given in the article by Andras Inotai in *Liberal* 4/1990, pp. 41–54, this on p. 41.

... **a quarter ... no less than half** ... ibid., p. 45.

... **joint ventures** ... this figure was given by Béla Kádár, Hungary's Minister for International Economic Relations, in Reforms in the Foreign Economic Relations of Eastern Europe and the Soviet Union (New York: Economic Commission for Europe, 1991) p. 77.

... **some eight per cent** ... a figure of 8.5 per cent is cited in *European Economy*, No. 45, December 1990, p. 154.

... **more than a quarter** ... see Table 4.2 in Angela Stent, 'Technology Transfer to Eastern Europe. Paradoxes, Policies, Prospects', in William E Griffith, ed., *Central and Eastern Europe. The Opening Curtain?* (Boulder: Westview Press, 1989).

... **some eighteen per cent** ... figures based on official Soviet statistics.

... **the largest single portion** ... see Teltschik, *329 Tage*, p. 232.

... **a common general dilemma** ... see my essay 'Reform or revolution?' in Garton Ash, *Uses*. The point is also stressed by William E. Griffith in the introductory chapter to William E Griffith, ed., *Central and Eastern Europe. The Opening Curtain?* (Boulder: Westview Press, 1989).

... **and the European Community in particular** ... on this, see now the valuable book by Peter van Ham, *The EC, Eastern Europe and European Unity. Discord, Collaboration and Integration since 1947* (London: Pinter, 1993).

... **the question of how to use that economic power** ... a lucid and stimulating introduction to the issues is Hanson, *Western Economic Statecraft*.

... **between Bonn and Washington** ... On this there is an extensive literature, dating mainly from the mid-1980s. Wörmann, *Problem*, is a thorough and thoughtful treatment, as is the slightly earlier study by Hanns-Dieter Jacobsen, *Die Ost-West Wirtschaftsbeziehungen als Deutsch-Amerikanisches Problem* (Ebenhausen: Stiftung Wissenschaft und Politik, 1983). See also Stent, *Embargo to Ostpolitik* and the same author's chapter in William E Griffith, ed., *Central and Eastern Europe. The Opening Curtain?* (Boulder: Westview Press, 1989), pp. 74–101. On the American side, Jentleson, *Pipeline Politics*, contains a wealth of useful detail on issues far wider than just energy trade. See also the relevant chapters in Kovrig, *Walls and Bridges*, Gordon, *Eroding Empire*, van Oudenaren, *Détente*, and the chapters by Gary K Bertsch and Steve Elliott-Gower, and by Heinrich Vogel, in Gary K Bertsch & ors, eds, *After the Revolutions. East-West Trade and Technology Transfer in the 1990s* (Boulder: Westview Press, 1991).

. . . 'If you want grain . . .' quoted in Kreile, *Osthandel*, p. 66.

Co-existence and Commerce . . . Samuel Pisar, *Coexistence and Commerce. Guidelines for Transactions between East and West* (New York: McGraw-Hill, 1970). Giscard d'Estaing wrote a glowing Preface to the French edition. One might note that the book was largely written in a château Pisar rented from Giscard. Pisar records this, and Giscard's praise, in his autobiography, *Of Blood and Hope* (New York: Macmillan, 1982), pp. 186–88.

. . . the 'romantics of eastern trade' . . . Otto Wolff von Amerongen, 'Aspekte des deutschen Osthandels', in *Aussenpolitik* 3/1970, pp. 143–48.

. . . including Franz Josef Strauss . . . conversation with the author, Munich, February 1985.

. . . 'light-switch diplomacy' . . . see Wörmann, *Problem*, pp. 47–48.

. . . Samuel P Huntington . . . some of the thinking behind this approach is laid out in Huntington's important article, 'Trade, Techology and Leverage. Economic Diplomacy' in *Foreign Policy*, Fall 1978, pp. 63–80.

. . . Richard Perle . . . see Jentleson, *Pipeline Politics*, esp. p. 19 ff, and Hanson, *Western Economic Statecraft*.

. . . a small set of sanctions . . . see Hanson, *Western Economic Statecraft*, pp. 1, 41.

. . . a massive pipeline system . . . on this, see the extensive discussion in Jentleson, *Pipeline Politics*, Wörmann, *Problem*, and the other general treatments listed above. The Deutsche Bank's leading expert in this field, Axel Lebahn, gives his account in *Aussenpolitik*, 3/1983, pp. 256–80.

'With equal insistence . . .' Josef Joffe, *The Limited Partnership. Europe, the United States and the Burdens of Alliance* (Cambridge: Ballinger, 1987), p. 12.

. . . a 'tension-reducing role' . . . in Hans-Dietrich Genscher, ed., *Nach vorn gedacht . . . Perspektiven deutscher Aussenpolitik* (Bonn: Bonn Aktuell, 1987), p. 121.

'The Europeans have been trading . . .' Helmut Schmidt, *A Grand Strategy for the West* (New Haven: Yale University Press, 1985), pp. 128–29.

'Mars must leave . . .' quoted in *Der Spiegel* 1/1988.

... as the historian Harold James points out ... see his very stimulating book *A German Identity 1770–1990* (London: Weidenfeld & Nicolson, 1989).

'In the West ...' Jürgen Ruhfus, 'Die politische Dimension der Wirtschaftsbeziehungen zwischen Ost und West', *EA*, 1/1987, pp. 1–10. Ruhfus was then the *Staatssekretär des Auswärtigen Amtes*, that is, the top career official in the Foreign Ministry. He subsequently became Ambassador to Washington.

... 'helping Gorbachev to succeed' ... notably in his famous Davos speech of February 1987, reprinted in Genscher, *Unterwegs*, pp. 139–50.

... the CoCom list ... on the Paris-based Co-ordinating Committee on export controls, which included representatives of Japan and all members of Nato except Iceland, see particularly the relevant chapters in Gary K Bertsch & ors, eds, *After the Revolutions. East-West Trade and Technology Transfer in the 1990s* (Boulder: Westview Press, 1991). Note, however, that dual-use or industrial-list items were not subjected to a blanket prohibition, but rather to case-by-case vetting.

What David Baldwin has called ... see David Baldwin, *Economic Statecraft* (Princeton: Princeton University Press, 1985). Hanson, *Western Economic Statecraft*, takes the term from Baldwin.

As we have suggested earlier ... see above p. 178 f.

... George Kennan ... in his *Memoirs 1950–1963* (New York: Pantheon Books, 1983), p. 297.

Kissinger argued ... see *Years of Upheaval*, pp. 25–51, 985–98.

... as Philip Hanson has argued ... see Hanson, *Western Economic Statecraft*, p. 12 ff, 71 ff.

... Adam Michnik told the author ... full text of the interview in *Encounter*, January 1985. Earlier in the same interview he observed that 'the Western sanctions against the Jaruzelski regime were generally seen as an act of solidarity with the Polish people and their aspirations'. One might note that similar sentiments were expressed by South African civil rights and opposition activists about Western economic sanctions against their country.

... Neal Ascherson ... *Observer* (London), 6 August 1989.

... Zbigniew Pelczynski ... communication to the author.

... $35 billion ... $18 billion ... see Table V.

... advocated by the IMF or World Bank ... interestingly, this is sharply and concisely described by the GDR's Balance of Payments experts, Gerhard Schürer, Alexander Schalck and others, in their memorandum of 28 September 1989, see Przybylski, *Tatort 2*, pp. 358 63, this on p. 362.

... what he called 'system-opening co-operation' ... see his speech reprinted in *Bulletin* 17 June 1987, pp. 525–29, and further discussion on p. 272 f.

A typical report from an East European visit ... see, for example, Chancellor

Kohl on his visit to Prague in *Bundestag Plenarprotokolle*, 11/58, p. 3987 (4 February 1988).

. . . 'an increase of people-to-people contacts . . .' John F Kennedy, *The Strategy of Peace* (London: Hamish Hamilton, 1960), this quotation on p. 93, from a Senate speech on 21 August 1957.

'We need . . . to seek forms . . .' A revised and expanded German version of the Harvard speech was published as Willy Brandt, *Koexistenz — Zwang zum Wagnis* (Stuttgart: Deutsche Verlags-Anstalt, 1963). Brandt quoted this passage himself in his Tutzing speech on 15 July 1963, see *Dokumente*, IV/9, p. 567.

. . . implementing the détente half of . . . Harmel . . . see, for example, the observation by Horst Ehmke in *Bundestag Plenarprotokolle*, 10/228, p. 17718 (10 September 1986), and by Richard von Weizsäcker in *Bergedorfer Gesprächskreis* 84 (25 March 1988), p. 68.

. . . ideas of Helsinki . . . among general works on Helsinki in English see particularly Mastny, *Helsinki I* and *Helsinki II*, Maresca, *Helsinki*, Davy, *Détente*, chapter 9 in Van Oudenaren, *Détente*, the relevant sections in Kovrig, *Walls and Bridges*.

Henry Kissinger, for example . . . for the next two paragraphs see Maresca, *Helsinki*, esp. pp. 11, 45, 77 ff, 120 ff, 158 f, 215, Mastny, *Helsinki I*, p. 4, and Kissinger's own account in *White House Years* and *Years of Upheaval*.

'We sold it . . .' quoted in Kovrig, *Walls and Bridges*, p. 123.

. . . historic purpose after the trauma of Vietnam . . . a point made by Maresca, and very forcefully by Robert W Tucker, quoted in Mastny and Zielonka, *Human Rights and Security*, p.112,

. . . Congressional and independent initiatives . . . the Congressional Commission on Security and Co-operation was established in 1976, largely on the initiative of Congresswoman Millicent Fenwick, see Maresca, *Helsinki*, p. 207. It played an important part in goading successive administrations. Arguably even more important was the independent New York-based Helsinki Watch committee, which was established in 1978, mainly as a response to the emergence of independent 'Helsinki monitors' in the Soviet Union and Eastern Europe. It was then mainly on the initiative of the New York Helsinki Watch that an International Helsinki Federation for Human Rights, with variously constituted European affiliates, was established in Vienna in 1982. See my article in the *Independent*, 18 April 1988.

American newspapers referred . . . as recalled by Richard Davy in his perceptive chapter in Nils Andren and Karl E Birnbaum, eds, *Belgrade and Beyond. The CSCE Process in Perspective* (Alphen aan den Rijn: Sijthoff & Noordhoff, 1980), pp. 3–15, this on p. 5.

Robert Legvold has aptly observed . . . quoted in Mastny, *Helsinki I*, p. 47.

. . . 'the favourite Soviet basket' . . . thus the chapter heading in Mastny, *Helsinki I*, p. 121.

... to collate the whole vast forest ... An obvious, basic starting-point is the official Foreign Ministry publication, quoted here as *KSZE Dokumentation*. A companion volume, quoted here as *KSZE Dokumentation 1990/91*, covers developments until early 1991. A combination of documentation and analysis from the pages of *Europa-Archiv* is given in the three volumes edited by Hermann Volle and Wolfgang Wagner, *KSZE. Konferenz über Sicherheit und Zusammenarbeit in Europa* (Bonn: Verlag für Internationale Politik, 1976) — here quoted as Volle & Wagner, *KSZE* —; *Das Belgrader KSZE Folgetreffen* (Bonn: Verlag für Internationale Politik, 1978); and *Das Madrider KSZE Folgetreffen* (Bonn: Verlag für Internationale Politik, 1984). Many further official statements are then to be found in such standard sources as the *Bulletin*, the *Bundestag Plenarprotokolle*, *Bundestag Drucksachen*, *Texte*, *EA* etc.

... a virtually impossible task ... at least until the opening of the official papers of the major countries involved. What could be done now, however, is a systematic interviewing of the politicians and officials involved.

... feeding ... into the common approach ... this is stressed by Karl E Birnbaum and Ingo Peters in their very useful article on 'The CSCE. A Reassessment of its Role in the 1980s' in the *Review of International Studies* 16/1990, pp. 305–19.

... really came to life ... a point made strongly to the author by Günther van Well, Bonn, 8 July 1991. On co-operation between the nine see the article by Frans Alting von Geusau in Nils Andren and Karl E Birnbaum, *Belgrade and Beyond. The CSCE Process in Perspective* (Alphen aan den Rijn: Sijthoff & Noordhoff, 1980), pp. 17–26, Ferraris, *Report*, and the statements on behalf of the EC 9, and subsequently twelve, reprinted in *KSZE Dokumentation*.

... 'attempt to cover (*abdecken*) ...' quoted from the 10 April 1977 typescript version of the Marbella paper in AdsD: HS 002.

... 'The Federal Government had no orginal interest' ... quoted from a typescript, annotated in Schmidt's hand, in AdsD: HS 295. From the context in the file it would appear that this was in preparation for his trip to Helsinki, to sign the Final Act.

... essentially defensive goals ... this can be seen clearly in the article of early 1972 by the then State Secretary of the Foreign Ministry, Paul Frank, reprinted in Volle & Wagner, *KSZE*, pp. 41–47.

... 'throughout Europe' ... in German: *in ganz Europa*. See Maresca, *Helsinki*, p. 84, who recalls that this clause was also for some time known among delegates as the 'Andorra Clause'.

... Henry Kissinger negotiated on Germany's behalf ... this remarkable story is well told in Maresca, *Helsinki*, pp. 110–16. The final outcome hinged on the placing of a single comma.

... placed in the list of principles before ... see Volle & Wagner, *KSZE*, p. 94. Hermann von Richthofen, London, 3 March 1992.

... **Hans-Dietrich Genscher singled out** ... his speech of 25 July 1975 is reprinted in *KSZE Dokumentation*, pp. 303–15, for this see especially pp. 309–10.

... **following intensive internal discussions** ... Günther van Well recalls in particular a working party chaired by Ulrich Sahm. Günther van Well, Bonn, 8 July 1991.

... **'common rules of the game** ...' this and subsequent quotations from Brunner's article in EA 13/1973, reprinted in Volle & Wagner, *KSZE*, pp. 49–54.

... **now common to the main participants** ... see for example the statement by Harold Wilson at the Helsinki Conference: 'Détente means little if it is not reflected in the daily lives of our peoples. There is no reason why in 1975 Europeans should not be allowed to marry whom they want, hear and read what they want, travel abroad when and where they want, meet whom they want', quoted in Maresca, *Helsinki*, p. 154.

... **'a net of co-operatic** ?' ... for this and following quotations see *KSZE Dokumentation*, pp. 303–15. See also the speech by Helmut Schmidt, reprinted there on pp. 316–20.

... **would explicitly berate** ... the precedent was set by the leader of the US delegation to the Belgrade review conference, Arther Goldberg, see the chapter by Richard Davy in Nils Andren and Karl E. Birnbaum, *Belgrade and Beyond. The CSCE Process in Perspective* (Alphen aan den Rijn: Sijthoff & Noordhoff, 1980), pp. 3–15. For a sample of intra-American debate about the wisdom of this approach see Mastny, *Helsinki I*, pp. 155–65.

... **'quiet diplomacy'** ... the view is eloquently expressed in Willy Brandt, *Menschenrechte misshandelt und missbraucht* (Reinbek: Rowohlt, 1987), especially pp. 89–101, where he makes it clear that this is a continuation of the line of 'small steps' developed in Berlin in the early 1960s. For a general discussion of this problem see Carola Stern, *Strategien für die Menschenrechte* (Hamburg: Fischer Taschenbuch, extended edition, 1983).

... **the German-American difference** ... see Kovrig, *Walls and Bridges*, p. 186 ff.

... **mapped out in basket two** ... for a highly critical account of the economic provisions of the Helsinki Final Act, see the article by Philip Hanson in *International Affairs* (London), 4/1985, pp. 619–29. The statements about economic relationships in the Helsinki Final Act, writes Hanson, 'are about as businesslike as the message in an average Christmas card'.

'Decisive is first of all ...' Weizsäcker, *Deutsche Geschichte*, p. 15.

... **on the subject of economic co-operation** ... on the Bonn conference on economic conference see *Bulletin*, 20 March 1990, pp. 285–88, and *Bulletin*, 19 April 1990, pp. 357–68. The concluding document is also reprinted in *KSZE Dokumentation 1990/91*, pp. 21–33. See also Mastny, *Helsinki II*, pp. 217–28, where the initially critical reaction of the United States to the West German proposal is noted.

... quietly to establish somewhat more autonomy ... see, for example, Schmidt's comments in *Bergedorfer Gesprächskreis* 76 (17–18 December 1984), p. 20, and his article, 'Europa muss sich selbst behaupten', in *Die Zeit*, 28 November 1986. This was also seen as an objective of American Helsinki policy, Warren Zimmermann, Washington, 15 April 1987.

Schmidt sometimes presented himself ... see Link, *Ära Schmidt*, p. 309.

... tacit co-operation with East Germany ... the phrase 'tacit co-operation' comes from Karl E Birnbaum and Ingo Peters in *Review of International Studies*, 16/1990, p. 316, summarising the conclusions of a larger study.

... a concluding document ... for a brief summary see my article in the *Independent*, 20 January 1989. The complete text is in *Bulletin*, 31 January 1989, pp. 77–105, and reprinted in *KSZE Dokumentation*, p. 189 ff.

... the greatest step forward ... see Mastny, *Helsinki II*, esp. pp. 11–18, 85–144, and the chapter by William Korey in Mastny and Zielonka, *Human Rights and Security*, pp. 77–105.

... clearly spelled out at the time ... ibid., pp. 89–90.

The German foreign minister tried to push ... information from members of several delegations. See also *Financial Times*, 5 January 1989.

... the Joint Declaration signed by Helmut Kohl and Mikhail Gorbachev ... text in *Bulletin*, 15 June 1989, pp. 542–44.

... 'no one can have a greater interest ...' speech of 25 July 1975, reprinted in *KSZE Dokumentation*, pp. 303–15, this on p. 303. The Foreign Minister quoted his own words in *Bundestag Plenarprotokolle*, 9/11, p. 6782 (9 September 1982).

'The comprehensive extension ...' this in an interview in *Der Spiegel*, 24/1989.

... 'through deepened co-operation ...' *Bundestag Plenarprotokolle*, 11/49, p. 3435 (10 December 1987).

'Our policy is today in harmony ...' speech on receiving the 'Thomas-Dehler-Medaille' in Munich, 3 January 1987, issued as: Der Bundesminister des Auswärtigen, Mitteilung für die Presse No. 1005/87.

'We do not want a technological division of Europe ...' this in a speech at the Evangelische Akademie in Loccum on 20 September 1985, reprinted in *Bulletin*, 24 September 1985, pp. 889–93, this quotation on p. 892.

'Every jointly erected desulphurisation plant ...' *Bundestag Plenarprotokolle*, 11/59, p. 4111 (5 February 1988)

... the Siemens computers ... information to the author.

... the American handcuffs ... Vladimir Bukovsky, *To Build a Castle. My Life as a Dissenter* (London: André Deutsch, 1978), p. 344.

'We all have only one alternative . . .' this in a speech to the Rotary Club in New York on 14 January 1971, *Bulletin*, 15 January 1971, pp. 25–28, the quotation on p. 27.

'The Federal Republic of Germany and . . .' *Bulletin*, 15 June 1989, p. 542.

. . . worse industrial pollution . . . see, for example, the map of sulphur dioxide levels in Keith Sword, ed., *The Times Guide to Eastern Europe* (Revised edition. London: Times Books, 1991), p. 280.

'. . . let us also direct attention to our common interests . . .' John F Kennedy, Commencement Address at American University in Washinton, 10 June 1963, in *Public Papers of the Presidents. John F Kennedy, 1963* (Washington, DC: US Government Printing Office), pp. 459–64, this quotation on p. 462. Compare also the comment by Chancellor Kiesinger in his 17 June 1967 speech to the Bundestag: 'We consider it to be a proven method first to seek areas that we can walk together, in order for the time being to put aside the great disagreements. This procedure, which is an important instrument in a policy of détente, has stood its test in the relations between states.' Quoted in Meissner, *Deutsche Ostpolitik*, p. 206.

. . . not so many French or British . . . a partial exception would be some French politicians in thinking about their relationship with West Germany. The underlying thought here was to anchor West Germany still more firmly against the temptations of eastward drift: interdependence as containment.

. . . the Kissingerite notion of the 'Gulliverisation' . . . Davy, *Détente*, p. 6.

. . . Klaus Ritter . . . see his article in EA, 15–16/1970, pp. 541–58, this on p. 558. Ritter was the long-time director of the *Stiftung Wissenschaft und Politik* in Ebenhausen.

. . . a speech to mark the fortieth anniversary of the Marshall Plan . . . delivered on 12 June 1987, and printed in *Bulletin*, 17 June 1987, pp. 525–29.

'We must find other "currencies" . . .' ibid., p. 528.

. . . 'under the sign of perestroika . . .' this speech, delivered on 27 October 1987, is reprinted in Theo Sommer, ed., *Perspektiven. Europa im 21. Jahrhundert* (Berlin: Argon, 1989), pp. 93–105.

. . . 'know that it's a matter of reforming their system . . .' ibid., p. 103.

'We too have our mistakes . . .' ibid., p. 104.

'Through our policy we don't want to change . . .' *Bergedorfer Gesprächskreis*, 84 (17–18 December 1988), p. 37.

'System-opening for me . . .' ibid., p. 38. The speaker was Dr Klaus Cantzler, a director of BASF responsible for dealings with East European countries.

. . . 'that is then system-opening co-operation . . .' ibid., p. 80. The speaker was Dr Friedbert Pflüger.

'I am inclined to believe...' this in the Preface to the English edition of *Eighteen Lectures on Industrial Society* (London: Weidenfeld & Nicolson, 1967), p. 13.

... 'is the result of a closed system...' *Bulletin*, 17 June 1987, p. 528.

... 'whoever recognises the social developments...' *Bundestag Plenarprotokolle*, 11/6, p. 293 (20 March 1987).

'The Conference on Security and Co-operation in Europe has...' this in a speech in Hamburg on 17 February 1989, printed in *Bulletin*, 22 February 1989, pp. 165–67, this quotation on p. 165.

'This attempt to pull over the divided Europe...' *Bundestag Plenarprotokolle*, 9/76, p. 4427 (14 January 1982).

... *auswärtige Kulturpolitik*... the best introduction to this aspect of West German foreign policy is the collection of essays and speeches by the veteran Foreign Ministry official in this field: Witte, *Kulturpolitik*.

... guidelines in 1970.... reprinted in *Vierzig Jahre*, pp. 230–33.

... as much as one third... figures from the Foreign Ministry.

Roughly half... Witte, *Kulturpolitik*, p. 233.

... *Sprachpolitik*... ibid., p. 233 f. See also the Preface by Hans-Dietrich Genscher to *Die Stellung der deutschen Sprache in der Welt. Bericht der Bundesregierung* (Bonn: Auswärtiges Amt, 1988). This official report was originally delivered to the Bundestag in 1985.

... 'decade of stagnation'... in a useful article specifically about Germany's cultural relations with her eastern neighbours in EA 7/1991, pp. 201–10, this on p. 201.

... only in 1988... see the reports by Hans Schwab-Felisch in FAZ, 26 March 1988, and by Carl Gustaf Ströhm in *Christ und Welt/Rheinischer Merkur*, 11 March 1988. Ströhm there laments that 'Hungary — and especially the younger generation — lies under the spell of the English-American civilisation-, language-, music- and culture-offensive!'

... the official map of German cultural establishments... in *Vierzig Jahre*, Karte 14.

... more than nine million... *Die Stellung der deutschen Sprache in der Welt. Bericht der Bundesregierung* (Bonn: Auswärtiges Amt, 1988), p. 29.

... explosion of interest... on the state of German in Central and Eastern Europe see the series of articles in the Feuilleton of the FAZ, 7 March, 11 March, 25 April, 15 May and 13 June 1991. See also Joachim Born & Syvlia Dickgiesser, *Deutschsprachige Minderheiten. Ein Überblick über den Stand der Forschung für 27 Länder* (Mannheim: Institut für deutsche Sprache im Auftrag des Auswärtigen

Amtes, 1989). The Bundestag passed a resolution on 30 October 1990 supporting the promotion of German, particularly in Central and Eastern Europe, see EA 7/1991, p. 204.

... to remain ... a *lingua franca* ... in EA 7/1991, p. 204.

... 'Those who speak and understand German ...' Witte, *Kulturpolitik*, p. 234.

... 'quangos' ... most of these are listed and briefly characterised in *Die Stellung der deutschen Sprache in der Welt. Bericht der Bundesregierung* (Bonn: Auswärtiges Amt, 1988).

... pioneering German-Polish projects ... The Bosch foundation started a major programme on German-Polish relations in the mid-1970s, see *Die Robert Bosch Stiftung und die deutsch-polnischen Beziehungen* (Stuttgart: Robert Bosch Stiftung, 1986). A notable element in this programme was also the support of publications and translations, including a small 'library' of translations from Polish literature, sponsored jointly with the Deutsches Polen-Institut (Darmstadt): the "Polnische Bibliothek" edited by Karl Dedecius and published by Suhrkamp.

... a large and increasing number ... thus a breakdown of Humboldt Research Fellowships granted in the years 1953 to 1990 shows that Poland had more than twice as many as any other European country, with Yugoslavia in second and Czechoslovakia in third place, *Alexander von Humboldt-Stiftung. Programm und Profil* (Bonn, 1991), p. 11. After noting the number of Polish visiting scholars the historian Gotthold Rhode observes 'it should be remembered that in the period of the Weimar Republic there was nothing remotely comparable'. See his article in APZ, B 11–12/1988, p. 15.

No Western country sent more tourists into the East ... In 1986, some 862,000 West Germans visited Hungary and 1.3 million visited Czechoslovakia. Nearly forty per cent of all Western visitors to Czechoslovakia in that year came from West Germany. Figures from *Press- und Informationsamt der Bundesregierung*, '*Deutsch-ungarische Beziehungen*' (Typescript, October 1987) and '*Die Beziehungen zwischen der tschechoslowakischen Sozialistischen Republik und der Bundesrepublik Deutschland* (Typescript, January 1988).

... than any other Western country ... Austria and Sweden, with no visa requirement for several East European countries, obviously let in *proportionately* more.

... more than 1.3 million ... figures supplied by the German Foreign Ministry. According to the Polish Interior Ministry, of 1.129 million Poles who travelled to Western countries in 1987, 405,000—that is, more than one in three—went to West Germany.

'It is important,' Kennedy had said ... this in his speech at the Free University in West Berlin on 26 June 1963, printed in *Public Papers of the Presidents. John F Kennedy, 1963* (Washington DC: US Government Printing Office), pp. 526–29, this quotation on p. 527.

... few Western societies were more open ... the exceptions are, once again Austria and Sweden.

... a minority also sought political asylum ... according to figures supplied to me by the Federal Interior Ministry, the figures for foreigners *officially registered* as resident in the Federal Republic as of 31 December 1988 included some 625,000 Yugoslavs, 200,000 Poles, 32,500 Czechs and Slovaks, 31,000 Hungarians, and 20,000 Romanians. These figures, from the *Ausländerzentralregister*, included those applying for asylum, but excluded people with dual citizenship.

... very few of them were actually sent back ... a 1966 resolution of the Conference of *Land* Interior Ministers determined that refugees from Warsaw Pact states could not be sent back against their will. This was modified by resolutions of 1985 and 1987, which raised the *possibility* of forcible repatriation to, for example, Poland or Hungary. Jürgen Haberland, Bonn, 15 March 1989.

... through the hard currency, goods or experience ... according to official Polish estimates, the total hard-currency remittances from all Poles living abroad in 1986 and 1987 was almost equal to the hard-currency trade surplus earned by the whole of the socialised sector. Estimate by the Ministry of Internal Trade and Services, quoted by Jacek Rostowski, 'The Decay of Socialism and the Growth of Private Enterprise in Poland', in Stanisław Gomułka & Antony Polonsky, eds, *Polish Paradoxes* (London: Routledge, 1990), pp. 198–223, this on p. 200. One can safely assume that a large part of this came from Poles working—legally or less so—in the Federal Republic.

... *na saksy* ... see under *Saksy* in W. Doroszewski, ed., *Słownik Języka Polskiego* (Warsaw, 1966), Vol. VIII, p. 16. There also a nice quotation from the work of the nineteenth-century novelist Władysław Reymont: 'Let those Germans come and see what they can do here ... I went *na saksy* for so many years that I've penetrated them.'

... an acceptance speech ... read on his behalf ... see FAZ, 16 October 1989, with the text of the speech on pp. 13–14. The texts are reprinted, in Czech and German, in Börsenverein des Deutschen Buchhandels, *Friedenspreis des Deutschen Buchhandels 1989: Václav Havel. Ansprache aus Anlass der Verleihung* (Frankfurt: Verlag der Buchhändler-Vereinigung, 1989). There also the following quotations. An English version of the speech can be found in the English-language edition of *Listy* 5/1989.

... 'a traffic accident on the road to détente' ... quoted by Pierre Hassner in Gordon, *Eroding Empire*, p. 197.

'That the Soviets found their way ...' Löwenthal, *Vom kalten Krieg*, p. 78.

... what the effect might be in the other direction ... see the illuminating discussion in Pierre Hassner, *Europe in the Age of Negotiation* (Beverley Hills: Sage, 1973 = Center for Strategic and International Studies, The Washington Papers, Vol. 1, No. 8), pp. 65–68.

'of all the Western states ...' Jacek Maziarski, 'My i Niemcy', *Poglądy* (Warsaw), 12/87, pp. 32–42, this quotation on p. 41.

. . . **not against the powers-that-be** . . . a clear statement to this effect was made by Hans-Dietrich Genscher in *Bundestag Plenarprotokolle*, 10/149, p. 11150, 27 June 1985. See also the comment by Peter Bender in Böll, *Verantwortlich*, p. 32.

. . . **these independent East Central European intellectuals** . . . for a general discussion see Garton Ash, *Uses*, and Garton Ash, *Solidarity*.

. . . **'the general idea of evolution in Eastern Europe** . . .' quoted in Garton Ash, *Uses*, p. 174. See also János Kis, *Politics in Hungary. For a Democratic Alternative* (Highland Lakes, NJ: Atlantic Research and Publications/Columbia University Press, 1989).

. . . **'the power of the powerless'** . . . see Václav Havel & ors, *The Power of the Powerless. Citizens against the state in Central-Eastern Europe* (London: Hutchinson, 1985).

. . . **Leszek Kołakowski's 'Theses on Hope and Hopelessness'** . . . first published in *Kultura* (Paris), June 1971, and in English in *Survey* (London), Summer 1971.

. . . **'the New Evolutionism'** . . . see Adam Michnik, *Letters from Prison and other Essays* (Berkeley: University of Califonia Press, 1985), pp. 135–48.

. . . **the Polish Workers' Defence Committee KOR** . . . see Jan Józef Lipski, *KOR. A History of the Workers' Defense Committee in Poland, 1976–1981* (Berkeley: University of California Press, 1985).

. . . **to compel the ruling** *nomenklatura* . . . It was, however, hoped that some of the more intelligent functionaries and leaders would support some, at least, of these reforms, out of enlightened self-interest. Arguably, this did happen to some extent in Hungary, and to a lesser degree in Poland, in 1988–89.

. . . **a strong civil society** . . . there is now a large literature on the concept and significance of civil society in the East European context. For a classic statement see Ralf Dahrendorf, *Reflections on the Revolution in Europe* (London: Chatto & Windus, 1990). A useful collection is John Keane, ed., *Civil Society and the State* (London: Verso, 1988).

. . . **more fundamental goal** . . . the crowds on the streets in the East German revolution of 1989 did not chant *'Wir sind die Menschen!'* They chanted *'Wir sind das Volk!'* and *'das Volk'* in this context comes close to the Polish or Czech sense of 'society': that is, the people getting together in spite of or against the so-called people's state.

. . . **it was better for him** . . . The Soviet satirist Vladimir Voinovitch once said to me: 'you have *homo sovieticus* in the West too'. And then he told me of a distinguished Western visitor to Moscow who declined to meet with Sakharov on the grounds that this might harm Sakharov. 'What he really meant,' said Voinovitch, 'was that it would harm him, the Western visitor.'

. . . **détente could not survive** . . . see above, pp. 94. But in a fragment of his diary from 29 October 1980, Zbigniew Brzezinski records: 'The Germans have told us at the Quad meeting that détente should not be the victim of such [Soviet] intervention [in Poland]: in other words,' Brzezinski goes on, 'the Germans are saying that in the event of a Soviet intervention the Germans would be prepared to continue with their East-West relationship. This was the best proof yet of the increasing Finlandisation of the Germans.' See *Orbis* (Philadelphia), Winter 1988, pp. 32–48, this on p. 34. A slightly different selection from this diary is given in the Polish edition of his memoirs, published as *Cztery Lata W Białym Domu* (London: Polonia, 1986), this on pp. 538–60. In an entry for 15 December 1980 he there records a disagreement between the Federal Republic on the one side and the United States, Britain and France on the other, about the imposition of sanctions against the Soviet Union in the event of a Soviet intervention. This, he writes, confirms his basic view about the Finlandisation of Germany.

. . . Solidarity was, by its very nature . . . see Garton Ash, *Solidarity, passim.*

. . . a 'result' of détente . . . see her article in *Die Zeit*, 29 August 1980. A similar argument was made by Kurt Becker in a leading article in the same issue.

. . . causes of Solidarity . . . see Garton Ash, *Solidarity*, pp. 16–19, 34–36.

. . . half million . . . 4 million . . . these figures include private and 'business' visits. As with the statistics on German-German travel, the record is of visits rather than visitors. See Holzer, *Solidarität*, p. 75.

. . . already borne some fruit . . . Willy Brandt formulated the claim quite cautiously. The 'normalisation' of external relations had, he said, removed the bogey of German revanchism, and perhaps made it easier 'to talk about reforms and debate. To this extent there is a certain connection, an indirect rather than a direct one'. Interview in *Die Welt*, 16 September 1980.

. . . only 10.7 per cent . . . this was one of a remarkable series of sociological surveys entitled 'Poles '80, '81, '84 and subsequently '88. See Garton Ash, *Uses*, p. 239, note 29.

. . . recognised by Polish activists . . . see, for example, Jan Józef Lipski, *KOR. A History of the Workers' Defense Committee in Poland, 1976–1981* (Berkeley: University of California Press, 1985), pp. 24–25; references in Peter Raina, *Political Opposition in Poland, 1954–1977* (London: Poets and Painters Press, 1978).

. . . 'without Helsinki . . .' Egon Bahr in conversation with Rainer Barzel in the *Magazin* of SZ, 27 September 1991.

. . . 'convention 87 . . .' see Garton Ash, *Solidarity*, pp. 46–7.

. . . above all . . . in the interpretation given it by the United States . . . See Garton Ash, *Solidarity*, p. 22. This is also the judgement of Holzer, *Solidarität*, p. 77 f.

. . . the direct linkage . . . see, for example, the announcement by President Carter of new credits on his trip to Warsaw in 1977, as described in R F Leslie & ors, *The History of Poland since 1863* (Cambridge: Cambridge University Press, 1980), p. 438.

...**Klaus Reiff**... see his *Polen. Als deutscher Diplomat an der Weichsel* (Bonn: Dietz, 1990), pp. 53–56.

... **'What would a German court say...'** AdsD: Dep WB, BK 92, note dated 7 December 1970. Kovrig, *Walls and Bridges*, pp. 171–73, notes that in the early 1970s Senator Fulbright led a campaign to have Radio Free Europe and Radio Liberty closed down on the grounds that they were 'outworn relics of the Cold War'. Zbigniew Brzezinski, *Power and Principle. Memoirs of the National Security Adviser 1977–1981* (London; Weidenfeld & Nicolson, 1983), p. 293, recalls Helmut Schmidt complaining to him about RFE as a hindrance to détente.

... **clearly not envisaged**... see the clear statement by Peter Bender in Böll, *Verantwortlich*, pp. 41–42.

... **one Western specialist**... Alec Nove, quoted in Davy, *Détente*, p. 258.

... **too far too fast**... Helmut Schmidt records himself saying in a private conversation with François Mitterrand on 13 January 1982 that Solidarity had wanted to press the process of change forward too fast, 'which had led to the recent reverse', see Schmidt, *Nachbarn*, p. 264. For a critical view of this judgement see Garton Ash, *Solidarity*, p. 297 ff.

... **some half billion D-Marks**... Schmidt, *Nachbarn*, p. 259.

... **the latter stressed the risk**... see, for example, comments by Brandt in *Bundestag Plenarprotokolle*, 9/49 (10 September 1981), p. 2753.

'Herr Honecker was as dismayed...' recorded in the Bundespresseamt transcript, BPA — Nachrichtenabt., Ref. II R3, Rundf.-Ausw. Deutschland, DFS/13.12.81/12.55/he.

... **'that it was a mistake...'** Bölling, *Die fernen Nachbarn*, p. 157. In his memoirs, Schmidt himself describes this as 'a not entirely happy choice of words', see Schmidt, *Nachbarn*, p. 74.

... **'I stand with all my heart...'** *Bundestag Plenarprotokolle*, 9/74, p. 4289 (18 December 1981).

... **a high-level Polish defector**... Colonel Ryszard Kukliński. See the interview with him, and additional material from Richard Pipes and Zbigniew Brzezinski, in *Orbis* (Philadelphia), Winter 1988. See also the discussion in Garton Ash, *Solidarity*, pp. 357–58.

An internal East German assessment... draft of 30 December 1981, now in ZPA: IV 2/2.035/86.

... **a storm of political and publicistic argument**... the best starting point is certainly Böll, *Verantwortlich*, although this collects contributions almost exclusively from left and centre authors. Also useful is the documentation by the independent, left-wing Berlin daily, *Die Tageszeitung* — the *taz* — which had consistently good and critical reporting on East Central Europe, and on German (especially SPD) policies towards it. See *Polen. "Euch den Winter, uns den*

Frühling" (Berlin: Taz-Verlag, 1982). Commentaries from the right and centre-right have not been so conveniently collected.

. . . **Herbert Wehner** . . . Wehner's visit, which caused a considerable stir at the time, and the embrace of Jaruzelski, is briefly described in Klaus Reiff, *Polen. Als deutscher Diplomat an der Weichsel* (Bonn: Dietz, 1990), pp. 302–06. For Solidarity activists' dismay at this, and the visit of Karsten Voigt, see the report by Gert Baumgarten in *Der Tagesspiegel*, 17 February 1982. A copy of Wehner's letter to parliamentary colleagues, dated 15 February 1982, and the enclosed appeal from the Bolivian 'consulate in resistance' (with handwritten note: 'Dear Herr Wehner, heartfelt thanks for the support you are giving us . . .'), is in the Wehner file in the press archive of the SPD.

. . . **also from French and Italian socialists** . . . see the sharp criticism of the line taken by Willy Brandt as Chairman of the Socialist International, reported in *Der Spiegel*, 1/1982.

. . . **from Poles who had actually been locked up** . . . see above, pp. 304–05.

. . . **and quite as emotionally** . . . the emotion was directed notably against the American advocates of sanctions. Thus, for example, the leading Social Democrat Erhard Eppler, after suggesting that 'above all we must take Jaruzelski at his word,' argued: 'Whoever now imposes sanctions, does not make it easier for Jaruzelski to keep his word, but more difficult. Whoever decrees such sanctions from the USA, must be told a thing or two by Europeans: Firstly, if you please, Poland lies in Europe and is therefore mainly a matter for the Europeans.' Quoted from Böll, *Verantwortlich*, pp. 84–85.

. . . **'wishing success** . . .' *Die Zeit*, 18 December 1981, p. 1.

. . . **'the highest priority** . . .' Egon Bahr in *Vorwärts*, 21 January 1982, but see also many contributions to Böll, *Verantwortlich*.

. . . **'even more important** . . .' *Vorwärts*, 24 December 1981.

. . . **'stability with a moderate continuation** . . .' ibid.

. . . **'the Hungarian model'** . . . interview in *Der Spiegel*, 1/1982, this on p. 24.

. . . **we have to think of our own German interests too** . . . 'Is it presumptuous today to make clear that in this ethics of détente there were and are also German interests?' Freimut Duve in Böll, *Verantwortlich*, p. 75.

'In the GDR . . .' Bölling, *Die fernen Nachbarn*, p. 121.

'Bonn depends on the Soviet Union . . .' Hendrik Bussiek in Böll, *Verantwortlich*, p. 60.

. . . **Rakowski could not simply be assumed** . . . although Marion Gräfin Dönhoff came close to it when she wrote, following Rakowski's visit to Bonn, of the satisfaction of people who ten years before could not have imagined 'that Bonn is the only capital in which *the Poles* seek help . . .' (my italics), see *Verantwortlich*, p. 68, reprinting an article from *Die Zeit* of 22 January 1982.

'I shall very much follow . . .' interview in *Der Spiegel*, 1/1982.

'When a freely-founded union . . .' *Bundestag Plenarprotokolle*, 9/74, p. 4296 (18 December 1981).

When Franz Josef Strauss visited Poland . . . This was part of a tour through East Central Europe in which, travelling ostensibly as a private tourist, Strauss nonetheless met political leaders including Jaruzelski and Honecker. In an interview with Radio Polonia, Strauss said: 'In Poland life had to be restored, that is, chaos had to be prevented. The fleeting impressions of a political tourist are that the situation has been consolidated . . .', although he did go on to say that he still sensed worries among the people, who wanted 'bread, peace, freedom'. See the transcript published in *Die Welt*, 29 July 1983. Strauss was there just as martial law was lifted and argued that his remarks were aimed at encouraging Jaruzelski to take further positive steps, see the long report in *Bayernkurier*, 6 August 1983.

. . . major power . . . most understanding . . . of the less important Western states, Greece under Papandreou showed even more demonstrative understanding, and thereby also complicated the co-ordination of public postures in Nato and the EC.

. . . 'the renormalisation of political contacts' Berthold Johannes, 'Mitteleuropa? Gesellschaftliche Grundlage der Entwicklung der Beziehungen zwischen der Bundesrepublik Deutschland und Polen', in *Frankreich – Europa – Weltpolitik. Festschrift für Gilbert Ziebura* (Opladen: Westdeutscher Verlag, 1989), pp. 227–36, this on p. 232.

. . . called off at twelve hours' notice . . . see Radio Free Europe Research, Background Report 4, 15 January 1988. A third reason for the cancellation was the Polish authorities' refusal to grant a visa for the visit to a well-known right-wing journalist, the *Die Welt* commentator, Carl Gustaf Ströhm.

. . . not . . . until January 1988 . . . although he did make a short stop-over visit, en route from Helsinki to Sofia, in March 1985.

. . . very difficult negotiations . . . see the authoritative but highly diplomatic account by the chief negotiator, Chancellor Kohl's foreign policy adviser, Horst Teltschik, in *Aussenpolitik* (English-language edition), 1/90, pp. 3–14. For background and further detail see Bingen, *Bonn-Warschau*, and Artur Hajnicz, 'Poland Within its Geopolitical Triangle' in *Aussenpolitik* (English-language edition), 1/89.

. . . more by good luck than by design . . . ibid, p. 8. The Bonn government did, however, deliberately delay the visit in the summer of 1989, following Solidarity's success in the June elections.

. . . but not of course only West German . . . a point made frequently and eloquently by the British political scientist George Schöpflin. See, for example, his trenchant 'Hungary: No Model for Reform' in *Soviet Analyst*, Vol. 12, No. 23 (23 November 1983), pp. 3–7. The British government was almost as fulsome as the Bonn government in the welcome it gave to Károly Grósz when he became party leader in 1988.

... **a DM 1 billion loan** ... see reports in FAZ, 8 October 1987, SZ, 9 October 1987

... **the communist Károly Grósz** ... in his case the label 'communist' may be justified, for, after the emergence of a multi-party landscape in Hungary, he remained as leader of the old Hungarian Socialist Workers' Party rather than joining the new Hungarian Socialist Party.

... **a contribution to further 'reform'** ... see Bulletin, 14 October 1987, pp. 881–83.

'We spent two thirds ...' This was quoted, without naming Németh, in an article by Joseph Fitchett in the *International Herald Tribune*, 24 March 1989, p. 2. Miklós Németh subsequently confirmed, in conversation with the author, that we was the speaker quoted, and that his view was that this loan had been substantially misused. He had said as much in the Hungarian parliament in December 1989 and also in conversation with West German leaders. Miklós Németh, Oxford, 22 January 1991.

... **the record is also complex** ... in the following few paragraphs I draw heavily on my own experience in this field. In this connection I would like to thank all those I worked with in the Central and East European Publishing Project, the Jagiellonian Trust, the Fondation pour une Entraide Intellectuelle Européenne, the International Helsinki Federation for Human Rights and the Stefan Batory Trust.

... **the German embassy had to ask the American embassy** ... information from the then American ambassador to Budapest, Mark Palmer.

The West German committee ... largely decorative ... This judgement might of course be disputed, not least by its chairperson, Annemarie Renger. A letter of 26 January 1984 from Annemarie Renger to a leading Christian Democratic member of the committee (and opponent of Ostpolitik) Werner Marx, now in ACDP: I-356-250, makes it clear that the founding of the German committee arose directly from the initiative of the International Helsinki Federation for Human Rights, in which the US Helsinki Watch group played the most dynamic part. The director of US Helsinki Watch, Jeri Laber, told the author, with regret, about the largely decorative role of the German committee. An even more critical verdict was given to the author by a disaffected former member of the German Helsinki committee, Martin Kriele (Leverkusen, 6 July 1991). In the Marx papers there is also a letter from Werner Marx to Martin Kriele, dated 27 February 1985, in which Marx writes that for at least eight months he has felt very unhappy to be the deputy chairman of a 'non-functioning association'. This in ACDP: I-356-250.

... **George Soros** ... 'Open Society Fund had an endowment of $3 million a year from 1979 on. Most, but not all, of this amount was spent in Eastern Europe.

In later years I made additional contributions.' Letter from George Soros to the author, 30 April 1992.

. . . 'you cannot have democracy without . . .' quoted from his article in the *Independent*, 12 August 1991.

. . . the 'stability commandment' . . . thus Eberhard Schulz in Ehmke, *Zwanzig Jahre*, p. 219.

. . . Volker Rühe . . . see *Bundestag Plenarprotokolle* 11/106 (10 November 1988), p. 7289.

. . . 'the process of reform . . .' reprinted in *Bulletin*, 12 June 1989, pp. 530–35, this on p. 532. It is noteworthy — and was noted by members of Hungary's democratic opposition — that the guest of honour at this inaugural meeting of a liberal party foundation was a foreign policy functionary of the Hungarian Socialist Workers' Party.

. . . 'Not only the Social Democrats . . .' Hans-Peter Schwarz, 'Auf dem Weg zum post-kommunistischen Europa', in EA, 11/1989, pp. 319–30, this on p. 326.

'the blessing of a late birth' . . . see his speech in the Israeli Knesset in *Bulletin*, 2 February 1984, pp. 112–13. The phrase was originally coined by Günter Gaus, see his *Die Welt der Westdeutschen*. (Köln: Kiepenheuer & Witsch, 1986), pp. 111–12.

. . . that Adenauer had achieved with France and Israel . . . for this comparison, see, for example, his statement in *Bulletin*, 13 July 1989, p. 653, and *Bulletin*, 9 September 1991, p. 96.

Richard von Weizsäcker recalls . . . in conversation with the author, Bonn, 30 September 1991.

. . . their 1965 report . . . this seminal document is reprinted in *Dokumente* IV/2, pp. 869–97. It is ably discussed and set in context by Erwin Wilkens, *Vertreibung und Versöhnung. Die "Ostdenkschrift" als Beitrag zur deutschen Ostpolitik* (Hannover: Lutherhaus Verlag, 1986).

'We forgive and ask for forgiveness . . .' The text of this remarkable letter, which is in large part an essay on the relationship between Polish Catholicism and Polish nationalism in the run-up to the millennium celebrations of 1966, is reprinted in *Dokumente* IV/2, pp. 940–47, this on p. 947. On the background to it, see now the article by Piotr Madajczyk in VfZ, 40/2 (1992), pp. 223–40.

'We, too, ask to forget . . .' see the text of the German bishops' letter in *Dokumente* IV/2, pp. 973–76, this on p. 975.

. . . many individual writers . . . for example, Hansjakob Stehle, *Deutschlands Osten — Polens Westen?* (Frankfurt: Fischer, 1965).

. . . historians . . . Gotthold Rhode, a venerable German historian of Poland, notes that the first post-war German-Polish historians' meeting took place as early as October 1956. Significantly, all the Polish historians came from the emigration. See his article in APZ, B 11-12/88, p. 12.

... **young Social Democrats** ... see the vivid short description in Bender, *Neue Ostpolitik*, p. 20.

..., **'the immediate gain ...'** This from a letter dated 9 December 1970, now in AdsD: Dep WB, BK6. Grass's letter of 25 November 1970 proposing that he, Siegfried Lenz and Marion Gräfin Dönhoff should accompany the Chancellor to Warsaw is in the same file. Marion Gräfin Dönhoff wrote on 7 December to explain why she could not bring herself to accompany him (BK4). On the same day Rudolf Augstein wrote to complain that he had not been included in the party whereas Henri Nannen of the rival *stern* had been (BK1). There was clearly some competition for the privilege of being allowed to be moved.

'... **recognise morality as a political force'** ... quoted in Bender, *Neue Ostpolitik*, p. 179.

'We want to be a nation of good neighbours ...' *Bundestag Plenarprotokolle*, 6/5, p. 34 (28 October 1969).

'The social-liberal coalition ...' *Bundestag Plenarprotokolle*, 9/111, p. 6760 (9 September 1982).

'We lived until 1945 ...' quoted in Kuwaczka, *Entspannung von Unten*, pp. 256–57.

... **the testimony of one unnamed German woman** ... in Theodor Schieder & ors, eds, *Dokumentation der Vertreibung der Deutschen aus Ost-Mitteleuropa*, (Munich: Deutscher Taschenbuch Verlag, 1984 = Reprint of original 1954 edition), Vol. I/2, pp. 439–41.

... **Konrad Adenauer was restoring German 'honour'** ... on this, see the vivid account in Schwarz, *Adenauer I*, pp. 897–906.

... **'In the relationship with Poland, too, ...'** *Bundestag Plenarprotokolle*, 6/93, p. 5044 (28 January 1971).

... **right through the 1980s** ... see Bingen, *Bonn-Warschau*, pp. 29–50, and, for the end of the 1980s, the excellent reports of Stefan Dietrich in the FAZ.

... **'An open letter to all Germans ...'** see the special German-language issue of *Kultura* (Paris), Autumn 1984, pp. 80–83. Also reprinted in Kuwaczka, *Entspannung von Unten*, pp. 140–43.

... **unreconciled or unrepentant** ... some of whom nonetheless also used the language of 'reconciliation'. See, for example, E von der Brahe, *Polen und Deutsche. Wie ist eine Versöhung möglich?* (Lausanne: Kritik-Verlag, 1986), which, on inspection, argues that such a 'reconciliation' is only possible if the Poles give back West Prussia — that is, part of Poland since 1918! — to the Germans. It may fairly be objected that these were marginal voices. Yet the author found this work prominently displayed in a leading Bonn bookshop, together with a map showing

Germany in the frontiers of 1937. See also the correspondence columns of the FAZ, *passim*.

... 'terrible things ...' *Bulletin*, 13 July 1989, p. 653.

'The consequences of war and war crimes ...' *Bulletin*, 30 August 1989, p. 713. A detailed, sensitive and even more carefully balanced statement was issued on this occasion by a group of prominent Polish and German Catholics, *Für Freiheit, Gerechtigkeit und Frieden in Europa. Erklärung polnischer und deutscher Katholiken zum 1. September 1989* (Bonn: Zentralkomitee der deutschen Katholiken, 1989).

... the West German *Historikerstreit* ... see the references given above, p. 541.

... if one sought 'reconciliation' with the rulers ... interestingly enough, precisely this point was made by Franz Josef Strauss in opposing the ratification of the Warsaw Treaty. 'The question of reconciliation with Poland,' he declared in the ratification debate on 24 February 1972, '... which we very much want, goes far deeper than the superficial support for their present powerholders, who want recognition and economic support as a means to strengthen their system.' *Bundestag Plenarprotokolle*, 6/172, p. 9911. The fact that this argument was advanced by Franz Josef Strauss does not *ipso facto* make it false.

... 'take him straight into the cabinet' ... Bölling, *Die fernen Nachbarn*, p. 157. See also the perceptive observations by Schmidt's former speechwriter, Jochen Thies, *Helmut Schmidt's Rückzug von der Macht. Das Ende der Ära Schmidt aus nächster Nähe* (Stuttgart: Bonn Aktuell, 1988), pp. 122–24. Schmidt's own account of his relationship with Gierek is in *Nachbarn*, esp. pp. 479 ff and 508.

... on the election of a Polish Pope ... *Bulletin*, 19 October 1978, p. 1097.

... asking Erich Honecker to use his good offices ... Bölling, *Die fernen Nachbarn*, p. 157.

His 'specifically German motive' ... this and subsequent quotations from Schmidt, *Menschen und Mächte*, pp. 306–07.

... 'with all his heart' ... *Bundestag Plenarprotokolle*, 9/74, p. 4289 (18 December 1981).

... Kazimierz Wóycicki ... see his article 'Hass auf die Deutschen?' in *Kursbuch*, No. 81, September 1985, pp. 131–35, the quotation on pp. 134–35.

... these *Hitlerowcy* ... the post-war Polish term which applies roughly to all Germans who did Hitler's bidding, i.e. rather more than merely 'Hitlerites' or 'Nazis', but less than simply 'Germans'.

... 'everything' would be '*kaputt*' ... quoted in *Der Spiegel*, 1/1982.

... 'that it made me angry ...' in the special German-language issue of *Kultura* (Paris), Autumn, 1984, p. 42.

... an appeal to Willy Brandt ... ibid., pp. 48–49.

Willy Brandt did come to Poland . . . for an excellent account of this visit, and reactions to it, see the article by Harry Schleicher, 'Hoffnung auf das "moralische Kapital" ', in *Frankfurter Rundschau*, 20 December 1985. For an account sympathetic to Brandt see the article by Gerhard Hirschfeld, 'Der Besuch Brandts in Warschau galt dem Volk', in *Vorwärts*, 14 December 1985. For criticism from the Polish opposition see, for example, *Le Monde*, 10 December 1985, where the leading Solidarity adviser Bronisław Geremek is quoted as saying 'The reasoning of many German leaders is limited to their own interests, not those of Europe'; the letter from the veteran Polish socialist, Edward Lipiński, quoted in FAZ, 30 November 1985; the open letter from the Warsaw regional executive, *Tygodnik Mazowsze* No. 148 (reprinted in Kuwaczka, *Entspannung von Unten*, pp. 148–53), and the subsequent commentary in *Tygodnik Mazowsze*, Nos. 149 and 150.

. . . **nor even on that of the murdered Father Popiełuszko** . . . starting with a visit by the junior (British) Foreign Office minister, Malcolm Rifkind, in November 1984, it had by now become regular practice for official Western visitors to pay their respects at the grave of the martyred priest. There was thus no objective obstacle to Brandt doing the same. The ommission was finally made good by Brandt's successor, Hans-Jochen Vogel, on his visit in the autumn of 1987, when he also had a very direct encounter with leading Solidarity advisers. See the reports in *Der Spiegel*, 41/1987, and *Vorwärts*, 3 October 1987.

He declined an invitation . . . Bronisław Geremek recalls drafting the letter of invitation from Wałęsa, which was sent via an intermediary, who returned with a verbal answer. As Geremek recalls, the message given from Brandt — or on Brandt's behalf — was that it would not be possible for him to accept this invitation, and the very fact of extending it was to put him, Brandt, under unacceptable pressure! When Geremek raised the issue with Brandt on a subsequent encounter, Brandt's response included the argument that, instead of making the public gesture of going to Gdańsk he was able to make a private appeal to Jaruzelski to issue a visa for Geremek to come to the West. (Bronisław Geremek, Oxford, 1 May 1992.) This was entirely in line with the Brandt approach since the mid-1960s — quiet diplomacy for humane alleviations rather than public demands for human rights — but entirely at odds with the real requirements of Solidarity, for which the public symbolic politics were infinitely more important than any small, individual humanitarian concessions, which the Jaruzelski regime was generally only too happy to concede. On a charitable interpretation, Brandt was thus mistakenly applying an approach developed in an earlier period, and for different circumstances.

As reported in *Tygodnik Mazowsze*, No. 157, Brandt subsequently wrote to Wałęsa, explaining his actions.

A singular and revealing account of this episode is given in Hans Gerlach, *Europa braucht Polen. Begegnungen, Gespräche, Reflexionen* (Frankfurt: Fischer Taschenbuch Verlag, 1987), pp. 135–39. Gerlach emphasises that as 'a German of the war generation', he may be inclined to view Poland 'in too rosy a light' (p. 175). On this episode he recalls that Brandt 'talked freely of the pressures (*Pressionen*) which had he had been put under even before the journey. There was an "invitation" from Wałęsa, which was not one at all, so Brandt said. Allegedly Wałęsa and a former press spokesman (*sic*) of Solidarity, Masowiecki (*sic*), had expressed their dismay that the SPD chairman would not go to Danzig and that he had come to Poland at this time at all.' None of Brandt's critics, Gerlach continues, 'seemed to have spared even one thought for the connection between the ability to reform, that is, concretely, generosity towards enemies of the regime, and the normalisation of the situation internally and externally. So long as the Polish government had to fear, with some justification, open or concealed enemies, they could not release those political prisoners who were dangerous in their view. Should one arrest them again, with all the adverse attention at home and abroad, if they again used their freedom for agitation? This question was posed again and again, not only by people like Press Spokesman Urban, but also by Rakowski.' Gerlach's understanding for the cares of the gaolers is almost touching. The spirit of reconciliation moves in mysterious ways, its wonders to perform.

. . . one of the most generous texts . . . 'Two fatherlands, two patriotisms', Polish text in *Kultura* (Paris) 10/1981. German translation in the German-language edition of *Kontinent*, No. 22, July 1982, with an introduction by Gotthold Rhode.

West German historians exercised heroic patience . . . see, for example, the hilarious footnote polemics on the historical chapters in Jacobsen, *Bundesrepublik-Volksrepublik*.

'Germans and Poles have found their way . . .' *Bulletin*, 2 February 1982, p. 69.

'People are often ahead of politics . . .' *Bulletin*, 30 August 1989, p. 714.

. . . 'We need a breakthrough . . .' *Trybuna Ludu*, 13 September 1989, p. 3.

. . . cultural, scholarly and youth exchanges . . . among these one should mention the regular series of German-Polish Forums held since 1977; the German Academic Exchange Service (DAAD) and the Alexander von Humboldt Foundation stipends that over the years brought hundreds of Polish scholars and intellectuals to the Federal Republic; the German-Polish Institute in Darmstadt, and the extensive German-Polish programme of the Robert Bosch Stiftung.

. . . a 1981 survey of Warsaw schoolchildren . . . reported in *German Politics and Society* (Harvard), No. 9, October 1986, p. 25.

. . . a major survey in 1991 . . . see the report in *Der Spiegel*, 36/1991.

. . . a pretty low opinion . . . see, the survey report in *Der Spiegel* 47/1990, which shows both East and West Germans giving a negative sympathy rating for Poland. An Infratest survey conducted for the Rand corporation in the autumn of 1991 produced a similar negative sympathy rating, see the report by Ronald D Asmus in Rand Paper P-7767 (1992), this on p. 3. In a perceptive article in FAZ, 9 November 1989, at the time of Kohl's visit, Stefan Dietrich reports Polish survey results placing the Federal Republic second to last in a sympathy table of eighteen countries, with forty-four per cent of those asked in a poll by *Gazeta Wyborcza* regarded 'Germans' (West or East) with hostility or distaste. Clearly many caveats should be entered about these data, but the general impression they give was by no means at odds with everyday experience.

. . . **as one independent Polish writer put it** . . . Jacek Maziarski in *Poglądy* (Warsaw), p. 39.

. . . **the nationalism of the victim** . . . see Garton Ash, *Uses*, p. 121.

. . . **his long-delayed official visit** . . . for the main texts see *Bulletin*, 16 November 1989.

A state visit by Richard von Weizsäcker . . . in an interview with *Der Spiegel* 18/1990, von Weizsäcker described this as 'my most important task in my office in foreign relations'. But the trip, though successful, was in the event quite low-key.

. . . **the first time in 990 years** . . . Stefan Dietrich in FAZ, 27 April 1990. In the year 1000 AD, Emperor Otto III visited Gniezno to participate in the funeral celebrations of the martyr Wojtech/Adalbert.

. . . **'once and for all'** . . . see *Bundestag Plenarprotokolle*, 12/39, p. 3256 (6 September 1991).

. . . **'stepping out** . . . **from under the shadow** . . .' see extracts from his speech in January 1987, reprinted in *Frankfurter Rundschau*, 14 January 1987 and Strauss's own article in *Bayernkurier*, 17 January 1987, which appears to be an edited version of the speech. But see also the interview in *Die Welt*, 17 January 1987, where Strauss explains what he meant.

. . . **'only just beginning'** . . . Eduard Neumaier in *Rheinischer Merkur*, 10 November 1989.

Chapter VI: A Second Ostpolitik

. . . **the proper study of public opinion** . . . for a study which pays particular and expert attention to the evolution of public opinion with respect to German foreign policy, see Schweigler, *Grundlagen*.

. . . **'a second phase of Ostpolitik'** . . . see Moseleit, *Zweite Phase*, p. 1, note 2 and *passim*. Moseleit's book is a careful but highly favourable account, by someone who was actively engaged in the formulation of the party's new thinking. Moseleit himself prefers the label 'second phase of détente policy'. For the more casual but also more catching usage 'second Ostpolitik' see, for example, Peter Glotz in conversation with Eric Hobsbawm in *Marxism Today*, August 1987, p. 14, and Glotz's comments at a press conference following a meeting with Jan Fojtik in Prague, reproduced in the press service of the SPD, 14 April 1988 (318/88).

Karsten Voigt . . . **January 1980** . . . see Moseleit, *Zweite Phase*, p. 1, quoting from NG, 1/1980. In a retrospective conversation with the author (Bonn, 20 March 1992), Karsten Voigt himself stressed the importance of going back to 1980 to understand the party's second Ostpolitik.

... what Horst Ehmke would call ... see his article in NG, 12/1987, pp. 1073–1080, this on p. 1073.

... 'the continuation of Ostpolitik ..' interview in *Zukunft*, 10 October 1986, pp. 8–9.

'... the key to everything' ... Bahr, *Zum europäischen Frieden*, p. 35.

... carried forward by a younger generation ... see Moseleit, *Zweite Phase*, p. 40, and *passim*.

... clearly influenced by ... movement ... on this see also the sharp observations in Baring, *Grössenwahn*, p. 78 ff and *passim*.

... first 'ventured' to formulate ... Bahr, *Zum europäischen Frieden*, p. 23.

... the Palme Commission report ... published in English as *Common Security. A programme for disarmament* (London: Pan Books, 1992).

... the need for a 'security partnership' ... see the full text of Schmidt's speech in *SPD Parteitag. 19–23 April 1982, München. Protokoll* (Bonn: SPD Vorstand, 1982), pp. 126–65, this on p. 149.

Egon Bahr ... respectfully referred ... ibid., p. 310.

... a specialist close to Bahr spelled out ... Dieter S. Lutz, *Security Partnership and/or Common Security? On the Origins and Development of a New Concept and on the Criticism and Reaction to it in the Federal Republic of Germany and the German Democratic Republic* (Hamburg: Institut für Friedensforschung und Sicherheitspolitik, 1986).

... as Bahr himself wrote ... quoted in ibid., p. 5.

... substantial elements of earlier Social Democratic plans ... a point well made by Stephen F Szabo in his article in *SAIS Review*, Summer-Fall 1987, pp. 51–62.

... Protestant theologians ... see, for example, the works of Dorothee Sölle. For some samples from the Hamburg church congress of June 1981, see Baring, *Grössenwahn*, pp. 290–92.

... security issues ... Moseleit, *Zweite Phase*, lists many of the publications in his extensive bibliography.

... Andreas von Bülow ... specifically on this see the useful article by Heinz Brill in *Neue politische Literatur* 1/1986, pp. 82–91. The commission actually produced several papers, but the one that became known as the 'Bülow paper' and caused a furore was a typescript of September 1985, published in *Frankfurter Rundschau*, 13 & 14 September 1985.

... 'structural non-offensive capacity' ... a very useful introduction to this particular concept is the Friedrich-Ebert-Stiftung paper by Christian Krause, *Strukturelle Nichtangriffsfähigkeit im Rahmen europäischer Entspannungspolitik* (Bonn, January 1987).

Liberation from the Bomb . . . *Die Befreiung von der Bombe. Welfrieden, europäischer Weg und die Zukunft der Deutschen.* (Köln: Bund-Verlag, 1986).

Fear of the Friends . . . Oskar Lafontaine, *Angst vor den Freunden. Die Atomwaffenstrategie der Supermächte zerstört die Bündnisse* (Reinbek: Rowohlt, 1984).

The critical distance . . . from the policies of the United States . . . on this aspect, particularly, see the excellent article by Ronald D Asmus, 'The SPD's Second Ostpolitik with Perspectives from the USA' in *Aussenpolitik* (English-language edition) 4/1986, pp. 40–55.

. . . the Selbstbehauptung Europas . . . a party working group under the chairmanship of Horst Ehmke actually produced a document in January 1984 entitled *Programm für die Selbstbehauptung Europas*, see Moseleit, *Zweite Phase*, p. 46. For Ehmke's article based on this paper see EA, 7/1984, pp. 195–204.

. . . coined . . . by Peter Bender . . . see his book *Das Ende des ideologischen Zeitalters. Die Europäisierung Europas* (Berlin: Severin & Siedler, 1981).

. . . 'relative vassals . . . ' quoted in Moseleit, *Zweite Phase*, p. 22.

. . . Mitteleuropa . . . on this see my article in *Daedalus*, Winter 1990, pp. 1–21 and the further references given there. As I note there, the word *Mitteleuropa* had, however, already appeared in the disarmament plans of the SPD in the 1950s — and notably in the 'Deutschlandplan' of 1959. As noted above, Brandt listed '*MI*' — that is, on his own reading, *Mitteleuropa* — top of his list of 'hopes' in his talks with Brezhnev in August 1970, see above p. 75.

The pioneer . . . Karl Schlögel . . . see his *Die Mitte liegt ostwärts. Die Deutschen, der verlorene Osten und Mitteleuropa* (Berlin: Siedler, 1986), and his contribution to Spangenberg, *Mitteleuropa*, pp. 11–31.

. . . 'the proclamation . . . ' this in Spangenberg, *Mitteleuropa*, p. 31. Schlögel here came out in favour of an 'antipolitical' revival of the concept, alluding to the notion of 'antipolitics' popularised by György Konrád.

'The renaissance of Mitteleuropa . . .' in Spangenberg, *Mitteleuropa*, p. 87.

'In the desire for détente . . .' ibid., p. 102.

'. . . divided from the margins in . . .' ibid., p. 103.

'We must win back Mitteleuropa . . .' NG 7/1986, p. 585. As chief editor of *Neue Gesellschaft/Frankfurter Hefte*, Glotz made it a forum for discussion on this theme.

'Let us use the concept of Mitteleuropa . . .' in *Niemandsland* 2/1987, p. 127. There also the following quotations.

. . . Eppler . . . leading an extensive exercise . . . see Erhard Eppler, ed., *Grundwerte für ein neues Godesberger Programm. Die Texte der Grundwerte-Kommission der SPD* (Reinbek: Rowohlt, 1984).

. . . nothing is more important than peace . . . this formula seems to have emerged in the peace movement in response to a comment by Alexander Haig to the effect that there are things more important than peace. See the interview with Heinrich Albertz in Böll, *Verantwortlich*, pp. 18–24, esp. p. 20.

. . . 'lifting ideology onto the same level . . . ' quoted by Heinrich August Winkler in his contribution to Jürgen Maruhn & Manfred Wilke, eds, *Wohin treibt die SPD? Wende oder Kontinuität sozialdemokratischer Sicherheitspolitik* (Munich: Günter Olzog Verlag, 1984), p. 31. He gives his sources as *Vorwärts*, 20 October 1983.

. . . 'deideologisation' . . . The notion was implicit in Peter Bender's title, *Das Ende des ideologischen Zeitalters*. Critics were charged with the heinous error of 'reideologisation', see the article by one such critic, Gesine Schwan, in *Rheinischer Merkur*, 20 July 1985. The 'end of ideology' had of course been proclaimed by Daniel Bell and others twenty years before.

. . . 'Peace is not everything . . .' the 'government programme 1987–1990' is printed in the *Protokoll vom Wahlparteitag der SPD in Offenburg 25. Oktober 1986* (Bonn: SPD Vorstand, 1986), pp. 107–54, this on p. 145.

. . . originated from the Social Democratic side . . . Moseleit, *Zweite Phase*, p. 25, suggests that it was first used by Rudolf von Thadden in 1981.

. . . 'Peace of Augsburg' . . . Gaus, *Deutschland, p. 275.*

. . . 'Peace of Westphalia' . . . thus Karsten Voigt in *Bundestag Plenarprotokolle*, 10/4, p. 135 (4 May 1983), 10/23, p. 1613 (16 September 1983), 10/35, p. 2449 (21 November 1983).

. . . the 'government programme' of 1983 . . . printed in *SPD Wahlparteitag-Dortmund 21. Januar 1983. Protokoll* (Bonn: SPD Vorstand, 1983), pp. 161–92.

'Humankind . . .' ibid., p. 88. There also the following quotations.

'never led Germany into a war' . . . A carping historian might, however, point out that the SPD had, famously, voted funds for war in 1914.

'The peoples in the East-West conflict . . .' the text of the resolution can be found in *Politik. Informationsdienst der SPD*, Nr. 8, September 1986. There also the following quotations.

. . . 'securing peace' . . . *Protokoll vom Wahlparteitag der SPD in Offenburg 25. Oktober 1986* (Bonn: SPD Vorstand, 1986), pp. 145–53. There also the following quotations.

. . . legitimised and facilitated . . . thus the report from the Soviet to the East German Party leadership on Willy Brandt's meeting with Gorbachev in May 1985 concludes by confirming the usefulness of increasing contacts with the Social Democrats 'as well as the possibility of actively involving the Social Democrats in the broad front of the struggle for preserving peace and banishing the danger of a new world war'. Quoted from the report ('Information') of 6 June 1985 in ZPA: IV 2/2.035/65.

... **supporting role** ... see also the pertinent observation of Moseleit, *Zweite Phase*, pp. 52–53.

... **ceremonious joint statements** ... the most ceremonious of these, a joint declaration with the Polish United Workers' Party on 'measures of mutual confidence-building', was published, with a joint preface signed by Brandt and Jaruzelski, on 25 November 1985. The joint group with the Hungarian Socialist Workers' Party produced a number of joint declarations, see for example the daily information service of the Social Democratic parliamentary party, 1845/1986, 533/1987.

... **vague joint proposals** ... see the statement of the joint working group led by Anatoly Dobrynin and Egon Bahr in the press service of the SPD, 13 October 1987 (842/87).

... **'many arguments ...'** Soviet memorandum of 15 October 1984, now in ZPA: IV 2/2.035/65.

... **the great schism** ... see Carl E Schorske, *German Social Democracy 1905–1917. The Development of the Great Schism* (New York: Harper Torchbook, 1972); Leszek Kołakowski, *Main Currents of Marxism* (Oxford: Clarendon Press, 1978), Volume 2; George Lichtheim, 'Social Democracy and Communism: 1918–1968' in *Studies in Comparative Communism*, Vol. 3, No. 1, January 1970, pp. 5–30. A very useful collection of documents is Weber, *Links*.

... **a Communist would tap furious polemics** ... this is recounted by Axel Eggebrecht, in his memoirs *Der halbe Weg. Zwischenbilanz einer Epoche* (Reinbek: Rowohlt, 1975), p. 273.

... **'demarcation resolution'** ... reprinted in Weber, *Links*, pp. 268–76.

... **drafted by Richard Löwenthal** ... In the 1930s, Löwenthal had himself been active in the '*Neu Beginnen*' group, which tried to join the efforts of Communists and Social Democrats against fascism.

... **amended** ... see the papers in AdsD: Dep WB, PV — *Theorie und Programmdiskussion/Beschlusspapier "Sozialdemokratie und Kommunismus"*. Even here, however, there were tactical concerns, notably about the date of publication. Thus in the first draft of a letter to Löwenthal in early September 1970, Brandt wrote 'if the party board (*Vorstand*) were to deliver, at the same time as the evaluation of the [Moscow] treaty, such a clear statement against the system which rules in the lands of our treaty partners, this could be interpreted as an attempt to tread on the brake out of fear of one's own courage. This would be bound to hamper our negotiating chances.' On 5 September 1970 a milder and more elusive version of this letter was sent, with Brandt thus self-censoring his suggestion of self-censorship. Baring, *Machtwechsel*, pp. 357–58, records that the Party leadership nonetheless passed the resolution on 14 November 1970, but other sources give the date of the final resolution as 26 February 1971. This is confirmed by the wording, which refers to the Moscow and Warsaw treaties.

... **an 'exchange of speakers'** ... see Bender, *Neue Ostpolitik*, p. 132 and Hildebrand, *Von Erhard zur grossen Koalition*.

. . . **reports of the Stasi's** . . . see, for example, the reports of the Central Evaluation and Information Group (ZAIG) on popular reaction to the results of the November 1972 federal elections and to news of Brandt's resignation as Chancellor, MfS: Z4083 and Z4088.

'**In my view** . . .' this from the copy of Wehner's untitled memorandum, datelined Bad Godesberg, 2 December 1973, in AdsD: Dep WB, BK 75.

. . . **the particular case of Honecker and Wehner** . . . see above p. 199 and notes.

. . . **a 'love-hate relationship'** . . . Moseleit, *Zweite Phase*, p. 51.

. . . '**now Ehmke and Bahr pose the same question** . . .' Report of 29 January 1979 on the conversation of Erich Honecker and B. N. Ponomaryev on 26 January 1979 in ZPA: IV 2/2.035/56. There also the following quotations.

. . . **on 2 November 1982** . . . ZPA: JIV 2/2/1972.

. . . **took over from Herbert Wehner** . . . Hans-Jochen Vogel, Bonn, 18 March 1992.

At their second such meeting, in March 1984 . . . On 14 March, and attended also by Wischnewski, Bahr, Voigt and the note-taker, Dieter Schröder. The establishment of the chemical weapons group seems not, however, to have been formally announced immediately following the Vogel-Honecker meeting. At its meeting on 29 May 1984, the Politburo discussed a report by Herbert Häber on the Social Democrats' Essen party congress, and approved a list of the measures to be pursued in relations with the SPD, of which this was the first. See point 5 and Appendix 4 to Protocol 22/84 in ZPA: JIV 2/2/2057. The deputy head of the Central Committee department for international relations, Manfred Uschner, who was to play a key role in the security policy working group, recalls starting work in the summer of 1984. Manfred Uschner, Berlin, 1 October 1992.

. . . **a remarkable document** . . . The Social Democrats published the document, together with the joint communiqué and a foreword by Karsten Voigt, based on his statement at the press conference in Bonn on 19 June 1985, in *Politik* 6/1985. The East German edition, including Axen's statement, was published as *Für Chemiewaffenfreie Zone in Europa. Gemeinsame politische Initiative der Sozialistischen Einheitspartei Deutschlands und der Sozialdemokratischen Partei Deutschlands* (Dresden: Verlag Zeit im Bild, n.d.).

. . . **by the Communist Party of Czechoslovakia** . . . see the joint statement reproduced in the press service of the SPD, 5 April 1988 (295/1988) and the commentary by Karsten Voigt in ibid., 296/1988.

. . . **a cordial summit meeting** . . . only a short report on this meeting is appended to the minutes of the Politburo meeting on 24 September 1985, in ZPA: JIV 2/2/2131. It should, however, clearly soon be possible to examine both the full record and that from the Brandt papers. (At the time of writing the author had access to the Brandt papers only up to 1981.)

. . . '**in accordance with** . . .' thus the wording of the Joint Communiqué of 21

October 1986, printed together with the text and preface by Egon Bahr in *Politik*, 19/1986. There also the following quotations. The East German version, with Axen's statement at the press conference, was published as *Für Atomwaffenfreien Korridor in Mitteleuropa. Gemeinsame politische Initiative der Sozialistischen Einheitspartei Deutschlands und der Sozialdemokratischen Partei Deutschlands* (Dresden: Verlag Zeit im Bild, n.d.).

. . . 'questions from the SPD . . .' Uschner, *Ostpolitik*, p. 137.

. . . would generally fly . . . Manfred Uschner, Berlin, 1 October 1992.

In his commentary, Bahr . . . *Politik*, 19/1986.

. . . for a 'zone of trust and security' . . . *Politik*, 6/1988. Also published in ND, 8 July 1988.

. . . the Soviet answers . . . the Soviet comments on Bahr's questions at the working group meeting, in Bonn on 27 January 1988, are now in ZPA: IV 2/2.035/60.

. . . 'social scientists' . . . In his book *Wie Feuer und Wasser. Sind Ost und West friedensfähig?* (Reinbek: Rowohlt, 1988), p. 13, Erhard Eppler talks of 'almost two years' of cautious exploration. See also Häber's report of 17 October 1983 on a trip, 9–16 October 1983, in ZPA: JIV 2/10.02/13. One should note that it was the East German 'social scientist' Otto Reinhold who had been charged with main responsibility for relations with the SPD already in the Politburo resolution of 2 November 1982.

. . . the summer of 1984 . . . this was one of the steps approved by the Politburo in its meeting of 22 May 1984, see the record and appendix 4 in ZPA: JIV 2/2/2057.

. . . delicately pitched . . . Moseleit, *Zweite Phase*, p. 63 ff.

. . . on the Scharmützelsee . . . Erhard Eppler, *Wie Feuer und Wasser. Sind Ost und West friedensfähig?* (Reinbek: Rowohlt, 1988), p. 98 f. See also the recollections of Carl-Christian Kaiser in *Die Zeit*, 21 August 1992.

. . . 'six theses on the relations . . .' published in the daily press service of the SPD, 17 March 1986.

. . . its party congress to coincide . . . on this, see the very useful summary by B V Flow in Radio Free Europe Research Background Report, 87/1986. Strictly speaking, the anniversary was on 22 April while the congress finished on the 21st.

For the first time . . . see report in FAZ, 18 April 1986.

. . . now merely 'non-communists' . . . Otto Reinhold in *Horizont*, 4/1986.

. . . their common paper . . . published in *Politik* 3/1987 and ND, 28 August 1987.

Gesine Schwan . . . see her article in FAZ, 23 September 1987. Egon Bahr responded in FAZ, 2 October 1987. See also the sharply contrasting commentaries of Gerd Bucerius and Marion Gräfin Dönhoff in *Die Zeit*, 11 September 1987.

'if it really happens . . .' . . . 'there is . . .' Erhard Eppler, *Wie Feuer und Wasser. Sind Ost und West friedensfähig?* (Reinbek: Rowohlt, 1988), pp. 77, 83.

. . . spokespersons for Western democracy . . . ibid., p. 100 f.

Richard Löwenthal . . . see his article in *Die Welt*, 2 September 1987.

. . . a rare argument . . . Egon Krenz, Berlin, 29 September 1992. Karl Seidel, Berlin, 30 September 1992. Kurt Hager, Berlin, 8 May 1992. Seidel, who was present to answer any detailed questions about preparations for Honecker's trip to West Germany, recalls Krenz — in the chair in Honecker's absence — ending the discussion with a comment to the effect that 'Erich wants it'. Here one also sees clearly the limitations of the Politburo minutes as a source, for in the minutes of the meetings on 18 August and 26 August there is no record of any such disagreement. ZPA: JIV 2/2/2235 and 2236. Rolf Reissig gives a slightly different account of how the paper was pushed through in *Berliner Zeitung*, 27 August 1992.

Kurt Hager, soon publicly qualified . . . see his speech reprinted in ND, 28 October 1987. On the reception and argument inside the SED see the useful article by Rüdiger Thomas in *DDR-Report*, 1/1988, p. 14 ff. *Der Spiegel*, 51/1987, reported an internal Party '*Information*', circulated to regional Party headquarters, which also gave a highly restrictive interpretation of the paper.

'There were, if you like . . .' Kurt Hager, Berlin, 8 May 1992. But if Reissig was a Social Democrat, then only in private or by Hager's definition. Egon Krenz says most emphatically that few if any traces of the 'social democrat' were visible at the time. Egon Krenz, Berlin, 29 September 1992.

. . . sharply contrasting testimonies . . . thus Manfred Uschner (Berlin, 1 October 1992) recalls lecturing to fascinated audiences even in a Party organisation of the frontier troops. Karl Seidel (Berlin, 30 September 1992), by contrast, recalls very little — and if anything rather critical — discussion in his Party organisation in the Foreign Ministry. Kurt Hager (Berlin, 8 May 1992) believed it had very little impact in the Party, but Egon Krenz (Berlin, 29 September 1992) believed it made a great impact. This is clearly a subject for further detailed research.

A September 1987 report . . . the eight-page report dated 24 September 1987 is in MfS: Z4230.

. . . Protestant Church . . . More critically, Hans-Jürgen Fischbeck in conversation with Thomas Meyer and Rolf Reissig in *Berliner Zeitung*, 27 August 1992.

A small group . . . this included Gert Weisskirchen and Jürgen Schmude.

. . . Gert Weisskirchen, himself says . . . Gert Weisskirchen, Bonn, 24 June 1992. See also his interview in TAZ, 21 February 1992, and his article in DA, 5/1992, pp. 526–30.

Eppler . . . genuinely affronted . . . this was also the impression of Carl-Christian Kaiser, see his article in *Die Zeit*, 21 August 1992.

'Those who refuse internal dialogue . . .' The statement is reprinted, together with Reinhold's response, in DA, 6/1989, pp. 713–16, this on p. 715.

. . . the traditional 17 June speech . . . see *Bundestag Plenarprotokolle*, 11. Wahlperiode [special session], pp. 11296–303 (17 June 1989).

. . . 'GDR-consciousness . . .' ibid., p.11299.

. . . 'neither side can prevent the other . . .' ibid., p.11300. The speech is reprinted in Erhard Eppler, *Reden auf die Republik. Deutschlandpolitische Texte 1952–1990* (Munich: Chr. Kaiser, 1990), pp. 31–46.

. . . 'We are pushing for . . .' typescript of Lafontaine's opening remarks at the 'Saarbrücken Conversation', 7 June 1989. It should, however, be pointed out that Lafontaine went on to warn against these conversations becoming a sort of *Friedenskumpanei* (i.e. ganging up in the name of peace), and against covering up the different views about democracy and the violations of human rights. Moreover, his guest, Egon Krenz (Berlin, 29 September 1992) recalls Lafontaine being quite tough and outspoken in his demands in private talks.

. . . extremely confused . . . some of the debate can be followed in the extensive collection of press cuttings in *Deutschland 1989*, Vol. 24.

'Nothing can be changed . . .' quoted in *Die Welt*, 30 August 1989. See also report in FAZ, 30 August 1989. Earlier in the year, Horst Ehmke had reacted critically to the founding of a social democratic party in Slovenia, see the report in FAZ, 30 March 1989.

. . . '*Wandel durch Anbiederung* . . .' *Bundestag Plenarprotokolle*, 11/156, pp.11723–733 (5 September 1989).

. . . Norbert Gansel . . . see his article in *Frankfurter Rundschau*, 13 September 1989.

. . . after Horst Ehmke let it be known . . . this is clear from an urgent message from the GDR's Permanent Representation in Bonn dated 12 September (1691/89), in which Ehmke's travel plan includes a formal meeting with Manfred Stolpe, and 'for the evening he points to a personal meeting with Bohley'. This in ZPA: IV 2/2.035/81. Extracts from the speech that Ehmke proposed to deliver are printed in FAZ, 18 September 1989.

From now on, contacts with the Churches and opposition . . . see report in FAZ, 20 September 1989.

. . . Bahr called for a stabilisation . . . TAZ, 30 September 1989.

. . . reforms leading to a third way . . . thus, explicitly, in ZDF's *Kennzeichen D* programme on 30 September 1989, transcript in BPA/KÜ I/31.08.89.

. . . 'a different GDR' . . . see his interview in *Der Spiegel*, 42/1989.

The people of the GDR . . . *Bergedorfer Gesprächskreis* 88 (6–7 September 1989), p. 62.

. . . 'homeopathic changes . . .' this in a radio interview on 8 October 1989, transcript in BPA/KU I/09.10.89.

. . . 'there's a principle that applies . . .' ibid.

. . . of a *new* unification (*Neuvereinigung*) . . . see the report of his conversation with a group of schoolchildren in FAZ, 6 Mai 1989.

'that which arbitrarily divides . . .' *Bundestag Plenarprotokolle* 11/150, p. 11193 (16 June 1989).

. . . 'how and how far . . .' *Bild*, 21 September 1989.

. . . discreetly let it be known . . . see *dpa* agency report, 18 October 1989.

. . . 'now what belongs together . . .' this famous phrase is to be found in the text of his speech before the Schöneberg City Hall on 10 November 1989 as printed in Willy Brandt, ". . . *was zusammengehört*", *Reden zu Deutschland* (Bonn: Dietz, 1990), pp. 37–41. It is interesting to note that Brandt referred in the previous sentence to the 'division of Europe, Germany and Berlin' and went on to say that what was growing together was 'the parts of Europe'. However, he seems in fact to have used the phrase earlier in the day in off-the-cuff remarks at the Schöneberg City Hall.

. . . then rallied at their party conference in Berlin . . . see *Protokoll vom Programm-Parteitag. Berlin, 18.–20.12.1989* (Bonn: SPD Vorstand, 1990), *passim*.

Had not Willy Brandt met with Tadeusz Mazowiecki . . . on this, see above, pp.306 and Notes. See also the article by an anonymous Solidarity representative in NG 6/1986, responding to Horst Ehmke's article in NG 11/1985.

. . . Vogel with Solidarity advisers . . . see reports in *Der Spiegel*, 41/1987 and *Vorwärts*, 3 October 1987. Several eye-witnesses report that this was a very difficult meeting.

. . . Erich Mielke reported to the Politburo . . . copy in ZPA: IV 2/2.035/81.

. . . Gerd Poppe . . . Bonn, 18 March 1992.

As Egon Bahr himself observed . . . see his interview in *Die Zeit*, 13 March 1992.

. . . a first, simple answer . . . ibid. So also Hans-Jochen Vogel, Bonn, 18 March 1992.

. . . the 'governmental' or 'statist' tradition . . . thus, for example, Gert Weisskirchen in TAZ, 21 February 1992, and in conversation with the author, Bonn, 24 June 1992. Somewhat surprisingly, Karsten Voigt (Bonn, 29 February 1988 and 20 March 1992) also identified this 'etatist' line, but suggested that he himself belonged to a different, reform and freedom-oriented line.

. . . Metternich of the left . . . to which charge Bahr himself once replied: 'Oh no. But even if it were true: Metternich achieved fifty years of peace in Europe. That was also not bad.' *Abendzeitung*, 24 November 1989.

. . . as the external dimension of détente . . . Horst Ehmke to a seminar of the Friedrich-Ebert-Stiftung in Bonn, 12/13 March 1988 (typescript), p. 6, referring back to his own contribution to the 1,000th volume of the Edition Suhrkamp edited by Jürgen Habermas in 1979. This seminar was a venture in dialogue with advocates of 'détente from below' from the Western left and peace movement, and with oppositionists from Eastern Europe, as Ehmke himself notes in *Vorwärts*, 20 August 1988. His article was in response to a powerful critique of the SPD's lack of support for the East European opposition by Sibylle Plogstedt in *Vorwärts*, 13 August 1988.

Karsten Voigt pinned his hopes . . . Karsten Voigt, Bonn, 20 March 1992.

'by our not . . .' This on the ARD programme entitled 'Als Erich auf dem roten Teppich stand . . .', 30 April 1992. He made the same argument in one of his most considered retrospective statements, a lecture in Dresden on 16 February 1992, circulated by the SPD Press Service, 85/92.

. . . original documents from the Party archives . . . See note on p. 526. The most important sources available for research on this particular topic were the papers of the office of Hermann Axen (*Büro Axen*), the minutes and working papers of the Politburo, and some other holdings in the internal archive of the Politburo.

Extracts from some of the documents from the *Büro Axen* appeared in an article by Christian von Ditfurth in *Der Spiegel*, 35/1992. A promised book-length treatment of this subject by von Ditfurth was not available when this chapter was written.

. . . a few from the SPD side . . . As this book was finished, the leadership of the SPD was still considering a request from the author for permission to examine the relevant documents. However, as already mentioned, Hans-Jochen Vogel took an exemplary initiative by making available to the author the records of his own regular annual meetings with Erich Honecker.

. . . Egon Bahr and Erich Honecker on 5 September 1986 . . . this and the documentation of the following developments are in ZPA: IV 2/2.035/89 (with some related material in IV 2/2.035/78). There the following quotations.

. . . the possibility of a tendentious record . . . The record is signed by Hermann Axen, 8 September 1986.

. . . fine-sounding (yet in fact still vague) . . . for what would 'full respect' of GDR citizenship in practice have meant? After all, the right of a GDR citizen to remain a GDR citizen, travel (if they could) as a GDR citizen, and return to the GDR as a GDR citizen *if they wanted to* was already fully respected by the Bonn government.

. . . evening television news . . . that is, the '*Tagesthemen*' on 18 September. The West German official transcript (BPA/Ku I/19.9.86) has a virtually identical wording. An excellent account of the effect of the announcement is given in *Neue Zürcher Zeitung*, 20 September 1986.

... 'the policy of the GDR ...' record of a conversation with Axen in Berlin, 6 April 1987, now in ZPA: IV 2/2.035/79. The note-taker was probably Günter Rettner.

... 'however it was the SPD's view ...' record of the conversation on 15 April 1987 in ZPA: IV 2/2.035/79.

... 'more firmly under control ...' But he really need not have worried. Just 9 days earlier, on 6 April 1987, Erich Mielke had sent out an additional executive instruction (*Durchführungsbestimmung*) to the basic service order of 1975, covering the control of Western visitors. This additional instruction was concerned specifically with the control of what it also referred to as 'polit-tourism', which it interpreted as being in the interests of Bonn's 'contact policy'. *2. Durchführungsbestimmung zur Dienstanweisung Nr. 3/75*, MfS Nr. 20187 (no new archival signature).

... records of his annual conversations ... photocopies in the author's possession.

... seventeen pages of them ... record of the conversation on 25 May 1989, typescript, p. 12.

... a cautious defence of Ronald Reagan ... record of the conversation on 28 May 1983, typescript, p. 13.

'Dr Vogel replied ...' record of the conversation on 15 May 1987, typescript, p. 17.

... near the end of the talk ... ibid., p. 19.

... the East German record ... in ZPA: JIV 2/2/2220.

... 'the administration slipped unprepared ...' record of the conversation on 29 April 1988, typescript, p. 10.

... 'The Social Democrats didn't want ...' ibid.

The East German version ... see the record (*Niederschrift*) of the conversation in the Hubertusstock on 29 April 1988 in ZPA: IV 2/2.035/80, this on p. 12. This may have been written by Günter Rettner or by Honecker's State Secretary in the Council of State, Frank-Joachim Herrmann. The usually reliable Karl Seidel did not attend this particular meeting.

... Oskar Lafontaine, Klaus von Dohnanyi and Klaus Wedemaier ... see the minute (*Notiz*) of the conversation on 23 October 1987 in ZPA: IV 2/2.035/79, also for the following quotations. The minute was probably written by Günter Rettner.

'Personally, Comrade Rettner continued ...' report by Günter Rettner dated 12 December 1987 of his talks in West Germany on 9–11 December 1987, in ZPA: IV 2/2.035/79. Rettner had taken over from Herbert Häber (who had retired 'on health grounds') as head of what was now euphemistically called the Central Committee Department for International Politics and Economics (IPW). Like the Institute of the same name, this — the West Department by another name — was essentially concerned with West Germany. Regrettably, Rettner declined to talk to the author.

. . . profound confidence in E. Honecker . . . as evidence, Lafontaine also pointed to his article on the occasion of Honecker's 75th birthday, in *Der Spiegel*, 35/1987.

Receiving Rettner again five months later . . . report by Günter Rettner dated 16 May 1988 of a conversation with O. Lafontaine in Saarbrücken on 13 May 1988, in ZPA: IV 2/2.035/80.

. . . 'note on a confidential [piece of] information . . .' dated 8 July 1988, this is now in ZPA: IV 2/2.035/80.

. . . hotly disputed . . . for some reactions see the article by Christian von Ditfurth in *Der Spiegel*, 35/1992. In conversation with the author (Berlin, 1 October 1992), Manfred Uschner suggested that the note — which is unsigned — may have been made, on Axen's instructions, by a diplomat at the GDR's Permanent Representation in Bonn who was also present at the lunch. Tendentious though the note may be, Uschner's own recollection is that Voigt did definitely speak of a possible expulsion.

In August 1988, Lafontaine . . . record (*Niederschrift*) of the conversation between Honecker and Lafontaine in the Hubertusstock, 18 August 1988, in ZPA: IV 2/2.035/80. On the atmosphere of these meetings between the fellow Saarländers, the East German note-taker, Karl Seidel, head of the Foreign Ministry department responsible for dealing with West Germany, comments: 'all that was lacking was the fraternal kiss'. Karl Seidel, Berlin, 30 September 1992.

. . . a tense exchange . . . in ZPA: IV 2/2.035/81.

. . . the Politburo agreed . . . the directive is in ibid., the actual Politburo decision in the minutes of the meeting on 8th August in ZPA: JIV 2/2/2340.

. . . an urgent message . . . in ZPA: IV 2/2.035/81. Lafontaine also sent his suggestions for defusing the situation, through an emissary, Hans-Peter Weber, despatched to talk to Günter Rettner in Berlin on 18 August 1989. According to Rettner's report of 21 August 1989 (in the same file) Lafontaine even suggested that the state government of the Saarland was considering not giving West German passports to East Germans who were visiting the Saarland and wanted them for trips to France and Luxembourg! According to Rettner's report, Lafontaine's emissary also made the helpful suggestion that East Germans who had taken refuge in the Federal Republic's Permanent Representation should be allowed by the East German authorities to leave the building with an assurance that they would not be prosecuted, while Honecker should give a private undertaking that they would then be allowed to leave East Germany 'after a longer period'. It must be emphasised, however, that this is a report of an emissary's report of Lafontaine's views, and both Lafontaine and the emissary in question dismissed it as false. See also the article by Christian von Ditfurth in *Der Spiegel*, 35/1992.

... a copy, courtesy of the Stasi ... in ZPA: IV 2/2.035/81, this comes attached to one of Mielke's confidential '*Information*' sheets, on SPD contacts with Church and opposition groups in East Germany.

... scholars and journalists also frequently indulged ... see above p. 211 and Note on p. 538.

... *kameradschaftlich* ... Erich Honecker, Berlin-Moabit, 27 November 1992.

... a note prepared for Hans-Jochen Vogel ... Note of 15 June 1990, final balance in the field 'Humanitarian help/GDR'. Copy kindly made available to the author by Dr Vogel.

'There is much to be said ...' '*Trotz allem — hilfreich. Das Streitkultur-Papier von SPD und SED. Fünf Jahre danach. Eine Stellungnahme der Grundwertekommission*' (Typescript, August 1992), reprinted in DA, 10/1992, pp. 1100–08. See also the article by Gode Japs in the same issue, pp. 1011–14.

... 'security is the key to everything' Bahr, *Zum europäischen Frieden*, p.35.

... 'you expected everything ...' *Die Zeit*, 9 February 1990.

'My real mistake was ...' in *Die Zeit*, 13 March 1992.

'There have been, if you like ...' this in the radio interview on 8 October 1989 already quoted, transcript in BPA/KU I/09.10.89. In an article in *Die Zeit*, 24 November 1989, the first of what were to be many sallies in defence of his SPD-SED paper, Erhard Eppler cited Willy Brandt to the effect that 'reform' was no longer an adequate word to describe what was now happening between the Bug and the Elbe. 'Reforms,' wrote Eppler, 'are changes or adjustments inside a power-system'.

... the breakthrough of the Leipzig demonstration ... see above, p. 345.

... the illusions of the Prague Spring ... It is interesting to find a foreign policy aide to the Social Democratic parliamentary party, Jutta Tiedke, taking the Prague Spring as a model for change in Eastern Europe as late as summer 1988. See her article in NG, 8/1988, pp. 712–17. Horst Ehmke told the author (Bonn, 19 April 1988) that he had nightly to defend the Social Democrats' Ostpolitik to his Czech wife. Ehmke could rightly claim consistency for his own approach; the question is, however, whether the consistent approach was right.

The Berlin programme ... *Grundsatzprogramm der Sozialdemokratischen Partei Deutschlands* (Bonn: SPD Vorstand, 1990). There all the following quotations.

... a *Sonderbewusstsein* ... see Karl-Dietrich Bracher, *Die totalitäre Erfahrung* (Munich: Piper, 1987), p.91 ff. See also the contribution by Kurt Sontheimer in the Festschrift for Bracher (to whom he attributes the term): Funke, *Demokratie und Diktatur*, pp. 35–45.

... 'in a large part of the young generation ...' in *Partisan Review*, 2/1984, pp. 183–198, this on p. 190. Alas, Löwenthal's own article quoted above (*Die Welt*, 2 September 1987) showed old-age symptoms of the youthful disorder he himself had analysed.

Martin Gutzeit recalls . . . Berlin, 29 June 1992.

Chapter VII: German Unification

. . . **329 days** . . . thus Teltschik, *329 Tage*.

. . . **as Peter Pulzer has suggested** . . . in a verbal contribution to a seminar by Catherine McArdle Kelleher at All Souls College, Oxford.

. . . **published sources** . . . the best single collection of the most important documents is in the last three volumes of *Texte*: III/7, 8a and 8b. The Foreign Ministry's *Umbruch* and the companion volume *Deutsche Aussenpolitik 1990/91. Auf dem Weg zu einer europäischen Friedensordnung. Eine Dokumentation* (Bonn: Auswärtiges Amt, 1991) provide some useful additional material on the diplomacy of unification, and Volker Gransow and Konrad H Jarausch, *Die deutsche Vereinigung. Dokumente zu Bürgerbewegung, Annäherung und Beitritt* (Köln: Wissenschaft und Politik, 1991) includes an interesting variety of less official documents. Among the already innumerable accounts of German unification, useful introductory surveys include Kaiser, *Vereinigung*, Jesse & Mitter, *Einheit*, and, in English, Szabo, *Diplomacy* and Grosser, *Unification*. Elizabeth Pond, *Beyond the Wall. Germany's Road to Unification* (Washington: Brookings for Twentieth Century Fund, 1993) appeared too late to be used in the preparation of this chapter.

. . . **writes Michael Wolffsohn** . . . in his contribution to Jesse & Mitter, *Einheit*, pp. 142–62, this on p. 142.

. . . **literally an iron curtain** . . . see Horn, *Erinnerungen*, p. 293.

. . . **more direct and conspiratorial means** . . . this, what one might call the 'hidden hand' theory, was of course the subject of endless speculation, especially among former Politburo members, concerning the role of the KGB, Markus Wolf, Hans Modrow and so forth. A fairly sober treatment of this aspect in English is Jeffrey Gedmin, *The Hidden Hand. Gorbachev and the Collapse of East Germany* (Washington: AEI Press, 1992).

'It began in the Caucasus' . . . Hans Klein, *Es begann im Kaukasus. Der entscheidende Schritt in die Einheit Deutschlands* (Berlin: Ullstein, 1991).

. . . **'refolution'** . . . see my articles 'Refolution: The Springtime of Two Nations' in *The New York Review of Books*, 15 June 1989, and 'Refolution in Hungary and Poland', *The New York Review of Books*, 17 August 1989.

. . . **Albert Hirschman's terms** . . . Albert O Hirschman, *Exit, Voice and Loyalty. Responses to Decline in Firms, Organisations and States* (Cambridge: Harvard University Press, 1970). Hirschman discusses the applicability of his own theory to what happened in the GDR in an article in *World Politics*, Vol. 45, No. 2, January 1993, pp. 173–202.

. . . 'who comes too late . . .' It is not clear whether he ever said precisely this. A letter in FAZ, 5 December 1991, suggests that what he actually said in public, in a spontaneous response to journalists, was 'it is dangerous for him who does not react to life'. His own official speech was extremely cautious, see *Texte* III/7, pp. 275–77.

What he said in private to the East German leadership was 'if we remain behind, life punishes us straightaway', but the immediate context was a discussion of the situation in the Soviet Union itself. See the record of his meeting with the Politburo on 7 October 1989, printed in Mittag, *Preis*, pp. 359–84. Several Politburo members told the author that they understood the remark to apply mainly to the Soviet Union.

In the protocol of his immediately preceding personal conversation with Honecker, Gorbachev is recorded as saying: 'E Honecker and the Party should seize the initiative, otherwise demagogues could suggest other ideas. From his own experience he knew that one should not come too late. He had very much liked E Honecker's speech [i.e. at the banquet the night before] because it said honestly and correctly what had to be done.' See the record (*Niederschrift*) in ZPA: IV 2/2.035/60. Here he clearly was applying the thought to the GDR. Interestingly, Honecker underlined the immediately preceding and the immediately following sentences, but not this one key sentence ('From his own experience . . .').

. . . a German revolution . . . witness countless speeches, headlines, book titles etc. A good first introduction to the subject in English is now Gert-Joachim Glaessner and Ian Wallace, eds, *The German Revolution of 1989. Causes and Consequences* (Oxford: Berg, 1992).

. . . 'the turn within the turn' . . . see, for example, Meuschel, *Legitimation*, p. 318 ff, and Eckhard Jesse in Jesse & Mitter, *Einheit*, p. 118 and note.

According to a transcript . . . published in *Der Spiegel*, 48/1990. The news magazine maliciously published this mildly embarrassing document on the eve of the all-German election on 2 December 1991.

. . . Chancellor Kohl's 'ten point programme' . . . see *Texte* III/7, pp. 426–33.

. . . partly a response . . . partly prompted . . . partly designed . . . Teltschik, *329 Tage*, pp. 42 f, 48 f, 55 f. Horst Teltschik, Bonn, 12 July 1991. Helmut Kohl, Bonn, 1 October 1991.

. . . real and very emotional breakthrough . . . Wolfgang Bergsdorf at a seminar in St Antony's College, Oxford, reproduced in an edited version in Grosser, *Unification*, pp. 88–106, this on p. 91. Helmut Kohl, Bonn, 1 October 1991. Teltschik, *329 Tage*, p. 87 ff.

. . . Round Table(s) . . . for one eyewitness account see Uwe Thayssen, *Der Runde Tisch. Oder: Wo blieb das Volk. Der Weg der DDR in die Demokratie* (Opladen: Westdeutscher Verlag, 1990). He summarises his argument in Grosser, *Unification*, pp. 72–87.

... 'dual power' ... the term is used by Gert-Joachim Glaessner, *Der Schwierige Weg zur Demokratie. Vom Ende der DDR zur deutschen Einheit* (Opladen: Westdeutscher Verlag, 1991), p. 89 ff.

... proclaiming his own commitment ... see *Texte* III/8a, p. 49 f.

Just three weeks before ... ibid., p. 13 f.

... nearly 350,000 ... Teltschik, *329 Tage*, p. 103, records Wolfgang Schäuble's report to the cabinet on 10 January, with a total of 343,854 registered as having come permanently as 'over-settlers' from the GDR, in 1989. In his entry for 12 February (p. 144) he records a rate of around 3,000 a day. See also the article by Hartmut Wendt in DA, 4/1991, pp. 386–95, especially the tables on p. 393.

... *Bleibt daheim!* ... see the interesting collection by Helmut Herles & Ewald Rose, eds, *Parlaments-Szenen einer deutschen Revolution. Bundestag und Volkskammer im November 1989* (Bonn: Bouvier, 1990), this on p. 26.

... had himself fled ... see his own account in Wolfgang Mischnick, *Von Dresden nach Bonn. Erlebnisse — jetzt aufgeschrieben* (Stuttgart: Deutsche Verlags-Anstalt, 1991), p. 249 f.

... if we don't take the DM ... thus Teltschik, *329 Tage*, p. 129, and countless other examples.

... negotiated by Wolfgang Schäuble ... see Wolfgang Schäuble, *Der Vertrag. Wie ich über die deutsche Einheit verhandelte* (Stuttgart: Deutsche Verlags-Anstalt, 1991).

... understanding/agreement/support ... In the debate about the wording of the CDU's Wiesbaden resolution in 1988, the words used were first *Einverständnis* (agreement), then, in the final version, *Verständnis* (understanding) and *Unterstützung* (support), see above, p. 446–47. The German word used most often after unification was *Einvernehmen*, meaning general all-round agreement. In an article explicitly making the comparison with 1871, Wolfgang Bergsdorf writes of 'the agreement and support of all Europeans', *German Comments*, No. 26, April 1992, pp. 35–41, this on p. 41.

... Bronisław Geremek ... *Rok 1989. Bronisław Geremek Opowiada, Jacek Żakowski Pyta* (Warsaw: Plejada, 1990), p. 328.

... 'perhaps two and a half' ... Hans-Dietrich Genscher, Bonn, 23 June 1992.

... the American side of the story ... beside the invaluable Szabo, *Diplomacy*, useful accounts are given by Elizabeth Pond, *After the Wall. American Policy toward Germany* (New York: Priority Press Publications, 1990) and Alexander Moens, 'American diplomacy and German unification' in *Survival*, Vol. XXXIII, No. 6, November/December 1991, pp. 531–45. See also Oberdorfer, *Turn* and Beschloss & Talbott, *Highest Levels*. Important details of the American role can also be gleaned from Teltschik, *329 Tage*.

... Vernon Walters ... Wolfgang Schäuble (Bonn, 17 March 1992) recalls Walters telling him on his arrival in Bonn in the late spring of 1989 that he would see German unification in his period as ambassador. Walters' memoirs will clearly be an important source.

. . . **Francis Fukuyama** . . . Szabo, *Diplomacy*, p. 12.

. . . **instrumental in winning** . . . ibid., pp. 24, 58 ff. See also the article by Elizabeth Pond in EA 21/1992, pp. 619–30.

. . . **the Nine Assurances** . . . ibid., pp. 61–62, 86.

. . . **'see to it that no harm comes . . .'** in his speech to a Central Committee plenum on 9 December, see Freedman, *Europe Transformed*, pp. 384–91, this on p. 385. Teltschik, *329 Tage*, p. 85, notes that Gorbachev subsequently wrote to Kohl emphasising this position 'in language tougher than the Central Committee speech'.

. . . **'quite impossible'** . . . quoted from an interview on ARD television on 6 March in Teltschik, *329 Tage*, p. 168.

. . . **domestic political consumption** . . . Gorbachev told François Mitterand in December 1989 that if Germany were to be reunited there would be a two-line announcement the next day, saying that a marshal had taken his place. He was exaggerating — but exaggerating a real danger, as the coup of August 1991 showed. ibid., p. 109.

. . . **matchless supremacy** . . . in talking to Kohl in Moscow on 15 July, Gorbachev described the Party congress, in allusion to John Reed, as eleven days that shook the world, Teltschik, *329 Tage*, p. 325. Without this success in consolidating his power inside the system, it is very doubtful if he could have risked making such concessions as he did over German unification.

. . . **the published day-by-day account** . . . Horst Teltschik emphasises, in response to a query from the author, that while the published version is closely based on his notes made at the time, and original documents, it only contains about half of his original rough diary.

. . . **a message** . . . **from Shevardnadze** . . . Teltschik, *329 Tage*, p. 100 ff.

. . . **52,000 tonnes of canned beef** . . . ibid., p. 114.

. . . **an important and very specific signal** . . . thus, also, Helmut Kohl, Bonn, 1 October 1991.

. . . **shape the last decade** . . . Teltschik, *329 Tage*, p. 139.

According to Teltschik's Russian counterpart . . . this in the lecture by Anatoly Chernyaev, printed in Gabriel Garodetsky, ed., *Soviet Foreign Policy, 1917–1992. A Retrospective* (London: Frank Cass, forthcoming). Chernyaev's direct quotations may be compared with the indirect quotations in Teltschik, *329 Tage*, p. 140.

. . . **a suggestion made** . . . **Boris Meissner** . . . ibid., p. 192.

. . . **'in the Bismarckian spirit'** . . . ibid., p. 206.

... Shevardnadze directly confirmed ... ibid., p. 218 ff.

... a secret mission ... ibid., p. 230 ff.

While James Baker discussed ... ibid., p. 241 f.

Writing to Gorbachev ... ibid., p. 244.

... 'chess move' ... ibid., p. 325.

... the edited and then retranslated Russian record ... this in *Gipfelgrespräche*, pp. 161–77. Note that this is a retranslation from the Russian record, which is presumably based on Chernyaev's notes, and perhaps those of the Russian interpreter. The account in Teltschik, *329 Tage*, is based on Teltschik's own notes, which he checked with those of the German interpreter, but unfortunately not quoted verbatim.

... 'we must turn to Europe ...' *Gipfelgespräche.*, p. 171.

... exchanging 'non-paper' drafts ... ibid., pp. 171–72.

... 'on the former territory ...' ibid., p. 175.

'The sovereignty of united Germany ...' ibid., p. 175.

... the security conditions ... summarised by Kohl in eight points on 16 July, and in ten on 17 July, see the statements to the press reprinted in EA 18/1990, pp. D480–90.

... 'Stavrapallo' ... The *Economist*, 21 July 1990. However, this article attributed the coinage to an East German official, and argued that the agreements did *not* add up to a Rapallo.

'We have acted ...' Gorbachev at the joint press conference on 16 July, EA, 18/1990, p. D481.

... eleven men in three capitals ... Szabo, *Diplomacy*, pp. 17 and 117 f.

'But,' he continued, ... *Gipfelgespräche*, p. 173.

'Genscher is mainly concerned ...' Teltschik, *329 Tage*, p. 339. This entry is perhaps not wholly without a touch of inter-departmental malice.

... diplomatic tactics ... for one observer's account of how the Polish Foreign Minister was actually treated at the Paris meeting see Ulrich Albrecht, *Die Abwicklung der DDR. Die "2+4 Verhandlungen". Ein Insider-Bericht* (Opladen: Westdeutscher Verlag, 1992), pp. 101–16. This and Szabo, *Diplomacy*, p. 72 ff make it clear that the Bush administration was rather impatient of Warsaw's specific diplomatic stance. Szabo quotes an American lawyer involved describing the Polish border issue as 'small potatoes'.

... 'sympathy' but ... Teltschik, *329 Tage*, p. 237

... the emotional decision ... 'Georgian games' Valentin Falin, Hamburg, 14 May 1992. Horst Teltschik (Bonn, 12 July 1991) notes that Falin was present at the Moscow meeting with Kohl in February, but no longer in the Caucasus. Clearly, the Georgian had won this particular game. This interpretation is confirmed by Falin's then deputy (and subsequently Gorbachev's spokesman) Andrei Grachev (Oxford, 24 January 1992).

... **haggled hard on the telephone** ... Teltschik, *329 Tage*, pp. 359–62.

... **no less than four** ... see Chancellor Kohl's statement on 12 September, in *Texte* III/8b, pp. 688–91. Negotiation of all four treaties only began after the Caucasus and Paris meetings in mid-July.

... **a last-minute British objection** ... this concerned the possibility of Nato forces carrying out manoeuvres in East Germany. See FAZ, 14 September 1990, and the resulting *Protokollnotiz* in *Texte* III/8b, p. 678.

... **'the historic changes ...'** text in *Texte* III/8b, pp. 672–78.

... **'Treaty on good-neighbourliness ...'** text in *Texte* III/8b, pp. 851–59.

... **'finally to have done with the past ...'** *mit der Vergangenheit endgültig abzuschliessen.*

... **'on several transitional measures'** ... text in *Texte* III/8b, pp. 795–801.

... **terms on which the Soviet troops** ... text in ibid., pp. 802–44.

... **'on the development of a comprehensive co-operation ...'** see *Bundesgesetzblatt*, 1991, Teil 1, pp. 798–809.

Gorbachev concluded ... text in *Texte* III/8b, pp. 848–51, this on p. 851.

... **Genscher would argue** ... Hans-Dietrich Genscher, Bonn, 23 June 1992.

In July 1987, Gorbachev had said ... see above p. 108.

In January 1989, Erich Honecker ... this statement, made partly in response to criticism of the Wall at the Vienna Helsinki review conference, is reprinted in *Texte* III/8b, pp. 24–25, from ND, 20 January 1989.

... **Reiner Kunze** ... in *Die Zeit*, 5 October 1990.

Chapter VIII: Findings

... **the most constructive answer** ... Michael Stürmer in a seminar at St Antony's College, Oxford, 24 February 1989.

... **Vertrauenskapital** ... see, for example, his Preface to *Deutsche Aussenpolitik 1990/91. Auf dem Weg zu einer europäischen Friedensordnung. Eine Dokumentation* (Bonn: Auswärtiges Amt, 1991), p. 7.

... **'the more European** ... this in a speech in the National Library in Vienna on 14 September 1989, Der Bundesminister des Auswärtigen, Mitteilung fur die Presse Nr. 1134/89.

. . . happily acknowledge . . . see the references on p. 441–42 above.

As with Stresemann . . . I draw here on the work of my colleague Jonathan Wright, of Christ Church, Oxford, who is preparing a new biography of Stresemann. For further references see the note on p. 442 above.

. . . an ongoing debate . . . a very useful introduction to the terms and assumptions of the debate within the academic subject of International Relations is Martin Hollis & Steven Smith, *Explaining and Understanding International Relations* (Oxford: Clarendon Press, 1990). The debate was much stimulated, particularly in the United States, by the end of the Cold War. See successive contributions to the journal *International Security*.

. . . 'complex interdependence' . . . thus Robert O Keohane & Joseph S Nye, *Power and Interdependence. World Politics in Transition* (Boston: Little, Brown, 1977).

. . . Feindbilder . . . thus in June 1989 the West German Foreign Ministry actually organised a colloquium on the analysis and dismantling of enemy-images, and the resulting booklet went into a second edition in 1991 'on account of the strong demand'. See *Abbau von Feindbildern* (2nd edition, Bonn: Auswärtiges Amt, 1991).

In this rhetorical world . . . on this see also Schwarz, *Gezähmten Deutschen*, *passim*.

. . . more concretely directed . . . notable in this connection, beside the extensive public record, is a note made by Alois Mertes on 23 August 1983, summarising a conversation with Kohl. 'It was a political task of historic dimensions,' Mertes summarised Kohl's view, 'that the FR Germany should make a new attempt in the direction of European unification.' After noting that Kohl preferred the word 'unification' to the technocratic 'integration', Mertes continued: 'the revitalisation of national reunification must be joined by the revitalisation of European unification — both in line with Western ideas of personal human rights and national self-determination'. Note of 23 August 1983, in ACDP: I-403, A-000.

. . . and cared as deeply . . . in his opening speech to the first sitting of the first freely elected Bundestag of united Germany, Brandt made a point of saying that the fulfilment of his political life would be the day when not just Germany but Europe was one. See *Bulletin*, 21 December 1990, pp. 1545–49, this on p. 1549.

When Helmut Schmidt says . . . Schmidt, *Menschen und Mächte*, p. 11.

. . . 'for all the importance . . .' letter of 31 May 1976, quoted from the copy in AdsD: Dep EB, 409.

Vladimir Semyonov . . . Köln, 21 March 1992.

. . . paid fulsome tribute . . . *Texte* III/8b, p. 849.

. . . 'my friend Ronald Reagan' . . . quoted in the *Daily Telegraph*, 5 May 1992.

... **Pope John Paul II** ... quoted in *Der Spiegel*, 11/1992.

In outward discourse ... classic examples in the speeches on the day of German unity, 3 October 1990, reprinted in *Texte* III/8b, p. 698 ff.

... *Helsinkipolitik* ... see for example the interview in *Die Welt*, 7 February 1992.

... **'human rights motor'** ... this in his speech on receiving the Heine Prize on 13 December 1991, reprinted in *Bulletin*, 17 December 1991, pp. 1165–70, this on p. 1169.

... **'the favourable atmosphere...'** Charter 77 Document No. 31, 1986, message to the participants of the Conference on Security and Co-operation in Vienna.

... **an internal memorandum** ... a copy of this memorandum, entitled 'Towards a new conception of Soviet-Central/East European Relations' (typescript, 26 pages) was kindly given me by Dr Marina Pavlova-Silvanskaya. Translation from the Russian by Tina Podplatnik.

... **the economic components of power** ... See the interesting reflections in Susan Strange, *States and Markets* (Pinter: London, 1988), and Joseph S Nye, *Bound to Lead. The Changing Nature of American Power* (New York: Basic Books, 1990).

... **at least since Ranke** ... see Hedley Bull, *The Anarchical Society. A Study of Order in World Politics* (London: Macmillan, 1977), p. 201 ff, and Martin Wight, *Power Politics* (Leicester: Leicester University Press, 1978), pp. 41–53, 295 f.

... **Paul Kennedy** ... *The Rise and Fall of the Great Powers. Economic Change and Military Conflict from 1500 to 2000* (New York: Random House, 1988). It is interesting to note how relatively little attention is paid specifically to the Federal Republic in Kennedy's last speculative chapter.

... **Bishop of East Berlin** ... Bishop Forck, quoted in FAZ, 23 April 1988.

... **'Whether Warsaw or Prague ...'** Brandt, *Erinnerungen*, p. 224.

... **Gyula Horn records** ... Horn, *Erinnerungen*, p. 308 ff.

According to Németh's recollection ... Miklós Németh, Oxford, 22 January 1991. See also Grosser, *Unification*, p. 9.

... **DM 1 billion** ... actually DM 500 million federal guarantees, and DM 250 million each from Baden-Württemberg and Bavaria. See report in FAZ, 9 October 1989.

'Do you realise ...' Horn, *Erinnerungen*, p. 322.

'The Germans ...' Dominique Moïsi, Jacques Rupnik, *Le Nouveau Continent. Plaidoyer pour une Europe renaissante* (Paris: Calmann-Levy, 1991), p. 134.

... **an 'exemplary' or 'model' character** ... see, for example, the remarks by Hans-Dietrich Genscher in *Bundestag Plenarprotokolle* 9/49, pp. 2767–69.

... a short leading article ... *Die Zeit*, 10 August 1984. Volker Rühe had earlier talked of the two German states developing 'a German model for a real détente across the dividing system frontiers' in the INF deployment debate, see *Bundestag Plenarprotokolle*, 10/36, p. 2515 (22 November 1983). In his 1987 state of the nation address, Kohl referred to the hope of developing 'an exemplary co-operation' between the two states, see *Bundestag Plenarprotokolle*, 11/33, p. 2162 (15 October 1987).

... one analyst has noted ... Michael Wolffsohn, in EA, 7/1991, p. 211 ff, and in a lecture at St Antony's College, Oxford, 1 March 1991.

... *sterben für Danzig* ... Günter Gaus at a seminar in the Free University, West Berlin, 4 February 1987.

... *mourir pour Dantzig* ... this in his speech (read in his enforced absence) to mark the centenary of Marc Bloch. Quoted in Carole Fink, *Marc Bloch. A Life in History* (Cambridge: Cambridge University Press, 1989), p. 344.

... his greatest satisfaction ... thus already in a letter to Bruno Kreisky dated 1 November 1971, in AdsD: Dep WB, BK11.

... Eugen Gerstenmaier ... see his *Streit und Friede hat seine Zeit. Ein Lebensbericht* (Frankfurt: Propyläen, 1981), p. 422.

... order ... an important value ... see Hedley Bull, *The Anarchical Society. A Study of Order in World Politics* (London: Macmillan, 1977), p. 96 f and *passim*.

... '*Vous aimez l'ordre* ...' Thomas Mann, *Der Zauberberg*. The French philosopher André Gorz said something similar in an interview in *Der Spiegel*, 4/1982.

... identification ... less complete ... At the end of his 1989 *Erinnerungen*, p. 500, Brandt said the real satisfaction of his life was to have contributed to the fact that the name of Germany, the concept of peace *and the prospect of European freedom* are 'thought [of] together'. But this was more true of peace than of freedom.

... 'vulnerable to blackmail' ... *Bergedorfer Gesprächskreis* 91 (7–8 October 1990), p. 16.

... this getting on with all sides ... the author has described Genscherism, in jest, as the attempt to have friendly relations with heaven, a deepening partnership with the earth, but also fruitful co-operation with hell.

... patience was the strongest weapon ... quoted by Klaus Gotto in his article 'Der Realist als Visionär', in *Die Politische Meinung*, Nr. 249, 1990, p. 6.

... 'German patriots in European responsibility' ... Brandt, *Erinnerungen*, p. 331.

... 'reunification of Europe' ... in Lutz, *Bahr*, pp. 249–51, Carl-Friedrich von Weizsäcker recalls an article he wrote in 1956 in which he argued that the reunification of Germany could only come as a consequence of the reunification of Europe, and if the reunification of Europe did not happen in the next three decades there would be war. 'Was I right?', he asks.

. . . 'under which we've lived quite happily' . . . see above, p. 2.

Epilogue: European Answers

In 1965, Konrad Adenauer . . . Konrad Adenauer, *Erinnerungen 1945–1953* (Stuttgart: Deutsche Verlags-Anstalt, 1965), p. 13.

. . . *Historikerstreit* . . . see the references given above, p. 541.

. . . *Literaturstreit* . . . this began in 1990 with the publication of Christa Wolf's *Was bleibt?*, and raged in the feuilleton sections of the FAZ, *Die Zeit* and other journals. The issues are briefly discussed in English by J H Reid in *The New Germany. Volume 1: Divided or United by a Common European Culture?* (Glasgow: Goethe Institut, 1992), with further references.

. . . agree with E H Carr . . . *What is History?* (London: Penguin, 1964), p. 108.

. . . old books . . . see, for example, J A R Marriott, *The Eastern Question. An Historical Study in European Diplomacy* (Oxford: Clarendon Press, 1917; 4th edition, 1940), R. W. Seton-Watson, *Disraeli, Gladstone and the Eastern Question* (London: Macmillan, 1935; reprinted by Frank Cass & Co., 1971).

They'll come again . . . from 'Tiananmen' in the song-cycle 'Out of the East'.

. . . Kinkel, visited China . . . quotations are from *Der Spiegel*, 46/1992, *Die Zeit*, 6 November 1992, FAZ, 3 November 1992. See also the interview with Kinkel in *Rheinischer Merkur*, 6 November 1992. Obviously stung by the criticism, the Foreign Ministry let it be known in early 1993 that Kinkel's quiet diplomcy had resulted in the release of four human rights campaigners, FAZ, 2 February 1993. Once again, the echo of Ostpolitik is very strong. It was also suggested that there might be an official or semi-official German-Chinese symposium on human rights.

. . . 'equipped not with more power . . .' speech of 30 November 1990, reprinted in *Bulletin*, 5 December 1990, pp. 1485–89, this on p. 1485.

. . . a new superpower . . . Antje Vollmer, quoted by Horst Teltschik in his own reflections on this subject in *German Comments*, 21/1991.

. . . 'world power against its will' . . . Christian Hacke, *Weltmacht wider Willen. Die Aussenpolitik der Bundesrepublik Deutschland* (Stuttgart: Klett-Cotta, 1988).

. . . a new great power . . . thus Gregor Schöllgen, *Die Macht in der Mitte Europas. Stationen deutscher Aussenpolitik von Friedrich dem Grossen bis zur Gegenwart* (Munich: Beck, 1992), pp. 169, 177, 182.

. . . a political scientist . . . Ludger Kühnhardt, in his inaugural lecture in the Albert-Ludwigs-Universität Freiburg, 27 November 1991, typescript, p. 16.

... 'we in West and Central Europe' ... quoted in *Der Spiegel*, 37/1991.

A leading contemporary historian ... Baring, *Deutschland*, p. 9.

A television newscaster ... this in the course of the ARD *'Tagesthemen'*, 2 July 1991.

Another analyst recalled ... Reinhard Stuth in *Aussenpolitik* (English-language edition), 1/92, pp. 22–32, this on p. 22.

In an interview on Austrian television ... ORF, 27 March 1991.

... 'the Western powers' ... Johann Georg Reissmüller in FAZ, 11 January 1993. In German, he referred to them as *die westlichen Mächte* but also once as *die Westmächte*, the term previously used for the Western occupying powers in Germany and Berlin.

In a great symbolic decision ... see Helmut Herles, ed., *Die Hauptstadt-Debatte. Der Stenographische Bericht des Bundestages* (Bonn Berlin [!]: Bouvier, 1991).

... the predictions of the economists ... see, for example, Leslie Lipschitz & Donogh McDonald, ed., *German Unification. Economic Issues* (Washington: IMF Occasional Paper No. 75, 1990).

... tied to a certain level ... of prosperity ... for a stimulating general discussion of the connections between prosperity and democracy, see Samuel P Huntington, *The Third Wave. Democratisation in the Late Twentieth Century* (Norman: University of Oklahoma Press, 1991).

... it just might face such a test ... the general point has of course been made many times, but for the specific concern see, for example, the interview with Ralf Dahrendorf in *Der Spiegel*, 3/1993.

... Bundesbank ... A very striking critical analysis of the conduct of Bundesbank policy in 1992, by Ulrich Cartellieri, a director of the Deutsche Bank, is given in *Die Zeit*, 26 February 1993. Despite its somewhat sensational sub-title, David Marsh, *The Bundesbank. The Bank that Rules Europe* (London: Mandarin, 1993) is an excellent introduction.

... projected budget deficits ... the official projections in February 1993 were: DM 132.5 billion for 1993, DM 108 billion for 1994, DM 100 billion for 1995, and a mere DM 75 billion or 1996. These were the total budget deficits, that is, including federal, state, local government and the special funds for German unity. Information from the Federal Chancellery.

... total public debt ... The official projection in February 1993 was DM 1,504.5 billion. Again, this included federal, state and local government debt, and the inherited debts of the former GDR. Information from the Federal Chancellery. Writing in *Die Zeit*, 13 November 1992, Helmut Schmidt found it instructive to spell the figure out, thus: DM 1,500,000,000,000.

... some of the largest armed forces in Europe ... since most of the military powers in the world were engaged in intense discussion of how and how far to cut their conventional forces, no figures are reliable. According to *The Military Balance 1992–1993* (London: Brassey's for the IISS, 1992) the total armed forces of Germany in mid-1992 were 447,000, compared with 431,700 for France and 293,500 for Britain (although the British army was of course a professional, not a conscript army). For very crude comparison: the United States had 1,913,750 on active service, and some 2 million in reserve, Russia some 2,720,000 on active service, and some 3 million in reserve, Turkey had a conscript army of 560,300, with more than 1 million reserves. The July 1992 final agreement of the negotiations on conventional force numbers in Europe (begun in Vienna in January 1989 — see above, p.265), set targets for 'land-based military personnel' (that is, army and air force) *in Europe* of 1,450,000 for Russia, 530,000 for Turkey, 450,000 for Ukraine, 345,000 for Germany, 325,000 for France, 315,000 for Italy, 260,000 for Britain, and 250,000 for the United States. See *Bulletin*, 17 July 1992, pp. 753–59. However, in early 1993 it appeared that leading Nato states might actually cut their forces still further, although perhaps at the same time making them more professional. See, for example, report by Michael Binyon in *The Times*, 10 February 1993.

... **more than \$6,500 million** ... this figure is given in a valuable article by Ronald Asmus, 'Germany and America: Partners in leadership?', in *Survival*, Vol. XXXIII, No. 6, November/December 1991, pp. 546–66, this on pp. 554–55. According to the official US government figures, this was 12.2 per cent of the financial contributions, compared to 18.7 per cent from Japan.

... **attractiveness** ... magnetism ... Joseph S Nye has tagged this 'soft power', see his *Bound to Lead. The Changing Nature of American Power* (New York: Basic Books, 1990), pp. 31–32.

... **'too big to play no role ...'** see above, p. 54 and the corresponding note.

... **Henry Kissinger** ... in conversation with the author, Berlin, 29 June 1991.

'Germany has become a normal state ...' quoted from *Bergedorfer Gesprächskreis* 91 (7–8 October 1990), p. 16.

... **'normalisation' of German foreign policy** ... this in a speech on 5 October 1992, devoted to the 'guiding principles of the foreign policy of united Germany', reprinted in *Bulletin*, 7 October 1992, pp. 1011–15.

... **it was argued** ... notably in the FAZ. As the path to the new Ostpolitik was beaten by 'published opinion' in the 1960s, notably in the Hamburg journals of the centre-left, above all *Die Zeit* and *Der Spiegel*, so it now seemed possible that the path to some of the new directions of German foreign policy was again being beaten by 'published opinion', but this time perhaps more of the centre-right, and above all by the FAZ. For the arguments for and against Bonn and Berlin see Alois Rummel, ed., *Bonn. Sinnbild deutscher Demokratie* (Bonn: Bouvier, 1990) and Helmut Herles, ed., *Die Hauptstadt-Debatte. Der Stenographische Bericht des Bundestags* (Bonn Berlin [!]: Bouvier, 1991).

... **by intellectuals of the centre-left** ... Jürgen Habermas went so far to define the idea that Germany was again 'normal' as the 'second life-lie of the

Federal Republic'. According to Habermas, the first life-lie had not been (as Willy Brandt had suggested) that of reunification, but rather the claim in the Adenauer that 'we are all democrats'. See *Die Zeit*, 11 December 1992. See also the article by Peter Glotz in NG, 9/1991, pp. 823–26.

. . . Hans-Peter Schwarz . . . *Rheinischer Merkur*, 7 September 1990.

. . . Nietzsche's famous dictum . . . in *Jenseits von Gut und Böse*, §. 244.

'Germany is our fatherland . . .' this in his government declaration of 30 January 1991, published as *Deutschlands Einheit vollenden. Die Einheit Europas gestalten. Dem Frieden der Welt dienen. Regierungspolitik 1991–1994* (Bonn: Presse- und Informationsamt der Bundesregierung, 1991), p. 78.

. . . 'the political unification . . .' ibid., p. 86.

'The *Staatsräson* of a united Germany . . .' Wolfgang Bergsdorf in Grosser, *Unification*, p. 106.

. . . amended in December 1992 . . . report and text in FAZ, 3 December 1992. But note that as this book went to press these changes were being challenged in the Federal Constitutional Court.

'Maastricht,' said President von Weizsäcker . . . article in FAZ, 13 April 1992, also reprinted in *Bulletin*, 15 April 1992, pp. 385–86.

. . . 'European century' . . . speech in honour of the President of Bulgaria, 2 September 1991, reprinted in *Bulletin*, 10 September 1991, pp. 769–70.

. . . General Naumann, said . . . interview on ZDF, 6 October 1991.

. . . 'German and European . . .' speech of 20 December 1990, reprinted in *Bulletin*, 21 December 1990, pp. 1545–49.

. . . asked by a weekly newspaper . . . *Rheinischer Merkur*, 28 December 1990.

. . . 'no single national, German . . .' quoted from the transcript of the Berlin Colloquium convened by Lord Weidenfeld, Berlin and Potsdam, 28–30 June 1991, this on p. 83.

. . . 'does not want more power . . .' *Kanzler-Kinderfest-Zeitung*, 26 June 1991.

As Henry Kissinger observed . . . *White House Years*, pp. 410–11.

. . . talking to students in Hamburg . . . Thomas Mann, *Schriften zur Politik* (Frankfurt: Suhrkamp, 1973), pp. 204–206.

. . . J P Stern wrote . . . see his *The Heart of Europe. Essays on Literature and Ideology* (Oxford: Blackwell, 1992), p. 3.

'The evil Germany . . .' this in his lecture on 'Germany and the Germans', reprinted in Thomas Mann, *Schriften zur Politik* (Frankfurt: Suhrkamp, 1973), pp. 162–183.

'There are a number of things . . .' William Hazlitt, 'On Cant and Hypocrisy', in *Sketches and Essays* (Oxford: Oxford University Press, 1902), this on p.26.

. . . a value in itself . . . see his celebrated essay 'A Kidnapped West or Culture Bows Out' in *Granta* 11, pp. 95–118.

. . . '*qui parle Europe a tort* . . .' this was a marginal comment on a letter from the Russian Chancellor, Gorchakev, in November 1876, see Johannes Lepsivs & ors, eds, *Die Grosse Politik der Europäischen Kabinette 1871–1914* (Vol. 2, Berlin: Deutsche Verlagsgesellschaft für Politik und Geschichte, 1922) No. 255, p. 87.

Thomas Mann . . . **an Oxford audience** . . . this in a lecture for the Goethe anniversary celebrations, 'Goethe and Democracy', reprinted in Thomas Mann, *Goethes Laufbahn als Schriftsteller. Zwölf Essays und Reden* (Frankfurt: Fischer Taschenbuch, 1982), pp. 283–308, this on p. 285.

. . . **wild Irish and Spanish** . . . the Irish reference was an article by Conor Cruise O'Brien in *The Times*, 31 October 1989, the Spanish, a book published in Germany: Heleno Saña, *Das vierte Reich. Deutschlands später Sieg* (Hamburg: Rasch & Röhring, 1990).

. . . '**which is bound to democratic** . . .' quoted from text in FAZ, 3 December 1992.

'**At the end of this decade** . . .' this in his New Year's speech for 1992, printed in *Bulletin*, 3 January 1992, pp. 1–2.

'**Now we must put Europe** . . .' *Die Zeit*, 21 September 1990.

. . . **the values of the West** . . . **easier to define** . . . which is not, of course, to suggest that they are *easy* to define. Interestingly, at their Malta meeting in December 1989, Gorbachev, Yakovlev, Bush and Baker had a little discussion about whether 'Western values' are actually *Western* values, or just 'democratic', 'humanist' or 'all-human' ones. See *Gipfelgespräche*, p. 128 f.

. . . **done extremely well out of the EC** . . . a stimulating discussion of this is the article by Andrei S Markovits and Simon Reich in *German Politics and Society*, Issue 23, Summer 1991, pp. 1–20.

Chancellor Kohl declared that . . . see his lecture at St Antony's College, Oxford, on 11 November 1992, published as Helmut Kohl, *United Germany in a Uniting Europe* (Oxford: St Antony's College & the Konrad Adenauer Foundation, n.d.), this on p. 2. German text in *Bulletin*, 25 November 1992, pp. 1141–45, this on p. 1141.

. . . **aggregated the sacred egoisms** . . . interestingly, Kohl himself hinted at this point in the same lecture, ibid., p. 9. In German text, p. 1144.

. . . **the aim of German foreign policy** . . . this at the second Berlin Colloquium convened by Lord Weidenfeld, 26–28 June 1992.

Helmut Kohl saw . . . **a European roof** . . . Helmut Kohl, Bonn, 1 October 1991.

. . . **Mitterrand expanded on his vision** . . . Teltschik, *329 Tage*, p. 208.

... **scribbled by Churchill for Adenauer** ... see Konrad Adenauer, *Erinnerungen 1945–1953* (Stuttgart: Deutsche Verlags-Anstalt, 1987), p. 512.

... **concentric** ... the image of concentric circles had first been given wide currency by an article by two advisers to Chancellor Kohl, Michael Mertes and Norbert Prill, in FAZ, 19 July 1989. It is reprinted in Michael Mertes & ors, *Europa ohne Kommunismus. Zusammenhänge, Aufgaben, Perspektiven* (Bonn: Europa Union Verlag, 1990).

... **European Communities** ... then still really in the plural. Readers will recall that the European Coal and Steel Community, Euratom and the European Economic Community were only merged in 1967.

... **Kohl once described Mainz** ... this in welcoming George Bush to the Rheingoldhalle in Mainz on 31 May 1989, see *Vierzig Jahre*, p. 586.

When Mitterrand launched ... in Prague, 12–14 June 1991. The author was one of those invited to participate in this curious event.

... **a large map** ... the map was a rather ingenious design showing Europe as the yellow foliage of a tree emerging from a blue tree trunk. The shade of yellow in the further eastern parts was, however, somewhat lighter — perhaps the Czech input to the design?

Josef Joffe summed it up ... this also at the Berlin Colloquium, 26–28 June 1992.

Kohl identified two great tasks ... speech to the International Bertelsmann Forum, 3 April 1992, printed in *Bulletin*, pp. 353–56, this on p. 353.

... *Kleineuropa* as *Kerneuropa* ... for a stimulating treatment of these issues see Ludger Kühnhardt, *Europäische Union und föderale Idee. Europapolitik in der Umbruchzeit* (Munich: Beck, 1993 = *Schriftenreihe des Bundeskanzleramtes*, Band 14). Interesting remarks can also be found in Peter van Ham, *The EC, Eastern Europe and European Unity. Discord, Collaboration and Integration since 1947* (London: Pinter, 1993).

... **'Ostpolitik mark-two'** ... The *Economist*, 29 February 1992.

... **'a moving moment'** ... this and the following quotations from Kohl's statement in the Bundestag on 4 September 1991, reprinted in *Bulletin*, 5 September 1991, pp. 749–752.

... **the dramatic headline figures** ... in September 1992, the government spokesman announced that some DM 80 billion had been provided since the end of 1989. But of this, more than DM 19 billion was directly related to unification (see the chapter on unification above), more than DM 17 billion was exports from the former GDR which had been paid for in transferable roubles, more than DM 28 billion was for export credit guarantees, and DM 2.9 billion costs for financing oil and natural gas investment projects. Figures taken from the overview provided in *Report from the Federal Republic of Germany*, 118/92.

... **in terms of direct grants and aid** ... the point is made by Ronald Asmus in *Survival*, Vol. XXXIII, No. 6, November/December 1991, pp. 546–66, this on p. 560.

. . . Kohl agreed with Yeltsin . . . report in FAZ, 17 December 1992.

. . . Hans-Dietrich Genscher called . . . in *Welt am Sonntag*, 10 January 1992.

. . . an *Ukrainepolitik* . . . on Foreign Minister Kinkel's first visit to Ukraine, see reports in FAZ, 17 February 1993.

. . . Yugoslavia . . . this deserves a longer treatment. A good short discussion is given by Harald Müller in Stares, *New Germany*, pp. 150–54.

. . . according to a credible source . . . private information to the author

. . . proceeded to do so itself . . . see the statement by the government spokesman on 19 December 1991, printed in *Bulletin*, 21 December 1991, p. 1183.

. . . public and especially published opinion . . . Germany also now had its equivalent of the 'ethnic lobbies' in the United States: in this case, some half a million Croats. See again Harald Müller in Stares, *New Germany*, p. 153. It is interesting to find that (in more general terms) Genscher mentioned the influence of this lobby in a speech calling for 'self-determination' for the Yugoslav republics, reprinted in *Das Parlament*, 15/22 November 1991.

. . . 250,000 refugees. . . . figures from the UN High Commissioner for Refugees and Federal Interior Ministry

. . . Helsinki process . . . golden bridge . . . see the Foreign Ministry documentation, *Deutsche Aussenpolitik 1990/91. Auf dem Weg zu einer europäischen Friedensordnung* (Bonn: Auswärtiges Amt, 1991). Dieter Kastrup, Bonn, 18 March 1992.

. . . 'Visegrád three' . . . this referred to the Visegrád Declaration following the trilateral Polish-Hungarian-Czechoslovak summit at Visegrád in February 1991.

. . . the bilateral treaties . . . the texts of these are conveniently collected in EA, 10/1992, pp. D369–402, with that with Poland in EA, 13/1991, pp. D310 ff.

. . . a Polish quality newspaper . . . leading article in *Obserwator codzienny*, 14 February 1992.

. . . the negotiation . . . with Czechoslovakia . . . Harald Müller in Stares, *New Germany*, pp. 148–50, once again gives a useful succinct account, and further references. Jiří Gruša, Bonn, 20 March 1991.

. . . 'see a future . . .' thus in his speech of 4 September 1991, *Bulletin*, 5 September 1991, p. 750.

. . . the numbers of out-settlers from Poland . . . see Table IX.

. . . as Hans Magnus Enzensberger . . . see his *Die Grosse Wanderung. 33 Markierungen* (Frankfurt: Suhrkamp, 1992), pp. 25–27.

. . . the total numbers . . . figures and detailed explanation from the Federal Ministry of the Interior.

... agreement was reached ... this paragraph is based on the text of the so-called 'asylum compromise' of 6 December 1992. The final law and administrative solutions might therefore be somewhat different.

... European burden-sharing ... the phrase *eine europäische Lastenverteilung* actually appeared in the text of the 'asylum compromise'.

... 'the *völkisch* worm' ... this in FAZ Magazin, 29 January 1993.

'That only those ...' ibid.

... Richard Schröder ... see his article in *Die Zeit*, 22 January 1993.

... state-nation ... that is, one in which belonging to the nation is defined by being a citizen of the state, rather than vice versa. The classic example is, of course, the United States. To some extent, however, this is also true of Britain. 'British nationals', in the language of the Home Office, are actually English, Scottish, Welsh, Irish, and now also often of Asian or Caribbean descent, heritage and tradition. But this is not for a moment to underestimate the immense difficulty of combining a heterogeneous 'multi-cultural' society with a strong, democratic state and the rule of (one) law, as the Rushdie affair in Britain and countless examples in the contemporary United States go to show. In the relative success of these examples of state-nations there clearly has been a strong element of homogenisation by one dominant culture, one language, one set of institutions and traditions: English, the flag and the constitution in the United States; English, parliament and the monarchy in Britain. Eugen Weber's study of 'Peasants into Frenchman' shows how there is a real sense in which in France, too, the state created the nation, rather than vice versa.

... not so restrained ... see, for example, the reports in *Der Spiegel* 24/1991 and 45/1992. The former report is sensationally entitled 'We want *Anschluss*'. However, the actual quotation in the text is 'we want to join Europe, to join progress' (*wir wollen Anschluss an Europa, Anschluss an den Fortschritt*).

Hartmut Koschyk ... see his article in *German Comments* No. 26, April 1992, pp. 19–25, this on p. 25.

... investment ... figures given by specialists at a conference organised by the Konrad Adenauer Foundation in Oxford, July 1992. In response to an enquiry from the author in April 1993, the German Foreign Ministry gave a significantly lower estimate: 37 per cent for the Czech Republic, 20 per cent for Poland, 18 per cent for Hungary.

... Andrzej Szczypiorski ... quoted in Baring, *Deutschland*, pp. 103–04.

'Nothing might do greater harm ...' Wiskemann, *Eastern Neighbours*, p. 295.

... 'the good traditions ...' see the treaty texts in EA, 13/1991, D310 ff, and EA, 10/1992, D369–402.

... German studies ... poisoned chalice ... see Burleigh, *Ostforschung*, passim.

... the territory of political science ... interesting discussion on the state of Soviet and East European studies in the Federal Republic could be found in the journal *Osteuropa*.

... 'the German-settled or German-permeated ...' quoted from the publisher's brochure for this *Deutsche Geschichte im Osten Europas. Eine Bilanz in 10 Bänden* (Siedler Verlag).

... 'again the hegemonial power ... leading power' Baring, *Deutschland*, p. 83.

... 'regaining her traditional role' ... ibid., p. 84.

'Bohemia and Moravia ...' ibid., p. 92.

'supremacy' ... 'key role' ... 'of course ...' ibid., pp. 105–06.

... 'cautiously and yet energetically ..' ibid., p. 106.

... 'colonisation task ...' ibid., p. 70.

... 'these, if you like, common territories' ... ibid., p. 40.

As early as 1988 ... see the report in *Frankfurter Rundschau*, 13 September 1989 and the interview with Christians in SZ, 27 September 1989. By Christians' own account, he first raised the subject in talks with the Soviet prime minister Nikolai Ryzhkov and Eduard Shevardnadze in March 1988. In this interview, he also supported the idea of resettling in the Kaliningrad region some of the ethnic Germans from other areas of the (then still) Soviet Union. In his preface to Christians, *Wege*, August Count von Kageneck summarises the basic idea of his friend Christians' proposal for the 'Baltic region K' (*Ostseeregion K*) as being to combine 'Russian workforce and German organisational talent' (quotation on p. 14).

... 'A Task called Königsberg' ... FAZ, 26 September 1992. There the following quotations.

Writing in *Die Zeit* ... 15 November 1991.

... 'One day the Germans ...' Winston S Churchill, *The Second World War. Volume VI: Triumph and Tragedy* (London: Cassell, 1954), p. 561.

... 'a good chunk of Silesia ...' this in *Die Zeit*, 9 February 1990.

... 'Centre of Lower Silesia' ... *Financial Times*, 26 October 1992.

'To be sure,' he replied ... the story is told in an 'Editorial' by Johannes Hampel in *Politische Studien*, Nr. 284, November/December 1985.

'Our time,' he wrote ... the message was addressed to the Socialist International, on his retirement from the Presidency. Text in FAZ, 16 September 1992.

... what the historian Fritz Stern has called ... this now well-known observation was made as part of the attempt by several historians, including the author of this book, to clarify what actually happened at a seminar of specialists on Germany convened by Mrs Thatcher at the Prime Minister's country residence of Chequers in March 1990. These are usefully reprinted, together with a number of other interesting observations by other historians, in Udo Wengst, ed., *Historiker betrachten Deutschland. Beiträge zum Vereinigungsprozess und zur Hauptstadtdiskussion (Februar 1990–Juni 1991)* (Bonn Berlin: Bouvier, 1992), with Stern's on pp. 139–43.

... had also to look south ... this is, however, definitely not to say that any of Germany's West European partners (or eastern neighbours) would be happy with the 'European division of labour' suggested at the end of Christians, *Wege*, p. 250, with Britons responsible for looking after 'the American cousins, the French and Italians for the African neighbours, Spaniards and Portuguese for their descendants in Latin America, and the Germans for Central and Eastern Europe'!

... lacked the 'internationalist élite' ... thus Robert Gerald Livingston in *Foreign Policy*, No. 87, Summer 1992, pp. 157–74, this on p. 172.

'I have the impression ...' interview in *Die Zeit — Magazin*, 17 July 1992.

... in an inaugural lecture ... Ludger Kühnhardt, inaugural lecture in the Albert-Ludwigs-Universität, Freiburg, 27 November 1991, typescript, this on p. 18.

Chronology

This chronology includes events that were relevant to the development of German Ostpolitik, of East-West relations in Europe more generally, and of the European Community. The terms 'Federal Republic' and 'West Germany' are used interchangeably, as are the terms 'GDR' and 'East Germany'. The label 'German-German' is applied, for the period 1970 to 1990, to talks or agreements between East Germany and West Germany, including those relating to West Berlin. Where reference is made to 'German-Soviet', 'German-Hungarian' etc, the word 'German' refers to the Federal Republic.

1945

4–11 February	Yalta Conference.
17 July–12 August	Potsdam Conference.
13 August	Russian agreement to final protocol of European Advisory Commission on division of Germany into occupation zones and Berlin into sectors.

1946

22 April	Forced merger of Social Democrats (SPD) with Communists (KPD) in Soviet occupation zone to form SED.

1948

24 June	Start of Soviet blockade of Berlin.

1949

25 January	Comecon founded.
4 April	Nato founded.
12 May	End of the Berlin blockade.
23 May	Basic Law of the Federal Republic of Germany promulgated: Founding of West Germany.
14 August	First election to Bundestag.
15 September	Konrad Adenauer elected first Chancellor.

21 September	Occupation statute for West Germany comes into force.
7 October	Constitution of the German Democratic Republic promulgated: Founding of East Germany.

1950

6 July	GDR recognises Oder-Neisse line: 'Görlitz Agreement'.
8 July	Federal Republic becomes associate member of Council of Europe.
5 August	Charter of the Germans expelled from Eastern and East Central Europe: 'Stuttgart Charter'.

1951

15 March	Establishment of the *Auswärtiges Amt*, the West German Foreign Ministry.
18 April	Founding of the European Coal and Steel Community.
20 September	Interzonal Trade Agreement between West and East German authorities.

1952

10 March	Soviet Union offers Western allies terms for a peace treaty with Germany: the 'Stalin Note'.
26 May	Signature in Bonn of *Deutschlandvertrag* (or 'General Treaty') with Western allies, linked to:
27 May	Signature of European Defence Community Treaty in Paris.
14 August	Federal Republic becomes member of IMF and World Bank.

1953

5 March	Death of Stalin.
17 June	Popular rising in East Germany.

1954

25 January–18 February	Berlin Conference of the foreign ministers of the Four Powers.
30 August	French National Assembly rejects European Defence Community.
23 October	Signature of 'Paris Treaties' including revised version of 1952 *Deutschlandvertrag*, linked to West German membership in Nato and West European Union.

1955

25 January	Soviet Union declares itself no longer in a state of war with Germany.
5 May	Paris Treaties come into force: the Federal Republic's 'Day of Sovereignty'.
9 May	Federal Republic accepted into Nato.
14 May	Founding of Warsaw Pact, including GDR.
15 May	State Treaty gives Austria independence on condition of neutrality.
17–23 July	Geneva Conference.
9–14 September	Adenauer in Moscow. Diplomatic relations established between Federal Republic and Soviet Union.
17–20 September	GDR premier Otto Grotewohl in Moscow. GDR given greater 'sovereignty'.
8–9 December	Introduction of so-called 'Hallstein Doctrine' in West German foreign policy.

1956

18 January	Creation of National People's Army out of Garrisoned People's Police in the GDR.
14–25 February	20th congress of the Communist Party of the Soviet Union: 'De-Stalinisation'.
19 March	General conscription introduced in the Federal Republic.
October–November	'Polish October' and Hungarian Revolution. Soviet invasion of Hungary.

1957

25 March	Signature of Rome Treaties (EEC and Euratom).
2 October	Polish Foreign Minister Adam Rapacki announces at the UN his plan for nuclear weapon-free zone in Central Europe: the 'Rapacki Plan'.
19 October	Federal Republic breaks diplomatic relations with Yugoslavia on basis of 'Hallstein Doctrine'.

1958

19 March	In conversation with the Soviet Ambassador to Bonn, Konrad Adenauer suggests an 'Austrian solution' for the GDR.
25 April	German-Soviet Trade Agreement, and agreement on repatriation of German citizens from the Soviet Union, signed during vist of Soviet deputy prime minister Mikoyan to Bonn.
10–27 November	Khrushchev's Berlin Ultimatum: Soviet Union

demands status of demilitarised Free City for West Berlin.

1959

10 January	Soviet proposal for a peace treaty with two German states.
18 March	SPD *Deutschlandplan*.
20 March	FDP *Deutschlandplan*.
May–August	Geneva Conference of foreign ministers of Four Powers, attended by delegations from Federal Republic and GDR. Western allies propose 'Herter Plan' for German unification.
13–15 November	SPD agrees 'Godesberg Programme'.

1960

30 June	In a Bundestag speech by Herbert Wehner, SPD expresses acceptance of the Federal Republic's integration in Nato and EEC as basis for future policy.
31 December	Signature of German-Soviet Trade Agreement in Bonn.

1961

14 June	All-party Bundestag resolution (based on so-called 'Jaksch reports') urges more active West German Ostpolitik.
13 August	GDR begins construction of Berlin Wall.
7 November	Konrad Adenauer elected Chancellor for fourth time. Gerhard Schröder (CDU) is new Foreign Minister.

1962

28 February	Publication of the Tübingen Memorandum by eight leading West German Protestants, suggesting abandonment of Hallstein Doctrine and recognition of the Oder-Neisse line.
22 March	Wolfgang Schollwer's first working paper on the Deutschlandpolitik of the Free Democrats.
6 June	Adenauer suggests to Soviet Union a ten-year 'truce' on the German Question.
17 August	Peter Fechter bleeds to death at the foot of the Berlin Wall.
October	Cuban missile crisis.
18 December	Federal Republic joins Nato pipeline embargo, breaking contracts with Soviet Union.

1963

22 January	Adenauer and de Gaulle sign Treaty on Franco-German Co-operation: the 'Élysée Treaty'.
7 March	West Germany agrees opening of trade missions with Poland.
11 March	Willy Brandt forms social-liberal (SPD-FDP) coalition government in West Berlin.
10 June	Kennedy proclaims 'strategy of peace' at American University in Washington.
23–26 June	Kennedy in Berlin delivers Free University lecture applying the 'strategy of peace' to Germany and city hall speech: *Ich bin ein Berliner*.
15 July	Willy Brandt and Egon Bahr speak at Evangelical Academy in Tutzing. Bahr's 'Tutzing speech' proclaims *Wandel durch Annäherung*.
15–16 October	Adenauer resigns after fourteen years as Chancellor. Ludwig Erhard elected to succeed him.
17 October	West Germany agrees opening of trade missions with Romania.
10 November	West Germany agrees opening of trade missions with Hungary.
17 December	First 'permit agreement' between West Berlin city government and East German authorities, allows West Berliners to visit relatives in East Berlin for Christmas and New Year holidays.

1964

6 March	West Germany agrees opening of trade missions with Bulgaria.
12 June	Treaty of Friendship, Co-operation and Mutual Assistance between Soviet Union and GDR.
14 October	Fall of Khrushchev. Leonid Brezhnev is new party leader, Alexei Kosygin is prime minister.
25 November	Introduction of compulsory exchange of hard currency for West German visitors to the GDR.

1965

8 April	Treaty on the fusion of European Coal and Steel Community, EEC and Euratom into single EC (effective 1 July 1967).
15 October	Memorandum of the Protestant Church in Germany (EKD) on 'the situation of the expellees and the relationship òf the German people to its eastern neighbours'.

| 18 November | Message of the Polish Catholic bishops to their German counterparts: 'we forgive and ask for forgiveness'. |

1966

25 March	Federal Republic sends 'Peace Note' to all states, including those in Eastern Europe, but not the GDR.
21 June–1 July	De Gaulle in Russia.
29 June	SED calls off proposed 'exchange of speakers' with SPD.
4–6 July	Bucharest Declaration of Warsaw Pact.
6 October	End of 'permit agreements' in Berlin, leaving only 'hardship post' for urgent family matters.
1 December	Grand Coalition (CDU/CSU-SPD) government formed in Bonn, with Kurt-Georg Kiesinger (CDU) as Chancellor and Willy Brandt (SPD) as Foreign Minister and Deputy Chancellor.
13 December	Chancellor Kiesinger's government declaration.

1967

31 January	Federal Republic opens diplomatic relations with Romania.
8–10 February	Warsaw Pact foreign ministers agree not to open diplomatic ties with the Federal Republic until it recognises the GDR: the 'Ulbricht Doctrine'.
3 March	Wolfgang Schollwer (FDP) produces another working paper proposing a major change in Deutschlandpolitik.
15 March	Poland signs friendship treaty with GDR.
17 March	Czechoslovakia signs friendship treaty with GDR.
12 April	Chancellor Kiesinger's government declaration on Deutschlandpolitik.
24–26 April	Karlovy Vary (Karlsbad) Conference of European communist parties.
18 May	Hungary signs friendship treaty with GDR.
May–September	Exchange of letters between Chancellor Kiesinger and GDR Prime Minister Willi Stoph.
17 June	Chancellor Kiesinger's speech on the 'day of German unity'.
3 August	Federal Republic agrees opening of trade missions with Czechoslovakia.
7 September	Bulgaria signs friendship treaty with GDR.

1967 *continued*

12 October	Beginning of diplomatic exchanges between Bonn and Moscow on possible renunciation-of-force agreements.
November	Egon Bahr becomes head of planning staff in West German Foreign Office.
6–12 December	De Gaulle in Poland.
14 December	Nato agrees Harmel report.

1968

29–31 January	FDP party conference elects Walter Scheel as party leader.
31 January	Diplomatic relations with Yugoslavia restored, puncturing 'Hallstein Doctrine'.
11 March	Chancellor Kiesinger delivers first annual 'Report on the state of the nation in divided Germany'.
17–21 March	SPD party conference in Nuremberg.
March–April	Repression of student protests in Poland. Anti-semitic campaign and purge.
11 June	GDR imposes visa obligation for travellers in transit between West Berlin and West Germany.
25 June	Nato proposes mutual balanced force reductions: the 'Reykjavik signal'.
11 July	Soviet Union breaks off talks on renunciation-of-force agreement with Federal Republic.
21 August	Warsaw Pact invasion of Czechoslovakia. End of 'Prague Spring'.

1969

20 January	Beginning of Nixon administration in USA, with Henry Kissinger as National Security Advisor.
2 March	Clashes between Soviet and Chinese border troops on the Ussuri.
17 March	Budapest Appeal of Warsaw Pact.
28 April	Soviet Foreign Trade Minister visits Hanover Trade Fair, and meets West German Economics Minister. Announcement of first German-Soviet natural gas pipeline deal since 1962 embargo.
10 June	Federation of Protestant Churches in the GDR begins its work.
3 July	Soviet Union and Federal Republic resume diplomatic exchanges on renunciation-of-force agreements.
24–25 July	FDP leader Walter Scheel in Moscow, with a delegation including Hans-Dietrich Genscher.

20–23 August	SPD parliamentary leader Helmut Schmidt with a delegation in Moscow.
12 September	Soviet diplomatic notes to Western allies suggesting negotiations about Berlin, and to the Bonn government suggesting negotiations in Moscow on renunciation-of-force agreement.
28 September	Elections to 6th Bundestag. CDU/CSU win 242 seats, SPD 224, FDP 30, thus giving SPD and FDP the chance to form a coalition with a majority of twelve.
21 October	Willy Brandt forms social-liberal (SPD-FDP) coalition government, with Walter Scheel as Foreign Minister.
28 October	Chancellor Brandt's government declaration.
17 November	USA and Soviet Union begin preliminary talks on strategic arms limitation (SALT).
28 November	Federal Republic accedes to Nuclear Non-Proliferation Treaty.
1–2 December	EC summit in The Hague. Resolutions on economic and currency union and foreign policy co-operation.
18 December	In a letter to Federal President Heinemann, Walter Ulbricht proposes negotiations on opening relations between the GDR and the Federal Republic.

1970

30 January	Egon Bahr begins talks in Moscow with Soviet Foreign Minister Andrei Gromyko.
1 February	Signature in Essen of German-Soviet natural gas pipeline agreement.
5 February	Ferdinand Duckwitz begins talks in Warsaw with Polish Deputy Foreign Minister.
19 March	Willy Brandt meets GDR Prime Minister Willi Stoph in Erfurt, East Germany.
26 March	Beginning of four-power negotiations on Berlin.
16 April	Beginning of Soviet-American SALT talks.
21 May	Willy Brandt and GDR Prime Minister Willi Stoph meet in Kassel, West Germany. Brandt offers his '20 Points'.
26–27 May	Nato meeting in Rome reviews state of bi- and multilateral East-West negotiations.
1 July	Confidential 'Bahr-paper' summarising results of German-Soviet talks is published in German press.

1970 *continued*

26 July–7 August	Walter Scheel negotiates final details of Moscow Treaty.
12 August	Signature of Moscow Treaty. Scheel hands Gromyko 'Letter on German Unity'.
3–13 November	Walter Scheel negotiates final form of Warsaw Treaty and 'Information' on German minority in Poland.
19 November	First meeting of EC foreign ministers for European Political Co-operation (EPC), in Munich.
27 November	Opening of German-German negotiations between Egon Bahr and State Secretary Michael Kohl.
7 December	Signature of Warsaw Treaty. Willy Brandt kneels at the memorial to the heroes of the Warsaw ghetto.
20 December	Strikes and protest demonstrations in Poland's Baltic ports lead to resignation of Party leader Władysław Gomułka. He is succeeded by Edward Gierek.

1971

26 February	Social Democrats pass 'demarcation resolution', defining their differences with Communism.
3 May	Walter Ulbricht replaced by Erich Honecker as East German party leader.
15–19 June	8th party congress of the SED.
3 September	Signature of Quadripartite Agreement on Berlin.
16–18 September	Brandt meets Brezhnev at Oreanda in the Crimea.
30 September	German-German agreement on post and telephone links, complementing Quadripartite Agreement on Berlin.
20 October	Brandt awarded Nobel Peace Prize.
17 December	German-German Transit Agreement, complementing Quadripartite Agreement on Berlin.

1972

23 February	Beginning of Bundestag debates on the Moscow and Warsaw treaties.
29 March	For the first time in nearly six years ordinary West Berliners are allowed to visit East Berlin.
23 April	SPD-FDP coalition loses majority in Bundestag.
27 April	Failure in Bundestag of Christian Democrats' 'constructive vote of no confidence' against Chancellor Brandt.
17 May	Bundestag ratifies Moscow and Warsaw treaties. 'Common Resolution' of CDU/CSU with SPD and FDP.

22–30 May	Nixon visits Soviet Union. Signature of SALT I arms control treaty.
26 May	Signature of German–German Traffic Treaty.
15 June	Egon Bahr and GDR State Secretary Michael Kohl begin talks on a general framework treaty between GDR and Federal Republic.
5 July	German–Soviet Agreement on Trade and Economic Co-operation.
July	Further German–Soviet natural gas pipeline agreement signed in Düsseldorf.
19 November	Elections to 7th Bundestag. SPD win 225 seats, FDP 41, giving them a majority of thirty-six over CDU/CSU, who have 230 seats.
21 November	United States and Soviet Union begin preliminary talks for SALT II treaty.
22 November	Representatives of all European states (except Albania), the Soviet Union, the United States and Canada begin preliminary talks in Helsinki for a Conference on Security and Co-operation in Europe (CSCE).
12 December	Willy Brandt re-elected Chancellor, continuing social-liberal (SPD–FDP) coalition government.
21 December	Signature of Treaty on the Bases of Relations between Federal Republic and GDR.
1973	
1 January	Britain, Ireland and Denmark become members of the EC.
31 January	Beginning of preliminary talks on Mutual Balanced Force Reductions (MBFR). Establishment of a German–German Frontier Commission.
23 April	Henry Kissinger proclaims his 'Year of Europe'.
11 May	Bundestag ratifies Basic Treaty with GDR, and legislates for Federal Republic to join the UN.
18–22 May	Brezhnev on state visit to the Federal Republic. New agreements on economic, technical and industrial co-operation and on cultural exchange.
28 May	Bavarian state government appeals to Federal Constitutional Court to test constitutionality of Basic Treaty with the GDR.
31 May	Erich Honecker receives the parliamentary leaders of the Social and Free Democrats, Herbert Wehner and Wolfgang Mischnick.
18–25 June	Brezhnev in the United States.

1973 *continued*

21 June	German-German Treaty on the Bases of Relations comes into force.
3–8 July	Opening in Helsinki of Conference on Security and Co-operation in Europe.
31 July	Federal Constitutional Court declares Treaty on the Bases of Relations with the GDR is compatible with the Federal Republic's Basic Law.
18 September	Federal Republic and GDR become members of the UN.
25 September	United States and Soviet Union begin SALT II arms control talks in Geneva.
18–20 October	Scheel in Poland.
30 October	MBFR talks begin in Vienna.
15 November	GDR doubles compulsory exchange of hard currency for West German and other Western visitors.
11 December	Prague Treaty signed. Diplomatic relations established between the Federal Republic and Czechoslovakia.
21 December	Federal Republic opens diplomatic relations with Hungary and Bulgaria.

1974

18 January	German-Soviet Economic Commission produces further accord on long-term co-operation.
2 May	Federal Republic and GDR open 'Permanent Representations' in their respective capitals.
6 May	Resignation of Chancellor Brandt, after the exposure of an East German spy in his office.
15 May	Walter Scheel elected Federal President.
16 May	Helmut Schmidt elected Chancellor in succession to Willy Brandt. Hans-Dietrich Genscher becomes Foreign Minister in succession to Walter Scheel.
20 June	Bundestag ratifies Prague Treaty.
27 June–3 July	Nixon meets Brezhnev in Moscow and Yalta.
7 October	Changes to GDR constitution on 25th anniversary of the state's founding. Reference to united Germany removed and GDR proclaimed 'for ever and irrevocably allied' with the Soviet Union.
26 October	GDR announces reduction of compulsory exchange for West German and other Western visitors from 15 November.
28–31 October	Chancellor Schmidt and Foreign Minister Gen-

scher in Moscow. Signature of third German-Soviet natural gas pipeline agreement.

1 November	German-Polish agreement on economic, industrial and technological co-operation.
11 November	German-Hungarian agreement on economic, industrial and technological co-operation.
23–24 November	President Ford meets Brezhnev in Vladivostok.
9–10 December	At a conference in Paris, EC heads of government agree to meet three times a year, together with their foreign ministers: the 'European Council'.
11–12 December	Signature of agreements between West Berlin and GDR agencies on the disposal of West Berlin's rubbish and sewage in the GDR.

1975

22 January	German-Czechoslovak agreement on economic, industrial and technological co-operation.
10–11 March	First meeting of EC's 'European Council', in Dublin.
14 May	German-Bulgarian agreement on economic, industrial and technological co-operation.
30 July–1 August	Ceremonial signature in Helsinki of concluding document of Conference on Security and Co-operation in Europe (CSCE): 'Helsinki Final Act'. Chancellor Schmidt has bilateral talks with Leonid Brezhnev, Edward Gierek and Erich Honecker.
22–30 September	CDU leader Helmut Kohl in Soviet Union.
7 October	New treaty of friendship, co-operation and mutual assistance between GDR and Soviet Union.
9–10 October	Genscher in Poland. Signature of agreements on a credit, pensions and accident insurance, and a protocol on emigration possibilities for the German minority.
10–16 November	President Scheel on state visit to Soviet Union.
24–28 November	Bulgarian Party leader Todor Zhivkov on state visit to Federal Republic.
19 December	German-German agreement on transit arrangements between West Berlin and the rest of West Germany. Federal Republic will pay annual lump-sum for 'transit fees', plus further sums for improvements to rail and motorway links.

1976

7 January	Publication of Tindemans report on further moves towards a 'European Union' of the EC.

1976 *continued*

January	First 'Parliamentary Symposium' of representatives of the Bundestag and Supreme Soviet.
19 February	Bundestag ratifies new agreements with Poland.
30 March	German-German agreement on postal and telephone links.
18–22 May	9th party congress of the SED.
8–12 June	Polish communist party leader Edward Gierek visits Federal Republic.
June	Workers' protests in Poland precipitated by food price rises. Violent repression in Radom and Ursus.
September	Formation of Workers' Defence Committee (KOR) in Poland.
3 October	Elections to 8th Bundestag. SPD wins 214 seats, FDP 39, giving majority of ten over CDU/CSU which have 243.
16 November	Balladeer Wolf Biermann deprived of his GDR citizenship during a tour in the Federal Republic.
15 December	Helmut Schmidt re-elected Chancellor.

1977

1 January	Charter 77 declaration in Czechoslovakia.
27–28 May	Schmidt in Yugoslavia.
13–15 June	Genscher in Soviet Union.
4–7 July	Hungarian Communist Party leader János Kádár visits Federal Republic.
4 October	Opening of CSCE follow-up conference in Belgrade.
28 October	Chancellor Schmidt's speech on Western security needs at International Institute for Strategic Studies (IISS) in London.
21–25 November	Schmidt in Poland.

1978

1 January	After five-year transitional period, Britain, Ireland and Denmark formally become full members of the EC.
6–7 January	Schmidt in Romania.
9 March	End of Belgrade CSCE follow-up meeting with further concluding document.
10–13 April	Visit of Czechoslovak Communist Party leader and head of state, Gustáv Husák, to Federal Republic.

4–7 May	Brezhnev in Federal Republic. Joint Declaration. Agreement on development of economic and industrial co-operation.
16–17 July	Summit of world's leading industrial countries (G7) in Bonn.
16 October	Cardinal Karol Wojtyła, Archbishop of Kraków, elected Pope John Paul II.
4–5 December	EC's European Council meets in Brussels. Agreement to introduce European Monetary System.

1979

5–6 January	Guadeloupe summit conference of Presidents Carter and Giscard d'Estaing, Prime Minister Callaghan and Chancellor Schmidt.
2–4 May	Schmidt in Bulgaria.
23 May	Karl Carstens elected Federal President.
2–10 June	Pope John Paul II visits Poland.
10 June	First direct elections to EC's European Parliament.
18 June	Carter and Brezhnev sign SALT II arms control agreement in Vienna.
21–24 November	Gromyko in Bonn.
12 December	Nato's 'double-track' decision to offer negotiations on intermediate-range nuclear forces (INF) with the Soviet Union, but to deploy new intermediate-range nuclear missiles in Western Europe from 1983 if these negotiations are unsuccessful.
27 December	Soviet invasion of Afghanistan.

1980

4 January	President Carter announces sanctions against Soviet Union, interrupts ratification of SALT II treaty, and threatens boycott of Moscow Olympics.
15 May	West Germany joins boycott of Moscow Olympics.
19 May	Giscard d'Estaing meets Brezhnev in Wilanów, near Warsaw.
12–13 June	EC's European Council in Venice.
22–23 June	G7 summit in Venice.
30 June–1 July	Schmidt and Genscher in Moscow.
10–12 August	Bundestag delegation in Soviet Union on tenth anniversary of Moscow Treaty.
22 August	Cancellation of planned meeting between Schmidt and GDR leader Erich Honecker on account of strike wave in Poland.

1980 *continued*

31 August	Signature of Gdańsk Agreement permits founding of Independent Self-Governing Trades Union 'Solidarity'.
5 October	Elections to 9th Bundestag. SPD win 218 seats and FDP 53, thus having a majority of 61 over CDU/CSU, who together have 226.
9 October	GDR announces increase in compulsory exchange for West German and other Western visitors.
13 October	Erich Honecker's 'Gera speech'.
17 October	Beginning of Geneva talks between Soviet and American representatives on intermediate-range nuclear forces (INF).
5 November	Helmut Schmidt re-elected as Chancellor.
12 November	Opening of CSCE follow-up conference in Madrid.

1981

1 January	Greece becomes tenth member of the EC.
20 January	Ronald Reagan sworn in as US President.
11 June	Richard von Weizsäcker elected Governing Mayor of Berlin.
29 June	Willy Brandt meets Brezhnev in Moscow.
10 October	Mass demonstration in Bonn against Nato double-track decision.
20 November	Signature in Essen of agreement between a German-led consortium and the Soviet foreign trade organisation on new natural gas pipeline to, and supplies from, Siberia.
22–25 November	Brezhnev in Bonn.
30 November	United States and Soviet Union resume talks on intermediate-range nuclear forces (INF) in Geneva.
11–13 December	Schmidt visits GDR. Summit meeting with Honecker at the Werbellinsee.
13 December	General Jaruzelski declares 'state of war' in Poland.
29 December	President Reagan announces sanctions against the Soviet Union as response to the declaration of martial law in Poland.

1982

5 January	Schmidt in America for talks with Reagan.
19–23 April	SPD party conference in Munich. Establishment of working group on 'new strategies' chaired by Egon Bahr.
May	Publication of Palme Commission report.

16 July	American and Soviet negotiators' informal 'walk in the woods' produces possible compromise formula on intermediate-range nuclear forces not accepted by their governments.
17 September	Social-liberal coalition ended with resignation of four FDP ministers.
20 September	German-German agreement on youth exchanges.
1 October	Schmidt deposed as Chancellor by a constructive vote of no-confidence, and succeeded by Helmut Kohl, who will lead a conservative-liberal (CDU/CSU-FDP) coalition government.
12–13 October	German-Soviet economic commission meets in Bonn.
November	Brezhnev dies, succeeded as Party leader by Yuri Andropov.
31 December	'State of war' in Poland is 'suspended'.

1983

16–19 January	Gromyko visits Federal Republic.
6 March	Elections to 10th Bundestag. CDU/CSU win 244 seats, FDP 34 seats, thus giving the conservative-liberal coalition a majority of 58 over the SPD, with 193 seats, and the Greens, with 27.
23 March	President Reagan announces Strategic Defense Initiative (SDI) research programme.
29 April	Honecker postpones his planned visit to West Germany.
28 May	SPD parliamentary leader Hans-Jochen Vogel has first of a series of annual meetings with Erich Honecker, in the GDR.
16–23 June	Pope's second visit to Poland.
29 June	Federal Government guarantees a DM 1 billion credit to the GDR, organised by Franz Josef Strauss.
4–7 July	Kohl and Genscher in Moscow.
15 July	End of Madrid CSCE review conference.
22 July	'State of war' in Poland is 'lifted'.
July	Franz Josef Strauss visits Czechoslovakia, Poland and the GDR.
1 September	In a joint letter on the anniversary of the outbreak of the Second World War, the Protestant Churches in West and East Germany appeal to the leaders of both German states to work within their alliances for arms reductions, especially in the Geneva negotiations on intermediate-range nuclear forces. Peace movement blockade of American military depot in

1983 *continued*

	West Germany. A South Korean jumbo jet is shot down by Soviet forces.
15 September	Richard von Weizsäcker, as Governing Mayor of (West) Berlin, meets Erich Honecker in East Berlin.
5 October	Lech Wałęsa awarded Nobel Peace Prize.
10 October	East German media publish letter from Honecker appealing to Chancellor Kohl not to go ahead with the deployment of new American nuclear missiles.
10 November	GDR celebrates Luther's 500th birthday.
10–16 November	German-Soviet economic commission meets in Moscow, chaired by Federal Economics Minister Otto Graf Lambsdorff.
18 November	SPD special party conference in Cologne votes by 583 votes to 14 (with three abstentions) against deployment of new American medium-range missiles in the Federal Republic.
22 November	Bundestag votes by 286 votes to 226 (with one abstention) for deployment of new American medium-range missiles in the Federal Republic, in line with Nato's double-track decision of December 1979.
23 November	Soviet delegation breaks off INF negotiations in Geneva.
24 November	Honecker tells his Central Committee the GDR should aim to 'limit the damage' done by the Bundestag decision.

1984

9 February	Bundestag Common Resolution of CDU/CSU, FDP, and SPD on Deutschlandpolitik.
9–13 February	Andropov dies. Kohl and Honecker meet for the first time at his funeral. Konstantin Chernenko succeeds him, and has talks with Kohl.
14 March	At their annual meeting, Erich Honecker and Hans-Jochen Vogel agree to establish joint SED-SPD working group on a chemical weapon-free zone.
17–21 May	SPD Essen party conference. Resolution on security policy incorporating 'new strategies'.
20–22 May	Genscher in Moscow.
27 June	A total of fifty-five East Germans take refuge in West Germany's Permanent Representation in East

	Berlin, hoping thereby to leave East Germany for the West.
1 July	Richard von Weizsäcker becomes Federal President.
25 July	Federal Government guarantees a DM 950 million credit for the GDR.
17 August	At a meeting in the Kremlin, the Soviet leadership express to Erich Honecker and his delegation their disapproval of his proposed visit to West Germany.
4 September	GDR announces the postponement of Honecker's visit to West Germany.
20 September	SPD and SED begin talks on a chemical weapon-free zone in Central Europe.
19 October	Father Jerzy Popiełuszko abducted and murdered by functionaries of the Polish secret police.
21 November	Last-minute cancellation of Genscher's planned visit to Poland.

1985

20 January	Ronald Reagan installed for second term as US President.
21–22 January	German-Soviet economic commission meets in Bonn.
10 March	Death of Chernenko.
12 March	Mikhail Gorbachev succeeds Chernenko as Party leader. Kohl meets Gorbachev and Honecker at Chernenko's funeral.
22–29 March	Lothar Späth visits Soviet Union in his capacity as president of the Bundesrat.
March	Resumption of American-Soviet arms control talks in Geneva.
18 April	Gorbachev receives F Wilhelm Christians, head of the Deutsche Bank.
8 May	Richard von Weizsäcker's speech on fortieth anniversary of the end of the Second World War in Europe.
16 May	Hans-Jochen Vogel meets Erich Honecker.
May	Willy Brandt meets Gorbachev in Moscow.
6 June	Herbert Wehner visits Erich Honecker.
14–16 June	Chancellor Kohl addresses meeting of expellees from Silesia.
May–June	Gdańsk trial of Solidarity leaders, Władysław Frasyniuk, Bogdan Lis, Adam Michnik.

1985 *continued*

19 June	SPD-SED draft treaty on chemical weapon-free zone in Central Europe.
2 July	Eduard Shevardnadze succeeds Andrei Gromyko as Soviet Foreign Minister. Gromyko becomes State President.
7 September	SPD defence specialist Andreas von Bülow publishes paper envisaging superpower disengagement and militia defence for West Germany by the year 2000: 'Bülow paper'.
8–11 September	Johannes Rau, Social Democrat prime minister of North Rhine Westphalia, visits Soviet Union and meets Gorbachev.
18 September	Willy Brandt, Egon Bahr and Günter Gaus visit Erich Honecker. Agreement to form joint working group on a nuclear weapon-free corridor.
19–21 November	First Reagan-Gorbachev summit meeting, in Geneva.
November	SPD joint declaration with Polish United Workers' Party on confidence-building measures in Europe.
29 Nov–5 December	Bundestag delegation visits Soviet Union.
7–8 December	Willy Brandt in Warsaw for fifteenth anniversary of Warsaw Treaty. Meets Jaruzelski but not Wałęsa.

1986

1 January	Spain and Portugal join the EC.
25 February	27th congress of Communist Party of the Soviet Union.
2–8 April	German-Soviet economic commission meets in Moscow.
17–21 April	11th Party congress of the SED.
22 April	40th anniversary of forced merger of Social Democrats with Communists to form SED.
26 April	Disastrous accident at nuclear power plant in Chernobyl, Ukraine.
6 May	German-German cultural agreement signed.
28 May	Gorbachev addresses top-level internal conference of Soviet foreign ministry. Hans-Jochen Vogel meets Erich Honecker in GDR.
25 June	Johannes Rau, prime minister of North Rhine Westphalia and probable Social Democrat candidate for Chancellor, in Soviet Union. Received by Gorbachev.

20–22 July	Genscher in Moscow, agrees with Gorbachev to 'open a new page' in German-Soviet relations.
25–29 August	Nuremberg party conference of SPD. Johannes Rau confirmed as the party's candidate for Chancellor.
11 September	Amnesty in Poland, includes virtually all political prisoners.
21–22 September	Conclusion of Stockholm Conference on Confidence- and Security-building Measures and Disarmament in Europe.
September–October	First German-German town-twinning agreement, between Saarlouis and Eisenhüttenstadt, is signed and ratified.
11–12 October	Second Reagan-Gorbachev summit meeting, in Reykjavik.
21 October	SPD-SED joint declaration on a nuclear weapon-free corridor in Central Europe.
4 November	CSCE review conference opens in Vienna.
10–11 November	At a meeting in Moscow, Gorbachev communicates in general terms to East European Party leaders a new and more permissive Soviet line towards them.
19 December	Soviet Union announces release of Andrei Sakharov from internal exile.

1987

January	Beginning of 750th anniversary celebrations in Berlin (East) and Berlin (West).
25 January	Elections to 11th Bundestag. CDU/CSU win 223 seats, FDP 34 seats, giving them a majority of 29 over the SPD, with 186 seats, and the Greens, with 42.
27 January	In a speech to the Central Committee of the Soviet Communist Party, Gorbachev demands the 'democratisation' of party and society.
25 March	Willy Brandt resigns as SPD party chairman.
15 May	Hans-Jochen Vogel meets Erich Honecker at Werbellinsee.
28 May	Matthias Rust flies his Cessna 172 to Moscow, landing on Red Square.
8 June	East German police clash with young East Germans on the Eastern side of the Brandenburg Gate.
8–14 June	Pope's third visit to Poland.
12 June	President Reagan speaks on the Western side of the Brandenburg Gate, calling on Gorbachev to open the gate and tear down the Berlin Wall.

1987 *continued*

14 June

Special party conference of the SPD elects Hans-Jochen Vogel as party chairman.

1 July

EC's Single European Act comes into force.

6–11 July

President von Weizsäcker in Moscow, together with Foreign Minister Genscher. Restatement of intent to 'open a new page' in German-Soviet relations.

26 August

Bonn government increases 'welcome money' for visiting East Germans from DM 30 to DM 100 a year.

27 August

Publication of SPD-SED Joint Paper on ideological argument and common security.

7–11 September

Erich Honecker makes his long-delayed official visit to the Federal Republic.

October

SPD joint statement with Communist Party of the Soviet Union on 'disarmament for development'.

25 November

State Security Service (Stasi) search of premises of the Zion Church in East Berlin, followed by further measures against dissident groups.

7–8 December

Third Reagan-Gorbachev summit meeting in Washington. Signature of treaty between the United States and the Soviet Union on the elimination of their intermediate-range and short-range missiles: the 'INF Treaty'.

28–31 December

Franz Josef Strauss flies himself to Moscow, and is received by Gorbachev.

1988

17 January

In East Berlin, an official demonstration in memory of Rosa Luxemburg and Karl Liebknecht is joined by unofficial demonstrators, many of whom are arrested.

17–19 January

Soviet Foreign Minister Eduard Shevardnadze in Bonn.

7–11 February

Lothar Späth, prime minister of Baden-Württemberg, in Soviet Union.

10 March

A West German cultural institute is opened in Budapest.

21–24 March

Rita Süssmuth visits Moscow as chairwoman of the CDU Womens' Union.

5 April

Joint declaration of the SPD, SED and Czechoslovak Communist Party, proposing a chemical weapon-free zone in Central Europe.

29 April

SPD chairman Hans-Jochen Vogel meets Erich Honecker for further talks.

April–May	Strikes in Poland, including major Solidarity strong-holds such as the Lenin shipyard.
May	János Kádár resigns as Hungarian party leader.
11 May	German-Soviet economic commission meets in Moscow.
29 May–1 June	Fourth Reagan-Gorbachev summit meeting, in Moscow.
13–15 June	Wiesbaden party conference of CDU passes extensive resolution on foreign policy and Deutschland-politik.
23 June	At a Church congress (*Kirchentag*) in Halle, Wittenberg pastor Friedrich Schorlemmer presents twenty theses for social and political renewal.
25 June	EC and Comecon open official relations.
28–31 June	19th conference (not congress) of Communist Party of the Soviet Union.
7 July	Hermann Axen for the SED and Egon Bahr for the SPD present joint proposal for a 'zone of trust and security in Central Europe'.
31 August	Wave of strikes in Poland leads to meeting between General Czesław Kiszczak and Lech Wałęsa. First formal discussion of Round Table talks with Solidarity.
30 Aug–2 September	SPD party conference in Münster.
1 October	Gorbachev becomes state President as well as Party leader.
24–27 October	Kohl in Moscow.
7 December	Gorbachev addresses the UN: principles of freedom of choice and renunciation of force. Gorbachev meets with Reagan and his successor George Bush.

1989

15 January	Vienna CSCE review conference ends with detailed provisions in concluding document.
16–18 January	Plenum of Central Committee of Polish United Workers' Party concludes with agreement in principle to relegalisation of Solidarity.
2 February	End of the sixteen-year long MBFR talks in Vienna.
6 February	Round Table talks begin in Poland.
10–11 February	Central Committee of Hungarian Socialist Workers' Party discusses reassessment of 1956 revolution and endorses the idea of a multi-party system.

1989 *continued*

21 February	Václav Havel sentenced to nine months' imprisonment.
19 March	Beginning of new talks on conventional force reductions, between Nato and Warsaw Pact, and on security and confidence-building measures, between all CSCE participant states; both in Vienna.
5 April	Polish Round Table talks conclude with agreement leading to relegalisation of Solidarity and semi-free elections to parliament.
6–7 April	German-Soviet economic commission meets in Bonn.
17 April	Legal (re)registration of Solidarity.
2 May	Hungary begins to dismantle the 'iron curtain' along its frontier with Austria.
7 May	Local elections in the GDR. Independent monitors point to rigging of the results.
12 May	In Texas, President Bush speaks of going 'beyond containment' in relations with the Soviet Union.
22 May	GDR and Poland sign treaty agreeing the exact frontier line across the Oder estuary.
29–30 May	Nato's fortieth anniversary summit, in Brussels.
4 June	First round of Polish parliamentary elections. Massacre on Tiananmen Square in Beijing.
12–15 June	Gorbachev in West Germany. German-Soviet Joint Declaration: the 'Bonn Declaration'.
13 June	Round Table talks begin in Hungary.
16 June	Ceremonial reburial of Imre Nagy and his associates in Budapest.
18 June	Second round of Polish parliamentary elections give Solidarity-led opposition all seats available to it in lower house (thirty-five per cent) and 99 out of 100 in the new upper house. In the EC, direct elections to the European Parliament.
6 July	Gorbachev addresses Council of Europe in Strasbourg.
7–8 July	Warsaw Pact meeting in Bucharest ends with declaration rejecting interference in the internal affairs of any state.
9–12 July	President Bush visits Poland and Hungary.
19 July	General Jaruzelski elected President of Poland.
July–August	Growing number of East Germans escape via Hungary to Austria, or take refuge in the West German missions in East Berlin, Budapest and Prague.

24 August	Veteran Solidarity adviser Tadeusz Mazowiecki is appointed Polish Prime Minister.
25 August	Hungarian Prime Minister Miklós Németh and Foreign Minister Gyula Horn visit West Germany for talks with Chancellor Kohl and Foreign Minister Genscher.
26 August	Initiative to found a social democratic party in the GDR.
9–11 September	Announcement of the founding of the New Forum opposition movement in the GDR.
10–11 September	Hungary announces the opening of its frontier to Austria for East Germans, at midnight on the 11th. From now until the end of October some 50,000 will leave by this route.
21–22 September	Shevardnadze meets with Bush in Washington and visits James Baker on his ranch in Wyoming.
25 September	Thousands in protest demonstration in Leipzig.
30 September	Some 6,000 East Germans who had taken refuge in the West German embassy in Prague are given permission to leave for the West in special trains, which pass through East Germany.
2 October	Some 15,000 in protest demonstration in Leipzig.
1–5 October	Some 1,500 East Germans who had taken refuge in the West German embassy in Warsaw are allowed to leave for the West.
4–5 October	A further 7,600 East Germans who had taken refuge in the West German embassy in Prague are allowed to leave for the West, in special trains which pass through East Germany.
5 October	Gorbachev arrives in East Berlin to take part in the GDR's fortieth anniversary celebrations. He warns against 'coming too late'.
7 October	On fortieth anniversary of the founding of the GDR, East German security forces break up demonstrations for reform in several East German cities. Founding of a Social Democratic Party in the GDR.
9 October	Some 70,000 demonstrate in Leipzig. Security forces gather, but do not intervene.
10 October	Hungarian Socialist Workers' Party dissolved, Hungarian Socialist Party succeeds it.
15 October	Václav Havel is unable to travel to Frankfurt to receive the Peace Prize of the German Book Trade.
16 October	More than 100,000 join in the now regular 'Monday demo' in Leipzig.

1989 *continued*

18 October	Erich Honecker resigns, succeeded by Egon Krenz.
23 October	Proclamation of the new Hungarian Republic in Budapest. Some 300,000 East Germans demonstrate in Leipzig.
28 October	Demonstrations in Prague to mark the seventy-first anniversary of the founding of independent Czechoslovakia are broken up by police.
30 October	More than 300,000 demonstrate in Leipzig.
4 November	Massive demonstration in East Berlin (estimates up to 1 million). Thousands more East Germans leave via Czechoslovakia.
6 November	Massive demonstration in Leipzig (estimates up to 500,000).
8 November	Bundestag resolution on Poland's western frontier.
9 November	Opening of the Berlin Wall.
9–14 November	Kohl visit to Poland, interrupted to return to Berlin to mark the opening of the Wall.
10 November	Resignation of Bulgarian party leader Todor Zhivkov.
13 November	Hans Modrow appointed Prime Minister of the GDR.
16 November	Hungary applies to join Council of Europe.
17 November	In Prague, police repression of a demonstration to mark the anniversary of the death of a student killed by the Nazis sparks what will be called the 'velvet revolution'. In East Berlin, the Modrow government proposes 'treaty community' with West Germany.
18 November	EC leaders meet in Paris to discuss response to developments in Eastern Europe.
20 November	Calls for unity as well as democracy at the regular Leipzig 'Monday demo'.
28 November	Kohl offers his '10-Point Programme' to overcome the division of Germany and Europe.
2–3 December	Bush-Gorbachev meeting in Malta.
3 December	Egon Krenz resigns as party leader, together with the whole Politburo and Central Committee.
6 December	Mitterrand meets Gorbachev in Kiev. Egon Krenz also resigns his state offices.
7 December	Round Table talks start in East Germany.
9 December	EC summit in Strasbourg reaffirms German right to unity through self-determination.
10 December	President Gustáv Husák swears in new Czechoslovak federal government, dominated by non-Communists, and then resigns as President. In

	Sofia, more than 50,000 people join in a pro-democracy demonstration organised by the newly-founded Union of Democratic Forces.
16 December	Special conference of the CDU in the GDR ends with commitment to unity. Lothar de Maizière elected chairman.
16–18 December	Kohl in Hungary.
19 December	Kohl in Dresden, greeted by large crowds demonstrating for unity. Agreement with East German Prime Minister Hans Modrow on moves towards a 'treaty community' of the two German states.
18–20 December	Special party conference of the SPD in Berlin votes for confederation between the two German states and passes new basic programme, replacing the Godesberg programme of 1959.
20–21 December	President Mitterrand pays a state visit to the GDR. He is the first and last head of state from one of the three Western Allies ever to do so.
21 December	In Bucharest, pro-Ceauşescu demonstration turns into anti-Ceauşescu demonstration.
22 December	Opening of the Brandenburg Gate.
24 December	Visa-free travel to the GDR for West Germans and West Berliners.
25 December	Alexander Dubček elected president of the Czechoslovak federal parliament. Nicolae and Elena Ceauşescu are executed.
29 December	Václav Havel elected President of Czechoslovakia.
30 December	Polish parliament changes the name of the state to Republic of Poland, and passes package of laws to begin economic transformation according to the 'Balcerowicz plan'.

1990

11 January	Gorbachev visits Vilnius, attempting to stop the movement to independence.
28 January	East German prime minister Modrow and the Round Table agree that Volkskammer elections should be brought forward to 18 March.
30 January	Modrow in Moscow for talks with Gorbachev.
1 February	Modrow presents plan for 'Germany, united fatherland'.
7 February	Bonn government forms cabinet committee called 'German unity' and agrees in principle to proceed with talks on German monetary union.

1990 *continued*

8–10 February	James Baker in Moscow, discussing, among other things, the '2 + 4' modality for talks on German unification.
10–11 February	Kohl and Genscher in Moscow. Gorbachev gives green light for unification of Germany.
12–14 February	'2 + 4' formula for negotiations on the external aspects of German unification is announced at Ottawa 'open skies' meeting.
13–14 February	Modrow in Bonn.
24–25 February	Kohl and Bush meet in Camp David.
2 March	Kohl appears to make signature of frontier treaty with Poland conditional on Polish undertakings on the reparation and German minority issues.
8 March	Bundestag resolution on the Polish frontier.
11 March	Lithuanian parliament votes to 're-establish' independence.
15 March	Gorbachev gains powers of an executive President.
18 March	Elections to the Volkskammer in the GDR. The Alliance for Germany, with the CDU as its leading member, gains 193 seats, the SPD 87 seats, with the former SED, now called the Party for Democratic Socialism, in third place with 65 seats.
19 March–11 April	CSCE conference on economic co-operation in Bonn.
9 April	Meeting in Bratislava of leaders of Czechoslovakia, Hungary and Poland, to discuss trilateral co-operation.
12 April	Lothar de Maizière forms coalition government in East Berlin. He declares his government to be in favour of joining the Federal Republic by way of Article 23 of its Basic Law.
18 April	Mitterand and Kohl send joint message to current President of the European Council of the EC, proposing an inter-governmental conference on 'political union' of the existing EC, as well as that already planned on economic and monetary union.
21 April	EC foreign ministers, meeting in Dublin, agree outline plans for the former GDR to join the EC when it joins the Federal Republic.
28 April	EC Dublin summit.
2–5 May	President von Weizsäcker on state visit to Poland.
5 May	First 2 + 4 meeting, in Bonn.

14 May	Kohl's foreign policy adviser Horst Teltschik takes bankers on secret mission to Moscow.
18 May	Federal Republic and GDR sign Treaty on Monetary, Economic and Social Union.
30 May–3 June	Bush-Gorbachev summit in Washington and Camp David.
5–8 June	Kohl meets Bush.
17 June	Joint session of Bundestag and Volkskammer to commemorate 17 June 1953 rising in East Germany.
21 June	Bundestag and Volkskammer ratify Treaty on Monetary, Economic and Social Union, and pass resolutions on the Polish frontier.
22 June	Second 2 + 4 meeting, in East Berlin.
1 July	German Monetary, Economic and Social Union comes into force. The DM comes to East Germany.
5–6 July	Nato's London summit.
1–13 July	28th congress of the Communist Party of the Soviet Union.
9–11 July	Houston summit of the G7.
14–16 July	Kohl and Genscher in Moscow and the Caucasus. Crucial agreements on the external aspects of German unification, with united Germany in Nato.
17 July	Third 2 + 4 meeting, in Paris. Discussion of the Polish frontier issue with the Polish foreign minister.
2 August	Treaty on all-German elections. Iraq invades Kuwait.
3 August	Árpád Göncz elected President of Hungary.
23 August	Volkskammer votes for the GDR to join the Federal Republic by Article 23 of the Basic Law on 3 October.
31 August	Signature of Unification Treaty between the Federal Republic and the GDR.
8 September	Bush and Gorbachev meet in Helsinki.
11–12 September	Fourth 2 + 4 meeting, in Moscow. Signature of the Final Treaty with Respect to Germany — the '2 + 4 treaty'.
13 September	Genscher and Shevardnadze initial bilateral German-Soviet friendship treaty.
17 September	EC Council of Ministers agrees measures for the accession of the former GDR to the EC on 3 October.
1 October	Formal declaration of the suspension of four-power rights in Germany.
3 October	The Day of German Unity. GDR joins the Federal Republic.

1990 *continued*

9 October	German-Soviet agreement on 'transitional measures'.
12 October	German-Soviet treaty on the arrangements for remaining Soviet troops and their planned withdrawal.
9 November	On the first anniversary of the opening of the Berlin Wall, Kohl and Gorbachev sign the German-Soviet friendship treaty and a further treaty on economic co-operation, in Bonn.
14 November	Signature of German-Polish frontier treaty.
19 November	Twenty-two member states of Nato and Warsaw Pact sign common declaration.
19–21 November	CSCE summit in Paris. Launch of the Paris Charter for a New Europe.
2 December	First all-German election to the Bundestag. In the resulting 12th Bundestag, the CDU/CSU have 319 seats and the FDP have 79 seats, giving the centre-right coalition government a majority of 134 over the SPD, with 239 seats, and the Bündnis '90/Greens (8) and PDS/LL (17).
9 December	Lech Wałęsa is elected President of Poland.
15 December	Beginning of EC's inter-governmental conferences on economic, monetary and political union.
20 December	First meeting of the all-German Bundestag. Shevardnadze resigns as Soviet Foreign Minister, warning of the danger of dictatorship.
20–21 December	EC begins negotiations with Czechoslovakia, Hungary and Poland on new association agreements.

1991

13 January	'Bloody Sunday' in Vilnius. Some fifteen Lithuanians killed following action by Soviet forces.
15 February	Visegrád Declaration of Hungary, Poland and Czechoslovakia.
25 February	Warsaw Pact agrees to dissolve its military structures on 1 April.
4 March	Supreme Soviet ratifies 2 + 4 treaty, together with the accompanying German-Soviet treaties.
13 March	Erich Honecker is transported by the Soviet military to the Soviet Union.
15 March	The Soviet ambassador to Bonn hands over the Soviet ratification document on the 2 + 4 treaty.
12–14 June	In Prague, President Mitterrand attempts to launch his European Confederation.

17 June	Signature of German-Polish treaty on good-neighbourliness and friendly co-operation.
19–20 June	CSCE Council of Foreign Ministers meets under Genscher's chairmanship in Berlin.
20 June	Bundestag votes that Berlin should remain the capital and become the seat of government of the Federal Republic.
25 June	Croatia and Slovenia declare their independence.
29 July–1 August	Bush-Gorbachev summit in Moscow. Signature of START treaty.
19–21 August	Attempted coup in Soviet Union.
28 August	Germany restores diplomatic relations with the Baltic states.
9 October	Signature of German-Bulgarian treaty on friendly co-operation and partnership.
18 October	Bundestag ratifies frontier and 'neighbour' treaties with Poland.
14 November	Bundestag passes law on the 'Stasi' papers, opening them for carefully regulated use from the beginning of 1992.
11–12 December	EC's Maastricht summit and treaty.
16 December	Signature of so-called 'Europe' agreements between the EC and Poland, Hungary and Czechoslovakia. Under pressure from Germany, EC foreign ministers agree to recognise former Yugoslav republics on 15 January, if certain conditions are met.
19 December	Bonn government announces that it is going ahead with the recognition of Slovenia and Croatia, as previously promised, before Christmas.
25 December	Gorbachev resigns as President, marking the effective end of the Soviet Union.
1992	
6 February	Signature of German-Hungarian treaty on friendly co-operation and partnership.
27 February	Signature of treaty on good-neighbourliness and friendly co-operation between Germany and the Czech and Slovak Federative Republic.
21 April	Signature of German-Romanian treaty on friendly co-operation and partnership.
18 May	Hans-Dietrich Genscher retires after eighteen years as German Foreign Minister. He is succeeded by Klaus Kinkel.
9 October	Death of Willy Brandt.

Maps

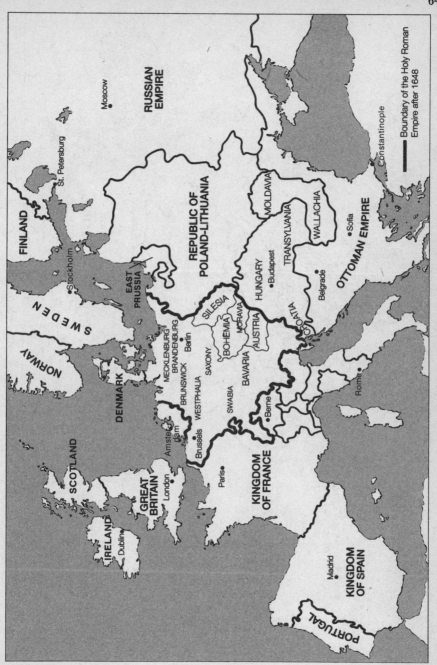

'Westphalia' Europe. Main frontiers c. 1700.

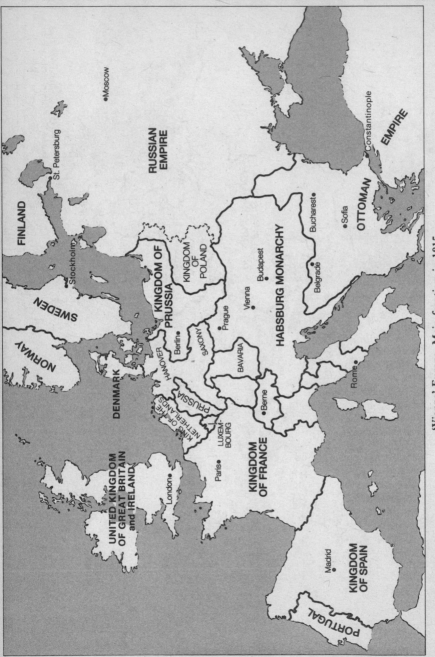

'Vienna' Europe. Main frontiers in 1815.

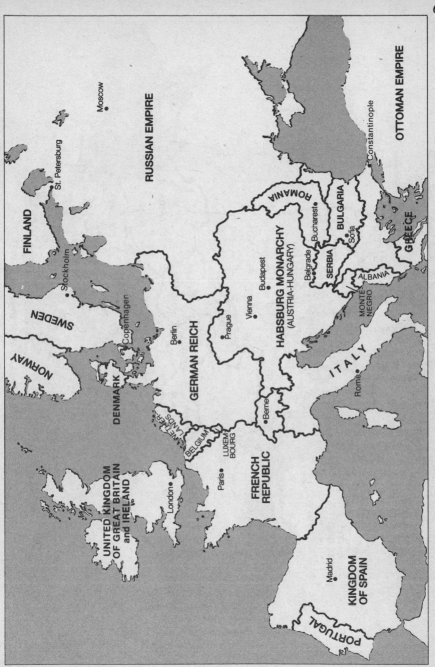

Europe after the first unification of Germany. Main frontiers in 1890.

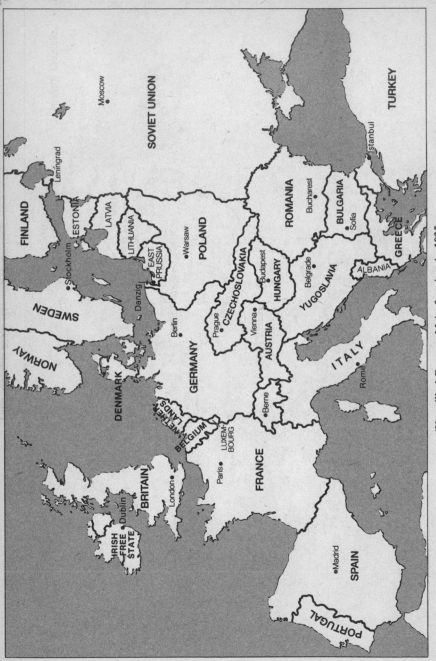

'Versailles' Europe. Main frontiers in 1925.

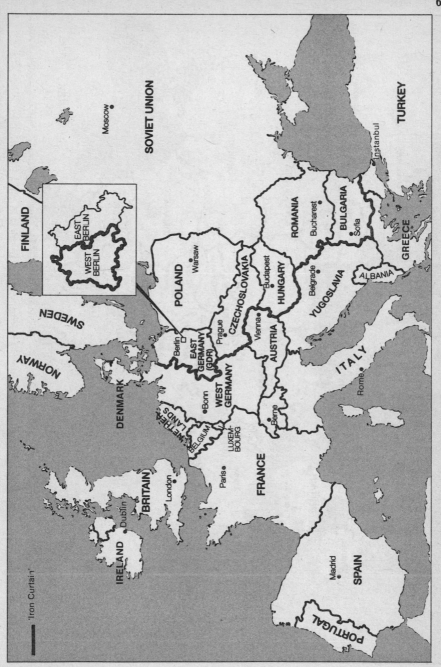

'Yalta' Europe. Main frontiers in 1961.

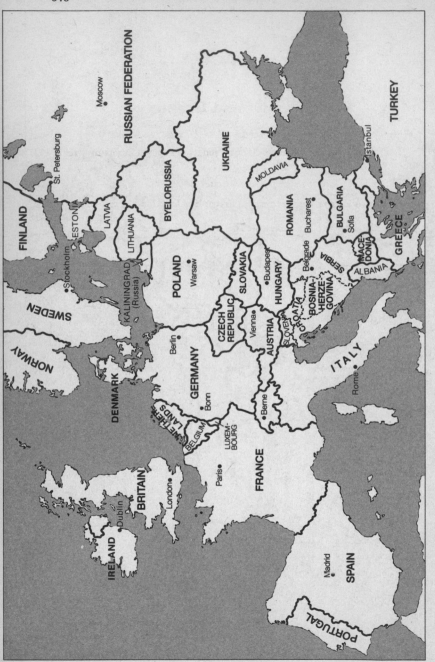

Europe after the second unification of Germany. Main frontiers in early 1993.

Tables and Graphs

650

I. ESTIMATED PER CAPITA GROSS NATIONAL PRODUCT OF SELECTED EUROPEAN STATES IN 1937 AND 1980

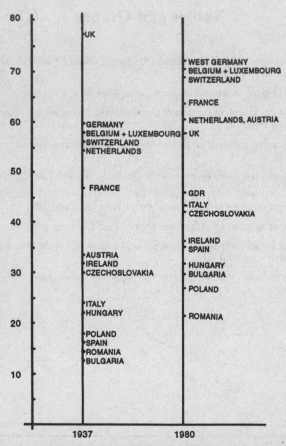

NOTE: This table shows estimated per capita GNP as a percentage of that in the USA. It is based on the work of the Hungarian scholar Eva Ehrlich. Individual entries seem questionable (for example, both the relatively low 1937 position for Czechoslovakia and its relatively high position in 1980) but the overall picture of the economic division of Europe emerges quite clearly.

SOURCE: Adapted from the article by Paul Marer in William E. Griffith, ed., *Central and Eastern Europe: The opening curtain?* (Boulder: Westview Press, 1989).

II. EASTWARD TRADE OF SELECTED WESTERN STATES
(millions of US dollars)

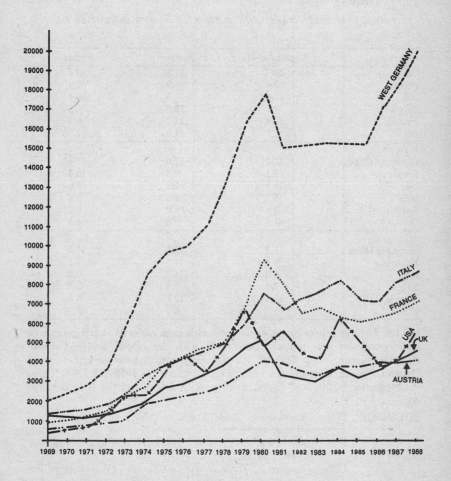

NOTE: This table shows volume of trade with the Soviet Union, Bulgaria,
Czechoslovakia, Hungary, Poland and Romania.

SOURCE: Comtrade Data Bank, United Nations. Calculations by Jerzy
Lisiecki.

III. MAIN WESTERN TRADING PARTNERS OF CZECHOSLOVAKIA, HUNGARY AND POLAND IN 1936, 1956 & 1986

(percentage of total trade with a set of Western industrial states)

1936	Czechoslovakia	Hungary	Poland
Germany	29.7	31.5	19.4
France	7.9	1.9	5.9
UK	11.6	9.0	24.4
Italy	1.7	13.5	2.6
Austria	10.4	21.9	6.9
US	11.7	4.9	12.5
1956			
Germany (West)	20.7	22.0	17.6
France	10.3	9.3	10.3
UK	11.9	10.3	18.0
Italy	5.2	8.3	2.4
Austria	9.6	15.0	8.2
US	1.4	0.8	4.3
1986			
Germany (West)	37.2	32.0	31.6
France	6.4	5.2	7.2
UK	6.0	4.8	9.7
Italy	7.9	9.0	7.7
Austria	12.0	17.6	6.8
US	3.2	6.7	5.5

NOTE: Figures represent the trade done with each major Western partner as a percentage of the country's total trade with the Unites States, Canada, Australia, Japan, New Zealand, Austria, Belgium, Luxembourg, Denmark, Finland, France, Germany (in 1936; West Germany for 1956 and 1986), Italy, the Netherlands, Norway, Spain, Sweden, Switzerland and the United Kingdom.

SOURCES: 1936—*International Trade Statistics* (Geneva: League of Nations, 1937)

1956—*Direction of International Trade* (New York: United Nations, 1960)

1986—*Direction of Trade Statistics Yearbook* (Washington: International Monetary Fund, 1989)

IV. MAIN TRADING PARTNERS OF CZECHOSLOVAKIA, HUNGARY AND POLAND IN 1991 & 1992

(shares in total exports and imports in per cent)

	Czechoslovakia				Hungary				Poland			
	Exports		Imports		Exports		Imports		Exports		Imports	
	1991	1992	1991	1992	1991	1992	1991	1992	1991	1992	1991	1992
Soviet Union	19.6	10.9	29.9	24.6	13.4	13.1	15.3	16.9	11.0	5.5	14.1	8.5
Czechoslovakia	—	—	—	—	2.2	2.7	4.1	4.3	4.6	3.8	3.3	3.2
Hungary	4.3	4.4	1.9	1.6	—	—	—	—	0.7	..	0.9	..
Poland	7.3	4.7	4.7	3.6	2.1	1.3	1.9	1.6	—	—	—	—
Germany	25.2	30.6	21.5	24.7	26.9	27.7	21.4	23.5	29.4	31.3	26.5	23.9
Austria	5.8	7.4	8.4	9.3	10.8	10.7	13.3	14.4	4.5	3.2	6.3	4.5
Italy	4.5	5.7	3.4	4.9	7.6	9.5	7.2	6.3	4.1	5.5	4.5	6.9
France	2.4	2.9	2.5	4.0	2.9	3.2	2.7	3.1	3.8	3.6	3.6	4.4
UK	1.9	2.2	2.0	2.2	2.0	2.0	2.5	2.9	7.1	4.3	4.0	6.6
USA	1.0	1.6	1.9	4.3	3.2	3.2	2.6	2.9	2.5	2.3	2.3	3.4
Japan	0.6	0.8	1.2	1.7	1.7	0.9	2.7	2.4	0.6	0.5	1.6	2.1

NOTE: Whereas until 1989 these countries' trade inside Comecon and that with the West was measured in different and strictly non-comparable units of account, for 1991 and 1992 it is possible to get an all-round picture. For 1992 it is, of course, the former Soviet Union.

SOURCE: Calculations by Dariusz Rosati, United Nations Economic Commission for Europe, on the basis of national statistics.

V. ESTIMATED HARD CURRENCY DEBT OF THE SOVIET UNION AND EAST EUROPEAN STATES
(billions of US dollars)

	1975	1980	1984	1985	1986	1987	1988	1989
Bulgaria								
gross	2.6	3.5	2.8	3.2	4.7	6.1	8.2	9.2
net	2.3	2.7	1.4	1.2	3.3	5.1	6.4	8.0
Czechoslovakia								
gross	1.1	6.9	4.7	4.6	5.6	6.7	7.3	7.9
net	0.8	5.6	3.7	3.6	4.4	5.1	5.6	5.7
GDR								
gross	5.2	13.8	11.7	13.2	15.6	18.6	19.8	20.6
net	3.5	11.8	7.2	6.9	8.2	9.7	10.3	11.1
Hungary								
gross	3.9	9.1	11.0	14.0	16.9	19.6	19.6	20.6
net	2.0	7.7	9.4	11.7	14.8	18.1	18.2	19.4
Poland								
gross	8.4	24.1	26.5	29.3	33.5	39.2	39.2	40.8
net	7.7	23.5	24.9	27.7	31.8	36.2	35.6	36.9
Romania								
gross	2.9	9.6	7.2	6.6	6.4	5.7	2.9	0.6
net	2.4	9.3	6.6	6.2	5.8	4.4	2.1	-1.2
Eastern Europe								
gross	24.2	67.0	63.9	71.0	82.7	96.0	97.0	99.7
net	18.8	60.5	53.2	57.4	68.1	78.4	78.2	79.9
Soviet Union								
gross	10.6	23.5	21.4	25.2	30.5	40.2	46.8	52.4
net	7.5	14.9	10.1	12.1	15.6	26.1	31.4	37.7
Comecon								
gross	34.8	90.5	85.3	96.1	113.1	136.2	143.7	152.1
net	26.3	75.5	63.3	69.5	83.8	104.5	109.7	117.6

NOTE: These figures are Western estimates based on officially reported data. In the case of the GDR, in particular, internal figures that became available after unification indicate that these estimates understated the net debt. The table nevertheless gives a sense of orders of magnitude.

SOURCE: Adapted from Vienna Institute for Comparative Economic Studies, *Comecon Data 1990* (London: Macmillan, 1991).

VI. ESTIMATED NUMBER OF VISITS FROM EAST TO WEST GERMANY, 1962–89
(in thousands)

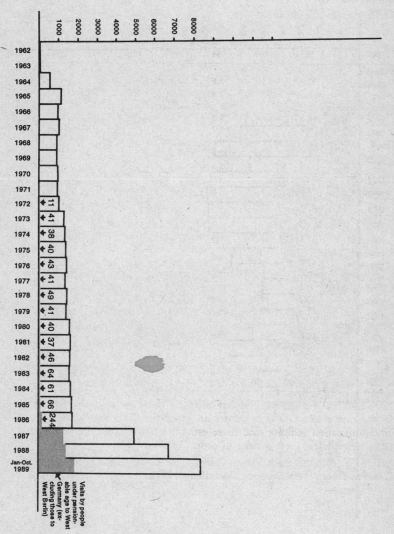

VII. ESTIMATED NUMBER OF VISITS FROM WEST TO EAST GERMANY, 1967–89
(in thousands)

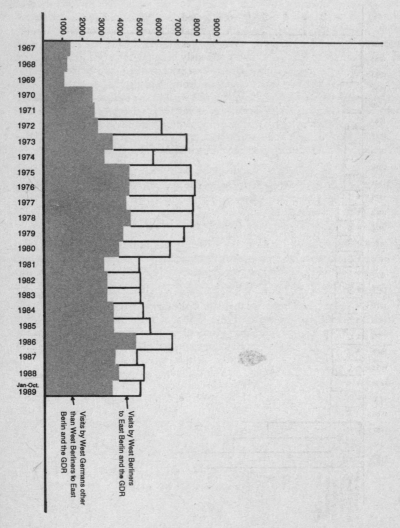

NOTES TO TABLES VI AND VII: The data on German-German travel are frustratingly incomplete. For a start, the records show the estimated total number of *visits*, but not the exact number of *visitors*. Moreover, just at the moment when the travel figures from East to West were soaring, the West German Ministry for Intra-German Relations changed its methodology. Whereas for the period up until 1986 it had collated information from frontier controls, supplemented by other sources, for the years 1987 to 1989 it relied mainly on a large-scale survey conducted by *Infratest Kommunikationsforschung*, based on interviews with West Germans. The resulting figures, starting with a pilot survey in 1986, suggested that there were actually more visits from East to West than had previously been thought, but less from West to East. So far as travel from East to West is concerned, one cannot therefore definitely say what part of the increase from 1986 to 1987 is due to a more permissive East German travel policy, and what to the change of methodology. Somewhere in the the East German archives there are presumably the precise East German figures, which would supplant all these. Note also that both tables deliberately give the figures only up to the end of October 1989, since the opening of the Berlin Wall obviously changed the picture completely.

On TABLE VI, note that the small black column, which gives the crucial figure of visits by people under pensionable age, allowed out of East Germany under the rubric of 'urgent family matters', does *not* include visits to West Berlin, only those to the rest of West Germany. The total number of such visits can therefore be assumed to have been larger.

On TABLE VII, note that in the earlier years some West Berliners were allowed to visit East Berlin by special permit (*Passierschein*). But the numbers were so small—some 60,000 a year from 1967 to 1969—that they would not show up on the scale on which this table is drawn.

SOURCES: For the period up to 1986: *Zahlenspiegel.* For the years 1987–89: author's estimates based on the 1987, 1988 and 1989 *DDR-Reisebarometer* of *Infratest Kommunikationsforschung* (Munich), supplemented by publications of the Ministry for Intra-German Relations and published East German figures.

VIII. ESCAPEES, LEGAL 'OVER-SETTLERS' AND POLITICAL PRISONERS 'BOUGHT FREE' FROM EAST TO WEST GERMANY, 1961–1989

	Total	Legal 'Over-Settlers'	%	Escaped via other countries	%	Escaped across the German-German frontier	%	Prisoners 'bought free'	%
1961	51 624		0.0	43 117	83.5	8 507	16,5		
1962	21 356	4 615	21.6	10 980	51.4	5 761	27,0		
1963	42 632	29 665	69.6	9 267	21.7	3 692	8,7	8	0.0
1964	41 873	30 012	71.7	7 826	18.7	3 155	7,5	880	2.1
1965	29 552	17 666	59.8	8 397	28.4	2 329	7.9	1 160	3.9
1966	24 131	15 675	65.0	6 320	26.2	1 736	7.2	400	1.7
1967	19 578	13 188	67.4	4 637	23.7	1 203	6.1	550	2.8
1968	16 036	11 134	69.4	3 067	19.1	1 135	7.1	700	4.4
1969	16 975	11 702	68.9	3 230	19.0	1 193	7.0	850	5.0
1970	17 519	12 472	71.2	3 246	18.5	901	5.1	900	5.1
1971	17 408	11 565	66.4	3 611	20.7	832	4.8	1 400	8.0
1972	17 164	11 627	67.7	3 562	20.8	1 245	7.3	730	4.3
1973	15 189	8 667	57.1	4 050	26.7	1 842	12.1	630	4.1
1974	13 252	7 928	59.8	3 255	24.6	969	7.3	1 100	8.3
1975	16 285	10 274	63.1	4 188	25.7	673	4.1	1 150	7.1
1976	15 168	10 058	66.3	3 010	19.8	610	4.0	1 490	9.8
1977	12 078	8 041	66.6	1 846	15.3	721	6.0	1 470	12.2
1978	12 117	8 271	68.3	1 905	15.7	461	3.8	1 480	12.2
1979	12 515	9 003	71.9	2 149	17.2	463	3.7	900	7.2
1980	12 763	8 775	68.8	2 683	21.0	424	3.3	881	6.9
1981	15 433	11 093	71.9	2 602	16.9	298	1.9	1 440	9.3
1982	13 208	9 113	69.0	2 282	17.3	283	2.1	1 530	11.6

	Total	Legal 'Over-Settlers'	%	Escaped via other countries	%	Escaped across the German-German frontier	%	Prisoners 'bought free'	%
1983	11 343	7 729	68.2	2 259	19.9	228	2.0	1 127	9.9
1984	40 974	34 982	85.4	3 459	8.4	192	0.5	2 341	5.7
1985	24 912	18 752	75.3	3 324	13.3	160	0.7	2 676	10.7
1986	26 178	19 982	76.3	4 450	17.0	210	0.8	1 536	5.9
1987	18 958	11 459	60.4	5 964	31.5	288	1.5	1 247	6.6
1988	39 845	29 033	72.9	9 129	22.9	589	1.5	1 094	2.7
1961–88	616 066	382 481	62.1	163 815	26.6	40 100	6.5	29 670	4.8
1989	343,85	325,054		17,073				1,727	

NOTE: Legal 'over-settlers' are those who left with the permission of the East German authorities. For 1989, the distinction between escapes across the German-German frontier and those via other countries can apparently no longer be drawn. Some of those counted as 'over-settlers' for 1989 would in earlier years have been counted as escapees.

SOURCE: FAZ, 21 October 1989, based on figures from the *Bundesausgleichamt*. Figures for 1989 from the *Bundesverwaltungsamt*.

IX. WEST GERMANY'S 'OUT-SETTLERS' FROM THE SOVIET UNION AND EASTERN EUROPE, 1950–92

	1950	1951	1952	1953	1954	1955	1956	1957	1958	1959	1960
Soviet Union	0	1,721	63	0	18	154	1,016	923	4,122	5,563	3,272
Poland	31,761	10,791	194	147	664	860	15,674	98,290	117,550	16,252	7,739
Czecho-slovakia	13,308	3,524	146	63	128	184	954	762	692	600	1,394
Hungary	3	157	30	15	43	98	160	2,193	1,194	507	319
Romania	13	1,031	26	15	8	44	176	384	1,383	374	2,124
Yugoslavia	179	3,668	3,407	7,972	9,481	11,839	7,314	5,130	4,703	3,819	3,308
Other areas	1,901	175	182	84	50	23	8	8	11	21	15
Total	47,165	21,067	4,048	8,296	10,392	13,202	25,302	107,690	129,655	27,136	18,171
Via third countries	332	3,698	9,321	7,114	5,032	2,586	6,043	6,256	2,573	1,314	998
Grand Total	47,497	24,765	13,369	15,410	15,424	15,788	31,345	113,946	132,228	28,450	19,169

	1961	1962	1963	1964	1965	1966	1967	1968	1969	1970	1971
Soviet Union	345	894	209	234	366	1,245	1,092	598	316	342	1,145
Poland	9,303	9,657	9,522	13,611	14,644	17,315	10,856	8,435	9,536	5,624	25,241
Czecho-slovakia	1,207	1,228	973	2,712	3,210	5,925	11,628	11,854	15,602	4,.702	2,337
Hungary	194	264	286	387	724	608	316	303	414	517	519
Romania	3,303	1,675	1,321	818	2,715	609	440	614	2,675	6,519	2,848
Yugoslavia	2,053	2,003	2,543	2,331	2,195	2,078	1,881	1,391	1,325	1,372	1,159
Other areas	9	12	15	6	13	33	14	6	5	9	23
Total	16,414	15,733	14,869	20,099	23,867	27,813	26,227	23,201	29,873	19,085	33.272
Via third countries	747	682	614	743	475	380	248	196	166	359	365
Grand Total	17,161	16,415	15,483	20,842	24,342	28,193	26,475	23,397	30,039	19,444	33,637

	1972	1973	1974	1975	1976	1977	1978	1979	1980	1981	1982
Soviet Union	3,420	4,493	6,541	5,985	9,704	9,274	8,455	7,226	6,954	3,773	2,071
Poland	13,482	8,903	7,825	7,040	29,364	32,857	36,102	36,274	26,637	50,983	30,355
Czecho-slovakia	894	525	378	516	849	612	904	1,058	1,733	1,629	1,776
Hungary	520	440	423	277	233	189	269	370	591	667	589
Romania	4,374	7,577	8,484	5,077	3,766	10,989	12,120	9,663	15,767	12,031	12,972
Yugoslavia	884	783	646	419	313	237	202	190	287	234	213
Other areas	6	11	18	15	19	5	9	21	15	19	16
Total	23,580	22,732	24,315	19,329	44,248	54,163	58,061	54,802	51,984	69,336	47,992
Via third countries	315	331	192	328	154	88	62	85	87	119	178
Grand Total	23,895	23,063	24,507	19,657	44,402	54,251	58,123	54,887	52,071	69,455	48,170

	1983	1984	1985	1986	1987	1988	1989	1990	1991	1992	1950 to 1992
Soviet Union	1,447	913	460	753	14,488	47,572	98,134	147,950	147,320	195,576	746,147
Poland	19,121	17,455	22,075	27,188	48,423	140,226	250,340	133,872	40,129	17,742	1,430,059
Czecho-slovakia	1,176	963	757	882	835	949	2,027	1,708	927	460	104,691
Hungary	458	286	485	584	581	763	1,618	1,336	952	354	21,236
Romania	15,501	16,553	14,924	13,130	13,994	12,902	23,387	111,150	32,178	16,146	401,800
Yugoslavia	137	190	191	182	156	223	1,469	961	450	199	89,717
Other areas	4	26	13	10	21	10	67	90	18	12	3,048
Total	37,844	36,386	38,905	42,729	78,498	202,645	377,042	397,067	221,974	230,489	2,796,698
Via third countries	81	73	63	59	25	28	13	6	21	76	52.626
Grand Total	37,925	36,459	33,968	42,788	78,523	202,673	377,055	397,073	221,995	230,565	2,849,324

NOTE: For the complicated definition of 'out-settlers' see the section 'Compatriots' in Chapter Five. For 1992, it is of course 'former Soviet Union' and 'former Yugoslavia'.

SOURCE: Federal Ministry of the Interior.

Acknowledgements

For permission to consult all or part of their papers in the archives, I am indebted to the late Willy Brandt, to Helmut Schmidt and Egon Bahr, to the heirs of the late Alois Mertes and Werner Marx, to Wolfgang Schollwer, and, in his capacity as chairman of the Free Democrats, to Hans-Dietrich Genscher. Invaluable assistance was then given me by the archivists of the *Archiv der sozialen Demokratie*, notably Frau Gertrud Lenz for the Brandt papers, Herr Christoph Stamm for the Schmidt papers and Frau Barbara Richter for the Bahr papers; by those of the *Archiv fur Christlich-Demokratische Politik*, notably Dr Günter Buchstab, Frau Kessler and Herr Dietmar Haak; and of the *Archiv des Deutschen Liberalismus*, led by Dr Monika Fassbender.

I owe a special debt of gratitude to the archivists of the *Zentrales Parteiarchiv* in East Berlin, notably Dr Inge Pardon, Frau Räuber, Frau Gräfe and the invariably cheerful Herr Muller and Herr Lange, all of whom made special efforts to facilitate my work during a difficult period of transition for that archive. Equally, I thank particularly Dr Hubertus Knabe for facilitating my access to the archives of the former Ministry for State Security, now under the so-called *Gauck-Behörde*, and Herr Förster and Frau Schulz for their detailed assistance.

Dr Hans-Jochen Vogel gave an example to his colleagues (in all parties) by making available to me his own records of his talks with Erich Honecker, so that these could be compared with those in the *Zentrales Parteiarchiv*. This was of course a valuable test of the veracity of those East German records.

The *Zentrales Dokumentationssystem* of the *Bundespresseamt* gave me invaluable assistance in tracking down the press and media reports which are so much the bread and butter of contemporary politics. I thank Professor Wolfgang Bergsdorf for opening the door to this wonderful resource, and Frau Anna Maria Kuppe for producing swift and meticulously researched answers to my often obscure queries. Equally helpful was the press archive of the SPD, which made available its rich files and tireless photocopier.

At a later stage in the work, the *Auswärtiges Amt* answered a number of detailed queries which could not readily be answered elsewhere. I am grateful to Dr Dieter Kastrup, the State Secretary of the *Auswärtiges Amt*, for suggesting this, and to Dr Martin Ney for organising the responses. The staffs of *Gesamtdeutsches Institut*, when it still existed, of the library of the ZI6 at the Free University of Berlin, of the Bundestag library and of the *Bundeszentrale für Politische Bildung* — there particularly Herr Rüdiger Thomas — were consistently helpful in providing books and information.

The many historical witnesses to whom I spoke provided one of the richest sources for this book. Their names appear at the appropriate places in the Notes, but I would like to thank them all for giving me their time and their selected memories. In addition, I would like to thank the following for their valuable help in discussing particular aspects or pursuing specific queries: Professor Egon Bahr, Dr Peter Bender, Dr Lev Bezymensky, Dr Brigitte Seebacher-Brandt, Dr Günter Buchstab, Lord Bullock, Richard Davy, Herr Roland Freudenstein, Herr Karl-Wilhelm Fricke, Professor Gabriel Gorodetsky, Dr Klaus Gotto, Professor Philip Hanson, Dr Hans-Jürgen Heimsoeth, Professor Sir Michael Howard, Professor Harold James, Professor Karl Kaiser, Dr Axel Lebahn, Professor Werner Link, Herr Manfred Meissner, Dr Sigrid Meuschel, Dr Marina Pavlova-Silvanskaya, Dr Jerzy Lisiecki, Dr Zbigniew Pelczynski, Dr Peter Siebenmorgen, Dr Wolfgang Stock, Herr Horst Teltschik, Dr Jochen Thies, Dr Armin Volze, Craig P Whitney, Professor Heinrich-August Winkler, Dr Stefan Wolle, Dr Jonathan Wright, Professor Hartmut Zimmermann.

Work on this book has been supported above all by extremely generous funding from the Ford Foundation, first for a research project based at St Antony's College, Oxford, then for a Senior Research Fellowship at that College. I should like to thank particularly Enid Schoettle and subsequently Shep Forman and Paul Balaran. At a later stage, the research was supported by the European Cultural Foundation, one of the few genuinely European foundations that exist, and my thanks there go especially to Franz Alting von Geusau and Raymond Georis. Further funding was provided by the Nuffield Foundation, by the Cyril Foster Fund at Oxford, and, at the last, by the Modern History Faculty of Oxford University. I am grateful to them all.

The very earliest drafts of the first part of this book were written during my time as a Fellow at the Woodrow Wilson International Center for Scholars in Washington DC, and I thank in particular the then director, James Billington, and the head of the West European Program, Michael Haltzel, for their assistance and support. A short stay at the *Stiftung Wissenschaft und Politik* in Ebenhausen, on the kind invitation of the Director, Professor Michael Stürmer, enabled me to discuss my ideas with the specialists there and to pursue some additional sources. A visiting fellowship at the Vienna *Institut für die Wissenschaften vom Menschen*, which has itself made a significant contribution to reducing the intellectual division of Europe, gave me an opportunity to discuss my ideas with Austrian and East Central European colleagues. I am grateful to Krzysztof Michalski for this opportunity.

The largest part of this book was, however, written in Oxford. I owe much to the wider community of scholars in the University, particularly to those in German and East European history, European politics and International Relations, and to the students who ask good questions.

The institution to which this book owes most of all is St Antony's College. It would, I think, be impossible to find a better place to pursue such a project. Virtually all my colleagues have provided a stimulus of one sort or another. For their assistance on particular points, I would like to thank specifically Andrew Walter, Alex Pravda, Anne Deighton, Archie Brown and Michael Kaser. I am especially grateful to Tony Nicholls, the Director of the European Studies Centre, who not only presided over many interesting seminars on related themes but also read and commented expertly on the whole typescript. The College librarians, Rosamund Campbell and Hilary Maddicott, have been unfailingly helpful and cheerful. Caroline Henderson gave me stalwart secretarial help in the early years, as did Anna Lever in the later ones.

I have been most fortunate in my research assistants, starting with John Connelly in Washington, and continuing in Oxford with Mark Smith, John Laughland, Tina Podplatnik, Frank Müller, Nikolas Gvosdev and, last but by no means least, Danuta Garton Ash. Their help was both invaluable and enjoyable.

Sir Julian Bullard, Pierre Hassner and Fritz Stern read the typescript, and greatly enriched it by their comments both at this and earlier points. I am much in their debt.

At the last editing stage, my publishers, David Godwin of Jonathan Cape and Jason Epstein of Random House, and my editor, Euan Cameron, encouraged the author and improved the text.

My final, very special thanks go to four friends who have, in their different ways, accompanied and shaped this book from its earliest days.

Werner Krätschell was for the first part of the writing still shut in behind the Berlin Wall, in Pankow. For the second part, he was free to visit his godson in Oxford at the drop of a hat. I have thought of him and his family often while working on what for most readers is history, but for them has been life.

Arnulf Baring, who crucially sharpened the definition of the subject at an early stage, has influenced me by the example of his own writing of contemporary history, by his encouragement, and, most of all, by his characteristic, restless and provocative questioning.

Michael Mertes has sustained a truly wonderful flow of information, ideas, suggestions and advice, by post, fax and telephone, culminating in an immensely helpful commentary on the complete typescript.

Ralf Dahrendorf has quite simply been godfather to this book, not just institutionally, as Warden of St Antony's, but even more intellectually and personally, informing, questioning, encouraging, sharpening at every step, with a unique perspective which is both German, British and, after all, European.

Index

Important terms such as Cold War, détente, Deutschlandpolitik, Europe (East, West and Central), Germany (West, East and united), Ostpolitik, socialism and the West have not been included in the following index since they appear so frequently throughout the book. Only the main text has been indexed.